HISTORY OF COLOR PHOTOGRAPHY

HISTORY OF COLOR PHOTOGRAPHY

BY

JOSEPH S. FRIEDMAN, PH.D.

1945

THE AMERICAN PHOTOGRAPHIC PUBLISHING COMPANY

BOSTON

Second printing, 1945

*Printed in the United States of America
by The Plimpton Press, Norwood, Mass*

PREFACE

This book has been produced in response to an insistent demand from color workers for exhaustive information on the many forms of research that have developed the various color processes of photography into the usable condition in which they are found today. This subject was covered very completely by Professor Wall up to the time of the publication of his famous book, "The History of Three-Color Photography," in 1925. But the demand for that work was so great that it has long been out of print and its information is no longer generally available. Even if it were, color photography has progressed so rapidly in the past twenty years that information as of that date could tell no more than half the story of today.

To the stupendous task of ferreting out and compiling into coherent and usable form all this accumulated data, Dr Friedman brings a splendid preparation. After graduating from Harvard and taking his doctorate at the University of Chicago, he plunged directly into color work on the staff of Technicolor which was then evolving its famous process in Boston Through the years he has been actively identified with the development of many forms of color photography, and is at present on the research staff of Ansco. He has long been known as a prolific and authoritative writer on this subject, and of late years his department in *American Photography* has been a general clearing-house of information about its latest aspects.

This book will be found invaluable to anyone who needs the complete record of what has gone before in any existing department of color photography. Starting with the earliest ideas of colorimetry, it traces the development of all the laboratory and commercial processes by which color has been evolved to its present-day applications, enumerating the underlying principles, describing the technique, and giving the history of the patents that have been issued concerning them. The record is as complete as it is humanly possible to achieve, and contains compactly compiled and correlated information that is nowhere else available without very extensive research. For anyone who wants to get a detailed and comprehensive picture of color photography as a whole, or who needs specific information about any of its special developments, no effort has been spared to make this book as complete and valuable as possible.

CONTENTS

INTRODUCTION

It is now almost twenty years since E. J. Wall published his monumental work "The History of Three-Color Photography." In that interval progress has been rapid. Viewpoints and emphasis have changed so much that the practice of 1944 uses techniques that received hardly any mention in 1925. Color photography passed from the use of the cumbersome one-shot camera with its delicate light-splitting device, to the monopack which could be exposed in an ordinary camera. It discarded the complicated positive processes which required precise registration of three separate images, and adopted the multi-layered material processed by color development or by silver-dye-bleach. It is somewhat ironic to recall that monopacks and color development were fully disclosed by 1913. And yet, while Mr. Wall was able to summarize the work done in this line up to 1925 in a few scattered paragraphs, it has since assumed such importance that these paragraphs are expanded to six chapters in the present text.

The use of monopack film leaves the operator with a color reproduction of an original scene. The ultimate object, for the motion-picture industry at least, is the conversion of this into any number of duplicates, all of uniform quality. The duplication of a color reproduction presents new problems whose solutions are indicated in the chapter dealing with masking. This is a procedure first introduced by Dr. Albert before the turn of the present century, for the photomechanical industry. Perhaps for that reason it was ignored by the photographer. When it was brought to his attention, he appraised it quickly as being "highbrow," and consequently scorned it. He made no serious effort until quite recently to study its possibilities. Consequently Wall, in his historical survey, found no reason to mention it by name, although he did describe procedures where masking was utilized. At this writing, there can be no further question of the usefulness of the technique. It complements the monopack film, for in combination with that material it seals the doom of the one-shot camera

The present text includes chapters on diazo and bleach-out photography. No great strides have been made in these fields to warrant the hope that they may some day offer a solution to the print problem. However they do suggest a possible extension of useful light-sensitive systems. The use of silver halides represents a constant challenge to the photographer and photographic chemist, for the silver halide system is extremely wasteful of light energy. When light is incident upon a photographic film, a large percentage of it is reflected off. Another substantial portion is transmitted. These represent sheer waste of light energy. Of the light that actually penetrates the emulsion layer, only a small part is utilized for the formation of the latent image. The rest is lost by scatter. In a system sensitized by dichromate or by a fugitive dye, only the useful light is absorbed, the rest is transmitted freely. This could be utilized for a similar or other purpose. Attempts have been made to combine the high efficiency of the diazo and bleach-out systems with the intensification possibilities of the silver halides. These are discussed in the chapters on diazo and bleach-out processes.

The history and development of color photography prior to 1925 has been very ably covered by Mr. Wall. Therefore in the present text it was deemed best to concentrate on the work done since that time However each subject has been traced back, as far as possible, to its initial introduction. This was done mainly to show that the basic principles which underlie nearly all our present-day procedures, are now in the public domain. The keynote of present research is not so much a search for something new. It is rather a search to improve and make useful the suggestions of yesterday. True, we need men of genius to create new scientific marvels. But more than that, we need the dogged plodder who can work through discouragement and who can analyze failure. It is this man who will make practical the brilliant achievement of the genius.

CHAPTER 1

COLORIMETRY

COLOR photography can be identified with colorimetry, the science that deals with the specification and measurement of color. It is, in fact, a system of mechanical colorimetry, where the amount of silver developed in a photographic emulsion, after it has been exposed to the light and color under consideration, is utilized as a measure of the intensity of a given primary present in that color. The fundamental ideas concerning colorimetry can therefore be of great importance in the practice of color photography.

The common practice with regard to both colorimetry and photography, is to regard the subject from the strictly psychological point of view. This is due to the fact that, as sensed by man, color is a sensation and not a substance. This fact was not recognized until very early in the nineteenth century, when Thomas Young read his famous paper to the Royal Society in 1802. The three-color theory bears his name because he was the first to emphasize this fact. Writing some forty years later, Maxwell had this to say, "It is almost a truism to say that color is a sensation, and yet by recognizing this simple fact Thomas Young realized clearly nearly forty years ago that the science of color must therefore be regarded as essentially a mental science." Stated broadly, the idea promulgated by Young was that the sensation produced by any one color could be matched by the proper mixture of three fundamental colors called primaries. Thus the infinite variety of hues present in the rainbow could each individually be matched by some mixture of three colors which are themselves also present in the rainbow. Young based his idea upon the hypothetical existence of three light-sensitive substances within the optical system of the human being. It is in this respect that he differed from his many predecessors who had actually experimented with trichromatic matching of colors.

The idea of primaries, from whose mixture all other colors could be compounded, is a deep-rooted one. The ancient Greeks taught that all colors could be compounded by the proper blending of white, blue, red, and yellow. Aristotle, noting that the rainbow was produced when only gray clouds and sunlight were present, advanced the idea that there were but two primaries, white and black. This idea dominated the thinking in this field up to the seventeenth century. Antonius de Dominis as late as 1624 propounded a like theory. Maurolycus (1494–1577) distinguished four principal colors in the rainbow. These were reddish yellow, green, blue, and purple, each of which blended into the next by means of an intermediate color. This was a clear anticipation of Newton, who also distinguished seven principal hues. Leonardo da Vinci, the genius of the Reformation, considered red, yellow, green, blue, white, and black as simple colors, and all the others as compounded from these. The three-primary-colors scheme was advocated by Lambert (1728–1777), Tobias Mayer (about 1775), and Brewster (1781–1868). It is significant that these scientists all chose red, yellow, and blue as the primary colors. From our later knowledge, we can assume that in these cases the red primary was considerably pinkish in hue, while the blue was quite greenish. Even today, when we have a more thorough knowledge of the fundamentals, we still call the minus-green red, instead of magenta, and the minus-red blue instead of cyan. This is a relic of the days when the hues of the secondaries were so far from the theoretical that they could truly be called red and blue, rather than magenta and cyan. We may therefore infer that the seventeenth and eighteenth century scientists did not distinguish between the additive and the subtractive colors. The colors used in the additive processes (red, green, blue) are termed primaries, while those used in the subtractive processes (cyan, magenta, yellow) are termed secondaries. The reason for this will be made apparent later. Most, if not all, the experiments with color matching were done by mixing pigments, and so those scientists who operated in this manner used secondary colors. This explains why an artist and scientist like Leonardo da Vinci, fell into this error Those who matched colors by mixing colored lights, used the primary colors, since they operated with additive systems Goethe in 1810, in his attack upon Newton, also fell into the same error of confounding secondary with primary colors.

Probably the first person who carried out extensive work upon trichrome color reproduction was Tobias Mayer. He left a notebook with copious notes in which he tried to determine the approximate number of distinguishable colors that could be compounded from three pigments. As stated above, he used red, blue, and yellow for his basic colors, but from the nature of his experimental work, it seems fairly obvious that his red and blue were really the red and blue of the printer, that is a pinkish red, and a greenish blue. His color chart represented each different hue by a formula of the type $r^{\alpha}y^{\beta}b^{\gamma}$, and for the most part $\alpha + \beta + \gamma$ equaled 12. The first person to put these ideas into practice was the printer J. C. LeBlon, who in 1722 used red, yellow, and blue printing plates to make colored reproductions. But none of these gentlemen realized that the matching of colors was purely a psychological process, that the fusion of the three primaries took place within the optic system of the human, and that the sensation of color was purely a figment of the imagination This was Young's contribution, and for this reason the three-color theory rightly bears his name.

The Young theory was extended considerably by Helmholtz in Germany and by Maxwell in England. Maxwell was the first to demonstrate that the then newly developed art of photography could be utilized to give a graphic and automatic method for the determination of the relative amounts of the various primaries that were present in any given color. In two lectures which he gave in 1857 and 1859 he demonstrated the photographic procedure. In his experimental work he used a blue filter made by interposing an ammoniacal solution of copper sulphate, a green filter which consisted of a solution of copper chloride, a yellow filter, and a red filter that was composed of iron sulpho-cyanide. Thus his primaries were the correct ones, although it is not apparent just why he used a fourth separation made behind a yellow filter. In this practice, however, he anticipated the four-color printers of modern times by fully fifty years. From his four negatives he made four positives, each of which he projected in superposition upon a white screen through the same filters that he used in making the negatives. The synthesis process was additive.

To Maxwell, the preparation of a colored photograph was but incidental to the study of colorimetry, in which he was keenly interested. He was quick to discover that colorimetry was identifiable with color photography, and that this last was merely applied colorimetry. But the state of the photographic art at that time was such that its practical application was a tedious job. There were no one-shot cameras available, so that the different "separations" had to be made one after the other. Collodion emulsions were the only ones which were known. The procedure, therefore, was equivalent to the wet-plate processes, hence exceedingly slow The exposure through the blue filter was six seconds; through the red it was eight; and through the green it was twelve seconds after the filter had been considerably diluted. It is no wonder that Maxwell was satisfied to treat the entire affair merely as an experimental confirmation of his work on colorimetry.

Since this is so closely allied to color reproduction, it is well to review some basic facts. It has its basis in the Young theory of color sensation, in that it stipulates that all color sensations can be matched by a suitable mixture of three widely differentiable colors. Young and his successors postulated that within the optic system of the human there were three receptors each of which was predominantly sensitive to the light of a single primary. Newton's discovery of the dispersion of light into a spectrum more thoroughly convinced the members of this school. In accordance with the Newtonian experiment, white light when passed obliquely into one side of a glass prism emerged from the other side, not as a beam of white light, but as a band of colors. This band was always constituted in the same manner. One end of it was colored blue-violet, while the opposite end was colored red, or rather an orange-red. Between these two extremes the colors all blended into one another, so that the blue-violet became blue, then blue-green, and this in turn became a green The green shaded off into a yellow-green, then yellow, orange, and finally turned red Each color differed in hue by an infinitesimal amount from the color that was situated immediately adjacent to it on the right and on the left. It may not be possible to distinguish two adjacent colors, so close is their match; but it is an easy matter to distinguish the color on the right of a given one from the color on its left, especially if the middle color remains between the two. The wave theory of light has made it very easy to differentiate the colors from one another. The wavelengths of each hue differ from each other, and these values can be determined to an accuracy of one part in ten million. Thus the wavelength of the D_2 line of sodium is 5889 977, while the wavelength for the D_1 line is 5895.944. These values are in Angstrom units, which are equal to 0.1 mμ. The eye is sensitive to colors that lie in the range between 400 and 700 mμ. Thus there are an infinity of colors and hues which the eye can distinguish Of course, if the eye is accosted by two colors whose wavelengths differ but slightly (and as far as the eye is concerned a difference of 5 mμ is very slight), it would be extremely difficult for it to differentiate between the two As a matter of fact Newton divided the band into only seven distinct colors. But the fact remains that theoretically a difference in hue does exist between two colors whose wavelengths differ by as little as one mμ.

Because physics demands the existence of this infinite range of different colors, color specialists have insisted upon a three-color theory. The eye cannot have present at every point of its sensitive area an infinity of light-sensitive elements each of which would be sensitive to light of but a single wavelength But the eye does distinguish between hues, and experiment has shown that a simple mathematical equation connects any four distinct colors, the only reservation being that no one of these should be matchable by a mixture of two of the others. The equation is as follows:

$$mA + nB + pC + qD = 0$$

where m, n, p, and q are constants that could be positive, zero, or negative (but not all of them could be equal to zero at the same time), and A, B, C, and D are the four colors. This means that it is possible to match any one color by some combination of the other three This is the real and experimental basis of the trichrome theory of colorimetry. It is independent of any hypothesis which attempts to explain why. Experimentally, the procedure can be carried out in this manner. One unit of the hue A is passed into one half of the photometric field of a color-matching instrument, while into the other half there are passed n/m units of the color B, p/m units of the color C, and q/m units of the color D. If any of the coefficients in the equation are negative, then these colors are added to the color A and the mixture is matched by a mixture of the remaining primaries.

When two colors are mixed together, the colors being in the form of light, a third color results The eye cannot distinguish in the third color either of the originals. In this respect the eye differs from all physical color-analyzing apparatus, in which the light is dispersed into spectra. These will always consist of the sum of the spectra of the component lights. The sum of two color sensations is also a color sensation, but it is not the linear sum of the other two sensations. Psychology does not have a conservation law of the type that plays so important a role in physics.

The mixture of two colors is a third color that is different from either of the other two, and in which it is not possible to detect them In particular, it is not possible for the eye to tell whether a given color is the sensation produced by monochromatic light (light of a single wavelength), or whether it is produced by the light of a whole range of colors For instance the color of the A filter is well known. It is red. When the light that this filter transmits is sent into a spectroscope it is seen that it consists of a mixture of all the colors whose wavelengths are greater than 600 mμ. The red due to the A filter is therefore a complex mixture containing an infinite number of hues If one half of the photometric field of a color-matching apparatus is illuminated by monochromatic light of wavelength 610 mμ, and the other half by the light transmitted by the A filter, the two will match perfectly. The eye will not be able to distinguish between them. In color-matching procedures it is immaterial therefore, whether monochromatic light or color blends are used as the primaries. The same results will be obtained in both cases.

Not all the colors to which the eye is sensitive appear in the spectrum of white light. In particular, the mixtures of the reds and the blues are not present in the spectrum. These are the pinks and the violets As a matter of fact, the mixture of two spectral colors gives rise to colors that can be matched in hue only by some color in the spectrum (if that mixture does not consist of red and blue). This brings us to a discussion of the other properties of color. Suppose we are given a large number of colored patches to classify. The first and most apparent classification is that of hue. All the reds can be grouped together, then all the greens, etc. But it is also possible to classify them in another manner It is possible to compare a red with a green and say that the intensity of red in the red is equal to the intensity of green in the green. By this classification we recognize that colors can have different degrees of intensity or brightness. It is also possible to consider the reds as a class and to compare two reds with identical hues, but which differ from each other in brilliance. Thus we may consider that one red appears to be quite pure, while another appears to be paler, as if it were a mixture of red and white. This type of classification is in terms of saturation. It is really quite significant that psychologists have arrived at a three-variable description of color, and at a trichrome analysis of color. Most probably the search for three variables was greatly influenced by the fact that three primaries were sufficient for color matching. Colorimetry attempts to give quantitative values to the three variables.

If monochromatic light is passed into one half of the photometric field and a suitable mixture of three independent colors (in that no one of them can be matched by a combination of the other two) is passed into the other half, it will be possible to match every monochromatic color in the spectrum. When this is done, it will be possible to draw a graph whereby relative intensities are plotted against the wavelength for each primary. This will give rise to three curves, which can be considered to be measures of the stimuli produced in the three postulated sensitive elements in the optic system. Such curves are called stimulus curves. Maxwell was the first to carry out such an experiment. He was followed by a host of others, notably by Konig and Dieterichi, Abney, Wright, Guild, etc. The results showed a remarkable similarity The International Committee on Illumination has adopted a set of such curves as a standard. It may appear that choosing one set of such values as a standard is rather arbitrary, but that is not so. It is true that the specific values for the coefficients depend upon the choice of the primaries, but then it is possible to determine these values for one set of primaries in terms of another. It will be found that this same relationship holds for any other color that may be matched in terms of the two sets Knowing the relationship between two sets of primaries makes the values determined by one set convertible into the other. The I C.I values have a definite significance in that one of the primaries has been chosen so that it corresponds exactly to the sensitivity of the normal average eye. This is termed the *Y* co-ordinate, and its value can be used directly as a quantitative measure of the brightness of any color. Thus one of the variables of color specification has been given a numerical value. The I.C.I. tristimulus values of the spectrum colors are given in the table below, to a degree of accuracy that allows their use in calculations for our purposes.

Wave-length	*X*	*Y*	*Z*	*Wave-length*	*X*	*Y*	*Z*
400	0.014	0.000	0.068	550	0.433	0.995	0.009
410	0.044	0.001	0.207	560	0.595	0.995	0.004
420	0.134	0.004	0.647	570	0.762	0.952	0.002
430	0.284	0.012	1.386	580	0.916	0.870	0.002
440	0.343	0.023	1.747	590	1.026	0.757	0.001
450	0.336	0.038	1.772	600	1.062	0.631	0.001
460	0.291	0.060	1.669	610	1.003	0.503	0.000
470	0.195	0.091	1.288	620	0.854	0.381	0.000
480	0.096	0.139	0.813	630	0.642	0.265	0.000
490	0.032	0.208	0.465	640	0.448	0.175	0.000
500	0.005	0.323	0.272	650	0.284	0.107	0.000
510	0.009	0.503	0.158	660	0.165	0.061	0.000
520	0.063	0.710	0.078	670	0.087	0.032	0.000
530	0.166	0.862	0.042	680	0.047	0.017	0.000
540	0.290	0.954	0.020	690	0.023	0.008	0.000
				700	0.011	0.004	0.000

These values may be interpreted as indicating the relative response which each of the three sensitive elements in the optic system gives when stimulated by monochromatic light.

The primaries used in any color-matching experiment are not restricted except that they must be independent of each other. It is therefore permissible to make a change of co-ordinates provided a linear relationship holds between the new and the old. This we proceed to do in the following manner. We define the co-ordinates x, y, and z by the equations $x = X/R$, $y = Y/R$, and $z = Z/R$, where $R = X + Y + Z$. A simple calculation will demonstrate that $x + y + z = 1$, so that only two of these are really independent. It is possible, therefore, to use two of the three co-ordinates as new variables, and for the third variable keep the Y component, since that is a numerical designation of the brightness. It is customary to choose x, and y. These can now be plotted as rectangular co-ordinates. From the table, the value of R for the wavelength 400 would be $0.014 + 0.000 + 0.068$, or 0.082. Then x will be given by 0.014/0.082, and y by 0.000/0.082. Thus x will have a value of 0.17 and y a value of 0.00. This will give rise to one point on the diagram. In a similar manner the wavelength 550 will give rise to a value of $0.433 + 0.995 + 0.009$ or 1.439 for R, and x will be equal to 0.433/1.439 or 0.30, while y will be equal to 0.995/1.439 or 0.69. This will give another point on the diagram. The values for x and y for the entire spectrum are tabulated below.

Wave-length	x	y	Wave-length	x	y	Wave-length	x	y
400	0.17	0.00	500	0.01	0.54	600	0.63	0.37
410	0.17	0.01	510	0.01	0.75	610	0.67	0.33
420	0.17	0.01	520	0.07	0.83	620	0.69	0.31
430	0.17	0.01	530	0.16	0.80	630	0.71	0.29
440	0.16	0.01	540	0.23	0.75	640	0.72	0.28
450	0.16	0.02	550	0.30	0.69	650	0.73	0.27
460	0.14	0.03	560	0.37	0.62	660	0.73	0.27
470	0.12	0.06	570	0.44	0.56	670	0.73	0.27
480	0.09	0.13	580	0.51	0.49	680	0.73	0.27
490	0.05	0.30	590	0.58	0.42	690	0.73	0.27
						700	0.74	0.26

It is to be noticed that at the two ends of the spectrum the points crowd each other severely. Had we carried the calculations out to the 4th or 5th decimal point, slight differences would be seen to exist between all the co-ordinates, but for our purposes it is not necessary to carry the calculations to any greater accuracy. The graph of the points due to the spectral colors is shown in Fig. 1. The point C in the diagram represents the locus of the light adopted by the International Illumination Committee as a standard white approaching daylight. A diagram such as is shown in Fig. 1 is called a chromacity diagram, for it indicates the dominant hue and the saturation of any given color. Pure white, which is a theoretical mixture of equal parts of the three primaries, would be located at the point $x = y = z = 0.33$. This is not far away from the locus of the point C.

A chromacity diagram is extremely useful in that it can graphically demonstrate all the known facts concerning additive color mixing. The points on the curve that depicts the spectral colors denote complete saturation or purity, and these are given a value of 100 per cent. Not all colors will be located upon this curve. In fact, the great majority of them will have positions within the area included in the curve. Suppose that the point A in Fig 1 denotes a color whose co-ordinates are (0.23, 0.39). To obtain the dominant hue of this color, a line is drawn from the point *C*, which represents the standard white, to the point *A*, and this line is continued until it intersects the spectral curve. The point of intersection *P* corresponds to a color whose wavelength is 506 mμ. This will be the dominant hue of the color whose locus is at *A*. To find the purity of the color *A*, we determine the ratio of the line *AC* to *CP*, roughly 2/9. The purity of the color is therefore 22 per cent. This color

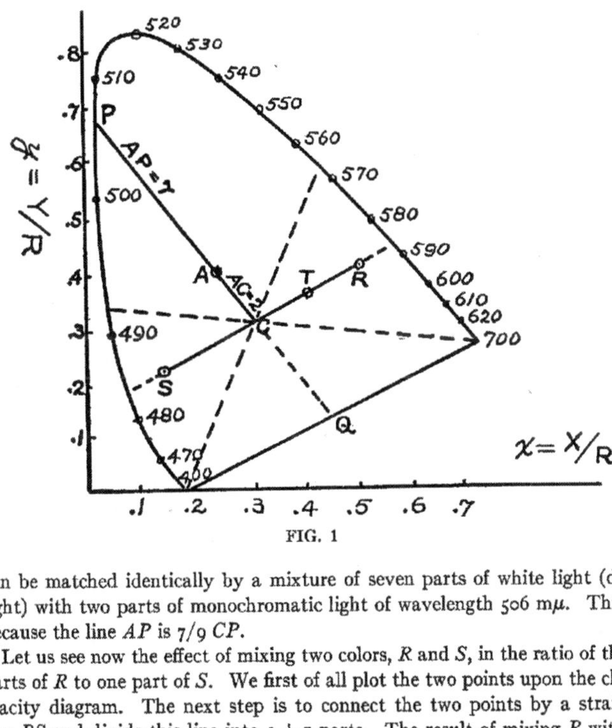

FIG. 1

can be matched identically by a mixture of seven parts of white light (daylight) with two parts of monochromatic light of wavelength 506 mμ. This is because the line *AP* is 7/9 *CP*.

Let us see now the effect of mixing two colors, *R* and *S*, in the ratio of three parts of *R* to one part of *S*. We first of all plot the two points upon the chromacity diagram. The next step is to connect the two points by a straight line *RS* and divide this line into 3 + 1 parts. The result of mixing *R* with *S* will be a color whose locus lies somewhere upon the line *RS*, say at a point *T*. This point will divide the line *RS* so that *ST* will be equal to three times *TR*. That is, the new color will be situated three-quarters of the distance toward *R*, the dominating color. It is seen that the line *SR* passes through the point *C*. The segment *SC* is roughly equal to the segment *CR*, so that white light of color *C* will result when equal parts of lights *R* and *S* are mixed. Thus the result of mixing two colors can under the proper conditions give rise to white.

Such colors are called complementary. It is readily seen that there are infinite numbers of such pairs of complementary colors. The line *SCTR* intersects the spectral curve in two places, one at a point which corresponds approximately to 586 mμ, the other at approximately 484 mμ. If equal quantities of monochromatic lights of these wavelengths are mixed, the result will be the sensation of white, despite the fact that from a physical point of view white light would contain all the wavelengths. In this manner it is possible to determine all the pairs of complementary colors Thus the point 700 mμ will lie on one end of the line through *C* while at the other end will lie the point 492. Since the two segments are not equal to each other, it will require more of the light of wavelength 492 than of wavelength 700 in order to obtain a white. In a similar manner the wavelength 400 mμ has for its complement a color whose wavelength is 567

It is seen that in the diagram in Fig. 1 the point 400 has been connected with the point 700 by a straight line. This line represents the locus of those colors that can be formed by a mixture of blue (400 mμ) with red (700 mμ). These are the pinks and violets which the eye can see as distinct colors, but which have no counterpart in the spectrum. There are no spectral matches to the colors which lie along this line, hence there can be no spectral complements to the colors in the range from 492 to 567 mμ. The color 492 is a greenish blue, while that of 567 is a pure lemon yellow. It is not possible to designate colors along this line by wavelengths, so it is customary to denote them by the wavelength of the complementary colors and place a small *c* after the number. Thus the color *Q*, which is complementary to the color *P* would carry the designation 506*c*, meaning that it is a color that is complementary to the color 506 mμ.

We have stated above that the eye cannot tell whether a given color is monochromatic or whether it is composed of a mixture of a great many colors This is made manifest when one plots the location of the hue transmitted by the A filter. The method of calculation is very interesting so it will be given here to serve as an example. We will consider that we are using daylight as our standard white. This is a color whose spectral distribution is well known. The intensity of each wavelength as it is present in this light is multiplied by the tristimulus value for that wavelength. This gives a measure of the stimulus intensity that each wavelength can give But the A filter passes only a definite percentage of the light, absorbing the rest. The product above must therefore be multiplied by the percentage transmission of that wavelength by the filter in order to obtain the tristimulus value due to the particular wavelength passed by the filter In this way there can be determined the values of the *X*, *Y*, and *Z* coefficients. If these values be determined for every wavelength that the filter transmits, and all the *X*'s added together, there will be determined the value of the *X* coefficient for the entire transmission of the A filter The *Y*, and the *Z* terms can be determined in a like manner. From these, the values of *x* and *y* can be calculated.

The transmission of the A filter begins at 570 mμ, where a total of 0.25 per cent of the light is transmitted. Light of this color has a relative intensity of 107.18 in daylight. The tristimulus values for this wavelength are $X = 0.762$, $Y = 0.952$, $Z = 0.002$ Hence the contribution of this wavelength to the total X value would be $0.0025 \times 107.18 \times 0.762$ or 0.20. The Y contribution would be 0.03, and the Z contribution would be completely negligible. In the table below is listed the rest of the values.

Wave-length	X	Y	Z	*Wave-length*	X	Y	Z
570	0.20	0.03	0.00	640	61.1	24.1	0.00
580	15.8	15.1	0.0	650	40.9	14.8	0.0
590	62.5	46.1	0.1	660	24.4	9.6	0.00
600	94.5	55.9	0.1	670	13.7	5.7	0.0
610	109.6	55.2	0.1	680	7.6	2.8	0.0
620	102.1	45.7	0.0	690	3.8	1.4	0.0
630	81.5	33.8	0.0	700	2.0	0.7	0.00
				Totals	619.5	310.0	negligible

The sum of X, Y, and Z, which is R, is 930. Therefore x is equal to 620/930 or 0.67, while y is equal to 310/930 or 0.33. This is the point A in Fig. 2. It is identically equivalent to monochromatic light of wavelength 610 mμ A similar calculation for the B and the C5 filters gives the following values:

B filter x is equal to 0.28 y is equal to 0.66
C5 filter x is equal to 0.14 y is equal to 0.07

These are the points B and $C5$ in Fig. 2. A glance at the diagram indicates that using daylight as our source, the A filter can be identified with monochromatic light of wavelength 610 mμ, the B filter can be matched by monochromatic light of wavelength 546 mμ mixed with approximately 15 per cent daylight, while the C5 filter can be matched by a mixture of one part of daylight and nineteen parts of light with a wavelength of 469 mμ.

Consider now a colorimeter where these are the primaries used. One half of the photometric field is illuminated by light of the unknown composition, and the other half is illuminated by a mixture of these primaries, the ratios being changed until a match is obtained. The question now arises how accurately will such combinations measure all the colors known to man. Of course it must be understood that the source of light behind the filters is daylight. Only those colors can be matched whose loci are located inside of the triangle $ABC5$. Any color which is located outside the confines of this triangle cannot be matched. A study of the triangle indicates that very accurate rendition will be obtained of all the colors, including the spectral, whose dominant wavelengths are greater than 540 Below that wavelength there is a very sharp decline in the accuracy of matching the purity of the colors. Thus a color with a dominant wavelength of 520 mμ will never be matched in a saturation or purity greater than 40 per cent. This continues until about the wavelength 485 mμ, when the best purity obtainable becomes 50 per cent. At 480 it is almost 70 per cent, and at 470 it is again at a maximum at about 90 per cent. Beyond this the efficiency falls off again. It is impossible to obtain accurate rendition of the pinks and violets, as far as purity is concerned, although the efficiency of reproduction never falls below 60 per cent. Very fortunately for us, colors as we are accustomed to experience them in nature, are never spectral in quality, so that it is very seldom necessary for

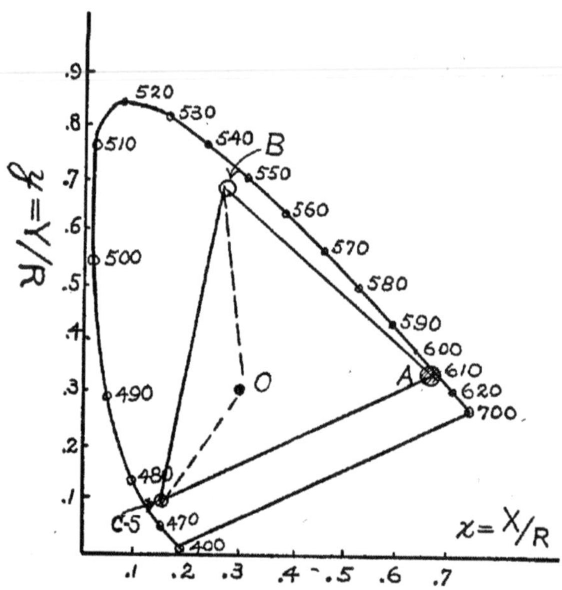

FIG. 2

us to attempt to duplicate colors outside of the triangle. The results in actual practice are therefore far better than would be expected merely from a glance at the triangle.

In the table below are listed the dominant wavelength and the purities of some Wratten filters, all of which have, at one time or another been recommended for separation work in color photography.

A. Red filters:

	Dominant Hue	*Purity*
No. 25	610	100%
29	631	100
70	628	100

B. Green filters:

	Dominant Hue	*Purity*
58	546	85
61	543	90
62	536	98
74	535	97

C. Blue filters:

47	469	95
49	466	99
50	566*c*	92

These filters are plotted on a chromacity diagram in Fig. 3.

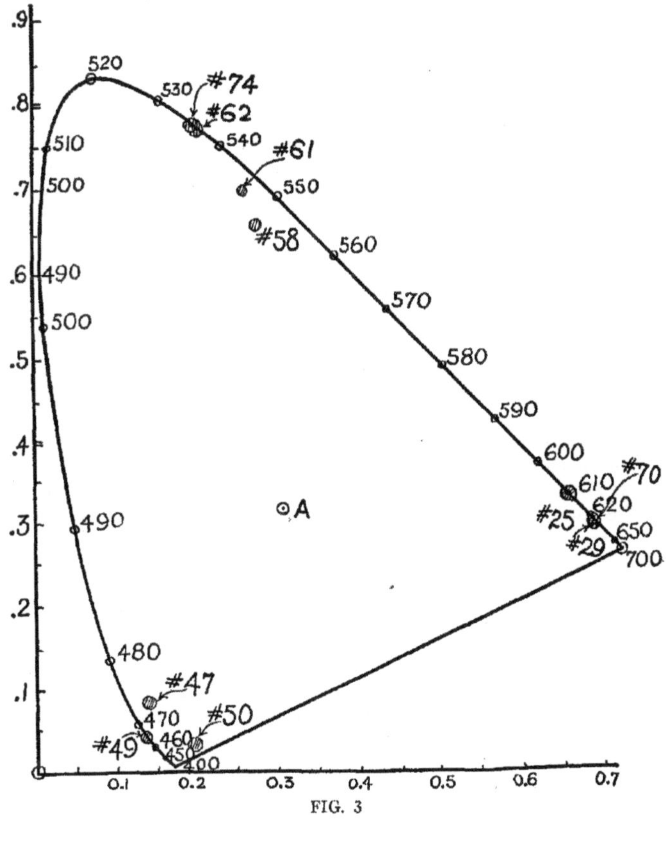

FIG. 3

CHAPTER 2

SUBJECTIVE COLOR REPRODUCTION

IN the previous chapter it was pointed out that any color whatsoever can be matched by the suitable mixture of three basic colors. This is an experimental fact that is not concerned with any possible hypothesis used to explain it. Young was the first to propound that the explanation lay in the human brain and that the optic system contained three sensitive elements which were differentially affected by the three primaries. In this respect Young differed from his many predecessors. Young's ideas were further developed by Helmholtz and Maxwell, the latter being the first to put into actual practice the consequence of the idea. But it is extremely interesting to note that the experimental procedure adopted by Maxwell was not a true application of the Young hypothesis He failed to recognize that the sensation curves which he obtained in the course of his work on colorimetry, were the basis for the theory of three-color reproduction. It was F. E. Ives who recognized this, and who incorporated it into his patent of 1890 (U S P 432,530). The curves Ives reproduced in his patent specifications were the color-mixture curves of Maxwell, who used an arbitrary set of primaries. Of course it must be remembered that there is no one set of basic colors, but an infinity of sets of such, each of which is convertible into the other. The Ives disclosure let loose a rather lengthy discussion from which very little seems to have resulted. The poor results that were obtained when using filters for color separation whose transmissions corresponded to the color-mixture curves, soon forced the subjective idea of color reproduction into the discard, and the further development of the subject of color photography appears to have proceeded along objective lines. But although the practical work in this field shifted away from the original Young theory, the interest in it continued. The literature is fairly replete with articles upon the theory of three-color reproduction. Especially, there has been a series of articles which re-opened the entire problem, and which bids fair to give the subjective processes a real test. Typical of these is the article by A. C. Hardy and F. L. Wurzburg, Jr, which was published in the *Journal of the Optical Society of America,* Volume 27 (1937), page 227.

In this study, use is made of the tristimulus values discussed in the last chapter. Let X_r, Y_r, Z_r, be the tristimulus values for unit quantity of the red primary, let X_g, Y_g, Z_g, be the values for the green primary; and let X_b, Y_b, Z_b, be the values for the blue primary Let the mixture of the three primaries at some point of the picture, be r units of the red, g units of the green, and b units of the blue. If X', Y', and Z' be the tristimulus values for the color depicted at this point, then we can write the following equation:

$$(1).\quad \begin{aligned} X' &= rX_r + gX_r + bX_r \\ Y' &= rY_g + gY_g + bY_g \\ Z' &= rZ_b + gZ_b + bZ_b \end{aligned}$$

Let the spectral distribution of the light that is reflected from the corresponding point of the subject be E, so that the tristimulus values at this point on the subject will be given by the form:

$$(2).\quad \begin{aligned} X &= \int_0^\infty E\bar{x}d\lambda \\ Y &= \int_0^\infty E\bar{y}d\lambda \\ Z &= \int_0^\infty E\bar{z}d\lambda \end{aligned}$$

where $\bar{x}$, $\bar{y}$, and $\bar{z}$ are the distribution functions of the observer. Perfect color reproduction will be obtained when X is identical with X', Y with Y', and Z with Z'. In practice there is allowable a certain tolerance, so that it becomes possible to write as a condition for perfect reproduction

$$(3).\quad X' = kX,\ Y' = kY,\ Z' = kZ$$

This must be true regardless of the form of the function E.

The first step is the preparation of separation negatives. Let the effective spectral sensitivity of the three photographic materials be S_r, S_g, and S_b. These values are defined as the products of the spectral sensitivity of the three emulsions, by the transmissions of the filters. Let the exposures impressed on the three emulsions when acted upon by E be Σ_r, Σ_g and Σ_b, where

$$(4).\quad \begin{aligned} \Sigma_r &= \int_0^\infty ES_r d\lambda \\ \Sigma_g &= \int_0^\infty ES_g d\lambda \\ \Sigma_b &= \int_0^\infty ES_b d\lambda \end{aligned}$$

Without making any assumptions regarding the subsequent procedure, let the process be one in which r, the amount of the red primary in the reproduction, depends only upon Σ_r and is independent of Σ_g and Σ_b. This can be done if the product of the contrast scales of the positive and negative processing be always equal to one, and if the processing is always maintained upon the straight-line portion of the H & D curve. Therefore it follows that

$$(5).\quad \begin{aligned} r &= k_r\Sigma_r = k_r\int_0^\infty ES_r d\lambda \\ g &= k_g\Sigma_g = k_g\int_0^\infty ES_g d\lambda \\ b &= k_b\Sigma_b = k_b\int_0^\infty ES_b d\lambda \end{aligned}$$

shall be able to prepare emulsions of this type. It is also an impossibility to prepare filters that have negative transmissions in a given range. But in their paper, Hardy and Wurzburg indicate several methods whereby such a net result can be obtained. Of these methods, the masking process is the only one of interest to us We shall have considerable to say concerning masking at a later time, but just now we will discuss their application of the technique. It is only the red-sensitivity curve that has a negative portion of sufficient moment to warrant reproduction The complete red curve is therefore split up into two different parts, one of which will utilize a filter whose transmission will start at 535 mμ, rise gradually to a maximum at 610, then fall gradually to zero at 700 mμ. This we will call the "normal" red separation.

In order to prepare the true red-sensitivity curve, the "normal" one must be corrected. This correction is made in the following manner. A filter is made which will have a transmission of zero at 400 mμ, and which will rise to a maximum at 510 mμ, a maximum that will have a relative transmission

VALUES FOR EQUATION 10

Wave-length	$\bar{x}$	$\bar{y}$	$\bar{z}$	S_r	S_b	S_g
400	0.01	0.00	0.07	0.00	0.03	0.01
410	0.04	0.00	0.21	0.00	0.11	0.02
420	0.13	0.00	0.65	0.00	0.35	0.05
430	0.28	0.01	1.39	0.00	0.74	0.13
440	0.35	0.02	1.74	0.00	0.91	0.15
450	0.34	0.04	1.77	−0.02	0.94	0.18
460	0.29	0.06	1.67	−0.03	0.92	0.19
470	0.20	0.09	1.29	−0.05	0.68	0.18
480	0.10	0.14	0.81	−0.07	0.43	0.18
490	0.03	0.21	0.47	−0.08	0.25	0.18
500	0.00	0.32	0.27	−0.08	0.14	0.23
510	0.01	0.50	0.16	−0.09	0.09	0.32
520	0.06	0.71	0.08	−0.08	0.03	0.43
530	0.17	0.86	0.04	−0.03	0.00	0.49
540	0.29	0.95	0.02	+0.04	−0.01	0.52
550	0.43	1.00	0.01	0.12	−0.01	0.52
560	0.59	1.00	0.00	0.23	−0.01	0.49
570	0.76	0.95	0.00	0.34	−0.01	0.42
580	0.92	0.87	0.00	0.46	−0.01	0.24
590	1.03	0.76	0.00	0.55	−0.01	0.24
600	1.06	0.63	0.00	0.58	0.00	0.25
610	1.00	0.50	0.00	0.62	0.00	0.09
620	0.85	0.38	0.00	0.49	0.00	0.05
630	0.64	0.27	0.00	0.37	0.00	0.00
640	0.45	0.18	0.00	0.22	0.00	0.01
650	0.23	0.11	0.00	0.16	0.00	0.01
660	0.16	0.06	0.00	0.09	0.00	0.00
670	0.09	0.03	0.00	0.05	0.00	0.00
680	0.05	0.02	0.00	0.03	0.00	0.00
690	0.02	0.01	0.00	0.01	0.00	0.00
700	0.01	0.00	0.00	0.00	0.00	0.00

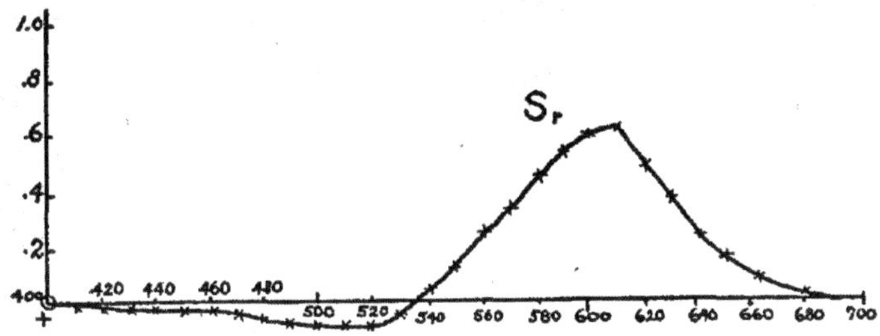

FIG. 4

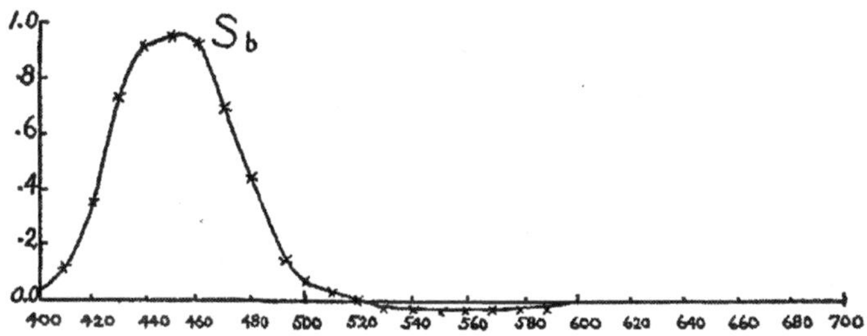

FIG. 5

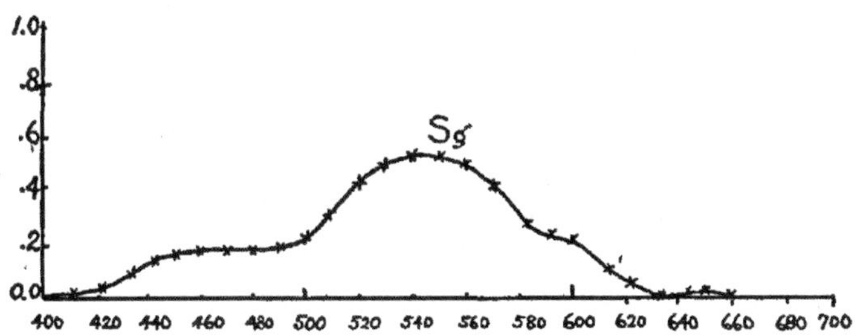

FIG. 6

of 0.09 as compared to a value of 0.62 for the maximum transmission of the "normal" filter at 610. Beyond 510 it will fall, reaching zero at 535. This will then be the exact negative of that portion of the curve that has minus values for the transmission, the range from 400 to 535. Instead of making three negatives, four will be made: one each through filters whose transmissions correspond to S_g, and S_b; a third through a filter whose transmission corresponds to the positive section of S_r, which we termed the normal red filter; and a fourth through the filter which is the exact negative of the other portion of S_r, whose specifications we have just outlined. From this last exposure, a positive is made, and this positive will be superimposed in exact registry upon the normal red-separation negative. A little thought will soon show that the combination of the negative taken through the "normal" red filter combined with a positive of the negative taken through the correcting filter, will yield a new masked negative that will approach the desired S_r sensitivity curve.

In the last chapter it was pointed out that as far as the eye is concerned, it cannot tell whether a given light consists of a blend of hues or is monochromatic. Thus, in a colorimetric apparatus there will be no distinction between the light that is transmitted by the A filter, and monochromatic light of wavelength 610 mμ. In the same manner, it should be possible to match the light transmitted by a set of filters whose transmissions correspond to S_r, S_g, and S_b. To determine the dominant wavelength and purity of each of these, we undergo a calculation identical to that made in Chapter 1 when the constants were determined for the various Wratten filters The transmission of the filter is multiplied by the relative intensity of each wavelength in the light source, then by the tristimulus value for that wavelength. The results are summed over the entire spectrum to give the X, Y, and Z values. From these the x, and y co-ordinates are determined, and the locus of the point corresponding to these values is plotted on the chromacity diagram The dominant wavelength and purity can be read off from the diagram. When this calculation is carried out, using light of daylight quality for our source of illumination, the red filter, S_r, has a dominant wavelength of 594.5 mμ and a purity of 100 per cent. The green filter, S_g, has a dominant wavelength of 520.5 mμ and a purity of 82 per cent. The blue filter, S_b, has a dominant wavelength of 468 mμ and a purity of 96 per cent. We compare three sets of filters, the standard A, B, and C5; the sharp-cutting 29, 49, and 61; the extreme set 50, 70, and 74, and the S_r, S_g, and S_b.

	Red		*Green*			*Blue*	
A	610 mμ	B	546 mμ	85%	C5	469 mμ	95%
29	631	61	543	90	49	466	99
70	628	74	535	97	50	566*c*	92
S_r	594 5	S_g	520.5	82	S_b	468	96

It is an extremely interesting phenomenon that of all the filter sets illustrated, the standard set approaches the ideal subjective curves most closely, but not sufficiently to be considered duplicates of them. It must be recalled, however, that the agreement cannot be too exact, as the ideal curves were developed upon the assumption that the product of the light intensity with the spectral sensitivity of the emulsion is a constant throughout the entire range from 400 to 700 mμ. This is only a very rough approximation.

Consider a colorimeter that contains filters whose transmissions correspond to those of S_r, S_g, and S_b. Such a colorimeter, of course, is an ideal that cannot be achieved, since it is not possible to make filters that have negative transmissions. Now compare this colorimeter with one in which the filters transmit monochromatic colors as follows: The red filter will transmit light of wavelength 594.5 mμ, the green filter will transmit light of wavelength 520.5 mμ and a purity of 82 per cent, and the blue will transmit light of wavelength 468 mμ and a purity of 96 per cent. As far as the eye is concerned, it would be impossible to distinguish between the two sets.

In this chapter we have adopted the point of view that color photography is merely applied colorimetry. Color analysis should then be an attempt to duplicate the mechanism by which the eye analyzes color, that is, in terms of filters such that the final result would be a spectral sensitivity that corresponds to the shape of the curves S_r, S_g, and S_b. It was indicated that as far as the eye is concerned these could not be differentiated from monochromatic filters whose transmissions are 594.5, 520.5, and 468 mμ respectively. Color photography in accordance with the subjective principles should be closely approached, therefore, if the analysis filters are made to correspond to these transmissions. This is an entirely different matter from the preparation of filters that correspond to S_r, S_g, and S_b. It should not be a difficult matter to prepare filters which would correspond to the above specifications. In fact the C5 filter is a very close approach to the proper blue. It must be borne in mind that it is not necessary to make true monochromats, for the eye cannot tell whether a given light is really monochromatic or whether it is a blend of many other colors. The red filters are very good examples of this, for as far as the eye is concerned these are true monochromats. From this point of view, it is also immaterial whether the range of transmissions of the three filters are mutually exclusive, or whether they overlap considerably at the edges, the only important thing being that the blend of the total transmissions must correspond to the specifications outlined above From the point of view of photography this means that broad bands could be used, a very useful concession, since this would allow greater speeds.

In additive processes, the same filters are used for taking and viewing. Thus in the line-screen and starch-grain processes the primary colors form a component layer of the sensitive material, and this is processed by reversal. Hence the same set of primaries is used in the final image. The above speculations are then at once applicable The starch grains, or the different lines that make up the filter layer, must be dyed to correspond to the specifications above It will be shown in a later chapter that by means of accurate processing it is possible to make the silver deposit correspond identically to the "density" of light that is reflected from the corresponding point in the original image.

But additive processes have a very limited application at the present time, since they are restricted to projection. The application of the above ideas to the subtractive processes is not so simple. In these procedures the positive that is made from the negative that is exposed behind the red filter, must be

CHAPTER 3

OBJECTIVE COLOR REPRODUCTION

IN the last chapter we discussed color reproduction from the subjective point of view. In that procedure the attempt is made to duplicate the processes by which color sensations are registered by the brain. Now we will discuss objective color reproduction, where the attempt is made to duplicate the processes which cause objects to appear colored This is purely a physical phenomenon, whereas the former is purely psychological.

The reason why any object appears colored, rather than a neutral gray, is that the object has a selective absorption or reflection of the light that is incident upon it. An object will appear to be colored yellow if it will absorb the blue and transmit the red and green rays. It is possible to draw a curve which gives the percentage transmission of each wavelength that is reflected from a colored object. This curve is called the spectrum of the color. In this case we no longer consider color to be a sensation sensed only by some mysterious forces within the human brain, but we must consider it a property of matter, the property of selective absorption of incident light. In this definition we can identify the color absolutely by its spectrum Two colors whose spectra are identical, will be identical under all conditions. If it be required to reproduce a given color, it is merely necessary to reproduce a color with an identical spectrum. This is the true aim of objective color reproduction.

There have been proposed many methods whereby the spectrum of a given color or set of colors can be duplicated automatically and precisely. The Lippmann process of interference photography is one elegant solution that received considerable attention at the beginning of the twentieth century. This process was first suggested or hinted at by J. Nicéphore Niépce (1829), but it was not until G. Lippmann used the grainless albumen emulsion described in Eder's *Handbuch* (Vol 2, p. 533), that any success was achieved. A grainless sensitive emulsion is coated upon a glass plate, and this is brought in contact with a highly polished mirror surface. When light waves pass through the glass plate and the emulsion and are reflected back by the mirror, the reflected light, will, in accordance with the principles of physical optics, be out of phase with the incident light by an amount equal to half a wavelength. The reflected and the incident light, traveling in opposite directions and being out of phase by one-half of a wavelength, will form stationary waves. These will be characterized by the fact that at the nodal points, situated half a wavelength apart, the two waves will just neutralize each other, and at these points the light intensity will be zero. At the crests, also situated a distance of half a wavelength apart, the light intensities will add to each other, and, at these points, the intensity will be doubled. If this takes place within the confines of an emulsion, then at the positions of the crests, there will be formed latent images, and after development, silver laminar deposits, capable of acting as mirrors. At the other points, there will be no photochemical action Each wavelength will deposit its own system of mirrors situated half a wavelength apart. When illuminated with light, each of these systems will reconstruct the original wavelengths, hence the original colors. But the illumination of these plates must be in accordance with the taking scheme; that is, with a mirror in contact with the print so that standing waves will be reformed. For this reason, the plates can be viewed only at a certain critical angle The process is very slow, because the use of grainless emulsions is necessary. These are about 10,000 to 1,000,000 times as slow as ordinary negative materials. For these reasons the Lippmann process has remained the plaything of the scientists The one very great contribution that work in this field has achieved, is the preparation of grainless emulsions that may be useful in fields more practical than interference photography. Their preparation is not essentially difficult. H. E. Ives (*Brit J Phot.*, Vol. 55 (1908), pp 942, 965, 979, Vol. 56 (1909), *Color Sup.*, p. 7), discloses the following procedure:

Solution A

25 parts Water (distilled)
1 part Gelatin

Solution B

50 parts Water
¼ part Potassium bromide
2 parts Gelatin

Solution C

5 parts Water
0.3 part Silver nitrate

Solutions *A* and *B* are warmed until the gelatin is melted, then they are cooled to 40 C, at which temperature solution *C* is added to *A*, and the mixture then added to *B*. After the addition of the sensitizing agents (pinacyanol, pinaverdol, cyanine, erythrosine, etc.), the emulsion is filtered, coated upon glass plates, washed for fifteen minutes in running water, then dried. R. E. Liesegang (*Kol Zeit.*, Vol 17 (1916), p. 36), disclosed a very convenient method for the preparation of such plates. Glass plates are coated with 6 per cent gelatin solution containing 3 per cent KBr. As soon as the gelatin has set, the plates are bathed for approximately five minutes in a 5 per cent solution of silver nitrate, after which they are washed with distilled water. The optical sensitization of these plates is not very easy. It seems that only erythrosine and cyanine could be used. Otherwise this method would be an extremely simple one

Another ideal solution to the problem of objective color reproduction is the "micro-dispersion" method. This was first disclosed by F. M. Lanchester

(Eng. P. 16548/95). In this scheme (Fig. 7), a lens L_1 projects an image upon a grating *G*, which consists of ruled parallel opaque lines, approximately 300 to the inch, with the width of the opaque lines about twice the width of the clear spaces between them. This image is then projected by a second lens, L_2, on to a screen. Between the second lens and the screen there is placed a prism whose angle of approximately 2 degrees, is sufficient to disperse the light traversing it into minute spectra that will just fill in the space between the images of the clear spaces in the grating. The axis of the prism is parallel to the lines in the grating.

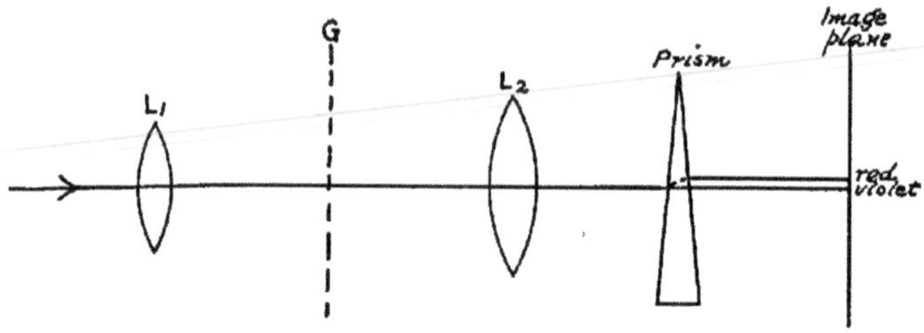

FIG. 7

By this scheme, the light that is reflected from the object is brought to a focus in the plane of the grating. This acts as a new original, composed of minute lines. The second lens will now image each one of the lines at a different point on the screen. When the image of one of the lines enters the prism, it is dispersed into a spectrum which is a true and absolute specification of the color of the light reflected from the corresponding point of the original. If the grating contains 300 lines to the inch, and if the second lens system magnifies the image three times, then the screen will contain 100 micro spectra to the inch, and the image on the screen will appear slightly coarser than the images in an ordinary magazine illustration, which breaks up the image into 133 units per inch. Now let us replace the screen by a panchromatic emulsion, and give this a balanced exposure. The negative, after development, will yield silver deposits whose densities will follow the spectral distribution of the light. Let us suppose that we are photographing a pure red light, consisting of all the wavelengths greater than 600 mμ. The negative will in that case have silver deposits only in that portion of each minute unit of 1/100 inch, which will correspond to the position of the red portion of the spectral band, say the upper third. The complete negative image will then consist of a series of lines, each one-third of 1/100 of an inch long, and running 100 to the inch. Let us now place this negative back into the original position, and this time project white light upon the grating, instead of colored light. The second lens will project this upon the screen, but upon the passage through the prism, the white light will be dispersed into a prism. In the position formerly occupied by the screen, we have placed our negative with its dot-like image. When this is synchronized with the grating, the image will just blot out that section of the minute spectra which will correspond to the wave-lengths that are greater than 600 mμ, hence the light that will emerge from the other side of this negative will be the exact complement of red.

Instead of processing the original to form a negative, it can be converted into a positive, taking great care that sizes are maintained in a strict one-to-one ratio. If such a positive be inserted in the position in exact registry with the image of the grating, then the color that will emerge will be red.

In an independent manner, and from a slightly different point of view, G. Lippmann (*Brit. J. Phot.*, Vol. 53 (1906), p. 644), whose contributions to color we have already discussed in this chapter, was led to formulate approximately the same scheme. Other workers who have disclosed similar or modified ideas, were P. E. B. Jourdain (*Brit. J. Phot.*, Vol. 46 (1899), pp. 232, 262), A. F. Cheron (Fr. P. 364,526), and M. Raymond (*Photo-Revue*, Vol. 19 (1907), p. 51), and J. and E. Rheinberg. These last used a line screen with 500 lines to the inch (*Phot. J.*, Vol. 52 (1912), p. 162). The clear spaces were three times as wide as the opaque. A direct vision prism giving a normal spectrum was used. Transparencies made from the negative had to be viewed in the taking apparatus. The Raymond disclosure appears to be of interest, as it indicates the use of a compensating prism in the viewing apparatus. A lens, L_1 (Fig. 8), projects an image of the object upon the grating G, which is similar to the one used by Lanchester. This image, consisting of lines a fraction of a millimeter in width, was then projected by another lens L_2 at

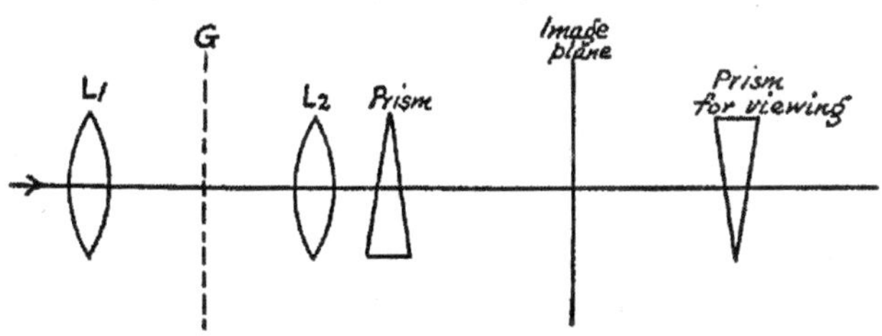

FIG. 8

a one-to-one ratio upon the sensitive material. Interposed between the lens L_2 and the emulsion was an appropriate prism to yield micro spectra that will just cover the spaces between the lines. Positives were made from the negative and positioned in the place formerly occupied by the negative. To view this, a compensating prism was placed between the eye and the positive.

The idea seems to have been dormant for some time. It was resurrected again by S. Prisner in 1931 (Eng. P. 341,078). In this scheme (Fig. 9), the light from a lens L_1 goes to a special lens L_2, which parallelizes it into a narrow beam, and causes it to fall upon a prism. The lens L_2, must obviously be of sufficient aperture to cover the entire image. The sensitive plate is placed with its emulsion side in contact or adjacent to the emergent side of the prism. For projection, the positive is placed between two prisms situated complementary to each other, and the entire assembly placed in the same relative position formerly occupied by the prism and the negative emulsion. F. Preinerstorfer (U.S.P. 2,088,399) disclosed an idea which appears to be a combination of the original Lanchester disclosure with that of C. Urban (Eng. P. 8723/07; Fr. P. 376,616). This last consists in placing the grating behind the second lens.

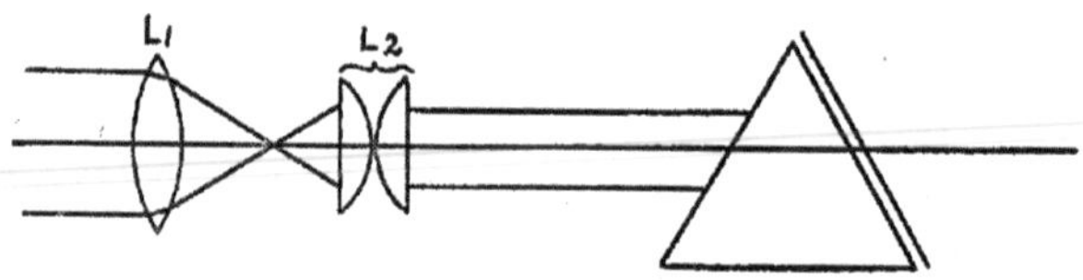

FIG. 9

The micro-dispersion methods of direct color reproduction are mere laboratory curiosities, principally because they are extremely slow, and because they call for very special apparatus both for taking and for viewing. In order to obtain satisfactory sharpness, the image must be broken up into at least five hundred lines to the inch. Thus each micro-spectrum must be less than 1/500 inch, and, in this extremely small space, there must be condensed the image of a spectral range of 300 mμ. A pure yellow would correspond to a silver deposit that covers only one-third of this area, so that the emulsion would have to be capable of resolving 1500 lines to the inch. I do not believe that many existing fast negative materials could give that resolution, and it must be remembered that this is but the minimum. Of course with grainless emulsions of the Lippmann type, this does yield an absolute solution to the problem.

It appears to me that the micro-dispersion methods may be utilized to prepare filters that have specified transmissions. In this case grainless emulsions can be used. Let us suppose that we desire to prepare a filter that will transmit 100 per cent of the remaining light. Then we set up a micro-dispersion system and photograph a white area, say a white opal glass. We illuminate this glass from the opposite side in the following manner. A source of light is dispersed into a broad spectrum by means of a wide-angled prism, and upon the emergent side of this prism is placed a template which will cut out all the undesired wavelengths. The template is made the "sandwich" filling between two prisms that are placed complementary to each other. The emergent light is projected upon the opal glass, and it is photographed to give a master from which duplicates can be made. These duplicates are then made the filling of a sandwich made of two complementary prisms identical to the one used in the photography. On the incident side of one of the prisms, there is placed a grating that is identical with the projection of the grating used in the original photography upon the prism when this is in the focal plane of the second lens. The completed sandwich will then act as a filter when illuminated by collimated light. Under ordinary circumstances, such filters would have very little application, and their preparation would merely serve as a convenient discipline But under certain conditions, as for example in investigations of a purely theoretical nature as to the effect of sharp-cutting or of widely overlapping filters upon reproduction processes, it may be essential to be able to prepare such ideal theoretical filters. It may be possible to prepare in this manner filters whose transmissions would correspond to S_r, S_g, and S_b. The masking process can be applied to the preparation of S_r in this case just as easily as in the case of ordinary photography, although much greater care must be exercised to maintain accuracy

The procedures outlined in this chapter up to this point are of only scientific interest, since their use involves conditions that are beyond the scope of ordinary practice. The successful application of objective principles that underlie methods of color reproduction, deals with attempts to approximate the spectral curves of the original colors, rather than with attempts to duplicate these curves exactly. The technique adopted to accomplish this is identical with the devices adopted by the mathematicians when they desire to determine the area under a complicated curve. The analogy is so close that it may be well to demonstrate the procedure in greater detail. Let us consider the spectral curve of the No. 30 Wratten filter, in the range from 400 to 700 mμ The transmissions are listed in the table below:

400	63 0%	500	0.0%	600	81 2%
410	61 4	510	0.0	610	84.5
420	57 6	520	0.0	620	86.0
430	52.8	530	0.0	630	86.7
440	45.8	540	0.0	640	87 4
450	38 1	550	0.0	650	87.7
460	29.5	560	4.0	660	88.0
470	18.2	570	31.6	670	88.0
480	8 0	580	63.1	680	88 0
490	1.3	590	75.5	690	88.0

The curve is shown in Figs. 10, 11, 12 and 13. The energy associated with the light transmitted by this filter is proportional to the area under the curve, and for that reason it is of interest to determine this value Incidentally the photographic effect of the light is directly proportional to the light energy. In order to determine this area, the mathematician will divide the curve into a series of rectangles whose upper side will be a straight line that is some average of the line that makes up the curve. The area under the curve will then be the sum of all the areas of the rectangles into which the curve has been subdivided. The area of each rectangle will be equal to the product

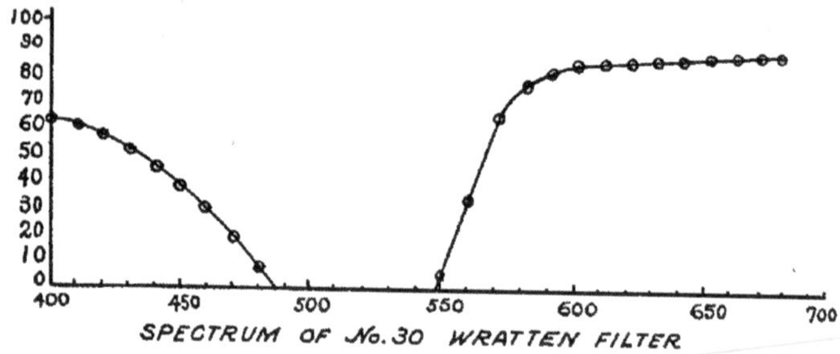

FIG. 10

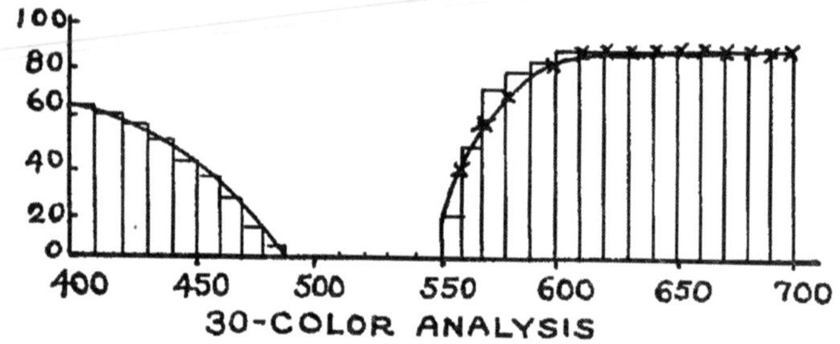

FIG. 11

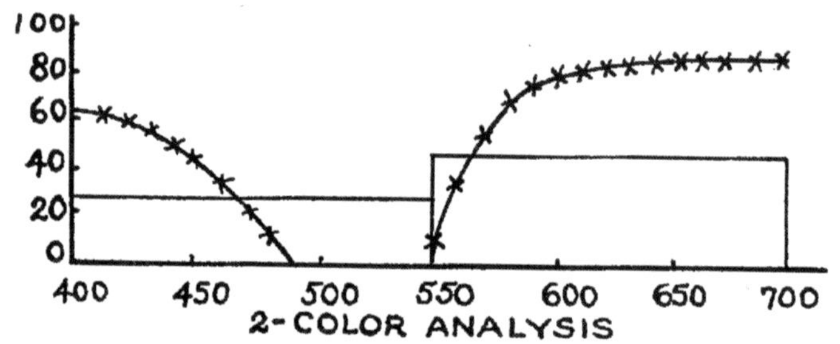

FIG. 12

of the width by the height, and if the first division is made into thirty equal parts, each 10 mμ in width, then the area will be ten multiplied by the value of the average transmission of the filter in that 10 mμ range. The rectangle bounded by the values 400 and 410 mμ will have an average transmission of $\frac{1}{2}(63 + 61.4)$ or 62.2 per cent, so its area will be 622 units. The areas in the other rectangles will be found in the same manner, and the sum will be a measure of the total area. Obviously the smaller the width of the rectangles, the closer will the approach be to the true value. The absolute value will therefore be obtained only when the curve is divided into an infinity of rectangles each infinitesimally wide. When this stage is reached, the mathematician says that he "integrated" the expression ydx, which represents the area under the curve if y represents the relative transmission of the filter, and x represents wavelength corresponding to the transmission.

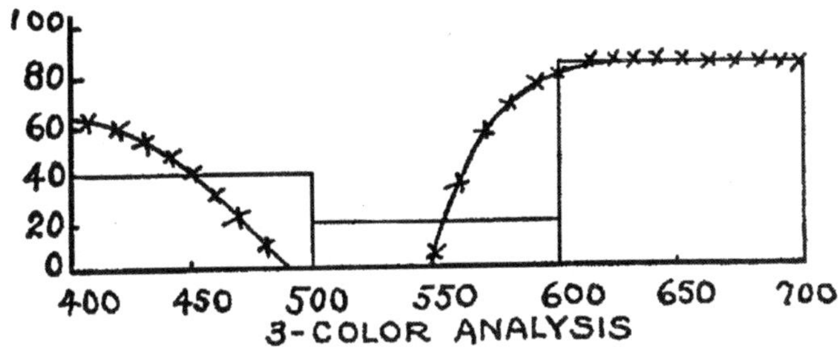

FIG. 13

It was stated above that the area under the curve is directly proportional to the energy associated with the light transmitted by the filter. This energy is also a measure of the photographic effect that the light transmitted by the filter will have upon an emulsion. When the photographer exposes a sensitive plate behind a filter, he is really making a determination of the light energy that the filter transmits. Hence a measure of the silver density produced by such an exposure is a direct measure of the area under the curve, and can be substituted for it. In order, then, to determine photographically the area under the curve, it becomes necessary to prepare a set of filters which will transmit only selected portions of the spectrum. If the analysis is to be made in terms of thirty elementary rectangles, then each filter must transmit completely the light in narrow bands of 10 mμ width, and absorb completely the remaining light. The light whose curve is to be determined is then brought into the lens of the camera, over which is placed these filters one after the other. Thirty exposures are required, timed to make up for the different relative sensitivities of the emulsion to the light passed by a particular filter. The plates are then all developed to the same contrast, and the densities measured. These values will be directly proportional to the relative transmissions in the filter, so that the thirty points will reconstitute the curve of the original color. Obviously to duplicate the curve exactly, there will have to be an infinity of such exposures through an infinity of filters, each of which transmits pure monochromatic light.

When the problem of objective color reproduction is restated in these terms, the question can be immediately asked into how few bands can the curve be divided so that the synthesized curve approaches the true one within the limits of accuracy attainable in reproduction processes Here eye tolerance plays a very large role. This is the only application of psychological processes that is used in the objective schemes This is made use of in the following manner. From each of the negatives prepared in the manner disclosed above, there is made a positive, so processed that the transmission through the positive will be identical to the transmission in the original filter, but this transmission is color blind. This can be done very easily, as will be made evident in Chapter 7. Each of these positives is then illuminated with the light that is transmitted by the filter behind which the corresponding negative was exposed, and the transmitted light is then projected in registry upon a white screen, or is led into the same half of a colorimetric apparatus. The other half is illuminated by the original light, and the two compared. The problem can now be stated as into how few bands must the color be analyzed in order that the eye will not be able to distinguish the duplicate from the original.

The smallest number of rectangles into which any curve can be divided is two, leaving out the trivial case of a single rectangle. To carry out this experiment, two filters must be prepared, the first of which transmits the light up to 550 mμ; the second transmits the light from 550 mμ on. The transmissions of the two filters must be mutually exclusive. When these requirements are met, and the colors compared in the colorimeter, it will be found that a surprisingly good approach to the truth will be obtained. There will be no inversion of colors; that is, there will be no cases where a red color would become duplicated as a green or blue, or vice versa. But no single color will be accurately reproduced.

The next simplest approach will be that of a three-band analysis. In this case the filter transmissions will be 400–500, 500–600, and 600–700 mμ. The hue of the first band will be a blue-violet, that of the second a pure green, and that of the third a red that verges upon the orange. When colors so duplicated are compared with the originals in a colorimeter, the approach will be found to be just within the limits of differentiation. It will be only when the original is placed directly beside the duplicate that a difference will be found between them. This very close correspondence, coupled with the hypothetical speculation of the Young-Helmholtz theories, gave rise to the belief that the one was an experimental verification of the other. But this is entirely an illusion. In the first place, the duplication was not made in accordance with the requirements of the subjective hypothesis, that is, in terms of filters whose transmissions correspond to S_r, S_g, and S_b. The two sets of filters differ very much, in that the ones suitable for the subjective processes overlap considerably, while the others are mutually exclusive. It may very well be that the dominant hues of the two sets of filters are not very far apart, as is seen from the table at the end of Chapter 2. It is this close approximation of the dominant hues of the two sets of filters that has given rise to so much loose talk, for when the different experimenters talked glibly of the three-color theory of reproduction as being based upon the Young-Helmholtz hypotheses, they utilized the mutually-exclusive filters for their experiments Hence their experimental work was not a test of their speculations — a fact realized very clearly by Hardy and Wurzburg in the paper detailed in the last chapter.

The very close approach which a three-band analysis makes to the original color makes speculation concerning a four-color analysis extremely interesting. The filter transmissions now must be 400–475 mμ, 475–550 mμ, 550–625 mμ, and 625–700 mμ. These colors are a violet, a bluish green, an orange-yellow, and a deep red, respectively. As far as is known this scheme has not yet been tested, but from the results of the three-color analysis, it may be inferred that the duplication of the colors by this system would be well beyond the ability of the eye to differentiate

So far we have discussed the analysis colors in color reproduction. The synthesis colors in objective systems must fulfill certain definite requirements as to transmissions and absorptions In the additive systems, the synthesis and analysis colors are identical, but in the subtractive systems they are complementary to each other. This was discussed slightly in the last chapter, but the same things are true here The positive print made from the negative that is exposed behind the red filter must be converted into a color that will absorb the red primary in proportion to the density of the image, and it must transmit completely the other two primaries Such a color will be a cyan, or blue-green Similarly the blue-filter positive must be converted into a yellow color which will transmit the red and the green, and absorb the blue The green-filter positive must be converted into a magenta hue, which will transmit the red and the blue, but which will absorb the green. Despite the high state of perfection of the dye industry, no dyes are known at the time of this writing which completely satisfy these requirements In fact, it is only the yellow colors that even approach the necessary transmissions to an extent of approximately 85 to 90 per cent. The other two colors are much worse. The blue-greens especially are poor in that they satisfy theory only to an extent of less than 50 per cent. The magentas are slightly better. Most of the very poor results in subtractive processes are due to this lack of satisfactory secondary colors. Some corrective measures have been disclosed in a procedure termed masking, but we will leave a discussion of this to Chapter 19. The ideal transmissions for the secondary colors in a three-color analysis scheme are listed in Fig. 14.

When the analysis of the color is made in terms of four bands, then the secondary colors must transmit three of these bands and absorb but one. The preparation of the secondary colors for a three-color analysis is far from perfect. The four-color secondaries would present a problem that is of a higher order of difficulty than the other Since no four-color color analysis has ever been attempted, there has not yet arisen the need for such secondary colors.

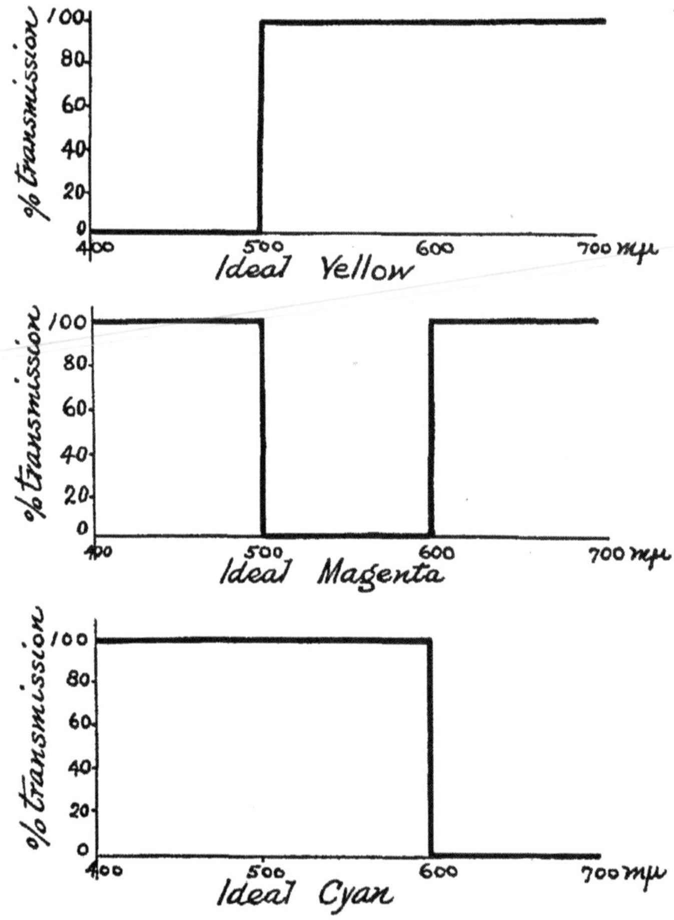

FIG. 14

The results outlined above can be generalized. Let us suppose we make our analysis in terms of n bands, which divide the spectrum into n equal divisions each $300/n$ mμ in width, and each of them mutually exclusive. As the number n increases, the need for exclusiveness is greater. The corresponding secondary color will in each case absorb one band that is $300/n$ mμ in width, and will transmit completely the remaining $n - 1$ bands.

CHAPTER 4

COLOR CAMERAS

FROM the discussion in the previous chapters it is evident that the first requisite for color reproduction is the preparation of color separations. When the subject matter is immobile, it suffices to photograph the object three times, each time through a filter which transmits but one of the primaries. In this manner three negatives are obtained such that each one of them represents the intensities of each primary at every point of the object But when the subject matter is such that it is not possible to effect this multiple photography, then the three exposures must be made simultaneously. This can be done by means of a one-shot camera.

Many variations of such cameras are possible, but in all of them there is one common factor. The light that is reflected from the object into the camera is divided into three sub-beams, and each one of the sub-beams is directed to a negative material that registers but one of the three primaries. It must be understood that the term primary is being used in a general sense, and not with the connotation current in subjective processes. By the term primary is meant the color or beam of light that is transmitted by one-third of the spectrum. The blue primary will therefore denote the ensemble of colors that have their wavelengths in the range between 400 and 500 mμ, the green primary will lie in the range between 500 and 600 mμ, and the red primary will lie in the region bounded by 600 and 700 mμ. Cameras differ from each other only in the design of this light-splitting mechanism.

The ideal camera will consist of a lens in combination with a light-splitting device which has the following properties. Let us suppose that a beam of white light enters the camera. It proceeds to the light-splitting mechanism which divides the beam into three sub-beams, and each of these is deflected to a different negative material. The ideal camera will so divide the main beam that all the red rays will constitute one of the sub-beams, all the green rays will constitute the second sub-beam, and all the blue rays will form the third sub-beam. Such a light-splitting device will lose no light due to the use of light filters, substances which lose at least 70 per cent of the incident light in three-color processes. Such an ideal camera is not an impossibility. It was disclosed by some scientists that by deposition of very thin layers of substances that have very high indices of refraction for certain colors with layers that have very low indices of refraction, it becomes possible to make reflectors which will transmit certain primary colors with great efficiency, approximately 90 to 95 per cent, and which will reflect other primaries with equally great efficiencies. Thus it will become possible to make reflectors which will transmit 90 to 95 per cent of the red and green primaries, and which will reflect 90 to 95 per cent of the blue. Our ideal camera will contain two such reflectors, one which will reflect the blue rays, the other which will reflect the green rays When a beam of white light enters the camera, the first reflector will transmit 90 per cent of the red and green primaries to the second It will reflect 90 per cent of the blue light There is thus a loss of only 10 per cent in light efficiency by the action of the first reflector. When the transmitted light reaches the second reflector, it will reflect 90 per cent of the green rays so that 80 per cent of the original green light will reach the green-sensitive negative material. This will also transmit 90 per cent of the remaining red rays so that 80 per cent of the original red rays will be deflected to the red-sensitive material. Since 90 per cent of the original blue rays will be effective, such a camera will have a light efficiency of over 80 per cent. It is permissible therefore to rate color cameras in efficiency, relative to this ideal.

The various light-splitting devices used in color cameras were classified by Adrian Klein in a very effective manner. In this discussion we will follow his classification, with a slight change in the order of numbering. This last is done to facilitate the discussion, rather than to attempt to improve his nomenclature. There are five main classes, of which two are of academic interest only. We will treat these first, so we designate them as Types 1 and 2.

1. Two or more lenses without beam division.
2. Two or more lenses behind inclined glass plates.
3. One lens in front of beam splitters.
4. Two or more lenses behind beam splitters.
5. A divergent lens in front of two or more lenses.

Before we begin our discussion concerning the various types enumerated above, it may be well to discuss briefly the elementary principles regarding lenses. When a beam of light passes from one medium (air), into another, which has an index of refraction that is different from the first, the direction of the beam is changed. The extent of this change is determined by the curvature of the interface between the two media and by the difference in the indices of refraction. From this fundamental fact, it is an easy matter to demonstrate exactly why the rays of light coming from a very distant point are brought to a point focus by means of a lens both of whose sides are convex. Such lenses are called convergent or positive lenses, and the ordinary lenses used in cameras are of this type. It is possible to grind the surfaces of a lens so that the beam of light that enters the lens is not brought to a point focus, but is spread out into another beam of light that is divergent. Such lenses are termed divergent or negative lenses. Both of these types are useful in camera design

In photography, the lenses commonly used have a focal length that varies from approximately one inch to twenty or more inches. In motion-picture work, and in candid cameras, where motion-picture film is used, the focal length of the lens is usually about 50 mm, or roughly two inches. This means that a beam of light that originates at infinity (relatively) will be brought to a point focus two inches behind the rear nodal point of the lens system. In still photography, when 5 by 7 inch film negatives are used the lens has a focal length of approximately eight inches. This means that the beam of parallel rays will be brought to a point focus exactly eight inches away from the rear nodal point of the system

Another characteristic of lenses is the aperture. This is a function of the effective diameter of the lens. It is customary to designate this property by a number like *f*:4 5, *f*:6 3, etc. This is the ratio that the effective diameter of the lens bears to the focal length, so that *f*:4.5 means that the focal length of the lens is 4 5 times the effective diameter Consider two lenses identical as far as structure is concerned, but differing only in *f* number, that is, one has a rating of *f*:4 5, while the other has a rating of *f*:9. This means that the effective diameter of the lens in one case is exactly twice that in the other How much light will enter the two lenses? The amount of light that enters a camera lens is determined by the effective diameter of the lens Suppose that the two lenses are of nine-inch focal length. The effective diameter in the case of the *f*:4.5 lens will be two inches, while in the case of the *f*:9 lens it will be only one inch The amount of light that will enter a lens is directly proportional to the area of the lens that is exposed to the beam of light This is proportional to the square of the diameter, so that in our case it becomes evident that the *f*:4 5 lens will receive four times the light that will be received by the *f*:9 lens.

Let us now consider what happens when we photograph an object situated about 25 feet away from the optical center of the lens system, with a camera that is equipped with a 9-inch focal length lens operated at an aperture of *f*:4.5. From every point on the object there will originate a cone of light, which, when it reaches the camera lens, will have a cross section equal to a circle with a diameter of two inches. The axis of the cone will be 25 feet in length, so that its angularity will be very slight. To all practical purposes we can disregard the fact that the beam of light is a cone, and consider it to be a bundle of parallel rays emanating from infinity. This bundle of rays will enter the lens of the camera at a definite inclination to the optical axis of the lens Since the bundle is to be considered as consisting of parallel rays, it will be brought to a focus at a point in the plane which is exactly nine inches behind the optical center of the lens, and perpendicular to the optical axis. This is the plane in which we place the negative material The exact position to which the rays will be focused is determined by only one fact, the angle which its axis makes with the optical axis. Two points on the object, that are separated by a very small amount, will generate two beams of light that will enter the lens system at different angles, hence the two beams will be brought to a focus at different points in the focal plane of the lens. This is a very important characteristic of lenses, and upon this property depends the entire system of lenticular processes.

We can now make short shrift of the devices that are classified in types (1) and (2). Consider the beam that originates from a point on the object, and which enters two lenses situated side by side, with their optical axes separated by a small amount Each lens will direct the beam entering it, to a negative material which is sensitive to but one primary. For the purposes of accurate registry, the relative positions of the point on the two negatives should be the same. Let us divide the two negative materials into squares, and call the point where the axis of the lens meets the negative material, the origin of a co-ordinate system which locates the squares. Now the position which the point under consideration will occupy in each of the two negatives, will depend only upon the angle which the beam of light that originates at the point, will make with the axis of the lens. But if the two lenses have their axes separated from each other, as they must have if they are not situated in the same place, then the angle which the beams make with the two axes must necessarily be different. Hence the relative positions that the point will occupy in the two negatives will be necessarily different. Absolute registry will therefore be impossible under these conditions. The practical requirements are so severe as regards registry, that even with a separation of a fraction of an inch in the optical axes of the system of lenses, the registry will be ruined and useless. But despite these insurmountable difficulties, inventors disclose cameras where the three separations are made through three lenses that are situated side by side, or in the form of a triangle, or in some other similar arrangement. It cannot be too strongly emphasized that correct registry under such conditions is impossible. Of course this is a great pity, since the use of three lenses would make possible the manufacture of cameras of great light efficiency, the only loss being that due to the absorption of the filters.

The early inventors in this field include Pfenninger (Eng. P. 25,908/06); Christensen (Ger. P. 203,110; Eng. P. 7,514/08, U.S.P 979,129); M. Maurich (Fr. P. 444,232; Ger. P. 264,085; Eng. P. 13,510/12); Featherstone (U.S.P. 1,034,006), Gaumont (Fr. P. 437,173, Eng. P. 3,220/12), and Ulysee (Fr. P. 459,669; Eng. P. 30,108/12). Later disclosures along these lines by G Griffith (U.S P. 1,589,754), Mannes and Godowsky of Kodachrome fame (U.S.P. 1,619,949); R. S. Alldridge (U.S.P 1,916,132; Eng. P. 322,801); C. L Fitz (U.S.P 1,931,983); and R. Thomas (U.S.P. 1,949,339). The disclosures of Thomas and Alldridge indicate some corrective measures to reduce the parallax caused by the non-identity of the optical axes, but at best these are of only doubtful value. Because of the inherent flaws, there is little need to continue the discussion of the various disclosures made in the above listed patents.

A more serious attempt to compensate for the parallax due to the use of several lenses adjacent to each other has been disclosed by A. J. Arnulf in a patent (Eng. P. 435,222) which forms the entire Type 2. Here parallel plates of glass are placed in front of the lenses at definite angles, and the claim is made that the consequent shift in the position of the image points will compensate completely for the parallax. We shall have reason to discuss in Chapter 5 devices which contain parallel-faced reflectors and transmitters, so that it would not be amiss to follow in the footsteps of Major Klein and treat this disclosure at some length. When light is incident upon a glass plate with parallel sides, at angle i, it will emerge from the other side of the plate at the same angle, but it will be displaced a distance d which can be determined from the following expression

$$d = E(1 - 1/n) \sin i$$

This expression holds when the angle i is less than ten degrees. The corresponding displacement δ on the negative for thickness E, will be given by

$$\delta = df/D = Ef/D(1 - 1/n) \sin i$$

Here D is the distance that the point is from the objective, and f is the focal length. When D is very large, that is, when the point being considered is at infinity, the displacement upon the negative will be zero. It becomes of considerable moment when the point is relatively near the objective.

Consider now the case depicted in Fig. 15, where the point A is photographed by means of two objectives, O and O_2. Let us consider the objectives to be ideal ones, and let O and O_2 be the nodal points. The rays that come from the point A and pass through O and O_2 will continue without deviation to the focal planes of the two objectives. The intersections will be the image points in the two cases. Thus the image of A will be A_1 when photographed by the first lens, and it will be A_2 when photographed by the second objective. The points B and C, situated directly behind the point A when the observation is made through the lens O, will yield images which will fall directly upon the image of A. But when observed through the lens O_2 these points will no longer be seen as positioned directly behind the point A, but somewhat on the side as well as behind. The lens O_2, will image these as three distinct points. This is the true meaning of parallax. There is no difference in image size, only a difference in the relative image position of the same point when photographed through two lenses. If the point A be moved back to infinity, the lens O would image it at A_1, but the lens O_2 will image it at the point Z_2 The distance A_2Z_2 is the extent of the parallax, and it is this amount that Arnulf attempts to correct for, by the use of a parallel plate glass placed in front of the two lenses. It is a very easy matter to compute the constants for a glass that will displace the image of the point A a distance equal to A_2Z_2, but this will not be sufficient to correct for the parallax. What is required is a scheme which will so distort the optical system of the lens O_2, that the images of the points A, B, C, D, E, etc., will all coincide, just as they

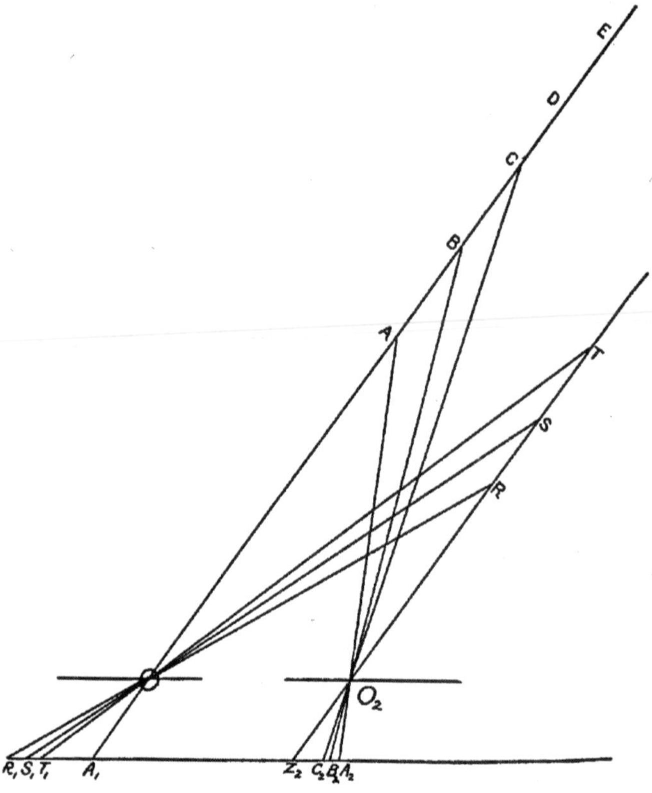

FIG. 15

do when the photography is done through the lens O. Not only must it compress the images from the points A, B, C, etc., into a single image, but it must also do the exact opposite with the points R, S, T, etc., which lie upon the ray that emanates from Z off in infinity, and which is imaged at the point Z_2 by the lens O_2 when no compensating devices are present. In the lens system O, these will give rise to the distinct image points R_1, S_1, T_1, etc. To escape from parallax, these should give rise to distinct image points in the second lens system. Thus the same optical device must compress the images of the points A, B, C, etc., into a single image, and it must spread out the image of the points R, S, T, etc., into distinct images. No effort is made in the patent disclosure to indicate that such would happen, nor is it indicated that such is even possible; all that is indicated is that it is possible to shift the relative position of the image any desired amount by placing a glass plate with parallel sides at an angle in front of the lenses. All the corrective measures that were disclosed in the earlier patents suffer from the same cause They shift the optical axes of the different lenses closer together, but they fail to correct for true parallax True parallax means that points which give rise to a single image in one lens system, give rise to distinct and separate images when viewed by means of another lens system.

CHAPTER 5

COLOR CAMERAS, TYPE 3

IN the Type 3 classification, there is included those cameras where the light-splitting devices are situated behind the lens. The lens beam is divided into two or more sub-beams, the intensity of each of which is a fraction of that of the original This type of camera is characterized by the fact that the sub-beams are all brought to a focus on different emulsions, but the points of foci all occupy the same relative positions in the three negatives. Thus there is completely eliminated the problems of parallax, provided the light-splitting mechanism itself does not introduce distortions. If due regard be taken of the optical requirements and properties of glass, such distortions need not appear.

The simplest type of light-splitting device is represented by a half-silvered mirror We will restrict the use of this term to designate reflecting surfaces that are uniformly coated with a thin deposit of metal, the deposit being so thin that it is partially transmitting and partially reflecting It is possible to construct another type of transmitting and reflecting mirror where a glass surface is only partially silvered and partially free from silver. The silvered portions of the surface are complete reflectors, while the non-silvered portions are completely transmitting. We will call this type of reflector a partially silvered mirror. While we speak of half-silvered or partially silvered mirrors, it must be understood that the coating need not be restricted to silver, but can also be made of gold, platinum, chromium, aluminum, etc.

The first camera disclosure was made by du Hauron in 1862. Here was disclosed the basic construction for a camera which utilized two semi-reflecting and transmitting mirrors, which divided the lens beam into three parts. This is illustrated schematically in Fig. 16. M_1 and M_2 are transparent mirrors, while M_3 is a completely reflecting mirror O is the optical center of the lens system The dotted lines represent the path traversed by the light rays. Let us consider the axial ray. This strikes the first mirror at b where it is partly reflected and partly transmitted The reflected beam is brought to a focus in the first image plane I_1 at the point p. The transmitted beam is again partly reflected and partly transmitted by the second mirror M_2. The reflected part is brought to a focus in the image plane I_2, giving rise to the point t, while the transmitted beam is directed to the mirror M_3 from which it is brought to a focus in the third image plane I_3 at the point i. The three points p, t, and i all occupy the same relative positions in the three planes,

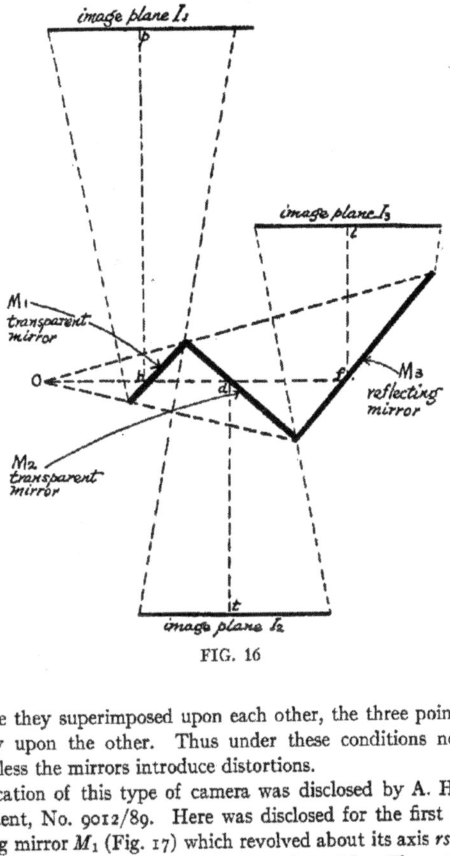

FIG. 16

so that were they superimposed upon each other, the three points would fall one directly upon the other. Thus under these conditions no parallax is possible, unless the mirrors introduce distortions.

A modification of this type of camera was disclosed by A. H. Cros in an English patent, No. 9012/89. Here was disclosed for the first time the use of a rotating mirror M_1 (Fig. 17) which revolved about its axis *rs*. Parallel to the plane of this mirror was a stationary mirror M_2. The rotating mirror was silvered only at certain sections, these being so arranged that the mirror transmitted light directly to the image plane I_1 part of the time, and the rest of the time it reflected the light to the mirror M_2. This reflected the light back again to the mirror M_1, but to a different segment of it, and the silvered and non-silvered sections of M_1 were so arranged that part of the time the beam that is reflected from the near end of M_2 will pass through a non-silvered portion of M_1, and the rest of the time it will be reflected again by M_1 to the far end of M_2. From here it is reflected to the image plane I_3. The transmitted beam is imaged at I_2. Thus the same lens beam gives rise to three image points in three different planes, which occupy the same relative positions in the respective negatives.

The original du Hauron chromoscope described above contains the really basic elements of camera design. In other patents, these elements were further developed. Thus in the original, du Hauron used silvered mirrors for his semi-transparent reflectors. In a later patent issued in 1874 (Fr. P. 105,881; Eng. P. 2,973/76) he disclosed another new idea. Instead of using a half-silvered mirror, one which is transmitting because of the thinness of the silver

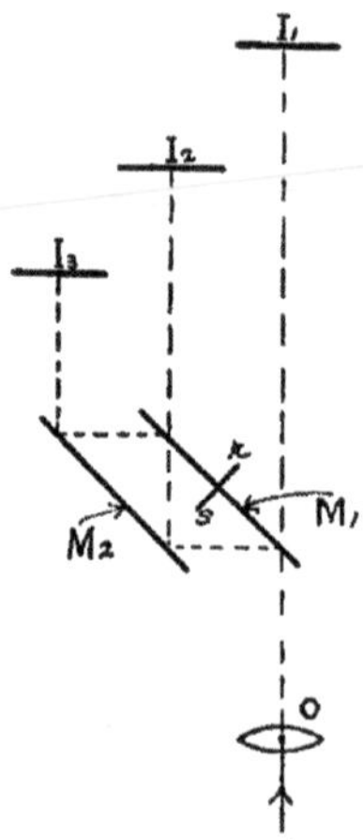

FIG. 17

deposit, he stated that it would be possible to achieve the same result if a mirror which was completely reflecting would be so treated that certain areas would have the silvering completely removed. These portions would then become completely transmitting, and the mirror would be composed of alternate areas that were completely transmitting and completely reflecting. The ratio of the transmission to the reflection could be governed by varying the respective areas of the silvered and non-silvered portions. The light efficiency of half-silvered mirrors is far from good. Thus, a mirror which has a surface coating of silver sufficiently thick to transmit twice as efficiently as it reflects will absorb about 30 per cent of the light that is incident upon it. This light is absorbed by the metallic deposit. If the deposit is made sufficient so that the mirror is completely reflective, then the amount of light that is absorbed by the metallic deposit is very low, not more than 5 per cent. Hence the du Hauron innovation gave a considerable increase in light efficiency.

The use of reflecting surfaces that are silvered only in selected areas has proven to be quite popular, and other inventors included such surfaces or modified forms of them in many successful cameras. Ives, for instance, a prolific inventor in the entire field of color reproduction, designed a camera where prisms instead of glass reflectors were used to split the light. The prism surface that actually divided the beam consisted of alternate bands of silvered and non-silvered portions (U.S.P. 703,929). A different form of the same idea is found in the French patent 350,004, issued to the Lumières. The beam divider consisted of two sheets of glass that had alternating silver and clear areas upon them. In one of the glasses the stripes ran horizontally, and in the other they ran vertically. The two sheets of glass were placed at right

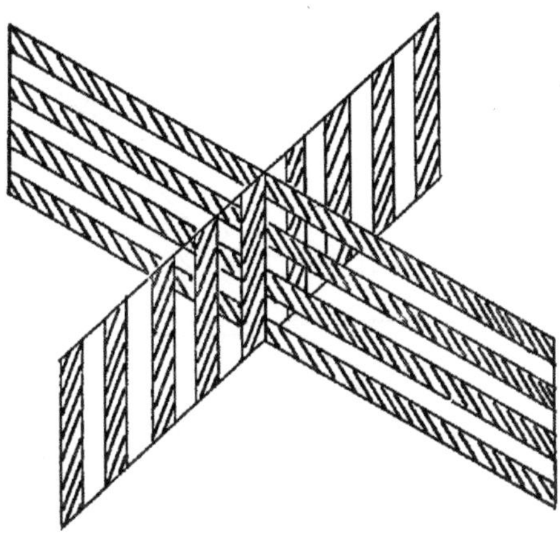

FIG. 18

angles to each other, forming a cross. The silver stripes were parallel to the intersection in one of the glasses, and perpendicular to it in the other (Fig. 18).

The idea crops up again in several of the very early Technicolor patents. In the English patent 101,972, and again in the United States patent 1,231,710, Technicolor disclosed light-splitting devices which utilized surfaces on which was spluttered metal in such a fashion that irregular patches of totally reflecting polygons were formed. This created a grid that consisted of minute areas that were totally reflecting, separated from each other by areas which were totally transmitting. This is a real improvement over the others since it removed any unevennesses that might be caused by the banded type of reflectors. A slight modification of this is disclosed in United States patent 1,451,774, issued to Holbrook and de Francisco. These gentlemen prepared the reflecting surface in the shape of a checkerboard, so that each transmitting area is surrounded by similar areas which are completely reflecting.

The disclosures discussed above all utilized glass surfaces or glass prisms to carry the metallic deposits. Where a glass surface is used, there is considerable danger that distortion is introduced. This is caused by the refraction of the rays as they penetrate the thickness of the glass. This is best illustrated in Fig. 19. Here *O* represents the optical center of a lens system, which would normally give an image in the focal plane of the lens. Now let us place a reflector in the path of the rays from *O*, at an angle of 45 degrees. Consider the axial ray *Ob*. In the absence of the reflector, this ray would give rise to the image point *m*, and the distance *Om* would be equal to the focal length of the lens. But when the glass reflector is present, the ray impinges the reflector at *b*, and instead of continuing on in a straight line to *s*, it becomes refracted and emerges at the point *e*, after which it continues along a line parallel to the

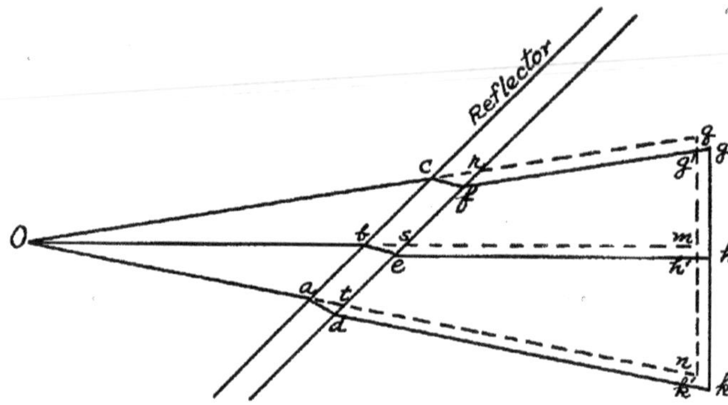

FIG. 19

direction *Os*. The optical path which this ray traverses must be identical to that of the normal ray. Let us suppose that the focal length of the lens is *p* inches. Then *Om* is equal to *p* inches, since the index of refraction of air is 1.000. The index of refraction of glass is 1.500. The optical path of the refracted beam is then equal to $Ob + be/1.500 +$ a distance along *eh* sufficient to make the sum total to *p* inches. Therefore the focal plane becomes moved back a trifle farther away from the lens. Not only is the focal plane moved back, but the axis of the lens drops a distance equal to *mh'*. This distance depends upon the angle which the ray makes with the reflector, and a glance at the diagram will quickly demonstrate that the terminal rays will make angles with the reflector different from that of the axial ray, and that all of them will be different from each other. Therefore *gg'* the distance which the upper terminal ray *Ocfg* is depressed will be different from *mh'*, the distance that the axial ray is depressed, and that is different from *nk'*, the amount that the lower terminal ray is depressed. If the thickness of the reflector is 0.10 inch, then the difference between *gg'* and *nk'* may be several thousandths of an inch, an amount that would cause serious registry trouble where the negatives are to be enlarged to any size at all. This defect was very quickly discovered by the various inventors, and many steps were taken to correct for it.

Ives (U.S.P. 622,480), and Strass Collins (Ger P. 102,206) suggested the use of wedge-shaped glasses, the thicker ends of the glasses being placed in the path of the rays which make the smallest angle with the glass Conrady and Hamburger (Eng. P. 28,722/12) would compensate for this distortion by tilting the focal plane somewhat. This has also been patented by W. Bermpohl (U.S.P. 1,951,896) in 1934, fully a generation later. Probably the best solution for this problem was offered by O. Pfenninger (Eng. P. 25,907/06). He placed a similar plate of glass in the optical path, but at exactly the opposite angle. Thus an equal but opposite distortion was introduced, and one negated the other. This distortion is completely absent when prism blocks are used instead of glass plates, but their expense does not make their use very popular. Besides the expense, the use of a prism block necessitates the use of special lenses, for the normal lens is corrected only for the glass distance that the rays travel through the lens. This distance would be multiplied by at least two in the case of prism blocks. The Pfenninger solution, while cheap and of little consequence upon the normal lens corrections, makes the camera somewhat bulky. It is not always convenient to place reflectors and compensators inside the limited space within the camera box

A very ingenious scheme which offsets this defect was disclosed by P. D. Brewster. Instead of using a glass surface for the reflectors, he used highly polished metal surfaces, and he made them partly transmitting by the mere expedient of drilling holes, so that only selected areas of the metallic mirror acted as reflectors, the remaining portions being open and devoid of metal. Because of their construction these reflectors were termed "Swiss Cheese Mirrors" (U S.P. 1,253,138; Fr P 483,761; Eng P. 100,082). In one form of the disclosure, the perforations in the metallic mirror were a series of parallel bands, duplicating the original du Hauron, Ives, and Lumière banded mirrors In another form the perforations were in the form of small holes, whose sizes changed toward the edges of the mirror. This is a duplication of the Comstock disclosures. In practically all of his many subsequent patents, Mr Brewster retained the idea of metallic mirrors rather than those of glass. There is one disclosure, however, in which Mr. Brewster designed a light-splitting device which used a glass plate surface coated with silver or platinum to make it semi-transparent. This plate was immersed in a cell which contained a liquid such as Nujol or other mineral oil, and which had an index of refraction that was the same as the glass. The cell sides were also made of glass with the same index of refraction. As is evident from the physics of this situation, the net result was the same as if a prism-splitter were being used. This little scheme made the cost of the light splitter a fraction of the cost of a similar glass prism. The defect of such a procedure lay in the fact that the lens corrections were completely negated. The use of prisms necessitates specially corrected lenses. This has been disclosed in United States patent 1,277,040.

Another method whereby the evils of refraction are eliminated is by the use of pellicle reflectors. A camera where this is used is disclosed by Reckmeier (U S P 1,895,555; Eng. P. 357,372). Here only one of the reflectors is of this type. The pellicle reflector is characterized by its extreme thinness, approximately 0 005 inch. It is usually made of cellulose, celluloid, or cellophane that has been stretched taut in a frame, so that the pellicle will lie evenly and without distortion. When they were first introduced, it was not possible to coat them with metallic reflecting surfaces, but there have lately been developed methods of metallic spluttering (Eng. P. 440,006) which give the proper metallic semi-transparent mirror surfaces. Methods of casting such pellicles have been disclosed by Adrian Klein (Eng. P. 380,938) The displacement of the image due to a pellicle that is 0.005 inch thick is completely negligible

The use of crossed mirrors has been disclosed in quite a few patents. Some American patents where such mirrors are used are the following: 1,217,391 to C. N. Bennett, 1,631,058 to H. Piloty; 1,812,765 to M. Astafiev; 1,857,578 to W. L. Wright; 1,897,097 to W L. Wright; and 1,986,425 to O. O. Ceccarini.

In camera systems where semi-transparent mirrors are used, each negative receives the light from the full beam that enters the lens, but at a greatly reduced intensity. This was not the case with the camera designed by A. H. Cros and described above. As will be recalled, Mr. Cros used a rotating mirror to deflect the full lens beam to another mirror, which then deflected it to the proper negatives. This camera was disclosed in 1889, a full generation before Mr. Brewster, who has sometimes been credited with the first introduction of rotating mirrors This is rather difficult to see since there have been several other predecessors Dallmeyer (Eng. P. 22,616/98) proposed to use a camera in which a single mirror was placed behind the lens, the mirror then being rotated to reflect the light to two sides of the camera. A similar idea was used by Gaumont (*Jahrbuch*, Vol. 16 (1902), p 543). In 1919 J. Dourlen and M. Chretien (Eng. P. 141,368) disclosed a camera which used rotating mirrors to deflect the lens beam to three sides of a rectangle, but this had evidently been previously disclosed by Gebay in 1913 (Fr. P. 464,637). Mr. Brewster's disclosure did not appear until 1930 (U.S.P. 1,752,477 and 1,860,525) In an article published in the *Journal of the Society of Motion Picture Engineers* (Vol. 16, p. 49), Mr. Brewster states the case for rotating mirrors. It has the advantage of not having to transmit the image through a block of glass, which results not only in a loss of light, but also in a loss of definition around the edges. But most important of all it makes possible the use of lenses with a focal length as little as 50 mm at an aperture of *f*: 2, allowing the placement of the lights fairly close to the object. This gives better efficiency for the light Just slightly later than Mr. Brewster, J A. Ball of Technicolor Motion Picture Corporation also disclosed the use of revolving mirrors (U.S.P. 1,871,649 and 1,924,901).

An entirely different principle for dividing the lens beam into two or more sub-beams is disclosed by Ives in United States patent 632,573 (1899). In this disclosure the cross section of the lens beam is divided into three parts by means of prisms which lie immediately behind the lens. Thus (Fig. 20) the pencil of parallel rays which enters the lens comes from a common point on the object being photographed. Immediately behind the lens there are placed two prisms. Part of the lens beam, marked *a* in the diagram, is incident upon the upper prism. These rays are deflected to the point *f*. Another part

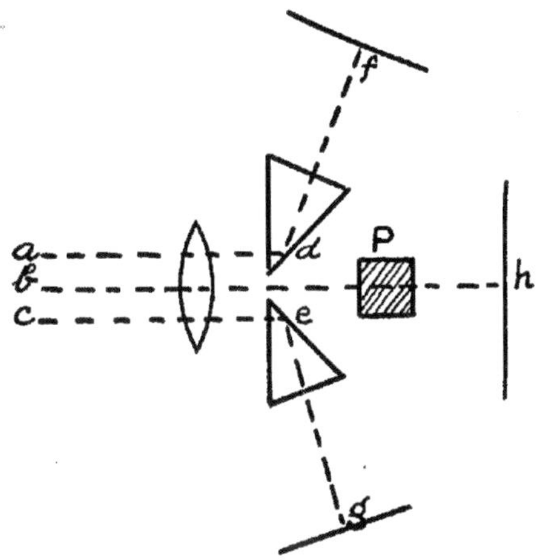

FIG. 20

of the lens beam designated by the letter *c*, is incident upon the lower prism, and these rays are deflected to the point *g*. The central portion of the beam passes through an opening between the prisms, and this is brought to a focus at the point *h*. In order to equalize the optical paths of the three beams, a glass block is placed in the path of the central rays which do not pass through any of the prisms.

Five years later, in 1904, O'Donnell & Smith (Eng. P. 4127/04) devised a camera where the same result is obtained by the use of mirrors directly behind the lens. This is illustrated in Fig. 21. Here again the lens beam *abc* emanates from a single point on the object being photographed, hence the rays are parallel to each other. That portion of the rays marked *a* is reflected by a total reflecting mirror *M* to the point *d*. Another portion passes through directly to the point *e*. The third portion marked *c*, is deflected by the mirror *N* to the point *f*. Hence a common point on the object becomes imaged at three different points, *d*, *e*, and *f*, all occupying the same relative positions in the three focal planes P_1, P_2, and P_3. Much more recently, the Jos Pé Company disclosed the same idea in several of its patents (U.S.P. 1,597,818;

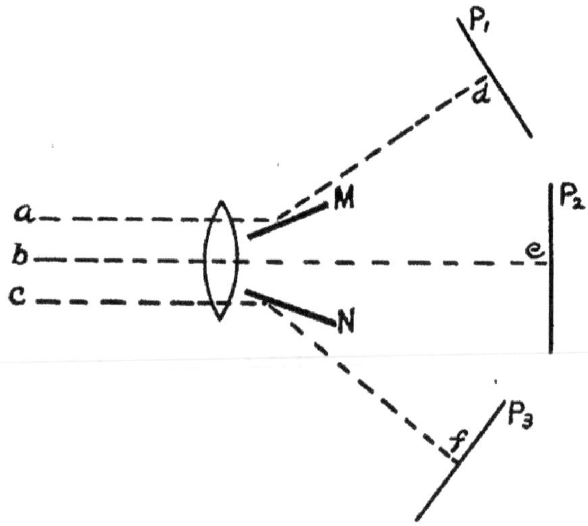

FIG. 21

Eng. P. 243,714 and 243,716 issued to H. Piloty; U.S.P. 1,801,143 issued to R. F. P. Defregger).

The Ives disclosure was somewhat changed in a patent issued to Dr. L. T. Troland of Technicolor (U.S.P. 1,843,007; Eng. P. 350,112). Here a prism block is placed immediately behind the lens system (Fig. 22). The prism block is designated by the shaded area in the diagram. The surfaces *M* and

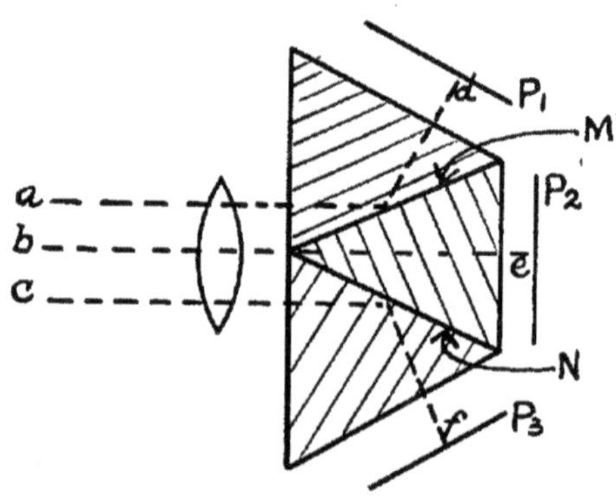

FIG. 22

N are semitransparent. Therefore the image in the plane P_2 is constructed from the entire lens beam. The upper portion of the beam, which is incident upon the surface M of the prism, is partly reflected to the image plane P_1, and there gives rise to the image point d. The image point f is similarly formed from the portion of the lens beam that is incident upon the surface N. Fundamentally, this does not differ from the original Ives disclosure, except in the details of construction. This disclosure has one great advantage over that of Ives in that the path of the rays through glass is identical in all three cases, so that there is no need to place corrective glass blocks in the path. Different only in structural details is the camera designed by W. M. Thomas (U.S.P. 1,957,371 and 1,988,882).

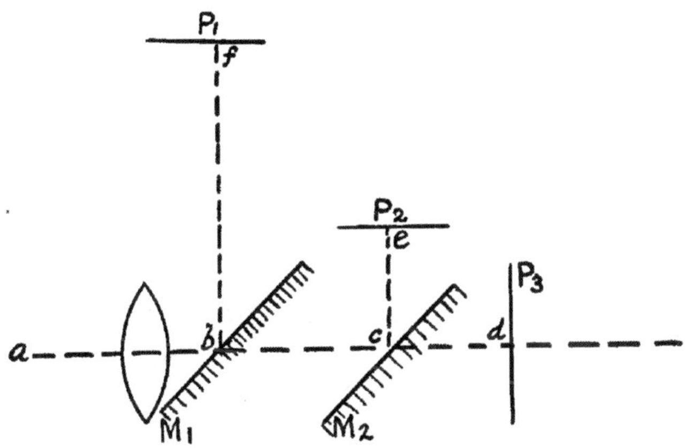

FIG. 23

The simplest and most popular types of cameras go back to the original design of du Hauron (cf. Fig. 16). Here the beam that enters the lens is made incident upon three reflectors one after the other, and each reflector deflects part of the beam to a different image plane. Edwards (Eng. P. 3,560/99) reduced the number of reflectors to two. He also disclosed the use of colored reflectors, thus eliminating the presence of double images. Part of the ray "a" which enters the lens (Fig. 23), is deflected by the top surface of the mirror M_1 to the image plane P_1, where it is brought to a focus at the point f. The remainder of the ray continues to the second deflector M_2. But the bottom surface of the mirror M_1 also acts as a reflector, and this would give rise to another image point in the plane P_1, which would not coincide with the point f since this image traversed two thicknesses of glass at the point b. But if the reflector M_1 be colored with a substance which absorbs the wavelengths that are to be registered in the image plane P_1, then this second image point would not be registered. Let us suppose that at P_1 we register the blue primary. Therefore in front of the emulsion, or somewhere in the path *bf*, there is placed a blue filter. Now if the mirror M_1 be colored yellow, the ray that will be reflected from the bottom of this mirror will be completely lacking in blue light, hence will not be able to register in the plane P_1. The ray *bf*, which is reflected by the front surface of the mirror will not be affected by the coloring matter. If the image plane P_2 is made to register the red primary, then the mirror M_2 should be colored green, so that no red rays will be reflected from the bottom surface of that mirror.

It is possible to arrange the mirrors in many different ways in order to obtain three images by this system. This has given rise to a large number of patents, each utilizing the same fundamental principles, but each having a more or less complicated arrangement of the mirrors. Nachet (1895); White (1896); Butler (1897); and Dawson (1912), were some of the other early inventors in this field. Somewhat later came Albert (U.S.P. 1,607,661); G. Cuenin (U.S.P. 1,637,294); Bermpohl (U.S.P. 1,951,896); Jacobsen (U.S.P. 2,082,579); and many others too numerous to mention.

Everything that can be done by means of mirrors, can also be accomplished by means of prisms, and every single disclosure which utilized a mirror has its counterpart in a patent which does the same thing by the use of prisms.

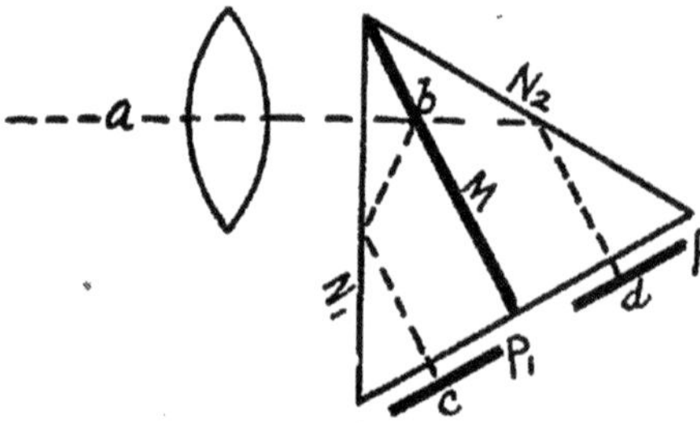

FIG. 24

Technicolor, outside of the few patents that concern themselves with metallic rotating mirrors, seems to have confined itself solely to the use of prisms for light-splitting devices. Thus Comstock and Ball disclosed a rather ingenious device which gave two images upon adjacent frames of a film (U.S.P. 1,451,325; Fig. 24). The prism block is in the form of a triangle. It is really composed of two right-angled triangular prisms cemented together along one side. This common juncture between the two prism components, marked *M* in the diagram, is semi-transparent. The lens beam entering the prism block is therefore divided into two beams when it strikes this surface. One of the beams continues on to the surface N_2, where it is totally reflected to the image plane P_2, while the other beam is reflected back to the surface N_1 from which it is again reflected to the image plane P_1. The application to three-color separation is of course obvious. The same idea crops up again in a patent issued to Dr. Troland (U.S.P. 1,821,680).

There may be some advantage if the three images can be placed upon the same piece of film, or upon the same plate. This means that the optical device must be such that the three image planes fall in a common plane. One of the very first to do this was Ives (U.S.P. 660,442) in 1900. The lens beam *a* (Fig. 25) first strikes the semi-transparent mirror M_1 at the point *b*. Here

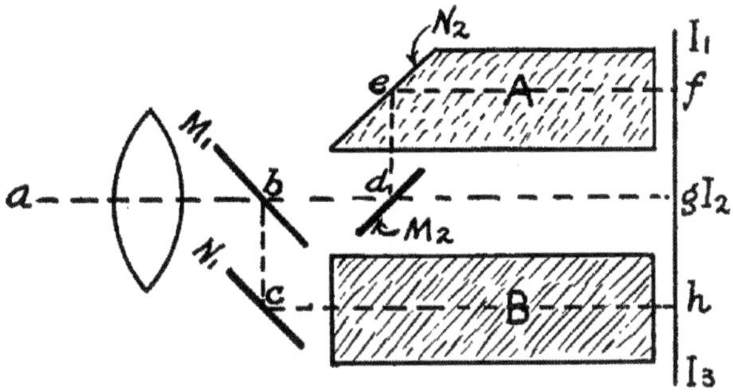

FIG. 25

it is divided into two beams. One of these continues to a second semi-transparent mirror M_2 where it is again divided into two beams. The total division is therefore into three beams. One of the beams is reflected off at *d* to the prism block *A* where it is totally reflected at the point *e* to the image plane I_1. Another beam continues from *d* in a straight line to the image plane I_2. The third beam starts at the point *b* and by means of a reflection by a mirror N_1, is directed to the image plane I_3. A glass block *B* is interposed in the path of this beam. The thicknesses of the glass blocks *A* and *B* are such that they equalize the three optical paths, and allow the three image planes to exist in a common plane. The three images could therefore be imaged upon the same piece of film or plate. Selle, in an early English patent (Eng. P. 12,514/99), used a similar system of mirrors to accomplish the tripartite division of the beam, but instead of using glass blocks to equalize the optical paths of the two outer beams, he put an auxiliary lens into the central beam to shift its focal plane forward until it lay in the same plane as the other two. Kunz (U.S.P. 1,319,292) combined the mirrors with the glass blocks so that a single block accomplished the same result. His scheme is indicated in Fig. 26, which is self-explanatory. Isensee (Ger. P. 334,776) accomplished a similar result, but instead of using a prism block made of glass, used a cell whose sides were glass, but whose interior was filled with cinnamic ether, which has a very high index of refraction. This is an obvious extension of the Brewster idea previously discussed.

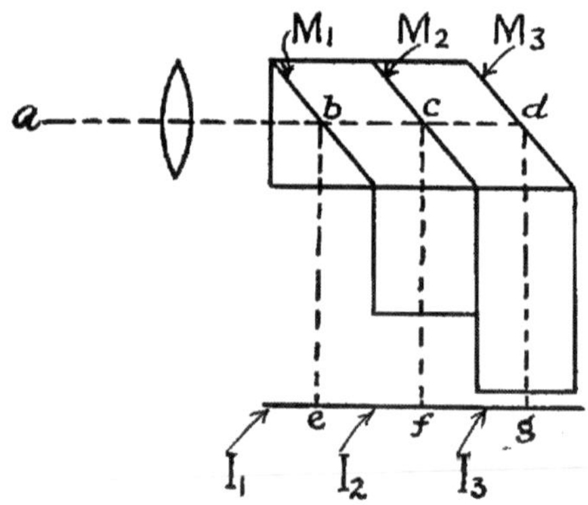

FIG. 26

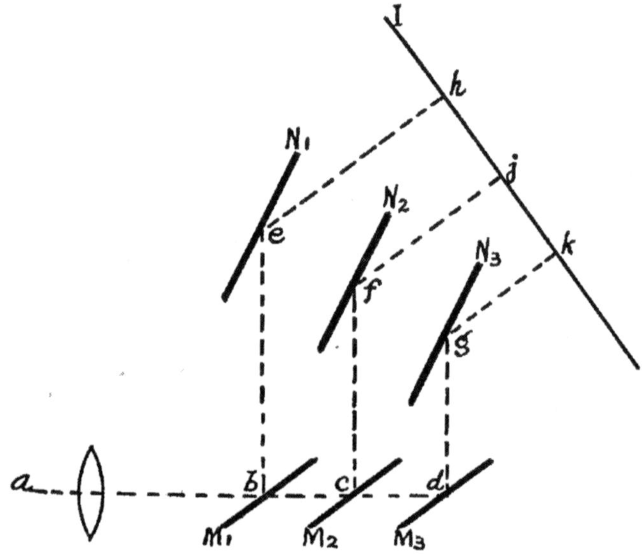

FIG. 27

A somewhat different arrangement was disclosed by L. Albert (Fr. P. 554,056; U.S.P. 1,607,661). Six mirrors were used. Of these (Fig. 27) two were semitransparent, M_1 and M_2, while the others were totally reflecting. The lens beam *a*, after reflections from the six mirrors, gave rise to the three image points *h*, *j*, and *k* all in the plane *I*.

CHAPTER 6

COLOR CAMERAS, TYPES 4 AND 5

IN a previous chapter it was pointed out that the cone of light which starts from any point on the object and enters the camera lens can, to all intents and purposes, be considered as a pencil of parallel rays. The position on the negative where these rays are brought to a focus is determined solely by the angle which the beam makes with the optical axis of the lens. If we have a system that utilizes two or more lenses, then it is incumbent upon the designer to see that the various sub-beams make identical angles with the optical axes of the separate lenses. It is only under those conditions that a given point will occupy the same relative position on all negatives.

Now let us consider a beam of light which emanates from a single point on an object, and which is split up into three beams by a system of semi-transparent mirrors. Each of the three beams will be made to enter a lens.

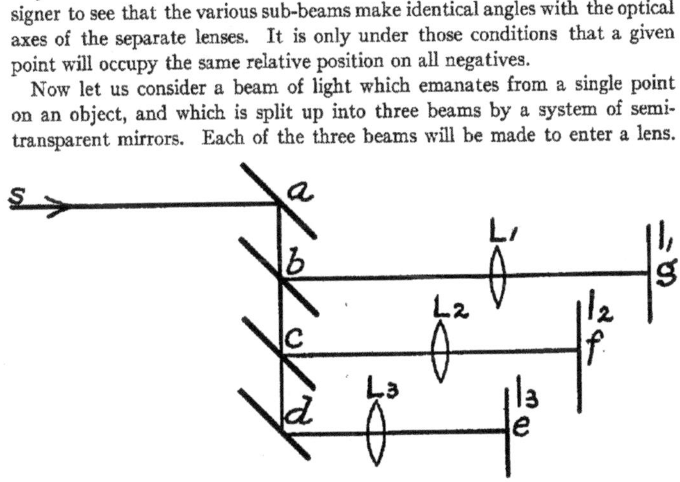

FIG. 28

This type of system, where the light-splitting device lies in front of the lens system, characterizes color cameras grouped under Type 4. A very simple scheme along this line was disclosed by Procoudin-Gorsky (Eng. P. 185,161/15). The beam of light, *s*, emanating from the object being photographed (Fig. 28) is first incident upon a total reflecting mirror *a*. The beam continues in the new direction at right angles to the old, until it strikes a semi-transparent mirror *b*. Part of the beam is again reflected at right angles, and is brought to a focus at the image plane I_1 by the lens L_1. The rest of the beam is transmitted to a second semi-transparent mirror *c*, where the same thing occurs. The reflected beam is brought to a focus in the image plane I_2 by the lens L_2. The transmitted part is totally reflected by the mirror *d*, and it is then brought to a focus by the lens L_3 in the image plane I_3. A glance at the diagram shows quickly that the three sub-beams make identical angles with the optical axes of the three lenses, hence the points *e*, *f*, and *g* all occupy the same relative positions in the three negatives.

Because this scheme is the first mentioned, it must not be inferred that it is the first mechanism disclosed which utilized a light-splitting device in front of the lenses. A similar type of technique was disclosed in 1900 by that

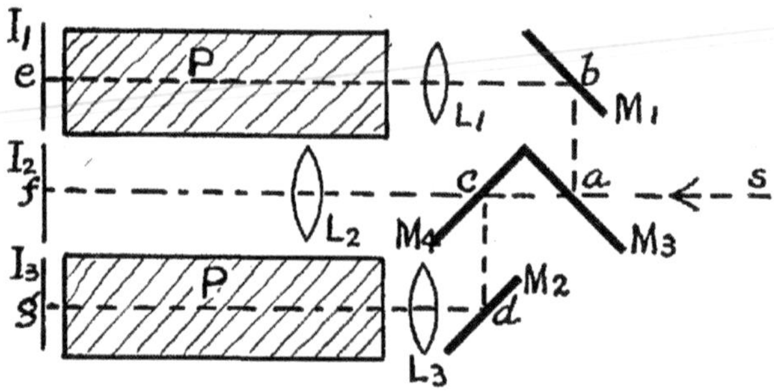

FIG. 29

prolific inventor in color photography, Ives (U.S.P. 660,442). The beam coming from the object strikes a semitransparent mirror (Fig. 29) M_3, and is partly reflected to the second semitransparent mirror M_4 which is at right angles to the first. The first part beam is reflected at *a* to the mirror M_1, which in turn reflects it to the lens L_1. The second part beam is again partly reflected at *c* to the mirror M_2, which reflects it in turn to the lens L_3. The transmitted beam at *c* is directed to the lens L_2. It is quite apparent from the diagram that the paths of the three beams are not the same, but that the two reflected beams travel somewhat greater distances than the direct beam. In order to equalize the three paths, Ives inserted blocks of glass, *P*, in the paths of the reflected beams.

The insertion of the blocks of glass created some problems, since they had a tendency to obliterate the lens corrections, which were calculated only for the glass distance in the lens system itself. Sacré (Fr. P. 460,310) disclosed practically an identical scheme, except that he left out the glass blocks which equalized the optical paths. This type of camera gave a slight parallax for the central beam, but if this is used for the blue filter image, it may not be very noticeable. Both Ives and Sacré place the three images upon the same negative, that is, in the same plane. This may be desirable from the point of view of convenience of operation; Horst (D.G.M. 757,468) accomplished this in a rather simple fashion, by merely by-passing the beams given distances, until the optical paths became identical. The diagram illustrating this (Fig. 30) is self-explanatory. *M* and *N* are total reflecting mirrors, *R* and *S* are semi-transparent mirrors.

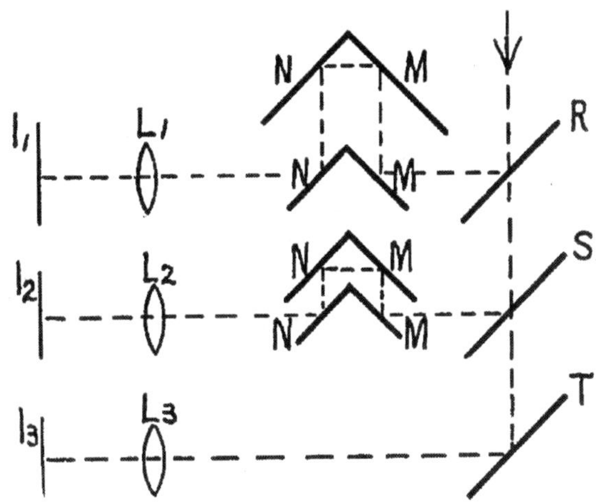

FIG. 30

A more complicated scheme is that of W. L. Wright and S. MacDonald (U.S.P. 1,641,466), and W. L. Wright (U.S.P. 1,688,606). In the second of these, the beam is made incident upon a series of semitransparent and totally reflecting mirrors (Fig. 31) which divide it into three sub-beams, each of which

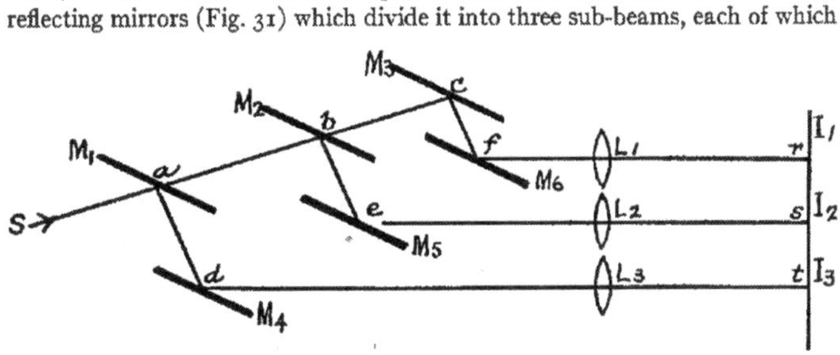

FIG. 31

is directed to a different lens. The three images lie in the same plane. A somewhat different scheme is disclosed by W. L. Wright in two patents (U.S.P. 1,730,712 and 1,930,498). Here the beam meets three mirrors, one after the other, so arranged that three images are formed in the same plane by means of one lens. The first semitransparent mirror, M_1 (Fig. 32) meets the beam at an angle that is slightly less than 45 degrees to the lens axis. The second mirror, M_2, is inclined at an angle of 45 degrees. The third mirror, M_3, is inclined at an angle slightly greater than 45 degrees. The three beams deflected by the three mirrors meet at the front nodal point of the lens system, L, and are imaged by L at the three points d, e, and f, all lying in the same plane. To equalize the optical paths, compensators c_1, c_2, and c_3 are placed between each mirror and the lens. These are blocks of glass of sufficient thicknesses to make up for the difference in the beam lengths. This means

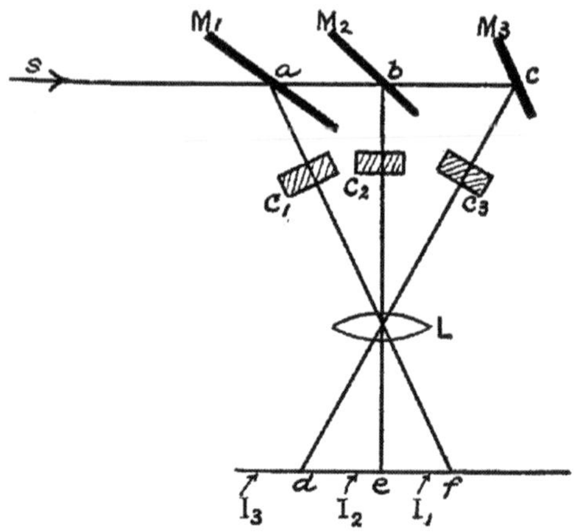

FIG. 32

that the distance *af* must be equivalent to *abe*, and these two must be equivalent to *acd*. Compensation is brought about by the fact that the optical distance that a beam travels through glass is equal to the thickness of the glass divided by its index of refraction, which is usually about 1.5000. Therefore if a beam travels for a distance of one and one-half inches through glass, it is equivalent to a distance of only one inch in air, which has an index of refraction of 1.000. Therefore the block c_3 must be much thicker than the block c_2, and this in turn must be thicker than the block c_1. This scheme may equalize the optical paths of the three beams, so that the points d, e, and f will fall upon the same plane, but it does not guarantee that the images due to beams at other angles will occupy the same relative positions with respect to each other, in all three images.

Most of the inventors in this field seem to have gone to great lengths to place the three images in the same focal plane, so that all three images could be photographed at different portions of the same plate. In certain respects this may seem like a good idea, in that but a single plateholder is required in the case of still pictures, and a single film-moving mechanism in the case of motion pictures. But this insistence leads to complications in the optics of what would otherwise be a very simple system. F. A. Bourges discards the idea completely, and very frankly couples three cameras behind a mirror light-splitter of the type disclosed by Procoudin-Gorsky. The three camera movements operate in unison, thus insuring registry. This is disclosed in an English patent (460,335). Another disclosure where three separate image planes are used was patented by R. E. Reason (U.S.P. 2,053,224; Eng. P. 418,671 and 423,190). Here there is a peculiar combination of types. The main beam (Fig. 33) is split into two by the semitransparent mirror M_1.

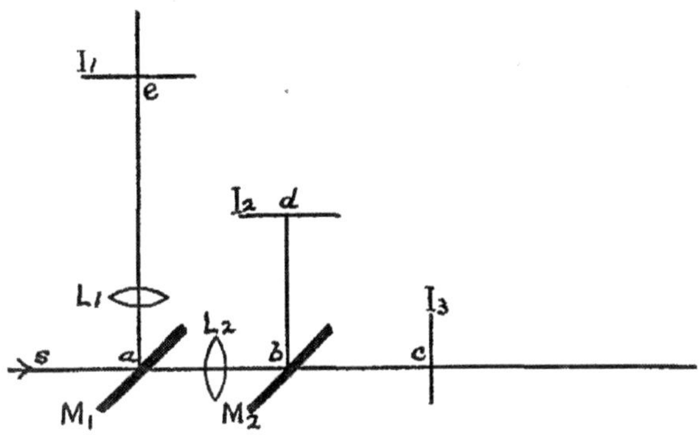

FIG. 33

The reflected beam is imaged by lens L_1 in the image plane I_1. The transmitted beam passes through lens L_2, then is split into two parts by the mirror M_2, giving rise to images in the planes I_2 and I_3. It is quite evident that regardless of the angularity which the beam makes with the optical axis of the lens L_1, it makes the same angle with the axis of the lens L_2.

A. G. Hillman, in a series of patents (Eng. P. 404,307, 414,059, 414,065, and 434,719) discarded the idea of equalized light paths. The light beam was split into two by means of a system of perforated and unperforated metallic mirrors, and each beam was deflected into a separate lens. The two lenses were situated one immediately above the other. Obviously the beam which entered the upper lens traveled a greater distance. The film (this idea was disclosed for use in motion pictures only), traveled past the two lenses one frame at a time. Two adjacent frames were exposed at one time. After each exposure, the film advanced one frame, and at the same time the filters changed, so that the filter which was in front of the top gate shifted to the bottom one. Let us suppose that at a given exposure, the red filter is on top and the green filter is on the bottom. In this manner, the top frame is exposed to the red primary, and the bottom frame to the green. After the exposure, the film advances one frame while the filters change positions. For the second exposure, the top frame is the same one which had previously received an exposure behind a green filter. In its new position, since the filters also changed, it is again behind the green filter. Thus each frame receives two exposures through the same filter. The film advances through the camera at the standard black-and-white rate. The separations, two-color, are present as alternate frames in the finished negative. It is claimed that because each frame receives two exposures, the parallax due to obvious inequality of optical paths is ironed out, and therefore not noticeable. This scheme can be used for three-color also, either by the use of three lenses, or by the use of two lenses but three filters.

Another rather ingenious scheme utilizes a single lens behind a mirror system, to give two images. This was disclosed by Bennett (Eng. P. 10,150/12) considerably before Wright. Here (Fig. 34) the beam of light falls upon a

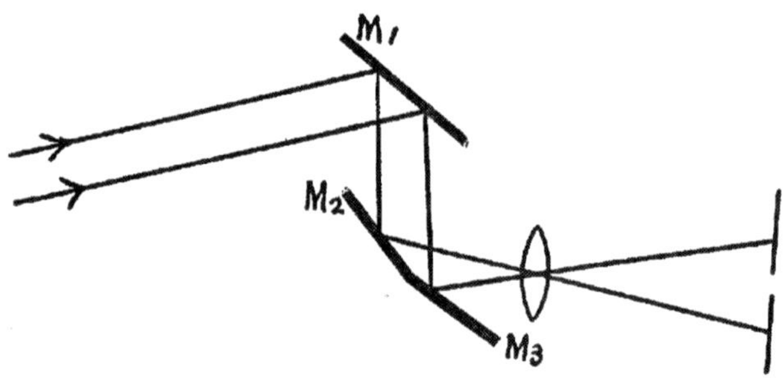

FIG. 34

totally reflecting mirror M_1 situated above the lens. This reflects the beam to two mirrors situated in front of the lens and at a slight angle to each other. The lens will image the beams from the two mirrors M_2 and M_3 at different portions of the same plane. By having the angle between the two mirrors at a proper value, it is possible to maintain the equality of the optical paths and also the equality of the angle which these beams make with the optical axis of the lens. In this case, the lens does not directly image the object being photographed, but images the reflection of the object in the mirror M_1.

Everything that can be done by mirrors can also be duplicated by prisms. The patent literature is fairly replete with disclosures of various prism designs which split the light into two or three beams. J. F. Romer, in a series of patents disclosed numerous designs of prisms which receive a single beam of light, and which transmit two, three, and four beams to an equivalent number of lenses. It is therefore possible to image two, three, or four images upon the same plate (U.S.P. 1,722,356, 1,722,357, and 1,765,882; Eng. P. 257,546,

257,547, 257,548, and 257,549). Twyman (Eng. P. 16,811/15; cf. also, 16,810/15) placed a simple prism block in front of the two lenses (Fig. 35), and a compensating block behind the lens which received the reflected beam. Practically the identical scheme, changed only to place another compensating

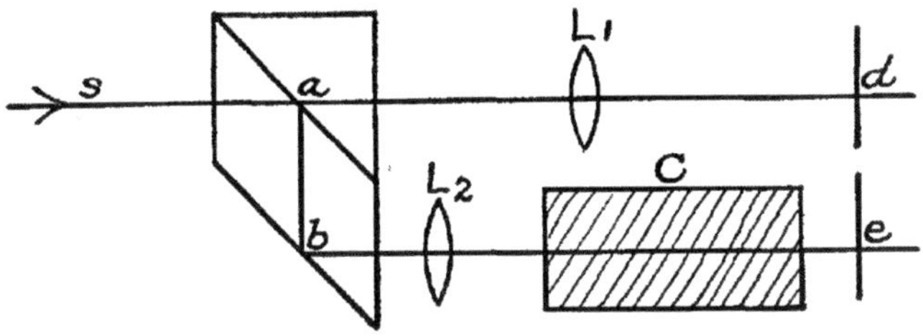

FIG. 35

glass block in the path of the transmitted beam, was patented considerably later by V. Hudeley (Eng. P. 444,051).

K. Martin and P. Tietze placed a simple prism block (U.S.P. 1,752,680; Eng. P. 276,591) in front of two lenses. Behind these lenses were deflecting prisms, designed to direct the two beams so that they emerge as parallel beams and are brought to a focus in the same plane (Fig. 36). Other prism

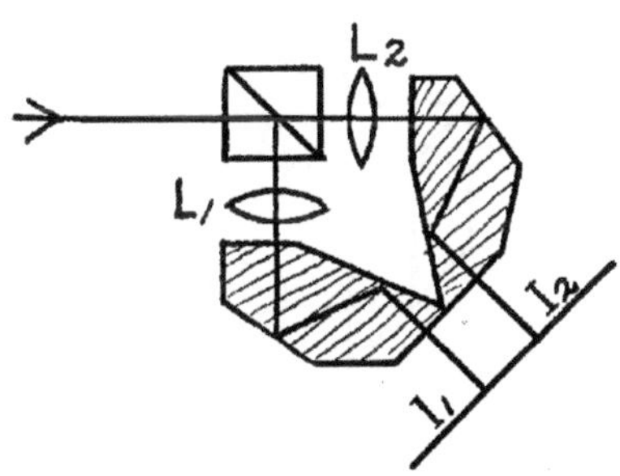

FIG. 36

devices were disclosed by A. Schustek (U.S.P. 1,845,062); D. Daponte (U.S.P. 1,945,029; Eng. P. 346,406); C. LeRoy Treleaven (U.S.P. 1,696,739); T. A. and R. T. Killman (U.S.P. 2,060,505); and A. Pilny (Eng. P. 342,036). Obviously there are infinite numbers of variations possible. F. E. Tuttle, of the Eastman Kodak Company, disclosed a novel method to equalize the optical paths of the different rays, by shifting the nodal points in the lenses. This is disclosed in U.S.P. 1,897,874. A simple prism divides the beam into two sub-beams, and directs them to two lenses. These lenses differ from each

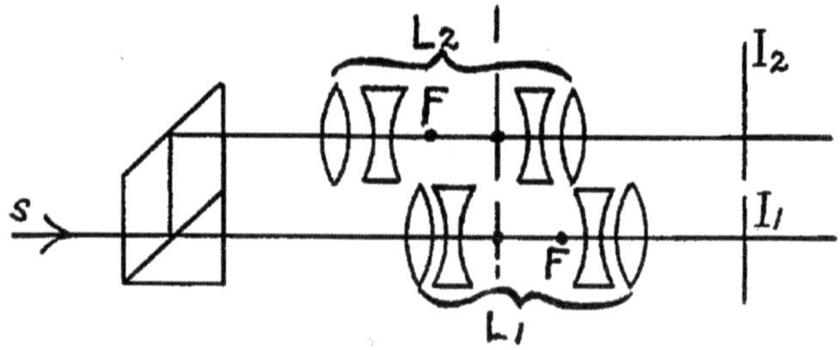

FIG. 37

other in that the front nodal point F on one lens is shifted a distance equivalent to the difference in the optical paths of the two rays (Fig. 37).

L. Didier placed a simple prism system in front of three lenses. Only two of the lenses (Fig. 38) received the light from the same beam, while the third lens received the light from a different beam. No effort was made to equalize the optical paths of the beams. Parallax was therefore present on two accounts (Eng. P. 306,329). Similar schemes were disclosed by J. M. Gutmann and P. Angenieux (Eng. P. 437,414, cf. also 385,141 and 419,894).

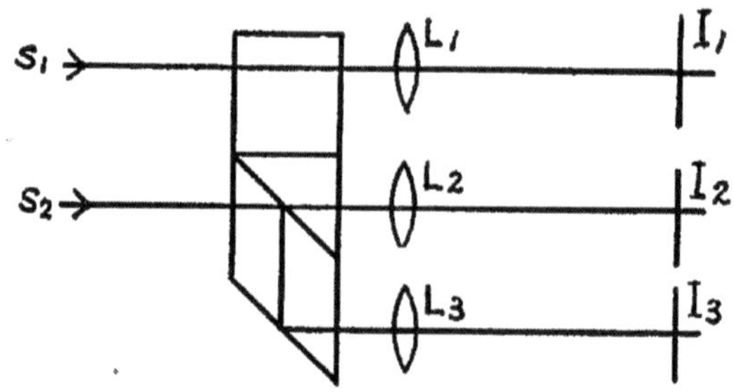

FIG. 38

A series of very important patents were issued to J. H. Dowell and Adam Hilger, Ltd. In these patents (U.S.P. 1,839,955; Eng. P. 349,107, 388,754, and 427,983) there is discussed the fundamental requirements for a prism system which will give two or more images that are identical in size and free from parallax, after transmission through a colored filter. Such prisms are constructed of glass, and it is usually found that the identity of sizes formed through these prisms is satisfied only for objects at infinity. When objects are not at infinity, it is found that the identity requirement is no longer satisfied.

In order that this be true for all objects, both near the lens and at infinity, two conditions must be satisfied. The first is the usual condition which practically all inventors satisfy, the condition that the reduced optical paths of the beams and sub-beams be identical. Thus if a given beam travels through air and glass, the following relationship must hold for each color. This is illustrated in Fig. 39. The beam enters the prism at a and proceeds to the semi-transparent mirror M_1. Here part of the beam is reflected to the totally reflecting mirror M_2, while the rest of the beam is transmitted to the mirror M_3, where it is reflected to the mirror M_4. The one beam travels through glass a distance equal to $ab + bc + cd$, then through air a distance dr, where

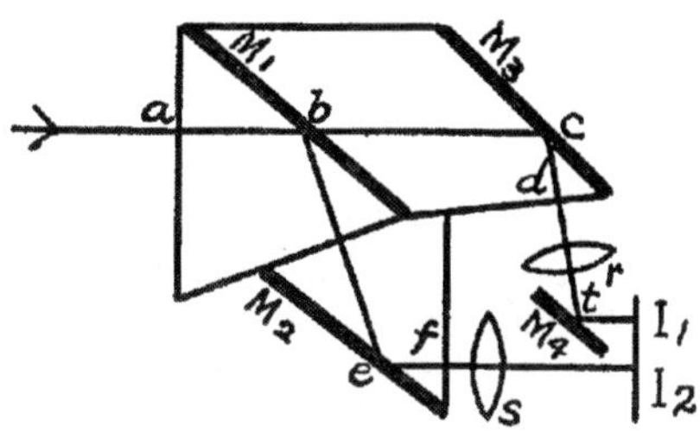

FIG. 39

r is the front nodal point of the lens. The total reduced optical path which this beam traverses will be, supposing that this beam registers the green image,

$$\frac{(ab + bd + de)}{N_g} + \frac{dr}{1.000}$$

where N_g is the index of refraction of the green rays for the glass used. The index of refraction of air is taken as 1.000. The other beam will traverse a glass path equal to $(ab + be + ef)$ and an air distance equal to fs, where s is the front nodal point of the second lens. This beam registers the red primary, so that the optical path traversed by this beam will be given by

$$\frac{(ab + be + ef)}{N_r} + \frac{fs}{1.000}$$

where N_r is the index of refraction for the red rays. The first condition to be satisfied is then the following:

$$\frac{(ab + bc + cd)}{N_g} + \frac{dr}{1.000} = \frac{(ab + be + ef)}{N_r} + \frac{fs}{1.000}.$$

The second condition that must be fulfilled deals with refraction. Whenever a beam of light enters a glass block at an angle, the beam is refracted, and not only is the whole beam shifted, but the amount of shift is different for each color. When the beam emerges from the prism, there will occur a lateral displacement of the beam, hence a lateral displacement of the image of that beam. The amount of this displacement is proportional to the distance which the beam travels through the glass, and to the tangent of the angle of refraction. Therefore, if L is the total glass distance which a given beam traverses, and r is the angle of refraction, then the second condition states that

$$\Sigma(L \tan r)_{\text{red}} \equiv \Sigma(L \tan r)_{\text{green}}$$

It can now be seen that if the distances which the separate beams travel through glass are not identical, then the displacement of the image due to refraction will be different, and the object will no longer be imaged in relatively the same positions in all negatives. The first condition does not state that the distance through glass must be the same for all beams, for it is possible to

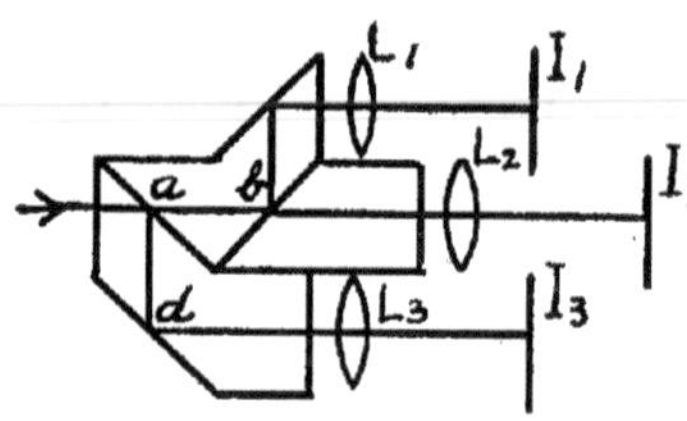

FIG. 40

compensate a distance through glass by some smaller distance through air. From the point of view of image size, it is the total optical distance which must be identical, and this condition, as has been stated before, is satisfied by most of the inventors. But very few inventors have taken the trouble to satisfy the second of these conditions, which most probably explains why practically all of the disclosures listed above have never left the laboratory stage. In their patents, Dowell and the Hilger company outline several schemes whereby these conditions are fulfilled. These are illustrated in Figs. 39 and 40. The patent disclosures give detailed calculations for these cases.

This brings our discussion to the fifth, and final, method whereby a beam of light emanating from a single point on the object, is divided into two or more beams, and brought to a focus upon two or more separate films. This method is characterized by the fact that it contains no mirrors, the beam division being accomplished by means of the lens system. We are confronted with the fundamental problem that a pencil or cone of rays, starting from a single point on the object, must be imaged as a single point. Why is it not possible, therefore, to pass this cone of rays through a lens which will maintain the cross section of the pencil of rays at a maximum, and then interpose a series of small lenses across that cross section, and grind these lenses so that they will bring the section of the beam which they encompass, to a point focus? Then it would be possible to divide the original beam into as many beams as there are lenses placed behind the first one. The germ of this idea was first disclosed by Berthon and Audibert (Eng. P. 24,809/11). It was improved by Audibert in 1912 (Fr. P. 458,040; U.S.P. 1,124,253). In its final form (Eng. P. 355,835; U.S.P. 2,096,665) a divergent lens, with its nodal points well in front of the lens system, is placed in front of three normal lenses (Fig. 41). Here O is the negative or divergent lens, whose nodal points are N_1 and N_2. The beam entering this lens is spread out slightly so that it will

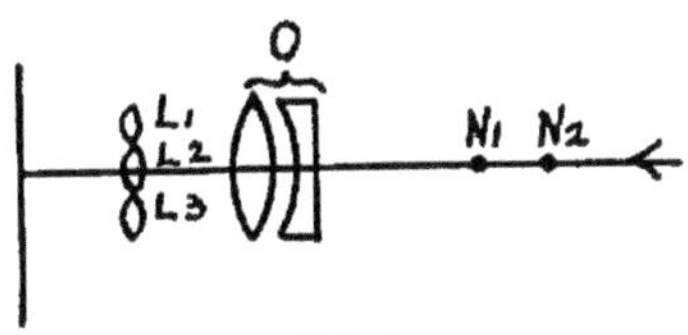

FIG. 41

cover completely the field of the three lenses which lie immediately behind O. These lenses are designated L_1, L_2, and L_3. H. N. Cox has done considerable work in this field. In the first few of his patents, he placed a lens at one end of a cylinder (U.S.P. 1,645,374, and 1,645,417), and at the other end he placed a quadrant-shaped achromatic prism and filters. This prism projected four images in the space of a single frame of motion picture film. In a whole series of other patents Mr. Cox develops the idea proposed by the Audibert disclosures. These patents are as follows:

United States	*English*
1,699,226	274,593
1,700,252	274,683
1,735,108	310,533
1,762,144	314,546
1,778,754	
1,781,496	
1,811,495	

Similar ideas were disclosed by J. A. Kienast (U.S.P. 1,843,642); M. de Francisco (U.S.P. 1,873,302); E. D. Goodwin (U.S.P. 1,921,918); L. M. Dieterich (U.S.P. 1,990,529); J. Szczepanik (Eng. P. 238,973); R. S. Alldridge (Eng. P. 322,801, 352,292, 352,293, and 352,294); and A. A. Arnulf and P. E. Bonneau (Eng. P. 418,562). A slightly different idea is disclosed by Paul Verola (Eng. P. 308,973). Immediately behind the lens (Fig. 42) there is placed a special trapezoidal prism of flint glass, with two sides made of crown glass. This divides the lens aperture into three parts, and the light through each part is refracted at a different angle, thus giving rise to three separated beams.

All of these schemes appear to be very good solutions of the problem of easy and fool-proof color separation, but they make the calculation of lens corrections an extremely difficult matter. For this reason, these systems suffer primarily from defects such as coma, etc. There seems to be always some group or other which utilizes them, but the group always appears to be in the experimental stage. At the present writing, the only commercially useful procedures for obtaining color separations appear to be restricted to a sys-

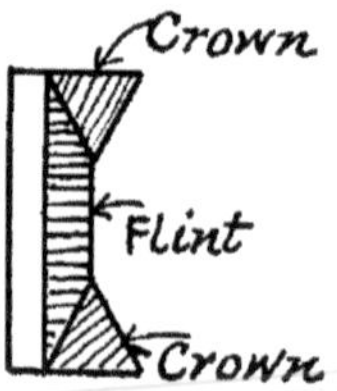

FIG. 42

tem of light splitters behind the lens, a system which we have discussed in Chapter 5 under the heading of Type 3. Types 1 and 2 we can immediately discard as being theoretically unsound. Type 4 presents the problem of matching two or more lenses, besides the problems inherent in the invention of a light-splitting device which satisfies the two conditions imposed by Dowell. Therefore, these systems offer no advantages over those of Type 3. In Type 5, there is the problem of designing a color-corrected negative lens of wide aperture, which could be coupled with matched lenses to yield a plurality of images in the space usually occupied by a single image.

CHAPTER 7

THE PHOTOGRAPHIC EMULSION

THE photographic negative material consists of a dispersion of micro crystals of silver iodobromide in gelatin. The term iodobromide is used to indicate that the composition of each grain is a homogeneous mixture of the two silver salts, the bromide and the iodide. Crystallographic studies have indicated that the structure within the individual grain is uniform, and that the distance of a negative halide from a positive silver ion is constant throughout each grain. But the grains are not identical to each other. They not only vary in size, but also in composition, and in their ability to react with light. It has been found that the faster grains were on the whole somewhat coarser and contained a greater percentage of iodide than the slower grains. It has also been found, that as the iodide content of a grain increased, the lattice distance between the ions increased It is apparent, therefore, that the ordinary photographic emulsion is a complex mixture of light-sensitive elements, dispersed in a binding medium, such as gelatin

The purpose of the gelatin is primarily to insulate the individual grains from each other, thus allowing each grain to act as a unit by itself The complete emulsion contains a large number of these grains, which exist in a statistical equilibrium. Uniformity in an emulsion is achieved only because the number of light-sensitive elements per unit volume is very great, and not because there is a uniformity of properties in the individual grains. This is very important to understand, as several of the important characteristics of the photographic material depend upon this point. It has been determined by Eggert and Biltz (*Trans. Far. Soc.*, Vol. 34 (1938), p. 892) that approximately 5 per cent of the silver bromide grains in an emulsion of moderate speed are developable upon the absorption of but a single quantum of light energy. But the average grain in the same emulsion will require the absorption of approximately two hundred quanta of light before development becomes possible, which indicates a wide variation in the sensitivities. This emulsion contains almost three billion grains to the square centimeter of surface area.

We can describe the negative material, then, as consisting of about three billion light-sensitive elements per square centimeter of emulsion surface, insulated from each other by a film of gelatin, and varying in their sensitivities to light over a wide range. When such an emulsion is exposed for a definite length of time, a certain number of the grains become developable. As the intensity of the light, or the time of exposure, is increased, a greater number of the grains becomes developable. The sole function of exposure to light is to make a definite number of the grains, per unit area of emulsion surface, developable. When a negative is exposed to the light that is reflected from an object, at each unit of surface of the negative there will be a certain number of grains made developable, the number depending only upon the intensity of the light which reaches that area. There is therefore a one-to-one correspondence between the intensity of the light which is reflected from any given point on an object, and the number of developable grains that is formed at the corresponding point on the negative.

When an emulsion grain is exposed to light, that grain is either developable, or it is not developable. This means that within the limits of fog-free development it is not possible to reduce to metallic silver a grain which has not received enough light to make it developable. What gives rise to density difference in a negative is the fact that a greater number of grains are being developed in one part of the emulsion than in another. It is true that as one develops longer, there will be a tremendous increase in the overall density, but this is not so much due to the fact that more grains are being developed, as to the fact that a greater proportion of each individual grain is being reduced.

The grain itself is a mixed micro-crystal of silver iodide and silver bromide, with an average cross-sectional area of 10^{-8} square centimeters. This would make the width of an individual crystal not far from one μ (one thousandth of a millimeter) The average crystal will contain one billion, seven hundred million molecules of silver halides. The true function of development becomes quite clear from these figures. The average grain will become developable upon the absorption of two hundred quanta of light, and upon development, these grains can yield approximately one and a half billion atoms of silver. There is therefore an intensification factor of almost ten million, due to the technique of development. This is the real difference between the printing-out and developing-out emulsions In printing-out emulsions, every atom of silver that is formed requires the absorption of one quantum of light. In developing-out emulsions there are ten million atoms of silver formed for every quantum of light that is absorbed. This explains also, the inherent slowness of dichromate printing, bleach-out, diazotype, and all other processes which use light-sensitive systems that yield the final image by the direct action of the light upon the sensitive elements. For this reason there may be a definite lower limit to grain size in fine-grain emulsions for negative purposes. The smaller the grain, the less the number of molecules of silver halides per grain, and therefore the less the number of silver atoms that may be formed by the complete reduction of such grains. It is silver that gives the density in a negative, so that if less silver is formed, less density results, and consequently a given amount of light yields a smaller quantity of final image

When an exposed negative is placed in a developing solution, the first thing that occurs is that the developer solution becomes absorbed by the gelatin. The rate at which this is accomplished depends upon the physical characteristics of the gelatin itself. This substance ranges in absorption properties from being completely waterproof, to acting as a sponge. The gelatin used for photographic purposes falls somewhere between these two extremes, although it is much nearer the sponge stage than the other. The solution absorbed by the gelatin then reacts with the exposed grains, and here again there is a preliminary adsorption stage, which takes some time. There is therefore a time interval in which no actual chemical activity takes place. This is called the induction period, and it was used by Watkins as a measure of the time required for complete development to take place The interval time is noted from the moment the negative is inserted in the developing solution, to the time that the image first makes its appearance. This interval, multiplied by a constant which is characteristic for each developer, denotes the proper time of development. This system of development is called the factorial system, and the constant is called the Watkins factor of the developer. In the days when panchromatic emulsions were not so common and negatives could be developed in red light, this system was a very handy one, but today, when the sensitivity of the emulsions is such that the development must proceed in total darkness, it loses its effectiveness.

The chemical reaction by which the silver halides are actually reduced to metallic state, does not proceed as rapidly as the neutralization of an acid by a base. Rather the crystal is slowly eaten away. This means that a considerable length of time must elapse before the grain is completely reduced. It is possible to stop the reaction at any point in this interval, and it is this characteristic that is used by technicians to vary the contrast of the finished negative. When a material is developed to gamma infinity, it means that it is developed to a point where all the exposed grains are completely reduced.

Consider a negative which has been exposed to a gray scale In this gray scale let us suppose that the first step is completely transparent, therefore transmits 100 per cent of the light that is incident upon it. The second step we will consider as transmitting 50 per cent of the light, the third step 25 per cent, etc., each step transmitting half as efficiently as the step before it. In the exposed negative we will have a series of stripes which contain varying numbers of developable grains. It must not be supposed that the number of exposed grains in the first stripe will be just twice the number in the second It must be recalled that the grains have a wide variation of sensitivities. The very first absorption of light will affect the extremely rapid grains, and the continued absorption will make the next fastest grains developable. The number of grains in each class is not the same, but is determined by the method used in the preparation of the emulsion. Fast negative emulsions contain a higher percentage of extremely fast grains. Such emulsions will give silver deposits upon the absorption of very small quantities of light. Slow emulsions, on the other hand, will not yield any visible amount of silver under the same conditions of exposure Therefore, as the exposure intensity is decreased, the number of grains containing a latent image may decrease at an entirely different tempo.

After the exposure, the negative is placed in the developer. In approximately three or five minutes, there will appear an image in the first step, a very faint one. As the development time is increased, the image will appear in the other steps, while that in the first step will grow much stronger. We can analyze the process in the following manner. As soon as the induction period is over, the reduction of the exposed grains starts. As a first approximation we can assume that all of the exposed grains begin to react with the developer. Before the silver can become visible, it must be present in a certain minimum concentration This can be achieved in two ways. There may be such a large number of grains made developable that when one-tenth of one per cent of each grain is reduced to metallic state, there will be sufficient silver precipitated to become visible. This is most probably the case in the first step of the gray scale. In the second and other steps, the concentration of the exposed grains per unit area of surface will be insufficient to yield a visible amount until a higher proportion of the individual grains is developed. Therefore no image will be visible in these steps until some time has elapsed, and the grain etched down to a much greater extent. In these cases, the distance between grain centers is much greater than it is in the case of the first step, but the area of each grain of silver deposit is greater Therefore the image in the first step would be considerably smoother than the images in the other steps, the difference corresponding to the differences that exist in pictures that are reproduced with a 40-line screen and those reproduced with a 60 or 120-line screen, in ordinary newspaper and magazine reproduction.

A silver deposit has a certain covering power; that is, it has a certain ability to absorb the light that falls upon it. If the grain is developed so that the area that the silver deposit covers is a relatively large proportion of the distance between grain centers, very little light will be transmitted by that image. If the development is so slight that only a very small portion of the space between grains is covered, then the image will be very transparent. It is possible, therefore, to achieve a certain percentage transmission in two ways. The exposure can be made sufficiently large so that the distance between exposed grain centers will be very small. Then, upon but slight development, there will be obtained a coverage due to distribution of minute pinpoint deposits quite close to each other. Or the exposure may be very short, but the development quite long. In this case the same amount of silver will be produced, but the silver will be in the form of relatively large dots situated at relatively great distances from each other.

This brings the discussion to the relationship which exists between exposure, development, and the resultant intensity of image. This intensity of image, really a measure of the concentration of silver that is deposited, can be measured by its ability to absorb light. We define, first, several terms that are in common use The ratio of the intensity of light that falls upon a silver image to the intensity of the light after it passes through that image, is termed the opacity. The logarithm, to the base 10, of this quantity, is termed density. Mathematically this can be written in the form

$$\begin{aligned} \text{Density} = D = \text{logarithm opacity} = \log O &= \log \frac{(I_o)}{I} \\ &= -\log \frac{I}{I_o} = -\log\left(100 \frac{I}{I_o} \times 1/100\right) \\ &= -\log (\%\ \text{transmission}) - \log 1/100 \\ &= -\log (\%\ \text{transmission}) + 2.00 \\ &= 2.00 - \log (\%\ \text{transmission}) \end{aligned}$$

I is the intensity of the light transmitted by the silver deposit; I_o is the intensity of the light which falls upon the silver deposit.

The term density is an extremely useful one. It denotes the degree of "blackness." Thus in a gray scale, as the steps increase toward the black, the density takes on higher values. A true black would have a density of infinity, for such a black would have a transmission of zero per cent, and the logarithm of zero is minus infinity. A transmission of 50 per cent is equivalent to a density of 0.30, since the logarithm of 50 is 1.70. In the same manner it can be shown that a transmission of 25 per cent is equivalent to a density of 0.60, a transmission of 12½ per cent to a density of 0.90, etc. As the transmission is decreased by 50 per cent, the density increases by 0.30. In photography, the intensity of a silver deposit is denoted by its optical density. A high density in a negative corresponds to a heavy silver deposit at that point.

It is possible to extend the use of this term to all surfaces which reflect or transmit light, in particular to the surfaces which are being photographed. It is not wrong, therefore, to speak of a given substance having a density equal to one, when we mean to say that the surface under consideration absorbs 90 per cent of the light which falls upon it. This is especially true of that small section of the picture which carries the gray scale. All pictures being photographed in color should carry a gray scale somewhere, for then the process of reproduction can be made into a science rather than an art. Let us center our attention upon this part of the picture. Upon exposure, there will be formed a series of areas in the negative in which there will be a progressive increase in the number of developable grains per unit area of emulsion surface. The relationship between the different steps in the gray scale is known, and for the moment we can assume that step number one is completely transparent or pure white, so that it transmits or reflects 100 per cent of the light that is incident upon it. Step number two will absorb 50 per cent of the light, step number three will absorb 50 per cent more than step number two, etc. Therefore, in the new nomenclature which we have just expounded, we may assign the density value of 0.00 to step number one, 0.30 to step number two, etc. If the gray scale contains ten steps, these will be the density values:

Step No. 1	0 00	Step No. 6	1.50
Step No 2	0.30	Step No 7	1.80
Step No. 3	0 60	Step No 8	2 10
Step No. 4	0 90	Step No. 9	2 40
Step No. 5	1 20	Step No 10	2 70

The last step will transmit only 0 16 per cent of the light which is incident upon it, while the first step will transmit all of it. There will be a ratio of 1 : 600 between the two, which is about ten times the ratio that one usually meets in practice. The ideal negative material would be such that there will be a continuous increase in the number of developable grains formed during the exposure in the entire scale of light intensities, ranging from 1.00 to 600. Unfortunately this is not true, the usable range of most negative emulsions being but a fraction of this

Upon development of the negative, it will be found that it will contain a series of ten steps, which should correspond to the ten steps of the original. When the transmissions of these steps are measured and their densities determined, it will be found possible to draw a curve in which the densities of the original scale are plotted horizontally, while the corresponding densities in the negative are plotted vertically, both in the same units. In a typical example, the density readings in a negative may be the following:

Step No 10	0 35	Step No. 5	1 40
Step No 9	0 40	Step No 4	1 70
Step No. 8	0.50	Step No. 3	1 85
Step No. 7	0 80	Step No 2	1 90
Step No 6	1 10	Step No 1	1 95

The heaviest density in the negative is obviously due to that step in the original which transmitted the most light, that is step No. 1 Therefore, the density 1.95 in the negative will correspond to the density 0.00 in the original. It is customary to arrange the scale of densities so that they increase as we proceed upward along the axis which denotes the densities in the developed negative, and from right to left, on the axis denoting the densities in the original Such a curve is depicted in Fig 43 Density has been defined as being equal to a constant minus the logarithm of the percentage of transmission But the percentage of transmission is identical to the intensity of exposure, therefore the density in the negative is directly proportional to the negative of the logarithm of the exposure Now it is quite apparent why the densities in the original were plotted in the reverse direction to that which one usually plots in diagrams.

An examination of the curve indicates that it can be divided into three parts. The first section is the part extending from the point E to the point A. Here the increase in the developed densities is not uniform for a corresponding increase in exposure. This section is called the toe of the curve, and it represents the region of underexposure. It can be interpreted to indicate that the number of developable grains per unit area does not increase regularly as the exposure intensity increases. It is only the extremely fast grains which are affected here, and the number of such grains is very small in proportion to the total number. Therefore, as the light intensity increases, only a slightly greater number of grains reach the developable stage, thus giving but a slight increase in the developed density. The increase in the number of developable grains becomes uniform by the time the light intensity reaches a value which

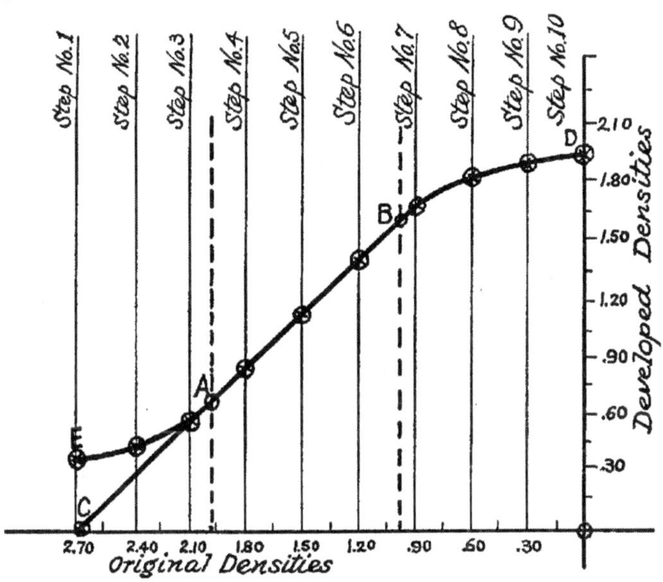

FIG. 43

corresponds to the point *A* on the curve. Now a given increase in exposure intensity results in a definite and uniform increase in the density. This condition holds until we reach a light intensity that corresponds to the point *B* in the diagram. This section is called the straight-line portion of the curve, and the useful range of the negative material lies in the region encompassed between points *A* and *B*.

The point *A* on the diagram corresponds to a density in the original of 2.00, while the point *B* corresponds to a density of 1.00. This means that the exposure intensity at *B* is just ten times that at *A*. The difference between *A* and *B* measured along the log-exposure axis is a measure of the latitude of the emulsion. In this case the emulsion was safe to use over a range of intensities of one to ten. This represents a very poor negative material since the light intensities in normal practice would have a ratio of one to fifteen or twenty for indoor photography, and one to forty or sixty for outdoor photography. In color work, the ratio would be even greater when measured through the different filters.

The third section of the curve is represented by the region between the points *B* and *D*. Here again there is no longer a uniform increase in developed density with a uniform increase in exposure. But this time, there is a slow

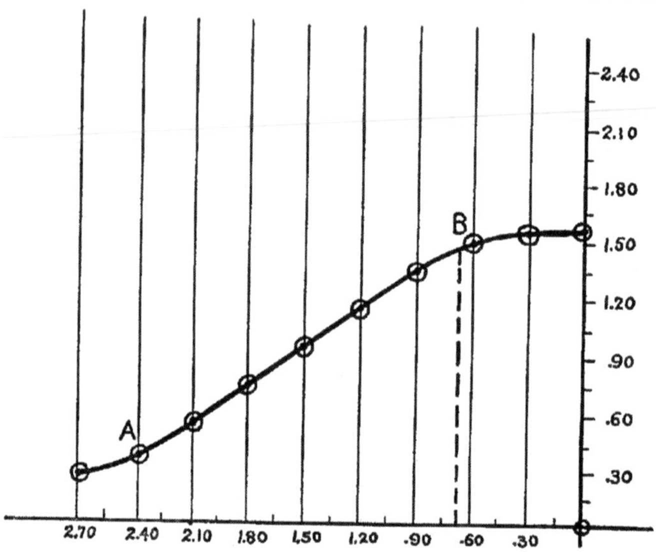

FIG. 44

and continuous reduction in the rate of increase, whereas in the toe of the curve, there was a slow and continuous acceleration. It is not quite so easy to explain the reason for the existence of this upper limit. Undoubtedly, there is a considerable diminution in the number of grains still available for latent image formation when light exposures of this intensity are being used. Therefore, the number of grains that are affected no longer follows the simple rule expounded above. Then there is the possible effect of reversion due to the sharp increase in the products of the photo-chemical reaction. This also would reduce the rate of increase. These are possibilities that affect the number of developable grains that would be formed.

There is one other possible explanation, which bears no relationship to the two mentioned above. It may very well be that even if the amount of silver deposit were in direct ratio to the exposure intensity, the opacity of the deposit, hence the optical density, would still be below theory In the normal negative emulsion, there are approximately thirty layers of grains present, and the grains in each layer are separated from each other by a thickness of gelatin. If every grain in the layer were completely reduced, there would be formed lamella of silver particles that are separated from each other by clear areas The silver deposit will absorb a certain percentage of the light, it will transmit a definite percentage, and it will reflect the rest. It has been estimated that the covering power of a single layer of silver deposit was such that it would have a density of 1.00. This means that ten per cent of the incident light will be transmitted or reflected. Let us consider the light that is reflected from the silver deposits. This will become incident upon other silver deposits lying either below or above the layer under consideration. If all thirty layers are completely reduced, there will still be some light reflected off the silver in the top layer which will be transmitted by the silver in the bottom layer, therefore there is a top optical density which can be measured from a lamellar silver deposit This top density will depend, not on the amount of silver that has been reduced, but upon the ratio of the area which the silver deposit covers in each layer, to the total area of the emulsion surface. This ratio, as was indicated above, depends to a great extent upon the relative areas of the silver halide grains. The larger the grains, the lower will be the maximum obtainable density, for in that case there will be relatively large spaces existing between the individual silver specks which make up the image.

Near this limit there could no longer be any effective increase in light absorption, and the definite ratio which existed between the intensity of exposure and the optical density of the resultant image, no longer holds In fact, this ratio begins to fall off, giving rise to the top or shoulder portion of the curve. It is very probable that the truth is in reality a combination of many causes, thus:

1. At high exposure levels, there is a reduction in the number of grains which become developable, due to the fact that a very large proportion of the available grains becomes used up before all the light is absorbed, and the remaining light affects grains of relatively low sensitivity. The concentration of these grains is less than the concentrations of the more sensitive grains. The failure of constant increase in this case is due to grain distribution.

2. When light acts upon the silver halide grains, metallic silver is formed, and halogen gas is freed. The free bromine or iodine is supposedly absorbed by substances present in the emulsion or by the gelatin. But if the halogen gas be formed in large quantities, the gelatin or the other halogen acceptors may not be able to effectively remove it, and the photolytic reaction which forms the latent image may become retarded and finally brought to an equilibrium state The failure of the constant increase is due in this case to the workings of the mass law.

3 It is usually considered to be sufficient to make it developable if one development center exists upon a single grain. These development centers are formed around flaws in the grain surface. The methods of their formation

are still not well understood, but current opinion accepts the following explanation. The light is incident upon the entire surface of the crystal or grain. Wherever the light is absorbed, silver is formed photolytically. But this silver does not become anchored at the points where it is formed. It instead travels about until it becomes trapped by surface flaws on the grain Here the silver accumulates to form a speck of rather large size (containing two hundred atoms for the average grain). This silver speck constitutes the development center. At extremely high exposure densities, many more than one sensitivity center may be formed upon each grain, some of these in the interior of the grain rather than on the surface. This will cause an effective reduction in the ratio of the light intensity and the number of developable grains formed.

4 The concentration of developable grains at one spot may be so great that during development there is a tremendous increase in halide content, due to released halide ions formed by the developer reaction. This will increase the halide ion concentration locally to a point where it will stop the chemical reaction which is taking place. This again is an application of the mass law, but now the application is to the secondary chemical reaction rather than to the primary photolytic reaction. The two cases must be carefully distinguished. In the first case it is the intensity of the latent image that is reduced, while in the second case it is the development reaction which is reduced.

5 There is no diminution in the intensity of the latent image formation, nor is there a reduction in the intensity of the silver deposit formation. In fact, there may be no diminution in the rate at which silver is formed. What is lowered is the covering power of the deposit, since that covering power depends (at this concentration of deposit) not so much upon the concentration of the silver present at any point, as upon the extent to which it covers the area in each layer.

The curve in Fig. 43 has other characteristics than the ones discussed above. The straight-line portion of the curve starts at the point A and ends at the point B. In this region there is encompassed a brightness ratio of 1 to 10, which is equivalent to a density differential of 1.00. This is a differential in the exposing light. When the negative was developed, we found that this density differential in the exposure light gave rise to a density differential of 1.00 in the silver deposit This ratio, the relationship between the logarithm of the exposure and the density in the resultant silver image, is termed contrast. In our example, the contrast has a value of 1.00, since a density differential of 1.00 in the original gave rise to a density differential of 1.00 in the duplicate. But if we had developed the negative but three-quarters of the length of time used to obtain the negative depicted in Fig. 43, we would have obtained a set of densities such as these:

Step No 10	0.20	Step No. 5	1.10
No 9	0.30	No 4	1.30
No. 8	0 50	No 3	1 50
No. 7	0.70	No. 2	1 53
No. 6	0.90	No. 1	1.55

The curve in Fig. 44 represents this result. Now we notice that the straight-line section of the curve starts at a density of 0.70 on the log exposure scale, and ends at a density of 2.40, so that the range of brightness which is correctly portrayed by the negative bears the ratio of 1 to 50 Corresponding to this density differential of 1 70 along the exposure axis, the negative deposited a density differential of 1.20. The ratio between the two is 1.20/1 70, or 0 70 This is the contrast of the negative development, in the second example From this point of view, it is seen that contrast is the degree to which a negative duplicates the brightness range of the original This can be carried over into the positive process to indicate the degree to which a positive duplicates the brightness scale of the negative. Since we are dealing with straight lines, this ratio becomes identical to the tangent of the angle which the straight-line portion of the curve makes with the exposure axis. This value of the tangent is normally designated by means of the Greek letter γ (gamma), therefore this letter has been universally adopted as a designation of contrast. Development is usually denoted as taking place to a gamma of, say, 0.80 By this is meant, that the development has been carried out until the brightness scale in the negative is 80 per cent that of the original. Up to very recently it has been customary to develop negatives to a value of gamma equal to 0.80, but with the advent of the more contrasty fine-grain emulsions, it is becoming increasingly more popular to push the value more closely to 1 00

We have stated before that the idea of contrast can be applied to the positive as well as to the negative. Consider, then, a positive that has been developed to a contrast of 1.50. This means that the positive reproduces the brightness scale in the negative to an exaggerated degree; it intensifies it by a factor of 1.50. If the negative had been developed to a gamma of 0 80, then what would be the relationship between the brightness scale in the original and in the final reproduction? Obviously it will be the product of the two gammas, that is 0.80×1.50, or 1.20. The reproduction will intensify the brightness scale of the original by a factor of 1.20 This is a general rule. When a reproduction is made by a series of steps, each step being capable of its own contrast scale, then the overall contrast will be equal to the product of the individual contrasts In color reproduction, there will be at least three steps, each of which is capable of changing the brightness scale. The first step will consist in the making of negative separations. This will usually be carried out to a contrast of 0.80, so that a density differential of 1.70 (the usual amount in outdoor photography), will be condensed to 80 per cent of this value, or to a differential of 1.36. The negatives will next be converted into positives, and here again the contrast may be varied at will. The final step is the conversion of the silver in the positive to color. This will again have its own conversion factor, and a density of 1.00 in silver may give a color density that is either a fraction of, or many times this value. In the iodide mordant processes, the silver density is multiplied by at least four when converted into a mordant and dyed with a basic dye. In metallic toning processes, the silver density is usually converted into a color density that is not far from the original value In the first case, if it is desired to maintain an overall contrast of 1.00, the silver density must be developed to a gamma that is one-fourth the gamma required in the second case

Another very important characteristic of the photographic emulsion, is the speed This is defined as the least amount of light that must be used before a suitable image is obtained in the negative. It is only the straight-line portion of the curve which is of interest to the photographer, since he must reproduce a whole series of light intensities, rather than a single one. Therefore any measure of the emulsion speed must take this into consideration. There are several methods for the designation of film or emulsion speeds, and of these, only one method is of value. This is the method based upon the researches of Hurter and Driffield They designated the speed by the value of the intercept of the straight-line portion of the curve with the exposure axis The Weston system of speed rating is directly proportional to this value There is another method which is very popular in Europe. This method is of value to the astronomer, and was in fact developed by Scheiner, an astronomer In this scheme, the emulsion whose speed is to be determined is exposed behind a gray scale, whose steps differ from each other by a value of 0.10 in density The steps are numbered 1, 2, 3, etc., so that the most transparent step bears the designation 1, and the other steps with a smaller transmission, bear the larger numbers The speed rating of an emulsion is the number which is just visible after it has been exposed and developed in a definite manner. An emulsion with a rating of 18 is exactly half as fast as one with a rating of 21, and this is half as fast as one with a rating of 24.

It is easy to see that speed rating according to this scheme is completely false as far as photography is concerned Consider the curves for two emulsions, both developed to the same gamma, and both having their straight-line portions intercept the exposure axis at the same point Photographically the two would be identical, and the reproduction obtained by the use of either of these emulsions, will be the same. But suppose that one of the emulsions has a toe which differs considerably from the toe of the other. One toe may be extremely short, and have a slope that is only slightly different from the main portion of the curve. The other may have a toe which is very long, and which has a very much lower inclination to the axis than the first. In the Scheiner system, this second emulsion would be given a speed rating which may be three or six units higher than the first. There will be a tendency to considerable underexposure if the Scheiner rating is used. In Germany, the emulsion speed is determined by a modified form of the Scheiner method. The speed is determined from that point on the curve which gives a density which is 0.10 above fog. The exposure and development are carried out under stated conditions. There is very little difference between this, the DIN specification, and the European Scheiner The American Scheiner ratings are determined in a manner that is completely analogous to Weston or H & D speeds.

For this reason, great care must be used not to confuse American Scheiner with the European

In the early days of photography it had been assumed, and most probably verified by the crude experimental procedures that were available at that time, that a reciprocal relationship existed between the intensity of exposure, the time of exposure, and the density of the final image This relationship could be expressed by the equation

$$I \times T = \text{constant.}$$

I is the intensity of exposure and T is the time of exposure This may be explained to mean that if the intensity of the exposing light is decreased by 50 per cent, it will be necessary to increase the time of exposure by a like amount, in order to obtain the same result in image intensity. An exposure of five seconds at f:11 is identical to an exposure of twenty seconds at f·22, since the intensity of exposure is four times that which it is at f 22. This is known as the Reciprocity Law. The general validity of this law was first questioned by Abney, and experimentally found to be not true by Schwarzschild. No adequate explanation has yet been made to explain why reduction in exposure intensity followed by an exact mathematically equivalent increase in exposure time, should yield an image density that is sometimes considerably lower than the one made at a higher intensity level. But the truth of this anomaly has been well established

Consider two emulsions, the first of which has a rating of Weston 40, while the second has a rating of Weston 4. We will suppose that we are making color separations from a still object, such as an oil painting. The object is illuminated in the normal manner, by means of two lights situated so that the lines from their centers to the center of the object make 45-degree angles with the plane of the object The intensity of illumination is such that it will require an exposure of approximately twenty seconds through the red filter, when using the emulsion with a rating of Weston 40 After exposure and development, it is found that a very flat negative results, indicating that the fast emulsion is not the proper material to use. The slow material will have a much higher contrast, and the apparent flatness can be overcome by a higher development gamma. In accordance with the relative speed ratings of the two emulsions, it would be supposed that an exposure ten times that of the other would be required. If that technique were followed, it would be found that the negative would be considerably overexposed. It will require an exposure only three or four times that given the first material to yield a usable negative.

This can be answered by the statement that the reciprocity law failed. The rating Weston 40 has been assigned to the first emulsion by a speed determination in which the intensity of illumination was such that an exposure of a fraction of a second was required. This will be identical to the conditions under which the emulsion would be used in actual practice The speed rating of Weston 4 was assigned to the slower emulsion by a test in which the intensity of illumination was quite low in comparison with the first, and exposures in the neighborhood of a minute or so, were used. These are the conditions for which this type of emulsion is intended. But when the first emulsion is used under the conditions intended for the second, the speed rating can no longer be applicable. A new determination is required, in which the lower intensity of illumination should be used. Were a test made under these conditions, it would be found that the speed rating would have been more nearly Weston 14 than 40.

A more practical effect of the failure of the reciprocity law may be had by a test of the extremely fast modern emulsions, under different lighting conditions. With these emulsions, the failure of the law is quite evident even with a drop in intensity levels of four to five times. The real speed of these emulsions is made apparent only when the exposure time is of the order of one-fiftieth of a second or less. When the exposure becomes as high as a tenth of a second, a loss of speed will become quite evident. It is this failure, which has given rise to the skepticism of the professional photographer to the speed values of the American film manufacturers. The distrust of the European speed ratings is due to a more fundamental fault, which was discussed above It is their insistence upon using threshold rather than actual values for the speed The photographer has no interest whatsoever in the ability of the emulsion to yield a density of 0 10 above fog, if that density lies in the region of underexposure or the toe of the curve. Up to the present writing, no emulsion has been made where the straight-line portion of the curve begins at a density value less than between 0 30 and 0.40. From this discussion, it becomes evident that an emulsion must be used only for the purposes for which it is intended, and at the light intensity level for which it is intended.

The last characteristic of the emulsion material in which the photographer is interested, is its spectral sensitivity. The silver iodo-bromide grain is light-sensitive only to the ultraviolet and blue regions of the spectrum. The emulsions that contain the greatest amount of iodide will have their sensitivities extend slightly into the blue-green region, say up to 540 mμ. But the sensitivity of the emulsion beyond the 500 mark is very much lower than it is up to there. The peak of sensitivity of such emulsions, when exposed to light of sunlight quality, is at 480. At 520 the sensitivity is about one-tenth of what it is at the peak, and falling very rapidly.

It has been found possible to add dyes to the emulsions just before they are coated upon the glass or film base, with the result that the sensitivity of the resultant material becomes extended to cover the absorption range of the dyed silver halide grain. This almost, but not quite, coincides with the absorption range of the pure dye. For this reason it has been inferred that a new light-sensitive material is formed by the action of the dye upon the silver halides, and it is this light-sensitive material that gives rise to the latent image. The number of dyes available for this purpose has been extended tremendously and it is possible to make emulsions whose sensitivity lies in almost any desired range. While it is true that with the extension of the sensitivity to regions beyond that of the absorption of pure silver iodo-bromide the sensitivity to the ultraviolet and the blue becomes diminished, it has not been found possible to completely reduce this native sensitivity to any considerable degree. In all cases of induced sensitivity, the speed of the emulsion to the blue rays remains considerably greater than the speed to the rays in the induced range. But this is neutralized to a considerable extent by the fact that even daylight, which is the bluest white light at our disposal, contains a tremendous excess of red and green over blue, and when an emulsion is exposed to such light, the intensity of red and green light exposure is several times that of the blue. Experiments upon the absolute sensitivity of panchromatic emulsions to light of selected wavelengths have shown that from 60 to 90 per cent of the total sensitivity of these emulsions still lies in the blue and ultraviolet regions, while the rest of the sensitivity is divided among the remaining two primary color regions.

In so far as color sensitivity is concerned, we can divide photographic emulsions into four classes. The first will contain those emulsions whose sensitivities coincide with the native sensitivity of the iodo-bromide grain. These emulsions are called blind, or non-colorsensitive, and their activity is limited to the ultraviolet and the blue end of the spectrum. The second class consists of the orthochromatic emulsions, those which have been sensitized to the green and the spectral yellow region. These emulsions extend their activity up to 600 mμ. Some of the older types of orthochromatic emulsions have their limits at about 560 mμ, but the later tendency is to sensitize for the entire green primary range, up to 600. The third class of emulsions is termed panchromatic, and as the term implies, these emulsions are sensitive to practically the entire visible range, up to 650 mμ. The visibility of the normal eye is very low beyond this point, so it is sufficient for most purposes to photograph only up to 650. The fourth, and last, class contains the emulsions that are sensitive to the infrared rays, beyond 700 mμ. These have but little application in color photography.

The ability of the emulsions to be sensitized to color depends to a great extent upon their composition and upon the size of the individual grains. In the main, the smaller grains sensitize much more readily. Also the grains with a minimum of iodide sensitize most readily. Unfortunately these are the conditions for slower emulsions. It is not possible then, to prepare an emulsion of the greatest possible sensitivity, and increase that sensitivity by the addition of dyes. To make color-sensitive emulsions that are very fast, it becomes desirable to make the individual grains quite fine, and with a minimum of iodide. It is perhaps for this reason that the blue sensitivity of extremely fast emulsions is appreciably lower than normal. It has also become the practice to prepare even the blue-sensitive emulsions in this manner; that is, to prepare the basic emulsion so that it consists of fine grains with a low iodide content, and to increase this sensitivity by the addition of yellow dyes which sensitize for the blue. This serves a dual purpose. First of all, it restricts the sensitivity to the blue and the ultraviolet, so that such emulsions can be used for the blue densities separation without filters. Secondly, the amount of blue light that is transmitted by the emulsion becomes reduced to an appreciable extent, so that the use of such an emulsion for the front element of a bipack, will make unnecessary the use of a yellow filter to remove the unused blue light before it reaches the rear element. We will discuss this to a greater extent in the next chapter.

CHAPTER 8

TRIPACKS AND BIPACKS

When color separations are made by means of a one-shot camera utilizing any one of the light-splitting devices which were discussed in the previous chapters, there is occasioned the loss of the greatest part of the light intensity. First of all there is a loss of at least 25 per cent of the light caused by absorption by the mirrors which make up the light splitter. Then there is a further loss of at least 66 per cent of the remaining light due to the fact that the lens beam is divided into three equal parts, and each sub-beam is used to make an exposure through a filter. Therefore only one quarter of the original intensity is present in each beam But this does not constitute all the losses. The standard camera is designed to use the A, B, and C5 Wratten filters. Of these, the A filter is the most efficient, transmitting almost 80 per cent of the available red light The other two are very inefficient, since they transmit less than 40 per cent of the other primaries. It is not difficult to calculate the efficiency of a one-shot camera which uses these filters. Let us suppose that we will use the fastest negative material that is available, and that this material has the following factors for the three filters when exposed to Mazda light:

A filter	4.0
B filter	6.0
C filter	10.0

In order that a balanced set of separations be made, it is necessary that the material behind the B filter be given one and one-half times the exposure given the material behind the A filter, and the C filter separation requires two and one-half times this exposure. But in a one-shot camera it is not possible to give to one negative a greater exposure time than to another, so that the difference in exposures must be made by dividing the light in such a manner that the beam which is deflected to the B filter has one and one-half times, and the beam which goes to the C filter has two and one-half times, the intensity of the beam which is directed to the A filter To achieve a correctly exposed set of negatives, it is necessary to direct 50 per cent of the light to the blue filter, 30 per cent to the green, and 20 per cent to the red filter.

It is possible to get some idea as to the amount of light that is lost in such a system by a determination of the number of times by which the normal exposure must be multiplied, in order to get a correct exposure by this means. The image behind the red filter receives but one-fifth of the total available light which enters the lens. This introduces a factor of five. Of this light, most is lost by the passage through the filter, which has a factor of four. There is therefore a lens factor of 20 A similar reasoning will demonstrate that this factor is true for the images behind the other two filters. A one-shot camera, working at maximum efficiency and utilizing the standard A, B, and C5 filters, will have a lens factor of 20 If the negative material that is used has a Weston speed rating of 96 for Mazda light, then the camera will have a speed rating of almost 5. This may be somewhat improved by using a different set of filters and special materials behind them, but we will leave a discussion of this for a later chapter.

The great inefficiency of a light splitter has given rise to efforts which will make their use unnecessary. One device which accomplishes this result is the tripack. This consists of a combination of three films, one situated on top of the other, and each coated upon its own base. Two of the films are placed with their emulsion sides in contact with each other, in the form of a bipack The third emulsion is placed behind this, with the emulsion side in contact with the rear of the bipack There is a separation between them equal to the thickness of the base of the center emulsion. This can be made as thin as 0.003 inch, but even this small amount is sufficient to give a slightly larger image, when the enlargement is several diameters

The three emulsions comprising such a pack, must fulfill certain definite requirements as far as color sensitivity is concerned The front emulsion must be color-blind, that is, it must be sensitive only to the blue rays of the spectrum. The native sensitivity of an emulsion that has received no treatment with dyes has its maximum at 480 mμ, after which it declines rather sharply so that at 520 mμ the sensitivity is only 10 per cent of what it is at the maximum. At 540 the sensitivity has declined to one per cent, so that for all practical purposes it can be assumed that the sensitivity of the blind emulsion has a limit at 530. The C5 filter transmits most efficiently at 440 mμ, and at 520 it has a transmission that is approximately 5 per cent of the maximum There is not a tremendously great difference between the two, although for really fine work the excess exposure in the green range occasioned when a color-blind emulsion is used without any filter, would result in a falsification of the blue-greens They would be rendered slightly greener or yellower. This film is the front element of the bipack, so that its base faces the lens, and its emulsion side is in contact with the emulsion side of an orthochromatic material. It is possible to choose a material such that it will have an almost uniform sensitivity from 500 to 580 mμ, after which there will be a very sharp decline, so that at 600 mμ the sensitivity will be practically negligible. It is customary to stain the emulsion side of the front element with a yellow dye, in such a manner that the yellow stain does not penetrate deeply into the depth of that emulsion but still is present in sufficient intensity to absorb any blue light which may reach the top emulsion surface of the front element. This will prevent the blue rays, that have not reacted with the silver halide grains to form a latent image, from reaching the middle and rear emulsions. Thus no blue light can act here to destroy the quality of these separations. Since the orthochromatic emulsions can be made to have very sharp cuts, the green separation made by this means should be every bit as good as a separation made behind a B filter.

The base of the orthochromatic emulsion is customarily stained red to absorb any green rays which have not reacted to form a latent image in the central film. This prevents these rays from registering in the rear element, and thus spoiling the quality of the red filter separation This rear element is a panchromatic emulsion but since only red rays can reach it, only the red record will be registered upon it. Here again, it is seen that the quality of the separation must be every bit as good as the one obtained behind a red filter. The tripack system suffers only in the quality of the blue filter separation, and even here, the loss is not very great

One defect of this system, as has already been pointed out, is that the rear emulsion lies several thousandths of an inch behind the plane of the other two emulsions. This gives rise to a slightly larger cyan image, which would be noticeable only at enlargements greater than three diameters. Where no such enlargement is desired, the differences in image size are negligible. But with this increase in image size there is also a lack of definition, and this is of greater consequence. The diffuseness of the rear image is highly aggravated by the fact that the emulsions are not optically clear materials which transmit completely the light which they do not absorb. The individual silver halide grain is a substance which has an index of refraction, relative to gelatin, whose value is 1.50. This means that approximately 10 per cent of the light will be reflected from the grain-gelatin interface. This reflection causes a certain amount of image diffusion to take place, for at the higher intensities the reflected light will form latent images upon grains which do not lie within the geometry of the image being photographed. Another cause of poor definition lies in the fact that the grain does not absorb all the light that passes through the interface. A considerable portion of the light is transmitted to the grains below. Here again the high index of refraction plays an important role, since it causes the transmitted rays to deviate from a straight line. But the diffusion introduced by this is considerably less than that produced by the scatter from the grain-gelatin interfaces.

The ideal type of tripack would consist of three emulsions arranged, as indicated above, in the form of a bipack plus a single film behind the bipack The emulsions that constitute the bipack should be completely transparent to the colors to which they are insensitive, and completely opaque to the rays with which they react. In the normal form, therefore, the first emulsion would be sensitive to the blue rays only. It would be completely transparent to the red and the green primaries, but completely opaque to the blue. Therefore no blue rays could penetrate beyond this emulsion. The second, or middle, emulsion would be sensitive to the green, in which case it would be completely transparent to the red rays, and completely opaque to the green The rear emulsion would be sensitive to the red. This emulsion need not be transparent, nor need its sensitivity be limited to the red, for since the blue and the green rays are completely removed before they reach this emulsion, they cannot register any image here. A pack such as this would be extremely fast and efficient in the use of the light. The blue component of the lens beam would register its image in the first layer, the green component would register in the second layer, and the red component in the last layer. No light would be lost, since each layer is completely transparent to the light to which it is not reactive.

Let us compare this with practice The normal negative emulsion consists of particles of silver iodo-bromide that have been color sensitized by treatment with certain types of basic dyes. The grains have a very high index of refraction relative to gelatin, so that when light is incident upon the top layer of grains in the emulsion, approximately 10 per cent of the light is reflected off. This 10 per cent cannot form an image upon the grain which lies within the geometrical limits of the image, but can form an image upon grains that lie outside of this Upon its passage through the entire depth of an emulsion, there will be approximately thirty layers of silver halide grains upon which the transmitted light will be incident. The net result is that a considerable portion of the light will be lost by scatter. Some preliminary tests indicate that an unexposed emulsion has a density of 0 60 to white light, and a value somewhat lower than this, about 0 40, to light to which, theoretically at least, it should be transparent. This means that an ordinary negative emulsion will lose by scatter from the grains and absorption by the gelatin at least 60 per cent of the light that falls upon it This loss of light effectively reduces the advantages of the tripack. Consider a practical case. We will use the fastest possible material for the rear element, a material to which we can ascribe a red filter factor of 2. This means that when exposed to Mazda light the emulsion will have 50 per cent of its entire sensitivity lying in the red region Up to 1940, the fastest emulsion had a Weston speed rating to Mazda, of approximately 100. The red sensitivity can be assigned a value of 50, since the red filter factor is 2. But this emulsion is to be used behind two other emulsions, and each of these will transmit only 40 per cent of the light which is incident upon it. Therefore only 16 per cent of the original light intensity will reach the rear element, and the speed rating will be only 16 per cent of 50, or 8. The best possible tripack can have a speed rating which is only 60 per cent higher than the best possible one-shot camera which uses the standard A, B, and C5 filters. This slight increase in speed does not in itself pay for the diffusion and lack of definition that is inherent in tripacks However, tripacks can be used in ordinary cameras, necessitating only a different type of plateholder, whereas one-shot cameras are intricate, cumbersome, and very delicate instruments. For these reasons, the interest in tripacks has never waned, and efforts are continuously being made to improve them, and to make the front emulsions more transparent so that better definition and more speed can be obtained. In the United States, there is at this writing one tripack being marketed, and this has a rating of Weston 3

The first disclosure concerning the possibility of this system was made by Ducos du Hauron, who was responsible for so many innovations in color photography. Du Hauron ("Handbook to Photography in Color," p 10) fully appreciated the difficulties that such a system presented In his book and in his patent disclosures (Fr. P. 250862) he discussed these problems. He pointed out the necessity for maintaining good contact between the three elements so that no anistropic media be interposed between them. The existence of such media would induce a loss of definition. He described the necessity for the use of transparent or almost transparent front elements, so that scatter be reduced to a minimum. Scatter is the cause of the greater part of the image diffuseness. He was also well aware of the fact that the rear emulsion lay a finite distance behind the image plane of the lens system, and that this gave rise to a slightly larger image as well as a slightly diffused one.

To offset the possible effects of poor contact between the various members of the tripack, J. H Smith coated the emulsions directly one on top of the other, but with an insulating layer of collodion between them. In this manner there was obtained a very compact pack, since the collodion layers could be made as thin as desired. Filter dyes could be placed in this insulating layer, so that there was removed the possible interaction between filter dye and sensitizer. The presence of the intermediate dyed collodion layers made it possible to strip the component emulsions apart, and process them individually. This scheme is disclosed in United States patents 781469 and 886883, German patents 165544 and 185888, and English patent 19940/04. The idea crops up again in a disclosure by S. Schapavoloff (Eng. P 205807) and more recently by W. T Tarbin (U.S.P. 1871479).

Biehler (U.S P. 2088145) accomplishes the same result by coating intermediate layers of soluble cellulose esters between the emulsion layers The surfaces adhere to each other merely by surface adhesion forces The Gevaert Company (Eng. P 481702) would separate the emulsion layers by means of paraffin. The melting point of the paraffin film separating the two upper emulsions would be quite a bit different from that of the paraffin layer separating the central from the bottom emulsion. In this manner it is an easy matter to strip the emulsions after exposure and process them individually after they have been transferred to other supports. Rowland S. Potter (U.S.P. 2126137) placed a thin transparent adhesive consisting of a soap solution, between the layers This permitted the pack to be processed as a single unit, since the soap film was permeable to aqueous solutions The members of the pack could be separated after the processing was finished.

E A. Lage (Eng. P. 183189) applied strong pressure to the pack. L von Tolnay and L. von Kovodsznay applied a vacuum to bring the members into close contact E. A. Weaver (U.S.P 1951043) would put a mild adhesive between the elements, the adhesive containing at least 60 per cent glycerin, so that as far as the ray was concerned, the complete unit, gelatin-adhesive-gelatin, would constitute an isotropic medium. Since the glycerin content of the paste was so high, there would be no tendency for any of it to penetrate into the depth of the emulsion. W. H. Moyse (U.S.P. 1900459) claimed to have obtained better contact by the mere expedient of surface coating the emulsion layers with a colloid. The one which was placed upon the front element could contain a yellow dye

But the problem of good optical contact can be solved most easily by the use of pressure plates. This is the procedure adopted by the Defender Company, who market a commercial tripack. The three elements are placed between two pieces of glass of appropriate thickness, which is determined by mechanical requirements. The sandwich is then loaded into the plateholder, the back of which has heavy springs which exert considerable uniform pressure upon the glass plates. This simplest of all devices proved eminently successful and altogether sufficient to overcome any flaws that might be due to poor contact.

A much more serious problem was the lack of balance that existed between the three elements unless special precautions were taken to prevent it. This lack of balance arose from two possible sources. The rear emulsions, having substances in front of them that lose a considerable portion of the light, are less fully exposed than the front. Shadow detail is much less defined, therefore, since these sections of the image would invariably fall upon the toe or underexposure side of the characteristic curve. As was indicated above, only 16 per cent of the light which enters the lens reaches the rear element. To obtain a perfect balance, it is required therefore to use an emulsion for the rear whose red sensitivity is at least six times as great as is the blue sensitivity of the front emulsion, and at least three times as great as the green sensitivity of the intermediate film. It is not a difficult matter to find emulsions whose sensitivities are at the required levels. The process emulsions have sensitivities that are one-tenth that of the slower negative emulsions, and it is possible to obtain any desired intermediate value. A certain prominent film manufacturer makes a fast negative material with a relative rating of 250. He also makes a moderate speed material rated at 150, a commercial type with a rating of 100, and at least three others whose values range from 10 to 80. But there is one bad feature of utilizing a mixture such as this. As the speed of the emulsion goes down, its contrast goes up, and its latitude becomes quite narrow. This is the second cause of poor balance. If we have a pack whose front emulsion has a relative blue speed of 10, a central film whose green sensitivity has a value of 25, and a rear material with a rating of 60 for the red, we would have a pack balanced for speed. But when the elements are developed it will be found that the front negative will be considerably more contrasty, and the rear negative considerably flatter than the central one. It is also a question whether by changing the development, both as to time and composition, it would be possible to really balance the three for contrast. And unless this balance is maintained, falsification of color reproduction will be obtained

This phase of the problem was recognized by F. E. Ives (U.S.P. 1173429). To maintain a correct contrast balance he insisted that it was essential that the same basic material be used for all three elements. The blue-sensitive emulsion would be non-sensitized, the other two sensitized for their region only E. J. Wall ("History of Three-Color Photography," p 163) points out that this device falls short of obtaining the correct result, since the contrast scale varies with the color of the light that is used for exposure. The silver halide grain itself has a greater absorption of the blue rays than of the other two primaries, so that the image due to the blue rays is situated on top. This, to a considerable extent, reduces the contrast. The red and green also give different gammas when developed for the same length of time, but to a very much more moderate extent. But this argument loses force because the differentials in the contrasts that are due to this cause are well within the range of the material It is possible to equalize the blue contrast by giving the blue filter negative from 10 to 100 per cent more developing time. The green negative requires at most 10 per cent additional development. It is important to note that Ives brought the three contrast scales to a point where their balance became possible.

While this solved the problem of contrast balance, it left completely open the problem of speed balance F. Thieme (Ger P 163282) reduced the speed of the front emulsion by staining it with acridin orange N. A. von Biehler (U.S.P. 1994627) adopted a similar idea. A highly sensitive basic emulsion was used for all three elements. The base of the film carried the emulsion on one side and a thin gelatin layer on the other. This layer contained one gram of tartrazine per 100 grams of gelatin if it was coated upon the blue-sensitive element. Thus the blue sensitivity was maintained at the same high level, but the intensity of the blue rays in the exposing light was reduced to a point where its action would equal the action of the other colors. The middle emulsion was sensitized to the green by means of erythrosin or pinaflavol The base of this emulsion carried a gelatin layer with 8 grams of tartrazine per 100 grams of gelatin. The rear element was sensitized to the red by means of pinacyanol blue.

In order for the heavy yellow backing of the central element to screen the green sensitive emulsion from the blue rays, it is necessary for this emulsion to be loaded with its carrier side to the lens. The bipack is now the rear element of the tripack, rather than the front This means that the central emulsion will be a definite distance behind the image plane, hence slightly out of focus. It may be assumed that this can be fixed up by making the image plane of the lens system coincide with the plane of intersection of the rear bipack, but this is a false hope. The true image plane is the first diffusing surface which intercepts the light rays, hence, under all conditions regardless of the lens optics, the front emulsion constitutes the true plane, and it is most desirable that this plane contain as many of the images as possible During its travel through the front element, the diffusion will be sufficient to reduce to a considerable extent the enlarging capacities of the negative, but it will still be sufficiently sharp to give a usable image in an adjoining emulsion that is in optical contact with the first But if there is a separation between the first diffusing surface and the second, the extent and degree of the diffusion becomes considerably enhanced.

This scheme should successfully reduce the blue sensitivity of the basic emulsion to balance. The green sensitivity is most probably controlled by the conditions under which sensitization takes place. It is rather doubtful whether or not, under such conditions, a proper balance is obtained without the loss of considerable light efficiency.

In a patent issued to T. T. Baker (U.S.P. 1867301) the balance in speed is obtained in a rather novel manner. At the same time an improvement in definition is also claimed in that the red filter negative, which yields the cyan image, is placed in front of the pack, followed by the green and the blue in that order The front element is a highly diluted, fine-grained, low iodide-content contrasty emulsion, sensitized to the red. These are the conditions for optimum action of the sensitizing dye upon the silver halide grain. The silver content of the emulsion is one-fifth that of the normal, so that great transparency results. The blue sensitivity of this element is further diminished by the inclusion of a slight amount of yellow dye. The middle emulsion is a similar one, diluted to contain one-fourth of the normal silver content, and sensitized with erythrosin. It should have a speed of 350 H & D. The rear element is an extremely high-sensitive, color-blind emulsion with a speed rating of 850 H & D.

It is apparent that this is an idealized procedure that is not capable of being really produced First and foremost, there is the disturbing fact that under the best of conditions it is not possible to sensitize an emulsion and attain a speed in the induced range that is sufficiently greater than the blue speed to make it possible to neglect the blue as insignificant. The blue sensitivity would have to be less than one-tenth that of the red in the same emulsion, in order to be able to discount its effect. If sufficient yellow dye be placed in the emulsion to accomplish such a result, there would not be enough blue light transmitted to the rear emulsion to yield an image there. Under normal working conditions, it is obvious that in this arrangement the red and green filter separations would be badly contaminated with blue. If the amount of this contamination be known, it will be possible to correct for it by a masking procedure. This discussion will be left for a later time.

In a later disclosure, Mr. Baker goes back to a more normal procedure (U S.P. 1910877). Here he adopts the fundamental idea disclosed by Ives, of using the same basic emulsion for all three elements. The front emulsion is diluted so that it is 50 per cent as concentrated as the normal, and it contains a basic yellow screening dye, such as auramine. The central emulsion is also diluted, but only by 25 per cent, so that it is 75 per cent as concentrated as the normal emulsion. It is sensitized with an excess of pinachrome, the excess dye acting to prevent any green rays from reaching the rear emulsion. The rear emulsion is sensitized to the red, and it is not diluted. In this scheme, which appears to be quite reasonable, the balance in speed is obtained by increasing the transparency of the emulsion by dilution. This also decreases the speed, since the number of grains per unit area becomes reduced. The balance in contrast scales is maintained within controllable range since the same basic emulsion is used for all three elements. E. Sanders Dolgoruki also used highly diluted emulsions (Eng. P. 452345). He found that this gave a very thin image that was not at all suitable for copy. To offset this serious defect, he intensified the silver image.

The inability to prepare emulsions that have no blue sensitivity makes it imperative to place a minus-blue filter somewhere in front of the central emulsion. F. Stolze (Ger. P. 179743) claimed that the emulsion itself is an efficient blue absorbent, but this is an overstatement. As much as 25 per cent of the blue rays will be transmitted by the normal emulsion. F. E. Ives (U S P 927244; Eng. P. 7932/08) proposed to deposit a surface layer of yellow dye upon the emulsion This would act as a filter without affecting the blue sensitivity of the emulsion itself. He proposed to do this by treating the front element with an alcoholic solution of the dye, a procedure that was previously disclosed by Husson and Bornot (U.S.P. 922908) in another matter Since alcohol does not wet gelatin, the dye cannot penetrate the gelatin surface to react with the silver halide grains beneath

Theoretically, the tripack should yield speeds that are but slightly lower than normal black-and-white emulsions, but due to the scattering properties of the photographic emulsion, the loss of light that results from the use of two emulsions in front of a third is about of the same order as the loss due to light-splitting devices. Efforts to increase the transmission do not seem to have been wholly successful, since the only commercial tripack on the market at this writing has a speed rating not greater than Weston 3. The rear element that is used with this pack is rated at ten times this amount. To retain some of the simplicity of the tripack system, with increased lens speed, there was introduced the bipack-plus-one assembly. In this scheme, first introduced by J. W. Bennetto (Eng. P. 28920/97) the lens beam is split into two parts. One portion is made incident upon a single plate, while the other is made incident upon a bipack. Thus three separations are obtained in a camera which splits the light into two beams. Of course any of the light-splitting devices mentioned in the previous chapters could be used here. We will forego, therefore, a discussion of the cameras used to achieve this. It is interesting to note that Technicolor utilized a bipack-plus-one camera to obtain its separations. In that procedure, the reflected beam registers the green separation. The main beam passes through a magenta filter which removes the green light, then is made incident upon a bipack the front element of which is a color-blind emulsion, while the rear element is a panchromatic one. It is even possible in this scheme to use an orthochromatic emulsion as the front element, since the magenta filter will remove all the green light. Such filters are very efficient transmitters of both red and blue, so excellent separation quality is achieved with a minimum loss of light efficiency.

It is possible to calculate the speed for a typical bipack, using the fastest materials available The rear element would therefore be a Super Panchro Press emulsion with a Weston speed rating for Mazda light of 64. The filter factor for the A filter, and incidentally for the red part of the magenta filter (Wratten No. 32) is two, therefore the red sensitivity can be assigned a value of 32. But the front element will transmit only 40 per cent of the light to the rear, so that the effective speed of the rear element is 13. To balance this, there must be used a front element, either color-blind or orthochromatic, which will have a like sensitivity when exposed through the No. 32 filter. This transmits approximately 55 per cent of the total blue, so that the speed of the front element should be approximately 24 The Ortho Press emulsion would qualify ideally. This emulsion or the Super Ortho Press, when photographed behind a K3 filter, has an effective speed of 16 Therefore the lens beam must be divided into two equal parts. This will introduce a factor of 2, so that it is possible to obtain a speed of Weston 6 by the use of a Super Panchro Press and two Super Ortho Press emulsions This is approximately the same speed as would have been obtained by the use of a tripack. But now the cut on the blue filter separation is exceptionally good, and there is a considerable increase in the quality of the definition. It is seen, of course, that it is possible to use other combinations than the one described above, but there will be no difference in the light efficiency of the result. Because of the danger that the optical system may not give absolute registry, it may be desirable to reflect off the blue-filter separation, and use an orthochromatic emulsion in front of a pan for the bipack. It will be impossible for the magenta and cyan positives to be out of registry in such a case.

An entirely novel approach to this problem of separations without the use of optical systems which divide the light into several beams, is disclosed by Ives (U.S.P. 1268847; Eng. P 112769; Fr. P. 487529). A bipack is used, the front element of which is a screen plate that contains yellow and magenta lines, and which is coated with an orthochromatic emulsion. The rear element is a red-sensitive or panchromatic emulsion. The screen elements are placed in front of the pack, so that all light that reaches the emulsions must pass through one or the other of the lines. Red light will be transmitted by both, but the emulsion coated over the screen elements is not sensitive to red, hence it will not register on the front element, but upon the rear, in the form of a continuous-tone negative. Blue light will pass only through the magenta line, hence these densities will be registered on the front element, immediately behind the magenta lines. Green will pass only through the yellow lines, hence the green densities will be registered on the front element only behind the yellow lines. The front element, therefore, yields two primary separations, while the rear element yields the third.

In this form the separations are of little value, since the front element contains two of them intermingled very closely. But it is a simple matter to separate the two primaries. Consider the effect of a print made from the front element by means of blue light. The yellow lines in the screen would prevent any blue light from penetrating But free passage to this light would be offered by the magenta lines, hence there will be printed only the densities that lie behind the magenta lines. If a print were made using green light, the magenta lines would prevent the passage of any light, but the yellow lines would permit complete transmission. Of course this print must be made upon a green-sensitive material. In this way it is possible to physically separate the two A system such as this is really an effective means for increasing the speed and the quality of color separations. The transmission of the red rays would be quite low, approximately 30 to 35 per cent, due to the absorption and scatter in the front emulsion and the slight absorption by the yellow and magenta lines. But using very speedy materials that have factors for the A filter of 2.0 and speeds of about 100 for the Mazda light, it is possible to obtain a pack with an overall speed of 16. A variation of the Ives' bipack has been disclosed by G. B. Harrison. He would use a pack in which a color-blind emulsion layer is coated on top of a two-line screen beneath which there is a panchromatic emulsion (Eng P. 471586).

It is rather hard to understand why this system did not immediately receive the attention it merited. Here was disclosed an easy and convenient method for making separations without the use of a complicated and costly optical system, and with a light efficiency that could not be equalled by any other method then known. True, the method for making successful line screens was not yet developed. Neither was there any great demand by the industry for an efficient means to make separations. Colored motion pictures had yet to be introduced. Colored illustrations in the magazines were just becoming popular, but these were mainly still shots. It was only after the success achieved by Technicolor, in the late 1920's, that people became conscious that color reproduction was a possibility. With this realization came increased pressure for colored illustrations and color photography. But even then, no effort seems to have been made to develop the Ives' scheme.

An optical equivalent of this scheme has been devised by the I.G (U.S P. 2093655, Eng P. 395124, 454788, 454842, 459027, and 460653). The screen is replaced by a lenticular film, coated with an orthochromatic emulsion. Over the lens is placed a two-banded filter, dyed yellow and magenta. The theory of the lenticular processes cannot be discussed at this time, but is to be left for a later chapter. It is merely sufficient to point out that the combination of a banded filter in the front nodal plane of the lens system, and a lenticular film in the rear focal plane, is an exact optical duplication of a line screen.

This disclosure accomplishes exactly what Ives does with his bipack, but with much less efficiency, and much more trouble, as will be made evident when lenticular film is discussed.

J. F. Shepherd (Eng. P. 169533) proposed to use a bipack in which the front element was orthochromatic and the rear panchromatic. The print from the front element was used to give the magenta image while the print from the rear was used to give the cyan image. The yellow was made from the combined negatives. Obviously this procedure is only a crude compromise to the true rendition It is impossible to obtain yellows, magentas, or purples, since these colors would yield equal densities upon both the front and the rear negatives. It is to be questioned if this procedure has any advantage over a two-color process A scheme somewhat along these lines was also disclosed by F. Rolan (Ger. P 406174) and W. R. Whitehorne (U.S.P. 1724445).

The fact that it is possible to obtain color reproduction by means of two-color separation instead of three was first recognized by du Hauron, and disclosed in the paper and patent noted at the beginning of this chapter. He was quickly followed by a host of others A. Gurtner (Eng. P. 7924/03; U.S.P. 730454), used a front element that was sensitive only to the blue, and a rear element that was sensitive up to but not including the red. He was the first person to suggest that the two films or plates be placed emulsion to emulsion, and have their edges pasted together to form a single pack Finnigan and Rodgers (Eng. P 140349) would dispense with a filter in the front element or before the rear, claiming that the emulsion itself acted as a filter. This is not quite accurate, as it merely acts as a filter with a density of 0.60, a value quite insufficient for practical results

To equalize the sensitivity of the rear emulsion with that of the front, A. F. Cheron (Fr. P. 444599) placed a filter in front of the lens that contained an inner circle that was clear, and an outer circle that was orange-colored. The front element was therefore exposed only by the cone of light that was transmitted by the inner clear area, while the rear element received this light and also the light transmitted by the orange-colored outer circle. A. B. Klein and T. S. Wilding (Eng. P. 449591) suggest a bipack that could be used for two- or three-color separations, in which the front element is red-sensitive, and the rear element is orthochromatic. The front element records, therefore, red and blue, while the rear element records the green When used with a yellow filter in front of the lens, there is eliminated the necessity of having the filter incorporated into the front element. But such a system, when used in two-color work, would record all the pure blues and purples as blacks and grays.

CHAPTER 9

MONOPACKS

THE most modern procedure for the elimination of complicated camera devices to achieve color reproduction lies in the use of monopacks. These substances are multi-layered films in which each layer contains an emulsion sensitized for a single primary color. The different layers are not separable, but must be treated as a single unit This means that a new technique must be used in order that the images in the different emulsion layers be separated from each other. The monopack film is merely an integral tripack.

The multiple coating of emulsion layers one on top of another has been known for a considerable length of time H Kuhn (Eng. P. 6921/91) disclosed such a system in 1891, although he made no attempt to utilize it for the purposes of color photography. A mount is made waterproof, and is then coated with an emulsion of barium sulphate in gelatin. On this is coated a series of sensitive gelatin or collodion silver bromide emulsions (print-out), mixed with aniline colors. One emulsion is coated on top of the other after the first has dried. Each layer is dyed a different color.

From this description it is not such a stroke of genius to make the system applicable to color photography. The dyes in each of the layers can be so chosen that they act as filters or color sensitizers. Therefore it is possible to coat one emulsion in its native state so that it will be blue-sensitive only. A yellow dye could be incorporated in this layer. The next emulsion layer is dyed with a green sensitizer. The yellow dye in the front layer can be used to prevent any blue light from reaching this or the third layer. This last is dyed with a red sensitizing dye. In 1891 the powerful carbocyanine and cyanine sensitizers were not known, so that the designation of aniline dyes may be taken to mean sensitizing as well as filter dyes. The specification does not disclose why the dyes were put into the emulsion, nor why the multilayered paper was needed But it does disclose the preparation of a monopack

The first specific disclosure of the use of a monopack for the purposes of color reproduction came from K. Schinzel (*Phot. Woch*, 1905, *Brit. J. Phot.*, Vol. 52 (1905) p. 608; Aust. P. 42478/08). The plate is coated with three silver-bromide emulsions colored complementary to their spectral sensitivities The individual layers must be dyed with colors that do not bleed, and which are insoluble in water. The top layer is colored yellow and is sensitive to the blue. The second layer, colored cyan, is sensitized for the red. The bottom layer is colored magenta and is sensitized for the green. This is as clear and as definite a disclosure of a multilayered monopack for color reproduction as it is possible to make.

The pack is exposed, developed, and fixed in the ordinary manner. In this condition each layer contains a silver image of a single primary, imbedded in a layer of a complementary-colored gelatin. Upon treatment with two per cent peroxide, it is claimed that the dye in the immediate vicinity of the silver image will be bleached, and in an amount directly proportional to the image density Therefore there remains a dye image in each layer which is the negative of the silver image. We will leave a critical discussion of the processing technique to a later chapter where we shall discuss the dye-bleach process of color reproduction. Here it is sufficient to point out that in 1905 there was disclosed completely the use of a Kuhn monopack for color reproduction purposes, thus anticipating Mannes and Godowsky, Troland, Gaspar, and a host of other inventors, who have made this system the best answer so far (1943) to the problem of original exposure.

Needless to say neither the state of the photographic art, nor that of the dye industry was sufficiently advanced to allow the Schinzel disclosure to be put to practical use. It remained for Dr. Bela Gaspar to accomplish this result. But the interest which it aroused was immediate, and the discussion that followed amplified the procedure. Neuhauss (*Phot Rund*, Vol. 19 (1905), p 239) pointed out that the use of peroxide was not advisable as this chemical would not discriminate very carefully between the dye lying adjacent to a silver deposit, and the dye that lay in non-image portions. Schinzel admitted the fallacy, and suggested the admixture of the emulsion with colorless substances which would afterward give rise to color formation (*Chem. Ztg.*, Vol 32 (1908) p 665; *Brit. J. Phot.*, Vol. 55 (1908) *Col. Supp.*, Vol. 2, p. 61).

Another suggested use of a monopack for color reproduction came in 1910, from F. Sforza (*Phot. Coul.*, Vol. 5 (1910) p. 209; *Brit. J. Phot.*, Vol. 57 (1910), *Col Supp.*, Vol. 3, p. 83) In this disclosure, the three layers were to be dyed with the primary colors that were mordanted to the gelatin. The dyes should have the added property of being catalytically destroyed in the presence of the silver Somewhat similar ideas were expressed by R. Luther (*Phot. Rund*, Vol 25 (1911) p 1).

From this, it is very evident that monopacks were well established by 1924 when Mannes and Godowsky were issued their first patent (U.S.P. 1516824). In this early patent there is disclosed a general two-layered monopack wherein the film base was first coated with a fast red-sensitive emulsion, then topped with a slower orthochromatic emulsion that contained a yellow dye dispersed throughout its depth. This prevented the blue rays from affecting the red-sensitive layer. The green rays would act only upon the top emulsion layer, since the bottom layer was not sensitive to the green. A two-color separation was achieved. If the two emulsions were correctly balanced, a single exposure yielded two equivalent latent images, one in each of the layers By development the latent images were converted into metallic silver. The pack was then fixed and washed. Treatment with ferricyanide converted the silver into reducible silver salts. A further treatment with a developer compounded to diffuse very slowly into the depth of the emulsion, made it possible to confine the developer action to the upper layer only. This achieved the separation of the two images, for one was now in the form of a metallic silver image that could be chemically or dye toned to any desired color, while the other was in the form of a silver salt which could be treated independently to form a different color. A slight variation of this was contained in a later disclosure by the same men (U.S P. 1659148).

At about the same time a large number of other inventors entered the field of monopack photography. Since the multiple coating of emulsion layers offered very little chance for invention, most of the disclosures differed among themselves only by the procedures which were adopted to separate the images in the different layers. J. F. Leventhal (U.S.P. 1697194) treated the pack, after development and fixation, with a chemical that retarded the action of a bleach. In that manner he was able to bleach the image in one layer without affecting the other. This left the film with one silver and one silver-salt image, which could be differentially dye or chemically toned.

The next advance came in 1931 in a series of patents issued to Dr. L. T. Troland, then director of research of the Technicolor Motion Picture Corporation (U.S P. 1808584, 1928709, and 1993576, reissue 18680, Eng. P. 370908 and 382320). These disclosed several methods for the preparation of the monopack, several uses for the material, and several methods whereby it became possible to separate the images. There is no novelty in the obvious coating methods for the formation of the monopack, so we shall discuss only the novel forms he disclosed. Dr. Troland recognized that it is very difficult to separate the images in a three-layered monopack, so he proposed to use a two-layered pack sensitized to yield the blue and the red separations. This monopack he then used as the front element of a bipack, the rear component of which was a green-sensitive emulsion This is merely a generalization of the Ives bipack disclosure where a screen plate is used as the front element.

Two methods were described for the formation of the monopack, which forms the front element. One is the obvious method previously disclosed by Kuhn, Schinzel, Sforza, etc., which consisted in physically coating properly sensitized emulsions, one on top of the other. There is very little to discuss here except that Dr. Troland preferred to have a separate filter layer, dyed yellow, between the two emulsion layers The second method was to treat a color-blind, blue-sensitive plate or film, with a sensitizing solution under the conditions of controlled diffusion. This can be done quite easily if the sensitizing bath be compounded with a high alcoholic content. Under these conditions the colloidally dispersed sensitizing dye (pinacyanol) does not penetrate deeply into the depth of the emulsion After drying to achieve thorough sensitization, the plate is bathed in a water solution of a yellow dye This penetrates more deeply than the sensitizing dye. By this method the emulsion thickness of an ordinary negative material is divided into a lower blue-sensitive zone, and an upper red-sensitive one. The yellow dye, dispersed much more deeply than the sensitizer, prevents the blue rays from penetrating into the zone of red sensitivity, hence there is no color contamination. This bathing method yields a product which is quite unstable, but which otherwise is altogether suitable

Dr. Troland was not the first person to disclose that stratification can be achieved by bathing the emulsion with the colloidal sensitizers. Indeed it was a well known and established fact that unless extra precautions were taken when sensitizing an emulsion by bathing, only a superficial layer of the coating would be affected But a very clear statement of this phenomenon, and a clear disclosure as to the effect that an increase in alcohol concentration would have, is contained in a sensitizing patent by G. Selle (Eng. P. 12516/99) who wrote: "To achieve my object I use a sensitizing bath, for instance, a solution of 0.002 per cent of cyanine blue and erythrosin in a fluid composed of 60 per cent water and 40 per cent alochol. By this means the red dye (erythrosin), which is more soluble in the water, is carried into the film, while the blue dye (cyanine blue), which is more soluble in alcohol, remains substantially on the surface of the plate. But other sensitizers having the same properties or results may be used." Pinacyanol or pinacyanol blue are red-sensitizing dyes that have the solubility properties of cyanine blue. Troland, therefore, did not discover the art of surface sensitization or stratification. But he appears to have been the first one to realize that this stratified emulsion could replace the screen plate in an Ives' bipack.

The Troland patent was issued in 1931, but it was applied for in 1921. For this reason Dr Troland was given priority to Mannes and Godowsky. Since the Eastman Kodak Company controls both these disclosures, the question of priority is merely academic and economic. The Troland patent is valid to 1948, while the Mannes and Godowsky patent expired in 1941

Independent of the above, Emil Wolff-Heide disclosed a similar scheme for surface stratification (Eng. P. 340278). He based his work upon the well known fact that pinacyanol was a colloidally dispersed dye when dissolved in a water-alcohol mixture, and that gelatin is an excellent semi-permeable membrane for colloids. Von Hubl ("Die Orthochromatische Photographie," (1920) p. 69) has the following to say in this respect: "Such solutions are colloidal and tend to flocculate; if one filters it, the dye remains on the filter paper and the solution comes through colorless. . . . (During sensitization) the dye separates out for the most part upon the surface of the film, and only a colorless solution, which does not sensitize well, penetrates into the innermost parts of the film." Mr. Wolff-Heide found it sufficient to bathe a film in a pinacyanol solution, together with filter yellow, rose bengal, and pinachrome. This is but slightly different from the Troland disclosure Since his patent was issued several years prior to that of Dr. Troland, he could not have been aware of the information contained in the latter. H. von Fraunhofer patented essentially the same (U.S.P. 2030903 and 2030904). In the second patent it is suggested that the sensitizing solution be placed upon the subbed film-base prior to the coating. The sensitization under those conditions would take place at the bottom of the layer, so that the zone of red sensitivity would be that part of the emulsion layer that lies adjacent to the base The two silver images were separated by treatment with a uranium toning solution The heavy uranium ion is ideally suited for use in controlled diffusion processes The time of treatment is so arranged that only the upper silver image becomes toned The lower image could be converted into a blue by any other method that would not affect the uranium-toned image.

A more detailed description of a sensitizing technique, which will yield a stratified emulsion, is contained in United States patent 2047022 issued to J. S. Friedman, and assigned to the Omnichrome Corporation. The sensitizing bath is concocted as follows:

Rapid filter yellow	1.0 part
Water	600 parts
Pinacyanol	0 015 part
Alcohol	400 parts

This bath contains 40 per cent alcohol. The time of sensitization is approximately two minutes at a temperature that is as close to 40 to 45 F as is possible It is also permissible to pre-wet the emulsion by immersion in a water solution made slightly alkaline by the addition of borax. This will swell the gelatin to a considerable extent and it will therefore give a greater degree of control to the diffusion of the sensitizing agents into the emulsion. A somewhat more effective reaction between silver halide and dye is also obtained when the emulsion is thus pre-wetted.

Another method whereby a stratified emulsion is obtained, is disclosed in a patent issued to J. S. Friedman and A. Bruck (U.S P. 2175836) and assigned to Color Processes Inc. Here advantage is taken of the fact that an alcoholic solution of a dye will not penetrate into the depth of the emulsion, but will leave a layer of dye deposited uniformly over the surface. Ives utilized this phenomenon to deposit a filter layer of dye upon the surface of an emulsion. In 1917 Koenig (*Phot. Korr.*, Vol. 55 (1918), p. 22, *Phot. Rund.*, Vol. 54 (1917), p. 257) recommended this as a fool-proof method for sensitization. But he did not recognize that with a slight modification, the procedure could be used to give color separations.

A blind emulsion is first bathed in an alcoholic solution of the red sensitizer containing 0.030 gram of dye to the liter of alcohol. Time or temperature plays no part whatsoever in this step, since all that happens is that a thin layer of the red sensitizer is deposited upon the surface. Only a sufficient quantity of dye is deposited to react with the upper half of the emulsion layer.

this time it will be the blue densities that will be seen. To separate the two images, it is sufficient to copy each side of the pack upon a different plate or film. In making these copies or "take-offs" it is desirable to use an orthochromatic process emulsion, and a K3 filter to offset the yellow stain of the silver iodide.

The reflection copies of the images on the pack will be positives. In some processes positives are required from which to print on to the coloring material. But in most cases it is desirable to have the separations in the form of negatives. It is possible, of course, to reverse the copies This can be done quite easily. After the copy has been exposed it is developed in a developer to which is added ten or fifteen grams of hypo per liter. A thorough wash removes excess developer. Treatment with acid dichromate or acid permanganate etches out the silver image. By this treatment the silver is oxidized to ionic state, in which condition it has a great affinity for gelatin The silver-gelatin complex must be destroyed and the silver ions removed before the next step is taken, otherwise this will be reduced to metallic silver again in the second development. A rinse in weak ammonia, or a bath of one per cent sodium sulphite usually accomplishes this. The washed plate is next exposed to light, or treated with thiourea or methylene-blue solutions which act exactly like light It is then developed in a second developer that does not contain hypo. Or, the plate after the treatment with sulphite can be treated with sodium sulphide, sodium hydrosulphite or any other reagent which will convert it to a black.

The original plate can be processed so that it yields a positive rather than a negative To this end it is possible, after the development of the two latent images is completed, to treat the plate with a strong sodium sulphide solution. This will convert the entire plate into a deep black, in which there is imbedded two silver images. The oxidation of silver to an insoluble salt proceeds much more rapidly, and at a considerably lower potential, than the oxidation of silver sulphide. It is therefore possible to find a mild oxidizing agent which will attack the silver and convert it into a white insoluble salt, and which will leave the silver sulphide intact. Mercuric chloride, cupric chloride, and ferricyanide solutions are substances that have this property By this treatment there will be formed a white negative image imbedded in a black background, and this is identical with the presence of a black positive image imbedded in a white background.

Another possible routine would take advantage of the mordant power of silver iodide for basic dyes After the monopack has been completely processed so that it contains two silver images imbedded in a background of silver iodide, the plate can be treated with a black basic dye, or with a mixture of methylene blue, rhodamine B, and auramine. The silver iodide will absorb the dyes deeply, especially if the iodide content of the final bath be increased to five or ten per cent. This treatment is to be followed by conversion of the silver to a white insoluble salt by treatment with mercuric, cupric, or ferricyanide ions, in the presence of halides or other cations whose silver salts are white and insoluble.

A further possibility would lie in the fact that soft gelatin is a strong absorber of certain dyes. After development of the monopack it can be fixed in alum-free hypo, thoroughly washed, and then treated with a bromoil bleach. This will harden the gelatin immediately surrounding the image, in which condition it will no longer absorb certain dyes like platinum black, or the pinatype dyes, while the rest of the gelatin will be very receptive of them. A uranium toning solution will affect the image gelatin in a similar fashion. Here again there will result a white negative image imbedded in a black background, or a black positive imbedded in a white background.

Dr. Bela Gaspar has disclosed a bipack which yields three color separations. The front element (Eng. P. 448161 and 450685) of this bipack was a monopack formed by coating two emulsion layers one on top of the other. What makes this pack differ from the one disclosed by Troland is that the layers contain dyes that are complementary to their sensitivity, and which by treatment with special chemicals become decolorized in direct proportion to the intensity of silver deposit. The preparation and chemistry of these solutions will be discussed in a later chapter, devoted to the Gaspar disclosures. The I.G. company also disclosed a bipack (Fr. P. 836173). The front element is a two-layered monopack that contains substances that react with the oxidation products of the developer to form insoluble dyes. These substances are called "couplers," and the process of development in which they are used is called "color-development." Because of the importance of this technique it will be discussed in a later chapter devoted exclusively to it. The tendency has been to utilize color-development almost exclusively with monopacks, so much so that the two appear to be bound in holy wedlock. This is a marriage of convenience, and it is not at all essential.

As was indicated above, monopacks are probably the most popular of all systems of photography at the present time, and this field is receiving considerable attention from all serious workers. Almost every film manufacturer has taken out patent upon patent to protect some supposedly novel feature in assembly or processing technique. But, truth to tell, there is very little real novelty in most of the disclosures. Gaspar (Eng. P. 421534; Fr. P. 753061) follows the lead of the I.G. company and adds substances to the emulsion that can be converted into colors. The duPont company would process the monopack film with color developers (U.S.P. 2133937 and 2140540; Eng. P. 497463 and 497698) In United States patent 2166617 Sease and Weber, of that company, disclose a scheme to treat the upper layer of the pack with concentrated solution of hypo (50 to 90 per cent). In English patent 505861, assigned to the duPont company, there is disclosed the following technique: A record is made of the combined images in the pack. These are then bleached to silver salts, and only the upper image is redeveloped. From these, the other image can be obtained by a system of masking.

Murray and Spencer in a series of disclosures also describe a monopack and a system for its processing to yield differentiable images. These disclosures (U.S.P. 2140847 and 2163325; Eng. P. 440422, 470074 and 489299) are not sufficiently novel to merit critical discussion.

A novel type of monopack is disclosed in a series of patents issued to D.K Allison and L. M. Dieterich and assigned to Detracolor (U.S P 2005790, 2014606, 2034220, 2034230, 2036994, 2151065 and 2161735; Eng P. 462232). The different layers of the monopack film contain the leuco bases of the more stable diphenyl methane dyes. These bases are unaffected by treatment with developers and hypo solutions, and they have no effect upon the sensitivity of the emulsions. The exposed, developed, and fixed monopack is finally treated with a bleach such as

Potassium ferricyanide	5 parts
Chromic acid	1 part
Copper sulphate	2 parts
Hydrochloric acid	5 parts
Water to	1000 parts

This oxidizes the leuco bases to the dyes and at the same time converts the silver image to a silver-copper complex that acts as a mordant. Bromine or chlorine water can also be used. It appears that the chemistry involved in the bleach solution may be a little weak. Unless a solution which contains both copper and ferricyanide ions is heavily loaded with citrate, oxalate or other organic polycarboxy or polyhydroxy acids, a precipitate of cupric ferricyanide is formed. But this is a minor defect in the disclosure, since it is possible to remedy it by the inclusion of the proper stabilizing ingredients.

CHAPTER 10

KODACHROME AND KODACOLOR

A SUCCESSFUL monopack film was introduced commercially in the spring of 1935 by the Eastman Kodak Company. It bore the trade name, Kodachrome This name is a little confusing since it was previously applied to another Eastman product, which had been abandoned for some time prior to 1935, and in which transparencies in color were made by a pinatype procedure. This will be discussed in greater detail in the section that deals with the pinatype processes. We will follow Eastman in restricting the term Kodachrome to the monopack The new process was an overnight success, and it helped make the photographic amateur color-conscious to such a degree that great pressure soon began to be felt in the entire industry to make color available to all, in a cheap and simple manner. Simplicity was perhaps a greater requirement than cost. For this reason, this discussion of the Kodachrome process will be rather detailed. A source rather high in the Eastman councils (E. R. Davies, of the British Kodak Research Laboratories) has expressed the opinion that the process can be ascribed to two men, L D. Mannes, and L. Godowsky, members of the Eastman research staff A discussion of the process becomes therefore, a discussion of the patents issued to these men. Of course not all the disclosures made by them are incorporated in the Kodachrome technique, but it is interesting to note exactly how the procedure evolved from a mere concept to a finished product.

The first application which Mannes and Godowsky made, and which terminated in the grant of a patent, bears the application date October 4, 1921. It is recalled that Mr. Mannes was at Harvard during the years 1917–20, so it is apparent that serious interest in color came at a very early period in his life This first patent (U.S.P. 1538996) does not disclose anything really new or very startling. It relates to the making of a colored positive from a set of separation negatives, and it uses the oft-discovered fact that when a lantern plate is exposed, not all the silver halide grains in that emulsion are used up in the formation of the latent or developed image. The plate, after exposure and development, is not fixed out, but is thoroughly washed, then bleached with ferricyanide. This converts the image into silver ferrocyanide. A subsequent treatment with ferric iron, converts it into a blue green. All this is done in the dark. The silver halide grains that remain are now exposed a second time, this time through another separation negative. The new latent image is then developed, and toned to a color complementary to the first.

It is very doubtful whether a procedure such as this can be applied in a practical manner. The treatment of the plate with oxidizing agents after the first image had been developed, no matter how mild, is not without effect upon the sensitivity of the remaining unexposed and undeveloped silver halide grains. These also are of a speed that is materially different from the grains that have been used to form the first image, since the faster grains will naturally be used up in the first exposure. The developer oxidation products also affect the speed of the unexposed grains, so that all in all the true speed of the plate after the first image has been toned a blue, is a thoroughly unknown quantity, and a quantity that would not be the same for two successive plates. Therefore, while it is possible to obtain some semblance of color by this procedure, it would be practically a miracle if accurate color rendition, or anything even approaching accuracy, could be obtained. However, it is from this humble beginning that Kodachrome can be traced.

Mannes and Godowsky quickly forgot this scheme when they hit upon the idea of multi-layered emulsions. The connection is not hard to see, for instead of finishing one image before starting the next, they felt that a better control would be obtained if the two images were done together. The only practical way to insure this, and to be able to color the individual images separately, was to segregate them. Then what is simpler than putting two layers one on top of the other, and printing an image in each of the two layers? Under these conditions it would be simplicity itself to develop the two images simultaneously, and in that way have absolute knowledge that the emulsion speeds in the two were completely independent of each other. The conversion of each image into a different color, could then be done at leisure under laboratory control. This type of emulsion is disclosed in their United States patent 1516824, which was applied for on February 20, 1923 and granted on November 25, 1924. Curiously enough, the second patent went through the patent office in a much quicker time than the first, so much quicker that it was issued exactly six months before the other.

In the second disclosure, a red-sensitive emulsion is coated upon a base such as glass or celluloid. Immediately on top of this, is coated an orthochromatic emulsion, which has been dyed yellow The dye prevents the blue light from reaching the lower emulsion when the exposure is made through the emulsion side of the pack The blue and the green densities would register upon the top layer, while the red densities would register upon the lower one After exposure, development, fixation and washing, the pack is treated with ferricyanide. This converts the two images into silver ferrocyanide, which can be very easily redeveloped Next comes the novel feature of the patent. The development of the ferrocyanide images was to be accomplished by means of a special solution, one whose diffusion into the gelatin could be controlled at will, so that only the silver salt in the top emulsion layer becomes reduced No formulas or other description as to how this was to be achieved is given. At the conclusion of this treatment, there is present a silver image in the upper layer and a silver ferrocyanide image in the lower. This last could then be toned blue with an iron solution (ferric ions must be used, not ferrous as is indicated in the specifications), and the upper one could be dye-toned red by Traube's silver-iodide mordant process. Of course it would have been just as easy to have compounded a ferricyanide bath that had the same properties as the second developer, and in that way convert only the upper image into silver ferrocyanide. Then a similar situation would result — one image would exist in the form of metallic silver and the other in the form of a silver salt. Each could be treated by an independent procedure to convert it to color

Several years later, a slight variation was disclosed (U.S.P. 1659148; Eng P. 245198). It was realized that because of the presence of the yellow dye in the top emulsion layer, that layer itself becomes stratified, for the blue densities would be completely restricted to the upper half of this layer, while the green densities would exist throughout the entire depth. The red densities would still be found in the bottom layer only. The preferred treatment in this case was to expose, develop, fix, wash, and treat with ferricyanide. The images in the upper emulsion layer are then developed. The red densities, still in the form of ferrocyanide, are next converted into an iron blue by the action of ferric salts, and the silver images in the upper emulsion are then treated with a mordant solution and dyed with a basic magenta dye. Up to this point the procedure is pretty much what it was in the original But if the magenta dye image be now subjected to the action of a basic yellow dye compounded so that it will not penetrate into the gelatin layer, the upper portions of the magenta image will be converted into a yellow. But it is only the upper portions of this image that correspond to the blue filter densities, hence true renditions of these are obtained. Of course complete accuracy is lacking, due to the fact that this image contains a considerable measure of green filter densities as well as blue.

Another advance was made in the next disclosure by these men (U.S.P. 1954452), which was issued in 1934 They had evidently given up the idea of obtaining color by toning methods and had turned to color-development, to which they subsequently clung with such a tenacity that monopacks and color-development appeared to be synonymous The fundamental principle of color-development is that the oxidized developing ions unite with some other substance present in the system, to form an insoluble dye. Two possible procedures were open. In one case, the emulsions were prepared with the coupling substances added. Thus an orthochromatic emulsion was prepared, and to it was added a yellow dye and tri chlor naphthol. A red-sensitive emulsion had added to it para-nitro-benzyl-cyanide and ethyl-aceto-acetate. The red emulsion was coated upon the subbed base, and the orthochromatic emulsion was coated on top of it. After exposure, the pack was developed with a paraphenylenediamine developer that contained no sodium sulphite The tri-chlor naphthol united with the oxidized diamine to form a cyan dye which was deposited in situ with the silver. The nitro-benzyl-cyanide and the ethyl-aceto-acetate also formed dyes with the oxidized developer, this time a mixture of a magenta and a yellow dye, so that the net effect was to deposit, beside the silver image in the bottom layer, a red dye image. Of course it was necessary that the ingredients that were added to the emulsion to effect this dye formation, be completely insoluble in water, and very little soluble in the alkalinity required for development, otherwise the materials would not stay put in their respective layers, and diffusion of the dye, with subsequent loss of definition would result. Ansco and the I.G. developed an entire industry in an effort to effect this insolubility, but this will be discussed at a later time. The silver images were removed by Farmer's reducer, leaving pure dye images.

In the other procedure, the red-sensitive emulsion was dyed yellow, besides having the coupling agents added, and the yellow dye was removed from the orthochromatic emulsion The dye used was such that it dyed the individual grain so that any light that struck that grain would first have to be filtered through the yellow dye. The grains of the two emulsions were then mixed in the proportion required to yield a balanced result. The combined emulsion was then coated upon a subbed base. After exposure, development was achieved by means of a sulphite free paraphenylenediamine developer, and the same result happened. The individual grain had associated with it the substance that would give the correct color by coupling with the oxidized developer. Other variations of this technique were disclosed in later patents (U.S.P. 1980941 and 1997493, Eng P 376794, 376795, 376838 and 451699).

Up to this time, the interest seemed to be centered mainly upon the fundamentals of monopack making and processing, with but little regard to the application to a three-color reproduction scheme. This was made apparent for the first time in United States patents 1969469 and 2059884, and English patents 427472, and 427516. The negative material was a two-layered monopack, such as the ones described above, but without having color formers present in the emulsion. It was proposed to use this in conjunction with a light-splitting camera which would yield two images in adjacent frames of the film. With the proper choice of filters, it became possible to register three separations upon the two frames If the exposure on one frame was made through a blue filter, then the blue densities would be registered upon the upper layer of the pack, since that layer was sensitive to both the blue and the green. Alternate frames were exposed through a blue filter. If the other exposure was made through a yellow filter, then in the upper layer of the emulsion there would be registered the green densities, while directly underneath it in the lower layer, would be registered the red densities The images in the lower emulsion layer were then processed to yield a magenta dye, while those in the upper layer were made to yield a cyan dye.

The monopack was made so that the individual layers were extremely thin. Hence the total thickness of the pack was no more than that of an ordinary negative material. This gave a considerable improvement to the definition and overall speed of the bottom layer. After exposure, the pack was developed in a solution which contained:

Amidol	5 parts
Sodium sulphite	10 parts
Sodium bisulphite	5 parts
Potassium bromide	1–4 parts
Water to	1000 parts

The development of the image in a developer of this type appears to start at the bottom, hence these are known as depth developers. They are indispensable with monopacks, where several layers have to be developed simultaneously and at equal rates. After a thorough wash, the pack was fixed, washed again, and then treated with the following bleach solution:

Potassium ferricyanide	10 parts
Ammonia 28%	10 parts
Water to	1000 parts

This converts the three images into easily reducible silver ferrocyanide. The next step, following a thorough wash, changed the silver salt to silver, and at the same time deposited a magenta image in situ with it

This was done by treatment with a solution whose composition was

Sodium sulphite	0.5 part
Sodium carbonate	10.0 parts
Diethyl-paraphenylenediamine hydrochloride	0.5 part
Water to	1000 parts

To every 100 cc of this add 0.5 gram of brom-thio-indoxyl, dissolved in a little acetone.

At this point the film contains images in the two layers that are a mixture of silver and magenta dye.

It is desired to treat the film in such a manner that the silver in the upper emulsion layer becomes converted into a silver salt, and the dye becomes simultaneously destroyed. This last is very easy to accomplish, since the dyes formed by coupling developers are all extremely unstable to acids, readily decomposing. It is necessary merely to make sufficiently acid the bleach solution that will be used to convert the silver into silver halide. The problem is how to confine the action of the bleach and the acid to the one layer only. This control of the penetration of the bleach is evidently a very important item in the processing of monopacks, for the solution of this problem forms the subject matter of a rather extensive series of patents (U S P 2019718 and 2059887; Eng. P. 427518, 454498, 454499 and 454622). It is achieved very easily by the inclusion of loading agents such as sodium sulphate, sugar, glycerin, alcohol, etc., in the solution. The action of the solution must be stopped by means of a solution whose penetration also can be controlled, if that stoppage is to be attained by the use of substances which have a deleterious effect upon the dyes. Since the penetration of the solution is to be limited, it is desirable that the time of treatment be held to a minimum, so that the concentration of reactive agents must be sufficiently high to effect reaction immediately Two such solutions are given.

A.	Chromic acid 10%	10 parts
	Hydrobromic acid 41%	3 parts
	Potassium bromide	2 parts
	Water	90 parts
	Alcohol	300 parts
B.	Glycerin	500 parts
	Isopropyl alcohol	1000 parts
	Water	75 parts
	Quinone	5 parts
	Hydrochloric acid 35%	20 parts

These solutions require approximately four minutes to penetrate through the upper layer. At the end of this time, the further action is stopped instantaneously by means of an alkaline short stop, such as

Alcohol	400 parts
Sodium sulphite	20 parts
Ammonia 28%	10 parts
Water to	1000 parts

The reformed silver bromide in the upper emulsion layer requires an exposure to light to make it developable. It is finally developed in a solution composed of 100 parts of *A* and 15 parts of *B*.

A.	Sodium carbonate	10 parts
	Sodium sulphite	5 parts
	Diethyl-paraphenylenediamine hydrochloride	2 parts
	Water to	1000 parts
B.	1:3 4 tri-chlor-naphthol	1 part
	Alcohol	150 parts

With this bath there is deposited a cyan dye image in situ with, and in direct proportion to the silver image. The film now contains a magenta dye plus silver image in the bottom layer, and a cyan dye plus silver image in the upper one. A treatment with Farmer's reducer (which is made by adding hypo to a ferricyanide solution), kept alkaline to prevent any effect upon the dyes, removes the silver from both layers, leaving pure dye images.

It is to be recalled that alternate frames in this film received blue and minus-blue exposures. If frame number one was exposed through a blue filter, then frame number two was exposed through a yellow one, and all the odd-numbered frames would be identical with the first, and all the even-numbered ones identical with the second The odd-numbered frames would contain a single image, colored cyan, and situated in the upper layer of the film All the even-numbered frames would contain two images — one cyan-colored situated in the upper emulsion layer representing the green filter densities; and the other magenta-colored, situated in the lower emulsion layer, and representing the red densities. Therefore the blue and the green densities lie in the upper emulsion layer, and are both colored cyan. They can be printed with red or infrared light, which would be modulated by the modulations in the cyan dye image. Since these images lie in alternate frames, their separation is very easily achieved by printing only alternate frames upon the same piece of film. The red densities can be separated from the others by using a minus-magenta light for the printing, that is, by printing with green light.

It may be wondered why the first development was not made to yield a color image directly. This would have saved two processing and two wash operations, four steps in all, namely the initial development and the conversion of the silver image into developable silver ferrocyanide. The reason for this extra labor is that were the development made directly in a color developer, a considerable loss in emulsion speed and in contrast would have resulted The exact reasons for this we will discuss in a later chapter, when the fundamental principles of color development are taken up. Since the monopack was being used in a camera, practical requirements demanded that all of the film speed be utilized. There is already a sharp loss due to diffusion of the red densities by their passage through the front emulsion layer The extra amount of light that is required to yield a sufficiently strong image could be given to the silver ferrocyanide or silver bromide formed by the bleach. At this stage, emulsion speed is no longer a criterion, for it is possible to use even a carbon arc, if necessary, to obtain sufficient exposure

The colored negative, prepared as above, was to be printed upon a specially coated three-layered monopack, whose structure and processing were disclosed in United States patent 2010459, and in English patents 427472, 427516, 427517, 427519, 427520, 440032, 440089, and 441325. On one side of the celluloid base there was coated a silver chloride emulsion that was sensitized to the infrared rays This was made waterproof by a coating of varnish, made by dissolving 150 grams of benzoyl cellulose (Eng. P. 327714, 339902 and 356308), in a mixture of solvents whose composition was

Benzene	1550 parts
Toluene	100 parts
Xylene	400 parts

The varnish could also contain a black pigment, in which case it would act as a non-halation coating. But this last was not essential, and would present certain complications in the printing On the other side of the base was coated a red-sensitive emulsion, a gelatin layer, and finally a green-sensitive emulsion. When the even frames in the colored negative were printed upon this with yellow light, the green component of the yellow would be modulated by the magenta image in the negative, and this would register in the green-sensitive emulsion of the positive. In a similar manner the red component of the yellow printing light would be modulated by the cyan image in the negative and would register in the red-sensitive layer in the positive. The blue densities lying in the odd numbered frames of the negative are printed with infrared light upon the silver chloride emulsion layer. Thus a natural disposition of the three primary densities among the three layers in the positive material, is easily obtained.

After the exposures have made been, the film is processed to yield a magenta dye image together with the silver. This will take place only in the two unprotected emulsion layers in which the red and the green separations have been printed, for the other layer is protected from the action of aqueous solutions by the varnish. The film is then fixed in hypo to remove the unused silver bromide, washed, and subjected to the action of a bleach whose penetration is limited to the upper emulsion layer only. The composition of the magenta color-developer and the bleach has been disclosed in a previous specification, so they need not be discussed at this time. We have present now a magenta-plus-silver image in one emulsion layer; a silver bromide image that requires an exposure to light before it can be developed, in the layer immediately above it; and a latent image in a silver chloride emulsion layer situated on the other side of the emulsion. All the reactions have been conducted in the dark up to this time. The next step is to remove the varnish layer from the chloride emulsion by means of an organic solvent. This is then developed in a yellow color-developer whose composition is

Diethyl-paraphenylenediamine hydrochloride	10 parts
Sodium sulphite	5 parts
Sodium carbonate	20 parts
Potassium bromide, molar solution	2 parts
Water to	1000 parts

To every 100 parts of this solution add 0.1 part of benzoyl-acetone, dissolved in a little acetone or alcohol.

After a thorough wash, the unreacted silver chloride is removed by treatment with a 4 per cent solution of ammonia. This will act as a fixing agent for silver chloride, but it will have no effect whatsoever upon the silver bromide Now the real reason for the use of this mixed type of emulsion is made apparent Some years later, in 1939, K. Schinzel, the same person who started monopack on its long history, took advantage of the differential properties of silver chloride and silver bromide, in a large number of disclosures all dealing with monopacks and monopack processing.

Now only the silver bromide positive image remains undeveloped. Before this can be developed, it must be exposed to light. Development is carried out in a cyan color-developer, whose composition is the same as that given in a previous disclosure. The silver present in each layer is removed by treatment with Farmer's reducer, leaving three dye images The yellow image was prepared by printing through the cyan image in the negative, which represented the blue filter densities. Therefore a correct rendition is obtained The magenta image was prepared by the red component of the yellow-light exposure. This was modulated by the cyan image in the negative. That image exists in the upper emulsion layer of the negative, and is the image of the exposure that was made through a yellow filter. It, therefore, must represent the green densities of the original, hence must be toned a magenta in the positive reproduction. A similar analysis will show that the cyan-colored image in the copy arose from the magenta image in the negative, and this is due to the red densities in the original.

The disclosures up to this point do not correspond to the use of a film which has emulsion coated only on one side, and which is processed by reversal. But it is not a great step from the two-layered negative to a monopack material that is capable of giving three dye images in three individual layers. This is disclosed in United States patent 2113329, and English patents 444198, 447092, and 455128. A transparent base of celluloid has an anti-halation layer coated on one side, and on the other, three emulsion layers separated by two gelatin layers. The bottom layer is a red-sensitive emulsion, made by the inclusion in it of naphthocarbocyanines. Above it is a layer of clear gelatin which serves to differentiate sharply the red-sensitive from the green-sensitive layer, and also to enable the green emulsion to be coated easily upon the other. It is very desirable that no intermixture of sensitized grains take place, and no diffusion of excess sensitizing dye from one zone to the next. The middle emulsion layer is sensitized by means of erythrosin. Above this is a layer of yellow-dyed gelatin, and this is finally topped with a color-blind emulsion. This last could also be, and preferably so, a very fine-grained emulsion that has had its blue sensitivity increased by the use of blue sensitizing dyes. This serves two purposes The main one is that such an emulsion would allow a much better transmission through it of the minus-blue light, since a fine-grain emulsion would not diffuse nor scatter that light in anywhere near the amount that a normal fast emulsion would. Another purpose would be to cut down as much as possible the ratio of the green sensitivity to the blue. All color-blind emulsions that have sufficient speed to be used for negative purposes, contain silver iodide, and this salt acts as an optical sensitizer for the emulsion, bringing the sensitivity up to approximately 520 mμ. The amount of the green sensitivity is not very great, but still enough to render certain shades of blue-green much lighter than proper. If the optical sensitizer has an absorption that falls short of 500 mμ, then the ratio of the green sensitivity beyond 500 to the blue sensitivity up to 500, is reduced considerably. No blue light can penetrate beyond the yellow filter layer beneath the top emulsion layer During the processing, the gelatin emulsion absorbs considerable water, probably twenty times its own weight. This results in a ten-time increase in the thickness of the layer Therefore, the presence of gelatin layers between the emulsions serves the third purpose of making much less critical the time of treatment with those solutions whose penetration into the emulsion layers must be controlled.

The initial exposure of such a film results in a clean-cut separation of the three primaries among the three layers of the pack. The blue densities are registered in the top layer only; the green in the middle, and the red in the bottom. These latent images are developed in a typical reversal developer, one that contains a silver-halide solvent such as hypo or thiocyanate. These developers will be discussed later when the screen plate processes are taken up. Such a developer is the following:

Metol	6 parts
Sodium sulphite	75 parts
Hydroquinone	10 parts
Sodium carbonate	30 parts
Potassium thiocyanate	1.75 parts
Potassium bromide	2½ parts
Formalin 40%	2½ parts
Water to	1000 parts

After development is complete, the film is washed thoroughly, then treated with acid permanganate to remove the developed silver image. This solution is made as follows:

Potassium permanganate 4%	5 parts
Sulphuric acid 20%	5 parts
Water to	100 parts

Another wash removes excess permanganate, then a bath in 2 per cent sodium bisulphite removes the permanganate reduction products, and restores the light-sensitivity of the remaining silver-halide salts. All of the treatments, except the development, require approximately four minutes time at 70 F. But the temperature of the bleach bath should be maintained at 65 F to prevent any too great softening of the gelatin. After an exposure to light whose intensity is sufficient to make all the remaining grains developable, the film is developed in a cyan color-developer such as:

A.	Diethyl-paraphenylenediamine hydrochloride	3 parts
	Sodium sulphite	5 parts
	Sodium carbonate	50 parts
	Potassium thiocyanate	½ part
	Water to	1000 parts
B.	Meta-hydroxy-diphenyl	2½ parts
	Methyl alcohol	100 parts

Add *B* to *A*

In this solution there was deposited a cyan dye together with the silver, in each of the three emulsion layers. The film was then washed, fixed, washed, and dried in preparation for the second stage.

This consisted of the conversion of the silver images in the two upper layers into silver chloride, with the simultaneous destruction of the cyan dye image It was accomplished by treating the film with the following solution for four minutes at 72 F.

Glycerin	500 parts
Isopropyl alcohol	1000 parts
Water	75 parts
Quinone	5 parts
Concentrated hydrochloric acid	20 parts

The action of this bleach was stopped by immersion in a stop bath whose composition was:

Sodium bicarbonate	15 parts
Isopropyl alcohol	1000 parts
Glycerin	1000 parts
Water	1000 parts

The time of immersion was 1½ minutes. After a thorough wash, the film was developed in a magenta color-developer.

A. Diethyl-para-toluylene-diamine hydrochloride	1 part
Sodium sulphite	10 parts
Sodium carbonate	30 parts
Potassium thiocyanate	½ part
Water to	1000 parts
B. Para-nitro-phenyl-acetonitrile	¾ part
Acetone	20 parts
Alcohol	100 parts

Add *B* to *A*

After a wash, the film is dried in preparation for the third stage

The film now contains a cyan-plus-silver image in the bottom layer, and magenta-plus-silver images in the other two. It is desired to convert the image in the top layer into a yellow. This is the function of the third stage. The magenta dye in this layer is destroyed, and the silver simultaneously converted into silver chloride by treatment with a bleach compounded like the one above. The action of this bleach is stopped in a stop bath, also like the one disclosed in the second processing stage. After a thorough wash the film is given its last development in a yellow color-developer.

A. Di-methyl-paraphenylenediamine sulphate	1 part
Sodium sulphite	2 parts
Sodium carbonate	30 parts
Water to	1000 parts
B. 4 nitro-aceto-acetanilide	2½ parts
Alcohol	100 parts

Add *B* to *A*

The silver can be removed by means of Farmer's reducer, leaving pure dye images. These are a cyan in the bottom, a magenta in the middle, and a yellow in the top layer

The box in which the 35 mm film is packaged carries on its cover a list of patent numbers, which presumedly disclose the structure and the processing of the material. The structure is supposedly disclosed in United States patent reissue 18680; for the other two numbers, 1638577 and 2019672, deal with the structure of a cartridge to hold the film. Reissue 18680 we have already discussed in the preceding chapter. It was issued to Dr. Troland, and assigned to Technicolor. It deals in general with a two-layered monopack film, with or without a filter layer between the emulsions. Nowhere in the specifications is there discussed the use of the material to yield a reversed or direct three-color transparency. It is certainly not an easy matter to trace any connection between the structure of the Kodachrome film and the structure of a Troland monopack. It is only in the reading of a few of the claims, worded in a very general manner, that any connection may exist. One such general claim deals with the existence of color-complemental latent images, in different strata of an emulsion. Another claim deals with the existence of color-complemental silver images in different strata of an emulsion. But a claim has validity only in so far as it is fully described in the specifications, and these mention only images formed in a two-emulsion-layered monopack Even if the more general view be taken, there is always the prior art to fall back on. In a Schinzel type of monopack (of last chapter), after the exposure has been made, it is impossible to have anything but three color-complemental latent images existing in different strata of an emulsion And after development, it is impossible to have anything else except three color-complemental silver images present in different strata of the emulsion

If this is not sufficient, then there is the patent (Eng. P. 15055/12) issued to R. Fischer, twenty years before Troland. Among other things, there is described a monopack in which three emulsions are coated one on top of the other. Between the top blue-sensitive emulsion, and the middle green-sensitive one, there is placed a gelatin layer dyed yellow. A colorless layer of gelatin is placed between the green- and the red-sensitive layers. We will discuss this patent in greater detail when Ansco Color is taken up. Here it need only be mentioned that a pack substantially like Kodachrome was disclosed in 1912, hence such could no longer be deemed a basic invention in 1921. The Schinzel disclosure was cited against Troland, but he was allowed the claim when he answered that Schinzel never put his disclosures into practice. The Fischer patent was not cited, hence no answer was required. This, of course, merely means that the Troland disclosures must still be tested from a legal point of view, in light of the more substantial Fischer disclosures.

The 35 mm film is evidently processed in accordance with United States patents, 1460703, 1900870, 1939231, 1954346, 1980941, and 1997493. Of these, only the last two were issued to Mannes and Godowsky. The first of these, 1980941, deals with an emulsion which contains a mixture of sensitized grains. Thus a blue-sensitive emulsion is mixed with a red-sensitive yellow-dyed emulsion, and the mixture coated upon a celluloid base. After exposure in the camera, the film is developed in an ordinary developer, and then washed. This procedure does not destroy the sensitivities of the dyed grains to red light, so that an exposure of the film at this stage to red light will produce a positive latent image only upon the red-sensitive grains. The exposure should be sufficient to make all the remaining red-sensitive grains developable. This last can be accomplished with a cyan color-developer. It is followed by a white- or blue-light exposure to make the color-blind grains developable, and these are developed to a red color. The silver images, both negative and positive, can be removed by Farmer's reducer. The procedure can also be applied to three color. The other Mannes and Godowsky disclosure (U.S.P. 1997493) relates to the processing of a two-layered monopack film. The upper layer can be developed using a surface developer, and the silver image here can be toned blue. Then the bottom latent image is developed and dye-toned to a complementary color. Or, both latent images are developed simultaneously, and the upper one toned blue with a solution compounded so that its diffusion could be controlled. The lower image is then dye-toned to a complementary color.

United States patent 1460703 deals with reversal in general, and has no reference to the treatment of color film. But the technique of etching out a silver image and exposing the remaining silver salts, is disclosed. This probably is used in Kodachrome processing. United States patent 1900870 was issued to M. Seymour. This discloses the use of an emulsion sensitized with a dye that withstands the action of acid dichromate A monopack is coated with such an emulsion for one of the layers, say the red-sensitive one After exposure, development, and removal of the silver by a bath in acid dichromate, the film is bathed in sodium bisulphite, exposed to red light, and color-developed with a cyan developer. This uses up the remaining red-sensitive grains Exposure to white light followed by development with a complementary color-developer, completes the processing. The silver is removed by Farmer's reducer. Another Seymour patent (U S. 1939231) included in the processing list, deals with reversal. The film after exposure and development in a non-staining developer, is re-exposed to light and developed in a blue-black or almost neutral gray color-developer. Two such are listed:

1. Alpha naphthol	½ part
Acetone	25 parts
Para-amino-diethyl-aniline	½ part
Sodium carbonate	7½ parts
Water	250 parts
2. 1:5 di-hydroxy-naphthalene	½ part
Acetone	20 parts
2:5 di-brom-4-amino-phenol	½ part
Sodium carbonate	7½ parts
Water	250 parts

The remaining patent in the list is one dealing with a two-layered monopack, in which one layer is sensitized with a stable dye. This patent was issued to Capstaff. It discloses a technique that is very much akin to that disclosed by Seymour. These patents do not appear to be wholly consistent with each other, and they certainly are considerably different from the description of the Kodachrome process outlined by E R Davies, a member of the British Kodak Research Laboratories (*Phot. J.*, Vol 76 (1936), p 248). In this paper the technique appears to be that disclosed in United States patent 2113329

Kodachrome cut film was introduced to the industry a year or two after the 35 mm film. On the box in which the film is packaged, patent reissue 18680 is noted, and this has already been discussed. The other processing patents noted on the package are 1460703, 1939231, 1954346, 1980941, 1997493 (all of which appear also on the 35 mm boxes), 1966330, 2019718, 2059887 and 2113329 One of these (1966330), issued to Burwell, discloses a method of processing a film that has single layers of emulsion coated on both sides This is the ordinary double-coated or duplitized positive film, so popular in the old two-color days. A primary separation is printed on each side of the film, and it is processed to yield silver-plus-cyan dye images. Then one side only is treated, after fixation and wash, with:

Potassium ferricyanide	2 parts
Potassium bromide	2 parts
Sulphuric acid	½ part
Water to	100 parts

This destroys the cyan dye and converts the silver into silver bromide.

Redevelopment with a red developer follows. The silver is removed by Farmer's reducer, leaving two pure dye images. The developers used have the following compositions:

A Cyan Developer	
3·5 di-brom-ortho-cresol	2 parts
Ethyl alcohol	20 parts
Sodium carbonate	7½ parts
Potassium bromide	0.3 part
Para-amino-diethyl-aniline hydrochloride	2 parts
Water to	250 parts
B. Red Developer	
Cyan-aceto-phenone	1 part
Ethyl alcohol	20 parts
Ethyl-alpha-chlor aceto-acetate	1 part
Sodium carbonate	7½ parts
Para-amino-diethyl-aniline hydrochloride	1 part
Potassium bromide	0.3 part
Water to	250 parts

If the ethyl-aceto-acetate be left out, a magenta rather than a red image would result. From this disclosure it does not seem that it is an important step in

Kodachrome processing. The last named patent (2113329) is apparently the true description of what actually takes place in the laboratory after the film is received there. The other two disclosures (2019718 and 2059887) deal with the all-important steps of controlled penetration of the bleach solutions into the film. These have been discussed in some detail above.

Some light as to the exact processing methods used was given by Dr. C. E K. Mees, vice-president of Eastman Kodak Company, and the director of research (*Am. Phot.* Vol 36 (1942) Mar. p. 8; Communication No 832, Kodak Research Laboratories) in a paper that disclosed just what Eastman was doing in the field of color. According to Dr. Mees, Kodachrome was no longer processed by the technique developed by Mannes and Godowsky, which utilized a controlled diffusion of a bleach bath. The newer method was to utilize the residual color sensitivity of the layers after they had been exposed and developed, to effect a layerwise separation of the complemental images

At this point the film contains three silver negative images imbedded in the three layers of unexposed silver bromide. The red and green sensitizers have been left unaffected by the development, hence the central layer remains green-sensitive and the bottom layer remains red-sensitive even after the exposed portions of these layers have been completely reduced An exposure to red light effects a reversal only in the bottom layer. Upon development with a cyan color-developer of the type noted above, a cyan dye plus silver image is formed in the bottom layer only The exposure and development must be sufficient to effect complete reversal, so that after this treatment the bottom layer no longer contains any light-sensitive elements. The next step is to expose the top layer with blue light, and color develop this with a yellow coupler-developer. The yellow-filter layer existing between the blue-sensitive and the green-sensitive emulsions must be insensitive to the developer baths, for it is essential that this layer be present during the time the top layer is completely fogged by the blue light. Otherwise a spill of blue exposure into the green layer would take place, and this would destroy the quality of the final color image.

After the blue layer has been reversed, there remains only the central layer This contains a silver negative plus a silver halide positive image It can be made developable either by exposure to light, or by treatment with such fogging agents as methylene blue, thiourea, etc Development is effected by means of a magenta coupler-developer. It remains now only to remove the silver images by treatment with Farmer's reducer or some other relatively mild bleaching agent which would leave the dye images unaffected.

In the same article, Dr. Mees disclosed another Eastman color process called Kodacolor. Like Kodachrome, the name had previously been used to denote an entirely different color process, that had been discarded. This will be discussed in a later chapter dealing with the lenticular processes. Kodacolor is a monopack film which yields a complementary colored negative as the direct result of the camera exposure. Strictly speaking, the discussion of

Kodacolor should be postponed until the subject of Ansco Color is taken up, since it has some properties in common with that product. But we will forego consistency for convenience, and continue our discussion at this point.

In Kodachrome, the couplers were added to the developer solutions. This made necessary the formulation of a processing technique which involved a stepwise processing of each layer. The film was developed in four separate stages. First was the normal development of the original exposure Next there was the development of the cyan image in the bottom layer, this being followed in turn by a similar processing for the top and the central layers. In Kodacolor a different procedure was adopted. The couplers were made part and parcel of the film itself. Each layer had associated with itself a coupler which would unite with the oxidized developer to deposit a pigment or insoluble dye. Ansco and the I G. had already disclosed one method to accomplish this (cf. Chapter 11). The procedure was to convert the coupling agents into non-diffusing components by alteration of the structure of the molecule Eastman adopted the procedure of grain isolation. The couplers were dispersed in water-insoluble but water-permeable resins, cellulose esters, ethers, or other polymers. The new bodies were then dispersed in the emulsion layer. The structure of a Kodacolor layer is quite different from anything that had previously been proposed The individual silver halide grains are dispersed in the gelatin and isolated from each other by walls of gelatin. Interspersed between them are resin particles These also are insulated from each other and from the silver halide grains, by walls of gelatin. There is, therefore, considerable granularity to the layer.

When an exposed grain is developed, the oxidized developer diffuses away from the developed grain. In its travels it will permeate the resin and once inside, will combine with the coupler present there. Therefore, a Kodacolor image cannot be as sharp as a Kodachrome, since the dye image is removed from the area where the light was originally focused. This effect might be offset by a more uniform distribution of the dye particles, hence a smoother, more homogeneous image might result.

Kodacolor evidently is based upon the disclosures of M. Martinez. In his first disclosure (U S P. 2269158, Eng. P. 505834) he proposed the general solution whereby the coupler was dissolved in a resin, and the result dispersed in the emulsion In a later patent (U.S.P. 2284877; Eng. P. 543606) he suggested that the silver halide grain also be dispersed in the resin, so that each resin unit contained all the ingredients necessary for image formation.

The extension of this principle was soon taken up by other members of the Eastman staff. Mannes and Godowsky (U.S P. 2304940; cf. also Eng. P. 524555) suggested cellulose esters as being suitable for coupler isolation. In English patent 524554 it was suggested that agents be added to the resin solutions to increase their porosity. The surface could also be treated to reduce light scatter since the index of refraction of the resin would be different from that of the gelatin. S. S. Fierke suggested other substitutes for the resin, notably polyvinyl acetate, polyvinyl acetal or polystyrene (U.S.P. 2272191). A diffusing coupler could be converted into one that was diffusion-fast by adding a water-soluble resin such as polyvinyl alcohol or phthalate. This suggestion was made by Peterson (U.S P. 2289803) Methods of dispersing the resin in gelatin or silver halide gelatin emulsions, were disclosed by Bennett and Fierke (U.S P. 2311020) and E. B. Knott (Eng P 540366, 540367, 540368, 544135)

The inverse procedure, the dissolution of a color former in gelatin, then dispersion of the gel into a cellulose ester silver halide emulsion, was disclosed by Leermakers and Fierke (U.S.P. 2279406; 2318788; cf. also English patent 524154). Such a procedure might be suitable for print or duplication purposes, since it is quite improbable that sufficient sensitivity could be obtained with other than gelatin emulsions.

The processing of Kodacolor involves merely a development with a solution containing practically no sulphite, and some derivative of paraphenylenediamine as the reducing agent. Color is deposited as the silver is reduced This is followed by a wash then by a bleach bath compounded so as not to harm the dye images. Fixation in hypo, and a wash complete the processing

CHAPTER 11

ANSCO COLOR AND AGFACOLOR

WHILE the Eastman Kodak staff has developed to a high degree of precision the controlled diffusion methods for processing monopack film, work has been going on apace on another procedure for obtaining a like result. Curiously enough, this method is the one originally disclosed by Fischer and Siegrist (Eng. P. 15055/12; U.S.P. 1055155, Ger. P. 257160). In accordance with these disclosures, three emulsions were prepared that were sensitized to the blue, blue and green, and blue and red respectively It was not possible to prepare a silver-halide emulsion whose sensitivity to the blue was repressed to a point where it would no longer matter. The three emulsions contained, besides the sensitizing dyes, the proper coupling agents, so that in the blue-sensitive emulsion there would be included substances which would yield a yellow dye by condensation with the oxidized developer, in the green-sensitive emulsion there would be a magenta, and in the red-sensitive emulsion a cyan, coupling-agent. The three emulsions were to be coated one on top of the other, with a layer of gelatin, dyed yellow, between the blue-sensitive and the other two layers, and a layer of clear gelatin between the green- and the red-sensitive layers. In this form, the disclosure might seem a prior conception of the monopack film as made in accordance with the description in the Mannes and Godowsky United States patent 2113329. The only difference between the two is that the earlier patent disclosed the inclusion of the dye couplers in the monopack, while the other preferred to put the couplers into the developer solutions. However, it is to be recalled that in one of the earlier Mannes and Godowsky efforts (U.S.P. 1954452) it is also suggested that the couplers be added to the emulsion directly. The green-sensitive emulsion has added to it para-nitro-benzyl-cyanide and ethyl-aceto-acetate, and the red-sensitive emulsion has included in it tri-chlor-alpha-naphthol After exposure, the pack is developed in a developer containing para-amino-di-ethyl-aniline or some equivalent substance. The ingredients in the green-sensitive layer combine with the oxidized developer to yield magenta and yellow dyes, so that the combined result would be red, while the ingredient present in the red layer yields a cyan dye. Treatment with Farmer's reducer removes the silver, leaving pure dye images. Thus it would appear that not only was the basic idea of the inclusion of the couplers in the emulsion layers previously disclosed by Fischer and Siegrist almost twenty-five years prior to Mannes and Godowsky, but that the type of ingredients used as couplers was also identical with that disclosed in the very early patents

No specific directions were given as to how these substances were to be put into the emulsion layers so that a stable result would be obtained. Fischer and Siegrist included the gelatin layers between the emulsions not only to serve as light filters, but also to completely segregate one layer from the next, so that the coupling agents in one zone would not interfere with those in another zone. This has evidently failed to satisfy the requirements for complete segregation, for the pack described by the early inventors never achieved commercial success. It is probably this slight difficulty that mainly directed the work of the Kodachrome group into controlled diffusion processes. But in some later patents, Messrs. Mannes and Godowsky return to this field, and in United States patent 1996928 they take advantage of the fact that when silver bromide is prepared in the presence of substances like alpha naphthol and its derivatives, or para-nitro-benzyl-cyanide and its substitution products, these will become adsorbed to the silver halide grain Thus it becomes possible to prepare an emulsion in which each grain contains associated with itself the coupling agents that are required to form the proper positive color, upon condensation with oxidized developer This adsorption, they claim, does not interfere with the sensitization of the grain with sensitizing dyes. A red-sensitive emulsion can therefore be prepared with alpha-naphthol derivatives adsorbed upon the grains, and a green-sensitive emulsion with adsorbed benzyl-cyanide derivatives. These can then either be coated in separate layers one on top of the other, or they can be tanned to isolate each individual grain, then mixed and coated as a single layer. In the first case it will suffice to include between the two layers a yellow-dyed filter layer. But in the second case, each grain of the red-sensitive emulsion must be dyed with a yellow filter dye, which will become mordanted to the gelatin surrounding the grain. Since this has been tanned, it is not a very difficult thing to accomplish. An idea such as this, but not to be used in conjunction with color formers, was advanced as far back as 1911, by Sforza and a little later by Luther. In a later disclosure (Eng. P. 503845) it is proposed to use color formers of the pyrazolone group. These have a labile hydrogen in the molecule, and can form silver salts that are very insoluble. The purified silver salt is dispersed in gelatin and then treated with potassium bromide. This converts the silver pyrazolone salt into silver bromide, and leaves the pyrazolone adsorbed upon the halide grain.

To prepare such an emulsion, the following procedure was disclosed: Two solutions were prepared, one containing a solution of pyrazolone in ammonia, and the other a solution of silver nitrate in ammonia.

A.	1-phenyl-3-methyl-5-pyrazolone	17 41 parts
	Ammonia 28%	30 parts
B.	Silver nitrate	8 495 parts
	Water	170 parts
	Strong ammonia sufficient to redissolve the precipitate	

Solution *A* is heated on a water bath to drive off the ammonia until precipitation of the pyrazolone salt starts, at which point 150 cc of water is added. Solutions *A* and *B* are then mixed at room temperature. The precipitate is allowed to stand overnight, the liquid decanted off, and the precipitate washed by decantation and centrifuging. It is finally dried in a desiccator at 55 C. The emulsion is made from this precipitate. Two solutions are again prepared.

A.	Silver pyrazolone salt	1 8 parts
	Water	10 parts
	Gelatin 15%	1 part

The salt is broken up, and suspended in the gelatin at 45 C.

B.	Potassium bromide	0.5 part
	Water	3 parts

B is added slowly to *A* with constant stirring, over a period of fifteen minutes. Then 15 cc of 15 per cent gelatin is added, and the emulsion is stirred. It is then set, shredded, washed for two hours, drained overnight, remelted, filtered, and coated. The speed of the plate is approximately the same as a lantern plate. It can be developed in a para di-ethyl-amino-aniline developer.

The fact that the later Eastman work deals with emulsions to which couplers have been added, would seem to indicate that this procedure has considerable merit. It remained for Ansco and the I G to develop it to a successful conclusion But it was not until after Kodachrome appeared on the market that they proceeded to develop their product, known as Ansco Color and Agfacolor Neue. The first English patent, issued in 1936, bears the number 455556. Here is disclosed a scheme to obtain an even dispersion of the couplers in the emulsion layers This is done with the aid of wetting agents, such as the sulphonated hydrocarbons, sulphonated castor oils, etc. A blue-sensitive emulsion has added to it, first a wetting agent like sulphonated taurine (sold by the I.G. under the name Igepon), then an alkaline solution of tere-phthaloyl-bis-acet-anilide. In the green-sensitive layer, with the aid of sulphonated castor oil, is dispersed the alkali salt of the symmetrical derivative of urea, prepared from para-amino-benzoyl-meta-amino-phenyl-methyl-pyrazolone.

But the true problem in the preparation of such layers is not the inability to obtain uniform dispersions of the couplers throughout the emulsion, but to prevent the couplers in one emulsion layer from wandering over into a neighboring layer By far the greatest efforts have been expended upon the solution of this problem. One method by which this can be done (Eng. P. 458400), is to attach substantive groups to the molecule, such as the residues of stilbene, azoxybenzene, di-phenyl, oxy-naphthoyl amides, benzthiazol, phenols with substitutions in the one and three positions, and amino phenols The coupler molecules will under these conditions attach themselves to the gelatin molecule, and apparently "dye" the gelatin with colorless and transparent "dyes." The preparation of such substances is covered in English patents 365531,

403915, 415945, and 417936 A typical monopack would contain three layers coated one above the other with gelatin filter layers between the emulsions, each properly sensitized and each containing diffusion-fast coupling agents The red-sensitive emulsion contains 3:5 di-(phenyl-amino)-phenol The green-sensitive layer contains para-(oxy-naphthoyl-amino)-phenyl-3-methyl-5-pyrazolone. The blue-sensitive emulsion has added to it tere-phthaloyl-bis-acetanilide. One gram of the coupler is dissolved in a little alcohol, then dispersed in 50 cc of 10 per cent gelatin. The dispersion is finally added to 100 cc of the sensitive emulsion.

In another disclosure (Eng P 464398), a slight variation is introduced. The yellow-image layer contains either tere-phthaloyl-bis-acetanilide, or benzoyl-acetanilide The magenta layer contains 1-(di-phenyl)-phenyl-3-carbethoxy-5-pyrazolone The third layer contains di-(2:8-di-hydroxy-3-naphthoic acid)-benzidide After exposure and color development, there is formed a silver-plus-dye image in each of the emulsion layers But the dye image is relatively low in concentration, since for every four atoms of silver that are formed, but one molecule of dye is deposited This results in a loss of speed and of contrast, after the silver image is removed To offset this tendency, the silver is converted into a silver anti-diazotate salt, by first converting it to silver chloride, then treating the chloride with sodium anti-diazotate In this form the diazo derivative cannot unite with the couplers present in the emulsion Therefore it is possible to wash out completely all the diazo compound from the non-image portions of the film, leaving it only at image portions in the form of a silver salt If the pack at this point be treated with a weak acid, the anti-diazotate becomes converted into the normal diazonium salt, and this immediately condenses with the coupling agents present in the film. Thus for every atom of silver that is formed by the development of the latent image, there will be formed one molecule of dye.

The formation of diffusion-fast couplers is tackled again in English patents 465823 and 488048. This time long-chain hydrocarbon residues are attached to the coupler molecule, as for example in the form of an amino substitution. This is utilized in the formation of a pack as disclosed in English patent 475191. To 1000 parts of emulsion is added one or the other of these solutions:

To blue-sensitive emulsion.	
Di-(benzoyl-acetic-acid)-benzidide	10 parts
Alcohol	30 parts
Sodium hydroxide, 20% aqueous solution	10 parts
To green-sensitive emulsion.	
1-(para-stearyl-amino-phenyl)-3-methyl-5-pyrazolone	10 parts
Methyl alcohol	10 parts
Sodium hydroxide, 20% aqueous solution	10 parts
To red-sensitive emulsion.	
Di-(1-oxy-2-naphthoyl)-benzidide	10 parts
Methyl alcohol	10 parts
Sodium hydroxide, 20% aqueous solution	10 parts

Rapid filter yellow could be added to the color-sensitized emulsions. The pack, after exposure, is developed in a para di-ethyl-amino-aniline developer.

In disclosure 476672 all the three layers of the pack contain the long-chain hydrocarbon residue The yellow layer contains para-capronyl-amino-benzoyl-acetamino-salicylic acid The cyan layer contains 1-hydroxy-2-carboxy-5-dodecoyl-amino-naphthalene. The magenta layer contains 1-(4′-oxy-3′-carboxy-phenyl)-3-(4″-dodecoyl-amino)-phenyl-5-pyrazolone. This did not complete the possibilities for the formation of diffusion-fast couplers, for they return to this problem again and again in a large number of patents. Thus it is proposed to use highly polymeric carboxylic acid derivatives (Eng. P. 479838) such as polyglucuronic acid, polyvinyl carboxylic acid, etc., as substitutions within the coupling molecule. In English patent 483000, it is suggested that sugars be used, and that one or more of the free hydroxy groups in the sugar molecule be esterified or etherized with coupler residues. It has also been proposed to use the degradation products of gelatin, albumen, or other colloids, causing these to combine with the coupling agents through a carboxyl or an amine group. The addition of a sterol, cholesterol, etc , group to the coupler through union with a carboxylic acid or an amino group, is described in English patent 489093 The presence of several coupler residues in a single molecule is again disclosed in English patent 489161 Recourse to heavy molecules is resorted to in English patent 489164. Here diffusion-fast couplers are made by replacing one or both of the hydroxyl groups in malonic acid ($HOCO \cdot CH_2 \cdot COOH$) with groups like NHR, where R is a heavy radical which would make the entire compound substantive to gelatin. Examples of such substances are $C_6H_5NH—CO—CH_2—CO—NHC_8H_{15}$ and

$$C_6H_5—C_6H_4—NH—CO—CH_2—CO—NH—C_6H_4—C_6H_5.$$

The heavy hydrocarbon attached to the nitrogen atom, can also contain a carboxyl or sulphonic acid substitution, to give the molecule water solubility in the form of an alkali metal salt Resin residues (Eng. P. 489274), or hydrogenated aromatic residues (Eng. P. 491958) when substituted into the coupler molecule, also gave it substantive properties.

In the preparation of these substances it is desirable to have the compounds soluble in the alkalinity required for development with substituted para-phenylenediamine compounds This, at first glance, may seem to be inconsistent with the requirements for diffusion-fastness, with the requirement that the molecule stay put in the position where it is lodged. But here good old colloidal chemistry comes to the rescue. Diffusion through a gelatin membrane is dependent to a large extent upon the particle size and molecular weight of the diffusing molecule. The larger the molecule and the greater its molecular weight, the less likely it is to wander to any great extent, in any given time It is for this reason that solutions of the simple inorganic salts, whose molecular weights are fairly low, diffuse with great ease through gelatin, and may be washed in or out of a gelatin layer. But when the molecular weight reaches well into three figures, the molecule becomes too heavy to respond to Brownian movement, or even to osmotic pressures. For that reason heavy dye molecules, once they stain gelatin, are very difficult to remove. This is taken advantage of in imbibition processes. There it is desired to have a water-soluble dye which has a tendency to stain gelatin, become imbibed by a matrix This is a gelatin relief carried by a celluloid base. The relief, at its deepest point, is of the order of 0.00001 inch. After dyeing, it is brought into contact with a plain gelatin film whose thickness may be from ten to one hundred times as much, and whose physical hardness is much lower than that of the matrix The two are brought into contact so that a layer of water, extremely thin, but still present, lies between them. The water dissolves out some dye from the matrix, since that dye is water-soluble. The solution then dyes the blank, since that is receptive to dyes. If the molecule is very large, it will move very sluggishly, once it is in the gelatin film, and hence excellent definition becomes possible. If the conditions of the water interlayer are made such that the solution of the dye becomes molecular and crystalloidal rather than colloidal, then the transfer will have very poor definition. This will take place if it is made alkaline. Much more of the dye will transfer, and in a much shorter time, but it will not stay put in the gelatin layer, and will continue to wander about until it has been made sufficiently dry to stop its traveling Treatment of the dyes with acids like acetic, is also based upon a similar idea.

We meet the same influence in the conversion of the silver image into a silver iodide mordant image by means of a bleach of the Miller type. There the iodizing solution is compounded to contain at least 7 per cent of potassium iodide. In so strong an iodide solution, silver iodide is quite soluble, and it is possible to fix out emulsions in solutions of potassium iodide. But if the silver image is imbedded so that it is completely surrounded by gelatin that has been hardened, the formation of the iodide will take place with the accompaniment of adsorbed potassium iodide. The new complex has a great molecular weight, and will move very sluggishly through the gelatin, so that in the short time which is required for the conversion of the image into the complex, it will have moved but an infinitesimal amount. That is the reason for the relatively fair definition of a silver-iodide, potassium-iodide, complex mordant. The same is true for the formation of the other complex mordant images of the Christensen type, which use thiourea and thiourea derivatives for the formation of the complex. But we can leave these questions for a later discussion They are being mentioned here only to illustrate the influence that high molecular weight has upon conferring substantive properties to any molecule. The I G. research workers have sought to "dye" the gelatin with the coupling reagent. This is a transparent and colorless dye, which will not have a tendency to wander about when the gelatin layer is made wet during the processing stages.

But this is not the only problem that is involved The presence of very heavy groups in the coupler molecule has a tendency to yield color shades that are distinctly duller than those obtained if the substitutions are left out It becomes extremely important, therefore, not to lose any brilliance in the remaining stages of the processing technique. One trouble spot in that connection may be overlapping color sensitivities in the three emulsion layers. This danger was recognized early, and considerable efforts were made to overcome it. It became necessary to develop new sensitizing agents whose spectral cuts would be sharp, and mutually exclusive, at least when used in connection with the proper filters. The red sensitizer must have a pronounced gap in the blue-green region of the spectrum. Pinacyanol fails completely in this respect, since it has a considerable activity in the green Sensitizers fulfilling these conditions are described in English patents 383486, 400951, 402521, 410481, 427887, 432969, 442160, 480778, 483548, and 486005. The exact requirements for the sensitivity of the various zones are described in greater detail in English patent 501190. The blue filter layer should have a sensitivity ranging from 400 mμ to 480 mμ. This indicates a considerably sharper cut than is generally used in three-color work, where the blue cut usually is allowed to extend to 510 or even to 520 mμ Since there is a yellow filter between the blue and the other two layers, the sensitivity of the green below 500 is of no account Light whose wavelength is less than that, will not be able to reach the green-sensitive zone Its sensitivity should not extend beyond 610 mμ, and the maximum should be at 540. The red-sensitive layer should have its maximum lying between 580 and 630 mμ. This would indicate that Agfacolor has a range extending from 400 mμ to approximately 650, and the sensitivities should separate from each other at 480 mμ and at 570 mμ. This again is quite different from standard procedure, which separates the three zones at 500 and 600 mμ.

The complete process is described in English patent 481501, issued on March 7, 1938. The monopack layers are formed as follows Upon the base is coated a red-sensitive emulsion layer to which has been added 1-N-stearoyl-4-N-(1′-hydroxy-2′-naphthoyl)-phenylenediamine-sulphonicacid, in the form of the sodium salt. It is interesting to note that this compound contains at least three conditions that would make it substantive to gelatin. One amino group of the paraphenylenediamine has been converted into a stearoyl-amide which, as has been pointed out, gives the molecule fastness to diffusion by the inclusion of an 18-carbon chain, hydrocarbon residue. The entire molecule is given an acid character by the inclusion of a sulphonic acid group. This makes it substantive to gelatin by virtue of its ability to form gelatin sulphonates. The third condition is the substitution of the phenylenediamine residue into the alpha-hydroxy-naphthoic-acid molecule, for it is the naphthol which combines with the oxidized developer to form the cyan dye. Any chance that the phenylenediamine molecule may have had to unite with the developer was destroyed when each amino group was converted into an amide, one by conversion into stearoyl amide, the other by conversion into naphthoyl amide. This explains the reason for the inclusion of an acid group into the naphthol molecule.

The second, or green-sensitive emulsion layer contains the sodium salt of 1-(5′-sulpho-3′-stearoyl-aminophenyl)-pyrazolone. Here again the substantive character of the pyrazolone molecule is taken care of, at least three times.

First, by the inclusion of the 18-carbon chain stearoyl residue, second, by the inclusion of a sulphonic acid radical; and third, by the substitution within the pyrazolone molecule of an amino-phenyl group. The coupling properties of this last group are destroyed by masking the amine group with the stearoyl residue The blue-sensitive layer contains the sodium salt of meta-stearoyl-amino-benzoyl-acetanilide-para'-carboxylic acid. The molecule is made substantive first by the inclusion of the very heavy stearoyl residue, second by the inclusion of the acid carboxyl group which would allow the formation of a gelatin-carboxylate salt, and third by the presence of an amino-benzoyl group whose coupler properties have been masked when the amine group has been converted into a stearoyl-amide It is to be noted that besides containing specific groups which yield substantive character, the molecules are all very heavy ones so that even if conditions are formed which would prevent their union with the gelatin, they would have a very limited range about which they could roam in the time during which they are sufficiently wet to be subject to diffusion. The cyan coupler present in the red-sensitive layer has a molecular weight of 613. The magenta coupler in the green-sensitive layer has a molecular weight of 543, while the yellow coupler present in the third layer has a molecular weight of 582 These are really giant molecules, which could hardly exist in solution except in colloidal state.

Despite all the efforts which have been made to find new agents which would yield color-coupled dyes, it is interesting to note that all the cyan dyes are formed either from the hydroxy benzenes, or from the hydroxy naphthalines This is true not only of all the coupling agents disclosed by Ansco and the I.G., but also of those disclosed by the members of the Eastman Kodak staff. And in the very early descriptions of Fischer and Siegrist, these substances were used for the formation of the cyan image All that has been done in the generation that has passed since that time, is to tack on certain side-chain substitutions into the molecule. And Fischer and Siegrist outlined in some detail what the effect of substitutions would be. The magenta couplers fall into two classes. First there is pyrazolone and the pyrazolone derivatives These couplers appear to be preferred by Ansco and the I G. Then there is benzyl cyanide and its derivatives These appear to be favored by Eastman The yellows, without exception, are all compounds which contain the central grouping —CO—CH_2—CO—. The only difference between the very many compounds that have been proposed, is in the nature of the groups which round out the molecule. Two such groups are needed to form the compound, and these can be anything from a simple hydrocarbon to a complicated substitution.

After exposure, the pack is developed for fifteen minutes in an amidol depth-developer.

Amidol	5 parts
Sodium sulphite	50 parts
Potassium bromide	1 part
Water to	1000 parts

A ten-minute wash removes excess developer. The negative image is next removed by treatment with a solution containing half of one per cent of chromic acid, or with

Potassium dichromate	4 parts
Sulphuric acid	2½ parts
Water to	1000 parts

The pack is washed again for a period of ten minutes. The treatment with acid dichromate or chromic acid desensitizes the silver halide salts remaining in the emulsion, so that it becomes necessary to restore the sensitivity by treatment for two minutes with a three per cent solution of sodium sulphite. After a further five-minute wash, the film is exposed to light until all the remaining grains become developable The second development is carried out in the amidol depth-developer noted above Instead of giving the pack an exposure to light to make the remaining grains developable, it is possible to treat it chemically with a fogging agent such as thiourea and thiourea derivatives. This is suggested in English patent 489845, but of course similar ideas have been suggested ever since reversal development became an established practice. The Eastman Kodak Company, in its procedure, mentions the use of these agents, as well as the use of dyes like methylene blue, etc. Thiourea was added to developers as far back as 1910 or thereabouts, when it was suggested to develop a positive image directly after the first exposure. Even at that time its action as a fogging agent of great power, was known. There is, therefore, but little novelty in this specific patent.

It may be wondered just why the second development was not carried out with phenylenediamine, so that conversion to color would take place immediately. That would have made unnecessary the patent which is being described now. But a more serious reason is that it may be desirable to see the positive in the form of a black-and-white silver image, and to note any corrections that may be necessary. Reduction, or intensification by means of silver salts, would then be possible. Since for every four atoms of silver there is formed one molecule of dye, the change in silver would change the dye content. But the only changes that would be possible would be overall changes in contrast, for it would be rather a difficult matter to treat the silver image, say in the bottom layer, without at the same time treating the silver images in the other two layers. After all manipulations have been carried out, the silver is converted into silver chloride by treatment with a bleach of the wash-off relief type

Chromic acid	5 parts
Sodium chloride	50 parts
Water to	1000 parts

or

Potassium dichromate	4 parts
Hydrochloric acid	2½ parts
Sodium chloride	20 parts
Water to	1000 parts

The silver chloride is now ready for color-development. This is accomplished by treatment of the reformed salt with a paraphenylenediamine developer made as follows:

Sodium sulphite	½ part
Di-ethylparaphenylenediamine	2½ parts
Potassium bromide	2½ parts
Potassium carbonate	30 parts
Water to	1000 parts

The time of development is twenty-five minutes. Since the coupling agents are already present in the film, it is not necessary to include them in the developer formula. Therefore the same solution is used to develop the three layers, and there is formed a magenta image in the green-sensitive layer (by condensation of the oxidized developer with the agent present in that layer), a cyan image in the red-sensitive layer (by condensation with the agent present there), and a yellow image in the blue-sensitive layer (by reaction with the substance in that zone). It is very important that the wash after this step be exceptionally good, so that no more developer is present in the film when it is subjected to the action of a 5 per cent ferricyanide solution to which has been added 5 per cent sodium chloride. Otherwise a general color stain will result. Hypo removes the silver chloride formed in the last step, and after a final wash the positive transparency is complete.

As outlined above, this process differs materially from the early Kodachrome. There a complicated system of processing was required before the three latent images were converted into their proper colors. Here all the complications have been removed, and only four simple steps are required to obtain the final result. The first is an ordinary development in a depth developer that is well known to photographic technicians Second there is the removal of the silver image by treatment with a silver solvent This step also has been well exploited by the average color technician who had previous experience with the older screen plate processes (cf. chapter on Screen Plates). The third step is redevelopment with a special developer, whose composition is well known. The last step consists in the removal of the silver image, and this can be done either in a single bath (Farmer's reducer) or in two stages, as described above.

CHAPTER 12

SCREEN PLATES

THE integral methods for the preparation of color photographs are not confined to the monopacks. Ducos du Hauron suggested a much simpler method almost fifty years before the first monopack was even conceived. This he disclosed in his French patent 83061 issued in 1868, and developed further in a series of papers which were later collected and published in book form, "Les Couleurs en Photographie," in 1869. If a base be completely covered with alternating lines of red, blue, and yellow, so that no empty spaces lie between them, they will not be seen at normal viewing distance as individual lines, if they are sufficiently fine., They will be seen as a gray, the hue that would result from the fusion of the three secondary colors. This effect can best be visualized by an examination of a halftone reproduction of a picture in newspapers and in magazines A newspaper picture is usually reproduced by means of 40 to 60 lines to the inch. At normal viewing distance the individual units could just be seen, giving rise to a picture with coarse detail. A magazine illustration utilizes a minimum of 120 lines to the inch, and these cannot be seen individually except under a small-power glass. The picture under these conditions appears smooth and continuous To make a motion picture equally smooth, it would require a minimum of 500 lines to the inch.

If the transmission through one of the lines were blocked out, the light that would result would be due to the fusion of but two primaries, and it would no longer be white or gray. Thus, in order to obtain a red color, it is sufficient to block out the blue and yellow lines. To obtain blue, the other two are blocked. It is possible to obtain any combination of colors by merely partially blocking out each of the lines, to a different extent. Black would be obtained by completely blocking out all three of the lines.

In making such a pattern, du Hauron pointed out that it is necessary that the fusion of the three lines, when none of them are blocked, give rise to a pure white. This was later described as the "first black condition" by Mees and Pledge. Then the uniform blocking of the three elements will give rise to neutral grays. If the elements of the screen are very coarse, it is possible to manually block out each primary color to the desired degree. But in the case where complete fusion is desired, the elementary cells would be too fine to enable an operator to deposit light-retarders behind each unit Du Hauron realized, however, that the rapidly growing art of photography enabled a person to make blocking-out a routine and automatic procedure. All that was necessary was to put a light-sensitive emulsion over the screen and allow the light to fall on the emulsion only after passage through the screen elements. The emulsion must be such that it can be processed directly to a positive, so that the different light intensities become immediately transformed into equivalent transparencies.

To make the procedure possible, the emulsion had to be sensitive to all the rays of the spectrum. If it was more sensitive to one group of rays than to another, it was possible to place in front of the areas occupied by the more sensitive colors, light retarders to such a degree that equivalent speeds resulted This was later known as the "second black condition" It is equivalent to placing neutral filters in front of the color elements. A more useful method for the balancing of the emulsion speeds to the three primary colors, was to vary the relative areas covered by each of the color elements

Up to this point du Hauron merely outlined, in general terms, a new method that could be used to make color photographs. He did not disclose how such a screen could be made until a considerable time had elapsed. It was not until 1897 that Alcide Ducos du Hauron, who was a brother of L. Ducos du Hauron, published a book, "La Triplice photographique et l'Imprimerie," in which he outlined two general procedures for the preparation of screens. These disclosures have great historical value, since they predate all other patents that disclose the formation of screens. The first method stated that it would be possible to rule the lines mechanically, using an obvious procedure. The second method is one which has been patented and repatented a countless number of times, not only in the exact form outlined by du Hauron, but with all possible variations And yet no successful screen plate utilizing this procedure has been marketed.

The scheme utilized the action of light upon dichromated gelatin which had been previously dyed a primary red, and which was coated upon a transparent base. It was exposed under a negative which consisted of a series of opaque and transparent lines, the width of the opaque ones being twice those of the others Upon exposure, the gelatin receiving the light becomes converted into insoluble form Hot water removes the gelatin protected from the light by the opaque lines. This leaves a series of fine red lines upon the base, which cover one third of the total area. The coloring matter is firmly fixed within the gelatin by a further treatment with mordants and tanning agents. After being thoroughly set and insulated, the base is recoated with sensitized gelatin, and this time dyed green. It is again exposed through a negative, but now the lines run at right angles to those previously formed, and the opaque regions are equal in width to the transparent ones. The sensitized gelatin is exposed through the red lines, so that these act also as opaque lines By this means, one-half of the areas between the red lines become converted into green areas. The remaining gelatin is removed by hot water, the green areas treated to fix the coloring matter in a permanent form, and the plate recoated again, but with sensitized gelatin dyed blue. The last exposure is made only through the base of the plate, the red lines and green squares acting as a negative. Since dichromated gelatin is insensitive to red and green light, only the regions free of them will be affected. In this manner the entire surface of the plate becomes covered with the color elements, no clear spaces existing between them, thus satisfying the fundamental conditions.

From the above it is seen that du Hauron had a very good conception of the procedure involved in screen plates. One curious fact stands out. In his very first disclosures, du Hauron speaks of the line elements being colored red, yellow, and blue. Thirty years later he makes the colors red, green, and blue The effect of loose terminology is quite apparent here The blue and red in the first set cannot be the same as the blue and red of the last. Yellow is a minusing primary, and in the set where it forms one of the colors, a magenta rather than a red, and a cyan rather than a blue, are required. Color photographers have fallen into the very bad practice of calling the "magenta" a red, and the "cyan" a blue. These misnomers arose from the fact that the printing inks available in the early days were poor. Even today, the actual color of the minus-green printing ink is much more nearly a red than a magenta, and the minus-red printing ink is almost a blue. We must assume, from the neutrality conditions that he himself set up, that in the first set du Hauron actually meant to use magenta, yellow, and cyan colored elements When such dots lie in juxtaposition it is possible to obtain a neutral, but if the magenta be replaced by a red, and the cyan by a blue, it will be impossible to obtain a neutral gray, but rather a highly diluted and unsaturated red.

The effect of photographing with magenta, cyan, and yellow elements, instead of the normal set, would be to dilute the colors with white. The image behind a yellow line, for instance, would contain a silver deposit that is due to the red and the green primaries. The red densities would be deposited also behind the magenta element, this time together with the blue. Thus there is no clear-cut separation of the primary colors A bright red color would yield deposits behind the yellow and the magenta lines, and no deposit behind the cyan. Upon conversion into a positive, the transmission through the cyan element would be zero, and through the yellow and magenta elements 100 per cent. But yellow contains equivalent portions of red and green, while magenta contains equivalent portions of red and blue. The fused beam would contain equivalent amounts of the blue and green primaries, and double that quantity of red One unit of red will combine with the blue and green to yield a white The final color will be red diluted with an equal quantity of white. It is significant that in his latest reference to the subject du Hauron no longer made that error, but utilized red, green, and blue.

In the preparation of a screened surface, several problems confront the technician First of all, the spectral characteristics of the individual line elements must be considered. The fact that the process is an additive one, should fix these rigidly, but the early workers in color photography were still under the influence of the psychologists, and considerable debate was occasioned by the lack of precise knowledge in this respect The physicists were strangely silent. Perhaps the apparent success of the Young-Helmholtz-Maxwell ideas concerning color mixtures throttled all other approaches in the field of color reproduction, just as it did in the field of color vision. It was only in the middle third of the twentieth century that the physical and biochemists began to challenge the other approaches to the study of color and vision. Unfortunately, color photography could not wait until a satisfactory solution to this fundamental problem had been found

The first experimenters utilized the data on color mixing that had been gathered by Maxwell, Koenig, and others. Prof J. Joly (*Brit J. Phot.*, Vol. 42 (1895), p. 774) rejected the Maxwell curves in favor of those by Koenig. His blue element approximated in color monochromatic light of wavelength 455 mμ. The red color was approximately that corresponding to a wavelength of 600 mμ, and the green corresponded to a wavelength of 550 mμ Actual measurements made on a Joly plate by Kaiserling (*Phot Mitt.*, Vol. 35 (1898), p. 273, Vol 36 (1899) p. 8, 14, 35, 46, 65) indicated that the red transmission began at 550 and extended to 670 with a maximum at between 580 and 600. The green began at 470 and extended to 570 with a maximum between 515 and 530. The blue ranged from 430 to 520 and had a maximum at 460 to 480. Thus, while precise specifications were laid down and theories accepted or rejected if they did not correspond to these specifications, the practice was really very much the opposite. The red overlap into the green appears to have been almost to the point of the maximum green transmission, and a very small gap existed between the limits of the blue and the red primaries, a gap sufficiently small to make these colors better suited for a two-color separation than for a three. The green transmission overlapped the blue up to the point of maximum blue transmission. The blue affected the green in a like manner. Such color separations may give plates with high speed ratings, and perhaps yield original color photographs that would appear quite pleasant, but the separations made from them would yield prints of very poor quality, unless color corrections were applied. Abney ("The Scientific Requirements of Colour Photography," 1897), also insisted that the elements correspond to the three fundamental color sensations, but because this would entail the use of a green highly diluted with white, he made a compromise upon this score. His green corresponded to a color with a wavelength of 527 mμ, which was but slightly diluted with white. The red, which according to his theory should correspond to a wavelength of 671, was also a compromise and actually corresponded to light with a wavelength of 656 The blue corresponded to a wavelength of 460 mμ

Mees (*Brit J. Phot*, Vol. 55 (1908), p. 41), and Mees and Pledge (*Phot J*, Vol 50 (1910), p. 197), made an exhaustive study of the entire subject. These men concluded that the practical requirements demanded that the red have a transmission which begins at 590; the green a transmission ranging from 490 to 590; and the blue, a transmission up to 500 mμ These are practically mutually exclusive filters that correspond very closely to the physical requirements for color analysis (cf. chapter on Objective Color). The F, N, and C4 filters, which are the Wratten filters Nos. 29, 61, and 49, approximate these transmissions As was indicated previously, their use would entail a tremendous loss of light efficiency, due to the inherent inefficacies of the dyes, so a compromise has been made in the use of the somewhat overlapping set, A, B and C5. The condition that the fused elements should yield a pure white, the first black condition previously pointed out by du Hauron, must be met by a variation in the ratios of the areas covered by the respective elements, rather than by change in the densities of the colors. These must give complete cutouts

Also very important in the manufacture of a screen, are the questions relating to screen pattern, and the size of the elements. W. Scheffer (*Brit J. Phot.*, Vol. 56 (1909), Col. Supp., p. 62, 70) tackled this last by a study of the relationship between object size and the resolving power of the eye. He found that black-and-white objects will be seen as distinct items if their period is 1/1000 of their distance from the eye. The period is the distance between two lines of like character in a screen containing opaque and transparent lines of equal width. E. J. Wall ("History of Three-Color Photography" (1925), p. 462) pointed out that color does not follow this rule. Color elements fuse much sooner The size under these conditions must be 1/600 of the distance of the object from the eye. With the irregular screen, the possibility of clumping further modifies these values. Mees and Pledge finally conclude that in geometrical screens the units should have a size varying between 1/300 to 1/600 of an inch. Irregular screens should have elements whose sizes fall between 1/900 to 1/1200 of an inch. This, of course, relates to screens to be used for normal viewing, and not for projection. The Autochrome plate contained colored starch grains whose average size was 0.015 mm. This corresponded to 0.0006 inch, or 1666 to the inch.

The first black condition demands that the entire surface of the plate be covered by the screen elements, and that no part of the area be free from color. If the screen is formed by mechanical dyeing or inking, there is danger that the color in one element will run over into an adjacent one. At any rate, the line formed by the juncture of two elements will contain both dyes, and to all intents and purposes, will be black. As these lines will have some dimension, in order not to lose too much light efficiency their length must be kept to an absolute minimum. C. W. Piper (*Brit. J. Phot.*, Vol. 50 (1909), Col. Supp , p 84), made a study of this phase of the subject. His results indicated that the length of the lines formed by the junction of two screen elements will be a minimum where the screen is composed of parallel lines. A close second to this is the case, used by Dufaycolor, where the elements consist of parallel lines of one color interposed with squares of the other two

Finally, there is the problem of putting a panchromatic emulsion on top of the screen. To make the emulsion stick, a substratum must first be coated directly over the screen. This serves two purposes. First it insulates the screen from the photographic emulsion and prevents the action of water or photographic processing solutions upon the ingredients in the screen elements Then it serves to bind the emulsion layer to the plate or film The thickness of this substratum must be as low as possible so that too great a separation will not exist between the screen and the photographic emulsion. The emulsion must be as rapid as possible, for there already is lost a considerable amount of light by absorption by the screen elements, etc. Therefore there is a limit to the fineness of the grains. On the other hand, they cannot be too coarse, for then too few of the emulsion grains would be located behind any one screen element to make it an average sample of the entire emulsion. Weird and uncertain results would be obtained This problem will be discussed in detail a little later.

The emulsion must be panchromatized in such a manner that when the exposure is made through the screen elements, equal times of exposure and development will yield equal densities behind each element in those regions which correspond to whites and grays. This is known as the second black condition. It is not a very easy matter to accomplish such a result, because it is difficult to make two batches of emulsion having identical characteristics One needs only to record the variations in the values of the filter factors of a given type of emulsion from coatings that are six months or a year apart, to determine this fact. A variation of the relative areas of the screen elements would probably be sufficient to maintain this condition, but it is a question whether a shift in these ratios made to fulfill the second black condition would not, at the same time, disturb the first black condition.

It has been suggested that the emulsion grains behind each screen element be sensitized only for the color which that element transmits. This can be done by adsorbing the sensitizer upon the colored screen element, and coating a blind emulsion directly upon this. Several problems are at once introduced. First there is no guarantee that a sufficient sensitization would be had by this technique, for only a few layers of grains would be affected. Secondly there is the problem of coating an emulsion directly on top of the screen elements with no substratum to bind the two together. Frilling and separation of the two are very likely to occur under such conditions. Finally there would be the problem of choosing the colors for the screen elements, so that they would not only adsorb sufficient sensitizing dyes to act upon the emulsion, but would also be completely impervious to the action of the processing solutions, of which one is acidified dichromate or permanganate, powerful oxidizing agents, especially toward the organic dyes.

A much better method has been disclosed by the I.G. (Eng. P. 459119). A basic emulsion is divided into three portions, and each portion is sensitized to a different primary. Portions of each emulsion are then tested behind filters that are identical with the ones in the screen plate itself. By this means the relative sensitivities of the emulsion to the three primaries are determined. The grains are then mixed thoroughly in the proportions required to yield exact balance.

The emulsion should be as fine-grained as it is possible to use with a given size screen element. The greater the area covered by each unit, the coarser can be the emulsion. It should be recalled that an emulsion is not a dispersion of homogeneous light-sensitive particles The sensitivities of the individual grains vary tremendously. It is only the fine-grained, very slow, and extremely contrasty emulsions that approach any degree of uniformity. An emulsion that has considerable latitude and wide covering range is possible only because of the existence of a large variety of sensitivities among the individual grains. It has been pointed out that in extremely fast emulsions, only five per cent of the grains are sufficiently sensitive to become developable by the absorption of but a single quantum of light. But it requires 200 quanta to make the average grain in the same emulsion developable. Therefore, there must be at least several hundred types of grains present, and the emulsion has properties which are a statistical average of the properties of each of these varieties. It is essential, therefore, in order to achieve uniformity, that behind each unit of screen there be present a sufficient number of grains to be representative of the emulsion as a whole. This number must be counted not in hundreds, but in thousands and tens of thousands And since it is desirable to keep the image as close as possible to the screen itself, each grain layer of emulsion must have this number behind each color unit.

Most of our information concerning emulsions comes from that brilliant team, Carrol and Hubbard, who did their work at the Bureau of Standards, in Washington, D.C. They used an experimental emulsion that represented a normal speed at the time they made their disclosures (*Bu Stand. J. of Res*, Vol 7 (1931) p 229). The projective areas of the grains in this emulsion ranged from 0 36 to 1 00 square μ, so that each grain had a linear dimension ranging from 0 6 to 1 0 μ These values have been corroborated by others, as representing the grain size in the average negative emulsion. The grains are dispersed in gelatin, and between any two grains there lies a wall of gelatin. The two substances, gelatin and silver halide, are present in equal amounts by weight, but gelatin is much less dense than silver, so that the volume of gelatin is much greater than that of halide. But we can assume exact equivalence. Hence the average distance between grain centers will vary from 1 to 2 μ, so that there will be from 500 to 1000 grains to the linear millimeter of emulsion surface, or from one-half to one grain per μ.

The Autochrome plate contained color elements that were about 1666 to the inch. It has sometimes been claimed to have 2000. Taking the last value, this means that the cell has a linear dimension of $12\frac{1}{2}$ μ, and an area of 156 square μ. In order for this space to contain 1000 grains, there would have to be 30 grains in $12\frac{1}{2}$ μ, or each grain would have to be at most 0.4 μ in size. This explains to a large extent why the Autochrome plate was sixty times as slow as the normal negative emulsion of that period. The Agfa plate was exactly twice as fast as the Autochrome

The Dufaycolor film contains color elements with a cross section of 0.002

inch or 50 μ Therefore between 625 and 2500 grains can lie beneath each screen element, per layer of emulsion. There are approximately thirty layers so that a total ranging from 20,000 to 75,000 grains will lie in each unit. This represents a good average for the emulsion as a whole, and the individual layers will also be fairly representative. Under these conditions, there is hope for latitude and range. The popularity achieved by this material can no doubt be ascribed in large measure to the fact that fast emulsions can be used in the preparation of Dufaycolor film, whereas screen plates with finer screen elements must use finer-grained, slower, and more contrasty emulsions. Unless our emulsion makers can make superfine emulsions, with high speeds, it is doubtful if screens with more than 500 elements to the linear inch can be made. The speed of an emulsion is to a large extent determined by the intensification factor of the developer. This term is defined as the ratio of the number of atoms of silver formed to the number of quanta absorbed by the grain to make it developable Under present conditions (1943), the fast emulsions have values of 10,000,000. If the grain is made materially smaller, the number of silver atoms in the grain becomes smaller. The problem is therefore to make the grains faster by an amount greater than the size decrease Considerable leeway is had in this respect, for in the fast emulsions, 200 quanta of light must be absorbed before the average grain becomes developable. Theoretically, only one quantum should be required

Many ingenious schemes have been formulated for the preparation of the screen These can be classified into a number of groups, the members of each group being related by the technique used. The groups are as follows:

1. Dusting-On Methods
2. Woven Fabrics
3. Blocks
4. Photographic Printing
5. Photo-Mechanical Printing
6. Ruled Lines
7. Resists
8. Miscellaneous

A critical discussion of these procedures will be given in the following chapter. Here will be offered only a generalized description.

In the dusting-on schemes, finely powdered colors are dusted over a tacky surface. A gentle blast of air removes the particles that are not directly adhering to the surface, and thus only one layer of the grains becomes attached. If the powders are properly mixed, each red grain will be surrounded by blue and green grains, and vice versa. In some schemes the dry powders are first distributed in a colloidal medium like gelatin, nitro cellulose, gums, etc., and this dispersion is coated upon the base in a thickness just sufficient to yield a single layer of colored particles. Obviously this is but an improved form of the dusting-on methods. All kinds of substances have been suggested for a source of the powders, including glass, nitro-cellulose, gums, varnishes, gelatin, pollen, microbes, bacteria, starch, oil drops, etc. In general, the substances are dyed, then ground or atomized to powder form, mixed to fulfill the first black condition, and coated upon the base

The rapid advances made by the textile industry in the making of extremely fine fibers soon brought the suggestion that such fibers, colored properly, could be woven into fabrics. The colored fibers would all be woven in one direction, while the fibers that would weave in the other direction to hold the fabric together, would be colorless and transparent. The artificial silk fibers, rayons, etc., were especially suitable for this purpose. The fibers could be drawn very fine, to the order of a few thousandths of an inch, hence screens suitable for normal viewing could be made.

One method for the preparation of the screens suggests itself naturally. Thus sections of nitrocellulose, gelatin, etc., are dyed properly, then placed one on top of the other until a solid block is built A cross section of this block will show a series of lines alternating in the three colors. The sections can be cast as thin as desired, even less than 0 0001 inch in thickness Any degree of fineness could therefore be obtained After formation, the block is cut across the layers by means of a microtome, giving sheets of screens suitable for immediate use. It is also possible to cross section a block of this type, reform the block, and cut it again from a different direction. Instead of lines, there will be obtained a checkerboard mosaic. Another possibility is to convert the block into a cylinder, and section this spirally, to yield a long continuous film of screen. It is not a difficult matter to cut sections 36 by 72 inches as thin as 0 005 inch Smaller sheets can be cut still thinner. Such film sections can be used not only as a screen, but also as the base upon which the emulsion is cast

The most obvious method for the formation of the screen is to rule the colored lines upon a base. This presents some technological problems, since it is essential that one element just touch its neighbor with a minimum of overlapping. Only slightly less difficult are the methods by which the screen is printed by photo-mechanical methods, such as letter press, lithography, or offset. Here, again, registry problems arise that are considerably more difficult than in ordinary printing In the present instance it is required to print screens with a minimum of several hundred elements to the inch, while in normal printing the screens have approximately 120 lines to the inch.

These difficulties are not met with when photographic printing is attempted. The more successful methods utilized dichromated gelatin. This was coated upon a base, and exposed under a black-and-white screen. The exposed gelatin became tanned and would absorb only certain types of colors. Or a pinatype dye could be put into the gelatin before the exposure, in which case it would wash out only from the non-exposed portions. Two procedures are open. The soft gelatin could be removed by hot water, and the plate recoated, this time with dichromated gelatin dyed another color. The new exposure is made at right angles to the first This fills up half the remaining spaces with a dyed gelatin The procedure is finally repeated to put on the third color. The other possibility is to take advantage of the fact that certain dyes will stain only tanned gelatin, while other dyes will stain only soft gelatin The plate, after the first exposure, contains a series of lines of tanned gelatin separated from each other by areas of soft gelatin. These could be dyed different colors, and the untanned gelatin again sensitized and exposed at right angles to the first. The dye is washed out of the soft gelatin, and this is dyed with the third color.

Anything that can be accomplished by the action of light on dichromate, could also be accomplished by means of a silver image It is possible therefore, to coat a plate with a silver emulsion, expose it to a line screen, and treat the silver to give lines of tanned gelatin interspersed with areas of soft gelatin The further procedure could be as above. It is also possible to convert the silver image into a primary color, by toning methods or by coupler development This would leave silver bromide in the areas between the toned lines, which could be treated in any desired fashion to yield the other two colors

The most successful of all screen processes, Dufaycolor, utilizes the resist methods for the formation of the screen Here a fatty ink is printed by mechanical means upon the surface of the dyed film The areas between the ink lines are subjected to a solution which dissolves out, or which destroys the coloring matter. These areas are next dyed a different color, the resist lines removed, and a new set printed at right angles to the first. Again the coloring matter is removed, and the third dye placed in the now colorless spaces. A variation of this would be to print, mechanically, a waterproof substance upon a photographic emulsion. The areas between the resists could now be treated with coupler developers. The resist is then removed and a new one put on, covering half of the remaining unreacted space; or, only half of the resist could be removed The newly exposed emulsion areas can be again developed to a different color The removal of the resist now exposes the last third which can be converted to the third primary. Instead of a series of color development, it is possible to convert the silver halide into silver iodide or silver iodide-thiourea complexes which are completely transparent and highly absorbent of basic dyes Or, the photographic emulsion, before the resist is put on, can be converted into a silver iodide complex and dyed uniformly one color. A resist could be printed upon it, and the dye halide complex destroyed by the action of acid permanganate. Treatment with sulphite removes the reduced manganous salts, and treatment with iodide reconstructs the silver-iodide complex. This is now dyed with another color, and the entire procedure repeated These last few ideas are discussed at this point rather than in the next chapter because they are not disclosed in the patent literature, and are only hypothetical processes.

The efficiencies of screen plates are not very high This is due mainly to the fact that the individual screen elements transmit but a fraction of all the light falling upon them. Measurements by Mees and Pledge made upon the plates commercially available in 1910, show that only 20 per cent of the light was transmitted by the most efficient of them all, the Dufay plate. This was not the final Dufaycolor film, but an early edition of the later product. Other color plates of the time transmitted as follows: Autochrome 7½ per cent; Thames (Finlay) 12 per cent, and Omnicolore 15 per cent. It is seen, therefore, that the Autochrome plate would have a factor of 14, were it able to use the normal emulsion. But its factor was 60

The introduction of Kodachrome, Ansco Color and Agfacolor dealt a severe blow to the popularity of the screen plates There are several basic advantages to the monopack schemes which would explain their immediate acceptance First of all, the lens speeds of the newer materials were at least equal to, and in all probability greater than, those obtained with screen plates. The popular demand has ever been for speed and more speed Secondly, the transparencies obtained by their use are continuous in tone, so that enlargement of four diameters or more can be made, whereas with the use of a screen plate, the enlargement is limited to not more than two diameters. In the matter of making separations from the transparencies, the use of monopacks is to be preferred, since the overlaps between the primary colors are much less There is one field, however, that appears to be ideally suited for the screen plate This is the use of a screened bipack in which the front element is a screen plate which registers two of the primaries, and the rear element registers the third. This procedure was first disclosed by Ives (Eng. P. 112769, Fr. P. 487529, U.S P. 1268847). The screen units in the front element were colored yellow and magenta, and these were coated with an emulsion sensitive only to the blue and green primaries. The blue densities would be registered only behind the magenta elements, while the green densities would register only behind the yellow lines. By the use of filters, it therefore becomes possible to copy the images behind these lines upon separate plates. Both the yellow and the magenta lines transmit the red rays with great efficiency. Since the front element is completely insensitive to this section of the spectrum, it will register only upon the rear element, and in the form of a continuous tone negative.

The making of a two-color screen is very much less complicated than the making of a three-color screen. It is rather surprising, therefore, that no one in the generation since Ives disclosed this idea, made any attempt to utilize it. J E Thornton (Eng P 238688) proposed to use a screen plate for two colors in a three-color process, but the third color was to be obtained by a separate beam. There is very little economy in this type of procedure. The same inventor also proposed upon many occasions to use a double-width film, each half of which contained a two-color line screen. A beam-splitting camera projected an image upon each half of the film, giving the possibility of a four-color process.

It was not until the Ives patent had almost expired, that the original disclosure became resurrected. G. S. Whitfield, of the Ilford company (Eng. P. 371009) proposed to use a bipack loaded celluloid to celluloid. The front element was blue-sensitive. The rear element was red- and green-sensitive, and carried a screen between the base and the emulsion. This scheme is different from the original, and also not nearly as effective. The existence of two thicknesses of celluloid between the front emulsion and the rear certainly does not tend to improve definition, already rendered somewhat inferior by diffusion through a front emulsion. Neither is complete registry possible, since this separation allows a further spreading of the rays, making the rear images slightly larger than the front

A method of printing from this bipack is disclosed by Mr. Whitfield in English patent 416114 Another variation of the Ives original disclosure is contained in English patent 419887, issued to J E. Thornton. He proposed to put a red-sensitive emulsion in front of a two-color screen which registers the other two primaries. As is the case with the Whitfield disclosure, this one is just so much wishful thinking. All the objections mentioned previously hold true here, and to these can be added the most serious one of all, that of poor color separation. It is not possible at this writing (1943), to prepare an emulsion in which the red sensitivity is so much greater than the blue that no interference will result. It has been proposed (cf. chapter on Tripacks and Bipacks) to dye a fast red-blue-sensitive emulsion, with a yellow dye in order to reduce the blue sensitivity. That most certainly can be done, but then very little blue light will reach the emulsion below. The loss of speed would be so great that even the most inefficient of one-shot cameras would be fast in comparison. The proposed improvement upon the Ives screened bipack is an improvement in name only, and represents merely someone's idea that it would be nice if the thing worked But it doesn't, not anywhere near as well as the original.

CHAPTER 13

FORMATION OF THE SCREEN

IN the previous chapter there were outlined eight general classes into which the techniques used for the making of the screen could be grouped Here will be discussed the specific methods contained in each of the groups The first to be discussed will be those procedures that do not yield geometrically patterned screens. Of these the most important are the ones utilizing "dusting-on" schemes. J. W. McDonough, who shares with Prof. Joly the distinction of being the first to put du Hauron's suggestions into practice, was the first to use this technique (Eng. P. 5597/92, U.S.P. 411186 and 471187) The surface of a plate or film was made tacky by a coat of varnish. On this was dusted a mixture of fine colored powders made of glass, pigments, stained gelatin, resins, or shellac The last was the preferred medium Three batches of shellac were dissolved in alcohol, dyed primary red, green, and blue respectively, dried, and finally ground into fine powders. These were mixed in the proportions required to fulfill the first black condition, then applied to the tacky surface If any colorless interstices showed up, heat was applied up to the point at which the colored powders fused together. He also suggested that the emulsion surface could be rendered tacky, and the colored particles dusted over it. This would allow the exposures to be made through the surface of the emulsion, in the normal manner. But if the colored particles consisted of shellac or other waterproof material, some difficulty might be met in the processing. Presumedly, in this case, it is the stained gelatin powders that were to be used

Soon after 1900 came the Autochrome plate which was the discovery and development of the Lumières, assisted by Seyewetz. This plate enjoyed a considerable popularity from the very beginning, and its use extended well into the nineteen thirties. The elements used were starch grains (Eng. P. 22988/04; U.S.P. 822532, Fr. P. 339223; Ger. P. 172851), ferments, yeast, bacilli, or powdered enamels The grains were dyed magenta, cyan, and yellow, mixed to yield neutrality, and then spread over a tacky surface On top of this was coated a second tacky surface upon which was distributed dyed grains such that the two together would yield red, blue, and green elements. The refractive index of the varnishes must be the same as that of the color elements, otherwise a loss of light by interface reflections would result The same result could be obtained by mixing particles dyed in six colors, red, orange, yellow, green, blue and violet (Eng. P. 25718/04, 9100/06 and 8153/11; U.S.P. 877351).

Some interesting details concerning the preparation of the plates were given by E. Ventujol (*Rev. franç. Phot.*, Vol. 4 (1923), p 80, E. J. Wall, "History of Three-Color Photography" (1925), p 467). The grains were sifted by elutriation, and dyed with triphenylmethane dyes The spaces between the colored particles were filled in with charcoal, which was applied by means of a special machine A daily examination of the plates was made to check the procedure, and one day the grains appeared to be much more transparent than usual This was traced to the application of pressure to the plate, a procedure that was finally adopted as routine About 5000 kilos (approximately 11,000 pounds) pressure per square centimeter was applied The emulsion was one rich in silver bromide, and poor in gelatin

The Lumières were not the only ones to use yeast or other dead cells. Borrel and Pinoy (Fr. P 373492) stained microbes, or staphylococci which had previously been killed by heat In French patent 379632 they also suggested yeast cells. A variation of this was disclosed by H. Clement (Fr P. 416700). He allowed the corpuscles to grow to the proper size, dyed them while still alive, then killed them. Dyed pollen was suggested by K. Campbell (Eng. P 224571). The pollen was bleached in peroxide, dyed, mixed to yield a neutral black, dispersed in a colloid, then spread upon a glass or film surface. Ten years later (U.S.P. 1965852) M. O. Miller patented practically the same procedure. The use of pollen, starch, microbes, etc, made unnecessary the grinding operation for the preparation of fine powders.

Many experimenters used gelatin as the color-carrying medium. McDonough, as was shown above, appears to have been the first person to suggest its use. Some years later J. Bamber (Ger. P. 233140; Eng. P. 3252/08 and 11147/09; Fr. P. 399320) disclosed a more specific procedure. Dyed gelatin was tanned by treatment with formaldehyde, ground to a fine powder, and then mixed to yield a neutral black. This was finally sifted on to a celluloid surface that had previously been made tacky by a coating of gum. In a later patent, however, (Eng. P. 15775/11) he suggested the replacement of the gelatin by gum sandarac J. Szczepanik (Ger P. 354317; Eng. P. 17065/08; U S.P. 1089602) varied the procedure somewhat Three batches of gelatin were dyed with basic dyes, then ground to powders When the dyed gelatin was dusted over a collodion surface and came into intimate contact with that surface, the basic dye transferred from the gelatin to the collodion When sufficient dye was thus transferred, the gelatin powder could be removed, leaving a dyed-screen pattern upon the collodion.

Powdered dichromate-hardened fish glue, dyed presumedly with a pinatype dye, was used by F. M. Duncan (Eng P. 50/09) for the preparation of the screen elements H. W. H. Palmer (Ger. P. 233167; Eng. P. 6279/11; Fr. P 406147) tanned gelatin, gum arabic, tragacanth, etc., with formaldehyde. These were dyed, then sprayed into a drying chamber. In this way there were obtained very fine powders. Or liquid glass, properly colored, could be blown into fine powders, then mixed and spread over a tacky surface In order to fill in the interstices, heat was applied to fuse the elements together This had been previously suggested by E. Gistle (Ger. P. 228597) who also added a final touch of grinding the glass elements smooth before coating them with an emulsion.

A slight novelty was introduced by H. N. Holmes and D. H. Cameron (U S.P 1429430) The dyed gelatin particles were dispersed in gum dammar, and the colloidal solution coated in a single-grain layer upon the plate or film base.

Atomization is evidently a very convenient method for the formation of powders, since so many inventors seem to turn to it. C Rusicka (Eng. P. 326764, 326779, 326780, and 326781) atomized dyed gelatins to form the powders. These were mixed to yield neutrality, then dispersed in nitrocellulose and coated upon the emulsion side of a panchromatic plate. This creates a serious problem of processing, for the screen elements would form a waterproof coating over the emulsion W R B Larsen (U.S.P 1918208) would atomize dyed gelatin to which the proper optical sensitizers had been added The dried gelatin powders were then mixed and spread on a film base. Over this would be coated a color-blind emulsion The liquid gelatin would dissolve the dye plus sensitizer, which would then diffuse into the emulsion Each emulsion grain would be sensitized and colored properly. One drawback of a scheme such as this is that only a few layers of emulsion grains would be sensitized and dyed, thus seriously reducing the already limited latitude of the plate

Instead of tanned gelatin, H W. H Palmer (Eng. P. 22228/07) proposed to use stained fluxes such as fused borax beads, or ceramics. These could be sifted on to a glass surface, then fired until fusion took place. A similar procedure was suggested by C. F. Bleeker (U.S.P. 1175224). He made colored powders from glass, mica, fused borax, etc. Zinc sulphide grains, upon which had been adsorbed aluminum hydroxide (a strong absorbent of basic dyes), was suggested by L. Paris and G Piard (Fr. P. 477173, addition 20019). A similar idea, except that calcined magnesia formed the dye-absorbing grains, was disclosed by B T Silverman (Ger P. 313008). Somewhat along these lines was the scheme proposed by A. A. Canton (U.S.P. 1828958). Iron particles were oxidized, then stained and spread on a surface receptive to the dye. The color transferred from the iron particles to the surface, after which the iron was removed by a magnet This last is a variation of a much earlier proposal by Szczepanik which was described above. M. Wieland (Eng. P. 137502, Ger. P. 353759, U.S.P. 1497747) proposed to use the synthetic resins made by the condensation of phenol with formaldehyde.

A rather novel scheme was suggested by J. Camiller and A. Hay. This was especially suitable for two-color processes, but could be applied to three colors as well Particles of one color (Eng. P. 154150 and 158670; U S.P. 1440373) were dispersed in a colloid dyed another color. The particles must not interact with either the dispersing medium or the dye it contained, otherwise faulty results would be obtained. The mixture was then coated on to a support in the form of a single-layered emulsion It is rather difficult to see how to prevent each particle from becoming completely surrounded by the colored dispersing medium. C. Schleussner (Ger. P. 293004) sifted the colored elements over a surface coated with acetic acid and glycerin. The acetic acid was then allowed to evaporate. The application of steam caused the particles to swell, thereby closing up any interstices left between the grains

Celluloid and the cellulose esters in general, could also be used. F. L. Dyer (U.S.P. 947965) atomized a solution of celluloid in amyl acetate, forming transparent colored particles that were very finely powdered. A similar scheme was outlined by I. Kitsee (U.S.P. 1206000). Solutions of dyed celluloid or gelatin were sprayed into a high compartment. Very fine particles were collected at the base. These were mixed and sprayed to a tacky surface. In another disclosure (U.S P. 1221457) he proposed to coat paper with gum, then with colored celluloid This was cut, after drying, into strips 0.00125 to 0.002 inches square. The pieces were soaked in water, which dissolved out the gum, then mixed and applied to a support R Lehner (Eng P. 7629/08) ground dyes into celluloid by grinding with alcohol-water solutions After homogeneity was achieved, the water was driven off, and the celluloid worked into a film. S. E. Sheppard, of the Eastman Kodak Company (U.S.P. 1290794) dyed nitrocellulose with basic dyes, and emulsified the result in a colloid. The dyes used were the Sudan colors which were alcohol-soluble Water-soluble dyes could be made spirit-soluble by precipitation with tannic acid. The action of this substance upon gelatin was prevented by a further treatment with antimony salts. The dyed nitrocellulose could be dispersed in gelatin dissolved in water, in which nitrocellulose was completely insoluble. C L A. Brasseur (U.S.P. 974464; Eng P 18750/08) formed threads out of colored celluloid. These were rolled on to a sheet of paper with a tacky surface, and transferred from this to a celluloid film.

A substance eminently fitted for use as a carrier for the color elements is resin, and its related compounds. Like nitrocellulose, it is a waterproofing material so that the colors held within it would be insulated from the action of the aqueous processing solutions. It can also serve well as a substratum for the emulsion, so that it can replace the usual subbing. One of the first to suggest this substance was McDonough (cf. above). Christensen appeared to have concentrated much of his effort along these lines. We will discuss his disclosures a little later, since they were adopted by the Agfa company in the production of its screen plate. This product was quite popular until the advent of the new monopacks, which, overnight, made all other color-transparency processes practically obsolete.

H. W. H. Palmer (Eng. P. 16313/09), two years after he proposed to use tanned gelatins, turned to dyed caseins and the gums, of which resin is a specific example. These were dyed, made insoluble, pulverized, mixed, and finally spread upon the tacky surface. Upon standing, the elements absorbed water, swelled, and in that manner closed any clear spaces left between them. Pressure applied to the screen elements, flattened them out evenly. A. Wiebking (Ger. P 250036) formed fine powders by spraying the colored resins into a liquid that would coagulate them. This was later adopted as a good working rule by S. E. Sheppard, who used nitrocellulose instead of resin, and who caused the precipitation to take place inside of a colloid such as gelatin, in which the nitrocellulose was insoluble, and with which it was immiscible. This was an improvement on the general Wiebking procedure. The Pathé Company also used resins to carry the color elements (Ger. P. 261161). K. Frohlich emulsified dyes in solutions of resins or oils. These were sprayed on to a support, and the dyes transferred themselves to the support through the emulsifying substance, which could be removed after the transfer was complete (Ger. P. 406706).

In 1908 J. H. Christensen proposed to dye dextrin and gum arabic, and emulsify the dyed substances in gum dammar which was thinned with turpentine (Eng. P. 20971/08, Ger. P. 224465; U.S.P. 994977). The particles were allowed to settle, after which they were suspended in benzene, carbon tetrachloride, or kerosine and asphalt. A mixture of the particles was poured over a support coated with rubber. The dyed globules could be tanned (Eng. P. 21007/08 and 7480/12) with substances that would have no action upon the material of the support. In some later disclosures (Eng. P. 163311 and 216853; U.S.P. 1486635; Ger. P. 403590) he proposed to form dye tannates, etc., in alcoholic media. The solutions were then atomized or emulsified, and the particles applied to a support. Again, in 1925 (U S.P. 1564202) he returned to the problem of making fine powders. This time he emulsified a liter of a dye solution in three liters of thick rubber solution, or rubber-resin mixture. The rubber was removed by carbon tetrachloride, leaving a finely-ground colored powder behind. After mixing properly, the powders were applied to the carrier. In 1929 (Eng P 309113) he prepared the screen elements by still a different method. Basic dyes and tannic acid were dissolved in alcohol, then emulsified in gasoline. The emulsions, properly mixed, were sprayed on to a glass surface. Upon drying, the dye and the tannic acid formed a transparent pigment. It was also possible to use acid dyes together with the basic. Suitable dyes were brilliant crocein, patent blue, sea green, erio-glaucine, and naphthalene green.

The Agfa company proposed (Ger. P. 254180; Eng. P. 9167/12) to atomize colored dextrin solutions, by means of compressed air saturated with water. The particles fell on a surface that was inclined, and over which flowed a layer of turpentine. This company controlled the Christensen screen-plate patents, and manufactured a plate which was quite successful up until the late nineteen-thirties.

A method which suggests itself immediately for the formation of a screen, is the use of colored transparent fabrics woven from threads. The silk industry has achieved a high degree of skill in the preparation of very fine fibers, and if this be composed of the artificial silks, they would be very transparent. It was Prof. J. Joly, one of the first independent workers to put du Hauron's ideas into practice, who suggested the uses of silk fibers for the screen elements (Eng. P. 19388/95). His first suggestion was to apply the colored threads to a tacky surface, a sort of dusting-on procedure But he also suggested that the fibers could be woven into a cloth, all the colored fibers running in one direction, while the fibers running across these were to be colorless and transparent. R. Berthon and J. Gambs (Eng. P. 20834/06, Fr. 357928, additions 5986 and 9464) also wove fabrics out of colored threads, making sure that the colored fibers lay adjacent to each other so that no clear spaces would exist between them

Instead of weaving the fibers into a fabric, Ratignier and Pervilhac placed them in celluloid just as that was being cast into a film. The comb, through whose teeth the fibers passed, was so arranged that the fibers touched each other at the point where they entered the celluloid solution. The fibers were thus kept in position by the solidified celluloid (Fr. P. 391785). A somewhat similar idea was disclosed by E. B. Smith (Eng. P. 139871). In this case a glass plate with a layer of gelatin was used instead of celluloid, and the comb was arranged so that the fibers touched each other just at the point where they came in contact with the gelatinized base.

F. Fritz, in a general discussion of the problem (Ger. P. 227130) pointed out that a woven fabric had the disadvantage of having a large number of clear areas not covered by colored fibers. He overcame this difficulty by the use of the artificial fibers. After the cloth was woven, he applied heat which softened and spread out the individual threads and caused fusion to take place. He also proposed to weave one thread of a transparent material and then imbed the cloth in a plastic dyed with the missing color (Ger. P. 231676).

Instead of using textile fibers for the weave, A. J. Jorelle (Fr. P. 460724) and A. N. Pierman (U.S.P. 1196718) suggested spun glass. The French patent appeared in 1912, while the United States patent did not appear until 1916, but it was applied for in 1908. Therefore the two inventors worked in complete ignorance of each other's contribution. Despite the apparent simplicity of this procedure, no successful plate made this way, was ever marketed

The next method to be discussed includes the processes in which a block is formed by cementing together layer upon layer of dyed gelatin or collodion sheets. This was apparently first suggested by H Snowden Ward (*Brit. J Phot.*, Vol 46 (1899), p 399). He proposed to stain thin gelatin sheets in the three primary colors, then superimpose them so that the colors alternated until a block was formed whose depth was at least equal to the length of the projected screen plate. If each sheet is to be 0.001 inch thick, it would require 1000 sheets to make a block one inch deep If the plate was to be seven inches long, then about 7000 sheets would be required. Technological progress in casting cellophane, celluloid, etc., has been so great that the making of large sheets that have a maximum thickness of one thousandth of an inch is commonplace. The gelatin emulsion layer, coated on positive motion-picture film stock, is only a half of a thousandth of an inch thick, and the individual layers used in a Kodachrome or Ansco Color monopack are even thinner. It is not a difficult matter to form such blocks The writer remembers a summer which he spent in the sheeting department of the Celluloid Company of America where it was a commonplace affair to cut sheets of celluloid, 36 by 72 inches, each 0 001 inch thick, and superimpose them to form a new block of celluloid that contained a complicated design The new block could then be sliced as desired. In order to form sections suitable for screen plates, the block must be cut in a direction perpendicular to the plane of the colored sheets.

At a later date (*Phot. J.*, Vol. 40 (1900), p. 141) Ward attributed the idea to Prof. Joly. However, sometime before this, O H Witt had already made a German patent application (Ger. P. Anm. 14,564 IV, 57a) for an idea identical to this, using stained celluloid or gelatin sheets for the elements. The application was abandoned on May 8, 1899 Some time later R E Liesegang (*Jahrbuch,* Vol 22 (1908), p. 147, *Phot. Almanach,* 1904, p 122) proposed the same idea However he suggested that each layer might be coated on top of the other, thus insuring good adhesion and the absence of clear spaces The idea was again suggested by Krayn, who marketed plates for a short period of time (Ger P. 167232; Eng. P 19202/05, Fr. P. 357895, additions 5375, 6534, 6536, 6537; 386772 and 409367). Or the colored sheets could be cast separately (Ger P. 167613) and then assembled to form a block that would be cylindrical in shape (Eng P 495/07, Ger P 188431, 190560; Fr. P. 388913) By this procedure long film strips could be cut If a block were formed, and this cut horizontally, then reassembled into a new block whose dimensions were exactly opposite to the first, the new block could be cut to give a screen consisting of a definite mosaic pattern, rather than a straight-line pattern (Ger. P. 193463; Fr. P. 405924; Eng. P. 2213/08). The Krayn disclosures were put into commercial use by the Neue Photographische Gesellschaft, who later attempted to put into practical use the Fischer and Siegrist color development ideas (cf. chapters on Color Development).

The same scheme of reforming the block and cutting again but in a different plane, was proposed once more by F. A. Fifield, (U S.P 990247) and somewhat later, by C L A Brasseur (Eng P. 28631/13; U S P. 1081484, Fr P. 466120). The last proposed to make some of his sheets 0 00025 inch thick. Since it was impossible to cut the sheets so thin, he sliced them as thin as he was able, then polished them to the desired dimension This made the process rather difficult and expensive. It is rather doubtful even with all our later ability to make fast fine-grained emulsions, whether elements as fine as 0.00025 inch could be used. Assuming that the average grain has a diameter of 0 5 μ, there would be approximately 12 grains of emulsion across each dimension of the element, or altogether 144 grains. This is by far too few to represent a good average of the emulsion, and also much too few to yield an appreciable density behind the element. This number of grains also fails to take into consideration the fact that the grains do not lie end to end, but are separated by a wall of gelatin whose dimension is at least equal to that of the grain itself Therefore it would be closer to the truth to state that in the area behind each screen element, which is 0 00025 inch square, there would be at most fifty emulsion grains. If the speed of the plate were of no consequence, much finer grains could be used, such as those present in the Lippmann colloidal emulsion. Then screens of much finer texture could be used.

W. C Masser and W. Hudson (Eng P 25730/07) also adopted the Krayn idea of making long films by cutting the blocks circumferentially. These two worked independently of Krayn and were obviously ignorant of his disclosures, since both patents were disclosed to the public in the same year. The Vereinigte Kunstseidefabriken cast color sheets, presumedly of cellulose acetate or artificial silk, that were approximately 0 13 mm in thickness, or 0 005 inch. These were superimposed before they were completely dry.

Perhaps this idea should really be classified under the miscellaneous procedures, but since the final screen is formed by cutting sections from a block, it is included here It was disclosed by F. Fritz (Ger. P. 218324 and 223819) in 1908. Artificial threads, such as those made from cellulose acetate, rayon, silk, etc., are woven into sheets. Or they can first be woven into strands, then combined to form a solid block that is finally cut into sheets by means of a microtome. The weaving technique enabled the formation of any desired mosaic pattern.

A variation of the procedures outlined above is contained in the disclosure of S. Schapovaloff (Eng. P. 389265). He placed between the colored sheets a sheet that had been dyed black, so that the order of the colors became red, black, green, black, blue, black, red, black, etc. The block was cut spirally to obtain long rolls of film The inclusion of black between the elements was to insure against distortion due to a spread of the light beam on its passage through a color element. But if the colors used were mutually exclusive, as they should be for best results, a green color-element would act just like black for the light that passes through either the red or the blue element.

The use of glass powders for the formation of the screen, has long been known. A. G. Oneil (U.S.P. 1892901) would cover an area with colored glass hexagonal rods, fuse them together by heat, then draw out the entire bundle of rods to the proper size, and slice off sections

The ability of the photographic emulsion, be it sensitized either with dichromated gelatin or silver halide salts, to reproduce fine details, was quickly seized upon for the formation of screens. It was first suggested by du Hauron ("Les Couleurs en Photographie Solution du Problem," 1869, p 54; "La Triplice photographique et l'Imprimerie," (1897), p. 336). A gelatin layer, dyed primary red, and sensitized with dichromate, was exposed through a black-and-white line screen, the blacks having twice the width of the whites. The action of the light tanned the gelatin that corresponded to the transparent areas of the master screen The soft gelatin was removed by a hot water etch This left a series of red lines, separated by transparent portions whose width was twice that of the reds. The plate was next recoated with gelatin dyed green, and sensitized with dichromate The second exposure was also through a black-and-white screen, but this time the width of the two was the same, and their direction was at right angles to the red lines. Since the red portions passed no light that was effective upon the dichromated gelatin, only the gelatin lying between the previously formed lines was affected, and of this, only one half of the total area became tanned Hot water treatment removed the unaffected gelatin, which was finally replaced with new gelatin dyed a primary blue, and as before, sensitized with dichromate. The last exposure was made without any master screen, only through the red and green areas formed previously. These acted as opaque lines for the blue rays to which the gelatin was sensitive. Between all coatings, it was desirable to further treat the plate to thoroughly fix the dyes or coloring matter in the tanned gelatin. Hence no diffusion of colors was possible

Although du Hauron completely outlined the methods, he did not put them into practice. E J Wall attributes to C L A. Brasseur the honor of being the first person to use dichromate photography for the formation of the screen ("History of Three-Color Photography," 1925, p. 483) The du Hauron technique was slightly changed in that after each printing a layer of varnish was put upon the plate to insulate one color element from the others (Eng. P. 21210/09, Ger P. 179378). This was in 1904, a considerable time after the first du Hauron disclosures E Sanger-Shepherd (Eng. P. 20384/07) did not depart in the least from the du Hauron specifications. A prolific patentee in this field was J. H Powrie. Instead of gelatin, he preferred to use fish glue (U.S.P. 802471; Ger. P. 215072, 222504 and 225004; Fr. P. 358746, 358747; Eng. P. 20662/05). The replacement of the gelatin by the fish glue allowed him to develop in cold water. The insoluble glue was then dyed up with an acid dye such as aurophenin This was then treated with a basic dye, either brilliant green, safranin or thiazine red. A reaction between the acid and basic dye took place which yielded an insoluble molecular combination of the two. Had Powrie used dyes of the same hue, an intensification of the color would have resulted. But in this case, the yellow served to convert the red or the green into shades that matched the primary colors. The dyed lines were further pigmentized by treatment with tannic acid, after which the plate was resensitized and exposed under the screen again, and the entire procedure repeated until three sets of lines were obtained.

In some later patents Mr. Powrie discloses a novel scheme for printing the screen lines in juxtaposition (U.S.P. 1605062, 1717404; Eng. P. 287188). A celluloid base was coated with a light-sensitive emulsion on one side, and on this was printed a master matrix in which the transparent lines had one half the width of the opaque lines. On the other side of the celluloid film base was coated a dichromated gelatin. The first printing was made with a beam of light whose axis was perpendicular to the plane of the celluloid base. Therefore there was impressed on the other side a series of lines consisting of tanned gelatin which lay directly below the transparent lines of the master matrix.

These lines were dyed with a primary color and were given an added stability by treatment with a tannic acid mordant. This was recoated with dichromated gelatin, and exposed again through the same matrix, but now, instead of using a beam of light whose axis was perpendicular to the film base, a beam was used whose axis was at an angle such that the zone of action of the light on the dichromated gelatin was adjacent to the line already formed. By this means, a line of tanned gelatin was formed next to the first one After removal of the unaffected gelatin the new set of lines was dyed in a second primary color, thoroughly tanned, and finally recoated with dichromated gelatin. The third printing was done after the master matrix had been buffed away, through the two sets of lines already formed. These were dyed red and green respectively, so that as far as their action on the gelatin was concerned, they were completely opaque. Screens with upward of 1200 lines to the inch have been made by Mr Powrie using this technique.

A really novel scheme was proposed by C. E. K. Mees (Eng P. 28406/07) and assigned to the Wratten & Wainwright company. A single exposure sufficed to give three differentially hardened lines This was accomplished by using a screen that was composed of an opaque, a semi-opaque, and a transparent line. Dichromated gelatin was then exposed behind this master, and after washing to remove unaffected dichromate, dyed up with patent blue. A thorough wash left the following condition. The completely tanned portion of the gelatin was dyed a deep blue. The partially tanned line absorbed considerably less dye, and this appeared as a blue-green, or cyan. The soft line (completely untanned) remained undyed. Upon soaking in a yellow pinatype dye, the medium and soft portions turned green and yellow respectively, while the hard line was unaffected. A final dyeing with a red dye, which would not take in tanned gelatin at all, completed the screen. This is really an ingenious scheme, and the only drawback would appear to be the fact that patent blue would always have some green transmission, and thus an impure blue primary rendition would result.

F. Faupel (Ger P. 216610 and 220154) also took advantage of the differential dyeing properties of soft and hard gelatin. Dichromated gelatin was exposed under a line screen and then washed to remove the unaffected salt. This gave a series of hard lines separated from each other by lines formed of soft gelatin. The tanned gelatin lines were then dyed with azorubin or crystal ponceau 6R, while the soft gelatin lines were dyed with methyl blue, brilliant wool blue G, or brilliant azurine After dyeing the two sets of lines, the plate was resensitized and exposed under a line screen, but at an angle to the first, then dyed with fast chrome yellow G. This converted the untanned portion of the lines into a green, which would indicate that the blue used was really a blue-green and not a primary blue The screen was composed of red, green, and cyan lines, a poor combination for color. The exposed and washed plate could also be dyed with a mixture of naphthol green and crystal ponceau. These dyes stained either tanned or untanned gelatin only, so that the tanned lines were colored

red, and the untanned were colored green, simultaneously. Resensitization with dichromate was followed by exposure to a master, but at an angle to the first. This tanned part of the green line The naphthol green of the untanned portions was removed by treatment with alcohol and water, after which it was dyed with brilliant azurine. This had no action on the tanned portions of the plate, dyeing up only the clear parts.

The same procedure was outlined again by C. Spath (Eng. P. 3601/09, U.S.P. 946470 and 1292347) Mr. Spath even fell into the same error of converting part of the blue line into a green by treatment with a yellow dye, indicating that he also used a blue-green rather than a primary blue for one of the elements

These procedures were slight variations of the one disclosed by Berthon and Gambs (Fr P. 358250) several years prior. Dichromated gelatin or other colloid, dyed "red," was exposed under a line screen. After the exposure, the dye was washed out of the unaffected regions, which were then dyed "blue." A protective varnish coating was put on this, and another layer of dichromated gelatin coated on top. This time a yellow dye was present. The exposure was made with the lines at a forty-five degree angle to the first The untanned portions of the second layer were dyed "red" These colors were not really red and blue, since the "red" by the superposition of yellow, became primary red, and the "blue" became green. Hence the "red" was really magenta and the "blue," cyan. Where the "red" and "blue" overlapped, there was formed blue-violet or primary blue. This was another indication that magenta and cyan were the true shades

Only slightly different from this is the procedure outlined by J M. Borrel (Fr. P. 393557) Dichromated gelatin was exposed under a screen. The tanned portions were stained with a red dye while the untanned portions were stained "blue." Resensitization followed, and this time the portions of the blue lines that remained untanned were stained with a yellow, which converted the "blue" into green. The last step was to treat the plate with a "red" dye which would affect only the hard gelatin areas Therefore the green areas were unaffected Staining a red area with a "red" (really magenta) dye left its shade unchanged But the "blue" or cyan areas were converted into primary blue. The loose usage of the terms "red," and "blue" leads to considerable confusion, and care must be taken to realize when a primary red or when a magenta or secondary red is really meant B Bichtler (Ger. P 292347) used a celluloid base coated on both sides with dichromated gelatin, and formed one series of color lines on each side. The third series was put on after one side of the film was recoated with dichromated gelatin.

A plate that enjoyed a large measure of success until Dufaycolor was introduced, was produced under the Finlay patents. The earlier patents utilized the dichromated gelatin technique, although later disclosures indicated that a resist method was adopted. This last will be discussed below. The earlier product was novel in that a mosaic of red and green circles upon a blue background was used. The screen was mounted upon a glass plate, and used as a front element in a bipack, the rear element of which was a panchromate emulsion (Eng. P. 19652/06, 4208/10; Fr. P. 426498; U.S.P. 1085727).

I Kitsee (U.S.P. 1383819, 1426995, and 1426996) took advantage of the fact that tanned gelatin would not swell. The soft lines did swell, so that they stood out in relief. These were dyed by means of a roller. After dyeing the swollen portions, the spaces between were filled with another color. A two-color screen is described by J. G. Zimmermann (U.S.P. 1579464). A prolific patentee is J. E. Thornton, who seemed to specialize in making screens for a four color process (U S P 1670671 and 1873673; Eng P. 224571, 253643 and 257836). He favored the use of fish glue rather than gelatin. After exposure, the dye was washed out of the soft areas, and they were then redyed with a pinatype dye The film base was double width, and only half as thick as the normal Each half contained two of the four colors. After processing, the film is slit in two and cemented together, either face to face, or celluloid to celluloid.

In a patent issued to the Durkoppwerke, A. G. (Eng P. 389843) it was suggested to have one half of the screen area undyed. To this end, a film of dichromated gelatin was exposed to a master. The untanned portion was dyed, then resensitized and exposed. The dye was washed out of the unaffected parts, which were then redyed in a complementary color. The use of such a screen would lead to poor color separations since both colors would be rendered behind the transparent line, indiscriminately. This procedure was also applied to the making of paper prints (Eng. P. 389844).

Instead of using dichromated gelatin for the light-sensitive medium in the preparation of the color elements of the screen, it is possible to use silver-halide salts. The first to suggest this appears to have been L Gimpel (Fr. P. 414953). A screen of parallel lines is photographed upon a fine-grained silver-halide emulsion. The silver image is then toned a primary red. After recoating, the screen was photographed again, but this time at right angles. The silver was then converted into a cyan color. After recoating the plate a second time, presumedly with an emulsion sensitive to the blue only, the plate was exposed through the lines already formed, so that behind the red line there would be formed no deposit, behind the cyan line a "half tone" deposit, and in the remaining area, a full tone. This was converted into a yellow. Although the process appears hopeful, the toning seems to be such that a very poor screen results Two of the elements are approximately correct. The initial exposure yielded a primary red, while the second exposure yielded a cyan which was converted into a green by the third treatment. But the third area in the unit will be yellow, whereas a blue color is demanded here.

A combination of dusting-on and chemical toning processes was adopted by E. H. Tarlton (Eng. P. 110993). A transparent support was coated with a layer that contained red particles dispersed in it, so arranged that they blocked out only half the surface area of the film On top of this was coated a red-insensitive silver-halide emulsion. The exposure was made through the red elements, so that silver images were formed that completely filled in the spaces between the red particles This was converted into an iron blue. Mr. Tarlton proposed his scheme for two-color analysis, hence the use of red and minus-red elements was correct G. Valensi (Fr P 536737) also used a base coated on both sides with silver-halide emulsions A line screen was photographed on each side, and the silver on one side converted into a yellow color, while on the other side it was converted into a "red." After resensitization, another series of lines were printed on the film, and toned "blue" Here again, a false color analysis would be obtained, since yellow forms one of the screen elements.

A silver-halide emulsion again forms the basis for screen formation in a disclosure issued to Naturfarben-Film G.m.b.H. The silver comprising the screen elements is treated with a tanning bleach. The soft gelatin is washed away, and the relief images remaining are dyed (Ger. P. 382575). This procedure is also utilized by H. Butschowitz (Ger. P. 389852), but instead of using a tanning bleach, he used a tanning developer. The chemical principles governing such processes will be discussed in a later chapter.

L. F Douglass (U S P. 1504465) printed a dot screen on to a silver-halide emulsion, and dye-toned the resultant silver image with a magenta dye. The clear areas between these were sensitized with ferric salts, and after exposure developed with ferricyanide, forming the well-known iron blue. The entire film was finally dyed yellow, which converted the iron blue into a green, and the magenta into a red. H Muller (U S.P. 2007282) exposed a silver-halide emulsion and obtained a screen composed of silver elements These were toned one color, and the clear areas between them, dyed another. It was also possible to use a tanning bleach, such as is used in the ozobrome processes, to convert the gelatin in situ with the silver to a tanned form. This can be dyed with a color which is retained by tanned gelatin, but which is washed out of the soft areas. These last can be treated with pinatype dyes. This is merely another form of the technique disclosed by Mees.

It is not a far cry from photographic to photomechanical printing methods, which by 1900 had been developed to a high state of mechanical perfection. Not many of the patent disclosures deal with such schemes, principally because the printing of more than 175 elements to the inch creates many problems whose solutions had not been solved up to forty years later. The one advantage of this procedure would be the possibility of copying a mosaic, made on a large scale, and reproducing this as fine as desired, over a large area, by the use of a step-and-repeat camera. The actual printing could be done by any of the photomechanical processes. For the formation of a continuous roll, rotogravure printing could be used.

J H. Smith, W Merckens, and H. B. Manissadjian (Ger. P. 197610) considered the problem quite carefully and came to the conclusion that steel or copperplate engraving was the best solution of the problem. The inks were to be printed on paper that was coated with nitrocellulose to form a stripping paper The inked nitrocellulose film was finally stripped on to a glass plate. C. L A. Brasseur (U S.P. 976148) came to the same conclusion, with regard to the printing methods.

In printing a screen, J S. Szczepanik (Eng. P. 6098/07) left areas completely devoid of color, and had areas which were printed in black. The need for these is not obvious, and it would seem to be completely unnecessary, for color dilution and unsaturation would result. The making of accurate color separations would also be made impossible. Other printing procedures were disclosed by A. Nodon (Fr. P. 372661) who printed two sets of lines horizontally, and two sets at an angle to these, choosing the colors so that a four-color screen with blue, green, orange, and red units, was formed. From the specifications it could not be determined whether the red and orange, and the blue and green were mutually exclusive in their transmissions, as would be required for a true four-color process C. E. K. Mees (U S P. 1666048) preferred to print the screen elements by offset.

The simplest type of plate with a geometric pattern is the one where the lines are ruled with colored inks This is the class which the late E. J Wall termed "linear screen plates," in his discussion (Wall, "History of Three-Color Photography," p. 475). The first plates of this type were prepared by Prof. Joly, and independently, by J McDonough. In 1893 Prof Joly was issued a patent in which he discussed color photography in a general manner (Eng. P. 7743/93). In the following year he disclosed a screen made by ruling the lines (Eng P. 14164/94). For the red line he used chrysoidine orange; for the green, a mixture of ethyl green and chrysoidine; and for the blue, water blue The screen was not coated with an emulsion, but was used as the front element of a bipack whose rear was a panchromatic plate Positives, made by contact from such negatives, were then registered with the screen. Machinery for ruling the colored lines was disclosed in English patents 7671/96, 8114/96, 8441/96, 9920/96, 18097/96, and 17900/97.

Following closely was J. McDonough (U.S.P. 561685, 561686, 561687; Eng. P. 12645/96) He also used the screen separate from the emulsion, and he suggested placing patterns in the corners of the plate to facilitate the registration of the positives with the viewing screens. Another modification of dubious value was to use more than three basic colors. One of his illustrations showed a pattern with six designations, *R*, *O*, *Y*, *G*, *B*, and *I*, evidently meaning red, orange, yellow, green, blue, and indigo. If these colors really represented a six-partite division of the spectrum of white light, the disclosure would have represented a true physical approach to the problem. But in that case, the description of the colors would have been in terms of spectral distribution. The yellow, for instance, would have represented a limited section of the band of colors whose limits would be 535 to 586 mμ. Orange would extend from 586 to 647, and the red beyond this. The green would extend from 492 to 535. Yellow filters, and in fact all yellow colors as we meet them in nature, transmit freely beyond 500 mμ. It is feared that the image behind the yellow line in McDonough's six-line screen would be the sum of the images as they appeared behind the green, orange, and red lines Machines for ruling the lines were disclosed by D. K. Tripp (Eng. P. 12922/01, and 15017/01), and by E. E. Flora (U S P. 676943 and 679070). It is hard to tell whether the English patents were issued to the original inventor, or to his English attorney, the English custom allowing anyone to whom a disclosure has been made to make application for a patent. The American custom is more rigid, so that only the inventor can apply for a patent. Paper prints made by the screen method were disclosed by McDonough in United States patent 611457, and in English patent 20417/98.

Not very much work seems to have been done along these lines, probably due to the fact that it was quite difficult to rule lines in exact juxtaposition. In 1930 J. N. Goldsmith, a member of the Spicers organization, which was interested in the Dufay disclosures, and which played a prominent part in the exploitation of Dufaycolor, proposed to rule lines with inks The Dufay disclosures dealt mainly with the ruling of resist lines upon dyed collodion. Goldsmith proposed that the resist inks also contain a color (U.S.P. 1877658, Eng P. 334243) which was capable of staining the collodion. The resist consisted of boiled linseed oil, or some other thickened vegetable drying oil. Red lines could be drawn by using an ink which contained

Williams oil red	20 parts
Thickened linseed oil	20 parts
Acetic acid	20 parts

Blue lines would be obtained from

Williams oil blue	10 parts
Thickened linseed oil	18 parts
Acetic acid	10 parts

A variation of this technique would be to put a dye component into the film base, then rule this with an ink that contained an ingredient which would unite with the other, to form a deep color of the desired primary. The ruled line would have to contain a sufficient concentration of the color-former to completely use up the ingredient present in the base. A second ruling, this time with an ink containing a component which forms a different primary color, could be made at right angles to the first. This creates a mosaic containing two colors, separated by clear areas which still contain color-forming ingredients. Treatment of the film with a substance capable of forming the third primary color, completes the screen The general idea for this is disclosed in United States patent 1818927, issued to J. N. Goldsmith, T T Baker, and C. Bonamico, all of the Spicers organization. Specific details are disclosed in English patent 352949. A film base is impregnated for several minutes in an alcoholic-sodium hydroxide solution containing beta naphthol. The excess is removed by means of a roller. If this be ruled with diazotized alpha naphthylamine, a series of red lines will be formed. At right angles to this can be ruled diazotized dianisidine to give blue lines.

In the preferred form, the film is impregnated with Naphthol A. S. This is the anilide of 2:3 oxy-naphthoic acid. If cellulose acetate is used as the base material, it is necessary to make the solution alkaline with one per cent alcoholic potassium hydroxide, otherwise the film will not take on the naphthol compound evenly. The excess is removed by means of a roller A series of parallel lines is then ruled, using for the ink a strong solution of diazotized 4-amino-4′-ethoxy di-phenyl-amine dissolved in 50 per cent alcohol, and buffered with sodium acetate. After three minutes the excess is removed and a second series of lines is ruled, perpendicular to the first The ink this time is a similarly constituted solution containing 2:5 di-chloro-benzene-diazonium chloride plus aluminum sulphate. The third color is obtained by dyeing the whole film with auramine. It is to be hoped that this is not the only ingredient of the third color, since that would indicate that yellow was one of the fundamental units, which would be entirely wrong.

The general idea of having a color-forming substance present in the base, then ruling it with a reactive material capable of color formation, is not original with Goldsmith and his co-workers. It had been previously suggested by F. Faupel in 1907 (Ger. P. 221231). He coated a base with a colloid that contained ferricyanide. Upon this he ruled lines of ferrous salts, forming a series of lines in iron blue. This, of course, is cyan and is more fitted for a secondary than a primary color But the shade of the color formed has no relationship to the disclosure of the technique involved. He also suggested that a colored untanned colloid be coated upon a film base, upon which there can be ruled lines with an ink containing chrome alum, tannic acid, formaldehyde, or other agents which would tan the colloid These would fix the coloring matter within the ruled spaces. The remaining color would be washed out, then replaced, and the procedure repeated after shifting the position of the lines.

M. Petzold (Ger. P. 279932) ruled lines of acid dyes plus an alkaline chromate, upon a gelatin surface. In this manner, colored lines were formed upon the surface, and these areas simultaneously tanned, so that they would no longer absorb a pinatype dye, or a dye such as rosaniline blue. Two sets of lines, red and green, could be ruled at an angle to each other, the third color being put on by use of pinatype dyes.

Perhaps the following should not be included in this section, but the ruling of lines carrying inks is one step in the procedure. It is the invention of A. Weckfort (Eng. P. 393797 and 402231). A series of blue lines in a greasy ink, is ruled on the surface of a color-blind emulsion. The ink base must be such that it will resist the action of water and sensitizing dye solvents. The clear areas are next sensitized to the green. After this, a series of green lines is ruled, also with a resist ink. The uncovered spaces are then sensitized to the red, and finally dyed red. In the meantime the coloring matter in the resist lines transfers to the gelatin surface. The removal of the resists completes the screen plate, which now consists of a pattern of parallel lines of blue, interspersed with red and green squares. Directly beneath each color element is an emulsion that is sensitive only to the color transmitted by that element. M. Zeller (U S P. 2009424 and 2061182), and H. Wilms (Eng. P. 436723) disclosed similar procedures These are but a modification of the O'Grady disclosures (U.S.P. 1402371) who ruled the screen elements on the surface of a panchromatic emulsion. After exposure, the lines were removed by washing. Positives made from the negative by contact were finally ruled in exact registry with a new set of colored lines. This presented a rather intricate registry problem.

The most successful methods for the preparation of screens have been those utilizing resists In these schemes, the screen base is given a partial coating with a resist medium. The spaces between the resist areas are then dyed. The first to utilize such a procedure was A. Baumgartner (Eng P. 22138/95). He printed red dots with lithographic inks, and these acted as resists against the further action of certain solutions. The areas between the dots were next dyed cyan. By this means, the entire surface became coated with red (magenta) and cyan dots. On top of this was printed in a haphazard fashion, a yellow dot. Where the yellow overlapped the red, an orange was formed, and where it overlapped the cyan, a green was obtained.

The color analysis obtained by a procedure of this type could not be accurate. Since the "red" became converted into an orange by the overlay of a yellow, it must transmit blue as well as red, so that in reality its color is magenta. The screen contains therefore four sets of dots, magenta, red, green, and blue-green. The blue primary would register under the magenta "red" and the blue-green dots simultaneously with the red and green primaries, respectively. The other primaries will also register together with one other color, under at least one of the four dots. No definite color separation results. Although there is no doubt but that a pleasing transparency can be obtained by this method, the subsequent separation of this into the proper negative separations, will be practically impossible to make. The same error, somewhat aggravated by the fact that a four-color process is claimed, is made by E. Scherpel (Ger. P. 375259, 375260, 375261). The process he used was to spray a colorless support with a resist, then bathe with a blue dye. The resist was removed and these portions dyed red On top of this was sprayed a yellow dye which converted the red into an orange wherever the two overlapped, and the blue with a green where these and the yellow overlapped. Thus red, orange, green, and blue dots were formed. Of course the same objections hold here, that were noted in the Baumgartner case.

G. S Whitfield (Eng. P. 9004/06) dyed the collodion base superficially, then applied a resist in the form of a spray of rubber, wax, or like material. The areas between the resist particles were then treated with a solution that bleached and removed the dye. A re-dyeing with a second color was followed by another application of a resist Presumedly the first spray covered but one-third of the total surface area, and the second spray covered one-half of the remaining exposed sections. The color was again removed, and the third primary applied. By this means it became possible to completely cover a surface with three colored areas, so that no overlaps and no undyed portions remain

Instead of using chemical agents to destroy or remove dye from a collodion surface, du Hauron and R de Bercegol (Eng. P. 194/07; Fr. P 387828; Ger. P. 218323; U.S.P. 995405 and 1005644) remove it by cutting it out. Thus a film base was given a coating of gelatin, and on top of this, a coating of green varnish. Through this last, is ruled a series of lines which cut completely through the varnish. Thus the dye was removed and the gelatin at these points laid bare. This now underwent a dyeing operation, after which a new coating of varnish was applied, this time colorless. The new lines were drawn through the varnish, cutting deeper into the gelatin so that the previously dyed portions which lay in the path of the new lines were removed. Now the third color was applied Or, superficially dyed celluloid was coated with gelatin. This was cut away in the form of a series of lines, the cuts extending to the celluloid layer below, and removing the dye A new dye, in acetone or alcohol, was applied. This did not stain the gelatin, since the dye solvent was not absorbed by it. Considerably later, after du Hauron died, R de Bercegol amplified this system. A sheet of film was colored an orange red. On this was spread a layer of wax and a series of parallel lines cut through the wax into the celluloid, so that the superficial dye in the celluloid was removed. These portions were then colored green, rewaxed and cut again, this time with a series of lines at an angle to the first The new lines were colored blue (Eng P. 189813, Fr P. 554912 and addition 27364 to this; Ger P. 392749; U S.P. 1673349 and 1706774). Machines for the ruling of these lines, were disclosed in French patent 557972, addition 27765 A similar procedure was outlined by I. Kitsee (Eng. P. 225659, U S.P 1449417, 1477880, 1477881 and 1477882) This time gelatin is used for the resist. The dyed celluloid is first coated with a layer of gelatin, and by means of a special cutting device (Fr. P 672827, U S P. 1477883) a series of broken lines, some running at right angles to the others, are cut through to the celluloid below, removing the dyed portions The lines are re-dyed, and the procedure repeated a second time to put in the third set of colors.

The cutting method is varied somewhat by the Vereinigte Kunstseide fabriken (Eng P 21739/08 and 21840/08; Ger. P. 218298 and 230387; Fr. P. 395165), and independently by A. Lehner (U.S.P. 1112540 and 1112541). A celluloid film is grooved, and upon the raised portion is printed a greasy resist. This allows the dyeing of the cut portions. The resist is removed, a new series of grooves etched in so that the dye in the first set is removed whenever the new and the old cross. A second dyeing is made. The resist is removed again, and a layer of dichromated gelatin put on Presumedly the first two colors were red and green, so that it becomes possible to expose through these to form tanned gelatin corresponding to those portions of the surface which were still uncolored. The tanned gelatin portions are dyed up. By the application of heat and pressure, the screen surface was made flat. A similar idea is utilized by C. Späth (Ger. P. 239486; Fr. P. 399676 and 421199; Eng. P 23138/10, U.S.P. 1069039 and 1108341). But this time rubber is used as the resist material. A series of parallel lines is ruled through the resist, laying bare the celluloid. This is dyed by treatment with a two per cent alcoholic solution of Victoria Blue. Now a new set of lines is drawn at right angles, and the new portions dyed with a mixture of ethyl green and auramine in 80 per cent alcohol The resist is removed and the remaining portions are dyed with a mixture of rubin and auramine in 60 per cent alcohol.

The Lumières are known for the successful marketing of the Autochrome plate, in which the screen elements consisted of dyed starch grains applied to a surface by a dusting-on process. But they also did some work with geometric patterns. A resist was printed or ruled on a dyed gelatin surface (Eng. P. 20111/08; Fr. P. 393296; Ger. P. 207750, U.S P 916467) The spaces between the resist areas were then subjected to the action of a solution which destroyed the dye. This was re-dyed and the process repeated until the entire area was covered with a series of three-color elements In a series of patents issued somewhat later, the procedure is extended (Eng. P. 29273/09, 4212/10 and 5377/10). Two-thirds of the area of a film surface is covered with a resist. The intervening space is dyed with eosine scarlet. The resist is removed, and a new series is put on which covers one-half of the undyed areas. The remaining half is dyed with cyanin V and metanil yellow to which have been added iron salts. These are present to prevent the dyes from affecting the areas previously dyed with eosine scarlet. The resist is removed, and this space is dyed with methyl violet.

At about the same time that this series of patents was being issued, R. Krayn also disclosed the use of iron salts in the dye solutions (Eng. P. 26911/09; Fr P. 409397; Ger. P. 221727; U S.P. 1055189). A gelatin surface was printed with a greasy resist, and the intervening areas colored with cinnabar scarlet, then fixed with ferric chloride. The first resist was removed, and a new one printed at right angles to it. The exposed surface was then dyed with methyl blue and fixed with ferric chloride. The resist was removed, and the remaining areas dyed with a mixture of patent blue A and yellow F. The fixing operation with ferric chloride was again applied. E J Wall ("History of Three-Color Photography," 1925, p. 494) reported that the red areas transmitted light having wavelengths greater than 560 mμ, the green areas transmitted in the range from 480 to 570 mμ, while the blue transmitted only below 490 mμ. These are ideal limits to the spectral transmissions of the three-color primaries in color reproduction. A slight variation to this technique is noted by F. May (Eng P. 201234). The dyes were fixed by treatment with ferric chloride, aluminum acetate, or formalin.

A slightly different procedure was adopted by J. Rheinberg (Eng. P. 9929/14; Fr. P. 476228, addition 19917, and 478117; Ger. P. 326710 and 326711; U.S.P. 1161731 and 1191034). A collodion base is dyed red, then coated with albumin containing 7½ per cent each of ferric ammonium citrate and uranyl nitrate. This was exposed to a line screen having transparent and opaque lines of equal width. A bath in acid alcohol removed the red dye from the portions that had received a light exposure. These portions were then stained green. A resensitization with iron and uranium followed. The plate was now exposed to a screen at right angles to the previous lines, and this time the opaque lines were twice the width of the transparent ones A wash in acid alcohol removed the dye in the portions that received an exposure, and these were finally dyed a blue.

The Finlay plate, which enjoyed a fair measure of success up to the advent of the latest edition of Dufaycolor, was prepared by the use of dichromated gelatin But, like the Lumières, Mr. Finlay also did some work with resists (Eng. P. 421771) A metal foil is coated with dyed collodion, then a series of resist lines is printed upon it. Treatment with alcohol removes the green dye from the interspaces, and these are dyed red. A new series of resist lines is then printed at right angles to the first. The red dye between the resist lines is removed by alcohol, and the spaces re-dyed blue. After completion of the screen formation, the collodion surface is stripped from the metal and transferred to a film base.

The most successful of all the screen processes was the one initiated by Louis Dufay. Today the product is known as Dufaycolor, but it was first introduced about 1910 as the Dioptichrome plate. The first Dufay patents were assigned to an organization carrying the quaint name "A Company for the Exploitation of the Process in Color Photography of L Dufay." This became the Versicolor organization. Some time later Spicers Limited became interested and such companies as Spicers-Dufay, Ltd., Dufaycolor, Ltd , and Dufay-Chromex, Ltd., were formed to exploit the disclosures. Finally the Ilford company became interested. In the United States there was but one organization, Dufaycolor, which marketed the product.

The first Dufay disclosures (Eng. P. 11698/08; Ger. P. 237755; U.S.P. 1003720) were concerning the preparation of the Dioptichrome plate, which combined dichromate printing and transfer *à la* wash-off-relief, for the formation of the screen. A variation of this was contained in English patent 18744/08. In another disclosure, the cutting through of a resist was adopted, thus following du Hauron and R. de Bercegol (Fr. P. 370956, addition 7138, 388616, additions 10541, 13132, and 13775; 408552, additions 11696, 118454, 442881, addition 19753; Eng. P. 15027/12 and 27708/12; Ger P. 273629; U.S.P. 1155900). This last group of patents was already assigned to Versicolor.

The modern Dufaycolor film is prepared in accordance with the disclosures in L. Dufay's English patent 217557 and United States patent 1552126, also assigned to Versicolor. A celluloid film is stained superficially with a "blue" dye, and on this is printed a series of parallel lines in a greasy ink. When this is treated with an alcoholic solution of a "red" dye, the "blue" is removed and replaced by the "red." This is accomplished instantaneously if the second solution is made alkaline. After the resist is removed, the entire film is dyed yellow. This converts the "blue" and "red" into green and orange, this indicating that the original colors were really cyan and magenta. A new series of resist lines is now printed at right angles to the first, and the places free from resist are treated with a blue-violet dye solution. This will remove the yellow dye completely, and the cyan and magenta but partially. These will become converted into a blue-violet or red-violet respectively. Dufay claims a four-color process here, but it appears a rather dubious claim, since the last two colors would have a tremendous overlap, hence are not really independent of each other. As an example, the first dyeing is made with methylene blue. The second is made with Rhodamine B. The yellow overall is made with auramine. At this stage the lines will be true primary red and green. After the final operation, the yellow becomes replaced with crystal violet, a dye that transmits much more blue than red, but still a significant amount of that primary. This on top of Rhodamine B will give a reddish violet, a color that will transmit red and blue freely, but no green. This certainly cannot be considered as a unit in a four-color process, since the same colors will be registered simultaneously under the red and the blue elements. These last will be formed at those places where crystal violet overlays the methylene blue. The first will prevent any green rays from being transmitted, while the second will prevent the red rays from being transmitted But both will transmit the pure blue. It is interesting to note that every claim made so far by the inventors of four- and more color processes, fails when analyzed in this manner. They only succeeded in destroying the purity of the color analysis.

The last patent issued to L. Dufay was the United States patent 1805361, issued in 1931, and assigned to H. Wade. The corresponding English patent 322432 was issued to H. Wade and assigned to Versicolor, a rather curious state of affairs. The American patent introduces a few names which later play a prominent part in the further development of Dufaycolor. The film base is prepared in accordance to the disclosures of H. J. Hands (Eng. P. 279139, 281803 and 294008). This is coated with a layer of collodion, dyed green by the addition of 2 cc of a stock dye solution to 30 cc of the collodion. This is a development of C. Bonamiço (Eng P. 321222). The stock dye solution has the following composition:

Malachite green	4 parts
Auramine	6.7 parts
Alcohol	100 parts

About 25 cc of collodion is used to coat an area measuring 100 by 25 centimeters, yielding a layer that is 0.01 mm thick when wet, and from 0.0002 to 0.0005 mm when dry.

On this is ruled a series of lines with a resist ink. This was done in accordance with the disclosures of H. Wade (Eng. P. 322454, U.S P. 1760048) Fifteen lines were drawn to the linear millimeter by means of a steel roller, at an angle of 23 degrees to the axis of the cylinder. This corresponds to 400 lines to the inch. The present material is somewhat finer, containing approximately 500 lines to the inch, and some screens were made in this manner with 750 lines to the linear inch The ruled lines were dried for one hour, and then bathed in a solution whose composition was as follows:

Alcohol	100 parts
Aqueous KOH, 10%	2 parts
Acetone	4 parts

Treatment in this solution removed the dye from the clear spaces, which are re-dyed by passing over a dye roller. The film base was thoroughly washed to remove excess dye, then it was passed through a solvent which removed the resist lines. A buffing action prepared the surface for a new set of lines, ruled at right angles to the old. The spaces clear of ink lines were again decolorized by the action of the alkaline-acetone-alcohol solution, and the un-dyed portions dyed blue by means of the following bath:

Crystal violet, 4% alcoholic solution	80 parts
Malachite green, 8% alcoholic solution	20 parts

The film base was cleared as before, then coated with a panchromatic emulsion. The further development of the Dufaycolor material was carried on by J N. Goldsmith, T. T. Baker, and C Bonamico.

Although Dufay no longer contributed to the solution, the procedure was not changed Rather, all efforts were centered upon the improvement of details. The first serious problem was that of putting a superficial coating of dye upon the film base, before the resists were applied. This coating must be absolutely uniform, and of sufficient density to act as a complete filter for one primary. The thickness of the coating must be kept to a minimum, otherwise the slight divergence of the rays after passing through the screen will cause the deposition of densities of one color under the areas intended for the other two. It is the screen which is in the rear focal plane of the lens system, so that divergence of the rays starts in the plane of the screen. Acid dyes do not stain collodion, so that the screen colors are limited to the basic dyes. But celluloid, which is collodion to which camphor and other plasticizers have been added, will not stain when treated with basic dyes. It seems that the addition of the plasticizer extensively changes the properties of the collodion

A whole series of patents, all issued jointly to the trio J N Goldsmith, T. T. Baker, and C. Bonamico, deal with the treatment of celluloid film to make it receptive of basic dyes. It is to be recalled that the basic patent (Eng. P. 322432) utilized a film base of cellulose acetate, and that this was coated with a layer of collodion dyed green. The first disclosure in which the attempt is made to prepare the film base itself for a superficial dyeing, is in English patent 333865 The base is treated with an alcoholic potash solution, ranging from one-half to five per cent of the lye After this treatment, it will take on dye uniformly from a bath such as

Malachite green	2 parts
Alcohol	60 parts
Water	40 parts
Acetic acid	4 parts

If the film base is celluloid, then this is coated with a thin layer of cellulose acetate, which is deposited from the following solution:

Cellulose acetate	1 part
Tetra-chlor-ethane	20 parts
Methyl alcohol	2½ parts
Acetone	2½ parts

A coating such as this readily takes up basic dyes from solutions that would have no effect whatsoever upon celluloid Therefore the coated film base could receive its superficial dyeing on one side with the absolute assurance that the other side would remain clear. This represents a tremendous simplification in the manipulations of the film base during the period of the screen formation. In a later patent there is disclosed still another scheme for putting a superficial coating of cellulose acetate on the film base (Eng P. 337073). The film passed around a roller which just dips into a solution of cellulose acetate in acetone, such as

Cellulose acetate	14–15 parts
Plasticizer	5–6 parts
Acetone	100 parts

The above treatment yields a layer which has a thickness of 4 to 8 μ (0.004 to 0.008 mm). Such a coating will not absorb the dye, but it can be given a surface coating of collodion which is already dyed. The cellulose acetate evidently acts as a subbing base for the dyed collodion layer.

The various difficulties encountered in the making of a uniformly dyed surface layer are discussed in English patent 339238. It is very difficult to apply a dye to a celluloid film, but once applied, the dye is retained with great tenacity. This makes its subsequent bleaching extremely hard. This can be overcome by the application of a coating of pure cellulose acetate to the surface, as is disclosed in English patent 334265. When a film base of cellulose acetate is to be used, other difficulties arise Too deep a stain is taken up, and one which does not discharge easily Coating such a film layer with collodion (Eng P. 322432) helped alleviate this situation In either case, however, the precautionary measures were nullified if the dye diffused beyond the superficial layer into the film base itself. To prevent this, the film may be dyed from a solution which is non-penetrating. This is accomplished by dispersing or dissolving the dye in castor oil, castor-oil-alcohol, or gum arabic mixtures.

To insure that the sound-track areas of motion picture film would be left free of screen pattern, C. Bonamico (U.S.P. 2008239, Eng. P. 356816 and 414761), and T T Baker (Eng P. 335899) so constructed the rollers which printed the resists that no deposits were made in those areas which, after slitting, would correspond to the sound-track region.

The next problem to be tackled was that of coating. Here it was necessary to insure the firm adhesion of a gelatin layer to another of rather complex structure, and one which contained basic dyes. These were not always neutral with regard to their action upon the photographic emulsion. Some of the dyes may act as sensitizers, while others may have the opposite action and act as desensitizers. So the simplest procedure to adopt was to insulate the screen layer from the emulsion. This was disclosed by T T. Baker (Eng P. 401719; U.S P. 1962679) and by H D Murray, H Baines, and R. A. S. Grist (Eng. P. 435484). A solution of resin in benzol to which some linseed oil had been added, was the Baker solution.

A complete specification for the formation of the screen is disclosed by T. T. Baker (Eng. P. 420824; U.S.P. 2030163). The reason for this patent is to protect the printing of the resist lines by means of a special roller, where non-printing areas contain an ink-resisting mercury-silver amalgam. The film base is prepared in the manner disclosed by H. J. Hands (Eng. P. 243032, 281803, 287635, and 301439). On this is coated a thin layer of collodion which is dyed green by the addition of 2 cc of a stock dye to 30 cc of collodion The dye is prepared by dissolving 4 parts of malachite green and 6.7 parts of auramine in 100 parts of methyl alcohol. A strip 100 by 26 centimeters requires from 22 to 25 cc of the dyed collodion solution. This had been disclosed previously by C. Bonamico and H Wade (Eng. P. 321222). Upon the dyed film is then printed a series of resist areas, which may or may not be in the form of a geometric pattern, by means of a special roller.

This is prepared in the following manner. A metal roller is first given a coating of silver. Upon this is deposited an even coating of chromium, also electrolytically. On top of the chromium is placed a sensitized tissue upon which the screen pattern has been photographically printed. The tissue used is a dichromated gelatin or other colloid. It is placed with the image portion adjacent to the surface of the roller. Treatment with hot water removes the non-image portions, leaving a tanned colloid relief image upon the surface of the roller. This is next subjected to the action of a solution which will etch the chromium wherever this surface has been laid bare, obviously between the tanned colloid relief areas. When the chromium surface has been etched away, leaving bare the silver, the etch is stopped. The tanned colloid resist is removed, and the roller treated with a mercury solution. Only the silver will form an amalgam, the chromium being insoluble in mercury. An amalgam surface has the extremely useful property of acting as a resist to greasy inks, while the chromium surface will adsorb the ink. Thus a matrix is formed by means of which a resist containing a superficial coating of dyed collodion can be transferred to the cellulose acetate film. This technique is a well established one in the photomechanical printing industry, especially in that section which uses planographic printing with mercury inks.

After the resist has been transferred, the dye in the areas between the lines is bleached by treatment with

Methyl alcohol	100 parts
Caustic potash, 2% solution	2 parts
Acetone	4 parts

The bleached areas are then re-dyed by treatment with an 8 per cent alcoholic solution of basic red N. The old resist lines are removed by treatment with a suitable solvent, and a new set of lines printed at right angles to the first. Decoloration is again accomplished in the areas between the greasy lines, this time both red and green being removed. At this stage the film base consists of a series of squares of red and green lying in juxtaposition, and running in lines. The lines are separated from each other by clear undyed lines that are free from grease, and which can therefore be stained from alcoholic solutions. This is accomplished by means of a blue bath, whose composition is the same as the one given above (cf. p. 168) A wash removes excess dye, while treatment with a solvent removes the greasy lines. The screen elements are then coated with an insulating layer of varnish, which also serves as a subbing for the panchromatic emulsion which is coated upon the varnish layer.

There are several schemes which cannot readily be classified in any group. F J. H Harrison (U S.P. 578147) used a band of celluloid that was colored solidly, and ruled with opaque lines which were twice the width of the transparent spaces between. The celluloid "ribbon" was divided into three sections, each of which was stained in a different primary color. The lines in each section were staggered with respect to those in adjacent sections The ribbon was moved by means of a spring motor across the front of the sensitive plate. The result was the same as if the plate were exposed behind a screen composed of colored lines lying in juxtaposition. It is hard to determine just exactly what advantage there was in this procedure outside of the fact that it is quite simple to prepare such a screened ribbon, for the subsequent separation or the preparation of a colored transparency would impose a very ticklish problem of registry. Similar ideas were expounded by C. L. A. Brasseur and S. P. Sampolo (Eng. P. 8390/96); and by F. E. Ives (U.S.P. 648748 and 666424). In the Ives procedure, the black-and-white screen was placed in front of the plate, and the three exposures were made through the three filters. Between the exposures, the position of the screen was shifted, so that a new area was exposed on the film each time, and through a different filter.

A rather simple procedure was adopted by M. Obergassner (Ger P. 263819; Fr P 438746). A plate was coated with dyed gelatin It was then grooved through to the glass in a series of parallel lines After recoating with another layer of dyed gelatin, a new set of grooves was cut through. The plate was recoated a second time, buffed even, then coated with a panchromatic emulsion. It is to be recalled that the earliest patents of du Hauron and Bercegol utilized a technique identical to this, except that they cut grooves through a resist surface This, therefore, is a simplification of the earlier disclosure C. L A Brasseur (Eng. P. 20909/08; Ger P. 219977; U.S.P. 976118) combined photo-mechanical printing methods with the dusting-on procedure He printed a tacky material upon a glass or film base, then dusted on colored powders. This was followed by another printing and dusting, until the film surface was completely covered. F. Faulstich also combined two methods (Eng. P. 152002). A base was sprayed with a dye so that only part of the total surface was covered The covered areas then acted as resists for a further dyeing operation. Somewhat similar in basic principle was the technique adopted by Keller (Eng. P. 244644). He sprayed a gelatin-coated base with colors compounded to contain alum or formaldehyde. These chemicals tanned the gelatin in situ with the dye powder, making that specific area no longer receptive of dyes, if these were of the pinatype group.

CHAPTER 14

PROCESSING SCREEN PLATES

(A). HYPERSENSITIZATION. — The early screen plates were extremely slow, from thirty to sixty times as slow as normal emulsions of their period. This lack of speed made itself felt very soon after their introduction, and much effort was expended in attempts to overcome it. One type of effort was to hypersensitize the emulsion just before use. At first the attempts were confined to an increase of the red sensitivity, but soon the attention became centered upon a general intensification of the plate sensitivity. No doubt the latter efforts were directly the results of the previous ones. Optical sensitization proceeds best when carried out in an alkaline medium, and this condition also leads to a large increase of general sensitivity. Later, when the screen-type materials could be made only a little slower than the normal, it was no longer necessary to resort to hypersensitization, but the discussion of this subject is included here mainly because of historical interest.

The photographic emulsion consists of a relatively coarse dispersion of micro crystals of silver iodo-bromide in gelatin The pure emulsion is sensitive only to the blue and violet portions of the spectrum. In 1873, H. Vogel discovered that when the silver halide grain was treated with certain dyes, the sensitivity of the grain became extended to the spectral regions absorbed by the dye. His discovery, accepted several years after the first disclosure, soon unloosed a veritable barrage of work, and after many years it became possible to prepare photographic emulsions whose sensitivities cover any desired range from the far ultraviolet, well below 200 mμ, to the extreme infrared above 1200 mμ The visible range extends from 400 to 700 mμ.

The first sensitizing experiments were carried out by bathing the finished plate in a dye solution. Plates sensitized by bathing in this manner were quite effective in the new range, but unfortunately had very poor keeping qualities. It was soon established that excellent keeping qualities would be obtained if the sensitizing dye were added to the emulsion just before it was coated But the degree of sensitivity induced was not quite so high in this case as when the coated plate was bathed and dried just before use. Bathing appeared to give a hypersensitizing effect. This was traced to the removal of the slight amount of soluble halide left in the finished emulsion to give it keeping qualities and freedom from fog. Carroll, Hubbard, and Kretchman made a special study of the effect that halides had upon the general sensitivity and the keeping qualities of emulsions Their conclusion was (*Bu. Stand. J. of Res.*, Vol. 12 (1934),

p. 223) that a finished emulsion should contain approximately one to five moles of soluble bromide per 1000 moles of silver bromide, in order for that emulsion to keep over a year. The presence of even this small amount of excess bromide was enough to materially decrease the general sensitivity of the plate, and to reduce to an even greater extent, the capacity of that emulsion to be optically sensitized.

When a finished plate containing the absolute minimum of soluble bromide requisite for good keeping qualities was bathed in a solution capable of removing some of the bromide, it was soon readily seen that the new plate was not only faster and more sensitive in the induced range, but that it also had poor keeping qualities. Efforts to replace the bromide resulted merely in a reduction of color sensitivity and general speed, although the keeping qualities did improve. This lack of stability was the stumbling block that lay in the path of the successful utilization of the Friedman Bipacks (cf. chapter on Monopacks).

A considerable intensification of the plate speed can be obtained by making the bath alkaline with ammonia. For a long time, bathing a plate in an ammoniacal solution was the recognized technique for hypersensitization. This action was first disclosed by Schumann (*Phot Woch.* (1885), p. 395; (1886) p. 49). It was soon verified by others, including Walters and Davis (*Bu. Stand. Sci. Paper* No. 422), Burka (*J Frank. Inst.*, Vol. 189 (1920), p. 25) and Jacobsohn ("Theorie und Praxis der Ubersensibilisierung"), who wrote a complete review that covered most of the work done prior to the contributions of Carroll and Hubbard (*Bu. Stand. J. of Res.*, Vol. 10 (1933), p. 211).

These men, applying the Donnan equilibrium relationship, have shown that the net effect of bathing a photographic emulsion with ammonia was to create an excess of silver ions in the emulsion, a condition that is very prone to fog as well as to increased speed. This they proved experimentally, using Seed 23 plates. The amount of excess silver ions ranged from 0.2 to 1 0 per cent. The same effect could be obtained if the plate were treated with silver solutions, hence the hypersensitizing action of solutions containing silver ions could be explained by exactly the same mechanism. It is a well-known fact that the basic sensitizers act much better in the absence of soluble halides, than in their presence. Hence it is to be expected that a plate sensitized with basic dyes will show an increased activity by treatment with soluble silver salts, which will remove the excess bromide ions completely, and leave the plate with excess silver ions. Bokinik (*Zeit. Wiss. Phot.*, Vol. 30 (1932), p. 322) reported that if a plate were dyed with a basic sensitizer, dried, then bathed with dilute silver nitrate solution, a considerable increase in the effective sensitization was obtained. Even some of the desensitizers gave definite sensitizing action under these conditions.

As soon as it was fully realized that the presence of halide ions affected the sensitivity of the plate to a great extent, efforts were directed to reduce this concentration to an absolute minimum, not by treatment with silver nitrate, which would leave excess silver ions, but by treatment with silver chloride solutions. One of the first to do this was F. Monpillard (*Bull Soc. franç Phot.*, Vol. 64 (1922), pp. 90, 130). The addition of silver ions to fluorescein sensitizing solutions has been known at least since 1884, when W Abney suggested that the silver salt of eosine be added to an emulsion to give it orthochromatic properties (*Phot News*, Vol. 28 (1884), p. 500). A short time later W. H. Hyslop substituted an ammoniacal solution of pure silver chloride for the silver nitrate (*Phot. News*, Vol. 31 (1887), p. 107) in the preparation of the silver salt of the sensitizer Silver nitrate (3 6 grams) was treated with excess hydrochloric acid. The precipitated silver chloride was washed thoroughly, then dissolved in concentrated ammonia and diluted with water to give a final volume of 10 cc. The erythrosine (5.4 grams) was meanwhile dissolved in 3 6 cc concentrated ammonia, and then diluted to 175 cc with alcohol. From these stock solutions, the sensitizing bath was compounded as follows:

Silver solution	1.85 parts
Dye solution	6 3 parts
Water to	1000 parts

The Monpillard technique merely substituted the cyanine dyes for erythrosine. Pinaverdol (1 part), pinachrome (0.5 part) and pinacyanol (0.5 part) were each dissolved in 1000 parts of alcohol. From these a stock dye solution was made containing 160 parts each of pinaverdol and pinachrome solutions, 80 parts of pinacyanol, and 600 parts of alcohol. A stock silver chloride solution was also prepared by dissolving 0.2 part of the silver halide in 8 parts of concentrated ammonia, then making up to 100 parts with water. The sensitizing solution was made by adding 100 parts of the stock silver to 100 parts of the stock dye, and diluting to 1000 parts with 50 per cent alcohol The temperature of the solution should be kept very low. After a five-minute treatment, the plates should be washed and dried as rapidly as possible. Since the emulsion would not keep for more than thirty-six hours, the technique was not commercially feasible. A thirty-fold increase in speed was claimed.

Approximately the same idea was disclosed by A. Ninck (*Bull. Soc. franç. Phot.*, Vol. 65 (1924), p. 345). He used pantochrome for the sensitizing agent (1:2500), and 2 per cent silver chloride containing 6.5 parts of concentrated ammonia per 100 parts of solution. The actual sensitizer contained:

Dye solution	20 parts
Silver solution	6 6 parts
Water to	1000 parts

Ninck claimed a speed increase of thirty times, and a keeping quality vastly superior to that of Monpillard. He also studied the effect of silver concentration (*Bull. Soc. franç. Phot.*, Vol. 66 (1924), pp 83 and 92). All the tests were made on the Autochrome plate, the exposures being made behind a Eder-Hecht wedge.

Test No	Silver Content in Sensitizing Bath	Relative Speed
1	Control	1
2	0 00 gram per liter	6
3.	0 07 gram per liter	17
4	0 18 gram per liter	23
5	0.20 gram per liter	33
6	0.53 gram per liter	40
7	1 69 grams per liter	17

The control plate was an Autochrome which received no treatment. Test No. 2 was made on an Autochrome which was treated with the sensitizing bath, but compounded to contain no silver. This test indicated the effect of bathing the plate in an ammoniacal dye solution. It is interesting to note that a maximum exists in the amount of silver that may be used. As the silver content of the bath increased, the keeping quality of the plate decreased Old plates, that were no longer fit for use because of their tendency to fog, could be revived by treatment with:

Chromic acid	5 parts
Potassium bromide	10 parts
Water to	1000 parts

After a five-minute wash, the plate could be hypersensitized. This treatment obviously destroyed the silver specks that were the cause of the latent fog

Many years later L. J Meker (*Bull. Soc franç. Phot*, for 1936, *Phot. Ind.*, Vol 35 (1937) p 12) disclosed an identical procedure for the renovation of old fogged Autochromes. His sensitizing bath was compounded as follows

Pinaverdol stock	30 parts
Pinachrome stock	30 parts
Pinacyanol stock	15 parts
Silver stock	1 part
Concentrated ammonia	3 drops

The dye stock solutions contained one part of sensitizer to 2000 parts of alcohol The silver solution was made by adding 15 parts of concentrated ammonia to 5 parts of a 10 per cent silver nitrate solution, and diluting with 25 cc of water.

Other systems of hypersensitization were based upon a reaction with the silver halide grain itself. It has always been felt that the latent image was composed of a grain of silver halide upon which there was adsorbed a speck of metallic silver. The brilliant photographic chemist Carey Lea had demonstrated that silver halide grains upon which there had been adsorbed colloidally dispersed silver, were developable without the action of light. But before developability could be conferred, a certain minimum size had to be reached by the adsorbed particle. It is possible to form the metallic silver particles by other means than by the action of light Mild reducing agents could be allowed to act on the grain for a period just sufficient to reduce a few molecules. Working along lines like these, Luppo-Cramer found that hydrogen peroxide intensified a latent image if the plate, after exposure, were treated with a weak alkaline solution of the peroxide (*Phot. Korr*, Vol. 52 (1915), p. 136). Sheppard and Wightman (*J. Frank. Inst.*, Vol. 195 (1923), p 337; Vol. 200 (1935), p. 335; Vol 203 (1927), p 261, Vol. 204 (1927), p 731; *Brit. J. Phot*, Vol. 74 (1927), p 447) studied this action critically, and found that the action would be obtained whether the plate was treated with peroxide before or after exposure They found that peroxide took the place of light in creating a latent image If the concentration of the peroxide was kept to a value that would produce an effect just sufficient to overcome the inertia of the emulsion (an effect equivalent to the toe of the H & D curve), then hypersensitization occurs. Schmieschek attempted to put this idea into practice by compounding an ammoniacal silver solution with peroxide present (*Phot. Ind.*, Vol. 28 (1930) pp. 445, 472), but the best opinion has it that his conclusions are unfounded.

More recently F. Dersch and H Duerr (*J Soc Mot Pict. Eng.*, Vol 28 (1937), p. 178) disclosed still another hypersensitizing procedure, one which had practically no effect upon any other photographic characteristic of the emulsion besides decreasing the inertia Their technique could be applied with equal results either before or after the exposure had taken place It was merely necessary to put a drop of mercury into the container holding the film, taking care that no part of the emulsion came in contact with the mercury. Where this happens, intense fog results Possible theories as to the mechanism of the reaction are contained in a discussion of this phenomenon by J. S Friedman (*Am. Phot*, Vol. 32 (1937), p. 738; Vol 34 (1939), p. 700). The hypersensitization that is obtained by the action of mercury is mild. The speed is increased, at most, approximately twice. This system has but little appeal, therefore, to screen-plate users But it does hold out the hope for better results.

The latent image consists of a speck of colloidally dispersed silver adsorbed upon a silver halide grain. But a grain that has colloidal gold, copper, or any one of many other metals adsorbed upon it, is also in a developable condition. From this point of view it can be considered that when a film is exposed to mercury vapor, some mercury atoms become adsorbed by the silver halide grains and in that way make them developable. The total number of grains thus affected may be just sufficient to overcome the inertia. Or the grains can adsorb an amount of mercury that is just insufficient to cause developability. It would require much less light, therefore, to bring these grains into a developable condition In either case a reduction of the emulsion inertia takes place.

The vapor tension of mercury at room temperature is very low, 0 00109 At 50 C the value is 0 0127, or twelve times as much. If the temperature at which the film is exposed to the mercury is maintained at 18 C, approximately 20 hours is required to effect a two-fold increase in speed. But at 50, only a few minutes treatment is required. This indicates a tremendous effect due to an increase in the concentration of the mercury vapor. Since the action can be carried out after exposure, it may be possible to duplicate the result by compounding colloidal solutions of mercury in water or other liquids, and subjecting the exposed film to this.

So much for the subject of hypersensitization. As pointed out at the first part of the chapter, Dufaycolor, with a speed rating of Weston 8, was sufficiently fast not to require this treatment.

(B). CHEMICAL REVERSAL. — Since the registry of the image with the screen elements must be so exact, the preferred method of processing screen plates has been by reversal. This popularized a form of technique mainly devoted to amateur motion-picture film. Briefly described, the procedure is as follows: The plate, after exposure, is developed in the normal manner, but it is not fixed out. Instead, it is treated with acid dichromate or permanganate, which dissolves out the silver image. The remaining silver halide grains are now present in the form of a positive, since a negative image has been removed. Exposure to light followed by a second development, yields a positive which is registered exactly with the screen elements There are several features in reversal development which make the procedure very useful not only for the processing of materials like Kodachrome, Ansco Color, Autochrome, Dufaycolor, etc., but for all types of work.

As has been stated so often in these pages, the photographic emulsion consists of a complex mixture of silver halide grains whose sizes and sensitivities vary over a wide range. In any one emulsion, the larger grains are the most sensitive ones During the initial development, a group of grains come together in some mysterious fashion to form a single silver grain which makes up the final image. The image that is developed during normal procedure will therefore contain grains that are fairly coarse and that are not too evenly distributed throughout the emulsion. But the grains that are left behind, after the initial image has been developed, consist of the finer grains of the emulsion; and these, during development, will not have as great a tendency to clump, since the individual particles are insulated from each other much more thoroughly. A reversed image is therefore universally much finer-grained and more evenly distributed than a direct image.

Another advantage is that a given emulsion will have a greater speed if processed by reversal than if processed normally. This is usually caused by the fact that the first development in reversible procedure is practically always carried out to gamma infinity. Every single grain that has received an exposure sufficient for the formation of a latent image, is reduced If this were done with normally processed plates, the developer would have to be compounded to contain a relatively high concentration of soluble bromide, otherwise intense fog would occur, which would ruin the printing qualities of the negative But in reversal procedure, the formation of a high fog level is of no importance whatsoever, since the silver that is formed initially is removed. This holds for the fog as well as for the image itself.

There are several disadvantages, however, in the use of this procedure.

There is first of all, a reversal of the image, as regards left and right. This means that the image must be copied with the base facing the emulsion side of the copying material. Secondly, the image is a positive transparency, and so before copies can be made it must be converted into a negative. In color photography, however, especially in the photomechanical field, it is sometimes necessary to use positives from which to print. In those cases, the printing image is one step closer to the original than would be true for the normal procedure

Reversal processing has received a considerable amount of study, and we cannot in these pages review all the work But since we are concerned with the technique from a practical point of view, we will discuss the disclosures of P. K. Turner, who made a special study of the working conditions best suited for reversal (*Brit. J. Phot.*, Vol. 84 (1937), pp 435, 449, 465). The problem that confronts the technician is best explained by Mr. Lloyd E. Varden (J. S. Friedman, *Am. Phot.*, Vol. 33 (1938), p. 283), who writes, in substance, as follows: The fact that an emulsion cannot be completely exposed and developed in one operation, would lead to degraded highlights in reversal processes if precautions in the first development were not taken. An emulsion can be exposed to a certain limit, at which limit some of the grains begin to solarize. The first developer is always a strong and highly caustic type of developer which reduces all the grains that have been exposed, but not exposed to the point of solarization. This development is prolonged beyond normal to make sure of this. If the exposure has been excessive and some of the grains became solarized, these grains will not be developable. Clear highlights in the final image depend upon the complete absence of developable silver-halide grains in these regions after the initial development is over To insure this, silver-halide solvents are added to the solution, such as ammonia, hypo, etc., but the preferred agent is potassium thiocyanate.

If a piece of film is exposed to the limit (not to solarization), and developed to the limit, there will still be some silver-halide grains left, which, after the removal of the developed silver, will give appreciable density. In reversal work, this silver-halide residue must be removed, and as stated before, this is accomplished by the addition of suitable solvents to the developer. Thus simultaneously with the reduction of the silver halide to metallic silver, it is also dissolved away preferentially in the regions of high density. The amount of solvent added should be sufficient to insure the complete removal of the silver halide left in the highlight regions of the film.

In his paper, Mr. Turner discusses the problem generally. There are four techniques available in reversal processing.

1. Controlled time of first development
2. Controlled exposure to light after reversal.
3. Controlled second development.
4. Use of a special type of first developer.

The first method can be discarded at once, as it is only for a single-exposure intensity that a sufficient number of grains become affected in highlight regions to enable a suitable density range to be covered in the final print. This makes its use by far too critical to be of practical value. The second method requires accurate measuring devices and processing conditions that are not readily available to the average technician. It is the method used by the Eastman Kodak Company. After the bleach treatment which removes the silver negative image, each frame in the film is metered by red light, photo-electrically, and then exposed automatically in accordance with this reading. It is seen that there must be had an accurate knowledge of the effect that the removal of the first image has upon the speed of the residual grains. This is complicated by the fact that not every frame will have the same proportion of the fast grains affected, so that a considerable variation of residual film speed exists The same objections may be noted for case three It is only the last technique that remains available for the average technician. This is the technique used by Autochrome and Dufaycolor.

Mr. Turner showed that with a sufficient quantity of bromide present in the developer to reduce the speed of the emulsion to one-fourth of its original, and with enough hypo present to allow the fixation to proceed at the rate that is one-tenth that of the development, it would be possible to obtain a brightness range in the positive of from one to thirty. To determine these constants more accurately, it is necessary to know the film speed of the emulsion for normal development A strip of the emulsion is exposed assuming twice the speed The developer is then compounded with no bromide present, so that complete development is obtained in five minutes Add 10 grams of potassium bromide and 16 grams of hypo, or 1.6 grams of potassium cyanide, per liter of solution Two strips of film, with identical exposure (half normal), are developed in this solution, one until the highlights appear as dense when viewed through the base as when viewed through the emulsion; the other strip fifty per cent longer. Of course the two film strips are desensitized to allow visual inspection during development. The strips are placed in the acid dichromate reversal baths directly from the developer bath, then cleared in bisulphite which removes the dichromate stain. Redevelopment in the first developer completes the operation. The two strips should have the same contrast. If they have different contrasts, the original exposure was wrong. If the strips appear too contrasty, more hypo should be added to the solution. If they are too soft, less hypo should be used. The developer suggested by Mr Turner, is the following one·

Metol	25 parts
Hydroquinone	50 parts
Sodium sulphite	200 parts
Sodium hydroxide	25 parts
Water to	1000 parts

For use, take one part of this, add one part each of 12½ per cent hypo and 10 per cent bromide, and 7 parts of water

The effect of adding silver halide solvents to a developer, was studied by H. D. Murray and D. A Spencer (*Phot J.*, Vol 77 (1937), pp. 330, 458) They found that in general the addition of substances like hypo or thiocyanate to a developer, caused an acceleration in the rate of development, if the concentrations were not too high. Mannes and Godowsky have found that the addition of approximately one gram of thiocyanate per liter of developer, gave a tremendous increase in the potential (U.S.P. 2091713) Other silver solvents that can be used are ammonia and its derivatives, such as the ethanolamines, ethylene diamine, etc. These have certain other advantages, such as the fact that they can also be used instead of the carbonate or other energizers.

The next step in the procedure is the removal of the silver image. This is usually called reversal, for after this step is accomplished, a positive residue remains, consisting of silver bromide. The removal of the silver can be accomplished by treatment with acidified dichromate or permanganate. The acid ion must be one that forms a soluble silver salt, such as sulphate, nitrate, or acetate, otherwise the silver will merely be changed into an insoluble silver salt. This, by the action of the second developer, will become reconverted into silver. Sulphuric acid is generally the most desired acid ion.

When gelatin comes in contact with silver ions, silver gelatinate is formed, a substance that will be easily reduced to metallic silver by the action of even very mild reducing agents. It is not possible to wash this substance out, so that regardless of how long the wash after the reversal is prolonged, the silver-gelatin complex will remain, and perhaps even grow This last may be due to the formation of excess silver ions by the hydrolytic action of water upon silver bromide.

$$AgBr \overset{H_2O}{\rightleftarrows} Ag^+ + Br^-$$

The bromide ions, having no special attachment to the gelatin, are easily removed by washing. This shifts the equilibrium to the right, causing more of the insoluble salt to go into solution, thus building up the silver-ion concentration Thus more and more silver gelatinate is formed.

Carroll and Hubbard (*Bu. Stand. J. of Res.*, Vol. 7 (1931), p. 811) made a special study of this reaction. They found that silver gelatinate was formed only in the absence of other substances, such as ammonia or sulphites, which also form complexes with silver ions. The gelatin-silver complexes are easily decomposed by the treatment with either ammonia or sulphite. The fogging effect produced when an emulsion is washed for a long time with water prior to development, can be traced to this.

It is very important, therefore, if the last ounce of perfection is to be obtained from the reversed screen plates, that the soluble silver ions be completely lacking in the emulsion after the treatment with acid dichromate. To insure one's self of this, it becomes desirable to give the reversed plate a bath in ammoniacal sodium sulphite, or if the volatile character of ammonia is objectionable, a sulphite bath to which ethylene diamine or mono-ethanolamine has been added

This operation can be carried out in light, so that the plate becomes developable at the same time that it is cleared of the objectionable gelatin-silver complex.

The final blackening of the remaining silver halides can be accomplished in many ways. One very simple method is to treat the plate with sodium sulphide solutions. This converts the silver halide remaining in the emulsion layer into a black silver sulphide. There are many other agents which can be used to sulphurize the halide. These are the compounds, containing the SH group, in which the hydrogen is in a labile form. Another direct method for converting the silver halides into a black substance is to use hydrosulphite, a substance that is not to be confounded with sodium hyposulphite, the ordinary hypo of the fixing bath.

However, the method most generally used is to give the remaining silver-halide salts a complete exposure to light, then develop them to form metallic silver. There may be some disadvantages to this method. The remaining grains are very slow, since all the faster grains have been used up to form the first image. Their sensitivity is still further decreased by the treatment with acid dichromate, which, while dissolving the silver, also etches out from the grain surfaces the sensitivity specks that were not previously affected by light. There is no telling, therefore, just what exposure is required to make all the remaining grains developable.

Many substances are known which produce intense fog when brought in contact with the silver-halide grain. One such was mentioned above, during the discussion of mercury hypersensitization. Thiourea, $S = C(NH_2)_2$, is another chemical that has this property. Indeed, so intense is its action that a concentration of one part in a million is sufficient to give considerable fog Many other compounds, all characterized by the – (CSH) group, in which the H is a labile hydrogen, will have this effect in alkaline solutions which favor the formation of the mercaptan salt. Many dyes also react in this manner. Methylene blue, janus green, capri blue, nile blue 2B, cyanine blue, Victoria blue, Bindscheller's green, malachite green, methyl violet, and crystal violet are all dyes which create considerable fog. Several patents covering the use of such fogging agents have been issued to Eastman Kodak Co. and to the I G., but the validity of such disclosures is open to doubt, as the phenomenon is a well known one and its application to reversal procedure very natural.

After the second development is complete, it is desirable to fix the plate to remove the last traces of undeveloped silver halides. It is an impossibility to develop all the remaining grains, so that some will always remain in the final image unless removed by treatment with hypo. Greater clarity will result, since the silver salt is a diffusing agent.

Some of the methods discussed in the chapter on monopacks can be readily applied to the processing of screen plates. Thus, after the first image has been removed, the remaining silver halides can be converted into silver iodide by treatment with the potassium salt of this halide In this condition, the salt will absorb basic dyes such as auramine, rhodamine B, and methylene blue.

These can be mixed in such ratios that a black image results. Or a black basic dye can be found which is absorbed by the silver iodide. Another possibility lies in the use of pinatype black M or platinum black, dyes which stain soft gelatin only. The silver image is not removed in this case by treatment with acid dichromate, but is converted into silver chloride by treatment with a bromoil bleach. This is compounded from dichromate, acid, copper sulphate, and a halide, such as sodium chloride or potassium bromide. Besides converting the silver into silver chloride or silver bromide, this tans the gelatin in the immediate vicinity of the negative image, making it no longer receptive of the pinatype dyes. The silver halide is then removed by treatment with plain hypo, which is without effect upon the gelatin. Treatment with platinum black, or pinatype black M, will then stain only the regions outside of the negative image, giving a black positive image, whose contrast can be controlled to a great extent by the concentration and other physico-chemical properties of the solution.

(C). Photographic Reversal Methods — These methods are at present (1943), merely laboratory curiosities, incapable of yielding images that are commercially acceptable. They are discussed here, because there is no telling when the procedures will emerge from the laboratory stage, and also because it is desired to make this discussion of reversal technique representative of the field. A plate or film is given a uniform overall exposure sufficient to yield a deep black of the desired shadow intensity were development to proceed directly. Instead of development, the plate is treated with a solution containing a light-sensitive substance whose degradation product is an oxidizing agent, capable of destroying the latent image previously formed The plate is then exposed in the camera. Where the light is incident upon it, the latent image formed by the first uniform exposure is reduced or destroyed, depending upon the intensity of the light. Development then yields a direct positive. The application to screen plates is of course obvious.

The idea can be traced back to Bayard, one of the founders of the Société française de Photographie. In 1839, several months before the Daguerreotype process was made public (Neblette, "Photography, Principles and Practice" second edition (1931), p 18), he exhibited prints that were made in accordance with the following technique. Paper, soaked with ammonium chloride, was dried, then floated on top of a silver-nitrate solution. After drying, it was exposed to light until a deep black resulted. It was then bathed in a solution of potassium iodide, and exposed in the camera while wet. Under the action of light, the potassium iodide decomposed to yield free iodine This united with the silver formed in the first printing-out operation, to form white silver iodide. Thus where the light had the greatest intensity, complete bleaching of the silver took place. A direct positive resulted.

The photo-chemical decomposition of a latent image is therefore at least as old as the idea of photography, and considerably older than any of the photographic processes now in use. It is extremely unfortunate that Bayard worked before developing-out emulsions were known, for then he would have been able to apply his reaction to a substance that was thousands of times as fast as the printing-out emulsion that he used. He would not have had to expose the paper until a suitable final image was obtained, but only until the released iodine became sufficient to destroy the developability of the grains in the highlights. The use of potassium iodide as the light-sensitive material would have forced him to utilize physical development, as silver iodide is not readily developed chemically. But then, there would have been an incentive for the photographic technician to devise methods to allow the chemical development of silver-iodide emulsions. Other substances whose photo-chemical decomposition products are oxidizing agents, are the peroxides, the alkali halides, dichromate, etc. Perhaps the dichromates could be compounded with a substance that yields an acid by photo-chemical decomposition, in which case local desensitization would occur by the action of acid dichromate upon the latent image. There are many other possibilities, some of which have been discussed by J. S. Friedman (*Am. Phot.*, Vol 33 (1939), p. 212).

The use of dichromate for the preparation of direct positives, was proposed by G. O't Hooft (*Brit. J. Phot.*, Vol. 85 (1938), p. 229) A piece of Kodak contrasty bromide is bathed in a 2½ per cent solution of potassium dichromate to which 10 drops of 10 per cent potassium bromide have been added for every 10 cc of solution. The excess liquid is removed by wiping, and a thin sheet of Kodaloid or other transparent waterproof film is placed over it The transparency whose copy is desired is then placed on top of this, and the exposure made through it. This will require approximately twenty minutes to daylight. The bromide is then washed for one hour to insure the complete removal of the dichromate, after which it is given a diffuse overall exposure. Where the light acted upon the dichromate, in the previous exposure, a reaction took place which released an oxidizing agent. This destroyed the sensitivity of the grain in its immediate neighborhood. The exposure through the transparency therefore formed an image in the bromide paper that consisted of insensitive silver bromide. The remaining silver bromide becomes developable, when exposed to light, which could be accomplished in the normal manner.

A variation of this technique would utilize a silver image. The plate or film is exposed in the ordinary manner. It is then developed normally, but instead of being fixed, it is treated with an acid-dichromate-alkali-halide solution, such as the one made by mixing equal portions of *A* and *B*.

Solution A.

Potassium bromide	30 parts
Copper sulphate	30 parts
Hydrochloric acid (1 10)	5 parts
Water to	500 parts

Solution B.

Ammonium dichromate	5 parts
Water to	500 parts

The time in this solution should not exceed ten minutes If the silver is not completely bleached, more of solution *A* should be added. After the image is bleached, the plate is rinsed in water, then bathed in dilute (1:200) sulphuric acid This is done to remove the stain. A twenty-minute wash removes all undesired soluble substances remaining in the emulsion layer. It is then given a diffuse flash exposure to make the silver-halide grains developable. But the new grains, which were formed by the action of the bleach upon the negative image, are very insensitive and require a considerable amount of light before they become developable Thus a positive image is formed by the final development

This reaction does not differ materially from one that has time and time again been proposed for the formation of a duplicate positive. A film or plate containing a silver halide emulsion is further sensitized by bathing in a 2½ per cent ammonium dichromate solution, and dried. It is then exposed, by contact, through the negative or positive transparency whose duplicate is desired. A thorough wash removes the excess dichromate, after which the plate is given an overall diffuse exposure. The grains that had received a previous exposure to light while sensitized with dichromate, have been rendered relatively insensitive and incapable of forming a latent image. Therefore, by the final step of normal development, there is formed a silver image which is of the same character as the one through which the first exposure had been made.

In his comments upon the O't Hooft reaction, J. S. Friedman (*Am Phot*, Vol. 33 (1939), p. 62) pointed out that if the photo-chemical decomposition of dichromate results in the release of nascent oxygen, it is possible to utilize the reaction in a different manner, to yield a direct positive. The silver halide emulsion is first given a diffuse overall exposure, one sufficient to yield a black of the desired intensity in the final image were development to proceed immediately. The latent image thus formed is a mild oxidizing agent, but one which is also capable of reacting with still more powerful oxidizing agents. This is because the latent image really consists of colloidal specks of silver, adsorbed upon a silver-halide grain. The mild oxidizing properties originate in the fact that such a system adsorbs reducing ions such as hydroquinone, metol, etc., and in that manner increases the local concentration of these ions to such an extent that reduction of the silver-halide grain takes place immediately The oxidizing properties are thus sort of indirect, due only to a favorable combination of ingredients. If some substance other than silver halide, which was not susceptible to reduction, was the constituent upon which the silver speck was adsorbed, then no reduction would be possible.

The strong reducing action of the latent image toward oxidizing agents of even the mildest character, is due to the fact that finely divided silver is very easily attacked by these substances, to form silver ions. One agent that has an action too mild even for the latent image, is dichromate that is strictly neutral or slightly on the alkaline side. But this agent becomes pronouncedly strong when exposed to light. What is more natural, therefore, than to combine the two? After the diffuse exposure, the plate or film is sensitized with a solution of potassium dichromate to which just sufficient ammonia has been added to change the orange color to a lemon yellow After drying, the plate is exposed to the negative whose duplicate is desired. It is then washed thoroughly to remove unreacted dichromate, and finally developed in the normal manner. A direct duplicate should result.

The Herschel effect represents probably the most interesting of all of these theoretical processes for the formation of a direct positive. By far the greatest contributor to this field has been Luppo-Cramer, and a summary of his contributions is contained in the latest edition of Eder's "Handbuch der Photographie" (Vol 2, part 1, *Grundlagen der photographische Negativeverfahren;* Vol 3, part 3, *Sensibilisierung und Desensibilisierung*). Carroll and Kretchman (*Bu. Stand. J of Res.*, Vol. 10 (1933), p. 499), K. Weber (*Phot. Korr.*, Vol. 75 (1939), p. 22) and J S. Friedman (*Am. Phot.*, Vol. 33 (1939), p. 848) have also disclosed interesting studies of this phenomenon.

When a plate is exposed to form a latent image, the exposed silver-halide grain takes on an added absorption in the red and infrared. If the latent image is exposed to light in this range, it becomes reduced in intensity, and may even be completely destroyed. Luppo-Cramer and many other experimenters have utilized this result to prepare positives directly. K. Weber proposed the following routine: A sheet of gaslight paper is exposed diffusely for three seconds to the light of a 60-watt bulb at a distance of 50 centimeters. It is then bathed for three minutes in a solution that contains one gram of pinakryptol yellow in two liters of water, and finally dried. A five-hour exposure in the camera through a red filter gave a direct positive, whose characteristics were typical of infrared emulsions.

But if an Ansco Brovira or other paper of equal speed is used, with a slightly different technique, a three-minute exposure becomes sufficient The paper is first diffusedly exposed as above. It is then bathed in Renwick's solution for 10 minutes.

Potassium iodide	10 parts
Sodium sulphite	10 parts
Hypo	30 parts
Water to	1000 parts

This is followed by a half-hour wash in running water, then by sensitization in a solution made as follows:

Malachite green	0 04 part
Potassium bromide	10.0 parts
Water to	1000 parts

The time of sensitization is 3 minutes at 65 F, followed by rapid drying. The exposed paper can be developed in alkaline amidol, which must be mixed just before use.

Solution A.

Amidol	5 parts
Sodium sulphite	50 parts
Water to	500 parts

Solution B.

Sodium carbonate	50 parts
Water to	500 parts

For use, mix equal quantities of *A* and *B*. It was Luppo-Cramer who discovered that the addition of bromide to the dye solution gave a greatly enhanced effect. Carroll and Kretchman proved that the effect is sensitized by desensitizing dyes In their technique, test plates of a special silver bromide emulsion were first given an overall diffuse exposure to white light. They were then bathed in the dye solution with and without bromide, the excess dye removed by wiping, and finally dried. The exposures were made in a spectrograph, to determine the color sensitivity of the result. The final development was with D-11, a process developer. In particular, one experiment is very interesting. A process plate was given uniform exposure to white light, then bathed in a solution that contained 2-*m*-nitro-styrrylquinoline dimethylsulphate 1:5000, and potassium bromide After drying, this was exposed for 2½ minutes under an Eder-Hecht wedge, at a distance of 30 centimeters from a 95-watt gas-filled lamp. Development was with D-11.

The effect of bathing with dyes is best illustrated by the following experiment, made by Carroll and Kretchman A pure silver bromide emulsion was pre-exposed for several minutes, then bathed in a one per cent solution of potassium bromide and no dye. After drying, this was exposed in the spectrograph through a red filter, to test the pure Herschel effect. It required a 150-minute exposure to produce even a limited reversal. But when dyes were added to the potassium bromide solution, very good reversals were obtained in ten minutes The opening paragraph of the Carroll and Kretchman paper states that positive images of passable gradation may be produced by this process, the sensitivity being about one-tenth that of a lantern slide.

(D). Lumière Filmcolor. — Of the four screen-plate processes (Lumière Filmcolor, Agfacolor, the Finlay Plate, and Dufaycolor) formerly available to the technician, Dufaycolor is the only one which at the present writing (1944) remains commercially available, but the methods of processing all these materials, which were carefully worked out by the manufacturers, are given for their historical value

Lumière Filmcolor, also known as Lumicolor, is supplied only in the form of film The speed of this material is one-twelfth normal, whereas the previous material had a speed that was one-sixtieth normal

After exposure, the film is developed for 2½ minutes in a special solution whose composition is as follows:

Metoquinone	15 parts
Sodium sulphite	100 parts
Ammonia (22 Bé)	32 parts
Potassium bromide	16 parts
Water to	1000 parts

For use, dilute with 4 parts of water. Metoquinone is a molecular combination of metol and hydroquinone, and is sometimes marketed under the trade name Quinomet. If desired, the exposed film could first be desensitized by treatment with a phenosafranine or pinakryptol green solution, then developed by inspection. If this be done, it is recommended that development be carried to a Watkins factor of 10 This means that the time from the start of development to the first appearance of the image (disregarding sky or other extreme highlights) is to be multiplied by ten. Since the recommended time is 2½ minutes, a correctly exposed film will have image appearance in fifteen seconds.

It is to be noted that the Lumières prefer to use ammonia as the silver-halide solvent. This necessarily has an influence upon the length of time of development, since the volatility of the ammonia would make the solution quite unstable. This can be overcome by the use of the non-volatile ammonia substitutes such as ethylene diamine, or mono-ethanolamine Dr. Troland overcame the defect by the use of caustic soda and ammonium halide. The two would react to yield free ammonia, but if the caustic be present in a molar concentration greater than that of the halide, the loss of ammonia will have but little effect upon the alkalinity of the developer.

After a minute wash, the film is placed in the acid dichromate reversal solution.

Potassium dichromate	2 parts
Sulphuric acid, concentrated	10 parts
Water to	1000 parts

In making up the solution, the dichromate is first dissolved in water, then the acid added cautiously. It must be carefully noted that the acid is to be measured out in a dry graduate, and added to the water, never the reverse. When a little water is added to sulphuric acid, tremendous heat is evolved, and there is great danger that the water will begin to boil and spatter this harmful agent indiscriminately. If the solution is warmer than 65 F it should be cooled to that temperature before the film is placed in it Four minutes is sufficient time for the silver to be completely removed, but there is no harm in letting it remain a longer time to insure this, as otherwise streaks will occur. At this point, if the film is examined, the highlights would be just barely veiled over. If a heavy deposit remains, it is evidence of underexposure After the film has been in this solution for a minute, white light can be turned on, and the rest of the processing done in bright light.

A rinse in water is followed by a second development which, in cold weather, can be done in the same developer used initially But in warm weather, when the temperature of the washes can rise well above 70 F, the use of a high-alkaline solution creates the danger that the emulsion may dissolve away, a defect known as frilling. If the second development be carried out in an amidol developer such as:

Sodium sulphite	30 parts
Amidol	5 parts
Water to	1000 parts

the danger of excessive swelling is eliminated. In this solution, the development is carried out to completion. A wash, and the drying operation, complete the procedure

If the original exposure has been too short, a heavy, dull transparency will result which it is very difficult to correct by reduction, since there will be not only blocked highlights but also a predominant blue hue, which is due to the fact that an excess of blue elements is present in the screen to overcome the limited blue component present in ordinary "white" light.

Overexposure will yield very transparent films that are weak and lacking in contrast. If the color of the highlights is not too warm, this defect can be overcome by an intensifying bath, whose composition is:

Sodium sulphite	10 parts
Mercuric iodide	1 part
Water to	1000 parts

The treatment is continued until the desired contrast is obtained, after which the film is washed, redeveloped in amidol for five minutes, washed again, and finally dried The intensified image will not keep unless the redevelopment is carried out The transparency and brilliance of the colors can be enhanced by a coat of varnish.

(E). Agfacolor. — The Agfacolor film is a screen material that is practically identical with Filmcolor in structure, but is slightly faster. The processing is also quite similar to the other. The preferred developer has the composition

Metol	3 24 parts
Sodium sulphite	25 parts
Hydroquinone	1 part
Potassium bromide	1 5 parts
Ammonia (0.91)	7.5 parts
Water to	1000 parts

Use full strength Develop three minutes at 65 F for the plate, and four minutes for the film. As with Filmcolor, Agfacolor can be desensitized by treatment with a 1:5000 pinakryptol green solution, for two minutes. In that case, the development can be carried out in a bright red light, to a Watkins factor of ten. The treatment beyond the first developer stage is identical with the one disclosed for Filmcolor, and the processing baths differ from those used in the first only in minor details

Reversal bath:	
Potassium dichromate	50 parts
Sulphuric acid, concentrated	108 5 parts
Water to	1000 parts

For use add 10 parts of water to one part of stock.

Second Developer:	
Sodium sulphite	57 parts
Amidol	11½ parts
Water to	570 parts

If the first developer be used for second development, it becomes unfit for further use, due to the carrying over of some reversal solution. But then, developers compounded with ammonia as the activating agents cannot be used too long, because of the volatility of the ammonia.

(F). Finlay Plate. — We will leave until last the discussion of Dufaycolor processing, and take up at this time the Finlay plate This is an entirely different type from the others in that the screen is separated entirely from the photographic emulsion. The screen is coated upon a glass plate, which is then used as the front element of the bipack, the rear element of which is a special panchromatic emulsion, prepared either by the Ilford Company (England), or the Eastman Kodak Company. The factor occasioned by the use of the screen, is six. Up to the advent of the Dufaycolor film, this was the most rapid screen plate made The results obtained by it were equally as good as those from Autochromes and Agfacolor material.

The separation of screen and emulsion enabled easy duplication of the transparency. Color-separation positives could be made directly from the original negative by use of "block-out-screens," which is a sort of masking procedure. Since the advent of the fine-grained and exceedingly fast emulsions, the Finlay plate should be able to give speeds that are far beyond the present scope of Dufaycolor or Kodachrome, but evidently very little is being done along these lines Perhaps the use of a screen that has but 175 elements to the inch is too coarse But where no enlargement is intended, the scheme offers untold possibilities. Instead of utilizing inefficient filters to make possible the use of the same plate under different lighting conditions, it becomes possible to use different emulsions, each made for use for a special type of illumination. Since the first appearance of the Finlay plate it has become possible to prepare emulsions with practically any desired characteristics.

The bottom of the Finlay plate screen carries a series of color-registration marks. If this area constitutes a highlight, the registration marks will be automatically registered upon the negative. If it constitutes a shadow, it is important to give the area a supplementary exposure to white light. This can be done by replacing the normal slide with one which has the corresponding section cut away, then exposing (through the camera), to the light reflected from a sheet of white paper. The registration marks in the Finlay screen consist of bands of red and blue, separated by green circles When the positive is registered on top of the viewing screen, these should appear in the complementary colors, that is as cyan and yellow bands, separated by magenta circles. Most of the texts give these colors as blue or green, yellow, and red respectively, but where this is done, it represents a lack of preciseness on the part of the writers

The original Finlay negatives are developed to yield the maximum coverage of the density range of the original. This means that a relatively low contrast is desired. Three types of developers are recommended

D-76

Metol	2 parts
Sodium sulphite	100 parts
Hydroquinone	5 parts
Borax	2 parts
Water to	1000 parts

Develop 12 to 14 minutes at 65 F.

Glycin Developer

Sodium sulphite	37½ parts
Glycin	15 parts
Sodium carbonate monohydrate	75 parts
Water to	1000 parts

For use dilute with an equal part of water. Develop 5 minutes at 65 F

Metol Developer

Solution A

Metol	12½ parts
Sodium sulphite	50 parts
Water to	1000 parts

Solution B.

Potassium carbonate	62½ parts
Water to	1000 parts

For use take one part of *A*, one part of *B*, and 5 parts of water. Develop for 6 minutes at 65 F This is the temperature best suited for materials to be used with the Finlay process At higher temperatures the gelatin will swell too much and after fixation there will be danger that the shrinkage will not be back to normal, thus throwing the image out of registry with the screen elements. The fixing bath should be compounded without alum, and should be used once and then discarded.

The negatives, when examined closely, will show the image to consist of minute squares of silver, varying in density. These correspond identically to the areas of the colored screen elements. No enlargement or reduction of the positives made from a Finlay negative is possible, as then the image squares would no longer correspond to the screen. Therefore, the positives are to be made by contact only. These should be brilliant and clear. Eastman Process or the equivalent Hammer plate are recommended. Ilford makes a special material, known as the Finlay-Ilford positive plate, for this purpose.

After exposure, the positive transparency plates are developed in D–72.

D–72 Stock solution.

Metol	3 parts
Sodium sulphite	45 parts
Hydroquinone	12 2 parts
Sodium carbonate	67.5 parts
Potassium bromide	1.9 parts
Water to	1000 parts

For use add four parts of water to one part of stock. If the negative is excessively flat, a hydroquinone-caustic developer should be used

Solution A.

Hydroquinone	25 parts
Metabisulphite	25 parts
Potassium bromide	25 parts
Water to	1000 parts

Solution B.

Potassium hydroxide	50 parts
Water to	1000 parts

For use mix equal parts of *A* and *B* Develop 90 seconds at 65 F.

The final colored transparency is made by registering the positive with a special viewing screen. These can be obtained in quantity, thus enabling the operator to make as many duplicates as are necessary.

Instead of making the positives upon process material, it is possible to make them upon a special positive emulsion that is coated on top of a viewing screen When this is done, the positive and negative must be registered in the darkroom The screened positive plate contains an extremely slow blue-sensitive emulsion, one which can safely be manipulated in the light of a Series OA safelight containing a 50-watt bulb. The two plates are shifted until the registration marks appear as a green outer band, a yellow inner band, and a red circle. It must be remembered that a minus-blue light is being used, so that the magenta will appear as red, and the cyan as green. Each patch must be completely devoid of the complementary color when viewed under a ten-power magnifier. When this is accomplished, the two are clamped together tightly, and exposed through the negative side. The color screen on the positive lies between the emulsion and the glass base, hence the exposing light does not go through this until after the emulsion has received a latent image. Then it acts as an anti-halation backing. There is no particular advantage in the use of a screened positive emulsion other than the possibility that loss of registry may result from faulty processing, due to an uneven expansion and contraction of the emulsion on the glass plate. But if there is any difficulty in obtaining registry, and a very long time is required before this is accomplished, there is grave danger of fog setting in, giving dull and lifeless prints.

(G). DUFAYCOLOR. — This is by far the most popular of all the screen processes It has a speed rating which is approximately the same as Kodachrome. While at the present writing, Kodachrome can be processed only in central laboratories, Dufaycolor processing can be accomplished immediately, giving the operator the opportunity to make immediate checks.

Dufaycolor can be processed in two ways. It can be reversed to yield a direct positive, from which separations can be made if paper prints or other type of duplicates are desired It can also be developed as a negative that is complementary in color as well as in tone. If copies are to be made on Dufaycolor material, the second is the preferred technique. G B Harrison and D. A. Spencer (*Phot. J.*, Vol. 77 (1937) April) made a detailed study of this, detailing the problems that are involved

The accurate rendition of screen processes depends upon the correct reproduction of densities behind each element of the mosaic. If a color-screen negative be projected upon another screen plate, one error arises due to the overlapping transmissions of the screen elements. Since it is impossible to accurately register the green elements in the master with the green elements in the copy, the projection of some of the green elements will fall on red and blue elements in the copy. If the three colors are mutually exclusive, no harm other than a loss in contrast (which can be overcome by a longer development) will result No deposition of green densities in areas that are reserved exclusively for red and blue, will take place. But the elements in Dufaycolor are not mutually exclusive The greens transmit considerable blue and red. Therefore, by such projection, green densities will register behind red and blue areas, thus diluting and desaturating the greens. The same is true for the other two elements, although to a smaller extent This, incidentally, is the one serious objection to Dufaycolor, but one which can be rectified by a procedure known as masking.

Another cause for poor results when making copies from the screen plates on screen material, is due to scatter of the exposing light by the silver-halide grain in the copy material. This type of error was discussed in an article published in *The Photographic Journal* (Vol 73 (1933), p 19) It was shown that the densities behind a given dot would spread a little due to this scatter, and yield densities behind adjacent dots of different colors. Two effects would be produced First the opacity behind a desired dot would be reduced, since some of the exposing light is not used; and second, the opacities behind adjacent dots would be increased. The net effect is a loss in color contrast, brilliance, and saturation. If developers are compounded with ammonia or other silver halide solvents present, a peculiar effect is obtained A reduction of density occurs immediately adjacent to a heavy-density region This is directly in opposition to the effect of scatter, so that the one neutralizes the other. In reversal procedure, the use of ammonia or thiocyanate (in amounts sufficient to obtain neutralization of the effects of scatter) is permissible, since the resultant high fog level is of no consequence. But where the film is to be developed as a negative, the presence of excess fog ruins the printing qualities, giving dull and lifeless prints. A substitute had to be found, therefore, for ammonia or thiocyanate. The following processing techniques were tried:

1. The film was developed in a very weak solution. In this manner, the grains closest to the screen elements developed first, since they were exposed first, and received the maximum intensity of exposure. The development of these grains used up the developer, so that the upper strata of emulsion grains could develop only after the lower ones were completely reduced. If the development was stopped short of this, the upper emulsion grains (representing the portions in which scatter is at a maximum) remained undeveloped. A very weak image resulted, but this could be intensified. However, the use of very weak developer solutions gave rise to variations, loss of speed, and other defects that forced the abandonment of the technique.

2. The negative is considerably overdeveloped and the image in the upper portions of the emulsion layer is removed by treatment with Farmer's reducer to which is added a considerable concentration of alcohol (up to 70 per cent), sodium sulphate (30 per cent), glycerin, or other substances which reduce diffusion. The difficulty in the accurate control of the diffusion forced the abandonment of this procedure.

3. The latent image in the upper strata of the emulsion layer was destroyed by treatment with oxidizing agents, prior to development.

4. A surface image is developed, then removed by treatment with acid permanganate, the film washed, and finally developed normally.

5. A surface image is developed with a non-tanning developer, and then the rest of the development is continued with a tanning developer. When this is treated with Farmer's reducer, the tanned gelatin will prevent the action in the lower portions. Thus only the surface image will be removed.

For proper results, processes 3 and 5 all depend upon controlled diffusion. With the use of thinly coated emulsion layers, this is faulty and unreliable.

6. The latent image is developed in a solution whose action is slowed down by the products of the development. Since the action starts at the bottom, next to the screen, this will give preferential treatment to this part of the image. A developer to accomplish this result could be concocted as follows:

Hydroquinone	12½ parts
Potassium metabisulphite	12½ parts
Potassium bromide	12½ parts
Potassium hydroxide	25 parts
Water to	1000 parts

This gave good results, but the contrast was too high for good printing quality.

7. The latent image is developed in a "depth" developer, whose composition

is altered as it diffuses through the gelatin. Consider a developer whose composition is as follows:

Amidol	15 parts
Sodium sulphite	125 parts
Potassium bisulphite	50 parts
Water to	1000 parts

As this solution diffuses into the gelatin layer, the bisulphite becomes absorbed by the gelatin. Therefore its concentration becomes diminished as the solution penetrates to the bottom. Thus there is no restraining action at the bottom, and development proceeds there in the normal manner. But the top strata are quite acid, so little action takes place there. This is why an acid amidol developer acts first at the bottom.

A developer compounded with hypo in the bath acts in a similar manner. The hypo is used up in the upper grain strata of the emulsion layer, so that the lower portions are not affected, and develop up in the normal manner. A very effective developer of this type for use with Dufaycolor film is:

Metol	10 parts
Sodium sulphite	30 parts
Sodium hydroxide	10 parts
Hypo	20 parts
Water to	1000 parts

The use of this developer gave a negative image that lay substantially close to the screen elements in the lower portions of the emulsion layer. Potassium iodide, and potassium or ammonium thiocyanate, if present in sufficient quantity, also give the same result. From negatives prepared in this manner, it was possible to print on to screen material after due precautions were taken to filter the printing light to correct for the overlaps in the transmissions of the screen elements.

The more normal procedure is to process Dufaycolor by reversal. The recommended technique differs but slightly from that described above for use with Lumicolor and with Agfacolor. But the differences are all in the direction of improved technique. The initial development is carried out in a developer compounded to contain potassium thiocyanate, thus:

Metol	6½ parts
Sodium sulphite	50 parts
Hydroquinone	2 parts
Sodium carbonate	37 parts
Potassium bromide	2¾ parts
Potassium thiocyanate	9 parts
Water to	1000 parts

Develop for three minutes at 65 F. If the film is desensitized, it can be developed by inspection to a Watkins factor of six.

After development, the film is washed in running water for a minute, then reversed in acid permanganate

Potassium permanganate	3 parts
Water	1000 parts
Sulphuric acid, concentrated	10 parts

The film should remain here until the silver is completely removed, after which it is washed again for two minutes, and cleared in a bisulphite bath (2½ per cent). This serves not only to remove the reduced permanganate, but also to break up the gelatin-silver ion complex. At this point the film can be given an exposure to white light to make all the remaining grains developable. Reduction of the silver salts can be accomplished by treatment in the following solution:

Metol	1 part
Hydroquinone	5 parts
Sodium sulphite	50 parts
Sodium carbonate	20 parts
Potassium bromide	1 part
Water to	1000 parts

It is also possible to use the first developer at this point, but in that case it can no longer be used with freshly exposed film. The silver halide grains that escape reduction at this stage can be removed by treatment with an ordinary chrome-alum hypo bath, or one compounded as follows:

Solution A	
Hypo	360 parts
Potassium metabisulphite	12 parts
Water	1000 parts
Solution B.	
Chrome alum	10 parts
Water	1000 parts

Add Solution *B* to *A*.

CHAPTER 15

SEPARATION NEGATIVES

UP to now we have discussed the problem of making an original color shot from the point of view of fundamentals, and apparatus required Very little was said about the actual act itself. To photograph an object in color, the operator has at his command a variety of methods. He can use a one-shot camera in which the lens beam is divided into three parts by any one of the many mechanisms described in previous chapters. In these cases he will have as his immediate product three negatives, each of which represents the intensities of a single primary as it is present at each point in the original. If this procedure represents limitations beyond his control, he can use one of the integral processes, such as Kodachrome, Ansco Color, Dufaycolor, etc. In these procedures he will have as his immediate end result a colored positive transparency, which he can use as a new original from which separations can be made.

Another possibility at his command is to photograph the subject through the three filters in succession. This represents the simplest of the methods, and the best, but unfortunately it can be used only in cases where the object remains perfectly immobile for the time required to make three photographs. This is a time long enough to enable one to expose three times, to change plates or films three times, and to change filters on a like number of occasions Mechanisms have been devised which do these operations automatically and mechanically. These are called repeating backs. A special plateholder is used in which the three plates are loaded side-by-side The three filters are placed so that each plate is situated immediately behind one filter By a single operation, the plateholder is moved so that one filter-plate combination is in position, the lens shutter is opened for the required time, and it is then closed; the plateholder is then moved so that a new filter-plate combination is brought into position, and the cycle is repeated until three exposures are made. It has been claimed that the entire act can be done in a period of a few seconds. The Autotype Company of England, makers of carbro and carbon tissue, market several types of such backs that can be used with the ordinary plate camera. The repeating back has a slight advantage over the normal one-shot camera in that it can be used under any type of lighting, for it is possible to vary to any desired extent the exposure behind any filter.

White light is largely a misnomer, for the normal Mazda light is very much on the red side, and carbon arcs are very much on the blue. Consider for instance, lights with color temperatures of 3000 K, 3200 K, 3435 K and 5400 K. The relative distribution of three primaries in these light sources is as follows:

Degrees K	*Red %*	*Green %*	*Blue %*
3000	54	32	14
3200	49	34	17
3435	46	35	19
5400	33	34	33

It is seen that as the color temperature of the light rises, the relative proportion of the red rays drops and that of the blue increases, until at 5400 K, which is the standard adopted for outdoor work, the ratios are practically identical. Ordinary Mazda light operates at a color temperature of 3000 K. Overvoltage lamps operate either at 3200 or at 3435 K. It becomes important to know, therefore, exactly what type of light is being used, since different light sources have different proportions of the three primaries present, and therefore will have different values for the filter factors.

In one-shot cameras, the filter factors are taken care of in the division of the intensities among the three sub-beams. Consider a camera designed to be used with Mazda light, and an emulsion which has filter factors of 2, 6, and 10 for the red, green, and blue filters respectively. In order to obtain balanced exposures, it will be necessary to direct five times as much light to the blue, and three times as much to the green, as to the red filter. Therefore the mirror reflectors are so arranged that 11 per cent of the lens beam is directed to the red, 33 per cent to the green, and 56 per cent to the blue filter. But if this camera is to be used for light of daylight quality, where the filter factors are 4, 6, and 4 respectively, the blue filter image will be considerably overexposed, and the red filter image considerably underexposed. Owners of one-shot cameras must be sure to use them only under the conditions for which they were designed. It is possible to put filters over the lens which will convert daylight into Mazda, and vice versa, but this results in a loss of light, and one-shot cameras cannot afford such loss. Some cameras can be converted easily from daylight to Mazda by merely shifting the position of the filters. This means that constant vigilance must be exercised to keep in mind what light is being used. However, this is no hardship, for color photography should not be attempted unless constant supervision is being exercised. With the repeating back, the relative exposure given to any one filter can be varied at will. But this can be used only on those occasions when the object can be held stationary for at least ten seconds

The relative exposures that have to be given through the different filters are determined by the values of the filter factors for the given emulsion and the given light source. Thus if the factors are 2, 6, and 10, it is necessary to expose ten times as long behind the blue, six times as long behind the green, and twice as long behind the red filter, as would be required were no filter used.

In making exposures, one other thing that must be considered is the failure of the reciprocity law. Theoretically the silver density that results from a one-second exposure at a light intensity of 100 units, should be the same as the density obtained from a 100 second exposure at a light intensity of one unit. The product of *I*, the light intensity, and *T*, the time of exposure, should be a constant A variation of a certain percentage in one, accompanied by the same variation but in the opposite direction, in the other, should give the same result But for some reason this is not so. The density obtained when the light intensity is high, is greater than when the exposure time is high. This makes itself felt in cases where time exposures are required.

Most speed ratings are made under the conditions for which the given emulsion is intended. For that reason a standard development in the developer solution recommended is also desirable, although use of the borax developer, D–76, is highly recommended for all cases where a moderate enlargement is required. For instance, a given emulsion is rated at Weston 100, and it is recommended that this emulsion be developed for fifteen minutes in D–76 at 65 F. This implies that when the light intensity is such that instantaneous exposures are being made, not over one second in duration, and the film or plate is developed as specified, exposure at a rating of Weston 100 would be correct. But if the light intensity is very low, or if the exposures are made through dense filters or at a low diaphragm opening so that from two to five minutes exposure is required, it will be found that the emulsion must be rated at Weston 25 or 35, rather than 100.

Of course, under the conditions specified above, it is quite immaterial whether the speed is 100 or 10, since speed is of no consideration. And it may be argued that it is ridiculous to use a fast negative emulsion, that is relatively coarse grained, for cases where a moderate-speed emulsion, prepared to be used under just these conditions, would suffice. But the object to be photographed may have a density range of 2.3. It is only when using the fastest known materials that this range may be successfully copied, so the use of such high-speed emulsions may be essential to the subject matter at hand. Then again, it may be desired to use Kodachrome film to copy a series of paintings or to make some still setups. Kodachrome can be obtained only in two grades, outdoor and indoor. There are no fast and slow Kodachrome materials, one suitable for instantaneous exposures, the other for long exposures. The same material must be used for both purposes In such cases, the speed of the Kodachrome should be rated at a maximum of one-half normal when time exposures are being made It is to be hoped that the reciprocity law failure is uniform for the three primary colors.

In the processing of the separations, it is desirable that the contrast ranges be identical in all three negatives. For this reason the inclusion of a gray scale is of the utmost importance. The densities in the gray scale should be at least equivalent to the densities encompassed in the subject matter itself, and preferably should overlap them. Then if the exposure and development be so arranged that all the steps in the gray scale lie on the straight-line portion of the curve, it is certain that this same absolute proportionality will exist with respect to the densities in the original subject

When such a gray scale is present the operator can completely forget the subject, and concentrate his attention upon the scale If this be identical in the three negatives, and if the different steps of the scale all lie on the straight-line portion of the H & D curve, then the three negatives are completely in balance and are correctly exposed. The existence of a toe would indicate underexposure. The existence of a shoulder would indicate overexposure. If the scales show both toe and shoulder, this is indicative that the density range in the gray scale is too great for the particular emulsion, and another type of material should be used.

The latitude of an emulsion may be considerably increased by a reduction in contrast. By this is meant that if the latitude is three octaves at a contrast of 1 20, it would possibly have a latitude of four or maybe five octaves at a contrast of 0 80, and six or more octaves at a contrast of 0 60. Three octaves would correspond to a density differential of 0.90. At a contrast of 1 20, the density differential would be 1.20 × .90 or 1.08. This means that at this high gamma, the differential in densities between the two extremities of the straight-line portion of the curve would be 1.08. The shoulder would be approximately .10 density unit above the upper value, and the toe approximately .20 below the lower value, so that the density differential in the negative would be 1 08 + 0.10 + 0.20, or 1.38. Six octaves correspond to a density differential of 1 80, but at a contrast of 0.60 the actual density differential in the straight-line portion of the curve would be 1.80 × 0.60, or 1.08. The toe and shoulder would add approximately 0.30 density unit, so that in this case, the negative would have a density differential of 1.38, but this differential correctly images six octaves. The same density differential in the case of a more contrasty negative images correctly only three octaves

The filter factors of panchromatic emulsions indicate that the red sensitivity of the emulsion is by far the greatest, the green next, and the blue least. A typical set of factors would be 2, 6, and 10, for the red, green and blue sensitivities. But the light for which these factors hold has a color temperature of approximately 2800 K It contains 60 per cent of its total intensity in the red, and only 13 per cent in the blue. It is a well-established fact that the sensitivity of the emulsion is predominantly in the blue. If the emulsion were exposed to equal quantities of red, green and blue lights, then it would be seen that well over 70 per cent of the total sensitivity of the emulsion lies in the blue. Therefore, the emulsion is a much better absorber of blue light than of red or green. This means that the blue image is much more of a surface image, hence it is flatter than the other two. To achieve the same contrast through the C5 filter as through the A or B, it becomes necessary to develop this negative for a greater length of time, from 25 to 50 per cent longer than the other two. Since a longer time of development means that the H & D curve becomes shifted somewhat to the left, a slight increase in emulsion speeds results so that a slightly shorter time of exposure could be used The exact amount of adjustment must be determined for each emulsion, but once determined, remains quite constant.

Ansco and the Eastman Kodak Company have set a good example to the rest of the industry by the publication of a pamphlet in which the physical and photographic characteristics of all their film materials are described. Not only are the normal properties listed, but there are given wedge spectrograms (both to daylight and to tungsten), filter factors for the more popular filters (which also include the A, B, and C5 set), exposure tables (including Photoflood and Photoflash data); recommended developer times for several developers, time-gamma, and time-temperature curves for these developers, and a set of H & D curves for one of the developers, giving the complete picture for values of gamma ranging from 0.50 to 1.00 One other very important bit of information that is given, is the resolving power of the emulsion. Thus the Super Panchromatic 35mm film is given a resolving power of 45 lines per mm with D–76. If the images of a series of parallel lines lie 45 to the millimeter, they will be distinct, but if they are more than 45 lines to the millimeter, they will not appear as individual lines, but as an indistinct gray area.

So much for the preparation of separations by the direct processes. Autochrome, Dufaycolor, and the other integral processes, give for the immediate products a single image in which the three color densities lie next to each other. To make reproductions, it is necessary to separate the three upon separate emulsions. The different integral processes allow this to be done in a variety of ways Kodachrome, Ansco Color, Agfacolor Neue have the three densities lying one over the other, differing from each other in their respective spectral absorptions and transmissions. Therefore, the different strata may be copied by the use of colored lights

The Kodachrome picture consists of a yellow image that lies in the top emulsion layer, and which depicts the blue densities. Below this, in a central layer, lies a magenta image depicting the green densities. In a bottom layer, lying adjacent to the celluloid, there is a cyan image giving the red densities Light that is transmitted through a film of this type must traverse all three layers If this be white light, then by its passage through a given point in the top layer the yellow image at that point will abstract a sufficient quantity of blue light to yield the requisite blue density. Such yellow dyes transmit (theoretically at least) the green and the red rays completely, so that no green nor red will be removed from the light source at this point. The remaining blue rays will pass unhindered (theoretically) through the magenta and cyan images. Hence the yellow image will form, or cause to be formed, only the blue densities The rest of the light will now proceed to the magenta layer Here just sufficient green light will be subtracted to yield the desired green density, the blue and red portions going through undisturbed. In a similar manner, by its passage through the final cyan layer, red densities will be formed to the proper degree. The light that reaches the opposite side will contain red, green, and blue densities, that, in combination, reconstruct the color as it was present at the corresponding point of the original

Now consider what happens if instead of using white light, there is used the light that passes through a C4 or C5 filter. This corresponds to the blue primary. Upon passage through the yellow layer, the intensities of the blue light will be varied at every point to correspond to the densities of the blue primary present at each point. We say that the yellow image modulates the blue light passing through it. No further action upon this light will take place upon its passage through the other two layers since they are both transmitters of the blue. Therefore, if this light is made to fall upon a photographic emulsion, it will register only the blue densities that are present in the Kodachrome. In this way a blue-filter separation is obtained. Similarly, if the color transparency is illuminated by the light that is passed through the green filter, it becomes possible to obtain the green-filter separation. By the use of red light, it is possible to obtain the red-filter separation. In other words, it may be possible to treat a color transparency as a new original and make separations from it in the normal direct manner.

The processes discussed up to this point are subtractive. Dufaycolor and the other screen plates are additive. But, the same end-result is true. It must be recalled that in the additive processes the different color densities lie in juxtaposition, and occupy a space small enough to register three elements as a single unit. Now consider white light falling upon one such elementary unit containing three elements, each in a different primary color. The red element will absorb the green and blue rays completely and will transmit the red rays to the extent allowed by the silver deposit lying below. Thus only red light, and this to a predetermined intensity, is passed. The green and blue dots act in a corresponding manner Through the entire set there will therefore be transmitted intensities which are the same as those reflected from the corresponding point in the original subject. Suppose, now, that the illuminating light is filtered so that it is a simple primary color, say blue. This will be transmitted only by the blue elements and will be modulated by the silver deposits lying beneath each blue element. Thus only blue intensities or transmissions will be photographed if the light is made to fall upon a photographic emulsion. Once again the colored transparency acts as if it were the original, and can be copied in the direct manner discussed above. In this discussion, the assumption was made that the colors were pure, and offered no interferences. This is only true in theory. The procedures to be used to overcome defects arising from the fact that the colors are not ideal, will be discussed later

The Finlay plate offers a slightly different problem. Here, it must be remembered, the image is separate from the screen. Of course it is possible to make a positive from the negative, and register this with a viewing screen In that event, a condition is had identical with those discussed above, and the separations can be made in the normal manner. Since it is a positive transparency that is being copied, the separations obtained will be negative in form If the negative is registered with the original taking screen, the transparency is a colored negative that is complementary in color as well as in tone. In this case the separations that are made by the use of filtered light, would be positives. This system would be recommended where separation positives are desired, as in pinatype and in certain photomechanical processes, where printing is done from positives.

Should one examine a Finlay negative closely, it would be seen to consist of a checkerboard arrangement of squares, each unit of which has a different density. Each square represents the density of a single primary color, and the four squares immediately adjacent represent the densities of the other two primaries. The Finlay company has prepared two black-and-white screens. These are used to block out the squares that correspond to a given primary One screen is used to prepare the magenta and cyan printers, the other for the yellow. This is done by registering the negative with the block-out screens, so that all the squares with the exception of those relating to one primary, become blocked out. When light goes through the combination, it will be stopped completely by the block-out screen from going through two of the elements, and will be modulated by the silver image of the negative in those spots corresponding to the third color-element.

To make the cyan printer, use the block-out screen marked "Red and Blue." It is rather a pity that the Finlay company should fall into the common error of calling the cyan, blue, and the magenta, red. The screen is registered with the negative so that the outer band of the registration edge at both ends appears opaque, and the circles and inner band appear transparent. It is then copied by projection upon a process or upon a Hammer Slow or Eastman 33 plate. To make the magenta printer, register the same screen so that the circles appear opaque and the outer and inner bands transparent. The yellow printer utilizes the other block-out screen, and this is registered so that the inner band appears opaque, while the circles and the outer band appear transparent. The block printer is made by binding the negative with a plain piece of glass whose thickness is the same as that of the block-out screens. It will require approximately one-sixth of the exposure given the others, this being the density of the screens.

The positives could be developed in any solution capable of giving good contrasts. The following formula is especially recommended:

Sodium sulphite	37½ parts
Glycin	15 parts
Sodium carbonate	75 parts
Water to	1000 parts

For use, dilute with an equal quantity of water. Develop five or six minutes at 65 F.

From the description of the working details of the block-out screens, it does not seem to be an extremely difficult matter to prepare them one's self. Consider the screen to be used to make the magenta printer. It is desired to opaque out the red and the blue elements, and to pass completely the green elements. This may be done by making a contact print of the taking screen upon a panchromatic emulsion, through a red and a blue filter The red filter would opaque out the areas immediately behind the red elements, and the blue filter would accomplish the same result behind the blue elements. Development should be carried out to gamma infinity, so that a density of at least 2 5, and preferably one of 3 5, will be obtained. The spaces behind the green dots should remain completely transparent. Therefore a process pan emulsion should be used The screen and the negative should face each other, hence the right and left positions in the screen must be opposite to those in the negative. The procedure outlined in the preceding paragraph would not give this reversal of direction

One method of accomplishing it would be to make master negatives of the taking screen by contact, through the three filters. To make the block-out screen for the magenta printer, the master negative is made through a green filter. If a positive is made from this, also by contact, the areas corresponding to the red and blue elements in the taking screen will be opaque, only the green will be transparent. The other two screens are made in an analogous manner. G B Harrison (Eng. P. 434434) disclosed a system of block-out screens, but these had been previously described by C L A Brasseur and S. P. Sampolo (Eng P 8390/96; U S P. 571314), C. L. A. Brasseur (Eng. P 15185/05, 710/07, U S.P. 897815), and G. S Whitfield (Eng. P 167793).

Two types of duplication are possible from screen plates Reproductions can be made upon a similar screen material, or separations can be made by means of filters, and the separations then used for the making of duplicate prints by any of the positive procedures A great deal of study has been made with regard to both of these types of duplication. Because of the impure transmissions and absorptions of the screen colors, it was early determined that only sharp-cutting filters could be used (C. L. A. Brasseur; Eng P. 4932/07, Ger. P. 214323 and 219821, Fr P. 367834; U.S.P 1163207). When printing one screen upon another, an interference pattern known as moiré is formed The intensity and visibility of this could be varied somewhat by angling the two screens relative to each other, a fact disclosed by A. Lehner (U.S.P. 1113359; Ger P 221916). This phenomenon is well known in the photomechanical industry, where the halftone negatives are screened at different angles to overcome moiré

The general problem of reproduction from screen plates, was studied by C. E. K. Mees (*Brit. J. Phot*, Vol 54 (1907), Col Supp., p. 49). He pointed out that when one screen plate is printed upon another, color dilution or degradation takes place. These findings were corroborated by C. Welborne Piper (*Brit. J. Phot*, Vol. 54 (1907), Col. Supp. p. 81; and by E. Stenger and F. Leiber (*Brit. J. Phot.*, Vol. 55 (1908), Col. Supp., p. 30, 69). More recently a detailed study of the problem was made by G. B. Harrison and R. G. Horner (*Photo. J.*, Vol. 79 (1939), p. 320. These men concerned themselves with the problem of making contact reproductions from Dufaycolor film.

We will first take up the Mees paper. Color dilution results from the fact that it is not possible to register exactly the screen elements in the master

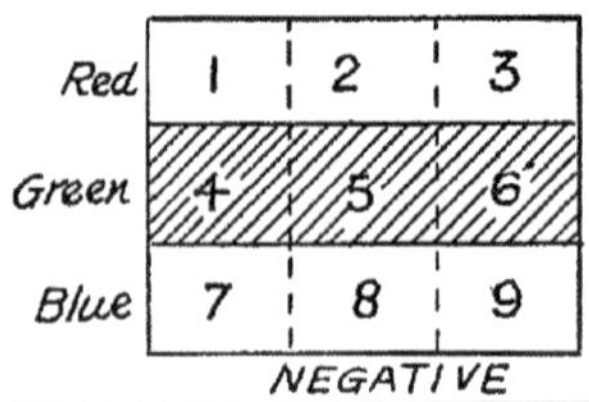

FIG. 45

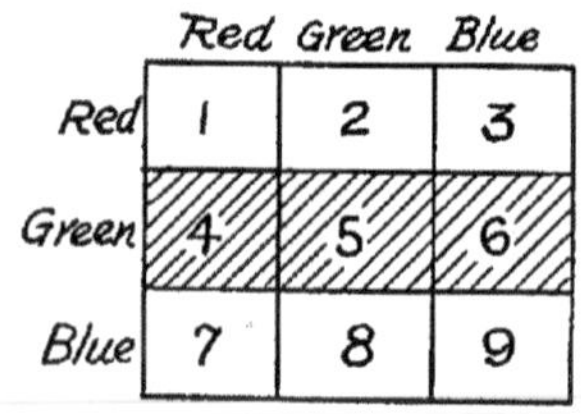

FIG. 46

and copy. Consider a line screen (Fig. 45) with red, green, and blue lines that is exposed to green light, and developed to form a negative. Therefore the green line will be opaque. Now print this negative upon another and similar line screen (Fig. 46), but with the lines at right angles to the other. This will divide the area into nine squares. In the negative, squares 4, 5, and 6 are opaque, 1, 2, 3, 7, 8, and 9 are transparent. Upon superposition of the positive we will have the following condition. Square No. 1, transparent in the nega-

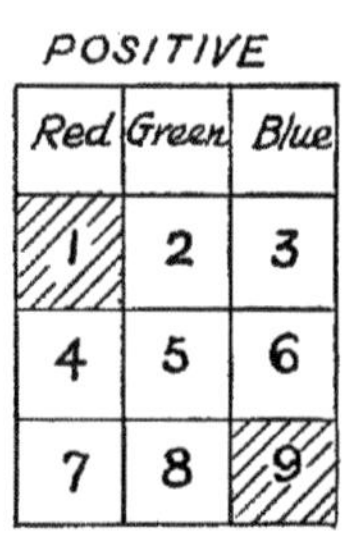

FIG. 47

tive, will transmit red light to the positive, and since it is over a red area an opaque deposit will be formed. Square No. 2 will project a red element over a green, hence no light will be transmitted to the emulsion below. In the positive (Fig. 47), square 2 will be transparent. Similarly squares 3, 7, and 8 will be transparent. Square 9 in the negative is a blue, and it is transparent. In the positive, it is also a blue, hence blue light will be transmitted to the emulsion below, so that this area will be opaque. Squares 4, 5, and 6 are opaque in the negative, hence these will be transparent in the positive. Since the positive is at right angles to the negative, the green line in it will correspond to squares 2, 5, and 8. These should be, and are, transparent in the positive. The areas behind the blue and red lines must be completely opaque, since these are transparent in the negative. The blue lines correspond to squares 3, 6, and 9, and of these only 9 is opaque, the other two being transparent because in printing differently colored elements fell upon each. A similar condition holds with squares 1, 4, and 7 where only square 1 is opaque. Therefore instead of three transparent sections, the positive contains seven, of which three are green, and two each are red and blue. The end result is a green diluted with two parts of white.

We proceed now to the Harrison and Horner paper. In making copies of a Dufaycolor film, it cannot be regarded simply as a new original. For one reason, the spectral composition of any color in the transparency is no longer the same as the original, but a visual match with it. The spectral transmissions of the elements, intended as analysis filters, will not act in this manner in additively produced reproductions. The result would be a considerable dilution of the colors This would be caused by the fact that the transmissions of the colors in the screen have considerable overlaps. Consider a pure green color in the original. In the colored negative transparency this would correspond to opaque densities behind the green element, and transparent areas behind the other two. When reproduced in the positive, it will be required to form opaque areas behind the red and blue elements, and complete transparency behind the green. Let us consider the red element. The projection of this part of the negative will fall upon not only red, but also upon green and blue elements in the copy, since it is not possible to register master and copy with respect to the screen elements If the blue and green did not transmit any red, no image formation would take place at these points. But the Dufaycolor blues and greens have appreciable red transmission, and vice versa Hence silver deposits will be formed behind the green and blue squares. In a similar manner the projection of the blue element in the negative will cause densities to form in the red and green areas. Hence there will be formed an appreciable silver deposit behind the green elements in the positive, which will reduce the brilliance and intensity of the green image. This is an effect that is caused solely by the presence of overlaps in the spectral transmissions of the screen elements This effect must be carefully distinguished from the one described by Mees, and discussed above.

To make a copy from a Dufaycolor film, no further analysis is required, as this has already been achieved during the first exposure. The color record consists of a set of three related densities which determine the proportions in which the three reseau colors should be mixed, when viewed. In order to preserve these proportions in the copy, it is necessary to insure that the light passing through one color-element of the first picture can affect the copying emulsion only behind elements of like color.

A second difficulty arises from the regular geometrical pattern of the screen. When two elements of like color fall on each other, opaque areas result in the positive. When they are different, transparent areas will form. Because of the regularity of the patterns, these interferences will form a regular mosaic that is distinctly visible and annoying. It is known as moiré.

Both of these disadvantages could be overcome if it were possible to register the screen elements of master and copy, but this is not possible. During processing, film shrinks slightly, so that the dimensions of the screen elements are no longer the same in master and copy. Besides being visible and annoying, the effect of moiré would be to dilute the colors, as pointed out previously by Mees (cf. above).

If the two screens are separated by the thickness of the celluloid base, and if the negative is illuminated by a perfectly diffuse light whose dimensions are large with respect to its distance from the negative, the negative reseau will become diffuse. The image also will be diffuse to a like degree, and this would make the results so poor in definition that they would be unusable. The problem is not so much to remove the moiré, as it is to reduce it to a point where it will no longer be noticeable, and this with a minimum loss of image definition.

In printing by contact, it is essential to have the negative and positive separated from each other by the thickness of the base, in order to allow the light that passed through the master to go through the reseau of the copy, before acting upon the positive emulsion. This separation between reseau elements can be utilized to effect complete removal of the master-screen structure. Consider first of all a pinhole camera (Fig. 48). The image B of the object A is a perfect reproduction, in so far as relative dimensions are concerned. The size of the reproduction is determined solely by the distance

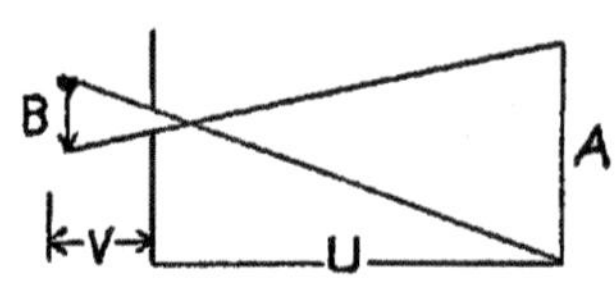

FIG. 48

of the object from the pinhole, and the size of the object. The Dufaycolor screen may be regarded as being composed of a number of juxtaposed squares each of which contains one red, one green, and one blue element. Each of these is of a dimension sufficiently small to act as a pinhole camera. Now consider the set-up in Fig. 49. The distance d is the length of one elementary cell in the reseau, and since there are 500 to the inch, this will have a dimension of 0.002 inch or 0.05 mm. The opening in the negative reseau has the dimensions of one of the color elements which make up the elementary cell, and which acts as the pinhole for the pinhole camera. D is the dimension of a uniformly lighted opal glass. The pinhole will image this upon the positive reseau. It is desired to make this image the exact size of the cell unit, which is equal to 0.05 mm square.

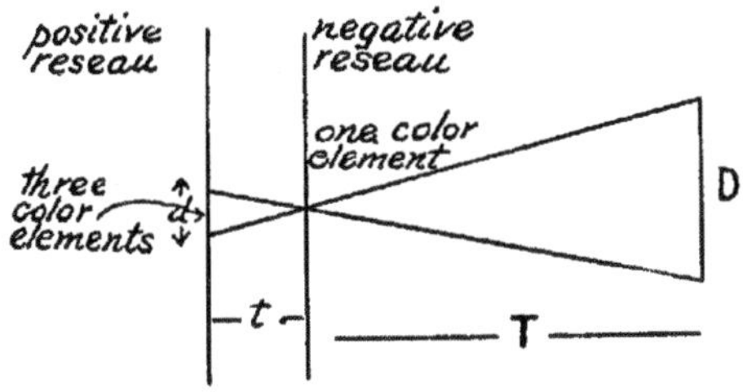

FIG. 49

Since the size (d) of the desired image, and the distance (t) between the two reseau patterns are constant, the ratio between D and T becomes fixed. The following relationship holds between the values d, t, D, and T.

$$\frac{D}{T} = \frac{d}{t/\mu} = \frac{\mu d}{t}$$

where μ is the index of refraction for the celluloid base. Assuming d = 0.05 mm, t = 0.005 inch or 0.125 mm, μ = 1.40, and T = 10 cm = 100 mm = 4 inches,

$$D = \frac{1.4 \times 0.05 \times 100}{0.125} = 56 \text{ mm} = 2\tfrac{1}{4} \text{ inches}$$

Hence the light source would have to be $2\frac{1}{4}$ inches square, situated a distance of 4 inches away from the master and copy, which are in contact with each other. Under these conditions each color element in the master will be imaged over the entire unit of three color elements in the copy. The adjacent color element will likewise be imaged over a full set, so that this scheme provides the exact amount of diffusion required to convert the screen into a continuous tone. Moiré is therefore completely eliminated.

In order to destroy moiré, it has been necessary to spread each color element in the master so that it covers an area containing three elements in the copy. Thus red light falls not only upon a red element in the copy, but also upon blue and green elements. Since it is required that a red element print only behind a red element, it is essential to examine the effect of red light transmission through the blue and green elements and vice versa.

The spectral transmissions of the screen elements are far from being mutually exclusive, and the colors are not completely saturated. The reasons for this were discussed in *The Photographic Journal*, 1937, p. 706. Because of the overlaps in transmissions, when a red color element falls upon a green element, an appreciable quantity of light is transmitted to the emulsion below, thus giving rise to silver deposits at these points. In making copies, it is this overlapping light that must be kept to an absolute minimum, to reduce color degradation and falsification.

Let P_λ be the sensitivity of the emulsion to light of wavelength λ, M_λ

the intensity of this wavelength in the printing light, and R_λ, G_λ, and B_λ the transmissions of the red, green, and blue reseau elements to light of this wavelength. Then R_λ^2, B_λ^2, and G_λ^2 will be the transmissions at the points where the color elements are in registry, that is, where a red falls upon a red, a green upon a green, and a blue upon a blue. And $R_\lambda G_\lambda$, $R_\lambda B_\lambda$, and $B_\lambda G_\lambda$ will be the transmissions of the overlapping portions, where a red falls upon a green, etc We have then six cases, as follows:

1 Red — Red	4. Red — Green
2. Green — Green	5. Red — Blue
3. Blue — Blue	6. Green — Blue

The photographic effect of light of wavelength λ upon the emulsion below, will be given by the product

$$M_\lambda \ P_\lambda \ X_\lambda \ Y_\lambda$$

where X_λ and Y_λ are the terms R_λ, G_λ, or B_λ. Where the red elements coincide, the expression becomes

$$M_\lambda \cdot P_\lambda \cdot R_\lambda^2$$

Where the red overlaps the blue, the expression becomes

$$M_\lambda \ P_\lambda \cdot R_\lambda \cdot B_\lambda, \text{ etc.}$$

To find the effect for the whole spectrum, these expressions must be integrated over the entire visible range, thus:

1 Red — Red $= \int_{400}^{700} M_\lambda \ P_\lambda \cdot R_\lambda^2 \cdot d\lambda = 100$ (arbitrary)

2 Green — Green $= \int_{400}^{700} M_\lambda \ P_\lambda \cdot G_\lambda^2 \ d\lambda = 100$ (arbitrary)

3. Blue — Blue $= \int_{400}^{700} M_\lambda \ P_\lambda \ B_\lambda^2 \ d\lambda = 100$ (arbitrary)

4. Red — Green $= \int_{400}^{700} M_\lambda \ P_\lambda \ R_\lambda \cdot G_\lambda \ d\lambda = 18\ 3$

5. Red — Blue $= \int_{400}^{700} M_\lambda \ P_\lambda \ R_\lambda \ B_\lambda \cdot d\lambda = 15.7$

6. Green — Blue $= \int_{400}^{700} M_\lambda \ P_\lambda \ G_\lambda \cdot B_\lambda \cdot d\lambda = 23\ 8$

The values for the cases where the colors coincide have been taken arbitrarily as 100, and equal to each other This is not strictly true, but serves our purpose The other values are those obtained when Mazda light is used for printing. The overlap of the red into the green is therefore 18 per cent. The blue elements have appreciable red transmission from 630 mμ on. The overlap in this case is almost 16 per cent. The worst offender is the blue overlap in the green, 24 per cent. This amount of desaturation cannot be tolerated, hence precautions must be taken to reduce them to a minimum.

A glance at the term

$$M_\lambda \ P_\lambda \ R_\lambda \ B_\lambda$$

which represents the amount of action due to overlapping colors indicates that only M_λ and P_λ can be varied, since R_λ, B_λ and G_λ are fixed by the spectral characteristics of the reseau colors. It remains, therefore only possible to make the product $M_\lambda \cdot P_\lambda$ a minimum in the range of the overlaps. Since P_λ relates to the photographic emulsion it becomes much simpler to vary M_λ, the spectral characteristic of the printing light. This can be done by means of filters. The overlap in the deep red, due to a dichroic transmission of the green and blue beyond 650 mμ, can be overcome by limiting the sensitivity of the emulsion to 650. This is the sensitivity boundary of the normal panchromatic emulsion. It is only the specially sensitized and the infrared emulsions that have sensitivities beyond this

The best method of changing M_λ in the desired ranges is to print through sharp-cutting filters whose transmissions are given by M_λ^R, M_λ^G, and M_λ^B. The Dufaycolor S and P filters are such. Using the sharp-cutting filters, the following conditions exist:

Color Combination	*Red Filter*	*Green Filter*	*Blue Filter*
Red — Red	100	9 6	5 4
Green — Green	2.5	100	2.5
Blue — Blue	2.0	4 5	100
Red — Green	6.7	4.1	2 3
Red — Blue	4.8	3.4	4 5
Green — Blue	2.5	5 8	7.3

This represents a considerable increase in efficiency over the use of unfiltered light

The regions in which the colors of the reseau elements are completely free from overlaps, are very narrow. Even with the use of monochromatic light, it is not quite possible to completely eliminate them. But a very good approximation can be obtained by the use of the red line of cadmium (λ = 6438Å) for the red, the mercury line (λ = 5461) for the green, and the two mercury lines (λ = 4047, 4358) for the blue. The yellow mercury doublet (λ = 5780) can be removed by use of a didymium filter. This absorbs strongly in the yellow, but transmits freely in the blue and the green. Since the use of the cadmium line is but slightly better than the use of the sharp-cutting red filter, and since the filter is so much more practical, it is inadvisable to resort to the very low luminosity occasioned by the use of a cadmium lamp.

The article in *The Photographic Journal* covers printing from Dufaycolor film, rather completely. It is surprising that no mention has been made of the previous work in this field. The problem of moiré was first discussed in a rather detailed manner by Mees, Piper, and Stenger and Leiber, as was pointed out above. Von Hubl also studied screen-plate printing. His work is reviewed rather fully in Wall's "History of Three-Color Photography" (1925), page 542.

The original articles appeared in the *Wiener Mitteilungen* (1910) and were abstracted in the *British Journal of Photography*, Volume 57 (1910) Colour Supplement, page 59.

When an Autochrome plate is printed so as to obtain a print in monochrome, the results are weak, since the light affecting the color-blind emulsion must come only through the blue elements. Hence, even in the deepest shadows, the blacks are diluted with two portions of white. The same difficulty is met when it is printed on another screen plate (since the chances of a blue dot falling on another blue dot are one in three). It is possible to obtain sharp images from Autochromes even if the emulsion side of the copy is placed against the glass side of the Autochrome, this occasioning a separation equal to 2 mm between them. The two are loaded into a camera (the lens of which is set at infinity so as to obtain parallel rays), and the camera then pointed to the sky, which must be covered with white clouds. This condition can also be duplicated in the laboratory, merely by exposing the combination in the camera to a large white area illuminated perfectly evenly. The image of this area must be sufficiently large to cover the entire surface of the Autochrome. Another way that this can be accomplished is to use a point source of light situated at the focal point of a set of condenser lenses whose diameters are larger than the diagonal of the Autochrome. The Autochrome plus copy material, is placed adjacent to the other side of the condensers.

Although procedures such as the above overcome the problem of definition loss due to lack of contact, the problem of color rendition still remains. Consider the case where a certain red color is composed of 300 transparent and 600 opaque grains. In copying this upon another screen plate, only 100 of the red grains will fall upon other red grains. The remaining grains will fall upon blue and green elements. No light will pass through these combinations. Therefore, in the copy, the reproduction will consist of 100 transparent grains and 800 opaque ones. If advantage be taken of the geometry of the situation, this can be overcome, although with a slight loss of definition. Consider first of all the case of a point source of light, as in Fig. 50. The

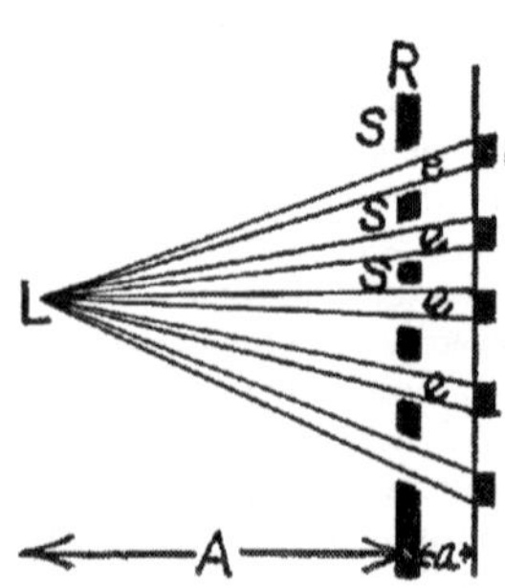

FIG. 50

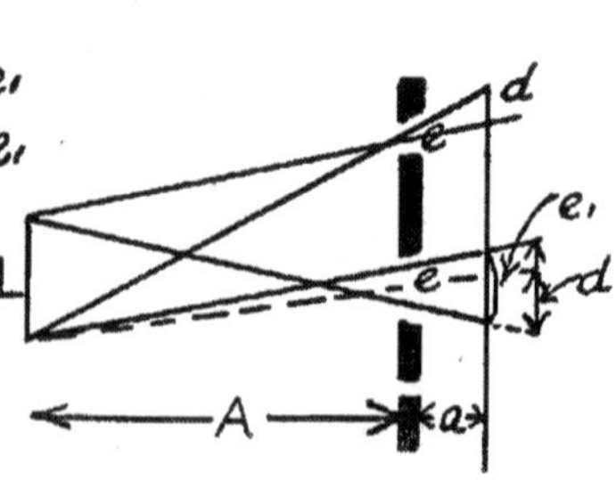

FIG. 51

elements S (opaque), and e (transparent) of the master screen will be reproduced sharply in the copy. But if the source of light is not a point, a different story is true, as is made evident in Fig. 51. Now the image e_1, of the transparent portion e in the master, will be enlarged, the degree of enlargement being d. This is also a measure of the unsharpness that is introduced by this method. From the geometry it is seen that conditions can be chosen so that the image e_1 is enlarged to cover a whole unit consisting of a red, green, and blue element in the copy screen. Then, if e represents a red dot in the master, it will have to fall upon a red dot in the copy, since its image, e_1, will encompass all three

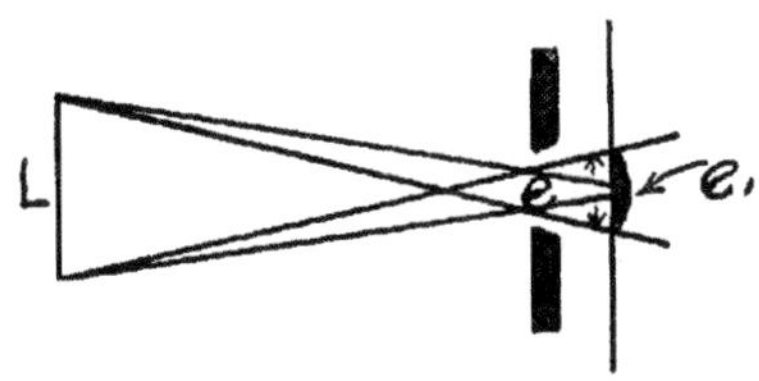

FIG. 52

colors. Instead of enlarging three times, which will be just sufficient to cover the spaces between the dots in the copy, Von Hübl suggests a four-time enlargement. Consider the nature of the image e_1, in its greatly enlarged form (Fig. 52). It is only the central portion that receives light from every point on the light source L. The edges, therefore fall off in intensity, hence the image e_1 of the element e is not uniform. But if the degree of enlargement is such that the edges overlap each other, their intensities will be increased. At a four-time enlargement this is sufficient to give a completely uniform density in the copy. Von Hübl made a mathematical analysis of the problem, much in the same manner as was done by Harrison and Horner, twenty-nine years later. He obtained the equation:

$$L = \frac{A(v - 1)}{a} \cdot e$$

where L is the size of the light source,
A is the distance the light source is from the material,
a is the separation between master and copy,
v is the degree of enlargement desired, and
e is the dimension of the dot in the master.

He also determined the degree of unsharpness, d. This is related to the other dimensions by the equation

$$d = \frac{L}{A} a$$

It has often been proposed to diffuse the image by racking the lens slightly out of focus. This will cause a slight diffusion which should be sufficient to cause the screen elements to fuse. J Tritton made use of the poor resolving power of the lens to effect a fusion of the elements It is a well-known fact that when light passes a sharp edge, it becomes slightly diffracted. The diaphragm of a lens is also a sharp line, and the light passing through the lens will be affected in this manner. If the circumference of the lens opening is made small, the diffusion caused by this phenomenon will be sufficient to fill in between the images of the elements When the copy is made one-to-one (*Brit. J. Phot*, Vol. 84 (1937), p 513) the aperture must be closed to at least *f*:45 or *f*:64.

The interposition of substances into the paths of the projected image to give a smoothing effect, has been a popular remedy. G. Heymer (U.S.P. 1879236) proposed to place a lenticular film base in the path. The lens elements of the film are such as to cause interference patterns which destroy the moiré. W. Chapman (U.S P. 1955715) placed a doubling image prism in the path of the rays The two images are spread sufficiently to fill in the space between screen elements This is extended to a quadruple image in a subsequent disclosure (U S P 2031032, Eng P. 389345) The same inventor also proposed to interpose in the path of the rays an element which will cause diffusion to take place, and in that way cause a fusion of the screen elements (U.S.P. 2049556) T. T. Baker accomplished the same result by interposing a sheet of glass with linear or circular depressions, 0.1 mm in depth (Eng. P. 337041) The same result could be accomplished according to T T. Baker (U S.P 1903971; Eng. P. 366958), if a lens be used at an aperture of at least *f*: 2. The lens is focused sharply upon the silver image of the master film. The depth of focus at this opening is so slight that the screen in the master will be sufficiently diffused to be negligible. This procedure is especially useful in copying a screen plate upon another screen plate.

F. A. Lindemann proposed to use two light sources at a slight angle to each other, and copy the screen plate by contact, but the emulsions in master and copy are placed a definite distance apart. The angularity of the two light beams is such that they cast adjacent images, thus filling in the spaces between the screen elements (Eng. P. 374891). Or a single light source could be used in front of a bi-prism, to yield the two beams. The method was originally proposed to overcome the moiré patterns formed when printing from a screen master to a screen copy film, but the application to separations is immediate. A somewhat similar idea is disclosed by S. D. Threadgold (Eng. P. 446679). He used a diffuse light source, and this gave an enlarged image, just sufficient to cover three elements. Thus the space between the elements becomes filled in. This is no different from the original von Hubl suggestion, or the Harrison and Horner technique Threadgold preceded the last mentioned disclosure by several years.

CHAPTER 16

THE LENTICULAR PROCESS

IN this chapter we turn our attention to one of the simplest and most elegant of all the proposals for the making of color reproductions. This is the lenticular process, which requires no special camera or special processing technique, except that a special type of film has molded on its back a series of lenticular elements which divide the surface into a honeycomb structure. For a long time after the idea was first proposed, nothing was done with it. But later it became extremely popular, and for a time it was thought that this scheme solved all problems of motion pictures in color. Some idea regarding the position which lenticular film held in the industry may be obtained from the fact that fully one-third of the patents dealing with color reproduction in the decade 1925–1935, dealt in one way or another, with this process. This interest waned considerably with the advent of the monopacks.

The principles which govern the use of lenticular film for color reproduction purposes, are purely optical in nature. Therefore, it may be of value to review at this point the fundamentals of lens and camera optics Consider the following situation. An object is being photographed at a distance of ten feet, with a 4 by 5 camera, equipped with an 8-inch lens, the exposure being made at an opening of f:8. The lens will have an effective aperture that measures one inch in diameter. From every point on the object there will radiate a cone of light, and the camera lens will intercept that portion of it which will have a cross section one inch in diameter (Fig. 53). Let us center our attention upon the cone of light which enters the lens. It has its apex on the object being photographed, 120 inches away from the camera. The base of the cone is a circle one inch in diameter. Therefore the angularity of the cone is very small. To all intents and purposes, it can be considered that the rays entering the lens are parallel to each other, and that their point of convergence is an infinite distance away Stated a little more scientifically, ten feet represents the infinity distance in this case. From every point on the object, then, there arises a beam of parallel rays, each beam making a different angle with the axis of the lens. That is the only difference between all the rays which enter the lens, and it is this difference which determines exactly where the image of any point will appear in the negative. But this is getting a little ahead of the story.

Lenses are possible because light travels at a different rate of speed through dense transparent substances, such as glass, than it does through air. The ratio between the velocities of light in vacuum and in any other medium, is called the index of refraction of the material. Now consider the case of

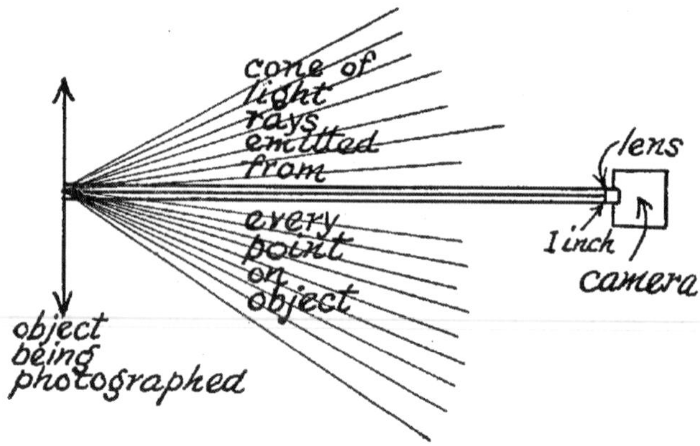

FIG. 53

a wave front AB, traveling in air, then entering a glass plate whose outer surface is depicted by the line CD in the diagram (Fig. 54). Let v be the

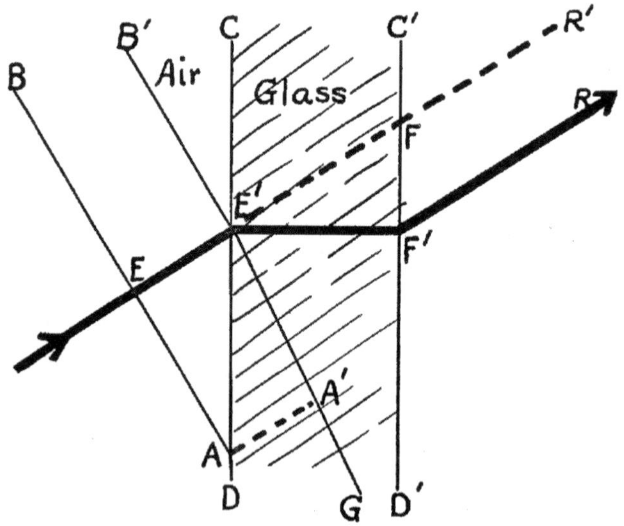

FIG. 54

velocity which the wave front has in glass, and C its velocity in air. The wave front is traveling in the direction EE', which is normal or perpendicular to AB. Consider the wave front from the moment the point A on it reaches the glass. As the beam moves forward, the point A moves into the glass where it travels with a velocity v. In a time t, the distance it will have traveled in the glass will be $vt = AA'$. During that same time, the wave front will have traveled in air a distance $Ct = EE'$, and the point E on the wave front will have reached the glass surface. Inside the glass, the wave front will take the form $E'A'G$, and the direction of its motion will be along a line perpendicular to the line $E'A'G$.

The direction of the original beam has therefore been changed when it passed from air to glass, as indicated by the line $EE'F'$. This break in the direction of a beam of light when it passes from one optical medium into the next, is called refraction, and the amount of change in this direction is measured by the index of refraction. It is quite easy to establish from geometrical considerations that the index of refraction is numerically equal to the ratio of the velocities in the two media. Glass, for instance, has an index of refraction ranging approximately between 1.50 and 1.70. The film base has a value of 1.40. Pure gelatin also has a value of 1.40 or thereabouts.

When a beam of light goes from air to a denser medium, its direction is always bent toward the normal to the surface of the denser medium. When a beam goes from a dense medium to air, it is always bent away from the normal to the interface between the two media. There is a cardinal rule in optics, the complete reversibility of action, and it is the one guiding principle in the entire study of the lenticular processes. Therefore the wave front $E'A'G$, upon emerging from the dense medium into air, will undergo the exact opposite direction transformation, provided the interface $D'C'$ is optically equivalent to the interface CD. This is true if the face $D'C'$ is parallel to the face CD. We can state the very important principle that is utilized in all beam-splitting devices, that when a beam of light passes through a sheet of glass with parallel faces, the direction of the beam is not changed, but its position is somewhat displaced Thus in our diagram, were no glass plate included in the path, the direction of the wave front would be along the line $EE'FR'$. But upon placing the glass plate in the path, the beam proceeds along the broken line $EE'F'R$. The line $F'R$ is parallel to FR' so that the direction is the same as previously, but the position has been displaced a distance FF'.

When a beam of light (this can be defined as the normal to the wave front, hence could be identified with the direction of the wave front) goes from air into a glass prism and then emerges from the prism, an entirely different story is true (Fig. 55). Consider the glass prism ABC, and the beam of light RD. Upon striking and entering the prism, the beam becomes refracted, and travels along the line DE until it reaches the new glass-air interface. Here the side AC is no longer the optical equivalent of the side AB, since it is not parallel to it. Hence upon emerging, the beam will be deflected away from the normal to the surface *AC*, and the new direction will be along *ES*. This is no longer parallel to, nor does it have any relationship to, the direction of

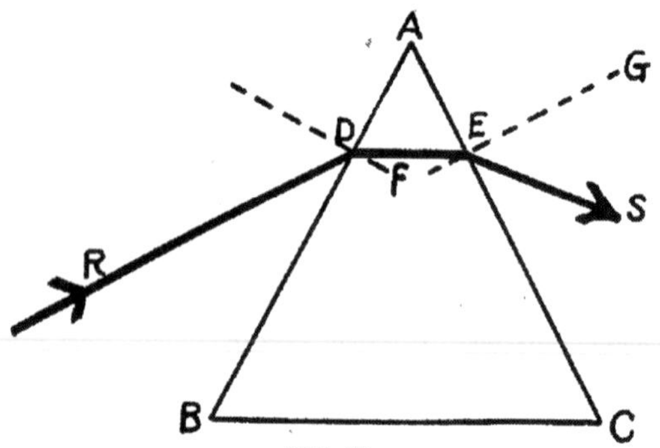

FIG. 55

the line *RD*, but is dependent mainly upon the angle of the prism, *BAC*. It is seen, therefore, that by properly designing a prism, it is possible to direct the beam to any desired place or direction.

Consider, now, a lens *LL'* (Fig. 56). This is a transparent substance whose outer faces have been polished down so that each point on the surfaces offers

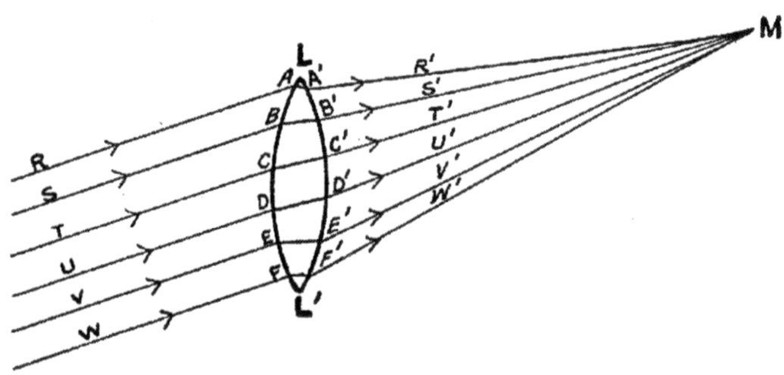

FIG. 56

a different angle to a beam of parallel rays. Such a beam is illustrated by the rays *R*, *S*, *T*, *U*, *V*, *W*, all of which are parallel to each other. If the surfaces of the lens are spherical, each of the rays, *R*, *S*, *T*, etc., will strike the front surface at a different angle. The ray *RA* will be refracted to the point *A'* by its passage through the lens. The angle which the refracted ray *AA'* makes with the other lens surface is different from the angle it makes with the first, hence upon going from the lens to air it will not proceed along the line parallel to RA, but along a different direction $A'R'$. A similar condition will be true for the ray WF. After passage through the lens, it will proceed along a direction $F'W'$, which is not parallel to $A'R'$, since the surface $LABCDEFL'$ is not parallel to $LA'B'C'D'E'F'L'$. The curvatures of the surfaces can be so chosen that the rays, after emerging from the lens, will intersect at some point, M. It has been found that if these surfaces are spherical in shape, and if the centers of these spheres lie on the same straight line, then a beam of parallel rays entering the lens will emerge in the form of a circular cone whose apex is at the point M. The line which joins the centers of the two spherical surfaces of the lens, is known as the optical axis (Fig. 57). From the geometry, this line must be normal to both surfaces at the points of intersection with them. A ray of light traveling along this path, will enter

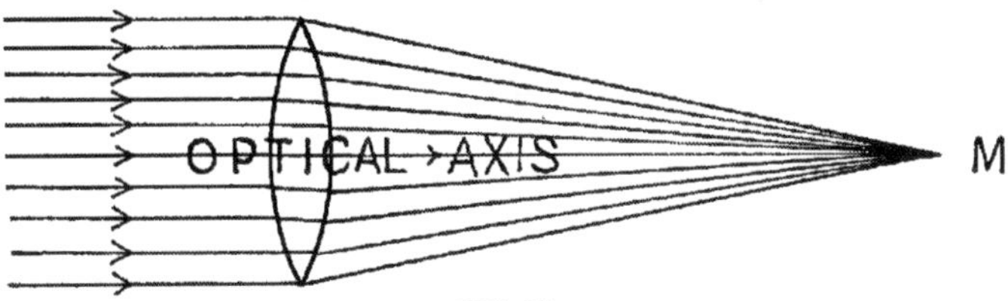

FIG. 57

and leave the glass medium normally, hence will not suffer any change in direction. If a beam of rays, all of which are parallel to the optical axis, enters the lens, it will converge at a point M which lies on the axis. This point is called the rear focal point of the lens. The plane through this point, perpendicular to the optical axis, is called the rear focal plane, or the image plane of the lens. This plane plays a very important role in photographic optics. The negative material is placed in this position.

If two beams of light, each consisting of rays that are parallel to each other, enter the lens from different directions, each beam will be brought to a focus at a different point. This is illustrated in the diagram in Fig. 58. The system of parallel rays B_1, B_2, B_3, enters the lens in the form of a beam, and leaves it in the form of a cone $B_1'\,B_7'\,B'$, with the apex at B', the point where all the rays B_1 to B_7 come to a focus. In a similar manner the system of rays A_1A_7 enters the lens as a beam but leaves it as a cone, coming to a focus at the point A'. The locus of the points A' and B' is determined solely by the angle which the rays make with the optical axis, RR'. The ensemble of all the points $A_1'B_1'\ldots'$, which are the apices of the cones that result when beams of light enter the lens at all possible angles, forms a plane which coincides with the rear focal plane or image plane of the lens.

The position of a point in this plane is determined by means of two entirely independent numbers. The direction which any line in space makes with a given standard direction is determined by three numbers. But these are connected by a relationship which states that the sum of the squares of these numbers (called direction cosines) must equal one. Hence only two of the numbers are independent. It is not a difficult problem for a mathematician to develop the connection between the two sets of numbers.

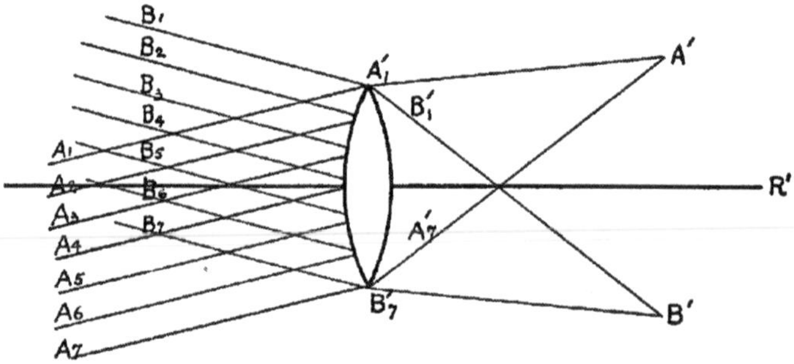

FIG. 58

A beam of light with parallel rays *A*, *B*, *C*, . . . *H*, entering a lens (Fig. 59) is brought to a focus at a point *O*, whose position in the image plane is determined by the angle which the beam makes with the optical axis *RR'*. The beam, after passage through the lens, will take the form of a cone of rays. In this cone, there will be one, and only one, ray whose direction is the same as that of the beam, and which will not suffer a change in direction by passage

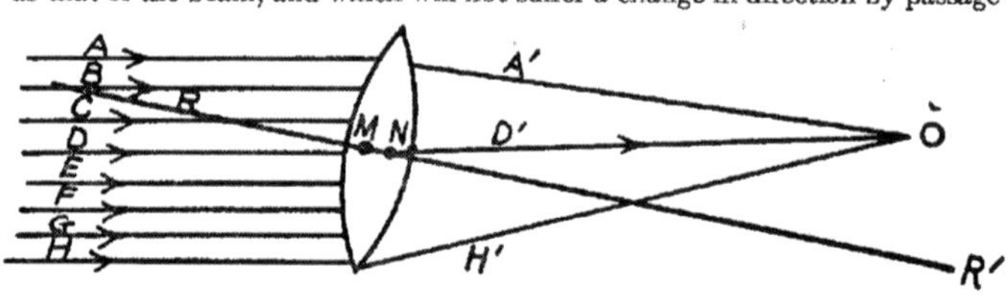

FIG. 59

through the lens. This is the beam *D'*. It intersects the optical axis at the point *N*, which is called the nodal point of emergence of the lens. The ray *D'* in the emergent cone corresponds to the ray *D* in the beam. This ray intersects the optical axis at the point *M*, which is called the nodal point of admission. Every beam of light, containing rays that are parallel to each other, will have one ray which proceeds from the source directly to the point *O*. The beam upon emergence from the lens, will appear as if it had emerged from the point *N*, and will have a direction parallel to that of the beam. The two nodal points *M* and *N* have a very important geometric property.

Draw a line from M in any direction, so that it intersects the entry surface of the lens RS (Fig. 60). This will be at the point B. At this point draw the tangent to the lens surface, BA. Now draw a line parallel to MB from the point N, to the emergent side of the lens. This will intersect the lens surface at C. Draw the tangent to the surface at C. This will be the line CD. The line CD will be parallel to the line AB. Now consider the ray LBM, whose direction is identical with the direction BM. This ray upon entrance into the lens will be refracted toward the normal to the surface at the point B. The refracted ray will pass through the lens to the point C, at which point

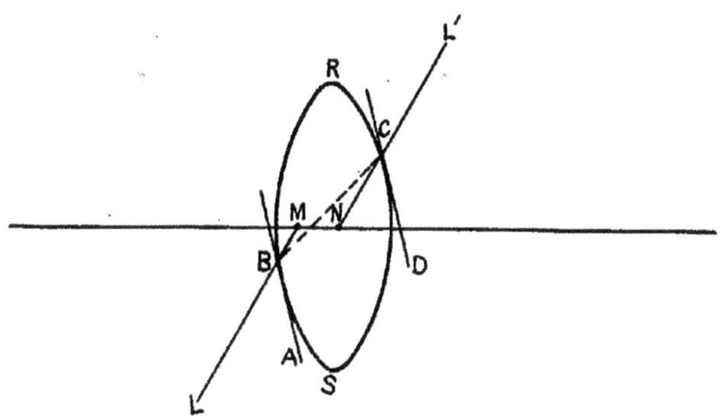

FIG. 60

it goes from glass to air, hence will be refracted away from the normal to the surface at the point C. As far as the ray LB is concerned (appearing to go through the nodal point of admission M) the lens is merely a glass plate with parallel sides AB and CD. Hence the ray will emerge in the same direction that it entered, but it will be displaced somewhat and appear as if it originated from the nodal point of emergence.

The existence of nodal points makes geometrical optics quite simple. Every lens can be classified exactly if the positions of the two nodal points and the rear focal plane be given. It has been noted above that from every point on an object being photographed, there radiates a cone of rays. That section of the cone which enters the lens aperture can be considered to consist of a group of parallel rays, hence the lens will bring these to a point focus somewhere in the focal plane of the lens. Among all the rays coming from a single point on the object, there will be one ray R, that will pass through the point M in the lens system, the nodal point of admission (Fig. 61). This ray will then translate itself from M to N, the nodal point of emergence, and continue from there in a parallel direction NR', until it intersects the focal plane F at the point P. This is the image point corresponding to the point on the object from which the beam characterized by the ray R, originated. In this manner, every point on the object gives rise to a single point in the image or rear focal plane. It must be understood that the discussion up to this point relates only to perfect and ideal optical systems, which serve as the goal toward which lens designers and opticians strive. Lenses are complicated

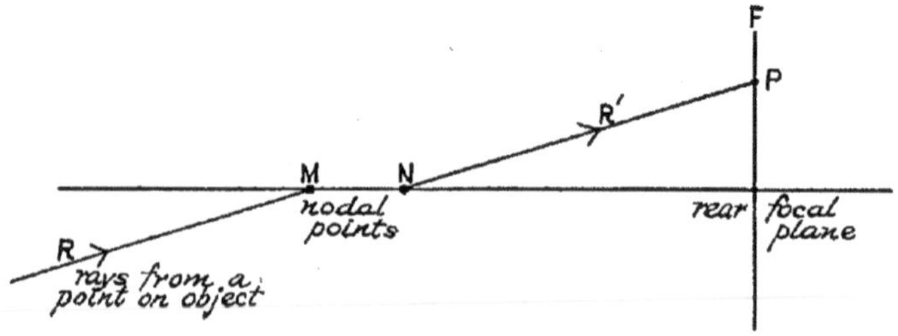

FIG. 61

affairs, the complications arising from the attempts to make them appear as close as possible to the ideal. It is only within the very limited and precise limits in which the commercial lens approaches the ideal, that they can be used; and one should never use them outside these limits, unless one is willing to accept poor definition and resolving power, or other inferior quality.

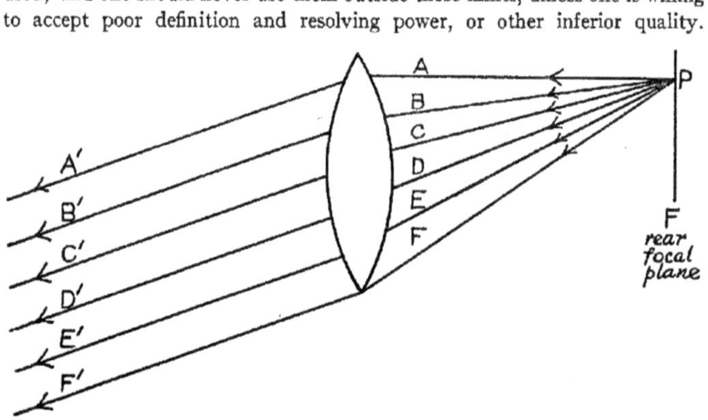

FIG. 62

Consider a light source at a point P (Fig. 62) which lies in the rear focal plane of a lens. This will radiate light rays in all directions and, in particular, will fill a lens aperture with a cone of light composed of the rays A, B, C, D, E, and F. One of the most important properties of the lens is that the cone of light originating at a point in the focal plane of a lens will emerge from that lens in the form of a beam containing parallel rays, which come to a point focus at infinity. This is the exact reverse of what happens when a beam of parallel rays enters the lens. There is therefore a complete reversibility in optical phenomena. This is the principle that makes lenticular processes possible.

Now let us consider the application of these principles to lenticular film. It was Gabriel Lippmann, the brilliant scientist who also developed the grainless Lippmann emulsion, who first suggested the possibility of a lenticular film material (*Compt. rend.*, Vol. 166 (1908), p. 446; *Brit. J. Phot.*, Vol. 55 (1908), p. 192). He suggested that a film base be impressed with a honeycomb structure, each element of which would act as a tiny lens. This will

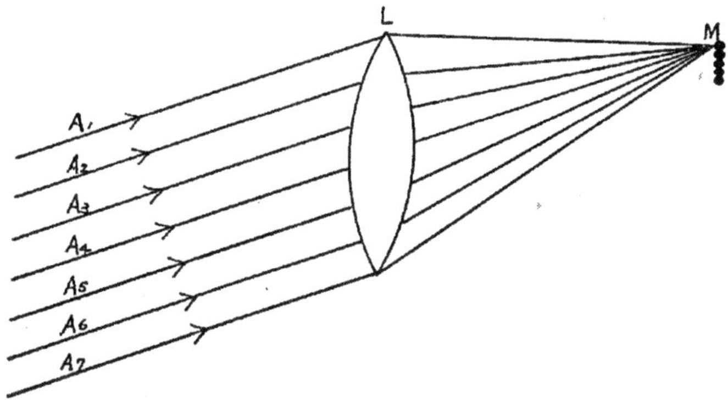

FIG. 63

image only that portion of light which is directly in front of it. In particular, it should be possible to make these lenses so small that they will see only the light that comes from a single beam. Thus in Fig. 63, the beam of parallel rays A_1, enters the lens L, and emerges in the form of a cone, coming to a focus at the point M. It is desirable to make the honeycomb structure on the base of such dimensions that each element of the honeycomb will receive the light from but a single cone, hence from but a single point on the object. The tiny lens at M will then form an image on the emulsion lying directly beneath it, of the intensity of the beam that enters the lens at that particular angle that will come to a focus at the point M. The entire picture would consist of a series of minute dots lying in juxtaposition, each dot being the image seen by the tiny lens immediately in front of it. If the dots are beyond the resolving power of the eye, they will not be seen as individuals, but as blends.

This description falls short of expounding a color process. To accomplish this each of the minute lenses must image three dots, one for each of the primary colors. It was R. Berthon, an astronomical optician, who showed how this could be done, just one year after Lippmann made his disclosures (Eng. P. 10611/09). Consider a beam of parallel rays $A_1A_2B_1B_2C_1C_2$, etc., entering the aperture of a lens L, in whose nodal plane of admission there is placed a special filter (Fig. 64). This consists of three bands lying side by side, each dyed the color of a single primary. Together, the three filters com-

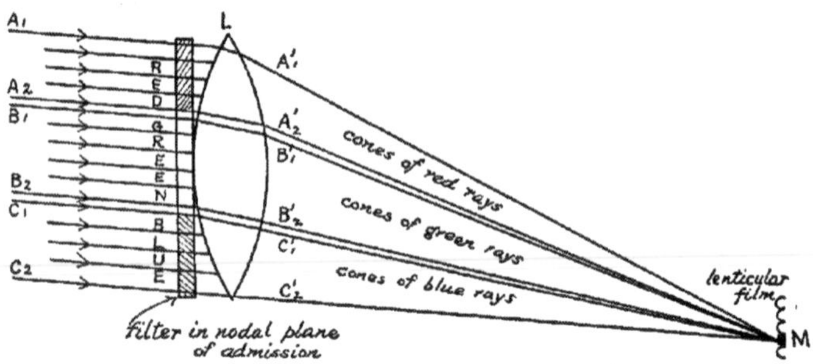

FIG. 64

pletely fill the lens aperture. The spectral quality of the beam $A_1, \ldots C_2$ is uniform, but only part of the beam will go through each portion of the aperture. Thus the part A_1A_2 will go through the red, the part B_1B_2 will go through the green, and the part C_1C_2 will go through the blue filter area of the aperture. After passing through the lens, the beam will be converted

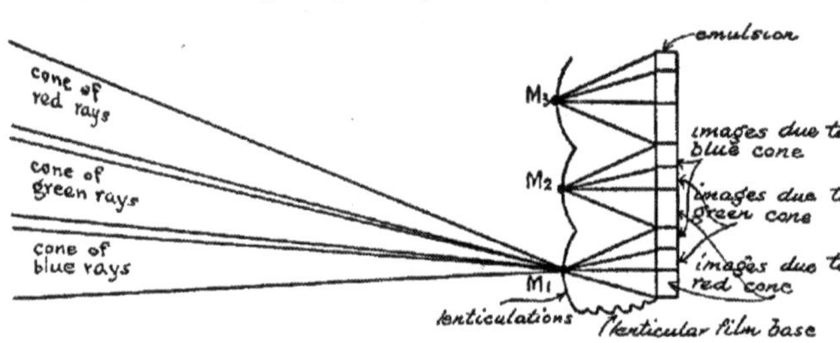

FIG. 65

into three cones, each of which comes to the same point focus, M, in the image plane. The cones will differ from each other in spectral quality, since they have passed through different filters. They will also differ in intensity, since the original beam had different intensities for the three primaries present.

Now consider the three colored cones from the point of view of the minute lens situated at the point of focus of the beam, that is, at the point M_1. This is illustrated in highly exaggerated form in the diagram in Fig. 65. The cone of red rays originates from the point on the object and passes through the red filter in the aperture of the taking objective, which sees it as a beam of parallel rays. The tiny lens, M_1, situated in the rear focal plane of the taking objective, will image this cone in the form of a dot that covers one-third of the area on the emulsion immediately behind M_1. The density of the dot will depend upon the intensity of the red rays present in the original beam The cone of green rays lies directly adjacent to the red, so that the lens M_1 will image this as a dot lying next to the red density image. The blue will in a similar manner be imaged adjacent to the green. The three dots together fill entirely the area directly beneath each tiny lens, and so, adjacent to the blue dot on the other side, will be the image of the red rays coming from an adjacent lenticule, M_2 These cones coming to a focus at M_2, originate from a point of the object that lies adjacent to the first.

Since the three dots arising from each beam take up a definite area, this becomes the unit of definition of lenticular processes. It is possible to make film with 20 to 30 such elements to the millimeter, or from 500 to 750 to the linear inch. It is seen, therefore, that the effect of a lenticular film, used in conjunction with a banded filter in the nodal plane of admission, is identical with a screen plate. In the first case the screen is formed optically, whereas in the second it is formed mechanically. It is considerably easier and cheaper to mold a lenticular film base than to rule or print colored elements. Therefore in this limited region, lenticular film has an advantage over screen plates. But this is offset by a large number of other disadvantages which served to sidetrack the lenticular processes as soon as screen plates and other color processes that were not too complicated, came into being.

Although Lippmann first suggested the possibility of lenticular film, and Berthon described the first successful application of the material to color, a somewhat similar idea had been current ever since 1895. F. N. Lanchester may be credited with the germ of the idea (Eng. P. 16548/95). A ray of light passing through a small opening in an opaque screen, and then through a prism, will be spread out into a spectrum. If instead of a small opening, the light passes through a slit with a definite width, the image will be in the form of a rectangular band of color. Now suppose that the slit be divided into three parts, and each part covered with a filter passing but one primary, then the image will consist of three bands colored red, green, and blue respectively. If these be projected upon a panchromatic film, there will be formed three silver densities corresponding to the intensities of each primary present in the beam that entered the slit at the given angle. In photography by this means, we replace the slit with a line screen.

The germ of the idea disclosed here is that in a screen that is placed in the rear focal plane of a lens system, each element acts as a pinhole camera. This breaks up the object into minute units, and each unit becomes photographed separately by means of a pinhole camera. Mr. Lanchester went on to disperse this light by means of a prism, achieving color photography by the micro-dispersion method. This has been described in detail in Chapter 3. Here we are interested in the one step of placing a screen in the rear focal plane of a taking objective, and having the elements of the screen act as individual pinhole cameras.

A further step in this direction was taken by R. E. Liesegang, who was apparently the first to suggest the use of banded filters in the aperture of a lens system (*Phot. Arch*, Vol 37 (1896), p. 250, *Brit J. Phot.*, Vol. 43 (1896), p. 569). In this article, he suggested the use of yellow, red, and blue filters It is rather surprising that so eminent and accomplished a photographic scientist as Liesegang should make so elementary an error as to confuse the subtractive or secondary colors with the primaries. Since the terms red and blue are used to designate two elements of each set, we can recognize which set is meant by the third color. Since Liesegang uses yellow, his red and blue must have been the red and blue of the printing inks, therefore really magenta and cyan. Although this set of colors, magenta, cyan, and yellow, does form a balanced unit, it is just exactly one hundred per cent wrong to use them for analysis purposes Each of these transmit two primaries, hence there will be no true color analysis. If he actually meant to use primary red and blue for two of his colors, then the use of yellow for the third color would again have destroyed true color analysis, for instead of obtaining a true evaluation of the green intensity, he would have obtained a green density mixed with an equal quantity of red.

But this error in the choice of colors does not mitigate against the soundness of his engineering and optical procedures. He writes in substance, as follows: Every element of a cross-lined screen acts as a pinhole camera, and reproduces an image of the aperture of the objective in whose rear focal plane it is placed. Thus, when using a square stop, the dots in the halftone produced will be square in shape; and when the stop is triangular, the dots produced will be triangles. If a diaphragm is used with several holes, each element of the screen will reproduce as many dots as there are holes in the diaphragm. If these holes be covered with red, yellow, and blue filters, the three dots will correspond in density to the intensities of the colors entering the lens aperture. In order to convert the negative into its natural colors, it can be converted into a transparency and projected through the three-color diaphragm and the original lens system.

The following year, J. A C Branfill (*Brit J. Phot*, Vol. 44 (1897), p 142) suggested the use of four openings in the diaphragm. Three of the openings were covered with the primary filters, and the fourth was left clear. The sizes of the openings were adjusted to yield balance by a simultaneous exposure Evidently Mr. Branfill had the photomechanical industry in mind, since it is here that a fourth (black) printer is demanded. The same idea was disclosed by Giesecke (Ger P 117598), Szczepanik (Eng P. 7729/99); F. E. Ives, (U.S.P. 648748); and J. de Lassus Saint-Genies (Fr P. 459566).

A further advance was made by Edward Russell Clarke (Eng P. 10690/02). He disclosed a method for the making of separations from the integral negative prepared as above. This was done by preparing block-outs made by exposing a plate to a uniform white area, with all but one of the openings closed. From such a negative, a positive was made. This had as solids all the area on the plate except those portions corresponding to the positions where the image of the one open stop would fall. If this were registered with the negative, it would block out all densities except the one corresponding to a single opening in the diaphragm, hence limit it to the densities of a single primary separation. In this manner, by the preparation of one block-out screen for each opening of the diaphragm, it is possible to isolate the dots corresponding to each color separation. It is also possible to project the negative through an identical optical system, and close all but one of the diaphragm openings. The resultant image will correspond to the densities of but a single primary.

From the foregoing it may be seen that the Berthon system was merely the optical analogue of the one described by Liesegang, and elaborated by Branfill and the other persons just mentioned, and fully described at least ten years before either Lippmann or Berthon. These men simply did optically what the others have done mechanically. Both of these schemes can be considered as the optical equivalents of the screen methods proposed by du Hauron, and first put into practice by Prof. Joly The pinhole camera or lenticular lens placed in the rear focal plane of an objective in whose front nodal plane is positioned three filters, projects a color screen upon the emulsion. The individual cell densities of this screen are determined by the composition of the light reflected from the object being photographed. In the screen plate, the cross-lined screen consists of elements each of which is colored in a different primary. In so far as the emulsion receiving the impression is concerned, the three are identical. It is interesting to note that Liesegang proposed his scheme frankly as a modification of the Joly screen process.

Lenticular film achieved a small measure of popularity in the United States. About 1928, the Eastman Kodak Company introduced it under the name Kodacolor, for amateur 16 mm movies. With the introduction of Kodachrome somewhat later by the same company, the lenticular process disappeared. It had a life of approximately seven or eight years. Its introduction may be ascribed to the terrific pressure that was being applied by the amateur for a color process, and it lasted only until a simpler procedure was introduced. Although the fidelity of color reproduction was quite high, the process had many inherent flaws that made its further use a matter of great inconvenience. These will be discussed at a later time.

Kodacolor was a transparency process, wherein the original film that was exposed in the camera was processed to yield a positive. By projection through a suitable lens, containing a three-banded filter in its aperture, a colored image was obtained on a white viewing screen Consider the path of a cone of rays originating at the silver image in the emulsion layer of a lenticular film shown in highly exaggerated form in Fig. 66. The base is approximately 0.005 inch in thickness. On this, opposite to the lenticulations, is the emulsion layer containing the silver images *r*, *g*, *b*, etc. These lie in the focal plane of the lenticular lens element *M*. The film is illuminated from behind by means of a beam of light with parallel rays. The aperture of the lens *M*, is the area covered by the image elements *b*, *g* and *r*. Since these are in the focal plane of *M*, the light passed by the silver deposits at *b*, *g*, and *r*, will be brought to a point focus. Let us concentrate our attention on the one ray from each of the silver deposits which passes through the nodal point of emergence *A*. This lies on the outer surface of the lens *M*, and therefore lies in the rear focal plane of the projection lens *L*. Consider the ray from the deposit *b*. After passing through *A*, it will continue in the same direction until it strikes the lens *L*. In a similar manner the rays from *g* and *r* will go through *A* and impinge on the lens *L*. As far as this lens is concerned, the three rays *r*, *g*,

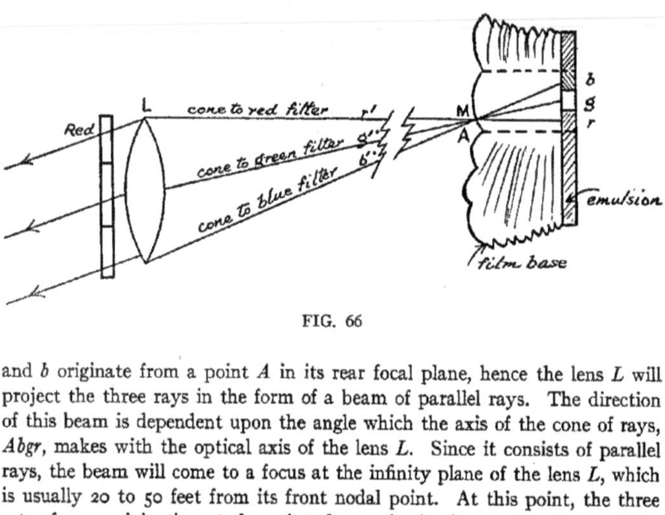

FIG. 66

and *b* originate from a point *A* in its rear focal plane, hence the lens *L* will project the three rays in the form of a beam of parallel rays. The direction of this beam is dependent upon the angle which the axis of the cone of rays, *Abgr*, makes with the optical axis of the lens *L*. Since it consists of parallel rays, the beam will come to a focus at the infinity plane of the lens *L*, which is usually 20 to 50 feet from its front nodal point. At this point, the three sets of rays originating at the points *b*, *g* and *r* in the emulsion layer of the lenticular film, will be fused into a single light point. The spectral characteristic, and the intensity of the light at this point, will be the sum of those of the three cones, symbolized by the rays *r*, *g*, and *b*.

Now let us consider more carefully the individual cones of light. The intensity of the light beam originating at the point *r* in the emulsion layer of the lenticular film (Fig. 66), will depend upon the density of the silver image at that point. Thus the three cones *r*, *g*, and *b*, will have different intensities, each depending upon the density of the image at *r*, *g*, and *b*. The three cones unite at *A*, so that in so far as the lens *L* is concerned, it is being illuminated by means of a point source of light situated in the rear focal plane.

But the lens *M* sees each cone from a different direction, hence will direct each cone in a different direction Therefore, by the action of the lens *M* the three cones of light *r*, *g*, and *b*, become directed to three different portions of the aperture of the lens *L*. The banded filter in this aperture can be so arranged that the light in cone *r* passes through a red filter, that of *g* passes through a green filter, and that of *b* passes through a blue filter.

If the lens *L* is equivalent to the lens used in the original photographing, the conditions for the exact reversal of paths will be satisfied, and the beam of light that passes through the filters in the aperture will be identical in composition to the beam that gave rise to the deposits *r*, *g*, and *b* As it leaves the lens *L*, the beam consists in reality of three sub-beams, each colored a different primary. But the three are brought to a focus at a point which corresponds to the infinity plane of the lens, so that here a blend will be formed. It is in this plane that the viewing screen is placed, or upon which the lens is brought to a focus.

The short life of the lenticular processes was due to the failure of opticians to make lenses that approach the ideal discussed above. To a minor extent the emulsion makers were also at fault, as it was necessary to make fast emulsions capable of resolving approximately 99 lines to the millimeter, if a film with 33 lenticules to the millimeter be used, and of a resolution of 75 lines to the millimeter if 25 lenticules be used. Fast emulsions, such as the Eastman Super XX, have resolving power of approximately 45 to 55 lines if developed in DK–20, the fine-grain developer. Slower emulsions have higher values. Thus, the high-contrast Safety Positive 35 mm film will resolve upward of 70 lines to the millimeter, while the Microfile 35 mm film will resolve 135 lines. The negative materials that have the speed desirable for color work fall just short of proper resolution. Instead of getting distinct separations between the densities representing the three colors, they will be more or less overlapping and indistinct.

It would take us too far afield to discuss at this point the theory of lens aberrations, or departures from ideal conditions and performance, but it is just these shortcomings that represent the biggest stumbling block in the path of successful utilization of lenticular processes. But we can discuss the effect produced, and indicate in that manner just what the nature of the problem is. The presence of a banded filter in the aperture of the lens means that the lens must be used at full opening, if only to allow the light rays from each filter area to reach each lenticular element. This means that the depth of field of the objective is very limited. It is true that each individual color is photographed only through one-third of the total aperture Hence as far as that particular image is concerned it will have a somewhat greater depth of field than the sum total of the three colors.

Consider a beam of rays entering a lens opened to full aperture, and coming to a focus in the image plane of the lens (Fig 67) For convenience let us consider the beam to be parallel to the optical axis. Theoretically the entire system of rays should come to a focus at the point *M* which is the rear focal point of the lens *L*. But this is far from the truth. In reality the different regions of the lens will bring the rays to a focus at different points, so that

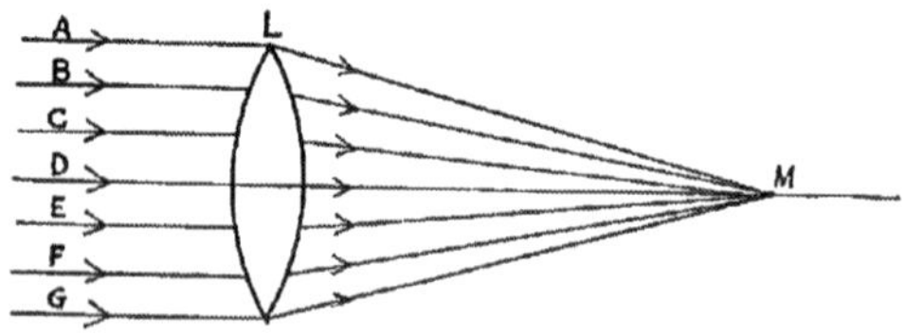

FIG. 67

instead of a center at which all the rays come together, there will be a definite area whose extent determines the circle of confusion. This is illustrated in Fig. 68, where it is seen that as the rays enter the lens further from the center,

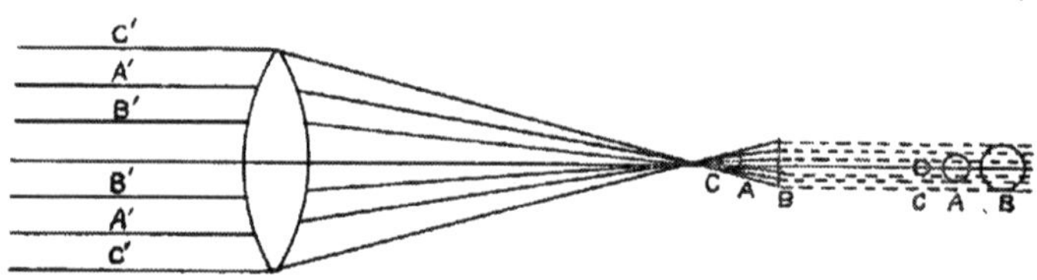

FIG. 68

they are brought to a focus nearer to the lens. Also the image created by the rays is not a point, but a circle as indicated at *A*, *B*, and *C*. The best result from all practical considerations would be if the focal plane were positioned at the point *C*.

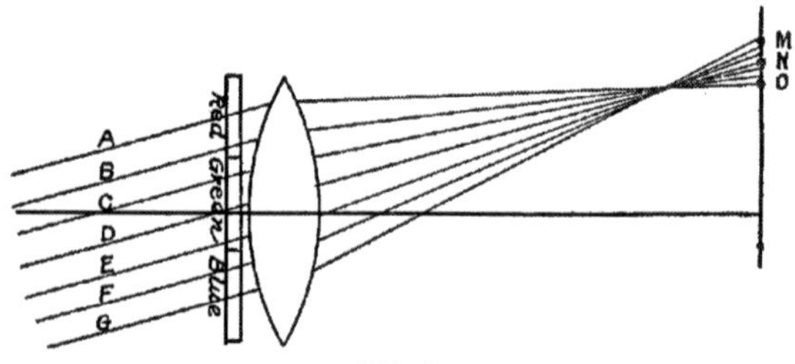

FIG. 69

In lenticular processes, this condition makes itself felt in this manner (Fig. 69). The rays *A* and *B*, will pass through the red filter area of the aperture. These being marginal rays, they will come to a focus at the point *O*, giving rise to a small dot with a definite area. The rays *C*, *D*, and *E* go through the central zone of the lens, where the green filter is positioned, and these rays will produce an image that does not coincide with *O*, but lies beside it at *N*. A similar story is true for the blue rays. Lenses are usually corrected to make the total area of the three images smaller than *f*: 2000, which is just beyond eye resolution at normal viewing distance. A 10-inch lens would have a circle of confusion of approximately 1/200 inch. A 2-inch lens should have a resolution of 1/1000 inch, but the best of our 50 mm lenses have a circle of confusion that is distinctly larger, approximately 1/500 inch. If a film be used with more than 500 lenticules to the inch, and if a 2-inch lens is used, it may well be that the red cones will come to a focus on one lenticule, the green upon a second, and the blue upon a third. In that event, the three densities will not lie adjacent to each other, and will not be projected upon a common point. Color falsification results. It is true, of course, that the densities will not be far apart, but they will interfere with each other, for the direction of the blue ray that strikes a lenticule adjacent to the one for which it was intended, may coincide with the red or green rays that strike that lenticule. The density that results will be due to both colors, hence impure

The fact that the circle of confusion of a lens is so large when the focal length is increased, is the reason why no success whatsoever was ever attained with the lenticular process with film sizes greater than 35 mm. Even here the lenses were just barely usable, since the best 50 mm lenses gave images whose units of definition were only 1/500 inch. This could be much improved by working at a low aperture, but if three filters had to be positioned in the lens aperture, there was a minimum of effective diameter that could be used. Also the loss of light intensity occasioned by the use of not too efficient filters and by a three-way split of the beam, made it imperative that as large an opening as possible be utilized.

This use of a very large opening makes itself felt in one other manner. It is well known that the depth of field is severely restricted when the lens is open wide. Hence the foreground is very sharp, but the background is quite diffuse, coming to a focus at an appreciable distance in front of the foreground. Thus the beam *A*, which originates in the foreground, comes to a focus at *M* in the image plane; but the beam *B* coming from the background, is focused well in front of the plane of *M*, at the point *N* (Fig. 70). By the time it has reached the focal plane, the rays have spread on into a cone *N BGR*, where *B*, *G*, and *R* represent the blue, green, and red sections respectively This cone may cover an area on the film which includes more than one lenticule, and therefore color distortion and degradation will take place. If to this is added background motion, then fringing is bound to occur, since the three colors will become imaged at non-adjacent portions of the lenticular film, and will therefore not re-combine upon projection

These are not the only optical difficulties that make lenticular processes difficult to handle, but they are typical of the others. It would take us too far afield to discuss all of them, and it would do very little good, since the problem of aberrations has now been known and discussed for almost fifty years without solution. Lenses have been tremendously improved by making corrections to minimize the effects of aberrations, but all efforts to completely remove them have so far been futile. Until that time, or at least until the diffusion caused by the aberrations in a lens operating at full aperture (*f*: 1.9), becomes considerably less than 1/500 of an inch, and until lenses can be made with a depth of focus at *f*: 1.9 equal to that at *f*: 32, lenticular processes will not be wholly satisfactory.

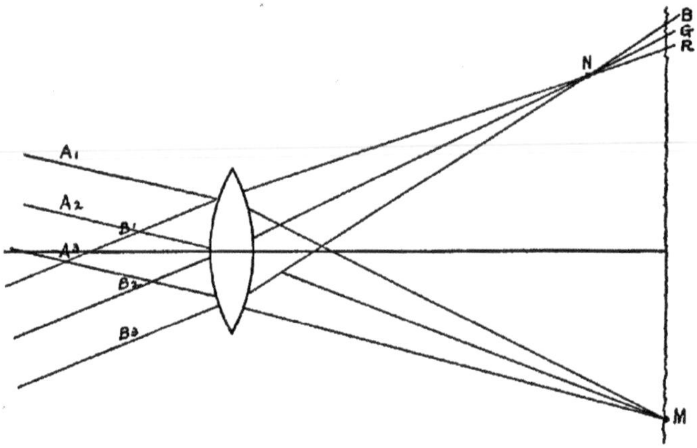

FIG. 70

These difficulties arise only when lenticular film is used for the original exposure. Up to the advent of the monopacks, this appeared to be the desirable technique, for the inconveniences of one-shot cameras, their bulk, delicacy, inefficiency, etc., made an integral process very desirable. This condition was rectified to a great extent by the introduction of Kodachrome and similar materials. The best position lenticular film can occupy would seem to be in the making of positive prints for projection purposes, from separations made in some other manner. It is possible to make separations of high quality from Kodachromes if a masking technique is used. These can be printed upon lenticular film, through lenses that are exactly equivalent to the projection lenses. This proposal has not received a very favorable reception, although the idea has been suggested many times. It will be discussed more fully in Chapter 18.

CHAPTER 17

LENTICULAR DISCLOSURES

THE patents dealing with lenticular processes can be classified into a number of sections, thus:

1. The Preparation of the Film Base.
2. The Properties of the Film.
3. The Lenses for the Taking System.
4. The Diaphragm and the Filters.
5. Projection Systems.
6. Duplicates by Projection Printing.
7. Duplicates by Contact Printing.
8. Separations from Lenticular Film
9. Printing Separations upon Lenticular Film.
10. Other Uses of Lenticular Film.

Of these, sections 1 to 4 deal with the raw material and auxiliary apparatus. These patents cover approximately one-third of the total number. The remaining sections, 5 to 10 inclusive, deal with the uses to which the film could be put. More than 65 per cent of the patents are distributed in these groups. Fully one-third of these deal with problems that arise in the duplication of the lenticular positive, by projection printing. Some idea of the popularity and esteem which this process had can be obtained when it is realized that in the ten years from 1928 to 1938, more than 250 patents dealing with lenticular processes, were issued in England. Because patents are issued later in the United States than in most other countries, not nearly that many were issued here. Evidently the sharp decline in interest in this method, coincident with the development of Kodachrome, Ansco Color, and color-coupling in general, resulted in the lapsing of many patent applications.

Although R. Berthon was the first to disclose the possibility of color reproduction by use of lenticular film, he did not disclose how he would prepare such a material. For this, we are indebted to A. Keller-Dorian, another Frenchman, who saw the tremendous possibilities of lenticular film, and who thereafter devoted most of his attention to its preparation and improvement. He proposed to pass celluloid sheets between two rollers (Eng. P 24698/14; Fr. P. 466781; U.S.P. 1214552). One of them was smooth, the other was engraved so that one side of the celluloid became embossed. The embossing could be in the form of hexagonal pyramids (Eng. P. 7540/15, 207836 and 207837; Fr. P. 472419) or hemispheres The interstices between elements were to be filled in with black (Fr. P. 516050), a procedure that could be accomplished photographically by the use of a special diaphragm (Fr. P. 547529, and 547530, Eng P. 180656).

The machine for embossing the film surface was the subject matter of many patents. J Audibert (U.S P 1625586) used highly polished rollers. A. Oswald (U.S.P. 1855198, Eng P. 395200) arranged to regulate the tension and temperature at those sections of the rollers that were in contact with the film. The same company, working under the Keller-Dorian original disclosures, disclosed other types of machines to accomplish this purpose (Eng. P. 298242, 298951, and 389830).

The Eastman Kodak Company was also interested P R. Ord, of its staff, proposed to make a model embossing roller, by winding a wire upon a temporary core, (U.S.P 1757543) This was plated, the core and wire were then removed, and the hollow left by the removal was filled in. H. E Hastings (U.S.P. 1813669; Eng. P 330151) proposed to make an embossing tool out of extra-hard drawn phosphor bronze. This was polished, then grooved with a series of closely spaced serrations. The grooves were polished, and finally chromium plated O. Wittel, also proposed to use wires (U.S.P. 1880632; Eng. P. 329214) But instead of using them as a model upon which to electroplate a shell, he used them as a tool to cut a spaced series of grooves into a metal cylinder that was to be used as the embossing roller.

Another method for cutting grooves in an embossing cylinder, was disclosed by P Brosse (U.S.P. 1703026; Eng. P. 265970). He used a diamond cutting tool, perfectly shaped, to cut through a gold or silver plating on a roller. The Agfa Ansco Corp. and the I.G., would also use a wire coiled around a cylinder as the cutting tool (U.S P. 1879237, Eng. P 341948, 375225). Or a cast from this could be used. In another disclosure, they proposed to use dichromated gelatin reliefs in the exact shape of the lenticules, with which to emboss the celluloid sheet (Eng P. 433875)

The Siemens and Halske Company, of Germany, was a prolific patentee in all phases of the lenticular processes. The preparation of an embossing machine was disclosed in a series of patents (U.S.P 1945586, 1945935, 1992279, and 1994054). They also were inclined to use wire with which to cut grooves in the embossing cylinders. Other types of machines were disclosed by A. Rodde, A. H. Herault, V. Hudeley, and J. Lagrave (U.S.P. 1955658; Eng. P. 406163), C. Roehrich (U.S.P. 2048816), and P. Fournier (Eng. P. 244740).

The shape and size of the lenticules were quite important, and it is no wonder that a number of patents were issued to regulate them. The Keller-Dorian disclosures have already been discussed. Berthon in his original patent did not dwell long upon this phase, but in later patents he disclosed the use of cylindrical lenticules (Fr. P. 402507) or prismatic surfaces (Fr P. 401342). He discussed the problem of number in a separate disclosure (Eng P 264123, U.S.P. 1707157). Two conditions must be fulfilled First, the lenticule must be optically perfect. Second, the diameter of the lenticule should be an accurate function of the relative aperture of the camera, the thickness of the film base, and the curvature of the lenticules. Thus with an objective operating at an opening of f: 2.5, a film base with a thickness of 120 to 130 μ, and a radius of curvature for the lenticules of 0.04 mm, the diameter of the elements should be 0.04 mm. This is equivalent to 22 to 23 elements per millimeter. But the limit of definition of an image should correspond to 50 elements per millimeter. This is possible only if the effective thickness of the base is reduced. This can be accomplished, without sacrificing any

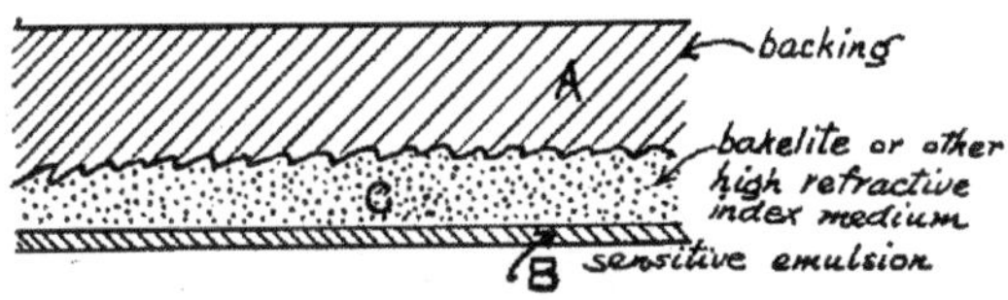

FIG. 71

film strength, by the following procedure. The thin lenticular base is coated on its lenticulated side, with a layer of transparent material whose index of refraction is considerably different from that of the film base. Thus in Fig. 71 a lenticulated celluloid surface C, has an emulsion B, coated on the side opposite the lenticulations, and has a layer of bakelite coated over the lenticulated surface. This is a material with a much higher index of refraction than celluloid. It is also possible to use for an overcoating, a material whose index of refraction is lower than that of celluloid, in which case the curvature of the lenticules would be in the opposite direction, as is illustrated in Fig. 72.

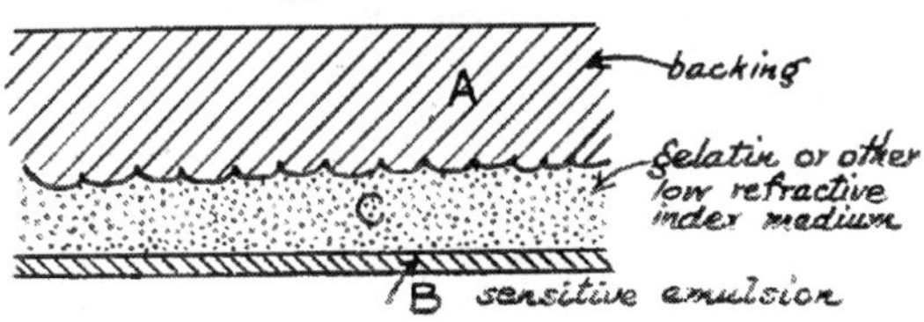

FIG. 72

The Keller-Dorian Company proposed to use differently shaped lenticules (Eng. P. 246829). In other disclosures, it was proposed to emboss more than 25 elements to the millimeter (Eng. P. 207836, and 207837), and to make the width of each lenticule from 10 to 40 per cent greater than the width of the image of the filter bands projected by each element on the sensitive surface (Eng. P. 261363). This would insure that the silver deposits would be distinct, with no overlapping of the images behind different lenticules. Before embossing, the film was partially dried. The exact opposite, treatment of the film base with swelling agents was proposed by G. Heymer (U.S.P. 1996868; Eng. P. 375229).

The use of a sensitive material other than silver halides, has also been proposed. R. Berthon (Eng. P. 274837) suggested diazotype, with gas development. In another disclosure it was proposed to use dichromated gelatin or diazonium salts (Eng. P. 289864). A feature of this last is that the lenticulations are present in the interface between the celluloid and the dichromated gelatin, hence the two outer surfaces are plane and parallel to each other (Fig. 73). A film of this type would have some advantage in projection as it would not be subject to scratching nearly as much as in the case where the lenticules are on one of the outer surfaces.

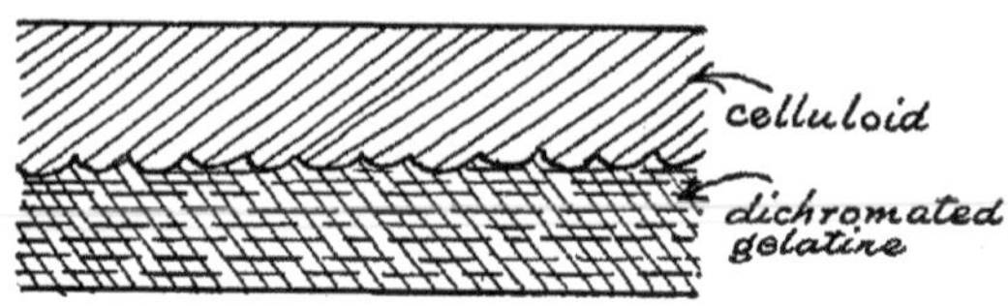

FIG. 73

The lenticular surface in conjunction with a proper lens system is the optical analogue of the screen plate. Therefore the objective and the filter system used with it, become a very important matter. Nor was this subject disregarded by the experimenters. The conditions were outlined generally, in the basic patents of R. Berthon (Eng. P. 10611/09; Ger. P. 223236; U.S.P. 992151; Fr. P. 399762 addition 11286, 413103 addition 12342, 430600 additions 14438 and 14439). Here was disclosed the use of a symmetrical lens

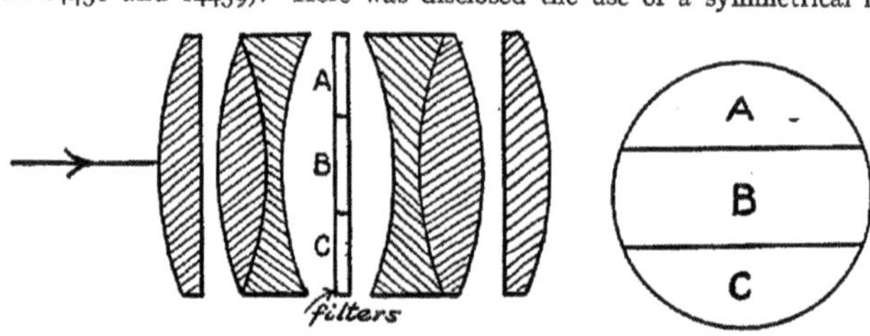

FIG. 74

system in whose center was positioned the set of banded filters. A beam of parallel rays entering the lens in the direction of the arrow (Fig. 74), will be divided into three beams each colored in a different primary, by the banded filter situated in the center of the lens system. The lens will convert each of these colored beams into cones whose apices coincide at the nodal point of admission of each lenticular element. Since, as far as this elementary lens is concerned, the three cones are not parallel, three images in juxtaposition will be formed on the photographic emulsion, on the opposite side of the lenticular surface.

Some of the intricacies involved in lens construction are outlined in the patent disclosures of I. Kitroser, of the Keller-Dorian Company (Eng. P. 348465 and 384009; U.S.P. 1897262). As shown in Figs. 75 and 76, he pro-

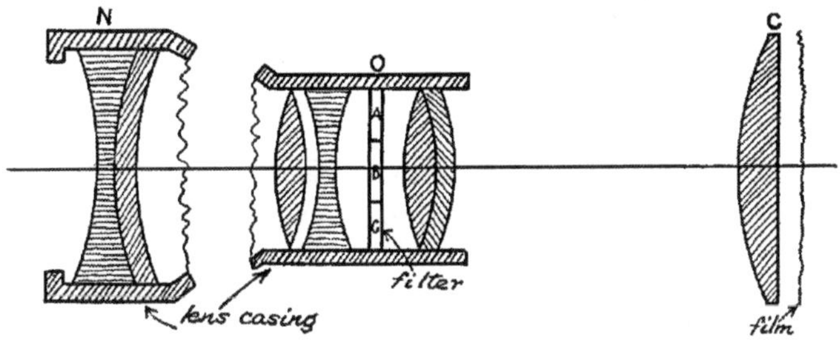

FIG. 75

posed to place a negative lens N, well in front of the objective O. In front of the lenticular film he placed a collimating lens C. The focal length of C is 50 mm, which is the same as that of O. The focal length of the negative lens will be $-f_{11}$, and it is placed a distance e in front of the nodal point of admission

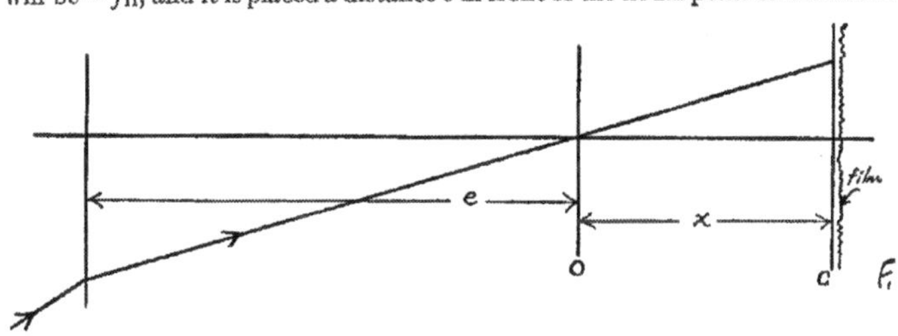

FIG. 76

of the lens O. If the collimating lens C is made of extra heavy glass with a refractive index of 1.8, the curvature of the field (Petzval curvation) introduced by it will be given by

$$D = -\frac{1}{f \times n} = -\frac{1}{50 \times 1.8} = -\frac{1}{90}$$

This means that the field will have a radius of curvature of 90 mm. In the corner of an 18 by 24 mm field that is covered by the objective at an opening of f: 2.5, the added circle of confusion will be approximately 0.5 mm. Now let the distance e be 100 mm, let f_{11} be 200 mm, and assume n equal to 1.50. The combined focal length of the lens N in combination with O, will be:

$$F = \frac{f \times f_{11}}{f_{11} + f - e} = \frac{50 \times (-200)}{-200 + 50 - 100} = \frac{-10000}{-250} = 40 \text{ mm}$$

The objective O, will be at a distance x from the film, such that:

$$\frac{1}{x} = -\frac{1}{e+f_{11}} + \frac{1}{f} = \frac{1}{300} + \frac{1}{50} = \frac{1}{60} \text{ or } x = 60$$

The collimating lens will need to have a focal length of 60 mm. The Petzval curvature of the combination will be the sum of the curvatures of the undivided units, and this will be:

$$P = -\Sigma\left(\frac{1}{f \cdot n}\right) = -\frac{1}{60 \times 1.8} + \frac{1}{200 \times 1.5} = \frac{1}{168.7}$$

or the radius of curvature will be 168.7 mm. This will give a circle of confusion at the edges of an 18 × 24 mm field that is equal to 0.25 mm.

The effect of placing a negative lens well in front of the objective is therefore quite evident. Ordinarily, a lens with a focal length of 50 mm will be situated so that 50 mm separate the film and the nodal point of emission of the lens. By placing a negative lens with a focal length four times that of the objective, a distance equal to half of its own focal length in front of the objective, the focal length of the combination becomes decreased to 40 mm. At the same time the film is to be placed a distance of 60 mm behind the nodal point of emission of the objective. This is a fact well worth remembering. Technicolor, who uses a solid glass prism to split the light beam with two sub-beams, made use of this property to eke out some free space between film and prism.

One other effect of such a system is worth noting, and that is the flattening effect it has upon the Petzval curvation. This, it must be remembered, arises from the fact that the oblique rays come to a focus somewhat in front of the rear focal plane. Thus in Fig. 77, the rays A which are parallel to the optical

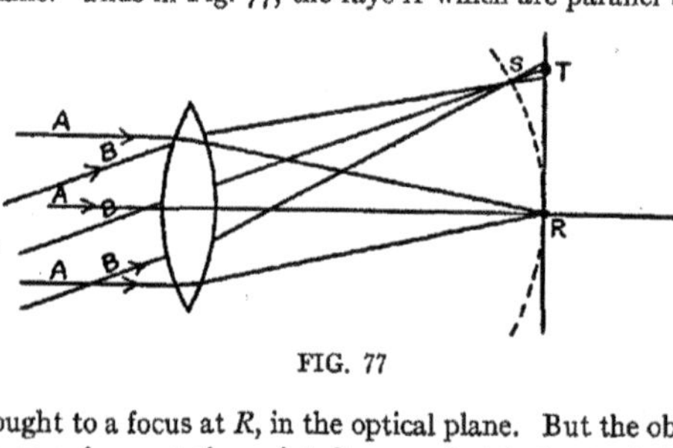

FIG. 77

axis, are brought to a focus at R, in the optical plane. But the oblique rays B, are brought to a focus at the point S, somewhat in front of the plane RT. By the time the rays reach the focal plane they are spread out, and instead of being a point, the image becomes a circle. If a line were drawn through all the points S, which represent the true foci of the light beams entering the lens, an arc would be formed. The radius of this arc is the Petzval curvature. It is determined by the focal length and the index of refraction of the lens, and is independent of all other constants. The greater the value of this radius of curvature, the flatter the image plane, and the smaller the circle of confusion for the uncorrected lens system. By use of a negative lens, this has been reduced from a value of 0.50 mm to 0.25.

It is a simple matter to determine what the circle of confusion would be in terms of the Petzval curvature. Let us take the case discussed above (Fig. 78),

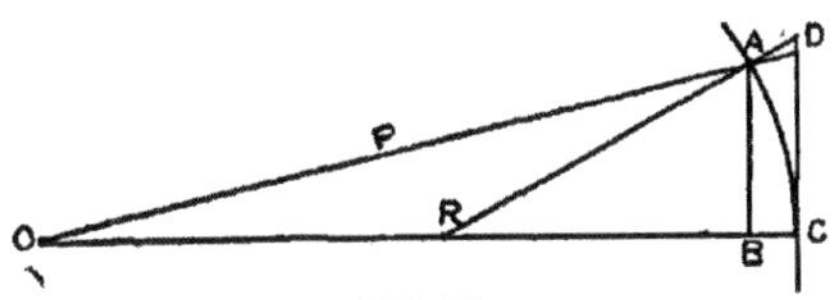

FIG. 78

where the Petzval curvature was equal to 90 mm. Then the distance $OA = OC$ is 90 mm. Let the point R be the optical center of the lens system so that $RC = 50$ mm. Since the point A is in one corner of the frame, which is 18 by 24 millimeters in size, the distance AB will be one-half of the diagonal, or 15 millimeters. The angle at D is then one whose sine is equal to 15/90 or 0.1667. Therefore the cosine would be equal to 0.986. The distance OB will be given by 90×0.986 or 88.74. Hence the distance BC will be equal to 1.26 millimeters.

Consider now the case of a beam of light A (Fig. 79), entering a lens system L, operating at an aperture of f:2.5, and giving rise to a Petzval curvature

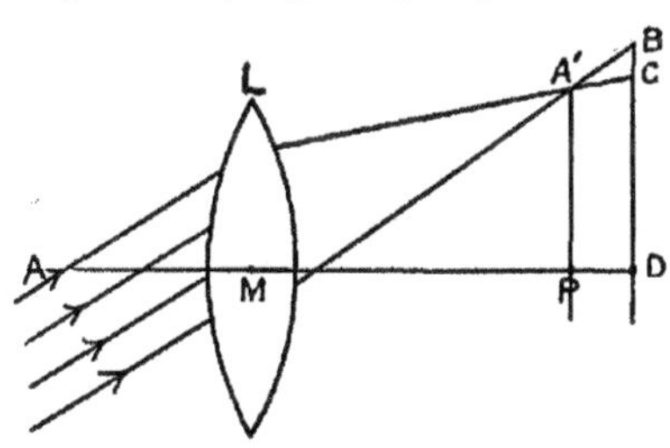

FIG. 79

at the point A equal to 90 mm. Then the distance PD will be 1.26 mm. In so far as the image BC of the rays A is concerned, the point A' will act as a pinhole camera, and will yield an image in the plane through D, of the aperture of the lens L. Therefore the size of the diameter BC of the circle of confusion, will be related to the aperture of lens L as the focal length of the lens A' is related to the focal length of the lens L. The focal length of the lens A' is 1.26 mm and of L it is 50 mm, so that the size BC is 1.26/50 of the size of the aperture of the objective, and since this is operating at f:2.5, it will have an aperture that is 20 mm in diameter. Hence the circle of confusion will have a dimension of

$$\frac{20 \times 1.26}{50} \left(= \frac{25.2}{50} \right) \text{ or } 0.504 \text{ millimeter}$$

The introduction of the collimating lens C, into the lenticular system (Figs. 75 and 76), caused the formation of a disc of confusion equal to 0.5 mm. But placing a negative lens well in front of the objective cut this down to half, to a value of 0.25 mm. This value for the size of the image dot gives some realization of the difficulties encountered with lenticular processes There are approximately 600 lenticules to the square mm, hence in an area 0.25 mm in diameter there will be approximately 30 lenticules. But for really accurate results, the image must fall on only one lenticule. That is why out-of-focus and marginal images are very poorly portrayed in lenticular systems.

The best lenses used in miniature cameras have a disc of confusion equal to 1/500 inch, or 0.05 mm. Lenses with longer focal lengths than two inches will operate with a disc of confusion that is more nearly 1/200 inch. Lenses of longer focal length operate at a disc equal to 1/200 inch. Since the size of a lenticule is approximately 0 04 mm or 0.0016 inch, it is seen that even the best of our lenses will give an image that is much coarser than the individual lenticule. The use of longer focal length lenses becomes highly undesirable in lenticular processes because the image of a single beam will encompass many more than one lenticule.

Other lens systems were disclosed by G Grosset, V. Hudeley, and J. Lagrave (U.S.P. 2003881; Eng. P. 411322), J. G. Capstaff (U.S.P. 2091699) and C. Nordmann (Eng. P. 411024, 424906, and 425058). The Capstaff and the last of the Nordmann patents are interesting in that they disclose the use of a light splitter behind the lens system. This splits the light into three sub-beams that are parallel to each other, and which first pass through a set of filters, then through another lens which brings all three to a common focus. This is illustrated in Fig. 80. The light beam R enters the objective O, where it is split into three parallel beams A, B, and C, by the light-splitting prism P. These go through the filters F, each sub-beam going through a differently colored section. From here the three parallel beams go to the lens L. Since this sees the three as parallel rays, it brings them to a point focus at S, the plane containing the lenticular film. The advantage which this procedure has over the normal one is that each sub-beam contains the rays from the entire aperture of the taking objective, hence can be modulated by means of an iris diaphragm, to regulate the light intensities. The two lenses must be carefully adjusted, however, to allow critical focusing for objects in front of infinity.

The original Berthon patent utilized a circular diaphragm, with the three filters completely filling the aperture. This was placed in the center of a symmetrical lens system (Fig. 74). Such a system created a problem of varying the lens opening in such a manner that the intensities of the three cones leaving the lens system became affected in a like manner. Obviously an iris

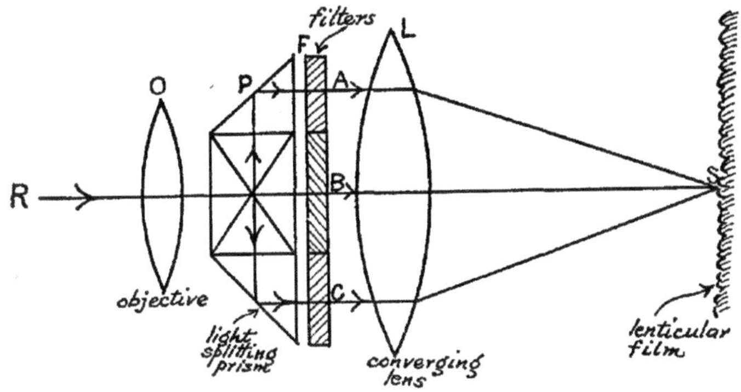

FIG. 80

diaphragm, operating by changing the effective diameter of the lens aperture, would affect the two outer zones much more than the central one, hence some other scheme must be adopted. This is strictly a problem in mechanical design. The most popular solution, patented by almost every worker dealing with this problem, was to make a rectangular diaphragm. This and other schemes are disclosed in the series of patents noted below:

U.S. Patent	
1687055	J. G. Capstaff, to Eastman Kodak Company
1688370	O. Wittel, to Eastman Kodak Company
1688441	D. H. Stewart, to Eastman Kodak Company
1689258	M. W. Seymour, to Eastman Kodak Company
1708371	M. W. Seymour, to Eastman Kodak Company
1754282	F. H. Owens, not assigned
1762143	J. G. Capstaff, to Eastman Kodak Company
1762938	D. H. Stewart, to Eastman Kodak Company
1769041	M. W. Seymour, to Eastman Kodak Company
1873758	A. J. Ginsberg, not assigned
1912700	E. C. Fritts, to Eastman Kodak Company
1944230	C. L. Gregory, Kislyn Corporation
1949414	C. L. Gregory, Kislyn Corporation
1989134	F. Fischer, Siemens and Halske
1989748	H. Frieser, Siemens and Halske
2029614	F. Fischer, F. Strecker, H. Neugebauer; Siemens & Halske
2041465	N. Gehrke & G. Strohmenger, to I.G.

English	
287488	Keller-Dorian Co.
295995	Kodak Ltd.
331971	Keller-Dorian Co
340881	Kodak Ltd.
350481	I G.
356977	Kodak Ltd.
366175	I G.
368970	I G.
373861	Kodak Ltd.
387159	I G.
401963	I G.
401982	I.G
406187	I G.
406304	E Leitz
440582	Opticolor
441713	Opticolor
454357	Opticolor
459634	Opticolor
492850	Opticolor

The use of gelatin filters was open to some objections, in that fading may occur. I. Kitroser would overcome this by the use of colored glass (Eng. P. 385680; U.S.P. 1878857), ground to the proper thickness to give correct spectral transmission. The three glass thicknesses were evened out by adding uncolored glass to each. In some other patents (Eng. P. 286223 and 303170) it was proposed to use liquid filters in tubes placed with their axes parallel to the lenticulations

Instead of using three bands (red, green, and blue), it was proposed to place a yellow band on one side of the set, and an orange one on the other (Eng. P. 294493). These were to act as compensators for the deficiencies of the three-color system. It is open to grave doubt whether any improvement would result from the use of the added yellow and orange bands. These would first of all divide into five, instead of three, the area covered by each lenticule, and this already requires an emulsion whose resolving power is approximately 1500 lines to the inch. To operate with five bands instead of three will require emulsions whose resolving powers would be approximately 2500 to the inch, and only the slower emulsions would have this resolution. Then again, the densities behind the orange and yellow lines, unless these colors be spectral yellow and spectral orange, would be the same as those behind the red and green, so that color degradation would result In English patent 314995, the same company proposes to use four bands instead of three, with the two outer bands having the same color. The I.G Company proposed to move the filters after each exposure, the distance of one band, but kept the colors in the same cyclic rotation (Eng P. 449762). This meant that the order red, green, blue, red, green, blue, etc. would be maintained, but if the central band were green in the first exposure, it would be red in the second, and blue in the third.

Instead of putting the filters in the optical center of a symmetrical lens, the Keller-Dorian Company proposed to put them well in front of the lens system. (Eng. P. 293047 and 331971). This was also proposed by B. E. Luboshez (Eng. P. 339511) who claimed that by this procedure the image of any one beam will cover more than one lenticule, thus smoothing out the final image.

L. Tissier would do away completely with the banded filters in the lens aperture. Instead, a special lens is placed in front of the lenticular film,

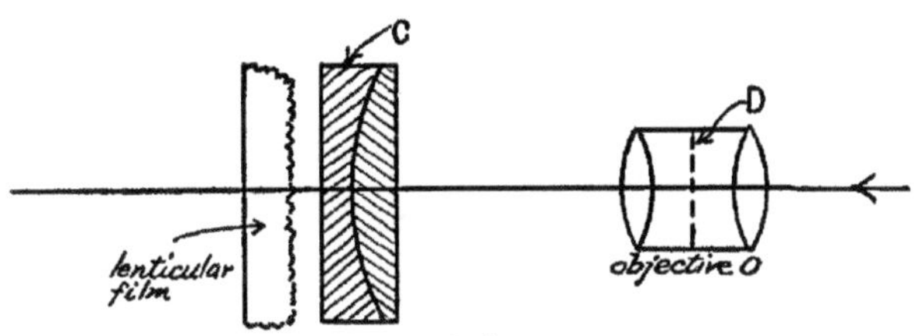

FIG. 81

which causes dispersion to take place (Eng. P. 24276/14). In order to insure that no rays reach this lens in a direction perpendicular to it, the central region of the camera objective is blocked out. Thus (Fig. 81) the light beam entering the camera objective *O*, is broken up into oblique rays by the diaphragm *D* in the lens aperture. The oblique rays then strike lens *C*, which is made of two components with widely differing indices of refraction. In effect, lens *C* is merely a direct-vision prism which disperses the rays incident upon it into their respective spectra. The spectrum of each beam is thus imaged individually by the lenticules. The use of the diaphragm *D* results in a considerable loss of intensity. It can be replaced by a lens situated directly behind the lens *C*, and having its optical axis different from that of *O* and *C*.

Another scheme to replace the filters was outlined by A. Keller-Dorian (Eng. P. 158511; Fr. P. 523336; U.S.P. 1372515). Behind the camera objective *O*, is placed a reflecting prism *P*, and adjacent to the reflecting surface of this prism, is placed a glass plate *R*, slightly separated from the prism at one end. The separation gives rise to interference bands, whose colors take the place of the filters (Fig. 82).

The rigid registry requirements of lenticular processes make the processing of the film by reversal the natural method for its treatment. Where but one copy is desired, as in amateur 16 mm motion pictures, lenticular processes do not create many problems. The curvature of the field, however, creates one such problem, and M. W. Seymour proposed to overcome this by making the gate of both the camera and the projector in the shape of a curve (Eng. P. 318040). The great loss of light occasioned by the use of gelatin or glass filters was minimized by the I.G. by the use of direct-vision prisms in front of the gate of the projection machine (Eng. P. 383795). This could be kept in constant motion (Eng. P. 446282 and 447490). Instead of prisms, it was suggested that gas-discharge lamps be used. Three are needed, and they are so positioned in the projector lamphouse that their images fill completely the areas that would be occupied by the filters (Eng. P. 419701). Projectors use lamps that give out great heat which may affect not only the film, but also the filters. The use of gas-discharge lamps reduces the heat tremendously. The colors so formed can be controlled by physical means to conform to the

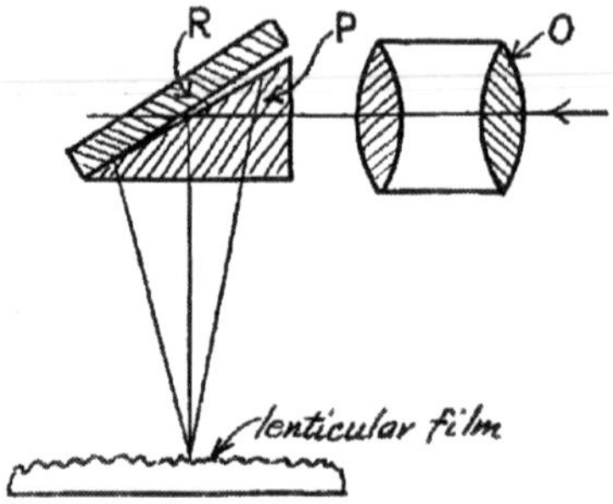

FIG. 82

three primaries, and the intensities would be much greater than those produced by means of a single light source behind gelatin filters. As far as the projection lens is concerned, it would see only three bright colored areas in the position that would ordinarily be occupied by a set of banded filters. These also would be seen by the projection lens as three colored areas, so the one system is identical to the other. The question of heat was solved by Opticolor by inserting a cooling coil in the lens and filter areas (Eng. P. 432401).

The projection of a film positive is usually carried out by means of lenses whose optical characteristics are different from those of the taking lenses. This creates quite a few optical problems. In order to recreate the original scene, the light that passes through any given dot in the film must be directed to the same filter that the original beam passed through in giving rise to this dot image. The exact conditions that must be fulfilled by projection lenses are described by I. Kitroser (Fr. P. 537508). Expressed briefly, these are that the filter, when viewed from any single lenticule, must subtend the same angle in the projection system that it subtended in the taking system. A somewhat more detailed discussion is contained in a disclosure by A. Averan and I. Kitroser (Eng. P. 308320).

For projecting lenticular film, the filter bands are placed in the lens diaphragm. Since the focal length of the projection system is considerably longer than that of the taking, this would mean that the filter bands are positioned a greater distance in front of the gauss points in the projection than in the taking system. It becomes necessary therefore, to find some means of bringing these points up nearer to the filters This can be done by the use of a supplementary lens, placed in front of the projection lens. The new optical system must fulfill the following conditions:

1. The diaphragm must coincide with the outgoing aperture, and must be positioned in front of the objective, at a short distance from the front optical element.
2. The filter band position must be made to coincide with this diaphragm
3. The new system must move the position of the film so that it will be the same optical distance behind the projection diaphragm that it was behind the taking diaphragm.
4. The opening of the diaphragm must correspond to the cross section of the beam projected by each lenticule upon the lens aperture.

In designing such lens systems, use is made of the fundamental law of optics governing the coupling of lenses This is expressed mathematically as follows·

$$f = \frac{f_1 \times f_2}{f_1 + f_2 - e}$$

Here f is the focal length of the coupled system, f_1 and f_2 the focal lengths of the individual lenses, and e the distance from the nodal point of emission of the first lens to the nodal point of admission of the second. From this expression it is seen that the focal length of a combination of lenses becomes equal to that of any one of the components if e is equal to the focal length of that lens. Thus if $e = f_1$, then $f = f_1$. If e is made less than the smaller of the two, then f becomes smaller than either, f_1 or f_2. If e is larger than the greater, then f is greater than either f_1 or f_2 If e is made larger than $f_1 + f_2$, then the character of the lens is changed, a divergent system becomes convergent, and a convergent system becomes divergent. The use of supplementary lenses for this purpose is disclosed by C. W. Frederick (Eng P. 294207, 330810, U.S.P. 1685600 and 1749278); P. Rehlander (U.S P. 1872501); C. Nordmann (Eng. P. 360524), and the I.G. (Eng. P. 342924) Other systems have been described by Pathé Frères (Eng. P. 17330/13), A. Dvornik (Eng P. 421120), and the I G (Eng. P. 436871 and 447834).

Of especial interest are the disclosures of Frederick, in that he reviews the optics of lenticular projection. The object which he set up for himself was to determine the position of the filters in a taking system, so that the images of the filters, as viewed from any point in the plane of the lenticulations, will appear to coincide in size and in shape with the filters in the projection system when viewed similarly. Every lens system has two gauss points, G' and G'' (Fig. 83). A ray AG', proceeding from the object to one of these, will appear to proceed in a parallel direction $G''A'$, from the other. There are two other points of importance. Light, coming from infinity and entering the lens system from either side, will be brought to point foci. These are the front and rear focal points, O and O', of the system. If G' and G'' are the front and rear gauss points respectively, then the distance OG' must necessarily be equal to the distance $O'G''$.

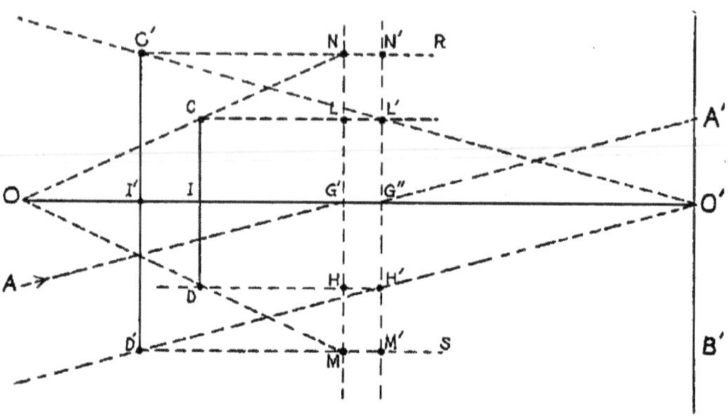

FIG. 83

Suppose that the lens has an aperture equal to $f{:}\,2$, and that HL represents the diameter of this aperture, which is situated at the front nodal point G'. From any point in the rear focal plane $A'O'B'$, this will appear to be positioned at G''. The aperture will subtend an apparent angle $H'O'L'$, with the axis. Stated another way, an object placed at G' will appear to be placed at G'' when viewed from the focal plane where the lenticulations are placed. If the object LH be moved nearer to O, its vertical image will appear in a plane that is determined by the expression:

$$\frac{1}{f} = \frac{1}{f_1} + \frac{1}{f_2}$$

where f is the focal length of the lens system, f_1 the distance of LH from G', (object distance), and f_2 the distance of the image $C'D'$ from G' (the image distance). This expression is the fundamental relationship in lens optics. If the object occupies the plane CID, where IG' is less than half of the focal length of the lens (less than half of OG'), then the virtual image, $C'D'$, will occupy a plane somewhere between O and I. When I moves close to G', its image I' is but a slightly larger distance from G''. As I moves away from G' to the left, its image will move away from G'' at a slightly faster pace, also to the left. When I reaches O, then the object distance becomes zero, and the image distance becomes infinite, so that the image becomes indeterminate. Thus a beam originating at a focal point of a lens system, will project a beam of parallel rays whose focus is at infinity, and vice versa. When I passes to the left of O, it changes its sign (f_1 changes from a positive to a negative number, or vice versa depending upon how the co-ordinate system is chosen). Since the focal length, f, of the lens is always a positive number, this means that the sign of f_2 must change, and instead of giving rise to a virtual image to the left of G'', there will be formed a real image to the right of the point

Although the size and position of an object placed at CID, somewhere between O and G', can be determined from the basic lens equations, it is also possible to do so graphically The rays that proceed from the focal point of the lens system, emerge as parallel rays. We assume that the position CID, and the points O, $O'G'$, and G'' are known. Along a line which represents the optical axis, mark off the points O, O', G', and G''. OG' must be equal to $O'G''$, and this is equal to the focal length of the lens system. Now mark off the line CID, to represent the position of the object whose image is desired. Draw lines through G' and G'' to represent the nodal planes. From O, draw the lines OC and OD As far as the lens is concerned, these are rays which originate at its focal point, so that they will proceed from the lens in the form of parallel rays. Since they originate on the optic axis, the emergent rays will be parallel to the optic axis. The rays intersect the nodal plane of admission (the plane through G') at the points N and M. When viewed from any point in the rear focal plane $A'O'B'$, these points of intersection will appear to be the points N', and M' in the plane through G'' (the nodal plane of emission). Therefore, through N' and M' draw lines parallel to the optic axis, to represent the emergent rays. These are the lines $N'R$ and $M'S$. The images of the points C and D must lie somewhere along these lines.

Another well-known rule of optics is that parallel rays entering a lens system will come to a focus somewhere in the rear focal plane If these rays are parallel to the optic axis, then the point focus coincides with the rear focal point. From C and D, draw lines parallel to the optic axis. These intersect the front nodal plane at L and H. From any point in the rear focal plane, they will appear to be positioned at L' and H', in the nodal plane of emergence. As far as the lens is concerned, the lines CL and DH represent parallel rays, which must come to a focus at the point O', and appear as if they emerged from the points L' and H' Therefore we draw the rays $L'O'$ and $H'O'$ and along these rays must be the images of the points C and D. Extend the lines $O'L'$ and $O'H'$ until they intersect the lines $N'R$ and $M'S$, which also contain the images of C and D. The intersections of these lines, C' and D', are the images of C and D respectively. Therefore, the object CID, placed somewhere between the front nodal point G' and the front focal point D, will appear, when viewed from a point in the rear focal plane, as if it were positioned at $C'I'D'$.

It is not always possible, in designing lens systems, nor is it always desirable, to place the filters in the front nodal plane of the lens system. The best position for them is in a plane that is just in front of the front surface of the lens system, such as the position CID in Fig. 83. In so far as the lenticular elements situated in the rear focal plane $A'O'B'$ are concerned, the filters will appear to occupy the position $C'I'D'$, and they will subtend the angle $C'O'D'$ with the point O' in the rear focal plane. The conditions laid down by Kitroser are that the image $C'I'D'$ must subtend the same angle with each lenticule during projection that was subtended during the original taking. Then, and only then, will the densities formed by the red portion of the beam become directed through the red section of the filter. If the same lens system is used for viewing as for taking, no difficulties arise, but if different lens systems are used, then complications begin to make themselves felt

It has been demonstrated that the apparent size and position of an object can be varied at will, merely by placing it somewhere between the points O and G in the lens system. Let us suppose that we are forced to use a projection system, such as was described in Fig. 83, and that the filters occupy the position CID. Let us suppose that we are likewise forced to use a taking system whose focal length is one-half that of the projection system, i.e., $og' = o'g'' = \frac{1}{2} O'G''$. The effective apertures of the two lenses are the same, $f{:}2$ so that

$$HL/O'G'' = \frac{hl}{o'g''} \text{ and } hl = \tfrac{1}{2}\, o'g'',\ HL = \tfrac{1}{2}\, O'G''.$$

The question is where to place the filters in the taking system so that the images of the filters will subtend the same angle in both cases, with corresponding points in the rear focal planes.

On Figs 83 and 84 the following data are known, the points o, o', g' and g'' and the angle $C'O'D'$. If we can position the filters c, i, d, in the taking system, in such a manner that the image will appear at $c'i'd'$, where $i'o' = I'O'$, and $c'd' = C'D'$, then the problem is solved. To this end draw the line oo' to represent the optic axis. Along this line, mark off the known points g' and g'', and then mark off the point i' so that $i'o' = I'O'$. At the point i', draw a line perpendicular to the optic axis, and on this line mark off the points c' and d' so that $c'i'd'$ becomes equal to $C'I'D'$. We desire now to find the position and size of an object, to be placed somewhere between g' and o', so that its apparent image, when viewed from the point o', will coincide with $c'i'd'$. From c' and d' draw lines parallel to the optic axis. These intersect the frontal plane at the points n and m. From these points draw the lines on, and om. The capital letters refer to the projection system (Fig. 83), while the lower case letters refer to the taking system (Fig. 84).

Somewhere along these lines will lie our object points. From c' and d' draw the lines $c'o'$ and $d'o'$. These will intersect the rear nodal plane at the points l' and h'. From these points draw lines parallel to the optic axis. These will intersect the lines on and om at c and d, which are the desired points. If

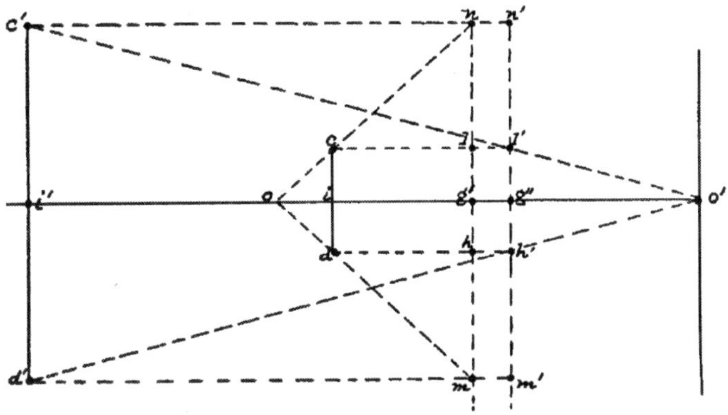

FIG. 84

the filters are placed in the position occupied by the object *cid*, then from any point in the rear focal plane, such as from the point o', they will appear to be positioned at $c'i'd'$, and to subtend an angle $c'o'd'$ with the lenticule at o'. This is identical to the view had by the lenticule at O, in the projection system. Hence the two systems are exactly equivalent. In his patents (cf. above) Dr. Frederick gives the complete data for the construction of lenses complying with these conditions.

CHAPTER 18

DUPLICATION OF LENTICULAR FILM

THE image in lenticular processes consists of a honeycombed series of densities. In each unit there lie three juxtaposed elements, each of which constitutes the density of a given primary color. Each unit lies adjacent to and touches the neighboring units It is an easy matter to duplicate the values for the densities at each point in the image space, but that is hardly sufficient for the purposes of forming duplicates of lenticular images upon lenticular film. It is necessary to duplicate the exact registry of the individual densities with respect to the lenticules, so that they will subtend the same angle with the nodal points of admission of each lenticular lens in both master and copy. This makes the duplication of the film a rather complicated optical problem. Unless this registry is carefully maintained, poor color separation results. When this problem has been overcome, the technician is confronted by the problem of moiré (arising when the pattern of the master film is placed on top of the pattern of the copy film), and the problem of wedging, which is caused by the fact that the marginal lenticules behave differently from the axial ones

One solution to these difficulties is to project the images upon a diffusing screen, to fuse the elements together, then photograph the colored image that has been projected on the screen. This scheme is utilized by A S. Howell (U.S.P. 1853683) and by H. E. Ives (U.S P 1985730 and 1985731). To remove all traces of moiré, the lenticulations on the master film are made to run at right angles to those on the copying material. This solution, while overcoming the flaw mentioned above, introduces a few new ones Only a small fraction of the light projected upon the screen is picked up by the copying system, so that exposures are long. Also the diffusion that is introduced by the screen is sufficient to make the definition of the copied image distinctly inferior.

The Eastman Kodak Company, very much interested in lenticular processes since they introduced it to the 16 mm field, offered several solutions to the problem of duplication Dr. M. W. Seymour (U.S.P. 1708370 and 1912661; Eng. P. 382974) proposed to use curved gates both in the camera and in the printer The curvature was predetermined so that when the film was supported therein, the microscopic elements would project the images behind each lenticule at identically the same areas in the copying system as in the taking.

Another person to take advantage of the fact that the lenticules are miniature lenses, was P. Brosse (U.S.P. 1878670; Eng. P. 303356). This scheme is illustrated in Fig. 85. The master film is illuminated by means of diffuse light from a lamphouse *B*, containing lamps L_1, and L_2, which illuminate a white reflecting curved surface *S*. The lenticular lens elements project this

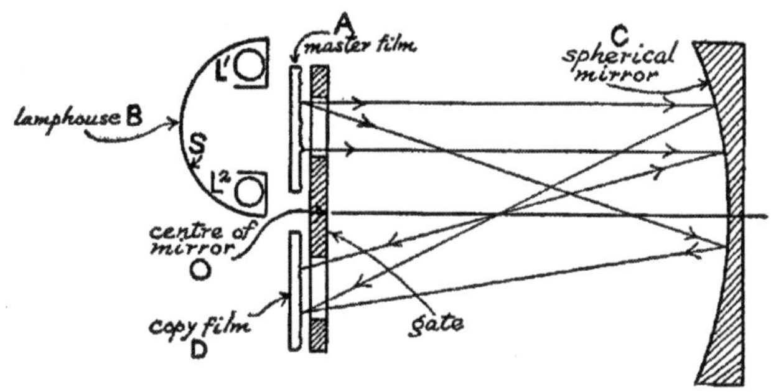

FIG. 85

light to a spherical mirror *C*, whose optical center is at *O*. This is in the plane containing the two lenticular films *A* and *D* (master and copy), and is symmetrical with respect to the exposed sections on each. After reflection from the mirrored surface of *C*, the rays coming from any point on *A* will recombine at the conjugate point on *D*. A special gate in front of films *A* and *D* prevents extraneous light from interfering.

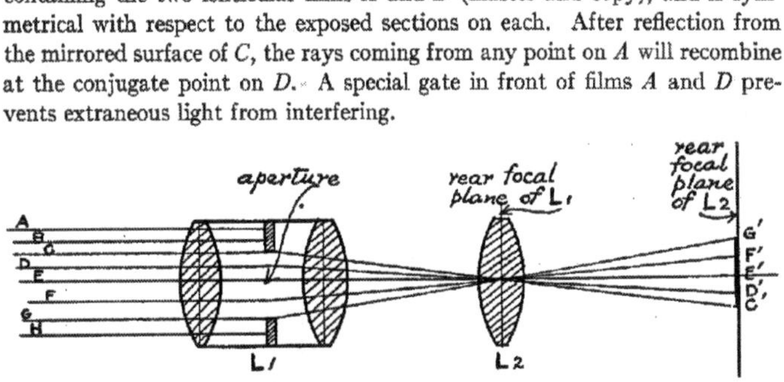

FIG. 86

The optical methods to solve the problem of duplication all make use of a few simple principles. One of these is that if a lens L_2, be placed so that its nodal plane of admission coincides with the rear focal plane of another lens L_1, then the lens L_2 will project upon its own rear focal plane the image of the aperture of the first lens system. Thus the rays *A*, *B*, *C*, etc. (Fig. 86), all of which arise from the same point on the original subject, enter the lens system in the form of a beam. Of these rays, *A*, *B* and *H* are intercepted by the diaphragm of the lens L_1, the remaining rays proceeding through to the rear focal plane, where they converge to a point. If a lens L_2 is placed at this point, the rays will be projected upon the rear focal plane of L_2, in the exact image of the diaphragm of L_1. This principle is, of course, the basic one which is utilized in the taking part of the process, but the lenses that are placed in the rear focal plane of the camera objective are the miniature lenses formed by the lenticulations.

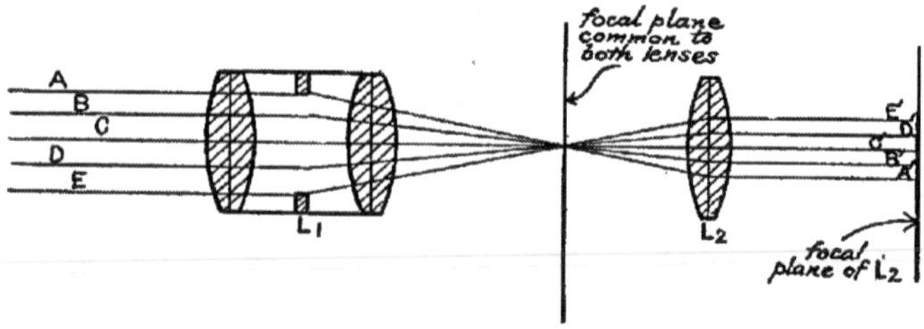

FIG. 87

Instead of placing lens system L_2 so that its nodal plane of admission coincides with the rear focal plane of L_1, it is possible to position it so that its front focal plane coincides with the rear focal plane of L_1. The results, however, are the same, for upon the rear focal plane of the second system will be projected the image of the aperture of the first system. This is made evident in Fig. 87. The rays A, B, C, etc., entering lens L_1 in the form of a beam, are brought to a point focus in the focal plane of L_1. But this is also the front focal plane of L_2, and as far as this lens is concerned, the rays originate at a point in its front focal plane. Therefore they are projected by the lens L_2 as a beam of parallel rays in the exact image of the aperture of the lens L_1, which determined their shape.

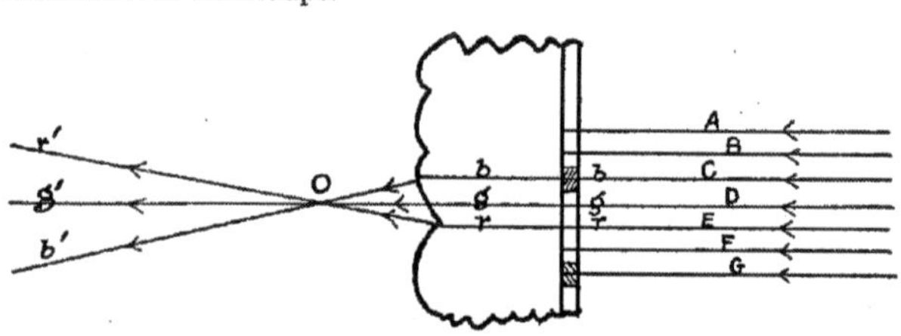

FIG. 88

When a lenticular film is illuminated from behind, depending upon the nature of the beam, the light that passes through any one lenticule will be either divergent or convergent. If the illuminating light is collimated, so that all the rays are parallel, then the beam is convergent, the point of convergence being in the front focal plane of the lenticular lens (Fig. 88). The rays of collimated light A, B, C, etc., strike the lenticular film at right angles. Therefore they are not deviated until they reach the curved interface between lenticular surface and air. They are converged to a point O, which lies in the front focal plane of the lenticular element immediately facing the image points r, g, and b. If the point O lies in the rear focal plane of another lens system, the rays will pass beyond O in the form of a divergent beam, and form an image in the nodal plane of admission (lens aperture) of the new lens system, of the images r, g, and b. The rays will emerge from the lens in the form of a beam whose cross section, taken normally to the axis, will be an accurate image of the densities r, g, and b.

It is also possible to use as a source of illumination, a cone of light whose apex is in the nodal point of the lenticular lens (Fig. 89). In this case the

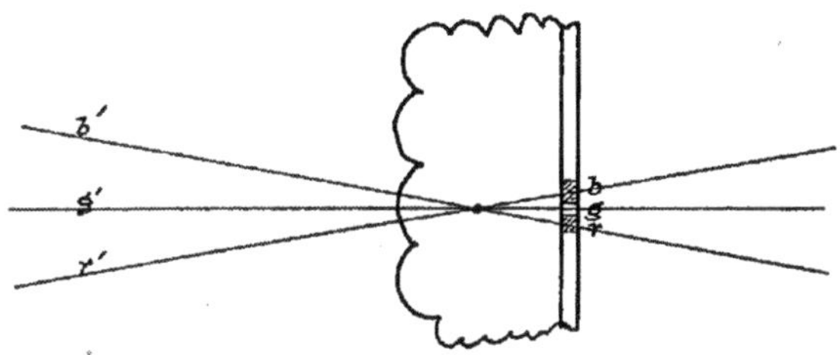

FIG. 89

light emerges from the system as a divergent beam. This principle is utilized by O. E. Miller of the Eastman Kodak Company, for the projection printing of lenticular film (U.S.P. 2095826). The image of the light source S, is projected by the lens system L_1, upon the master lenticular film which is placed behind a slit that is just sufficient to allow a single lenticule to be illuminated at any one time (Fig. 90). This is the lenticule A, situated on the optical axis

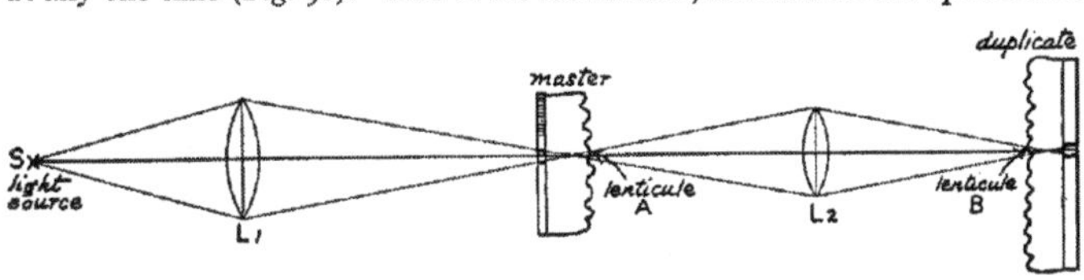

FIG. 90

of the entire system. The nodal plane of lens A lies in the focal plane of lens L_2, therefore, in accordance with the principle enunciated above, this lens will project in its own rear focal plane the image of the aperture of the lens A. But this image will correspond identically to the three densities that lie in the emulsion layer directly behind lens A. Thus at B there will be produced the duplicate of what lies in the rear focal plane of A. Since there will be an inversion of the image at *B*, the copy film could travel in the opposite direction from the master. This will at the same time provide a slight relative omtion between the two which will destroy any moiré pattern that may be inclined to be formed.

A somewhat more complicated system is described by G. Chretien (Eng. P. 286684). The objective has three separate positive optical systems, *O*, *C*,

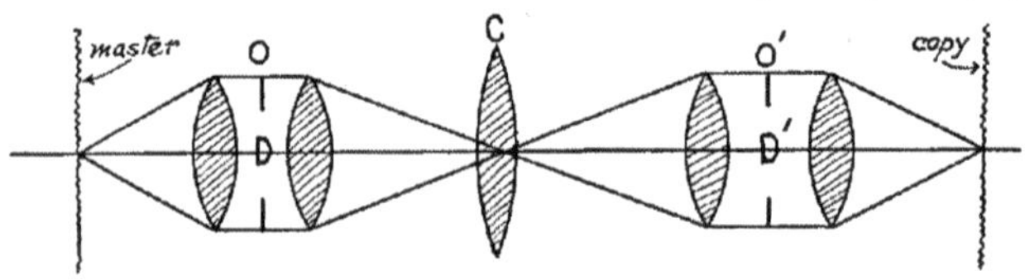

FIG. 91

and *O'*, so arranged that the diaphragm *D* of the system *O*, has for its image (beyond the intermediate system *C*), the anterior image *D'* of the lens system *O'*. Thus *D* and *D'* are conjugate (Fig. 91). Here again it is seen that *C*, being in the focal planes of system *O* and *O'*, will project an image of the diaphragm of *O* in the nodal plane of admission of the system *O'*. This of course, coincides with the position *D'*, the diaphragm of the lens system *O'*. If the diaphragm *D* is illuminated by a cone of light originating from a single horizontal or vertical lenticule, then the diaphragm *D'* registers accurately the intensity of the cone of light, and it will accurately image this intensity in its own rear focal plane in which the copy film is situated.

A similar idea is disclosed by the I.G. in a series of patents (U.S.P. 1915418; Eng. P. 356701, 364559, 369262, 399984, and 449954). An objective is used

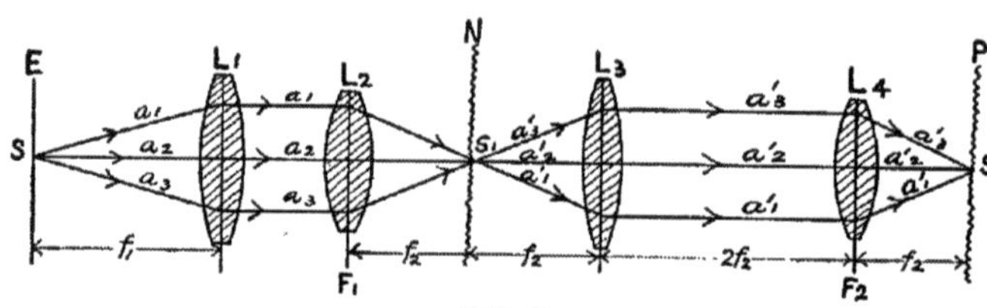

FIG. 92

which is equal in function to the original taking lens. This means that the images of the set of filters, when viewed from the rear focal planes of both systems, will appear to be situated the same distance in front of these planes. One of the schemes is outlined in Fig. 92. A luminous plane *E* is situated in the focal plane of a lens system L_1. Every point on *E* can be considered as a source of light. Consider the cone of rays originating at the point *S*. Since *S* is in the focal plane of L_1, this lens will project the cone originating at S, in the form of a beam of light with parallel rays. Three of the rays are marked a_1, a_2, and a_3. These proceed to a lens system L_2 which is equal in function to the original taking lens. Since the rays a_1, a_2, a_3 enter lens system L_2 in the form of a beam, they will be brought to a point focus in the focal plane of L_2. At this point the master lenticular film is placed

The aperture of the lens system L_2, is therefore illuminated by a whole series of beams each consisting of a pencil of parallel rays, and each making a different angle with the optical axis. These beams originate from the different points on the luminous plane E. Since the lens L_2 is equal in function to the original taking lens, each one of these beams will be brought to a focus on a different lenticular element on the film N, and when viewed from these lenticulations each cone of light will have the same angularity that the corresponding beam had in the original taking system Each beam will also cover, behind each lenticule in N, the same relative area that was covered in the original. The two systems differ in but one important respect, and that is that in the original system the intensities of the beams were determined by the reflection characteristics of the original. In the present case the intensities of the beams are all equal. Hence in the focal plane N, there is projected a uniform sheet of light, every portion of which makes the same angle with the optical axis that the corresponding portion made in the original.

Now place at N, the master positive film. Let us consider the path of the cone of rays originating at the point S. After passage through L_1, these will emerge as a beam of rays that are parallel to each other, and to the optical axis This beam is equivalent to a beam which originated at a point on the original object that lay on the optical axis of the original taking system. Upon passage through that system, one portion of the rays went through the red filter, another through the green, and the rest through the blue. In the copying setup, the equivalent portions are designated by the letters a_1, a_2, and a_3, and for the sake of argument let us assume that the rays a_1, went through the red, the rays a_2 through the green, and the rays a_3 through the blue filter areas. The intensities of the rays after they passed through the filters were different, and depended upon the spectral composition of the beam of light of which they are the components. The three rays gave rise to three different densities behind the lenticule S_1 in the original.

In the copying system, the rays a_1, a_2, and a_3 are reconstructed in every particular except that the spectral compositions and the intensities of the three are identical. The angle that a_1 makes with the optical axis is identical with the angle made by the red rays after passage through the filter in the original taking system. Therefore the rays constituting a_1 will come to a focus in the same relative area behind the lenticule S_1 that the red rays did in the original. The same is true with the rays a_2 and a_3. If the master lenticular film is placed at N, then the rays a_1, a_2, and a_3 will become modulated upon passage through the lenticule S_1 to a degree that corresponds to the original. Therefore the rays a_1', a_2', and a_3', immediately after their passage through

S_1, are no longer identical in intensity, but have intensities that correspond to those of the red, green, and blue portions of the corresponding original beam. When viewed from a point to the right of N, the original scene is reconstructed in so far as light intensities are concerned It becomes necessary merely to rephotograph this scene in order to make duplications. This is the function of the lens system L_3 and L_4, in conjunction with the lenticular film P.

Here again, advantage was taken of several optical principles in order to make the reproduction easier. Ordinarily, if an object A is to be copied one-to-one, it is placed in front of a lens system so that the distance between it and the nodal plane of admission is twice the focal length of the copying lens. At a distance twice the focal length away from the nodal plane of emission, is placed the copy material. But it is extremely difficult to copy accurately silver images that are of the same order of magnitude as the disc of confusion of the lens and the resolving power of the copy material. It is much easier to copy a beam of light making a definite angle with the optical axis. This is the dodge adopted above. Consider the beam of light which is exemplified by the rays a_1, a_2, a_3, at the moment it enters the nodal plane of admission of the lens L_2. If it is desired to photograph the image of this plane on a one-to-one ratio, it becomes necessary to place a lens L_3, where its nodal plane of admission is a distance twice its focal length from F_1, the nodal plane of emission of L_2 This will project an image of the aperture F_1 upon a plane F_2, which is twice the focal length of the lens F_3 away from the nodal plane of the lens L_3 The plane F_2 is the rear focal plane of L_3 in the position occupied by L_3 under the present circumstances The intensity of the ray a_1' as it enters the plane F_2, corresponds to the intensity of that portion of the original beam which passed through the red filter. Hence at F_2 the beam is reconstructed identical in all respects except that of spectral composition, and this plays no role here, since the emulsion on the film P is sensitive only to the blue. If a lens L_4 is placed at F_2, it will project upon a film P, in its own focal plane, the image of the aperture of the lens L_3. If the film at P is a lenticular film, the lenticulation, being in the rear focal plane of the lens L_4, will image the aperture of L_4, thus reconstructing the densities as they are at N. Since the rays at N and P are reversed with respect to each other, the film at P could move opposite in direction to that of N.

A different scheme, but based upon the same principles, is outlined in English patent 295313. In Fig. 93, a condensing lens B registers the image of the light source A, in the nodal plane of admission d of the compound lens D, which is equal in function to the original. The diaphragm d is movable. Placed immediately behind D is a lens E, whose characteristics are such that the focal length of the combination of lenses D and E is one-half that of D alone. Hence if the copy film F be placed in the rear focal plane of D, considered individually, it is a distance twice the focal length of the system D plus E If D is accurately focused on C, then the images at F and C will be identical in size. The size and dimensions of E must be such that no rays through *d* are intercepted by *E*. As the individual rays originating at *A* pass through the film *C*, they become modulated so that the rays reaching *F* have the proper intensities. *F* and *C* being conjugate to each other, the lenticules at *F* will reconstruct the images behind the corresponding lenticules at *C*. Hence duplication is achieved. Abbé's experiments have shown that if *d*

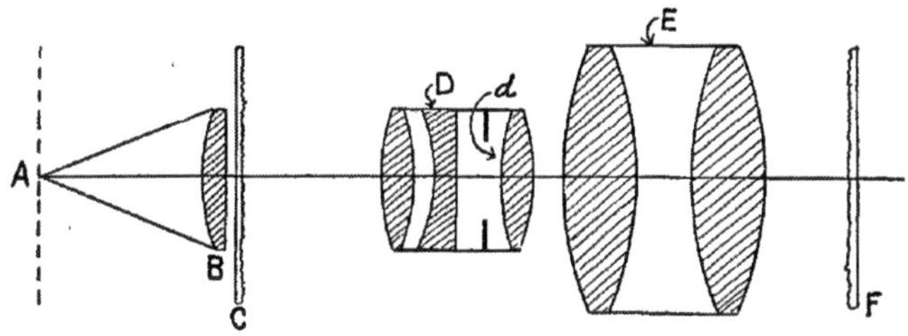

FIG. 93

allows only the central image of the light source to pass through, the image of the network at *C* cannot be formed at *F*. Hence no moiré patterns can arise. This scheme is also suitable for use in duplicating screen plates.

A very popular type of printing objective utilizes a symmetrical lens. This can be formed by coupling two identical lens systems. Because of the complete reversibility of light paths, one lens will completely reverse the other. The aperture of the coupled system would be exactly in the centre. A system

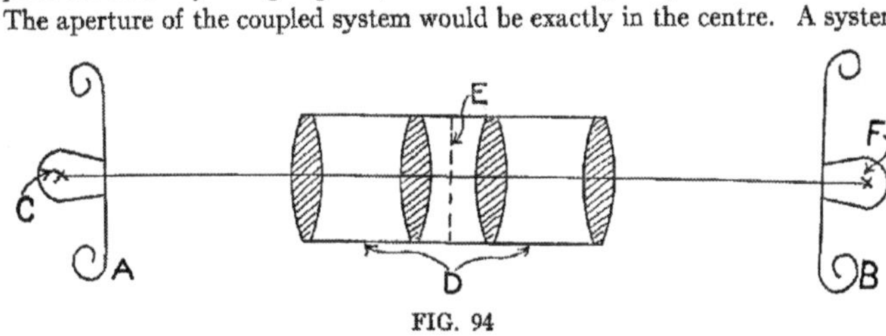

FIG. 94

such as this has been disclosed in English patent 274848, issued to "Société Civil pour l'Étude de la Cinématographie en Couleur." A master lenticular film *A*, is illuminated by means of light *C* (Fig. 94). The front portion of the symmetrical lens system *D* starts to project this image, but the rear portion reverses the procedure and reconstructs the rays at *B*, the copy film. The films *B* and *A* are conjugate to each other, so that the miniature lenses at *B* will reconstruct the apertures of the miniature lenses at *A*. The aperture *E*, of the lens system *D*, corresponds to the position, with respect to the front portion of *D*, that would be occupied by the filters were *D* allowed to project the image in the normal manner. Hence *E* also corresponds to the position of the filters, as far as the rear portion of the system *D* is concerned. The lens *D* is characterized by two properties:

1. The aperture *E*, of the system *D*, must afford passage to a pencil of light rays whose angle must be the same as that of the corresponding beam in the original taking system.
2. None of the rays received by the lens will be intercepted before reaching the copying film, *B*.

F is a lamphouse that fogs the copying film *B*, so that color dilution, due to the blocking of light by the interstices between the lenticular elements at *A*, will be overcome.

Dr. M. W. Seymour, of the Eastman Kodak Company, likewise used a symmetrical lens system (U.S.P. 1976300). In the plane of the common

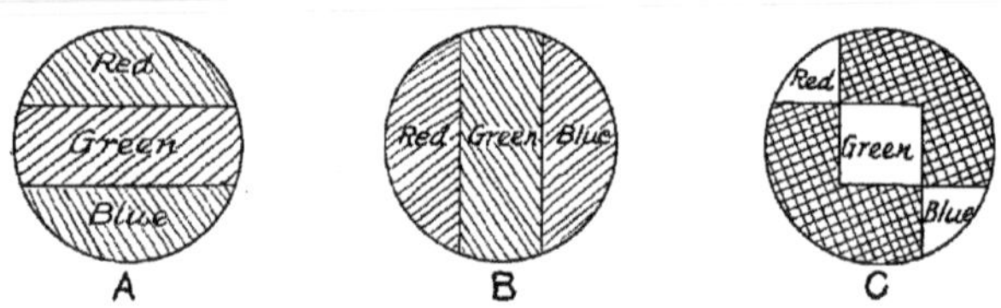

FIG. 95

diaphragm to the two portions of the symmetrical objective, is placed a special diaphragm, thus enabling him to place the lenticulations of the copy at an angle to those of the master. This reduced moiré. In lenticular processes, it is essential that the filter bands be parallel to the lenticulations. In Fig. 95, let *A* be the filter bands parallel to the direction of the lenticules in the master, and *B* the filter bands parallel to the direction of the copy. Then *C* will be the shape of the diaphragm used. In the diagrams *A* and *B*, the shaded portions indicate different colors. But in diagram *C* the shaded areas represent opaque portions, while the clear areas represent transparent portions. J. L. Vidal (Eng. P. 349276); A. Dervieux (Eng. P. 451283); K. Rantsch, of the Siemens and Halske Company (U.S.P. 2009816); the Société française de Cinématographie (Eng. P. 294579); the Keller-Dorian Co. (Eng. P. 284995); and F. E. Tuttle, of the Eastman Kodak Company (U.S.P. 2039691; Eng. P. 411407 and 446752) also disclosed similar ideas.

The Tuttle disclosures deserve some special attention because a principle in optics is disclosed that is used considerably in other schemes. The printing is done in three stages, one color at a time. A different light source is used for each color. These are marked numbers 17, 18, and 19 in Fig. 96. Consider first the case where the printing is done by means of light source 18. This lies on the optical axis of the entire system. In front of the three light sources, is placed a diaphragm shutter (20) which is coupled with another shutter

(21) placed on the same shaft, and which rotates between the two symmetrical elements of the copying objective (16). The plane containing the light sources 17, 18, and 19 lies in the front focal plane of the collimating lens (23), behind which is placed the master lenticular film (10). Immediately behind the film is a lens (24), which directs the rays to the symmetrical copying objective (16). The master film, lying between the two lenses (23 and 24), acts like a diaphragm for the combination, modulating the intensities of the individual rays. The copying objective (16), projects an image of these rays upon the copy film (13), through a compensating lens (25).

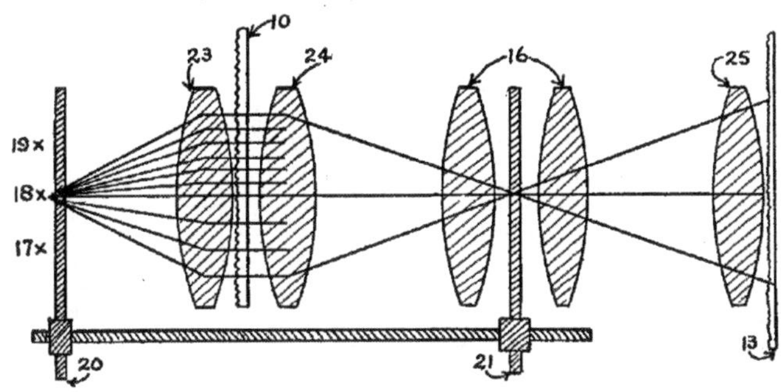

FIG. 96

Since the light source (18) lies on the front focal plane of the lens (23), and on its optical axis, the cone of rays emanating from this point will be converted by the lens (23) into a beam that is parallel to the optical axis. Therefore every lenticular element in 10 will be illuminated by a pencil of rays that are parallel to the axis of the lenticular lens. Each pencil of rays will be brought to a focus on only one image point behind the lenticular element, this being the image of one color density. In a similar manner, the cone of rays starting at 17 or 19 will also give rise to beams with parallel rays, but these make different angles with the optical axis. Therefore these will illuminate the lenticular elements with pencils of rays that make different angles with the optical axes of the miniature lenses, and they will be brought to foci at different points behind the lenticules. The positions of the points 17, 18, and 19 are such that the pencils of rays will assume the same angularity with respect to the optical axis that was originally assumed by the rays after they passed through the red, green, and blue filters in the original. Each pencil will be brought to a focus at a point behind the lenticular element, corresponding to a single color element.

In Fig. 96 only the axes of the pencils passing through each lenticular element have been indicated, hence the reason for the presence of a diaphragm shutter (21), positioned between the elements of the copying objective (16), is not clear. Let us consider the case of the entire pencil of rays, taking into consideration also, the optical properties of the lenticules. This is indicated in Fig. 97. The cone of rays originating at 17 becomes converted into a beam with parallel rays. The lenticules in 10 become illuminated by the parallel rays, hence they will bring the rays to point foci in the image plane of 10. There the pencils become modulated by the image due to a single color element. After passage through this point, the rays diverge again into a broad pencil. The lens (24) directs them into the copying objective. Here they cover much more than the area that would normally correspond to a single

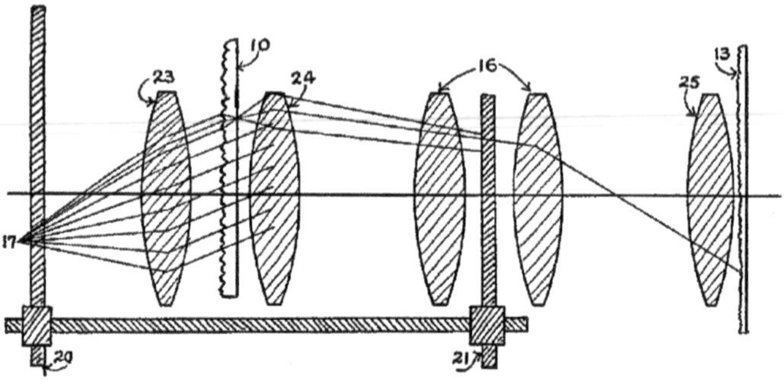

FIG. 97

beam, hence the diaphragm (21), coupled with 20, eliminates all those rays which extend beyond the proper confines. Therefore the lenticulations at 13 become illuminated by cones of light whose axes make the same angles with the axes of the lenticules, as the rays through the red filter made with the lenticulations in the original exposure.

This principle of illuminating the master lenticular film by three different light sources, so arranged that the optical system converts the rays from these sources into three pencils bearing the same angularity to the lenticular axes that the filter areas bore to them in the original taking, is disclosed in a number of patents issued to J. Eggert and G. Heymer (U.S.P. 2013178; Eng. P. 367414 and 399977). Three gas-discharge lamps, or one lamp with three filaments, are used, so positioned in front of a lens system that their images appear to occupy the positions occupied by the filters during the original exposures.

The pencils of rays after passing through a plane that lies in the focus of a lens system, will diverge again into a broad beam. Wherever complicated optical schemes are used, such as the ones disclosed by Dr. Tuttle, the breadth of the beams may be such that overlapping of images occurs. It is to be recalled that he introduced a special diaphragm to confine the limits of these beams. Dr. Tuttle was preceded in this by P. Fournier (Eng. P. 236204) who utilized only that portion of each beam that corresponded to the central portion of the filter areas. G. Heymer (U.S.P. 1915418; Eng. P. 400057) also adopted a similar procedure.

The use of a separate pencil of rays to print each color element behind each lenticule, is disclosed by K. Rantsch in a whole series of patents, the earlier of which were issued to the German engineering concern, The Siemens and Halske Company (U.S.P. 2022978 and 2036499), and the later ones to Opticolor A. G. (U.S.P. 2061088, 2070179, 2071764). All the corresponding English patents were issued to Opticolor. These bear the serial numbers 421084, 422983, 422991, 430467, 430503, 435859, 436465, 436466, 436608, 438356, 438748, 440273, 440809, 441028, 441709, 443266, and 508219. In general, these disclose a system where a light source is situated in front of a system of mirrors which directs three pencils of light rays, at different angles, into three objectives which in turn direct the rays to the same point in the common focal plane of the lenses. The master lenticular film is placed between the light source and the mirrors, so that for all intents and purposes this can be considered as the light source. Every lenticular element on the master film will direct a pencil of rays to each of the mirrors and objectives. The mirrors are so positioned that each pencil represents the rays proceeding from one of the three color densities behind each lenticule.

A rather simple scheme is outlined in Fig. 98. If the master lenticular film, *M*, is illuminated with diffuse light, each of the densities behind each lenticule

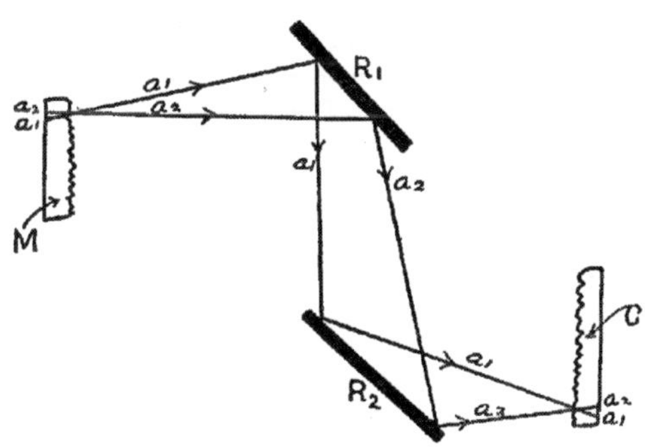

FIG. 98

becomes the origin of a point source of light. Due to the optical properties of the lenticules, the ray from the points a_1 and a_2 behind a single lenticule, converge to a common point from which they then diverge. Therefore it is seen that the light from the three-color densities gives rise to three beams of pencils of light, a_1, a_2, a_3 (only two of these are indicated in the diagram). By a proper choice of the mirror reflectors R_1 and R_2, these widely divergent rays are reunited upon a single lenticular element in the copy film *C*. Since the elementary lenses see only three pencils of rays converging upon them, each of the pencils will be imaged as a distinct point behind each lenticule.

A somewhat more complicated arrangement which accomplished the same result is depicted in Fig. 99. Here again the light originating at the three image densities behind each lenticule, gives rise to three pencils of rays which intersect each other in the focal plane of the lenticules of the master film *M*. The widely divergent pencils (two of which are indicated in the diagram) a_1 and a_2, are then reunited by a system of lenses L_1 and L_2 and reflectors R_1,

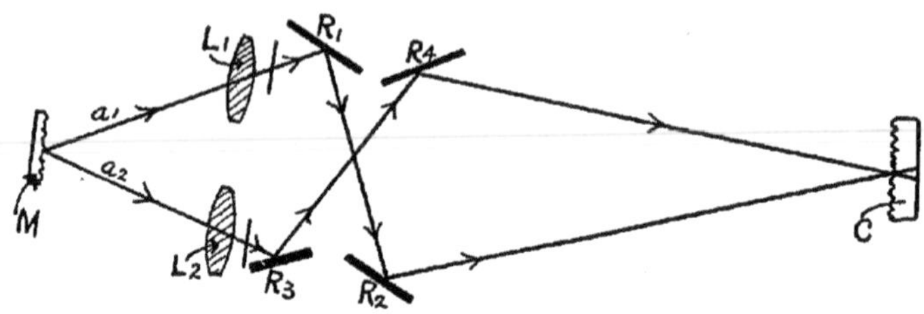

FIG. 99

R_2, R_3, and R_4, so that they reform at a single lenticule on the copy film *C*. Since this lenticule sees the rays from widely differing angles, it will image them as separate densities. In United States patent 2062146, K. Rantsch discloses some other very general processes.

The Keller-Dorian Company (Eng. P. 247168) disclosed a projection printer which used an objective whose pupil of emergence was at infinity. Therefore the images of the three filters in the lens aperture are independent of the focal lengths of the objective, since the rays passing through them emerge as three beams, each containing rays parallel to each other, each beam making a different angle with the optical axes of the lenticular elements. F. Strecker (U.S.P. 2040280) would place filters in the copying objective to correspond to the filter areas in the original objective. But these filters would pass the ultraviolet, violet, and blue-green regions respectively. Therefore ordinary colorblind emulsions could be used for copying, since the sensitivities of such materials extend slightly into the green, just beyond the blue-green. In order to prevent the light from a given point in the master from reaching two lenticular elements in the copy, F. Fischer (U.S.P. 1984471) placed a grid or other refracting surface, in front of the silver image. Anne Henri Jacques de Lassus Saint Genies disclosed several projection printing schemes in a series of patents (Eng. P. 457656, 460533, 462996, and 464723). These appear to be modifications of schemes already discussed. Other schemes were disclosed by A. Blondel (Eng. P. 462655); E. M. Sandoz, (Eng. P. 495348); Kapella, Ltd. (Eng. P. 373938); E. Leitz (U.S.P. 2055237); and C. Nordmann (Eng. P.

364627 and 410609). The last two are important in that they discuss fundamental principles from the point of view of general optics, and they lay down the conditions that must be fulfilled when the image sizes or the optical characteristics of original and duplicating systems differ from each other.

The usual conditions met during the taking of photographs with lenticular film are depicted in Fig. 100. A pencil of rays a_1, a_2, a_3, enters the lens. In the aperture of the objective, is positioned a filter F containing three filter zones r, g, and b, colored red, green, and blue respectively. After passage through the lens, the three colored pencils a_1', a_2', a_3', are recombined upon

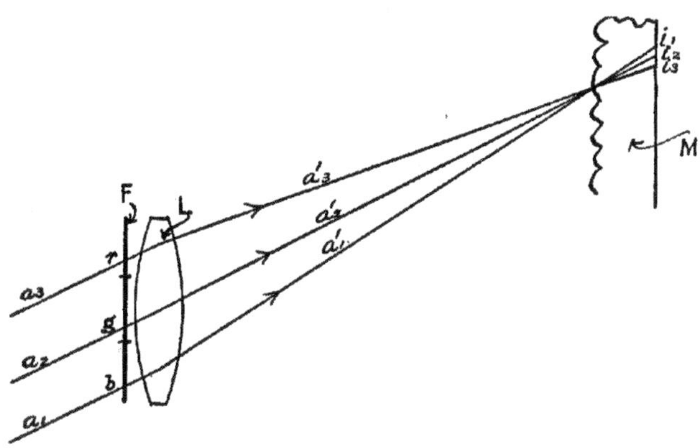

FIG. 100

the front surface of the lenticular film M, and give rise to three images i_1, i_2, and i_3, in the emulsion layer of M. To reconstruct the image in its original state, the paths of the light rays must be identically reversed.

In order for this to happen, it becomes necessary and sufficient that the light which illuminates the film from behind be broken up into three pencils by each set of image densities behind each lenticule. The ray in each pencil proceeding from the center of the image to the point on the lenticule which represents the nodal point of emission for the miniature lens, can be considered as the elementary axis of the pencil. Therefore from each lenticular element, there proceed three axes. This is illustrated in exaggerated form in Fig. 101. The relationship of the image dots i_1, i_2, i_3, m_1, m_2, m_3, to the lenticular elements A and B is determined by the shape and number of lenticules in the master film M, and by the optical properties of the lens through which the initial exposure has been made. It is the focal length of the lens and the dimensions of the filter bands occupying its aperture, which determine the angularity which the rays b_1, b_2, b_3, a_1, a_2, a_3 (Fig. 102), make with the optical axis of the entire system. But one thing is true regardless of what the lens characteristics are. The rays a_1 and b_1, which pass through the same section r of the filter band F, in the aperture of the lens system L, intersect each other in the exact center of the filter zone r. The same is true of the rays a_2 and b_2, and the rays a_3 and b_3. We can therefore make this very general

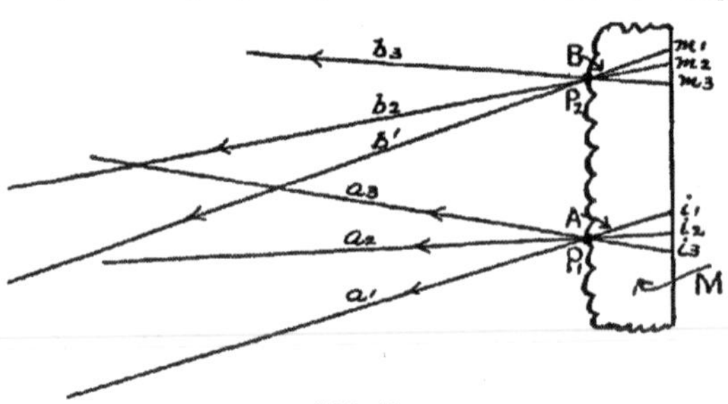

FIG. 101

statement: When a lenticular film is illuminated from behind, the elementary beams proceeding from corresponding points behind each lenticular element, will, in the absence of an optical system, intersect each other at points which correspond to the center of the filter zones present during the original photography. The distance x, of these points of intersection, from the lenticular surface of the film is therefore a definite characteristic of the master film,

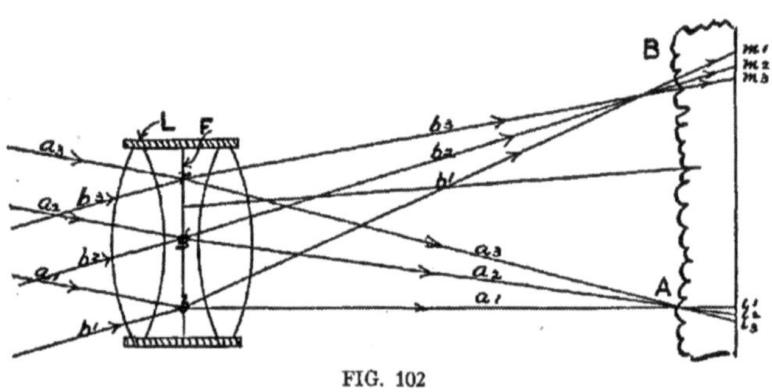

FIG. 102

and is fixed by the optical properties of the lens system in the original camera exposure. If it is desired to project a lenticular film in natural color, it is necessary and sufficient that the filters be placed in the plane of these points of intersection, and the centers of the filter zones must coincide with these points. If there is interposed an optical system in the path of these rays before the points of intersection, and if the nodal planes of admission and emission are separated by a distance equal to l, then the points of intersection of the elementary axes are moved forward a distance equal to l, so that the new position of the filter zones is at a distance $x + l$ from the lenticules.

Since the optical properties of the projection system are always different from those of the original taking system, it is not always possible to have the plane of the points of intersection clear so that a filter system can be installed there To overcome this difficulty, Keller-Dorian (Eng. P. 247168, cf. above) proposed to make these axes parallel to each other, by placing a special optical system between the color filters and the film not only during the copying, but also during the projection. In this case the exit pupils will intersect each other at infinity. This makes the system independent of the focal length of the objectives used. In order to project this film, it becomes necessary to interpose between the film and the aperture of the projection lens which contains the filters, such an optical system that the elementary axes will intersect in the centers of the filter zones A system of this type is known as a collimation system

The Nordmann disclosures represent a different attack upon the same problem, and one which does not utilize the expensive added optical equipment. It is necessary to know the position of the filters in the projection system. Suppose this be a distance of $y + l$ from the lenticular surface, where l is the distance between the nodal planes of admission and emission of the projection objective In making copies, it is necessary to use an optical system which will cause the elementary axes to intersect at a point y in front of the lenticular surface. If the master lenticular film is such that these axes intersect each other at a point X, which is a distance x in front of it, then a definite relationship must hold between X and Y, the point of intersection of the corresponding beams in the copy material. It is known that X is a distance x from the lenticular surface of the original, and Y is a distance y from the front surface of the copy film or a distance $y + l$ if an optical system lies between Y and the copy film, l being the separation between the nodal planes The relationship is that the points X and Y are conjugate to each other This means that the rays that go through X, must coincide with rays that would ordinarily go through Y.

This will become clearer as we analyze the problem in greater detail (Fig. 103). It is desired to make copy and master identical in size. Hence if the focal length of the lens system used in copying is f, the master film C is placed a distance equal to $2f$ in front of the nodal plane of admission P_1, of the system. The copy film I, is placed a distance $2f$ behind the nodal plane of emission P_2 of the system. The planes P_1 and P_2 are separated a distance l from each other. The axes of the elementary beams from the lenticules A and B, intersect at three points which represent the centers of the filter zones Consider the rays that would normally go through the central zone. These rays will intersect at a point X, which is a distance x in front of the plane containing A and B. The ray a, from the lenticule A, after going through the point X continues until it intersects the nodal plane P_1 at the point S. The ray b

from the lenticule B, intersects the nodal plane P_1 at R. The two rays then translate themselves parallel to the optical axis OO', until they reach the nodal plane of emission P_2. This they do at the points R' and S'. From these points the rays b' and a', continue until they reach the rear focal plane of the lens system. To determine the exact points A' and B' where these rays intersect the rear focal plane, we draw from the points A and B the rays c and d, which go directly to the nodal point of admission M. From here the rays translate themselves to the nodal point of emission N, then continue in the

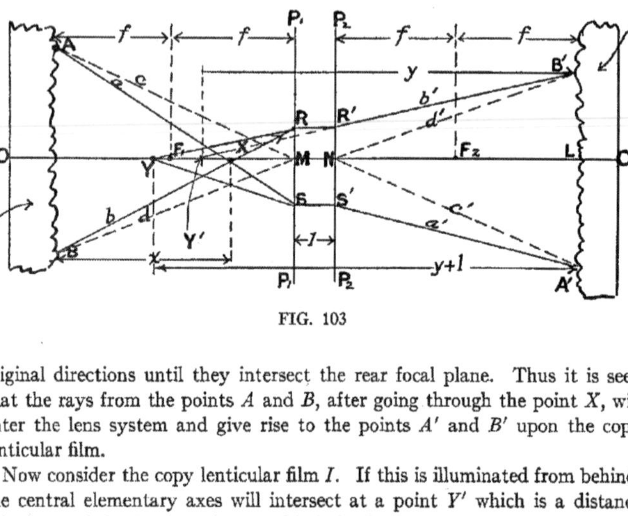

FIG. 103

original directions until they intersect the rear focal plane. Thus it is seen that the rays from the points A and B, after going through the point X, will enter the lens system and give rise to the points A' and B' upon the copy lenticular film.

Now consider the copy lenticular film I. If this is illuminated from behind, the central elementary axes will intersect at a point Y' which is a distance y in front of the lenticulations. This is in the absence of a lens system between the two films. In the presence of a lens system, the distance of the point of intersection will be moved forward a distance l, which is the separation between the nodal planes of admission and emission. This is the point Y in Fig. 103. Let us illuminate the two films C and I, both from the side carrying the images. Let us center our attention upon the central pencils of rays through each lenticule. The axes of these pencils will intersect at the point X or the point Y, depending upon whether they originate at C or I. We say that X and Y are conjugate to each other if the following conditions hold: A' and B' are the images of the points A and B. The axes of the central pencils of rays from the lenticular elements A and B, are the rays a and b. The axes of the corresponding pencils from A' and B' are a' and b'. The rays a and b intersect at the point X since no optical system lies between X and C. The rays a' and b', in the absence of such a system, would intersect at the point Y', but since there is a lens between I and the point of intersection, this moves forward to the point Y. If the rays a and b, after passing through the lens system, coincide with the rays a' and b', then the points X and Y are conjugate to each other. These conditions determine x and y. Since Y is the virtual image of the point X, the relation

$$\frac{1}{p}+\frac{1}{q}=\frac{1}{f}$$

must hold, where p is the distance of the point X from the nodal plane of admission, q the distance of the point Y from the nodal plane of emission, and f is the focal length of the lens. The distance p is XM, and this is equal to $2f - x$. The distance q is YN or $YL - NL$. But NL is $2f$ so that $q = y - 2f$. But q is positive if it is measured to the right of N, and negative if it lies to the left, hence q is negative. Substituting these values in the equation above, we have

$$\frac{1}{2f-x}+\frac{1}{-(y-2f)}=\frac{1}{f} \quad \text{or}$$

$$\frac{1}{2f-y}=\frac{1}{f}+\frac{1}{x-2f}$$

In this equation the value of x is known, since it is a characteristic of the master film. It is equal to the distance between the lenticulation and the plane of the filters in the camera during the original exposure. The value of y is also known, since this is the distance between the plane of the filters and the lenticulations in the projection system Therefore there is but one unknown, f, the focal length of the lens that is used for the copying system. If during the original exposure the object was at the infinity distance, and if the screen projection is arranged so that a life-size enlargement is obtained, and if the filters are placed in the front nodal planes of the systems, then x is the focal length of the original lens system in the camera and y is the focal length of the projection system. Thus these three optical constants are related to each other in a very simple manner

In the second of his patents (Eng. P. 410609) Mr. Nordmann takes up the more general problem of making duplicates a different size from the original. Thus it may be desirable to make the initial exposures upon 35 mm film, and the duplicates upon 16 mm material, or vice versa. With the recent introduction of 8 mm film as a standard material, this field is greatly enlarged. The relationship that holds now is the following:

$$\frac{1}{p}+\frac{1}{p'}=\frac{1}{f} \quad \text{and}$$

$$g=\frac{p'}{p}$$

where p is the distance from the master lenticular film C (Fig. 104) to the nodal plane of admission, p' the distance of the copy lenticular film I from

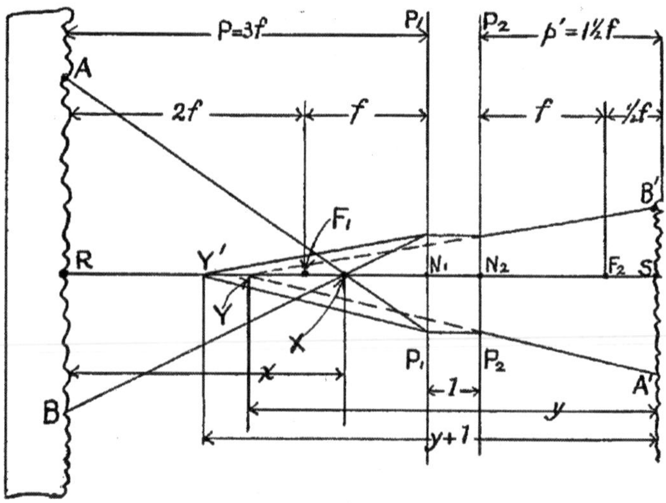

FIG. 104

the nodal plane of emission, f the focal length of the lens system, and g the degree of enlargement. Let us suppose $g = \frac{1}{2}$, then

$$\frac{1}{2} = \frac{p'}{p} \quad \text{or} \quad p' = \frac{1}{2}p$$

The master film is twice the distance from the nodal plane of admission that the copy film is from the nodal plane of emission. Substituting this value for p' into the lens equation, there results:

$$\frac{1}{p} + \frac{1}{\frac{1}{2}p} = \frac{1}{f}, \quad \frac{3}{p} = \frac{1}{f}, \quad p = 3f$$

Therefore the master film is placed a distance equal to three times the focal length in front of the nodal plane of admission, while the copy film is placed one and one-half times the focal length behind the nodal plane of emission. For a 2-inch lens, these are six and three inches respectively. Between the point of intersection X of the elementary axes of the central pencils of rays from the lenticular elements A, B, etc., of the master C and the copy film I, is placed an optical system whose focal length is f, and whose nodal planes P_1P_1 and P_2P_2 are a distance l apart. As before, it is desired to use a projection system in which the filters are placed a distance $y + l$ in front of the lenticular surface. This fixes completely the focal length f of the copying system, since this must be such that the axes of the central pencils of rays from each lenticule A', B', etc., must intersect each other at a point Y, which is a distance y from the lenticular elements, when no optical system is interposed between Y and the film. In the presence of such a system the point Y is moved to Y', a distance equal to the separation between the nodal planes.

The points X and Y' are conjugate to each other. Therefore the standard lens equation is applicable to these points. The distance X from the nodal plane of admission is XN, which is equal to $RN_1 - R$ or $p - x$. The distance Y' from the nodal plane of emission is $Y'N_2$ which is equal to $Y'S - N_2S$. But in the distance $Y'S$ is included the distance between the two nodal planes, l. From the point of view of optics, this distance is completely neutral, hence must be subtracted from the total. $Y'S = y + l$, hence the optical distance is y. The distance N_2S is p'. Therefore the equation may be written:

$$\frac{1}{p - x} + \frac{1}{p' - y} = \frac{1}{f}$$

If the point X lies on the other side of N_1, x will be greater than p, and the relationship will then take the form:

$$\frac{1}{x - p} + \frac{1}{y - p'} = \frac{1}{f}$$

Since s and y are known constants, and p, p' and f are related to each other ($p = 3f$, $p' = 1\frac{1}{2}f$, for a reduction to $\frac{1}{2}$ size), only the value of f is unknown, and determinable from the equation:

$$\frac{1}{x - 3f} + \frac{1}{y - \frac{1}{2}f} = \frac{1}{f} \quad \text{or}$$

$$\frac{1}{x - 3f} + \frac{2}{2y - 3f} = \frac{1}{f}$$

The patents by Nordmann are very general in scope. They disclose the most general conditions that have to be satisfied in order to make duplicate copies from a master lenticular film. The original taking system may differ from the projection system not only in the focal length of the objective used, but also in the effective aperture of the lens, the width of the filter zones, etc. The I.G. in several disclosures (Eng. P. 434206 and 444191) outlines systems which compensate for these and other characteristics of the camera and projection systems. The Keller-Dorian Company (Eng. P. 297773) would solve most of these problems by first reproducing the images on non-lenticular film, then copying the reproductions upon lenticular film through an appropriate optical system, to yield the desired properties. In copying film of this type, it was found that the interstices between the lenticules in the master did not transmit light. This leaves the corresponding sections in the copy blank, leading to color dilution. The Keller-Dorian Company remedied this by giving the film a supplementary exposure through the lenticular elements using a special annular diaphragm (Fig. 105), having the central portion completely blocked out. This portion corresponds to the space directly behind the lenticule. The clear portion would affect only the regions beyond the central zone (Eng. P. 245118).

It is also possible to print the lenticular film by contact. Here the main problem is to avoid the formation of moiré. This will take place whenever the pattern of the master fails to register completely with the pattern of the copy material. The effects of moiré are identical in this case with those in the case of screen plates. It may be recalled that a very successful solution was to have the emulsion of the master separated from the emulsion of the copy film by the thickness of one film base. This has its counterpart in the schemes

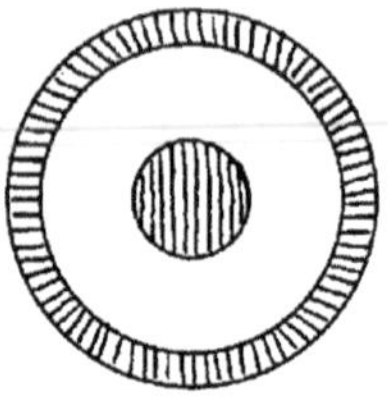

FIG. 105

disclosed by the I.G. where a glass plate with parallel sides (Eng. P. 317051), or a clear lenticular film (Eng. P. 435813) is placed between the master and copy, the entire group forming a sandwich.

The printing of the copy upon a film whose lenticulations are at a definite angle to those of the master, has been proposed quite often by a number of people, among whom are H. Arni (U.S.P. 1876442); Eggert and Heymer (U.S.P. 2072396); Capstaff (U.S.P. 2058409); J. L. Vidal (U.S.P. 1935422); the Keller-Dorian Company (Eng. P. 211486 and 391110); the Société française de Cinématographie (Eng. P. 317051 and 329899); and the Kislyn Corp. (Eng. P. 371546). In some of the disclosures the lenticulations were at right angles to each other, in others the angle could be as low as one or two degrees.

The projection printing of lenticular film was also complicated by the problem of moiré. The I.G. proposed to place a piece of clear lenticular film in the path of the rays (Eng. P. 367411). This had also been proposed by O. E. Miller of the Eastman Kodak Company (U.S.P. 2008989). The Keller-Dorian Company disclosed many schemes to solve this problem. Direct vision prisms (U.S.P. 1982187; Eng. P. 378249 and 391908), parallel plate glass at an angle to the optical axis (U.S.P. 1884996 and 1904671; Eng. P. 288290 and 378245), prisms which deflected the images (U.S.P. 1884995; Eng. P. 265069 and 304643), doubly refracting elements (Eng. P. 374993) and diffraction gratings (Eng. P. 303357) were placed in the path of the light rays, to cause a sufficient deflection of the beam to remove the moiré.

The Société française de Cinématographie (Eng. P 310320) and the Kislyn Corp (Eng P. 377717) proposed to reflect the exposing light off a rocking mirror. In another disclosure this company suggested that the copying objective could be vibrated (Eng. P. 309540) The Keller-Dorian Company used the inefficiencies of the optical system to eliminate the moiré (Eng, P. 317060) operating under a circle of confusion that was beyond the structure of a lenticular element. The I G (Eng. P. 434205) used a cylindrical lens in the copying system to effect a spread of image. Other proposals were made by Räntsch (U.S.P. 2011263) and S. B. Colgate (U.S.P. 2026376).

In printing lenticular film by contact, the lenticules at the edges of the image receive light at a different angle from those in the center. Unless this is neutralized, the effect is to give the image a dominant line. C. Nordmann studied this problem and suggested a number of solutions (Eng. P. 360524, 362490, 363387, 363409 and 363447). The I.G. also disclosed various schemes by which lenticular film could be printed by contact (Eng. P. 392987, 417020, 417096, 440567 and 447317).

The many intricate problems that beset the technician when he attempted to print duplicates upon lenticular film naturally forced his attention to the possibility of making color separations from a lenticular master film. The separations could then be used to prepare any type of color positive that was available to him There were many advantages to this idea in the days before monopacks and condensed tripacks were disclosed It made the camera man independent of the whims of balky and temperamental one-shot cameras and one-shot camera owners, and it was not necessary to carry three times the quantity of film. But best of all it enabled him to use the short-focal-length lenses to which he was accustomed in black-and-white work, thus making it unnecessary to shift his lighting arrangements. No registry problems remained to hound him. In short, all the headaches of color became removed to the precision laboratory where they belonged.

A very obvious method of accomplishing the separation was to project a colored image upon a screen and copy the projected picture through the separation filters. This was disclosed by A. Blondel (Eng P. 462794). Any of the proposals outlined above for the projection printing of lenticular film could be used also if special diaphragms were placed in the paths to block out the rays that would correspond to two primaries. Thus but one color is printed at a time. Similar proposals were disclosed by H. T Kalmus and J. A. Ball (Eng. P. 343369); H. E. Ives (U.S.P. 1970936); and by the I.G. (U S P 1874529; Eng. P. 353121, 402902, 440187).

A rather novel system, based upon the principle of masking, is outlined by the I.G. in a series of patents (U.S.P. 2064058; Eng. P. 412021, 428875, 435994 and 440025). When a lenticular film is illuminated by means of a uniformly lighted area equal in size to one of the filter bands, and arranged at a substantial distance from the plane of the lenticules, there is obtained a line running parallel to the lenticules. The line will cover an area that is one-third of the space behind the lenticular element, and the exact portion that the line covers depends upon the angle which the axis of the beam makes with the elementary axes of the miniature lenses. Since the source of illumination is substantially at infinity, the light reaching the film consists of parallel rays Three such films are made, one each with the angle to correspond to that of a single primary color If these are printed by contact upon a smooth-based film, registry being maintained by use of the perforations on the side of the film, there will be obtained a line which corresponds to the width of two color densities. The contact prints are called stencils. The master positive or negative is now printed by contact upon a smooth-based film with a stencil lying between the master and the copy film. This will completely block out the densities corresponding to two color primaries, leaving the third one to come through to print upon the copy film. Since there will be the thickness of a base between the master and the copy, no trace of moiré will be present if the source of illumination be properly chosen This was discussed in some detail in the chapter dealing with screen plates

In order to avoid the lateral inversion that takes place when lenticular film is printed, G. Heymer (U.S P 1874529; Eng P. 353121) would print the film with the emulsion sides in contact If the printing is done by projection the original objective can be used, and the zones occupied by two of the filters are to be blocked out. This is practically identical to the schemes proposed by Ives and Kalmus and Ball P. A. Richard (U.S P 1750358) also disclosed a similar scheme.

The reverse procedure, printing color separations on to lenticular positive film, has also been disclosed. Several schemes were proposed by V. Hudeley and J. Lagrave (U.S P. 2030795; Eng P 408109, 421582 and 430585) The negatives were made in a special triple-lens camera, which gave three images in a single frame. This created the problem of enlarging and properly registering each of the three part-images in a single frame of lenticular film. The I.G. Company (Eng. P. 392987) would print the separations on to the lenticular positive by contact. The color record is placed in contact with the lenticular side of the copy film, and the beam used for exposure is given the proper angle with respect to the elementary lenticular axes so that the image will be formed in the proper zones behind each lenticule. In a subsequent patent, a stencil such as is disclosed in English patent 412021 is placed between the color record and the lenticulated side of the copy film. Here again the angularity of the incident light is controlled to deposit the image in the proper zone.

Dr. Bela Gaspar (Eng. P. 343369, 406013 and 409270), and the I.G. (Eng. P. 375338, 451175 and 460653) proposed to print lenticular master positives upon other types of monopack film, and process them to color transparencies by means of dye-destruction or dye-coupling methods.

In line with the use of lenticular film as a negative process, the I G has disclosed its use as the front element of a bipack (U.S.P 2093655; Eng. P. 395124). The film is coated with an orthochromatic emulsion. In the lens aperture there is placed a two-banded filter with a yellow and a magenta zone Both of these transmit the red rays. Since the front emulsion is not sensitive to the red, these will not register here, but upon the rear red-sensitized film. A continuous-tone record of the red densities will be obtained. The front lenticular film will register but two densities behind each lenticular element, since but two filter zones are present in the lens aperture. One zone transmits blue and red light, therefore only blue will be registered by this beam. The other zone transmits red and green, hence only green will be recorded by it upon an orthochromatic emulsion. The subsequent separation of the two color densities is a much simpler job than the separation of three densities.

CHAPTER 19

MASKING

NO discussion of the negative processes would be complete without mention of the subject of color correction by masking. This technique was first introduced by Dr. E. Albert in the eighteen-nineties (Ger. P. 101379 and 116538) to improve the qualities of the black printer in four-color reproduction. The use of a key plate to give the final print more contrast and better blacks, had been firmly established about ten to fifteen years before this, and the practice introduced several problems that did not exist previously One of these problems was that all the bright colors became degraded because black was printed into them by the key plate Dr. Albert proposed to eliminate this trouble by making a weak positive from the black printer negative and placing it in registry with the three-color negatives. The combination was used to print the positives. This had the effect of removing black from each of the color-printing plates The general procedure of combining a positive of one separation with a negative of another is termed masking.

Another method for producing the same result was disclosed in the *Process Photogram* (Vol. 8 (1901), p. 114). Here it was proposed to combine each separation negative with positives made from the other two negatives. This was later patented by L O. van Straatten (Eng. P 353151). Schelter and Giesecke (Ger. P. 152799) patented the use of secondary masks; that is, masks made from negatives that were exposed behind magenta, cyan, and yellow filters. It is therefore seen that the van Stratten technique is but a modification of this one In all of the disclosures made up to this point, the main objective was to eliminate black from the color printer Thus the combination of a red negative with a minus-red positive will increase the densities in the masked negative at those points where green and blue densities are being deposited by the other two plates. Therefore less red densities (less cyan color) will be deposited here. Black, where it is required, will be deposited by the black plate, so that no loss of density or definition will take place The net effect will be to brighten up all the colors, thus increasing brilliance and saturation.

It was O. Pfenninger and E. C Townsend (Eng P 26608/10) who first proposed masking as a corrective for the poor transmissions of the magenta printing ink. We have met Mr. Pfenninger previously in our discussions concerning one-shot cameras In order to compensate for the poor blue transmission of the magenta ink, they combined a weak positive of the green-filter (magenta printer) negative, with the blue-filter negative to form a masked yellow printer. This was later patented by J. A H Hatt (U S.P. 1349956), but in a different form. The green-filter negative was placed in a special camera which allowed registry to be carefully maintained The red-filter negative was then projected upon this in exact registry. The position of the green-filter negative was carefully marked, and the plate then removed and coated with a collodion emulsion. It was finally replaced in the camera, and a red-filter positive printed upon it. By this means there was formed a green-filter separation that had a weak positive of the red-filter separation combined with it. The extension to three colors was proposed by J. Keenen (U.S.P. 1866556). Mr. Keenen also pointed out that the masks could be made upon separate plates that could then be bound in exact registry with the different negatives F. H. Hausleiter (Eng. P. 360441) also proposed a like technique, as did Wilkinson (U.S.P. 2004144), R. Mackay (U.S P 2060816); J R. Elsworth (Eng. P. 440086), and Feeny (Eng P. 444229). Other complicated arrangements utilizing special types of plateholders and cameras that allowed the removal and replacement of plates in exact positions, were disclosed by E. H. Gamble (Eng. P 6768/12); E. A. Raschke (U S P. 1373020); J. A. H Hatt (U.S.P. 1518426 and 1569124), S. J. van Straatten (Eng. P. 427234); L. Nerót (Fr. P. 780364); and Boettger and Kronschnabl (Ger. P. 592003 and 601484, Eng. P. 402082; U S P. 2020688) A complete disclosure as to the working details of a masking process is contained in the Eastman Kodak booklet "The Modern Masking Method of Correct Color Reproduction." Here is disclosed one novel feature. The black printer is prepared by exposure through an infrared filter This is based upon the disclosures of A Murray of the Eastman staff that most pigments used in paints are transparent to or highly reflective of the infrared rays Other discussions of the subject are contained in articles by F J. Tritton (*Phot J*, Vol 78 (1938), p. 732); H. H. Lerner and W Perelstrus (*Phot Tech*, Vol 1 (1939), November, p. 25, December, p. 35); and J. S. Friedman (*Am. Phot.*, Vol. 30 (1936), pp. 692, 771, 837; Vol. 31 (1937), pp. 129, 584; Vol. 33 (1939), pp. 372, 928), from which this historical abstract has been compiled.

The necessity for masking arises from the poor spectral characteristics of the colors used in the synthesis processes The red filter separation is a record of the red densities as they are present in the original. The positive made from this must deposit red densities at every point of the reproduction, to the extent determined by the relative transmissions at each point of the red-filter negative This is the sole function of the red filter or cyan positive But the cyan colors available to the color technicians are extremely poor in their green and blue transmissions Instead of transmitting 100 per cent of the blue and green rays, the average transmissions will be in the neighborhood of 45 per cent. Therefore the cyan image will deposit not only red densities, but also blue and green densities. In the same manner, the magenta colors suffer as far as the blue transmissions are concerned It is only the yellow pigments which have a sufficiently high transmission of the desired primaries to be practically perfect. The average magenta will transmit upwards of 85 per cent of the red rays that are incident upon it, but only 45 per cent of the blue. Let us take these figures for our general average.

Consider a point on the original that contains a color that reflects 75 per cent of the total blue rays which fall upon it, 30 per cent of the green, and only 3 per cent of the red. We can convert these transmissions into densities by use of the formula Density = 2 − log (% Transmission). The blue therefore can be assigned a density value of 0.13, the green a value of 0.52, and the red a value of 1 52 If the processing of the negatives and the positives has been done accurately, the magenta positive which deposits the green densities will have a value of 0 52, the cyan a value of 1.52, and the yellow a value of 0.13, after they have been converted into color. But now the effects of poor transmissions of the colors to light of their own ranges become evident. Suppose that the cyan dye transmits but 45 per cent of the green and blue. When this dye is present in sufficient quantity to give a density equal to 2 00, there will be a considerable amount of blue and green light absorbed, with consequent deposition of considerable quantities of blue and green densities Since at maximum concentration but 45 per cent of the green and the blue is transmitted, it becomes a simple matter to calculate the amount of undesirable density that is deposited To obtain an accurate determination, it is only necessary to measure the densities of a heavy cyan image through all three filters. Let us suppose that when the value through a red filter is 1 55, the value through the green filter is 0.31, and the value through the blue filter also 0.31.

Theoretically the values should have been 1.55 through the red, and zero through the other two filters. Therefore at each point of the cyan image, there have been deposited green and blue densities equal to 20 per cent of the red. These deposits bear no relationship whatsoever to the requirements of the picture, because the true green densities will be put down by the magenta image. Since the transmissions of the blue and green are 45 per cent of theory, and a transmission of 45 per cent is equivalent to a density of 0.35, this will be the maximum amount of undesired densities that the cyan dye could deposit. Applying these results to the point in question, we see that the cyan dye will deposit these densities

Red	1.52
Green	0 30 (= 20% of 1 52)
Blue	0 30

The magenta dye, transmitting practically 100 per cent of the red rays, will deposit no red densities But it transmits only 45 per cent of the blue rays, hence it will deposit a considerable quantity of blue densities. Since the inefficiency of the magenta to the blue is the same as the inefficiency of the cyan to this primary, we can assume that here also 20 per cent will be deposited. Hence the magenta dye will give these densities:

Red	0.00
Green	0.52
Blue	0.10 (= 20% of 0 52)

The yellow image, being practically perfect, will deposit merely blue densities, and these to a value of 0.13 The final color will have the composition, in terms of densities:

Red	1.52 + 0.00 + 0 00 = 1.52
Green	0 30 + 0 52 + 0 00 = 0.82
Blue	0.30 + 0.10 + 0.13 = 0.53

These densities will correspond to the following transmissions:

Red	3%
Green	15%
Blue	30%

The color is still a blue, but now it has a very pronounced bluish-green tint, and is extremely dull. The original color was an extremely bright blue, with but a slight greenish tint. The shade, therefore, has been made considerably greener, and the saturation reduced to a very low value

This degradation of color can be corrected if some means can be found to reduce the deposition of blue densities by the yellow printer to an amount equal to 20 per cent of the red densities at each point, and an added amount equal to 20 per cent of the green densities at each point. Apparently O. Pfenninger and E. C. Townsend (see above) must be given the credit for first disclosing how this can be done

Let us suppose that our negatives have been developed to a gamma of one The cyan printer is made from the red-filter negative, and it deposits the red densities. For all practical purposes, this printer is the only one which deposits red densities, since the magenta and the yellow inks or dyes transmit the red with great efficiency. Now if another positive is made of this printer, but developed to a contrast equal to 20 per cent of the contrast of the first, each point on this positive will have a density which is 20 per cent of the density of the corresponding point in the true cyan printer. These are the densities that must be subtracted from the yellow printer. The subtraction is carried out by registering the weak positive with the yellow printer or blue filter negative. Center our attention again at the point where the red density is 1 52 and the blue density is 0.13. The corresponding point in the blue filter negative has a very heavy silver deposit, since but a very thin deposit is required in the positive. Let us suppose that the value of this deposit is 1.75 in the blue-filter negative. The true cyan positive has a value of 1.52 at the same point, hence the mask has a value of 20 per cent of 1.52 or 0.30. The combined mask and blue-filter negative has a value of 1.75 + 0 30 or 2.05 at this point, and when the yellow printer is exposed through such a masked negative, and developed to a gamma of one, there will be a corresponding reduction in the image at this point. Therefore we have succeeded in subtracting the desired densities from every point of the yellow printer.

However, there is one point to be brought out The original color calls for a deposition of a blue density equal to 0 13. We have added a density equal to 0 30 to this point on the blue-filter negative. Our exposure is such that without the inclusion of the mask there would be formed a density of 0.13, so that with the mask added, the exposure would be insufficient to print through the added density If more exposure is given there will be distortion all along the line Therefore this is no solution We conclude, therefore, that masking can correct only when the color densities are sufficiently high, so that they are greater than the densities deposited by the inefficient transmissions of the dyes themselves In our present example, the cyan, which is the principal color at this point, will deposit a blue density of 0.30 The magenta, which should shade the cyan so that it becomes somewhat less green, also gives a deposit of blue to the value of 0 10 It is therefore impossible for us to obtain a value for the blue density which is less than 0 40. This much falsification and degradation of colors must be accepted

When a negative having a contrast of 1.00 is registered with a positive whose contrast is 0.20, the result will be a negative whose contrast is 0.80. This is evident from the following example Included in the picture is a ten-step gray scale whose steps have a constant differential of 0 15 If the lightest step has a value of 0.30, the second will have a value of 0.45, etc. The gray scale will be reproduced in each of the three separations. The blue-filter negative, if developed to a gamma of 1.00, will have values for the different densities as follows:

Step	*Density*	*Step*	*Density*
1	0 30	6	1.07
2	0.45	7	1 20
3	0 61	8	1 35
4	0 75	9	1.49
5	0 90	10	1 60

The other negatives, also developed to the same gamma, will have values very close to this The original scale had the following values:

Step	*Density*	*Step*	*Density*
1	1 65	6	0.90
2	1.50	7	0.75
3	1.35	8	0.60
4	1.20	9	0.45
5	1.05	10	0.30

The positive made from the red-filter negative has densities:

Step	*Density*	*Step*	*Density*
1	1.60	6	0.89
2	1.50	7	0.76
3	1.35	8	0.61
4	1.20	9	0.47
5	1.05	10	0.35

The weak positive made from the red-filter negative has densities that are only 20 per cent of these, thus:

Step	*Density*	*Step*	*Density*
1	0.32	6	0.18
2	0.30	7	0.15
3	0.27	8	0.12
4	0.24	9	0.09
5	0.21	10	0.07

The combined mask and yellow negative, will have values:

Step No.		*Step No.*	
1	0.30 + 0.32 = 0.62	6	1.07 + 0.18 = 1.25
2	0.45 + 0.30 = 0.75	7	1.20 + 0.15 = 1.35
3	0.61 + 0.27 = 0.88	8	1.35 + 0.12 = 1.47
4	0.75 + 0.24 = 0.99	9	1.49 + 0.09 = 1.58
5	0.90 + 0.21 = 1.11	10	1.60 + 0.07 = 1.67

This, when plotted against the original (Fig. 106), is seen to have a gamma of 0.80.

This can be made into a general rule. The combination of a negative with gamma a, with a positive whose gamma is b, will be a negative with a gamma $a - b$, if b is less than a. If it is greater, then the result will be a positive with a gamma equal to $b - a$. Since it is essential to preserve equality of gammas in the three printers, the use of a mask on one negative will necessitate the extra development of the positive through that masked negative, in order to maintain balance. Therefore, if a 20 per cent mask is in order, there will be required a development to a gamma $\frac{1.00}{.80}$, or 1.25.

There is another method for maintaining this balance. The operator knows beforehand that he is to deliver a set of masked negatives, and that the magenta printer is to receive a single mask from the cyan negative equal to 20 per cent of the cyan printer, and the yellow negative is to receive a mask from both the cyan and the magenta printers equal to 20 per cent of the densities deposited by those printers. He develops the red-filter negative to a contrast of 1.00. The green-filter negative is to be developed to that contrast which, when combined with the contrast of the cyan mask, will yield an overall contrast of 1.00, at the same time preserving the 1:5 ratio between the contrasts of the green-filter negative and the cyan mask. If x is the value of the contrast of the mask, then $5x$ is the contrast of the green-filter negative. We can set up the equation $5x - x = 1.00$ which stipulates that the differences in the contrasts of the green-filter negative and cyan mask must be 1.00. Solving, we get $x = 0.25$, so that the mask must be developed to a contrast of 0.25, while the green-filter negative must be developed to a contrast five times that, or 1.25. When the two are combined we will have a

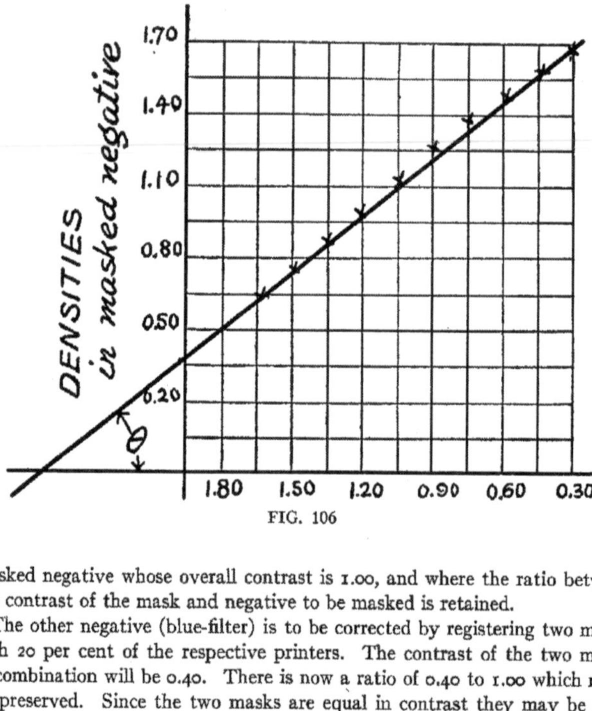

FIG. 106

masked negative whose overall contrast is 1.00, and where the ratio between the contrast of the mask and negative to be masked is retained.

The other negative (blue-filter) is to be corrected by registering two masks each 20 per cent of the respective printers. The contrast of the two masks in combination will be 0.40. There is now a ratio of 0.40 to 1.00 which must be preserved. Since the two masks are equal in contrast they may be considered as one. If x is the contrast of the combined masks, then $2.5x$ is the contrast of the negative. Therefore the equation takes the form:

$$2.50x - x = 1.00$$
$$1.5x = 1.00$$
$$x = 0.67$$

Under these conditions, the contrast of the masks must be each 0.33 and the contrast of the blue-filter negative 1.67.

This result can also be obtained in another manner which does not call for such drastic measures. Since masking is confined today practically completely to still life or to separations made from copy, speed is of no value The yellow printer is to be masked by equal red- and green-filter masks. Therefore, if a special negative is made, either by giving a plate exposures through both the red and green filters, or by exposing through a minus blue (yellow), there will be obtained a negative combining the red and green densities. This can also serve as the black-printer negative. The mask for the yellow printer is made from this negative and it is developed to an overall contrast that is equal to two-fifths the contrast of the blue-filter negative. The printer made from this is developed to an overall contrast of 1 67. Thus if the original blue-filter negative has a contrast of 1.50, not an impossible value except with the fast negative materials, the mask will be developed to a contrast of 0.60, and the yellow printer to a contrast of 1.10, so that the overall contrast is (1 50 − 0.60) × 1 10, or 1.00

The necessity for masking in the photomechanical trade arose from the need for eliminating the very expensive and time-consuming operations of re-etching and hand retouching Not only are these operations costly, but they give a mechanical appearance to the picture, removing all such aspects as are now grouped together under the term photographic quality. When a study was made of the properties of the printing inks and the deficiencies of the spectral characteristics noted, the idea of photographic re-etching or subtraction of densities by use of masks became immediately apparent. For a short space of time the photoengraving industry, never noted for scientific approach to its problems, went overboard for this technique without inquiring too closely as to possible discrepancies between working conditions and conditions under which masking is possible The net result was that in a very short time it became evident that although masking helped, it did not by any means eliminate the re-etching. This caused a reaction to set in, and far too many of the shops gave up the practice and returned to the use of their good right eyes. But the brief introduction of the technique had one good effect. It made the shop technicians realize the value of densitometric control.

From the surface, it would appear that masking should be an excellent corrective technique to use under any conditions But the failure obtained in the industry cannot be lightly dismissed. Let us examine what conditions must be preserved in order to be able to apply a masking technique intelligently. First of all, the masks and the negatives to which they are applied, are both continuous in tone. When a correction is to be applied at a given point, it is because at the same point there has been or will be deposited some unwanted densities. This is of course axiomatic in subtractive processes—and masking can be applied only to subtractive processes.

Now consider the photomechanical product. When the halftone negatives are made, the different separations are angled differently with respect to the screen so that the imposition of the three screen patterns, one on top of the other, will not cause an annoying moiré pattern to form This solved the moiré problem, but it created another which is seldom mentioned but which probably explains the existence of the most of the headaches in that industry. This problem is that it separates the undivided color dots so that in practically all areas with the exception of the blacks and the very dark colors, the color dots fall side by side, rather than one on top of the other. An examination of the various tones in a magazine illustration under a moderately powered glass, will quickly show what is meant In the highlights and the lower middle tones, we do not operate under a subtractive system, but under an additive one This, more than any other reason, explains why the cyan and the magenta approach more nearly the green and red of the two-color processes than the cyan and magenta of a three-color process.

In the middle tones, the sizes of the dots become sufficiently large to occasion some overlapping. In this region, which extends to the region of the deep grays and the dark colors, the system is operating partly additive and partly subtractive. It is only in the deepest shadows that it acts subtractively, and even here due to the common practice of maintaining a dot structure, there will be a slight region where the additive principle is working. The finer the screen, the greater the mixture between the two, for then the additive portions will blend more smoothly It must be recalled that in tone values the halftone system is strictly additive in operation. Grays are obtained by mixing white with black (regions of pure white are mixed additively with regions of pure black). Under these conditions it is no small wonder that masking fails to eliminate all re-etching and, depending upon the subject matter, may not even eliminate a large proportion of it. This explains the claims of some technicians that masking eliminates from fifty to seventy-five per cent of the hand work, and of others, who state that it accomplishes very little.

Although of dubious value in the photomechanical industry, masking properly applied can play a great role in the field of photographic reproduction Here there are no complicating problems of tone separation. The different color densities of corresponding points fall directly one on top of the other. The application to photography can be traced back at least to 1915, when two patents were issued to W. F. Fox (U S P. 1166121 and 1166122) Here was disclosed a method for increasing the color contrasts in a two-color process The negative of one color separation is united with a positive of another, to make a masked printing negative. In his all-inclusive patent (Re-issue 18680) Dr Troland also utilized masking, but for an entirely new and novel purpose. It is to be recalled (Chapter on Monopacks) that the front element of a Troland or Friedman bipack, was a stratified emulsion. The lower half contained the blue densities, and the upper half, the red. Between the two, and acting as an opaque barrier between them, were the unfixed silver halide salts

A copy of the red densities is made by reflection printing of the upper image. The copy is made so that the size is identical with that of the original, and the contrast is made equal to that of the red-density image. When these are registered with each other, the positive reflection copy just neutralizes the negative of the red densities. If this combination is printed, only the blue densities will modulate the exposing light In this way the blue densities are obtained. This technique would yield separations of a quality much superior to those obtained by copying.

This type of masking technique has been suggested by J. S. Friedman, (p. 274) as a means of greatly increasing the lens speed of a one-shot camera. In order to achieve this, the filters in a one-shot camera are replaced by an A, a Wratten No. 12, and a Wratten No. 32 respectively. Behind each of these filters is placed a panchromatic emulsion. The image behind the A filter will represent the red densities. The image behind the yellow filter will represent the green and the red densities, and to an equal extent. If the contrast of the No. 12 negative be 1.50, then the mask made from the A filter should have an overall contrast of 0 75. The combination of the two will be a negative having a contrast of 0.75. The mask will subtract red densities from the No. 12 negative to a contrast of 0.75, but the red densities present in this negative have a contrast that is equal to 0.75. Hence the masking positive will just neutralize the red densities in the No 12 negative, leaving only the green densities to come through. In a similar way the combination of a mask from the A filter negative, developed to an overall gamma equal to one-half that of the contrast of the No 32 filter negative, with that negative will neutralize the red densities here, and allow the blue to come through. By this technique there is obtained, after masking, the three color separations

The filter factors of the Nos. 12 and 32 filters are 2. The filter factor for the A filter is also 2 (for light of Mazda quality, 3200 K) We have, therefore, to divide the light intensity entering the camera lens equally into three parts. If this is done, and if emulsions with a Weston rating of 50 are used, there will be obtained speeds of approximately Weston 9. This measures quite favorably with the speeds of 1 to 2 that would be obtained under similar conditions, using the more normal technique.

The Eastman Kodak Company, in their booklet describing the Wash-Off Relief Process, describe a method for masking that can be generalized to all other types of processes. This scheme is also discussed in United States patent 2169009 issued to M. W. Seymour of the Eastman Kodak Co., and in English patent 517020, issued to R. F. W. Selman, of Kodak, Ltd., England. We will first discuss the special scheme outlined in the booklet, then the generalization. The Wash-Off Relief dyes are very efficient in their red transmissions, hence the red-filter negative need not be masked. This negative is printed by contact upon Wash-Off Relief material, and processed to form the cyan matrix which is dyed up to the extent required for the final cyan image. The magenta matrix must be corrected for the green densities deposited by the cyan image.

The cyan-dyed matrix is placed in registry with the green-filter negative, and the combination is printed by contact upon Wash-Off Relief material. The automatic character of the masking now becomes evident. The masked negative should be printed with green light. Therefore the intensity of the light at any one point is first reduced to the extent to which the cyan image deposits green densities at that point, and then is modulated by the green-filter negative lying below the mask. This would require that the Wash-Off Relief emulsion be green-sensitive, which it is not. But the amount of green masking is approximately the same as the blue, so that but very little difference would be obtained if the printing of the magenta matrix were done with blue light instead of green. This is taken care of by the emulsion itself, since it is truly blind The magenta matrix is processed to completion, and is dyed to the exact extent that would be used in the final image. The two matrices, dyed cyan and magenta, are combined and the combination placed in registry with the blue-filter negative Now a contact print made from this combination will be correctly masked for the poor blue transmissions of both the cyan and magenta dyes actually used, because the exposing light must first pass through the cyan and magenta positive images before passing through the blue-filter negative. Therefore the light is modulated, first of all to the extent of the blue densities deposited by the dyes, then by the blue-density negative.

As disclosed by the Eastman technicians, this semi-automatic scheme is useful only in the case where same-size images are made. The scheme is termed semi-automatic because the green densities are corrected by the blue absorptions of the cyan dye, rather than by the green absorptions. But as noted above, the two approximate each other very closely. It is possible to generalize the technique to make it useful for enlargement. The masks, in this case, are made by contact and registered with the negatives in the manner disclosed above. But these are not used for the final print. New matrices are made by projection through the masked negative, so that enlargements to any desired degree can be obtained.

Should one use other methods of making the positive prints, a similar type of technique could be evolved Let us suppose that the print is to be made by color development. The red-filter negative is first printed by contact upon a film, and this is converted into a cyan image by coupler development (cf. chapters on Color Development for details). The colored image is registered with the green-filter negative, and the magenta image printed by contact from this combination, etc. With different systems, it may be advantageous to mask the red-filter negative, as well as the others. This is a rather obvious extension of the present technique

The current popularity of the monopack films typified by Kodachrome, bids well to extend the idea of masking to still another field, the making of separations from monopack transparencies. Here more than anywhere else, a masking technique is desirable. This matter is discussed rather critically by J S. Friedman in several of his columns in *American Photography* (cf. l.c., and Vol. 34 (1940) p 128). It also forms the subject matter of a patent by Dr Bela Gaspar (Eng. P. 494341). A colored image in a transparency consists of three dye part-images lying in three superimposed emulsion layers. One image is magenta in color, hence gives the green densities. Another image is cyan, while the third image is yellow. These give the red and blue densities respectively.

When the composite is illuminated by means of red light, the rays will pass completely undisturbed through the magenta and yellow layers, provided these are theoretically correct. Upon passing through the cyan, absorption will take place to correspond to the image density Thus the red light becomes modulated in accordance with the amount of red densities present in the transparency. In a similar manner it is possible to obtain the green and the blue densities, by exposing with green and blue light respectively. Provided the dyes in the transparency are accurately chosen, it becomes possible to obtain excellent color separations from this type of color transparency. But no dyes are known that are perfectly correct in their absorptions and transmissions. Every magenta dye absorbs some red and blue. Hence when the red light passes through the magenta image, some of the red rays become absorbed. The light becomes modulated to correspond to the green densities to the extent to which absorption takes place. Therefore there is imposed upon the record of the red densities a weak record of the green densities and the quality of the separation becomes materially reduced. A similar story is true with respect to the green and the blue densities, and unfortunately, to a considerably greater extent Masking, therefore, is in order.

If the amount of correction is known, it will be possible to subtract this amount from the negatives, by adding positives from the other negatives to each separation. This would be the normal manner of procedure, corresponding to the technique disclosed above Dr Gaspar, however, adopted a more suitable method. In general, the red-filter separation need not be corrected. This is made by contact printing with red light, and the negative is processed to yield a cyan dye image whose gamma, measured through a red filter, is 1 00. After drying, the colored negative image is registered with the original transparency. Where this is done, the cyan positive image in the transparency becomes completely neutralized by the cyan negative mask and, in so far as the exposing green light is concerned, the transparency has overlayed upon it a uniform cyan fog. Just as much green light will be restrained in the shadows as in the highlights. Now if an exposure be made with green light, the light will be modulated correctly by the magenta image, and uniformly reduced in intensity by the cyan image plus mask. The efficiency of the yellow to green light is quite high, so but secondary or tertiary effects will be noted here.

To correct for the blue it is necessary to use two masks, one a cyan made as above, and the other made from the cyan-masked transparency by means of green light. This last yields the magenta mask, hence it must be colored a magenta. The combined cyan and magenta masks, registered with the original transparency, are now used to make the blue-filter separation.

This method when applied to Kodachrome transparencies, gives automatic correction provided the colors used to dye the negative masks are the same as those used in the original Kodachrome. Dr. Gaspar proposed his scheme for use with Gasparcolor, and the materials upon which the masks were made could be identical with those used in Gasparcolor. But the Kodachrome dyes are not known The patents list a number of different magentas, cyans, and yellows However, no tremendous differences lie between the various colors A good set to use would be para-nitro-phenyl-aceto-nitrile for the magenta, di-chlor-alpha naphthol for the cyan, and aceto-acet-anilide for the yellow. These are the coupling agents that are added to a developer containing 2-amino-5-di-ethyl-amino-toluene-mono-hydrochloride. A complete discussion of color development is contained in Chapter 23, but since this procedure is of increasing importance, the modus operandi will be discussed now.

Coupler developers yield dye images together with the silver, so that after the removal of the silver, a pure dye is left behind The developer is concocted by mixing three stock solutions

Stock Solution A.	
Water	1000 parts
Potassium metabisulphite	10 parts
2-amino-5-di-ethyl-amino-toluene-mono-hydrochloride	5 parts
Potassium bromide	10 parts
Potassium thiocyanate	5 parts
Stock Solution B	
Water	1000 parts
Sodium carbonate	100 parts
Stock Solution C (for magenta)	
Para-nitro-phenyl-aceto-nitrile	1 part
Acetone	100 parts
Stock Solution C (for cyan).	
Di-chlor-alpha-naphthol	2 parts
Acetone	100 parts
Stock Solution C (for yellow).	
Aceto-acet-di-chlor-anilide	10 parts
Acetone	100 parts

For use, take 100 parts of solution *A*, 100 parts of solution *B*, 5 parts of solution *C*, then make up with water to 1000 parts. Develop for three minutes at 70 F. Each exposure must be developed in a fresh solution, which should be immediately discarded after use, as the solutions do not keep except in the stock form described above After development the images are fixed in hypo to which a little metabisulphite has been added. Care must be taken that the acidity is maintained at a minimum, as acids destroy the dye image A thorough wash removes the hypo. Treatment with one per cent ferricyanide plus one per cent bromide converts the silver to silver bromide, which can then be removed with hypo. After a wash, the images can be dried and registered with the original. It should be noted that this type of masking is analogous to the masking described by the Eastman Kodak Company, and described above. But there the masking is accomplished by registering the dyed matrix with the separation negatives, while here it is achieved by registering a colored separation with the original copy. This type of masking allows separations to be color-corrected for the deficiencies of the dyes in the original while making the separations, after which the ordinary type of masking can be applied to correct for the deficiencies of the synthesis colors

It is not essential, of course, to use color masks if the amount of correction to be applied is known. In that case, it is sufficient to prepare black-and-white masks of the proper intensity, register these with the original, and make the separations through the combined black-and-white masks and colored transparency.

A scheme along these lines is outlined in the Gevaert "Graphic Art Handbook," where it is proposed as a dodge to be used to reduce the excessive contrast in Kodachromes. Instead of making three separations, three masks are first made through filters that are complementary to the separation filters Thus the mask for the blue-filter separation, is made through a yellow (Wratten Nos 9, 12, 15, or 16). The mask for the red-filter separation is made through a cyan (Wratten Nos. 43, 44, 44A, 45, 64, 65, or 65A). The mask for the green-filter separation is made through a magenta filter (Wratten Nos. 31, 32, 33, 34, or 35). The contrast to which the masks are developed, is determined by trial and error Upon completion, the mask made through the cyan filter is registered with the original, and the combination exposed through the red filter to yield a cyan printer negative. The other two separations are made in an analogous manner, the masks being changed before each exposure.

In his discussion of this procedure, J S Friedman (l.c.) suggested that it is possible to combine the Gaspar, with the Gevaert schemes. Instead of using a yellow filter, the mask can be exposed partially through a red filter, and partially through a green, the proportion of the two exposures being in the inverse ratio to the sensitivity of the emulsion to these colors In that way it is possible to obtain equivalent red and green contributions to the mask. By this means, there have been copied upon the same mask the images in the cyan and magenta layers of the original The mask is color-developed a magenta as disclosed above. It is fixed, washed, and treated with ferricyanide-bromide, but instead of being fixed, it is thoroughly washed to remove the last traces of bleach solution, then color-developed a cyan. By this means there will be prepared a blue-colored mask, which, after the silver has been removed, is registered with the original Kodachrome When light is transmitted through this combination, the yellow image will modulate the blue rays and allow the other two colors to pass through unhindered. The cyan positive in the Kodachrome will be completely neutralized by the cyan negative image in the mask, so no modulation of these rays will take place. Similarly the magenta image in the Kodachrome will be neutralized by the magenta positive image in the mask. Therefore, the light, after passing through the Kodachrome will represent the image present only in the yellow layer of the Kodachrome. Since the red and green rays pass unmodulated, though reduced in intensity, it is necessary to make the exposure through a blue filter, to avoid loss of brilliance and formation of excessive over-all ground density.

This appears to be a rather long-drawn-out procedure to accomplish a desired result. It is possible, of course, to mix the cyan and magenta couplers in the proper ratio, so that equivalent amounts of cyan and magenta dyes are formed in the first development. Or, if the degree of absorption of blue by the cyan and magenta be known, the mask could be developed to that extent, as a black and white. A still simpler, though slightly less thorough way, would be to process the plate a magenta, or a cyan, and let it go at that. The green-filter separation is to be masked by means of a magenta filter or by partial exposures through the blue and red filters. Theoretically, this should be converted into a green by color development, but a more practical practice would be to leave it cyan or yellow in color. Similarly, the mask for the red filter separation is made through a cyan filter or by partial exposures through the blue and the green filters. This mask should be processed to yield a red. The simplified technique would be to leave it magenta or yellow in color. This type of masking is termed secondary, since each mask is made by exposure to secondary colors rather than to primary.

Since the colors used in the original Kodachrome are quite deficient, much better results would be obtained were it possible to mask these colors during the preparation of the original. A scheme to accomplish this is disclosed by N. E. Brookes (Eng. P. 496997). It is to be recalled that the Kodachrome transparency contains three layers, the bottom of which contains the cyan image, the central layer the magenta image, and the top contains the yellow. After the original exposure, the film is developed, the silver image is removed, and the remaining silver halides developed a cyan color. A bleach destroys the dye in the two upper layers, and converts the silver to silver halide, which is then developed to a magenta. This process is repeated, this time the bleach being confined to the top layer, which is developed a yellow.

This is the normal procedure. The Brookes modification is to expose the reformed silver halide salts in the second and third layers, by means of green light, through the already formed cyan image. Therefore the intensity of the latent image produced in the magenta- or green-density layer, will be reduced to the extent that green is absorbed by the bottom image. This is developed a magenta, and the procedure is repeated, this time using blue light and exposing through the images already formed. Thus the intensity of the latent image produced in the top layer is modified to the extent that blue is absorbed by the magenta and cyan images in the other layers.

In general, the practice of masking involved the use of several plates or films, registered with respect to each other. Special cameras were suggested, as pointed out above, which enabled one to register the mask with an unexposed negative plate, so that the final result would be a single emulsion layer. There have been other suggestions that accomplished the same result. One of them has been discussed in detail, and involved the use of negative masks registered with the original, if that is a transparency. The I G. (Ger P. 593666) suggested the following scheme: The separations were processed to retain the gelatin in a soft condition. The final step consisted in bathing them with a light-sensitive dichromate solution. Since the red-filter separation requires no correction, this is not so treated The green-filter separation, after sensitization with dichromate, is registered with a red-filter positive, and exposed to arc light. Where the light is incident upon the green-filter negative, tanning of the gelatin takes place. After exposure the excess dichromate is washed out, and the plate dyed with a black pinatype dye. Since this is not absorbed by tanned gelatin, a positive is formed, thus creating the mask in the same emulsion layer as the negative. The contrast of the positive is governed by the acidity of the dye bath, giving the operation a wide latitude.

The Interchemical Corporation (Eng. P. 501661) would use a double-coated emulsion upon which to make the exposures. One of the emulsions is a negative material, the other a positive The plates are not fixed out, with the exception of the red-filter separations, but are registered with the red separation, and a positive printed upon the second emulsion layer. A rather novel scheme, is the one suggested by L. T. Troland of the Technicolor Motion Picture Corporation (U.S.P. 2098441 and 2098442). Use is made of the Herschel effect, where the intensity of a latent image becomes reduced by exposure to red or infrared light. The procedure is applied to the printing of the matrix. This is first normally exposed to the negative under consideration. It is then exposed through the proper mask by means of red light. The loss of latent image will correspond to the mask. Other techniques of masking are disclosed by E. A. Weaver (U.S.P. 2183598 and 2186053) and by J. A. C. Yule (U.S.P. 2176518). A tremendous number of patents in this field are applicable only to the photomechanical trades. Of these, only a very few received consideration in this chapter.

It was stated above that masking has its real appeal in the making of separations from color transparencies such as Ansco Color or Kodachrome. A rather naïve treatment of the subject was outlined. At this point we will reconsider the problem from a more sophisticated point of view.

The usual procedure used in making color reproductions, be they purely photographic or photomechanical in nature, is to copy the original through the three separation filters. These, as was pointed out in Chapter 3, have mutually-exclusive transmissions, so that they have no interdependence whatsoever. When a red-filter copy is made, the image produced can be represented mathematically by the form

$$a_1r + 0.00g + 0.00b.$$

This means that the photograph is a graphical representation of the red densities to the value of a_1. If the photograph is a negative, then the constant a_1 is written with a negative sign in front, so that in the case above, since the red separation is a negative of the original, we should write

$$-a_1r + 0.00g + 0.00b.$$

Let us make another simplification. We will focus our attention upon one point in the original, a point that has a density of 1.00 when measured through each of the three filters. Then the value a_1 or $-a_1$ will be the contrast to which the negative was developed. In a similar manner we can write for the green and blue-filter separations, the forms

$$0.00r - a_2g + 0.00b,$$

and

$$0.00r + 0.00g - a_3b.$$

Taken as a unit, they give rise to the mathematical "color matrix" whose elements are the coefficients in the three equations, thus

$$\begin{pmatrix} -a_1 & 0 & 0 \\ 0 & -a_2 & 0 \\ 0 & 0 & -a_3 \end{pmatrix}$$

For a truly balanced set of separations a_1, a_2 and a_3 must have the same value. Thus the ideal balanced set of separations can be represented by a color matrix such as

$$\begin{pmatrix} -a & 0 & 0 \\ 0 & -a & 0 \\ 0 & 0 & -a \end{pmatrix}$$

Now suppose we photograph the same object by means of a film like Ansco Color or Kodachrome. We obtain a color image that is a reproduction of the original, which is composed of three monochrome images superimposed upon each other. Each monochrome is supposedly the image of a single primary. Thus the cyan image gives the pattern of the red densities, the magenta gives the pattern of the green densities, and the yellow the pattern of the blue densities as they have been registered on the transparency. Such a transparency can serve as a new original for the purposes of reproduction, provided it is possible to isolate each of the individual part images. The beauty of such a procedure would be that it would eliminate the expensive, intricate, and exceedingly delicate one-shot camera, and project the problem of separations into the precision laboratory where it belongs.

In order to make separations, we photograph the transparency through the three separation filters. If the absorptions of the cyan were ideal, i.e. if the cyan absorbed no blue or green light, and if the other two colors absorbed only the light they were meant to absorb, this scheme would work perfectly, and one-shot cameras would immediately be relegated to the scrap heap. But the colors are all impure, and in general absorb not only the primary they were intended to absorb, but also the others. A typical set of secondaries or subtractive primaries is the following

$$\begin{aligned} \text{cyan} &= 1.00r + 0.50g + 0.30b \\ \text{magenta} &= 0.15r + 1.00g + 0.45b \\ \text{yellow} &= 0.05r + 0.10g + 1.00b \end{aligned}$$

The cyan dye, when it is present in sufficient quantity to yield a density of 1.00 through the red filter, yields a density of 0.50 through the green, and a density of 0.30 through the blue filter. Similarly, when the magenta is present in a quantity sufficient to give unit density through the green, it also gives a density of 0.15 through the red and 0.45 through the blue. When the yellow is sufficiently strong to give a density of 1.00 through the blue, it also gives a density of 0.05 through the red, and 0.10 through the green filter

A color transparency is processed in such a manner that a gray scale is reproduced as a gray, and presumedly a density of 1.00 in the original is reproduced as a density of 1.00. This is the goal, and the departure from it is slight, so it will represent second-order corrections. We will therefore ignore them in this analysis. Given a reproduction process using the secondaries noted above, there is one, and only one, combination of the three which will yield a density of 1.00 through the three filters Let us suppose this is the combination which utilizes a concentration x of the cyan, y of magenta, and z of yellow. This is exposed and processed to yield a density of 1.00 through each filter.

Consider the red filter. The cyan will contribute an amount $-1.00x$, the magenta will contribute an amount $-0.15y$, and the yellow $-0.05z$. Together the total density will be -1.00, the negative signs indicating that the image obtained will be a negative. A similar result will be obtained from the green and blue-filter separations, so we have the three equations

$$\begin{aligned} -1.00x - 0.15y - 0.05z &= -1.00 \\ -0.50x - 1.00y - 0.10z &= -1.00 \\ -0.30x - 0.45y - 1.00z &= -1.00 \end{aligned}$$

Solving for x, y, and z, we obtain $x = .90$, $y = .50$ and $z = .50$. Substituting this in our equations, we get for the dyes as they are actually present in the film for a density of 1.00

$$\begin{aligned} \text{cyan} &= 0.900r + 0.450g + 0.270b \\ \text{magenta} &= 0.075r + 0.500g + 0.225b \\ \text{yellow} &= 0.025r + 0.050g + 0.500b \end{aligned}$$

The color matrix for the set as the dyes are actually present in the film, is therefore

$$\begin{pmatrix} .90 & .45 & .27 \\ .07 & .50 & .23 \\ .03 & .05 & .50 \end{pmatrix}$$

We have rounded out the values, since a third-place accuracy is meaningless in photographic sensitometry

A color matrix such as this is a veritable fountain of information for the photographic technician. Let us suppose that these are the dyes to be used in a monopack process utilizing color development. The emulsions must then be balanced for contrast so that the red-sensitive emulsion will yield a cyan image whose red contrast is .90. The green-sensitive emulsion must be such that the magenta image it yields has a green contrast of 0.50. The blue-sensitive emulsion must yield a yellow image whose blue contrast is likewise 0.50. Thus the color matrix of a reproduction process specifies completely the characteristics of the emulsions used in the monopack.

Let us now set up the problem of separations from such a transparency To compete with the one-shot camera, the transparency must yield separation negatives characterized by the matrix

$$\begin{pmatrix} -a & 0.00 & 0.00 \\ 0.00 & -a & 0.00 \\ 0.00 & 0.00 & -a \end{pmatrix}$$

Consider the blue-filter separation It will be represented by the expression

$$-0.27r - 0.23g - 0.50b$$

since the cyan and magenta both absorb blue light indicative of densities 0.27 and 0.23 respectively. Thus, superimposed upon the pattern of the blue densities (yellow image) will be the pattern of the red (cyan) and green (magenta) densities. In fact, the blue densities will only contribute 50 per cent of the total in this separation negative. To this extent we have correct blue rendition.

Suppose by some method, it is possible to make a negative characterized by

$$-0.27r - 0.23g + 0.00b$$

and this negative is registered with the transparency. The blue filter will see the unmasked transparency as a picture whose density at the reference point is represented by

$$0.27r + 0.23g + 0.50b$$

In combination with the mask, the transparency will be represented by the expression which is the sum of the two, i.e.

$$(0.27 - 0.27)r + (0.23 - 0.23)g + (0.50 + 0.00)b$$

or

$$0.00r + 0.00g + 0.50b$$

Thus by registering a special type of masking negative with the transparency, we were able to color correct it, in so far as the blue-filter separation is concerned.

The correcting negative contains both red and green densities, in the ratio of 27 to 23. Were we to make a negative through the green filter, we would copy the densities in the inverse ratio. The red-filter separation copies the densities in the ratio of 13 to 1. Obviously, some combination of the two is needed. If the ratio of the two is m of the red to n of the green, we can formulate these equations

$$.90m + .45n = .27$$
$$.07m + .50n = .23$$

Solving these for m and n, we get

$$m = .075$$
$$n = .45$$

Our correcting masks will be a red-filter negative represented by

$$-0.07r - 0.01g - 0.00b$$

plus a green-filter negative represented by

$$-0.20r - 0.22g - 0.02b$$

These are made by developing the red-filter mask to a gamma of 0.08, and the green-filter mask to a gamma of 0.44, these being the sum of the densities imaged in each mask.

The complete mask can also be made by giving the film two exposures, first through the red filter, then through the green. This is done to eliminate any possible latent image reduction by a Herschel effect. The combined masks register a total density of 0.08 as a result of the red exposure, and 0.44 as a result of the green exposure, when the development is carried to a gamma of 0.52. The difference between them is 0.36. Were the development carried to a gamma of 1.00, this difference would be $0.36/0.52 = 0.70$. This, then, is the logarithm of the relative exposures that must be given through the two filters. Therefore the green filter exposure is 5 times (which is the antilog of 0.70) that of the red. If the material being used requires an exposure of 10 seconds, with no filter, to yield the correct densities at a gamma of 0.52, and if the filter factors are 4 for the red and 6 for the green, then 40 seconds through the red, or 60 seconds through the green, would be the total exposures needed. But of the total exposure, the red constitutes only $\frac{1}{6}$, and the green $\frac{5}{6}$. Therefore the mask is made by first giving it a red exposure equal to $\frac{40}{6}$ or 7 seconds, followed by a green exposure equal to $60 \times \frac{5}{6}$ or 50 seconds. The exposed film is developed to a gamma of 0.52.

The mask will contain densities that will be the sum of the two masks, so that we can express it as

$$-(0.20+0.07)r-(0.22+0.01)g-(0.00+0.02)b$$

or

$$-0.27-0.23g-0.02b$$

This in combination with the transparency, when viewed through the blue filter will have for its mathematical form

$$0.00r+0.00g+0.48b$$

Thus we have succeeded in masking out the deficiencies due to the poor blue transmissions of the cyan and magenta images.

In a similar manner the other two colors can be corrected to yield the equations

$$0.82r+0.00g+0.00b \text{ for the red}$$

and

$$0.00r+0.45g+0.00b \text{ for the green}$$

The corrected transparency (when masked with the proper negative, and viewed with the proper separation filter) has the color matrix

$$\begin{pmatrix} 0.82 & 0.00 & 0.00 \\ 0.00 & 0.45 & 0.00 \\ 0.00 & 0.00 & 0.48 \end{pmatrix}$$

This is but half the job. We have succeeded in correcting for the poor spectral characteristics of the secondaries used in the transparency. Now we must balance the contrasts

The answer is obvious Let us suppose we desire our separation negatives to have a gamma of 0.80. This means our negative should have the color matrix

$$\begin{pmatrix} -0.80 & 0.00 & 0.00 \\ 0.00 & -0.80 & 0.00 \\ 0.00 & 0.00 & -0.80 \end{pmatrix}$$

We know now that a separation through the blue filter will yield a density of 0.48 where the original had a density of 1.00. We must bring this value up to 0.80. Therefore we must develop our blue-filter separation to a gamma equal to 0.80/0.48 or 1.67. Similarly the green-filter separation must be developed to a contrast equal to 0.80/0.45 or 1.78 The red-filter separation must be developed to a gamma of 0.98, or practically 1.00. This means that a process emulsion is in order for the making of the separations

If these separations are converted into positive prints by the reproduction technique symbolized by the color matrix

$$\begin{pmatrix} 0.90 & 0.45 & 0.27 \\ 0.07 & 0.50 & 0.23 \\ 0.03 & 0.05 & 0.50 \end{pmatrix}$$

the reproduction will be identical with the transparency. Thus by printing the separations on to a monopack material of the same type as used for the original transparency, or one equal in function to it (having same color matrix), identical duplication is achieved. This is of great importance in those fields where multiduplication is required.

If the spectra of the secondaries are known, two of the masks can be made by a single exposure upon a single piece of film. Consider a set of curves such as those indicated in Fig. 107. These curves are not the same as those which give rise to color matrix A. This is done expressedly to forestall any possible

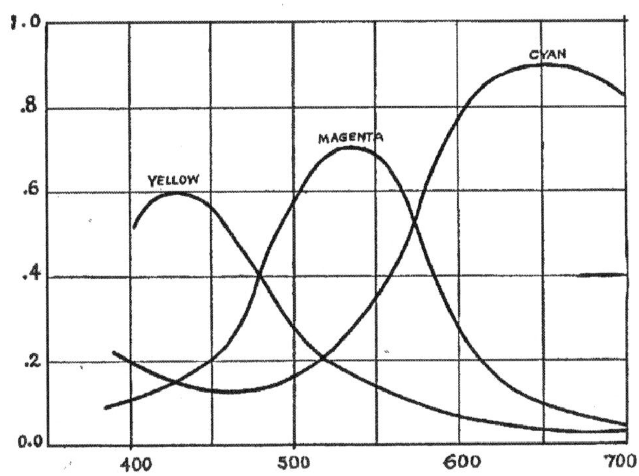

	Cyan	Magenta	Yellow
400	0.19	0.11	0.50
425	.15	.15	.60
450	.12	.20	.55
475	.13	.37	.28
500	.16	.58	.28
525	.23	.68	.19
550	.35	.68	.12
575	.55	.50	.09
600	.78	.25	.06
625	.88	.15	.05
650	.90	.09	.04
675	.88	.06	.03
700	.81	.04	.03

FIG. 107

use of the data developed here, for an actual case. We are interested only in showing how the problem can be solved for the general case, not for a specific instance.

The curves indicate that the cyan and magenta intersect in the region of wavelength 572. If we use monochromatic light of this wavelength, or a combination of Wratten filters, the center of gravity of whose transmission (in a very narrow band) is the wavelength, we would copy the cyan and magenta images in equal proportions Our mask requires a proportion of 27 of the cyan to 23 of magenta, i e. the cyan is to be copied to a slightly greater extent This will be true if we shift the center of gravity slightly, say to 575 mμ At 600 mμ, the ratio of cyan to magenta will be almost 3 to 1. At 550 mμ the ratio of cyan to magenta is .35 to .68 or 1 to 2. So it is seen that depending upon the wavelength used, we can get almost any ratio desired of cyan to magenta

The magenta and yellow curves intersect at about 480 mμ. Using light of this wavelength, we copy the yellow and magenta images in equal amounts. At shorter wavelengths we would copy more yellow than magenta, while at longer wavelengths the reverse is true. Since the yellow and cyan curves do not intersect in the regions of their high absorptions, we cannot make a mask for the green-filter separation in this manner.

In the analysis above we used a negative density. This density is a value arrived at by a simple calculation. Consider the negative made of a gray scale whose densities vary from 0 00 to 2.00. That portion in the negative which corresponds to a density of 0.00 in the original, will be the blackest. Suppose we developed the negative to a gamma of 0.80, and that we were very careful to expose so that we are on the straight-line part of the curve. Suppose the straight-line portion starts at a density of 0.30, so that this point corresponds to the point in the original with a density of 2.00. Then the point corresponding to 0.00 on the original will have a density of $0.30 + 0\ 80 \times 2\ 00$ or 1.90. The point in the negative which corresponds to the density of 1.00 in the original, will have a density of $0\ 30 + 0.80 \times 1.00 = 1.10$. The difference between these densities will be $1.10 - 1.90 = -0.80$. This is the negative density which we used in our equations above It is the difference in the densities in the negative, between a pure white and the point under consideration. If that point has a density of 1.00, then the actual value obtained is likewise a measure of the contrast to which the negative was developed. In the case of separations made from transparencies, where light is absorbed by all three layers, each layer will contribute to the total, so that the negative contrast to which a film was developed which has for its form

$$-0.90r - 0\ 07g - 0\ 03b$$

would be $0.90 + 0\ 07 + 0.03$ or 1.00.

CHAPTER 20

CHEMICAL TONING

THE black-and-white photographic image is composed of finely divided silver In such condition it is an excellent reducing agent If the oxidation is carried out in the presence of a silver ion precipitant, the metallic image becomes converted into one composed of silver salts. These can be made to undergo other reactions, such as conversion into a salt of a different metal. In this manner it becomes possible to convert the silver into practically any desired insoluble salt, which may itself be colored, as are the heavy metal ferrocyanides, or can be converted into such, as is the case with nickel ferrocyanide. Processes depending upon this type of procedure, are known as "chemical toning."

By far the most popular form of toning starts with the conversion of the silver image into a mixture of silver and some other insoluble metal ferrocyanide. The reaction between silver and ferricyanide proceeds in accordance with the following scheme:

$$4Ag + 4K_3Fe(CN)_6 \rightarrow Ag_4Fe(CN)_6 + 3K_4Fe(CN)_6$$

For every atom of silver, one molecule of potassium ferricyanide is needed. As a result, the silver is precipitated as silver ferrocyanide, which localizes but one of the four ferrocyanide groups formed. The other three pass into solution and are washed out of the film. Therefore this method is very inefficient, since the greatest part of the desired reaction product is lost. No harm is done if it is desired to re-develop, since it is the silver salt which reacts here, and all the silver is used up. But if the purpose is to form the colored ferrocyanide salts of iron, copper, uranium, nickel, vanadium, etc, then only a 25 per cent efficiency is achieved

The early experimenters evidently recognized this fault, for efforts were soon made to overcome it by concocting solutions which would precipitate the ferrocyanide ions as fast as they are formed. This is accomplished by having soluble salts of the desired metal present in the solution. If it is desired to form nickel ferrocyanide, the solution is compounded to contain nickel nitrate. In that case, the reaction would go in accordance with this equation:

$$4Ag + 4K_3Fe(CN)_6 + 6Ni(NO_3)_2 \rightarrow Ag_4Fe(CN)_6 + 12KNO_3 + 3Ni_2Fe(CN)_6$$

Both silver and nickel ferrocyanide are insoluble, so that all of the ferrocyanide is precipitated. But not all of it exists in usable form. For instance, if the color itself consists of a nickel compound, then only three of the four ferrocyanide molecules are used. This is much better than the first case, where only that part of the total is available which exists as part of the silver ferrocyanide molecule

If an ion is present in the toning solution which precipitates silver more easily than the ferrocyanide, then it becomes possible to use up all the ferrocyanide. The reaction then proceeds according to this schedule:

$$4Ag + 4K_3Fe(CN)_6 + 8Ni(Br)_2 \rightarrow 4AgBr + 4Ni_2Fe(CN)_6 + 12KBr$$

Now all four molecules of ferrocyanide are precipitated as the nickel salt, which can then be converted into the color by reaction with di-methyl-glyoxime. We can now compare the three possibilities In the first case only one molecule of ferrocyanide is available, since all the rest is removed in the wash which must always follow the treatment with ferricyanide. By treatment with nickel halides, the silver ferrocyanide becomes converted into the nickel salt thus

$$Ag_4Fe(CN)_6 + 2NiBr_2 = 4AgBr + Ni_2Fe(CN)_6$$

In the second case, three molecules of nickel ferrocyanide are formed directly. If the print be then further treated with nickel bromide, the fourth molecule is formed In the third case, the four molecules become formed immediately.

It is apparent that this procedure can be utilized to intensify a weak silver image. It is merely necessary to treat the nickel-silver ferrocyanide image with silver nitrate, to cause the nickel salt to become converted into the silver salt. Since in the second case there are three nickel ferrocyanide molecules, containing six nickel ions, there will be required twelve silver ions, thus multiplying the silver content four times

Not only are the heavy metal ferrocyanides insoluble, but the corresponding ferricyanides are also This makes the devising of toning baths a difficult matter, but by the application of a few elementary principles of physical chemistry, their formation becomes possible Let us consider these principles. A salt like NaCl can be represented as a union of a positively charged sodium ion, Na^+, with a negatively charged chloride ion, Cl^-. This can actually be shown to be the case by the imposition of a strong electric field about liquid NaCl. It will be found that the sodium will migrate to the negative pole, while the chlorine will migrate to the positive pole. When salt is dissolved in water, this type of dissociation also takes place, and if an electric field be imposed upon a solution of NaCl in water, it will be found that the sodium will migrate to the negative pole, while the chlorine will go to the positive. This indicates that under the imposition of the field, the two electrically charged ions dissociated to form free positively and negatively charged particles The strength of the field required to completely dissociate the ions, depends upon the surroundings. Thus to dissociate molten sodium chloride will require very strong currents, while relatively weak ones will suffice in the case of a solution. The reason for this is that water has a dielectric constant equal to a value of approximately 80.

When two charged particles, of opposite sign, are a distance d apart, the force of attraction between them is given by Coulomb's law:

$$F = \frac{1}{c} \frac{e_1 \times e_2}{d^2}$$

where F is the attractive force, e_1 and e_2 the numerical value of the charges, and c, a constant, called the dielectric constant, of the medium in which the charges are dispersed. This law holds true not only for isolated charges in space, but also for ions in solution It is therefore seen that the force which holds the sodium and chloride ions together in the solid state, will be much greater than when the salt is dissolved in water, for air has a value of 1.00 for the dielectric content.

That property of water, which gives rise to a value of 80 for the dielectric constant, acts upon all charged particles which are dispersed in it The action is to weaken the bond between the ions. In many cases, this weakening may be sufficient to allow the ions to become entirely free from each other, especially under the constant impacts received from collisions due to Brownian movement. This phenomenon is called dissociation, and the extent to which this takes place is called the degree of dissociation. Very weak solutions of salts are usually considered to be dissociated 100 per cent. Strong solutions are very seldom completely dissociated. Water, HOH, also dissociates very slightly to form hydrogen ions H^+, and hydroxyl ions OH^-. When a substance in its pure form dissociates, just as many negative as positive ions are formed, so that the solution remains in an electrically neutral condition.

When a substance AB, dissociates in water, an equilibrium is set up, which may be expressed by the equation:

$$\frac{(A^+) \times (B^-)}{(AB)} = \text{a constant}$$

The value for the constant is specific for each substance, and it is a function of temperature only Here (A^+) is the measure of the concentration of the ion A^+, (B^-) of the ion B, and (AB) of the undissociated molecule AB. If water is the substance considered, then (AB) or (H_2O) is a constant, and the equation can be written:

$$(H^+) \times (OH^-) = 10^{-14}$$

Since $(H^+) \equiv (OH^-)$, this equation can be solved for (H^+),

$$(H^+)^2 = 10^{-14}, \text{ or}$$
$$(H^+) = 10^{-7}$$

Water at a temperature of 25 C will dissociate to such an extent that the solution will have a concentration of hydrogen ions equal to 0.0000001 N. There will also be an equal concentration of hydroxyl ions.

Chemists have adopted a very convenient nomenclature for this value. The logarithm to the base 10 of this number, is minus seven. The negative of the logarithm is plus seven. This value, the negative of the logarithm of the molar concentration of hydrogen ions is written pH,

$$pH = -\log (H^+) = \log \frac{1}{(H^+)}$$

A neutral solution will have a pH value of 7.0.

The most general law of solutions can now be stated. Whenever any substance is dissolved in water, the product of the concentrations of the hydrogen by the hydroxyl ions must always be 10^{-14}. Since the first is measured by pH, and the second by p(OH), and since these represent logarithms,

$$pH + p(OH) = 14$$

In a neutral solution, pH = p(OH), so we must have pH = 7.0. If the hydrogen ions predominate, then the value of pH will be numerically lower. Acid solutions will have pH values that are less than 7.0 If the (OH) ions predominate, then p(OH) will be less than 7, so that the pH, in order to maintain the constancy required by the equation above, will be greater than 7.0. Alkaline solutions will be characterized by a value for the pH that is greater than 7.0.

Every solid substance has a definite and limited solubility in water Let us center our attention upon the substances with very low solubilities, such as the silver halides, which have the following solubilities.

AgCl	Silver chloride	8.9×10^{-5}	0.62×10^{-5}
AgBr	Silver bromide	8.4×10^{-6}	0.44×10^{-6}
AgI	Silver iodide	3.0×10^{-7}	10.3×10^{-7}

The values in the third column represent the solubility (in grams) of the substance in 100 cc of water. The values in the last column represent the molar concentrations. For ions in solution, in equilibrium with solid matter, we can write the following equation:

$$(A^+)^a + (B^-)^b = \text{constant},$$

where the chemical formula of the substance is A_aB_b. In the case of AgCl, both a and b are equal to one. The value for the constant would therefore be:

$$0.62 \times 10^{-5} \times 0.62 \times 10^{-5} \quad \text{or} \quad 0.37 \times 10^{-10}$$

since the molar concentrations of Ag^+ and Cl^- are identical in a pure saturated solution of AgCl in water. The values for the solubility product for some typical insoluble silver salts are:

AgCl	0.37×10^{-10}	AgCNS	0.49×10^{-12}
AgBr	0.20×10^{-12}	Ag_2S	1.6×10^{-49}
AgI	0.12×10^{-15}	HgS	4×10^{-53}

The importance of the concept of solubility product lies in this statement. If two solutions each containing one of the ions of a difficultly soluble salt are mixed, no precipitate will be formed unless the product of the ion concentrations in the mixture is greater than the solubility product. Thus, when a solution of silver nitrate is added to a solution of potassium chloride, no precipitate will take place until the concentrations of Ag^+ and Cl^- are sufficient to satisfy the equation

$$(Ag^+) \times (Cl^-) = 0.37 \times 10^{-10}$$

It must be carefully borne in mind that the equation above demands the silver to be present as a silver ion If something is added to the solution which represses that ionization, a buffering action can be noted. Let us consider the case of silver hydroxide formed by the addition of ammonia to silver salts. The very first addition of ammonia causes this reaction to take place ;

$$AgNO_3 + NH_4OH \rightarrow AgOH + NH_4NO_3$$

The solubility product of silver hydroxide is 1 52 $\times 10^{-8}$ Since silver nitrate is completely dissociated in a solution whose concentration is 0 1N, the molar concentration of silver ions would be 10^{-2}. Therefore if the ammonia dissociates to produce hydroxyl ions to the extent of 10^{-7}, a precipitate would form. Ammonia, in normal solution, dissociates to the extent of 0 4 per cent, so that a molar solution of ammonia would give rise to 0 004 moles of OH ions The (OH) concentration would then be 10^{-3}, which is considerably greater than the value required to satisfy the solubility product law. Therefore precipitation would take place But immediately a second reaction takes place, typified by the equation

$$AgOH + 2NH_3 \rightarrow [Ag(NH_3)_2]OH$$

This new substance is extremely soluble, but in solution it dissociates in a peculiar manner

$$[Ag(NH_3)_2]OH \rightleftarrows [Ag(NH_3)_2]^+ + OH^-$$

No longer are there present silver ions, except to the extent that is demanded by a new relationship

$$\frac{(Ag^+) \times (OH^-)(NH_3)^2}{(Ag(NH_3)_2OH)} = k,$$

The addition of ammonia reduces to a very small fraction the concentration of the silver ions present in solution. This disturbs the equilibrium condition between (Ag^+) and (OH^-) so that the product must necessarily become less than 10^{-8}. In order to preserve this value, some silver hydroxide will go into solution If the concentration of ammonia is sufficient to react with the dissolved silver, it will immediately go back into solution and more silver hydroxide will be forced to dissolve In this manner it becomes possible to dissolve completely all the silver. The solubility of silver chloride in ammonia, potassium cyanide, sodium sulphite, potassium iodide, hypo, etc., can all be explained in a similar manner There are formed substances with very limited dissociation into silver ions, but which, nevertheless, are very soluble in water.

When silver ions are added to a solution that contains two groups that form insoluble salts with the silver, the salts will be formed in the inverse ratio to the solubility products of the two. This comes into play, for instance, in the case when a silver image is oxidized by means of a solution of ferricyanide Both silver ferrocyanide and ferricyanide are insoluble, but since there are four silver atoms in the ferro salt and only three in the ferri, the solubility product for the first varies with the fourth power of the silver concentration, and for the second it varies with the third power. Therefore the value for the ferro salt will be much lower than the value for the other As the silver and the ferri react, silver ions are formed together with ferrocyanide ions. In solution, at the instant of reaction, there will be ferricyanide, ferrocyanide, and silver ions present, the first being present in relatively high concentrations, the other two in very small amounts Equilibrium between the ions will quickly be established, in accordance with the relationships

$$(Ag^+)^4 \times (Fe(CN)^{\equiv}_6) = k_1, \text{ and}$$
$$(Ag^+)^3 \times (Fe(CN)_6^{\equiv}) = k_2$$

As soon as enough silver and ferrocyanide ions are formed to satisfy these relations, the two insoluble salts will begin to be precipitated inversely to the ratio of the values k_1 and k_2. Thus if k_2 is 10^3 times as great as k_1, the silver ferrocyanide, corresponding to the constant k_1 will be precipitated 10^3 times as rapidly as the ferricyanide. The final image will consist of 999 parts of ferrocyanide and one part of ferricyanide For all practical purposes, this can be considered as consisting of pure ferrocyanide

When a silver image is treated with a mixture of potassium ferricyanide and chloride, the image will consist of silver chloride only This would indicate that the solubility product for silver chloride, which is 0.37×10^{-10}, is considerably lower than the value for silver ferrocyanide. The value for the bromide is 0.20×10^{-12}, a value that is about sixty times less than that of the chloride. Therefore when both chloride and bromide ions are present in a solution it will be predominantly silver bromide that will be precipitated, with an appreciable mixture, approximately $1\frac{1}{2}$ mole per cent, of the chloride. The value for the iodide is $0\ 17 \times 10^{-15}$, a thousand times less than the value for the bromide.

These principles can be applied in another manner. The conversion of a silver image to one of silver chloride is very easily accomplished by use of copper salts plus sodium chloride But it may be desirable to have an image of thiocyanate, or iodide, since these substances can absorb basic dyes while the silver chloride will not. If the silver chloride image be treated with a solution of potassium thiocyanate, or potassium iodide, a reaction will take place in this manner· As soon as the solution has saturated the film, enough silver chloride will dissolve to satisfy the equation

$$(Ag^+) \times (Cl^-) = 0.37 \times 10^{-10}$$

But since there are present iodide ions, a new equilibrium will be established, namely:

$$(Ag^+) \times (I^-) = 0.17 \times 10^{-15}$$

The less soluble silver salt of the two, the one with the lower value for the solubility product, will be precipitated and as long as there is AgCl left this reaction will continue, until finally practically all the chloride will have been converted into the iodide It is not possible to convert the iodide into any salt whose solubility product will be greater than 0.17×10^{-15}, unless there are added substances to the solution which form non-dissociated silver complexes with the iodide Under such conditions the value for (Ag^+) can be made so low that even with iodide present in the solution, the product will be less than 0.17×10^{-15}. This happens when silver salts are treated with hypo, cyanide, thiourea, thiocyanate, very large excesses of iodide (to the order of 10 per cent or more), and many other salts In these cases there are formed silver complexes in which ionization into silver ions becomes reduced to a value that is a minute fraction, one thousandth or less, of the former value. Then, regardless of whether this non-dissociated silver complex is soluble or not, the silver ions become depressed to practically the vanishing point.

The principle just enunciated is used to a considerable extent in compounding single-solution copper and iron toners Cupric and ferric ferricyanides are insoluble in water. Therefore should ferric or copper salts be added to ferricyanide solutions, an immediate precipitate is formed But both these metals form non-dissociated salts with citrates, oxalates, etc. Therefore when it is desired to form single-solution toners which contain cupric or ferric salts together with the ferricyanide, it is essential that citrates or oxalates be present The most convenient method to use with ferric salts is to utilize ferric ammonium citrate or oxalate. With copper salts it is necessary to have present from fifty to one hundred grams of potassium oxalate or citrate per liter of solution. Then the ferric or cupric ferricyanide will no longer precipitate

A similar scheme is used with iron developers. It will be recalled that when exposed silver halides are treated with ferrous salts, metallic silver is formed, the ferrous ion being simultaneously converted into ferric ions in accordance with the equation:

$$Ag^+ + Fe^{++} \rightleftarrows Ag^0 + Fe^{+++}$$

This is a reversible reaction. When halides are present, the concentration of the silver ions will be considerably depressed, causing the reaction to proceed to the left. Therefore ferrous sulphate cannot be used as a developer, since the tendency would be for the ferric salts formed to immediately attack the silver to yield silver halides again But when potassium oxalate is added to ferrous sulphate in sufficient concentration, there is formed the ion $Fe(C_2O_4)_2^{=}$, present to the extent required by the equilibrium

$$K_2Fe(C_2O_4)_2 \rightleftarrows FeC_2O_4 + K_2C_2O_4$$

The ferrous oxalate is present in free form, only to a very mild extent, but in sufficient quantity to have present an appreciable amount of ferrous salts The complex $K_2Fe(C_2O_4)_2$ is quite soluble, but very, very little dissociated, sufficiently low to enable the otherwise insoluble ferrous oxalate to remain in solution The corresponding ferric salt $K_3Fe(C_2O_4)_3$ is also soluble, and but slightly dissociated to form ferric ions. A condition similar to the one noted for the use of the silver ferro- and ferricyanides, is true here. The instability constants in the two cases

$$Fe_2(C_2O_4)_3 + 3K_2C_2O_4 \rightleftarrows 2K_3Fe(C_2O_4)_3 \quad \text{and}$$
$$FeC_2O_4 + K_2C_2O_4 \rightleftarrows K_2Fe(C_2O_4)_2$$

depend upon the third powers of the concentration of potassium ions in the case of ferri salts, and upon the second power in the case of the ferrous salts. Therefore the ionization of the ferric ion will be considerably reduced in a mixture of the two salts, leaving the concentration of the ferrous ions to be a maximum. Now when a silver image is treated with potassium ferrous oxalate, there will be sufficient ferrous ions formed to react with the silver salts. As fast as the ferric salts are formed, they unite with excess oxalate ions to form the complex ferric oxalate ion, that is relatively unionized. As fast as the ferrous salt is removed by the conversion into the ferric ion, more of the ferrous oxalate ion will dissociate, since equilibrium must be maintained. Therefore the presence of a large quantity of the very weakly dissociated complex, $Fe(C_2O_4)_2^{=}$, acts as a reservoir of ferrous ions This is called a buffer action. Its greatest use is in the control of the pH of a solution.

As was pointed out above, whenever water is present, in the water phase there must exist this equilibrium

$$(H^+) \times (OH^-) = 10^{-14}$$

If a mole of an acid which is completely dissociated, is dissolved in water, there will be present 10^0 or 1 mole of hydrogen ions. In that case the value for (H^+) will be 10^0 or 1, and the value for the (OH^-) will be 10^{-14} We can write this in the form (cf. above)

$$pH = 0$$
$$p(OH) = 14$$

Consider the case where 6 2 grams of boric acid are dissolved in water. This is sufficient to make a tenth-molar solution. Were this acid completely dissociated, the pH of this solution would be approximately one. But boric acid in this concentration dissociates only to the extent of 0.01 per cent Therefore instead of being tenth-molar with respect to hydrogen ionization, it is 0.01 per cent of tenth-molar, or 0 00001 molar. This would correspond to a pH of approximately 5 00. Despite the fact that a sufficient quantity of boric acid is dissolved in solution to be tenth-molar, the hydrogen ions are present only to the extent of 0 01 per cent of the total. Suppose now that to this solution is added something which uses up the acid or hydrogen ions.

Since equilibrium must be maintained under all circumstances, as soon as some hydrogen ions become used up, more boric acid will dissociate. The dissolved but undissociated boric acid acts as a reservoir of hydrogen ions, feeding these to the solution as rapidly as they are used up This principle is made use of in the concoction of buffered developers, a subject which does not concern us at this particular moment

We have indicated above how the principles of dissociation, ionization, solubility product, and instability constant, are applied to the preparation of single-solution toners It would sound well were it possible to state that the persons who developed the toning processes were fully familiar with these ideas, and that their work was the result of a careful analysis of the various constants involved But that would be a gross mistatement The solutions were compounded empirically. It was discovered that the addition of oxalates prevented the deposition of insoluble ferrous oxalate It was natural therefore to apply the same technique to the preparation of other solutions that would form insoluble iron salts Surely in 1840, when Herschel first discovered the cyanotype process (now known as blue printing), these ideas were unheard of And yet he used ferric ammonium citrate in solution with potassium ferricyanide.

This disclosure represents probably the first case in history where an image in color was produced. True, the color was a monochrome, blue-green, but it paved the way for all the others. This reaction, in this or some modified form, has been patented and repatented a countless number of times. As soon as it was generally recognized that the silver of the image could replace light, the reaction was again patented in any number of new variations By 1881 and 1882, when C. R. Woods published his notes concerning the conversion of the silver image into colored metallic ferrocyanides (*Brit J. Phot.*, Vol 28 (1881), p. 675, Vol. 29 (1882), p. 248) the reaction was so well known that it did not create any more than a passing notice The Woods technique was to treat the silver image with a solution of ferricyanide This, as was indicated above, formed an insoluble silver ferrocyanide, which was next converted into the corresponding copper, molybdenum or other heavy metal salts. Iodides could also be used. Mr. Woods did not propose his procedure to be used for the purposes of color photography.

This was done by R. Namias (*Phot Korr.*, Vol. 51 (1894), p. 323). Prof. Namias used the light-sensitive properties of the toning solutions. A paper was sensitized with a saturated solution of lead lactate to which had been added 10 per cent of potassium ferricyanide The lactate ion maintained the lead ferricyanide in solution by depressing the ionization into lead ions After exposure, the ferricyanide became reduced to ferrocyanide Since the solubility product for the ferrocyanide salts is considerably lower, as a rule, than the values for the corresponding ferricyanide, the presence of the lactate ions did not interfere with the precipitation of that salt. After exposure, the paper was washed clear of unreacted ferri, then treated with sodium or potassium dichromate The lead ferrocyanide reacted with this substance to form the yellow lead chromate, probably the finest yellow pigment that could be used in three-color photography. The paper was washed free of dichromate, then sensitized with a standard blue printing solution containing ferric ammonium citrate and potassium ferricyanide. This was exposed under the red-filter negative, to yield the blue-green image The paper was finally sensitized with copper lactate and ferricyanide. Here were noted some difficulties It was not possible to prepare a completely clear copper ferricyanide solution unless alkalis were present. But this also had a solvent action upon the brick-red image that was formed For this reason, it was not possible to completely fix the red image.

If the paper were sensitized with the lead lactate solution used for the yellow image, this difficulty was overcome because then an insoluble but fixable image of lead ferrocyanide would result. This could be converted into the brick-red copper salt by treatment with cupric acetate or sulphate. Another possibility, also pointed out by Prof Namias, would be to prepare silver images from the three separation negatives. The one made from the blue-filter negative was treated with the lead lactate-potassium ferricyanide solution. The silver reduced the ferri to ferro, forming a mixture of the lead and silver salts, as indicated above The red-filter positive was treated with the usual cyanotype solution, and this gave a blue-green image directly. The image from the green-filter negative was converted first into silver ferrocyanide, then into copper.

Many variations existed for the formation of the yellow and magenta images, but only one general reaction was used to form the blue-green impression. This was to convert the silver into ferric-ferrocyanide, or Prussian blue. The reaction was first disclosed by that early photographic scientist, Sir John Herschel, in 1840 He discovered that a mixture of ferric ammonium citrate and potassium ferricyanide was sensitive to light, especially in the presence of organic matter, such as paper A paper, sensitized with this solution, and exposed under a negative, gave a blue-green image of Prussian blue wherever the light reacted with the chemicals The unreacted salts could be washed out, leaving clear white areas The Herschel idea was utilized by J. Lewisohn (U S P 1071559 and 1126495, Eng. P. 2474/15) for all three images. Thus each component is first printed upon a cyanotype emulsion. Three blue-green iron ferrocyanide images result The print made from the red-filter negative is left undisturbed The blue-filter positive is dyed with aurantia, then treated with silver nitrate. This decomposes the cyanotype image, and fixes the dye in the image-bearing portions. The green-filter positive is dyed with eosine red and then treated with silver nitrate.

It was soon discovered that the action of light could be replaced by a silver image Generally it is sufficient to treat the silver image with

Ferric ammonium citrate	10 parts
Potassium ferricyanide	10 parts
Acetic acid	10 parts
Water to	1000 parts

As pointed out above, this solution would utilize only three-fourths of the ferrocyanide formed. The remaining 25 per cent is present as the opaque colorless silver salt, which should be removed in order to have brilliant images. But it can also be used to change the tones from a blue-green to blue or green. For instance, if the blue-toned image is treated with vanadium chloride, the remaining silver ferrocyanide becomes converted into the yellow vanadium ferrocyanide. This represses the blue transmission, yielding a green image. R. Namias (*Jahrbuch* (1903), p 158), utilized a mixture of iron and vanadium chlorides to obtain a green tone. After converting the image into silver ferrocyanide it was treated with:

Ferric chloride	4.8 parts
Vanadium chloride	4 parts
Ammonium chloride	10 parts
Hydrochloric acid, conc.	10 parts
Water to	1000 parts

The silver chloride that is formed can be removed by treatment with hypo.

A great deal of fuss seems to have been made with regard to the presence of halide in the toning solution. In the absence of such salts, part of the ferrocyanide is prevented from functioning, since it becomes converted to the translucent but ineffective silver salt. The opacity of silver chloride or bromide cannot be very much greater than that of the ferrocyanide, but Prof. E. J. Wall was sufficiently impressed by it to concoct a solution for green tones, that contained no halides (*Phot J.*, Vol. 68 (1921), p. 96; *Am. Phot.*, Vol. 16 (1922), p 396) A solution of vanadium oxalate was first prepared. To this end 100 grams of ammonium metavanadate is treated with 460 grams of oxalic acid, and 500 cc of water. Upon heating, the mixture first forms a paste which finally becomes very fluid, the color changing in the meantime from white to orange-red, and finally to a gray-green. Water is added until solution is achieved, at which time the color changes to a brilliant blue. If the volume is then made up to 1477 cc, there will be obtained a 20 per cent solution of vanadium oxalate, containing a slight excess of oxalic acid. If the sulphate is desired the oxalic acid is replaced by 197 cc of sulphuric acid, this being added to the ammonium metavanadate dispersed in 200 cc of water.

Sufficient heat will be generated by the addition of sulphuric acid to the water, to cause solution to take place, but more heat should be applied if the color is not the brilliant blue. The toning bath is compounded as follows:

20% Vanadium solution	50 parts
Oxalic acid, saturated solution	50 parts
Ammonia alum, saturated solution	50 parts
Ferric oxalate solution	as desired,
Glycerine	50 parts
Potassium ferricyanide, 10%	10 parts
Water to	1000 parts

The amount of ferric oxalate to be added is determined by the tone desired. Greener tones are obtained with less ferric salts, bluer tones with more.

It is to be noted that three insoluble ferrocyanide salts can be formed here — silver, iron, and vanadium. The exact amount of each will be determined by the relative insolubility products, at least as far as the iron and vanadium salts are concerned. Since this value is not a true constant, but varies with the temperature, no exact relationship, except under controlled condition, will be possible This is the great danger that is ever present when it is desired to modify the tone of a ferrocyanide image by the formation of mixed ferrocyanide salts For the people who are interested in the making of two-color prints, the iron-vanadium toned image can be highly recommended for the green image.

For three-color work, the pure vanadium image can serve for the yellow impression, although it is somewhat too far on the orange side. It was R Namias (*Jahrbuch* (1901), p. 171) who first proposed vanadium for toning. His technique was to oxidize the silver to ferrocyanide, then convert that into the vanadium salt In a later article, he suggested that the tone could be made greener by treatment with a citric acid solution of ferric alum (*Rev. franç. Phot.*, Vol 5 (1924), p 76). In this case the iron replaces some of the vanadium salt, so that the action could be stopped at any stage from the yellow of the pure vanadium to the cyan of the pure iron ferrocyanide.

Besides the lead chromate or vanadium ferrocyanide images, other types, such as an image composed of silver and mercury iodides, could be used for the yellow. A Hamburger, inventor of the Polychromide process, claimed to be the first to utilize this (*Brit. J. Phot.*, Vol 70 (1923), p 183, Eng. P. 20880/11; U S.P 1059867; Ger. P. 329273), but Wall, in his monumental "History of Three-Color Photography," (p. 416 ref No. 36) points out that C. R. Woods had suggested a similar idea in his 1882 paper, and that G Brunel, in his book "La Photographie en Couleurs," published in 1891 (p. 108) suggested that a lead-ferrocyanide image could be toned yellow by treatment with a potassium-mercuric-iodide complex. But even before this, C. Glissenti (*Phot. Times*, Vol. 17 (1887) p. 68) proposed to convert a cuprous iodide image into a yellow by toning with mercury iodide complexes. The Hamburger technique converted a silver bromide or lead ferrocyanide image into a yellow by treatment with the following bath:

Mercuric chloride	24 parts
Potassium iodide	48 parts
Water to	1000 parts

The print remains in this solution until the desired tone is obtained. The action can be stopped by an acid bath. H E Rendall also used an iodide image for the yellow (*Brit. J. Phot*, Vol. 70 (1923), p. 167). The silver was bleached by treatment with a 2.3 per cent solution of dichromate containing 1.25 per cent hydrochloric acid. After washing it was treated with a solution prepared by adding mercuric chloride to 12½ per cent potassium iodide until precipitation started. E. C. G. Caille (Eng. P. 15050/08) converted a silver iodide image into a yellow, by bathing with tartar emetic, then with mercuric chloride. J. F. Shepherd (Eng. P. 175003) in his Triadochrome process treated the silver image with mercuric iodide, ferricyanide, and bromide. The cyan was the usual cyanotype image, but he resorted to carbon to prepare the magenta. E. A. Lage (U.S.P. 1623123; Eng. P. 188692), used lead chromate for the yellow. This was formed by toning a bromide print made from the blue-filter negative. The paper was then sensitized with a cyanotype solution, and exposed under the red-filter negative. The magenta was formed by sensitizing the bromide with dichromate, and after exposure and removal of the unreacted dichromate salts, it was inked with a greasy magenta ink which took only in the exposed regions. M. S. Procoudin-Gorsky (Eng. P. 168100) converted the blue-filter image into a yellow by treating with potassium ferricyanide, potassium iodide, and ammonia. In the same disclosure he speaks of converting the yellow-sensation positive into a blue. This would indicate a very poor knowledge of the fundamental principles of color separation. It is the red, and not the yellow impression which must be so colored. A pure yellow impression has no place in color reproduction, since it would be equivalent to the combined red and green sensations.

A very close second to lead chromate for the yellow impression, lies in the use of cadmium sulphide. This is disclosed by Snyder and Rimbach in several patents (U.S.P. 2171609; Eng. P. 469133). Two stock solutions are used.

Solution A	
Cadmium nitrate	40 parts
Water to	200 parts
Solution B.	
Potassium citrate	300 parts
Citric acid	30 parts
Formalin	100 parts
Water to	800 parts

Solution *A* is added to *B* under rapid stirring, which is continued until a clear solution results. The bleaching bath is compounded by adding 20 parts of a 15 per cent solution of potassium ferricyanide to every 100 parts of the above. The print is bleached in this to completion. Since there are no halide ions present, some of the ferrocyanide will exist as the silver salt. To completely convert this into the corresponding cadmium salt, the print is removed from the solution and replaced there after the addition of 10 parts of 7 per cent hypo for every 50 parts of toning solution. The weak hypo slowly dissolves out the silver ferrocyanide, which is immediately precipitated as the cadmium salt. A very delicate balance must be preserved between the rate of solution of the silver salt and the rate at which precipitation of the cadmium salt takes place, otherwise there is danger that not only will loss of density result, but also loss of definition. This will take place if the silver is removed much faster than precipitation can take place.

After a thorough wash, the cadmium ferrocyanide is converted into the sulphide by treating with·

Sodium sulphide	5 parts
Sodium bicarbonate	7 parts
Water to	100 parts

A yellow image of cadmium sulphide is formed Any yellow stains in non-image portions that are not caused by deposition of cadmium sulphide, can be removed by treatment with a one and one-half per cent solution of hydrochloric acid. This is the yellow that is used in the Chromatone process, which is based upon the disclosures of Snyder and Rimbach More will be said concerning this, below

The magenta or red image can be prepared directly by toning with uranium. This substance was first used in 1859, when J. C Burnett (*Eder Handbuch*, IV, 4, (1929), p 159) prepared prints by exposing a sheet of paper sensitized with uranium salts, under a negative The light reduced the uranium. The image was developed by treating this with ferricyanide, silver nitrate, gold thiocyanate, etc. When potassium ferricyanide was used as the developer, a reddish brown image resulted, that was much more suitable for two-color photography than for three.

A comprehensive study of uranium toning was published by Dr. Sedlaczek (*Phot Ind.*, (1924), p. 234, *Am Phot*, (1925), p. 8). The tones obtained vary from a dark brown to a bright brick red. The brown tones are obtained from a solution containing a minimum of oxalate,

Uranyl nitrate	5 parts
Ammonium oxalate	10 parts
Hydrochloric acid, 10%	10 parts
Potassium ferricyanide	2 parts
Water to	1000 parts

By increasing the oxalate content to a maximum, such as the use of 100 parts of saturated oxalic acid, the tone becomes much brighter. He recommended especially the following formula:

Uranyl nitrate	5 parts
Potassium citrate	5 parts
Potassium ferricyanide	2 parts
Ammonia alum	10 parts
Hydrochloric acid, conc.	0 3 part
Water to	1000 parts

Since hydrochloric acid is used, the silver is converted into silver chloride. Hence fixation should follow the treatment. If cobalt salts be added to the hypo, colder tones are obtained, possibly by the formation of some cobaltous ferrocyanide, which is gray-green in color. A typical bath would be (Neblette "Photography, Principles and Practice," p. 448)

Hypo	5 parts
Potassium citrate	1 part
Cobalt nitrate	1 part
Water to	1000 parts

Mannes and Godowsky in their earlier patents, (U S.P. 1516824 and 1538996; Fr. P. 587395) utilized toning to separate the two images in their monopack. This, it should be recalled, consisted of a plate with two emulsions coated one on top of the other. The bottom emulsion was panchromatic, while the upper one was orthochromatic. After development and fixation, the two images were converted into silver ferrocyanide. Then the upper one only was redeveloped This left the lower image in the form of silver ferrocyanide, while the upper one consisted of metallic silver. Treatment with ferrous salts converted the lower image to a cyanotype, after which the upper image could be converted into a red by means of copper, uranium, or vanadium toning followed by a bath with a basic dye. The chemistry here is a little weak, since silver ferrocyanide when treated with ferrous salts would not produce an iron blue. The ferric salt must be used to accomplish this result, and ferric salts would be dangerous, since they would reduce the intensity of the silver image in the upper layer. Burwell of the Eastman Kodak Company, also used uranium to form one image in a monopack (U.S.P. 1966330). The exposed plate was developed with a dye-coupling developer which yielded a cyan dye plus a silver image in the two emulsion layers.

3·5 di-brom-ortho-cresol	2.0 parts
Alcohol	20 parts
Sodium carbonate	7½ parts
Potassium bromide	0.3 part
Di-ethyl-paraphenylenediamine-hydrochloride	2 parts
Water to	250 parts

The dye in the upper emulsion layer is destroyed and the silver image simultaneously toned a red by treatment with:

Uranyl nitrate	5 parts
Potassium oxalate	5 parts
Potassium ferricyanide	2 parts
Ammonium alum	12 parts
Hydrochloric acid, 10%	10 parts
Water to	2000 parts

This is practically identical to the uranium toner disclosed by Sedlaczek A uranium toning solution that was supposed to yield a true magenta tone, was disclosed by J. N. Thompson and Friese-Greene (Eng. P. 160540).

Potassium ferricyanide	12.5 parts
Uranyl nitrate	12.5 parts
Rose bengal	0.013 part
Naphthol yellow	0.013 part
Iodine	0.013 part
Acetic acid	12.5 parts
Water to	1000 parts

It is quite difficult to understand why a yellow dye is needed in the preparation of a pink

Copper salts could also be used for the preparation of the magenta or red image. As is true with uranium, it is much more suitable for use in two-color work than in three. Its use can be traced as far back as 1876, when Eder and Toch wrote a paper about it in the *Photographische Korrespondence.* Namias (cf. above) suggested the use of copper lactate, but he was unable to prepare a clear solution. In 1900, Eder (*Phot Korr.*, Vol. 36 (1900), p. 537), suggested that clear solutions could be had by use of ammonium carbonate, but the copper ferrocyanide image was also soluble in this, so that loss of image resulted. Ferguson, (*Phot. J*, Vol. 25 (1900), p. 133) succeeded, by having present potassium oxalate. The *British Journal Almanac* gave the following technique, which used two stock solutions.

Solution A:

Copper sulphate	6.25 parts
Potassium citrate	25 parts
Water to	1000 parts

Solution B:

Potassium ferricyanide	5.2 parts
Potassium citrate	25 parts
Water to	1000 parts

Just before use, mix equal parts of *A* and *B*. Sedlaczek also examined copper toning with the rigor he had applied to uranium, and he disclosed a number of solutions which gave tones varying from red to violet-brown. Since both copper and uranium toned images are so poor for the purposes of color photography, they need not be discussed at this point. A further discussion will be had in the chapter dealing with dye toning.

The convenience of the direct toning processes made it highly desirable to find a suitable method by which to produce a magenta image. T. T. Baker applied the finding of Feigl (*Zeit. Anal. Chem.*, Vol. 74 (1928), p. 382) to the solution of this problem (Eng P. 444773). Feigl had found that a magenta precipitate was formed when an ammoniacal solution of para-di-methyl-amino-benzal-rhodanine was added to silver salts Baker proposed first of all to bleach the silver image with copper chloride, forming an image of cuprous and silver chlorides. These are soluble in ammonia, forming cuprammonium and silver-ammonium complexes. Hence when treated with an ammoniacal solution of the rhodanine compound, a magenta precipitate will replace the metal salts. The rhodanine compound, although quite expensive, can be obtained from the Organic Chemical Division of the Eastman Kodak Company

Karl Schinzel proposed another attack upon the problem of toning directly. Just as the rhodanines can form colored insoluble salts with many heavy metals, so can the mercaptans (Eng. P. 500716). These are the thio-alcohols, and contain the —SH group. The hydrogen attached to the sulphur is quite acidic and can be replaced by many of the heavy metals, in which case colored insoluble products are formed. The silver is first converted into silver chloride then treated with alkaline solutions of the mercaptans. Most of the colors produced are reds and yellows, but it is claimed that cyans and magentas could also be obtained. The substances can be prepared by means of the well-known diazo reaction, where a diazonium salt is added to a boiling solution of the cuprous salt of the desired acid ion. Or some other salt can be used, in which case powdered copper should be added. The acid ion replaces the diazonium group in the compound. In this case it is suggested that a xanthogenate be used. This is a molecular mixture of carbon disulphide and an alkali sulphide After the addition, the reaction product is subjected to a saponification, which yields the free thio-alcohol or mercaptan. A yellow image is obtained by using the naphthalide of thio-glycollic acid, while thio carbine yields a red. It should be mentioned that the mercaptans are very undesirable substances with which to work. Not only are they very poisonous, but they have a very disagreeable odor. The well-known odor of the skunk is due to a derivative of mercaptan.

The most successful solution for the preparation of the magenta image lies in the use of di-methyl-glyoxime This was devised independently by Anton Jasmatzi (Eng. P. 402619), F Lejeune (U.S.P. 1963707) and Snyder and Rimbach (U S.P. 2100224 and 2171609; Eng. P. 469133). The Snyder and Rimbach disclosures are incorporated in the Chromatone process for three-color prints by toning, a technique that was marketed in the United States by the Defender Photo Supply Co. Colin Butement (*Brit. J Phot.*, Vol 84 (1937), p. 113) gave rather simple directions for the formation of the magenta image using this technique. The image must first be converted into an insoluble nickel salt, since the magenta compound is nickel di-methyl-glyoxime. This is accomplished by treating the silver image with the following bath:

Nickel nitrate	5 parts
Potassium citrate	15 parts
Potassium ferricyanide	2 parts
Nitric acid, conc	½ part
Water to	150 parts

The time of treatment is five minutes. It should be noted that a large quantity of potassium citrate is present in the solution to prevent the precipitation of nickel ferricyanide. This is in accordance to the principles discussed in the first part of this chapter. After a ten-minute wash, the nickel is converted into the magenta compound by the action of alkaline di-methyl-glyoxime,

Saturated solution of di-methyl-glyoxime	5 parts
Sodium hydroxide, 0 4%	5 parts
Water to	50 parts

The print is left in this solution until no further reaction takes place, after which it is washed in water for two minutes, fixed in 5 per cent hypo for a like period of time, and washed in water again. The acid treatment is necessary since this image may come in contact with the blue-toned image, and partially destroy it.

Snyder and Rimbach (cf above) use an entirely different chemistry They point out in their specifications that in order to successfully convert the silver of an image into a different salt of ferrocyanide, it is necessary to have in the solution an acid which is stronger than hydroferricyanic acid. This means that equimolar solutions of the two should give a lower pH for the added acid than for hydroferricyanic acid. There must also be present a salt which will prevent the precipitation of the ferricyanide, but not the ferrocyanide Suitable acids are oxalic, tartaric, acetic, nitric, etc. Suitable salts are the citrates, malates, oxalates, tartrates, benzoates, succinates, etc , all of which must be present in relatively high concentrations Since it is quite easy to replace the nickel in nickel ferrocyanide with ferric ions, to form a cyan image, and to replace the ferrocyanide ion by means of di-methyl-glyoxime to form the magenta, it is possible to use nickel ferrocyanide for both the magenta and cyan impressions The silver images are treated with:

Nickel chloride	50 parts
Potassium citrate	300 parts
Citric acid	30 parts
Formaldehyde	100 parts
Water to	1000 parts

To every 100 parts of this solution, there is added just before use, 20 parts of a 15 per cent solution of potassium ferricyanide. Because this solution will not keep, it is best to mix just enough for immediate use, and discard immediately afterward. Because chloride ions are present in this solution, the silver will be wholly converted into silver chloride, leaving all the ferrocyanide free to unite with the nickel.

To convert the nickel ferrocyanide into the rose-colored nickel-di-methyl-glyoxime salt, the bleached print, after a thorough wash, is treated with a di-methyl-glyoxime solution made alkaline, since nickel ferrocyanide is somewhat soluble in caustic. Instead of ammonia, Snyder and Rimbach used mono- and tri-ethanolamines. These are ammonia-like substances which are not volatile, hence can be stored.

Di-methyl-glyoxime	10 parts
Tri-ethanolamine	150 parts
Mono-ethanolamine	50 parts
Water to	1000 parts

The mixture of the ethanolamines and di-methyl-glyoxime is heated to 100 C, and kept at that temperature for 15 minutes. A red-brown solution results, which is then diluted with water to form 1000 parts of final solution.

Di-methyl-glyoxime is the simplest substance in a family characterized by the grouping

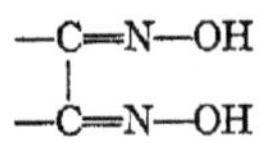

These are the dioximes of the ortho diketones. This grouping appears to be specific for nickel and palladium The reaction between nickel and dimethyl glyoxime was first discovered by Tschugaeff (*Z anorg Chem.*, Vol. 46 (1905), p 144, cf. also "The Application of the Dioximes to Analytical Chemistry," H Diehl, published by the G. Frederick Smith Chemical Co.), and immediately applied by him as a test for nickel It was soon developed that all substances containing the ortho dioxime grouping gave a red precipitate with nickel and a yellow one with palladium. Other metals also gave precipitates but not with such characteristic colors.

The statement that all compounds with the dioxime group yield the insoluble metal salts, must be somewhat qualified. Three types of compounds could be formed, depending upon the special relationship of the two hydroxyl groups, thus:

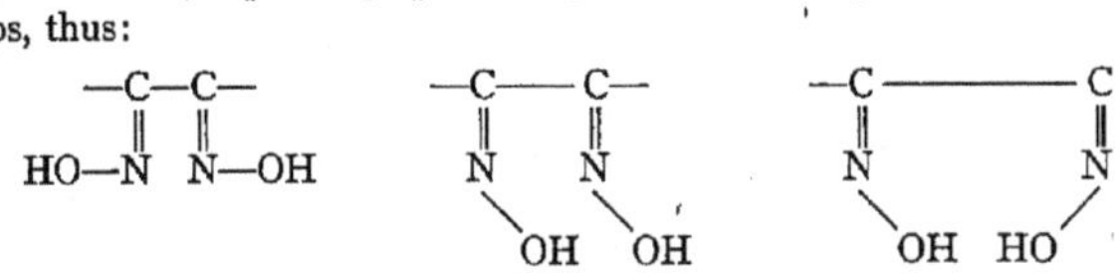

Anti form Amphi form Syn form

It is only the anti form of the dioxime which gives the red precipitate with nickel salts. Each nickel atom unites with two dioxime molecules to give a compound, with the structure:

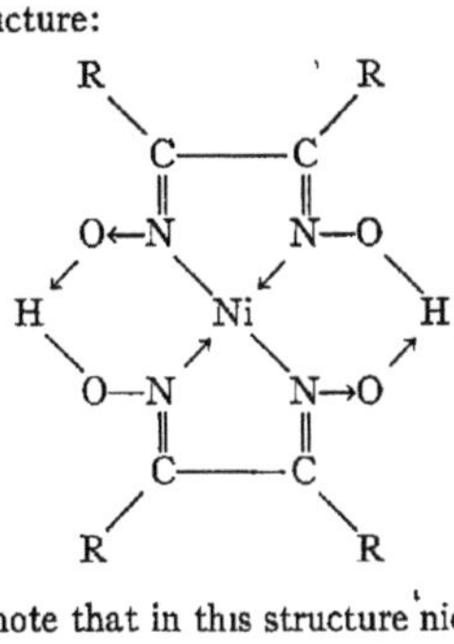

It is very interesting to note that in this structure nickel is quadrivalent, consisting of two covalences and two secondary valences.

The color of the precipitate is a red with enough blue transmission to make its use as the magenta in a three-color process just passable, but not preferable. The fact that the *R* in the formula above can be made different from a methyl group, gives rise to the possibility that the red may be somewhat bluer with other substitutions. This possibility should not be overlooked by the technician. Also the reaction with other metal salts is very interesting. Palladium gives a precipitate which has been described as being lemon yellow. This would seem to be ideally suited for the minus-blue impression. The disadvantage of the expense of using palladium would be offset by the simplicity of operation, and by the fact that no poisonous or disagreeable substances are involved

The enterprising chemist can investigate all compounds which contain two hydroxyl, amino, oxime, and other groups with a labile hydrogen, situated on adjacent atoms, for such groups always yield the possibility of a chelate ring formation The chemistry of the chelate rings has been discussed rather fully by Dr. H Diehl in an article which appeared in *Chemical Reviews* (Vol 21 (1937), p. 39) It is interesting to note that the blue-green pigment recently hailed as the answer to the printing-ink problem, is the copper salt of a complex containing a chelate ring, and composed of phthalic acid units It is known, for that reason, as a phthalocyanine.

Gold was suggested for the magenta image by W. Reichel (Eng. P. 6356/03; Ger P. 163326) The separation negatives were printed upon stripping paper and then toned Vanadium ferrocyanide, or lead chromate served to form the yellow image Iron ferrocyanide formed the cyan. No novelty can be found up to this point. But to form the magenta, the print is toned with gold sulpho-cyanate in conjunction with sodium iodide and potassium carbonate.

Complete systems for the preparation of color prints by chemical toning methods have been disclosed time and time again, with but little variety in the technique involved. A prolific patentee in this respect was F. E. Ives (U.S.P. 1170540, 1188939, 1225246, 1278667, 1278668, 1376940, 1499930, 1538816 and 1695284, Eng. P. 9954/15, 113618 and 119854). In one type of disclosure a yellow-dyed emulsion was used One separation was printed through the base, forming an image that did not penetrate deeply into the depth of the emulsion. This was toned cyan by treatment with:

Oxalic acid	4.25 parts
Potassium ferricyanide	1.75 parts
Sodium chloride	4.25 parts
Potassium bromide	0 35 part
Ferric chloride solution, U.S.P.	1.0 part
Water to	1000 parts

After this conversion, the film was resensitized by treatment with bromides, and it was exposed again, this time through the emulsion side. Development was accomplished with an acid amidol solution, which would not affect the blue-toned image already present. The second image was toned red with copper or uranium

Instead of printing the second image by means of resensitized silver bromide, Mr. Ives suggested that the print be sensitized the second time with dichromate. After exposure and removal of the unreacted dichromates, the film could be colored with dyes that stain only soft or only hard gelatin. Such dyes were well-known, being sold by the I G. under the trade name of "pinatype." Fast red would stain only those portions that received light. A procedure not very different from this was disclosed by S. J Cox (Eng. P. 15648/14) One record was printed and developed with a non-staining developer such as ferrous oxalate or amidol. This image was toned blue. After sensitization with dichromate, the print was exposed to a positive of the other separation, forming non-staining portions wherever the light penetrated. A positive image could then be obtained by staining with a pinatype dye. If a third color is desired, the pinatype dye is fixed by the action of copper sulphate, the print coated with sensitized gelatin, and the process repeated Several years prior to this, T. A. Mills disclosed a two-color process which called for recoating the film with a silver chloride emulsion (U S P. 1172621; Eng. P 28081/11; Ger. P. 275683). The film, after exposure, development, and toning with iron, was recoated with a printing-out emulsion. This, after exposure, was toned red with a mixture of vanadium and copper or uranium

In 1907 F. W. Donisthorpe utilized a uranium, iron, lead, or vanadium-toned image for the formation of a resist against the staining of a gelatin film by certain acid dyes (Eng P. 13874/07 and 158021; U S P. 923030 and 1517200). The solutions recommended were the following:

Uranium nitrate	1 part
Potassium ferricyanide	1 part
Water	45 parts

After toning in this solution for ten minutes, the negative was treated with:

Ferric chloride	1 part
Glycerin	1 part
Water	50 parts

The preferred bath, however, was:

Vanadium chloride	2 parts
Potassium ferricyanide	2 parts
Ferric chloride	1 part
Glycerin	1 part
Ferric oxalate	1 part
Saturated oxalic acid	100 parts
Water	900 parts

After toning, it was found that the gelatin about the silver image resisted the action of the pinatype dyes In 1913 (Eng. P. 7368/13; U.S.P. 1193879;

Ger. P. 329509) he discovered that these solutions could serve to tone positive silver images, for the preparation of color prints Simultaneously and probably with complete ignorance of this work, W F. Fox disclosed practically the identical procedure (U.S.P. 1166121, 1166122, 1166123, 1187241, 1187422, 1187423, 1207527 and 1256675; Eng. P. 552/14, 8728/14 and 3666/15). The full routine of both the Donisthorpe and Fox techniques, is as follows: A weak positive of one record is registered with the negative of the other. This is probably the first application of masking to continuous-tone color reproduction. From such a masked negative, a print is made. Let us suppose that it is the red negative that is used for printing. The positive is toned green by treatment with one of the solutions noted above. This will harden the gelatin immediately surrounding the toned image. The film is then dyed generally with a pinatype dye, complementary in color to the toned image The dye will take only in the non-image portions of the film. If there is registered with this another film that contains a silver record of the other separation, the dyed portion of the film will be modulated by this added silver image. This technique was improved at a much later date, by Emil Wolff-Heide (Eng. P. 340278). Mr. Wolff-Heide surface-sensitized a color-blind negative emulsion by treatment with colloidal sensitizing agents (cf. chapter on Monopacks) The image produced in the upper stratum of the emulsion was toned red with a uranium toner. This not only converted the upper image into a red, but it also hardened the gelatin in the image portions, so that they would no longer absorb pinatype blue In this manner a negative was produced in which densities in the upper emulsion layer modulated the green rays, while the black-and-white silver densities in the lower layer modulated the dye that gave a general stain to the rest of the gelatin. In the English patent Mr. Wolff-Heide proposed to place the dyed and toned negative in contact with the emulsion side of a positive. If this were exposed through the negative by means of blue light, the uranium-toned image would modulate the light, so that in the regions corresponding to the red-toned image there would be produced a latent image in the positive At the same time the pinatype dye would transfer to the positive. The film was developed, and the developed silver image toned red.

During a small part of 1931, the writer acted as consultant for the Wolff-Heide Photochemical Company. By this time the entire processing was changed. The negative was prepared, as previously, by surface sensitization of a color-blind emulsion. This gave a red-sensitive stratum in the upper half of the layer, and blue in the lower half After exposure, the film was developed, giving two images in the two emulsion strata. The top image was toned red with uranium, then the rest of the film was dyed blue with pinatype blue D. The colored negative was contact-printed upon another surface-sensitized film. The red rays, modulated by the silver image plus pinatype dye, would yield a latent image in the upper stratum of the positive film. The blue rays, modulated by the red-toned uranium image, gave a latent image in the bottom portion The processing technique was identical with the one used for making the negative In the final print, therefore, there was a red-toned image that was supposed to represent a copy of the bottom or blue density image in the negative, while the blue stain modulated by the silver image was a record of the red tones in the colored negative. It is, of course, very obvious that the silver image lying in the bottom portion of the negative will modulate both red and blue light passing through it, so that upon copying it will be impossible to obtain a correct rendition of the red densities lying in the uranium-toned portion of the image. To obtain a true copy of these densities, it is necessary to print with a light to which the other record is completely transparent. Since it remains as a black-and-white silver image, that is impossible.

The Ives technique of printing one image, toning it, then resensitizing the film with dichromate, was patented again by C. F. Jones (Eng. P 165380; Ger. P 349944), and in a slightly varied form, by M. S. Procoudin-Gorsky (U.S.P. 1435283, Eng P 135161). L. Dufay, of Dufaycolor fame, started with a thin base which had an emulsion coated on each side (Eng. P. 197912). It was thus possible to print two images, one on each side, and tone them separately. Upon completion, the duplitized film, as such double-coated film is called, could be mounted on a paper base. The application of this type of film to motion pictures was made by Hernandez Mejia (U.S.P. 1562828). W. V. D. Kelley (U.S.P. 1753379) printed an image on one side of duplitized film, toned it a blue, then converted the silver to silver bromide and printed two more images, one on each side. These were developed with amidol, then toned yellow and red respectively. Previously Mr. Kelley had patented other modifications of the Ives's technique (U.S.P. 1561168 and 1787201; Eng. P. 228887). These related to two-color prints in which iron was used to tone one image and uranium to tone the other. The procedure was patented once more by the Colour Film Ltd., in the late nineteen-thirties (Eng. P. 400251). The treatment of a silver halide emulsion with acid ferricyanide solutions, essential in toning, destroys a good deal of the sensitivity of the film. This can be restored by treatment with sulphite, bisulphite, hydrazine, or hydroxylamine (Eng. P. 404856 to I.G.) Kelley, Ives, and the Eastman Kodak Co., in many of their patents, noted this fact J. B. Harris Jr, printed an image through the base, converted the silver to copper ferrocyanide, then printed an image on the surface of the emulsion, and toned it with iron (U S P. 1825863). In a later disclosure (U S P 1848717) the bottom image was converted into a copper-mordant image. The sensitivity of the emulsion was restored by treatment with a solution containing NH_4Br and dichromate. This destroys the latent image left in the emulsion. The second image was developed, then the first image converted into a blue by treatment with basic dyes, and the second toned a red.

For a time, motion pictures in two colors were made by Multicolor and its successor, Cinécolor. These utilized duplitized film. The two separations were exposed in a camera simultaneously, in the form of a bipack. One separation was then printed on each side of the duplitized positive stock, which was dyed yellow to prevent any printing light from penetrating from one emulsion to the other. After development and fixation the film was floated on top of a solution (so that only one side was treated) which contained:

Ferric ammonium oxalate	9 parts
Potassium ferricyanide	4 parts
Ammonium chloride	8 parts
Hydrochloric acid	4 parts
Water to	1000 parts

At the end of five minutes, all the silver in the one layer became converted into a blue-toned image. The film was then washed, and treated with a uranium toner, such as:

Uranyl nitrate	3 parts
Potassium oxalate	8 parts
Potassium ferricyanide	2½ parts
Hydrochloric acid (conc.)	8 parts
Water to	1000 parts

Uranium ferrocyanide has the peculiar property of adsorbing basic dyes in direct proportion to the image density The blue-toned image does not have this property, hence upon treatment with solutions containing safranine, chrysoidine, rhodamine B, auramine, etc, it becomes possible to modify the color of the red-toned image to any desired degree, without affecting the other.

The silver of the image becomes converted into white translucent silver chloride, since chloride ions are present in both toning solutions. To make the picture more brilliant, it becomes desirable to remove this, a procedure which is accomplished by treatment with a hypo bath, such as:

Hypo	904 parts
Sodium bisulphite	22 6 parts
Chrome alum	16 8 parts
Potassium alum	16 8 parts
Potassium iodide	21.6 parts
Water to	3400 parts

This concoction contains two mordants for basic dyes, chrome and potassium alum. The presence of potassium iodide would indicate that the first step would be the conversion of the silver chloride to the corresponding iodide, a substance utilized by Traube as an adsorbent of basic dyes But it is open to doubt whether the silver iodide, even in combination with dyes, would remain untouched by so strong a hypo bath. The process is disclosed in United States patent 1897369 issued to W. T. Crespinel and H. K. Fairall, and in English patents 339323 and 384334.

A completely integrated process for the making of prints in color by toning methods, was marketed about 1936 by the Defender Photo Supply Company.

The process is based upon the disclosures of Snyder and Rimbach. The separation negatives were printed upon a special stripping paper supplied by Defender. It has been determined by actual test that the conversion of the silver image into the nickel-di-methyl-glyoxime compound resulted in no loss of density, but the conversion into the cyan resulted in a loss of 15 per cent, and the conversion into a yellow in a loss of 30 per cent (the "Defender Chromatone Process," seventh edition, p. 19). In making the exposures, it becomes necessary therefore to increase the cyan and yellow printing by 15 and 30 per cent respectively. Masking is recommended to improve the rendition of the reds and greens. For this purpose, weak positives are made from the red-filter negative, and developed to a gamma equal to one-third that of the separation negatives. These are superimposed upon the negatives. When printing from masked separations, the bromides should be developed approximately thirty per cent longer. The use of a densitometer makes the gauging of exposure very easy.

The green-filter negative is placed in the enlarger, and the instrument set for the desired size image. It is then locked in place. The negative is replaced by a negative of a gray scale, and a print made with a guess timing. This is processed to the final stage, including toning with di-methyl-glyoxime. The strip is then placed upon a white surface, and the step is noted where a pure white still persists. Let us suppose this to be the step which has a density of 1.50 in the negative gray scale A point is picked out in the negative which would correspond to a white in the final picture. This is read Suppose the reading is 1.15. There is a difference of 0 35 between the two densities. Since the density in the negative is lower than the one in the gray scale, less exposure must be given in order to preserve a pure white. The antilogarithm of 0.35 is 2.24. This is the factor by which the guess timing must be divided in order to obtain a pure white, so that if the original exposure was 150 seconds, the desired exposure would be 150/2.24 or 62 seconds. Let us suppose now, that the corresponding points in cyan and yellow printers are 1 25 and 1 05, respectively The density differential between 1.15 and 1.25 is 0.10, the antilogarithm of which is 1 26 Since the cyan negative is heavier than the other, more exposure will be required, so that 62 must be multiplied by 1.26 to obtain the correct value This gives an exposure of 78 seconds. To this must now be added the 15 per cent to compensate for the loss involved in toning The final exposure will then be 78 × 1.15 or 90 seconds

The yellow negative has a density of 0.10 less than the standard. Therefore the exposure time will be less by a factor of 1.26. The correct value was 62/1.26 or 50 seconds. But on top of this must be added the thirty per cent required by the toning technique. The final exposure will be 50 × 1.30 or 65 seconds. Therefore the magenta will require an exposure of 62 seconds, the cyan 90, and the yellow 65.

After exposure, the bromides are developed in 55–D for 1½ to 2 minutes at 70 F if unmasked, and up to 2½ minutes if masked separations were used:

55-D

Metol	2.4 parts
Sodium sulphite	36 0 parts
Hydroquinone	10 parts
Sodium carbonate, anhydrous	36 parts
Potassium bromide	4-13 parts
Water to	1000 parts

For use, dilute with two parts of water Normally it would be preferable to use the larger quantity of bromide, since that would insure fog-free development The bromides are fixed for at least five minutes in an acid hypo bath, which contains no alum:

Hypo	250 parts
Potassium metabisulphite	25 parts
Water to	1000 parts

After fixation, the prints are placed in water and allowed to stay until the film strips off the paper base. If this is not forced, smooth non-curling tissues result. After the tissues are stripped, they should be washed in not less than six changes of water At this stage they can be toned.

As indicated above during the discussion of the Snyder and Rimbach disclosures, the magenta and cyan tissues are bleached in the same bath. This is prepared by adding 25 parts of the solution marked *Red and Blue Toner A*, to 25 parts of water, then add 5 parts of the standard potassium ferricyanide solution. This is made by dissolving 11 parts of the crystals in 100 parts of water. The time of treatment is fifteen minutes, after which they are washed again through six changes of water. In the meantime, the yellow tissue is bleached in its bath compounded by adding 25 parts of the solution marked *Yellow Toner A–No. 1*, to 25 parts of the solution marked *Yellow Toner A–No. 2*, then adding 5 parts of standard ferricyanide solution. The addition of toner No. 1 to toner No. 2 should be accompanied by vigorous stirring, to prevent the precipitation of cadmium salts. In this solution, the yellow tissue is bleached for ten minutes. It is removed, washed once, during which time 10 parts of a 7 per cent hypo solution are added to the above, and returned for a further treatment of three minutes. At this time the bleach solution is discarded, and the tissue is washed through five changes of water.

To convert the bleached images to color, the washed magenta tissue is treated with the solution marked *Red Toner B*, until no further change is observed. The cyan image is treated with the contents of the bottle marked *Blue Toner B*, and the yellow tissue, with the contents of the bottle marked *Yellow Toner B*. The yellow image is now complete, and after five changes of water, is ready for assembly. The magenta-toned image is fixed in 7 per cent hypo for three minutes, and is then washed in six changes of water, rinsed in 1 per cent acetic acid, and washed again This completes the magenta image. The blue image is treated with dilute hydrochloric acid, washed in five changes of water, fixed in 7 per cent hypo for five minutes, then washed again in five changes of water. All three tissues are now ready for assembly.

Since the yellow image is the most opaque, it is placed on the bottom of the pack. A piece of gelatinized paper is soaked thoroughly until it has stretched to a maximum. It is then placed gelatin side up, upon a sheet of plate glass or masonite board. The yellow image is placed upon this (after a pool of water has been thrown on the surface), and squeegeed down thoroughly. The operator can mount the images either gelatin side up, in which case a mat surface is obtained, or collodion side up, which will give a glossy surface. After a few minutes to allow the surfaces to cohere somewhat, the magenta image is placed on the yellow. If a pool of water is placed on the surface of the yellow, the magenta tissue will slide very easily over it. After registry is achieved, the tissues are again squeegeed together, and the entire procedure repeated with the cyan.

After assembly, the print is allowed to set for a while, then the edges are taped down firmly to the board or glass with gummed tape that is at least one or one and one-half inches in width. Several layers of tape should be used because a terrific pressure will be exerted upon the sides during drying This should require eight to twelve hours, at the end of which time the print may be cut away from the board and mounted in the usual manner.

A novel toning procedure which should be capable of extensive generalization was outlined by Dr. Bela Gaspar, of Gasparcolor fame, in one of his earliest contributions to color photography (U.S.P. 1956017, Re-issue 21513; Eng. P. 379679). The main idea is that the silver image is converted into an oxidizing agent which is then made to act upon the ethers or ester salts of the leuco vat dyes We will have more to say concerning the chemistry involved, in the chapter dealing with color development

In the specifications, Dr. Gaspar points out that it has already been proposed to use leuco dye bases in emulsions, and these can be oxidized to the dye in situ with the silver image But the leuco bases are very unstable substances. The emulsions containing them could not be stored long, without air oxidation taking place. These difficulties could be overcome by the use of ethers, esters, and ester salts of the leuco bases. To oxidize these to their respective colors, the silver image is transformed into a compound which will act as an oxidizing agent. To make a blue picture, leuco indigo derivatives may be used. The substance di-acetyl-leuco-indigo is insoluble in water, hence may be added to the emulsion. It will be unaffected by alkaline developers, and neutral fixing baths.

The plate containing this substance dispersed in the emulsion, is exposed, developed, fixed, and washed in the normal manner. This will yield a silver image imbedded in gelatin containing di-acetyl-leuco-indigo The image is next converted into lead chromate, which may be accomplished in the following manner. Treatment with a ten per cent solution of potassium ferricyanide will oxidize the silver to silver ferrocyanide. No acid can be present, since this would saponify the acetyl groups and form the dye with no regard to the silver image. After a thorough wash, the image is treated with lead salts to form lead ferrocyanide. Another thorough wash removes excess lead ions, after which, treatment with a ten per cent solution of potassium chromate will convert lead ferrocyanide into lead chromate, a yellow pigment If this be treated with dilute hydrochloric or sulphuric acid, chromic acid will be released

$$PbCrO_4 + 2HCl \rightarrow PbCl_2 + H_2CrO_4$$

This is a strong oxidizing agent, and it will act upon the leuco derivative to saponify and oxidize it to the blue dye indigo. The untreated leuco base can be removed by treatment with acetone and hypo solutions. Instead of leuco indigo, the alkaline salts of the sulphuric acid ester of indoxyl can be used. These substances have the structures:

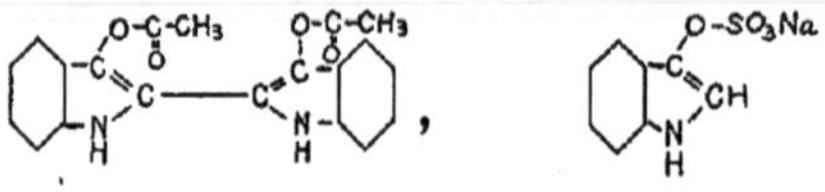

Di-acetyl-leuco-indigo Sodium indoxyl sulphate

It is also possible to use oxidized forms of the indigos, such as di-acetyl-indigotine. Under these conditions the silver image must be processed to yield one consisting of ferrous salts, after which it is made to react with the indigotine to yield indigo. In the first example dye formation took place by a procedure which involved saponification and oxidation. In the second example there was utilized saponification and reduction.

In another example, the silver image is converted into one composed of manganese dioxide The Gaspar specifications do not describe how that may be accomplished. For this step we must go back to the disclosures of the Neue Photographische Gesellschaft (Eng. P. 18370/03, 10898/04 and 21584/-06). A silver image is treated with:

Potassium ferricyanide, 0 5%	100 parts
Manganous sulphate, 2%	20 parts
Potassium bromide, 10%	15 parts

or

Potassium ferricyanide, 0.5%	100 parts
Manganous sulphate, 2%	25 parts

After the silver is completely bleached, the print is washed, then converted into the manganic dioxide by treatment with:

Potassium ferricyanide, 2%	9 parts
Sodium hydroxide, 4%	10 parts

This technique was evolved by the Neue Photographische Gesellschaft for the formation of colored images by the subsequent action of these solutions upon aromatic amines and other color formers, but it can also be used to tone prints by the Gaspar procedure. If the manganese dioxide image be treated with acids, manganic acid will be released, which could then act upon the sodium salt of the sulphuric ester of leuco-thio-indigo to form a red image. The yellow could be formed from helindon yellow.

Vanadium salts can act as an oxygen carrier or as a catalyst for the oxidation of the leuco derivatives of the vat dyes. The formation of a vanadium ferrocyanide image has been discussed in some detail, above. When such an image, imbedded in gelatin containing the leuco derivatives, is bathed with:

Potassium dichromate	0 1 part
Sodium chlorate	0 1 part
Sulphuric acid, 20%	1 part
Water to	50 parts

the leuco base will be saponified and simultaneously oxidized

The sulphate esters of the leuco vat dyes possess a strong affinity for gelatin, so that under normal conditions no fixing agent is required. Where this affinity fails, they can be pigmented with cinchonine or other alkaloids The affinity for gelatin can be increased if tartaric acid or tanning agents such as chrome alum, are present. The sulphate esters of the vat dyes are also known as indigosols.

The I.G. also disclosed a toning procedure which utilized the indigosols (U.S.P. 1945658; Eng. P. 365661). The silver image is treated with the following solution:

Ammonium persulphate, 5%	15 parts
Sulphuric acid, 10%	2 parts
Copper sulphate, 10%	1–2 parts
Potassium bromide, 10%	5–20 drops
Indigosol pink J R, 2%	5 parts
Water	50–70 parts

The time of treatment is four to six minutes. The claim is made in the specifications that the milder oxidizing agents, such as ammonium persulphate, etc , will not attack the indigosol even in acid solution. The silver of the image acts catalytically to cause this oxidation. Perhaps the true reaction is the release of nascent oxygen by the interaction of ammonium persulphate and the silver image, a fact first noticed by R E. Liesegang (*Brit. J Phot*, Vol. 44 (1897), p. 774, 814; Vol 45 (1898), p 2, 646). If such is the case, then the solution used in the formation of gelatin reliefs by the etching process (cf. chapter on Transfer Processes) could be used instead of the one given above.

The I.G. disclosed another application of dye chemistry to toning, in a series of patents (U S.P. 1963197, 2127257 and 2179228; Eng. P. 387197). The silver image is converted into silver diazotate, and this is made to undergo a coupling reaction to form a dye. The chemistry of the amines and diazonium salts will be discussed in detail in the chapter dealing with diazotype photography, so here only a few highlights will be referred to.

The diazonium salts are formed by the action of nitrous acid upon aromatic amines

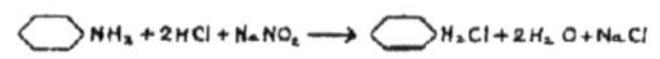

Aniline Benzene diazonium chloride

When treated with amines or phenols, in neutral or slightly alkaline media, a condensation occurs, by which a dye is formed

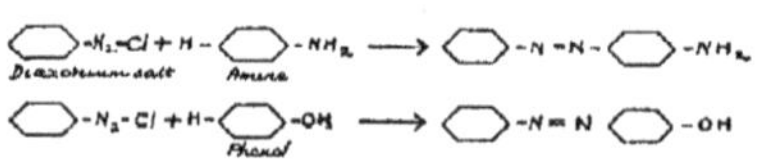

The number of dyes that can be formed runs into the millions, hence practically any shade or hue can be obtained.

Among other reactions of the diazonium salts, is one in which a metal-diazotate is formed,

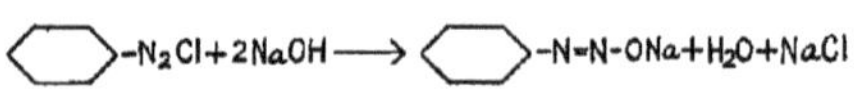

Sodium diazotate

The diazotates are characterized by a dynamic tautomerism, of the syn-anti form

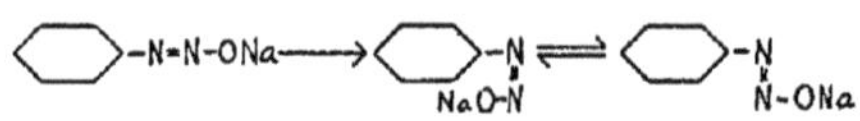

Syn diazotate Anti-diazotate

These two forms can be distinguished from each other by the fact that the anti-diazotate does not couple, while the syn form does The sodium diazotates are quite soluble, but the silver salts, especially of para nitro compounds, have but little solubility. Therefore it becomes possible to convert a silver image to one which is composed of silver-anti-diazotate To accomplish this, the silver is first converted into silver chloride by well known methods. It is then treated with sodium anti-diazotates. The excess is washed out. The reason for the use of anti-diazotate rather than the syn form is to prevent any coupling with gelatin. After the image has been completely converted, it is treated with the proper coupler and at the right pH. The anti-diazotate becomes converted into the syn form and couples to form the dye.

In another variation, aromatic amines with free —SH, —C≡CH, or =NH groups are used. These form insoluble silver salts. Thus an image composed of silver bromide, is bathed for five minutes in the following solution:

6-amino-2-mercapto-benzthiazol	1 0 part
Sodium sulphite	1.0 part
Sodium hydroxide	0 1 part
Water	100 parts

In this solution will be formed an insoluble image composed of silver-mercapto-6-amino-benzthiazol

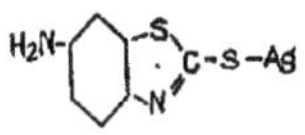

It is washed for fifteen minutes in water containing some sulphite, and is then converted into the diazonium salt with acid nitrite.

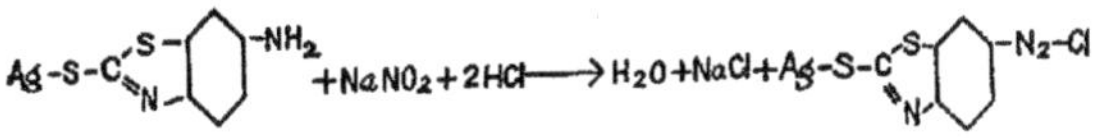

This will remain anchored because it is in the form of a silver mercapto salt. Upon treatment with the proper coupling agent, dyes are formed.

Images composed of azo dyes are formed by still another method by F. Lierg (U.S.P. 1758572). Here the silver image is converted by devious methods into an image consisting of complex nitrite salts. These can be made to react with amines to form diazonium chlorides, which are then coupled to form dyes. The silver image could be treated with thallic chloride. This will form thallous and silver chloride. Upon treatment with sodium-cobalti-nitrite, there will be formed cobalt-thallium-nitrite complexes which are insoluble. Treatment with acids will release the nitrite.

The dye that is formed should be as insoluble as possible. This is accomplished by use of 2:3 hydroxy-naphthoyl-anilides

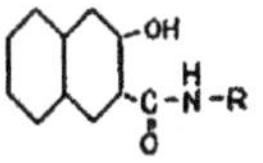

These compounds can couple in but one position, the one that is ortho to the hydroxyl group. There is evidently formed the hydrozone form of the dye, since despite the presence of a free OH group, no solubility in alkali is obtained. The structure of the dye can therefore be written:

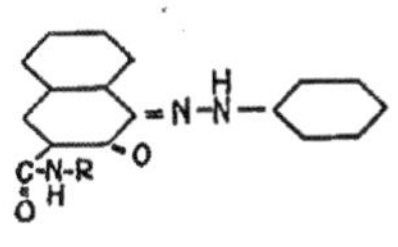

The shade of the dye can be varied at will by the proper choice of amine.

CHAPTER 21

DYE TONING

A CLEAR piece of film, when bathed in solutions of basic dyes, can be washed clear of all coloring matter But if the film be given a previous bath in chrome or potassium alum, it will no longer be possible to wash the dye out The chromium or aluminum ions unite with the gelatin to form stable salts or complexes. These can unite with the dye to form insoluble or "laked" pigments. Many other substances beside alumed gelatin, have this property of mordanting dyes. Since it is so easy to transform the silver of a photographic image into a variety of other insoluble salts, it is apparent that a further reaction with dye becomes possible, provided a correct choice has been made with regard to the conversion. This is the fundamental principle underlying the dye-toning processes. Slightly more general in scope, since they are not limited by the previous formation of a silver image, are the mordant processes. Here the mordant images are formed either from silver or by exposure of a non-mordanting light-sensitive system, which forms mordants or products that can be converted into mordants, by the action of light.

Dyes can be classified into a number of groups depending upon their chemical behavior, reaction with fiber, chemical constitution, etc. A dye is called direct, if it is absorbed by the fiber without the aid of a mordant. A chrome dye requires the fiber to be previously treated with chromium salts before a true staining can occur. Among other classifications are those of acid and basic dyes An acid dye is one whose chemical constitution is such that it unites with a base to form a salt Such dyes usually contain an acid group like —COOH, —SO_3H, —OH, etc., which contain a hydrogen that can ionize. With bases, these form metal salts which ionize in solution to yield a negatively charged dye, and a positively charged metal ion. A basic dye is one which unites with an acid to form a salt. These usually contain the basic group —NH_2, or —NR_2, where R is a hydrocarbon residue. By virtue of the presence of the amino group, such dyes form ammonium-like salts which ionize in solution to yield a positively charged dye, and a negatively charged acid ion.

When an acid unites with a base, neutralization occurs In chemistry, this means that the hydrogen ions of the acid unite with the hydroxyl ions of the base to form a substance which does not ionize readily, and which yields equivalent quantities of the two ions when dissociation does occur. An analogous reaction takes place when acid and basic dye solutions are mixed in equivalent amounts. It is not necessary for the acid and basic dyes to be present in the forms which yield hydrogen and hydroxyl ions. Thus in a solution of methylene blue hydrochloride, no hydroxyl ions are present, the methylene blue ion being in the form of an ammonium salt Similarly in a solution of acid fuchsine, the hydrogen has been replaced by a metal ion such as sodium. When equivalent quantities of the two dyes are mixed, the dye ions unite with each other (if the solution is maintained at a predetermined pH) to form a new unit that is electrically neutral, and generally insoluble. The new unit will be formed by the union of the positively charged acid dye ion with the negatively charged basic dye ion.

It may be wondered why the metal or acid salts of the dyes do not act in the same manner. After all, the sodium salt of a dye like acid fuchsine, is also a union between the negatively charged dye ion and a positive sodium ion. But now colloidal chemistry comes into play. It is an open question whether a heavy dye molecule can exist in solution, except in the form of a colloid. This is a system in which the special properties of the particular chemicals involved become modified perceptibly by the surface forces which arise from the interaction between large surfaced particles, and the medium in which they are dispersed. The charge arising specifically from the dissociation of the dye molecule into dye and metal ion, may be translated to the dye particle as a whole, so that a solution of a dye can be represented as a dispersion of charged particles in water. The mixture of two dye solutions, one containing particles with a net positive charge, the other with a net negative charge, will cause an interaction between the heavy ions which will result in a neutralization of the charges, and mutual precipitation of the particles. This principle is utilized in the determination of the strength of dye solutions.

Many other substances dissolve in water with the formation of heavy particles that carry charges. Tannic acid, for instance, will act in this manner and in solution, if not present in large excess, will precipitate a basic dye. It may be stated generally that the precipitation of a dye from solution, can be accomplished by the addition to the solution of an oppositely charged colloid.

When a substance is dissolved in water, the solution can be either crystalloidal or colloidal in nature. In crystalloidal solution, the dissolved particles are present in no larger than molecular state. If the dielectric constant is sufficiently high, and if the valence bonds in the dissolved molecule are sufficiently loose, dissociation will take place, with the formation of positively and negatively charged ions. The surface charges on the particles arising from such dissociation must be fairly high, since the particle size is very small. But under other conditions, it is possible that the dissolved particles exist in the form of conglomerations of many molecules This gives rise to very large particles, upon which charges may reside due to external conditions, such as adsorption of ions, etc. But now the intensity of surface charge is relatively low, since a given charge becomes distributed over a large area. When the intensity of the adsorbed charges reaches a sufficiently high level, the particles maintain themselves in a state of suspension by virtue of mutual repulsion of like charges. Such particles are called peptized

It is possible to peptize many insoluble substances to cause them to go into colloidal solution. Silver iodide, cuprous iodide, and the corresponding thiocyanates are all very insoluble. Upon the addition of large excesses of the negative ion, adsorption upon the surface of the insoluble particles takes place, with the formation of either molecular or colloidal complexes that are highly charged. Since it is the acid ion which is adsorbed, the molecule takes on a net negative charge. When such particles, either in colloidal solution or coarse dispersion, are added to a solution of a basic dye, neutralization of charges takes place, and mutual precipitation results. The precipitation of dyes by the alums, tannic acid, and all the other mordants can be explained by this theory. The failure of a substance to mordant the dyes whose charges are not opposite to that carried by itself, is a very strong argument in favor of this colloidal theory of dyeing It is only fair to state that many other explanations have been offered, but for the purposes of dye-toning none of the others appear to be so generally satisfying. An explanation somewhat along these lines was proposed by E. R. Bullock of the Eastman Kodak Company, (*Trans Far. Soc.*, (1923) p. 327).

The ability of various insoluble metal salts to adsorb dyes was tested by A. B. Clark (*Abr. Sci. Pub.*, Kodak Research Laboratory, Vol 2 (1915–1916), p. 130). Suspensions of many metal ferri- and ferrocyanides, and the silver halides were treated with dyes, and the staining properties of the dyes were noted. The dyes were both of the acid and basic varieties. The silver halides were found to be very poor in this respect. The halides of manganese, cobalt, nickel, and iron also were poor mordants. Practically the only dye which was absorbed by these halides was alizarin, a dye which is known to form lakes very easily with heavy metal ions. Somewhat better were the corresponding salts of bismuth, cadmium, ceric, cuprous and cupric, stannous and stannic, vanadium, and uranyl ions. The heavy metals like mercury and thorium gave the strongest action. Abnormal in its action was zinc, which, being a relatively light metal, should have but little attraction for the dyes, but actually has a strong affinity for them Clark concluded the following:

1 When the ferricyanide ion is present in slight excess, all ferricyanides mordant basic dyes better than acid dyes;
2. Under like conditions, with excess ferrocyanide present, the same is true with all ferrocyanides except lead and thorium;
3. Ferricyanides mordant better than ferrocyanides

It is rather peculiar that these findings have found practically no application. In fact the practice has been to use silver iodide as the mordant image. Under proper conditions it is possible to prepare this salt in a form whose absorption of basic dyes cannot be matched by any other type of mordant This is the form in which it is utilized in the Brewster Color process.

The first efforts with mordants did not utilize a silver image, but one composed of the reduction products of dichromate The action of light upon dichromate and its application to photography was first observed by Mungo Ponton, a Scotchman (*New Phil. J.*, (1839), p. 169). The first use of this product as a mordant for coloring matter came sometime in the late eighteen-fifties, and the credit can be divided between Testud de Beauregard and Masson (*Photo J*, Vol. 2 (1855), p. 197), Hunt, Perry (who took out a patent on February 6, 1857), and V. Joseph Sella, who, in a letter published in *Photographic Notes* (Vol. 2 (1857), p. 242), suggested that it may be possible to treat a plate that contains an image of reduced chromium salts with logwood, madder, sumac, etc. These are dyes, and the inference is that they would become mordanted upon the reduced chromium salts, and in that way intensify the image. But after that, the letter goes on to describe a process that was quite similar to that of Perry.

Perhaps a clearer exposition of the principle of dye toning was contained in the article by E. Kopp (*Phot. News.*, Vol. 8 (1864), p. 147). In this paper Mr. Kopp discussed the use of a mixed salt of ammonium and potassium dichromate, as the light-sensitive element. After exposure the plate was to be washed Three alternative methods of intensifying the image were then proposed. First, if the wash is sufficient to remove all the dichromate, but not sufficient to cause the brown image to disappear, it becomes possible to treat it with salts of lead, silver, bismuth, mercury, etc., to form the corresponding opaque and highly colored chromates. Secondly, it is possible to treat the image with aniline, naphthylamine etc., and form intense colors by the action of the chromic oxide upon these amines. This is a clear anticipation of dye formation via the oxidation of amines, now utilized in color development. Third, if the wash has been very complete, it is possible to treat the image with logwood, alizarin, Brazil wood, purpurine, etc., in which case the coloring matter will become adsorbed upon the reduced chromium image

The following year Carey Lea (*Brit. J. Phot.*, Vol. 12 (1865), p 162) made the suggestion that if a silver image is treated with mercuric chloride, a mordant will be formed for murexide. He specifically mentioned that the procedure might be generalized to include other mordants and other dyes. Nothing much further appears to have been done for some time In 1892 A. Villain presented pictures to the Société française de Photographie which appear to have been made by the Kopp procedure, although instead of using pure dichromate as his light-sensitive medium, he used this mixed with ammonium vanadate. After exposure and washing, the prints were dyed with alizarin, isopurpurine, alizarin blue, etc The application to three-color photographic reproduction appears first to have been made by G. Selle (Eng. P. 12517/99; Ger. P. 117134). Koenig, in his book, "Die Dreifarbenphotographie" (1904), page 54, gives Selle's disclosure some rather undue attention. He says that this disclosure is really an original process, since it does not depend for its action upon the insolubilization of gelatin, but upon the reduction of dichromate to chromic oxide, in the presence of organic matter. But it is apparent that Kopp was keenly aware of this, and that he took advantage of this very reaction when he intensified his images with coloring matter

Von Hübl, on the other hand, disagrees with the Koenig estimate. Because the action of the dye upon image portions is only slightly more pronounced than it is upon non-image portions, he claims that some different explanation must be had. He states (*Brit. J. Phot.*, Vol. 46 (1899), p. 538) that gelatin readily absorbs dyes without a mordant, hence there can be no question of the chromic oxide acting in that capacity. Rather, the dye washes out with greater difficulty from the hardened portions of the gelatin than from the non-hardened portions.

This explanation is not wholly satisfactory. It is evident, since von Hubl mentions the ability of gelatin to act as a mordant, that he had acid dyes in mind These are the only ones for which untreated gelatin acts in this manner. But as indicated above, gelatin containing reduced chromium salts will retain basic dyes. Where this is true there may very well be a true mordant action. However the von Hübl explanation is not to be discarded lightly. Some of the later patents by Ives and Kelley, would appear to be in the same category. The Ives disclosures would convert the silver image into one of silver ferricyanide by treatement with:

Potassium ferricyanide	1.39 parts
Chromic acid	0.35 part
Glacial acetic acid	50 parts
Water to	1000 parts

In this solution the silver is oxidized either by the chromic acid and precipitated as the ferricyanide, or it is oxidized first to ferrocyanide by the ferri and then to ferri by the chromic acid. In either case, reduced chromium salts would be formed, and these would unite directly with the gelatin to form a tanned image. Basic dyes such as safranine, aurantia, malachite green, methylene blue, fuchsine, and chrysoidine, are used in concentrations of 0.25 to 0.75 per cent, acidified with a little acetic acid (U.S.P. 1376940; Eng. P. 193069). Since basic dyes are used, unquestionably there must be present some mordant action, due either to silver ferricyanide, which Clark (cf. above) has shown to be a good mordant, or to reduced chromium salts. The Kelley disclosures (U.S.P. 1411968; Eng. P. 160137; Ger. P. 378959), falls in a slightly different category since acid dyes may be used. The silver image, after development, fixation, washing, treatment with 10 per cent formaldehyde, and washing, is then treated with:

Potassium dichromate	4.75 parts
Potassium bromide	9.5 parts
Copper sulphate	14 parts
Hydrochloric acid	10 parts
Water to	1000 parts

After the image is bleached it is washed, then fixed, and washed again, before it is subjected to the action of the dyes.

In a later patent (Eng. P. 193069; U S P 1810180) Mr Kelley proposed to use a yellow-dyed emulsion. One image was printed through the base, developed, and then treated with the bleach solution as above. The emulsion was next treated with chromic acid plus bromide to restore the sensitivity, and the other image printed on the surface. After development, the film was fixed, the lower image was dyed, and the upper silver image was toned to a complementary color. Since the dyeing operation was preceded by a fixing bath, there can be no question here that silver salts are acting as a mordant. Cuprous bromide, the other salt that may be formed, is not known to be a good mordant. However Kelley suggests that acid dyes be used, hence these would be acted on by the gelatin itself The combination between acid dye and gelatin is a very loose one which can be destroyed by excess washing. Naturally the water will not have as strong an action in the tanned portions where it is absorbed to approximately one-tenth the extent to which it is in the unhardened portions. Hence the dye will remain there preferentially

The Ives procedure was again revived by J. Guardiola and Harmonicolor (Eng P. 450877) Duplitized film, colored with basic dyes, and containing silver images, is treated with a solution containing chromic acid and potassium ferricyanide. This fixes the dye in the image portions of the film where silver was previously present Of course the silver is present in the form of silver ferricyanide. Detracolor (cf. chapter on Monopacks) disclosed a monopack along these same lines. The emulsion contains stable leuco basic dyes After development, fixation, and washing, the film is treated with a solution containing copper salts, chromic acid, and potassium ferricyanide. The leuco dyes are converted into the respective colors and are immediately mordanted upon the silver-copper ferricyanide formed.

The Curtis Neotone process apparently works upon the Kelley scheme, although no formulas or details other than strict working directions are given. The separation negatives are printed upon stripping paper and developed in a modified Eastman D-76 formula.

Metol	2 parts
Sodium sulphite	100 parts
Hydroquinone	5 parts
Kodalk (sodium metaborate)	4 parts
Water to	1000 parts

After development, the prints are stopped in a solution containing one-half per cent glacial acetic acid, after which they can be further processed in white light. The prints are bleached in a special solution whose composition is not disclosed by the makers, the Thomas S. Curtis Laboratories, Huntington Park, California. After bleaching, the prints are washed for three minutes, then fixed in an acid fixing-bath that contains no hardener

Hypo	200 parts
Potassium metabisulphite	10 parts
Water to	1000 parts

After fixation, the films are dyed in special baths which must also be obtained from the Curtis organization. The dyeing time is five minutes. Care must be taken that the tissues do not fold over, as dye transfer will take place wherever two dyed gelatin areas touch each other. This indicates that no true mordant action takes place. Before registering, the dyed tissues must be washed in water at 70 degrees F, to clear the highlights At higher temperatures, the dye will wash out of the densities; at lower temperatures, too long a time will be required for clearance to take place These are conditions typical of the Kelley type of pictures. Registry of the three images completes the process.

J M Blaney suggested stannic ferrocyanide as a mordant (U.S.P. 1331092) . The image was first treated with

Hydrochloric acid	2 parts
Glycerin	75 parts
Water to	1000 parts

It was next converted into stannic ferrocyanide by treatment with:

Oxalic acid	4 7 parts
Ammonium nitrate	2 parts
Glycerin	50 parts
Stannic chloride (sp gr 1 50)	13.9 parts
Potassium ferricyanide	3 5 parts
Water to	1000 parts

The silver chloride formed in this reaction is removed by fixation with acid hypo

Iron salts have been suggested a number of times, especially in connection with textile fibers and cloth. The first to use this mordant appears to have been J. Mercer, according to W. H. Harrison (*Brit J. Phot.*, Vol. 42 (1895), p. 55). He toned monochrome prints to various shades. The blue-green iron image was decomposed by treatment with lime, and the iron hydroxide thus formed was able to fix a large number of vegetable dyes. Mr. Mercer exhibited prints made this way in 1858, a long time before color photography was a practical reality. It should be recalled that the fundamental disclosures of Ducos du Hauron had not been made at that time. Even then the use of iron hydroxide was well established, for a patent disclosing its use was issued to J. Perry in 1856 (Eng. P. 1983/56). This is the same Perry who questioned so bitterly the priority of the process disclosed by V. Joseph Sella (cf. above). In 1864 A. Baudesson and P. Houzeau (Eng P. 2526/64) also disclosed the use of iron as a mordant. More than a generation later, Stewart J. Carter (*Brit J. Phot.*, Vol. 45 (1898), pp. 445, 449 and 806) used an iron printing process, which he then converted into the iron hydroxide and toned with dyes, or formed inks with gallic acid Fabrics were sensitized with ferric ammonium citrate and potassium ferricyanide. Upon exposure and washing, this gave a blue-green image. Treatment with alkali decomposed the Prussian blue to yield red iron hydroxide, which then acted as a mordant for such dyes as resorcine green, logwood, alizarin, etc.

Others who suggested similar processes were A F. Hargreaves (Eng. P. 25043/98); F. Dommer (Ger. P. 114923, Fr P. 281659); and J. Ephraim (Ger. P. 166832). L. F. Douglass applied the method to a silver image which he first toned blue-green by treatment with a standard blue-toning solution (U.S P. 1450412; Fr. P. 450412). The blue-green image was then converted into one consisting of ferric hydroxide and toned to any desired color by use of basic dyes. Somewhat different in technique was the procedure outlined by J. I. Crabtree of the Eastman Kodak Company (U.S.P. 1389742). The silver image was first converted into one consisting of silver ferricyanide, by treatment with:

Potassium ferricyanide	20 parts
Potassium permanganate	20 parts
Water to	1000 parts

or

Potassium ferricyanide	71 parts
Chromic acid	29 parts
Water to	1000 parts

After a thorough washing, the image was treated with:

Ferrous sulphate	50 parts
Hydrochloric acid	50 parts
Water to	1000 parts

In this bath, the silver ferricyanide was converted into ferrous ferricyanide and silver chloride, which could be removed by fixation. By treating with alkali, the iron is converted into ferrous hydroxide which can be toned with dyes. The iron hydroxide can be removed with oxalic acid.

The mordant action of a uranium-toned silver image was noted in the previous chapter. Since this substance yields an image that is so deeply stained, it is limited in its use to the formation of the orange red that is required in two-color work. Silver sulphide, as a mordant, was suggested by Michael Robach (*Brit. J. Phot.*, Vol. 70 (1923), p 363; Vol. 71 (1924), p. 183). The silver image was first converted into a sepia by the action of two baths. The first was the following:

Ammonium dichromate	2 6 parts
Sodium chloride	5 2 parts
Hydrochloric acid	5.2 parts
Water to	1000 parts

It converted the image into silver chloride. The second, a one per cent solution of sodium sulphide, converted the silver chloride into the sepia silver sulphide. A clearing bath after the dichromate was advised. This consisted of a 3 per cent solution of sodium sulphite. After a thorough wash, the sepia-toned print could be dyed a red with:

Rhodamine B	5.6 parts
Chrysoidin Y extra	0 93 part
Auramin	9 3 parts
Oxalic acid	3 parts
Acetic acid	50 parts
Water to	1000 parts

Instead of using sodium sulphide for the formation of the sepia tone, Mr. Robach suggests either of the following:

Potassium sulphurata	1.5 parts
Hypo	0.3–0.75 part
Water to	1000 parts

or

Sodium sulphantimoniate	0.75–1.5 parts
Ammonia	0.3 part
Water to	1000 parts

This disclosure created some discussion. A. Seyewetz (*Bull. Soc. franç. Phot.*, Vol 12 (1925), p. 204) reported that his attempts to duplicate the Robach findings ended in failure, and he concluded that silver sulphide had no mordant action toward basic dyes Mr Bullock in "Chemical Reactions of the Photographic Latent Image," p 113, states as his opinion that silver sulphide, prepared in an excess of soluble sulphides, is not a mordant for basic dyes, but that in this case the mordant action may be sought in associated molecules. Chromium salts must be present, and also antimony sulphide if sulphantimoniate were used. In a footnote to this discussion, Mr. Bullock pointed out that it is generally possible to convert a silver image into one that is composed of a negatively charged colloid, in which case it would mordant basic dyes A silver ferrocyanide image bathed in 0.1 per cent tin, antimony, or arsenic sulphide, kept in solution by the presence of a slight excess of ammonium sulphide, will form a colloidal image that will mordant basic dyes In his paper before the Faraday Society (cf. above) Mr. Bullock pointed out that silver cyanide is much more soluble in normal cyanide than the iodide is in normal iodide solution. This in turn is greater than the bromide. Under similar conditions, the sulphide is the least soluble of the four. From these facts it can be concluded that silver cyanide forms the complex with the largest charge, with the iodide being next in intensity, and the sulphide least The mordant action should follow in the same order. Therefore both Mr. Robach and Dr Seyewetz are correct.

Copper salts form very potent mordants. The first use of this salt as a mordant for dyes appeared to have been made by J. Helouis and C. de Saint-Père (Fr. P. 247065) in 1895 Fabrics were sensitized by bathing in a solution containing dichromates, and uranium, iron, lead, and copper salts. Under the action of light these gave the "ous" salts, which acted as mordants for cochineal, alizarin, the tannins, logwood, etc. R. Namias published a comprehensive study on the use of copper and other metals as mordants, in 1909 (*Brit. J. Phot.*, Vol. 56 (1909), Color Supp., Vol. 3, pp. 68, 91). Cobalt ferrocyanide he found to be completely negative, copper very unsatisfactory, and lead the best of all. The image was converted into lead ferrocyanide by treatment with a solution containing lead acetate, acetic acid, and potassium ferrocyanide. To remove the last traces of non-image lead (this metal is held very tenaciously by gelatin) the washing had to be thorough, and a further treatment with ten per cent nitric acid was found to be very beneficial. The silver salt formed was removed with hypo The lead ferrocyanide was converted into the sulphate by the action of a five per cent solution of sodium sulphate, containing one-half per cent sulphuric acid. Dyeing was very slow, several hours being required from a one per cent solution. For three-color work, safranine served for the magenta, auramin for the yellow, and methyl blue for the cyan. The opaque lead sulphate could be removed with concentrated hypo solutions containing 7 per cent boric acid. Since lead hydroxide is more transparent than the sulphate, the ferrocyanide could be converted into the hydroxide by treatment with alkalis. This image must be stained in an acid solution of the dye, preferably acetic acid.

The Namias findings seem rather strange in the light of subsequent experience The action of the copper ferrocyanide formed by him must have been exceptionally poor, if a lead mordant, requiring several hours for complete dyeing, was much more satisfactory. It is not necessary to treat a mordant image for a period longer than five to fifteen minutes, and then only if the dye solutions are extremely weak, in concentrations that are less than 0 1 per cent For this reason it is rather hard to see why the German government rejected Traube's application for a patent (Ger. P application T20656) on the ground that Namias had priority. The English and French governments did not take this limited view and granted Traube the protection he merited (Eng. P. 147005, 147103 and 163337; Fr. P. 491927 and 520111). A later modification was allowed by the German government (Ger. P 403428) in which the claim was made for the presence of excess ferricyanide ions. Since it is not possible to compound a bath where this substance would not be present in a ten-thousandfold excess over the silver, the granting of this and the rejection of the original claim, appear to be somewhat inconsistent. Traube pointed out that the copper ferrocyanide (Namias to the contrary) possessed a very high potency as a mordant, and consequently the images used should be extremely thin, but full of detail. This means that ample exposure should be given to the print, and that the development should be very soft. A 0 1 per cent solution of the dye required but five minutes for complete staining. The silver should be removed with weak hypo, which will not affect the copper salt. Traube commercialized this process under the name of Uvachrome.

Traube was followed by several others who made slight changes in the chemical composition of the bleaching solutions J. I. Crabtree (U.S.P 1305962) treated the silver image with

Copper sulphate	12 parts
Potassium ferricyanide	12 parts
Potassium citrate	57 parts
Ammonium carbonate	6 parts
Water to	1000 parts

The presence of ammonium carbonate created the danger that a slight loss of image might result, a fact which would be felt mainly in the highlight region. R. Namias (cf. chapter on Chemical Toning) pointed out that both cupric ferri- and ferrocyanides are soluble in solutions made alkaline with ammonium salts. After rinsing, to remove excess bleach solution, the material could be dyed in 0.1 to 0.2 per cent solutions of basic dyes, with 0.1 per cent acetic acid present Suitable dyes were rhodamine 6G, thioflavine, methyl green, or methylene blue. The silver ferrocyanide formed could be removed by treatment with hypo to which was added 0.25 per cent of tannin and sodium acetate

A neutral solution of copper sulphate and potassium ferricyanide was proposed by F. E. Ives Two stock solutions were prepared. These were mixed in equal amounts just before use (U.S.P 1278667 and 1300619, Eng. P. 113617 and 113618).

Solution A:	
Potassium ferricyanide	5.7 parts
Potassium citrate	27.68 parts
Water to	1000 parts
Solution B:	
Copper sulphate	7.14 parts
Potassium citrate	27.68 parts
Water to	1000 parts

Since the citrate is present to repress the ionization of the copper sulphate into cupric ions, it is hard to see why it is required in the ferricyanide solution. After bleaching, the image is dyed with:

Fuchsin	0.026 part
Auramin	0.026 part
Acetic acid	1.6 parts
Water to	1000 parts

It is seen here that extremely weak dye baths are used The presence of the yellow dye indicates that a two-color process is intended. In a subsequent disclosure (U.S.P. 1499930 and 1655182; Eng. P. 119254) Ives proposed to print two images in the same emulsion layer. A yellow dyed film is used. The red-filter image is printed through the base, giving an image that lies adjacent to the celluloid, and which penetrates but a short distance into the film. This is toned blue-green by means of iron. The green-filter separation is printed in registry, in the normal manner. This gives a surface image that does not penetrate deeply, so does not reach the lower one. The upper image is converted into a red by use of the technique just disclosed. The same idea is utilized by L F. Douglass (U.S P. 1632278); W V. D Kelley (U.S P 1712439 and 1810180); Max B. Dupont (Eng P 360109), and W. H. Peck (U.S.P. 1840524).

In all of the above disclosures, it is cupric ferrocyanide that is used as a mordant As E J. Wall points out in his "History of Three-Color Photography" (p. 371) it is perfectly possible to accomplish the same result by first treating the silver image with ferricyanide, then with copper salts. What is not pointed out, is that a tremendous loss of image density results. But this is not an unmixed blessing, since it allows the operator to make a more normal print for toning. After dyeing, the dye image may be fixed with tannic acid or some stronger mordant than copper ferrocyanide, and this last removed by treatment with alkali. This use of two-bath toning was suggested by F. J. Ventujol (Fr P 558699). A two-bath solution proposed by the Naturfarben Film g.m b.H. (Ger. P. 393790) differs from the above in that cuprous ferricyanide is the mordant. This is formed by the action of cupric chloride upon the silver image, followed by a ferricyanide bath.

Equal in potency to the ferrocyanide, but free from the color of this image, is cuprous thiocyanate, first proposed by J. H. Christensen (U.S.P. 1447759; Eng. P. 132846 and 135477, Ger. P. 319459, 319477 and 334277). The silver image is treated with the following solution:

Potassium citrate	55.5 parts
Copper sulphate	41 75 parts
Potassium thiocyanate	20 parts
Acetic acid	25 parts
Water to	1000 parts

This formula was modified to a slight extent by Seyewetz, in a paper dealing with mordant processes in general. Dr. Seyewetz is quite partial to the cuprous thiocyanate mordant. His modified formula (*Brit. J. Phot.*, Vol 71 (1924), p. 609) is the following:

Copper sulphate	40 parts
Potassium thiocyanate	20 parts
Potassium citrate	60 parts
Acetic acid	30 parts
Water to	1000 parts

The bleached print is a dirty gray in color. This does not modify the shade of the image, although it leads to a slight degradation. An improved formula, in that keeping qualities are much better, was given by Lyman Chalkley.

This is characterized by the presence of high concentrations of potassium citrate

Copper sulphate	40 parts
Potassium citrate	250 parts
Acetic acid	30 parts
Ammonium thiocyanate	25 parts
Water to	1000 parts

The ammonium thiocyanate could be replaced by the potassium salt, of which 29 parts should be used.

This formula can be further modified to advantage to yield practically an invisible image (Joseph Friedman, *Am. Phot.*, Vol. 32 (1938), p. 212). This is accomplished if the thiocyanate concentration is increased It is possible to have a sufficiently high concentration to completely fix a silver-bromide emulsion. But true fixation occurs in two steps, the first of which is the formation of a complex silver salt whose index of refraction is the same as that of gelatin At this stage the film becomes completely transparent If the size of the complex salt is such that it is very mobile, it will quickly diffuse out of the gelatin, but if its mobility is greatly restricted, it will remain fixed It is to be recalled that Ansco and the I.G. in their successful solution of the monopack problem utilized this principle in the preparation of their film If the concentration of the thiocyanate be carefully determined, and if the time of treatment be controlled, it is possible to convert a silver into a silver-copper-thiocyanate image that is practically invisible, and one whose dye absorption properties are at a maximum.

Probably the best mordant of all, and the simplest to operate, is the iodide. This can be either the silver or the copper salt, it being immaterial which is used. The first public disclosure of silver iodide as a mordant came from Dr. A. Traube (Ger. P. 187289 and 188164; Eng P. 10258/07, U.S P. 1093503) The silver image is treated with oxidizing agents in the presence of the desired ion, in which case it becomes possible to precipitate either silver iodide, silver-copper-iodide, the corresponding bromides, chlorides, ferrocyanides, or the corresponding silver-mercury compounds, etc. Upon treatment with basic dyes, these became fixed to the bleached image. In order to obtain transparency the insoluble silver complexes must be removed, a procedure that could take place only after the dye had been treated with tannic acid and sodium acetate. The final image was not a silver-iodide-dye complex. Traube suggested that stripping celluloid film could be used. This is very interesting since Chromatone and other stripping papers take on a general dye stain This is probably because the product is not celluloid, but collodion, and this is a mordant for basic dyes, a fact utilized by Dufaycolor (cf. chapter on Screen Plates). Evidently the addition of considerable quantities of the plasticizer camphor causes a complex formation with the cellulose nitrate micelle to take place, in which the negative charge becomes considerably reduced or converted into a positive charge In this condition, a basic dye will not be absorbed by the base.

Traube's claim to priority was soon contested by Tauleigne and Mazo, whose own disclosures came in 1909 (Fr. P. 420584; Eng. P. 27818/09; U S P. 1059917). But they claimed that their first experiments were made in 1897. However they did make an improvement. The silver image is first converted into the ferrocyanide by treatment with ferricyanide. Or it can be converted into a mixture of cuprous and silver chloride by the action of cupric chloride. The bleached image is next acted on by a weak potassium iodide solution, 2 to 3 per cent, which converts it into a mixture of cuprous and silver iodide. This absorbs dye better than pure silver iodide, but it is equally opaque. A real contribution came in the next step, which consisted in treating the dyed image with a solution containing 20 per cent of potassium iodide As was indicated above, silver iodide is quite soluble in a strong solution of potassium iodide. This rendered the iodides transparent, but, as they were careful to note, did not remove them, thus maintaining the dye in its proper position. This is a very clear anticipation of the formation of the silver-iodide hydrosol which forms the basis of a patent issued later to Hoyt Miller (U.S.P. 1214940; Eng. P. 100098; Fr. P. 483764; Ger. P. 405962) Tauleigne and Mazo did not realize, of course, that the transparent substance into which the mordant was converted was itself a far better absorbent for basic dyes, than was the cuprous-silver iodide.

The Miller disclosure represents a distinct advance in mordant procedure, and is worthy of special attention Unlike most patentees, Mr. Miller gives full acknowledgment to the earlier experimenters, Traube, Tauleigne and Mazo, and Thornton (Eng. P. 25084/12), and he pointed out that the first and last named workers formed opaque mordants that had subsequently to be fixed out, and that the second group dyed an opaque mordant which they later converted into a transparent material. Mr. Miller then discusses the work of Bancroft, (*J. Phys Chem*, Vol. 14 (1910), and Lottermoser (*J. Pract Chem.*, Vol. 68, p 341; Vol. 72, p. 39; Vol. 73, p. 324), where the principles involved in the formation of silver-iodide "hydrosols" are discussed. These gentlemen point out that the insoluble salt, silver iodide, absorbs potassium iodide, the degree of absorption being dependent upon the concentration of iodide ions. The silver iodide particle with the adsorbed iodide ions begins to go into colloidal solution, the extent depending upon the amount of iodide present. Therefore, it becomes possible to form colloidal solutions, or hydrosols, of silver iodide with almost any desired degree of dispersion. The very coarse dispersions are formed in the presence of slight excesses of potassium iodide These are turbid solutions When the concentration of potassium iodide is sufficiently high, the dispersion becomes extremely fine, and completely transparent. This is the form desired by Mr Miller.

Acting upon the ideas disclosed in these papers, and having the Tauleigne and Mazo example before him, Mr Miller decided that if the silver of the image is converted into silver iodide in the presence of high concentrations of potassium iodide, a completely transparent silver iodide–potassium iodide mordant is formed. The solution he proposed was the following:

Potassium iodide	50–70 parts
Iodine	0.7–3.0 parts
Acetic acid	15 parts
Water to	1000 parts

When bleached in this solution, a completely invisible image composed of a complex potassium silver iodide, is formed, an image which absorbs dye to a degree many times that of the opaque mordant. Since the gelatin becomes softened by the action of so high a concentration of potassium iodide, it becomes desirable to first harden the gelatin with formaldehyde. Alum, tannic acid, or other agents which harden gelatin and which also precipitate basic dyes, cannot be used. Fomaldehyde has no such action upon basic dyes, but the formaldehyde gelatin must first be dried before any tanning takes place. Not only does this procedure preserve the gelatin, but it also gives much improved whites, since tanned gelatin will not absorb dyes as readily as the soft variety. But the absorption by the image will not suffer materially since here there is a mutual attraction between dye and mordant.

The silver iodide complex is completely soluble in concentrated potassium iodide solutions. But if it is formed so that a layer of gelatin lies between it and the solution, then dissolution must be followed by diffusion before it is removed from the locality of formation. The mobility of the complex cannot be very high, since the particle is colloidal in nature, and is quite heavy. To insure the presence of a relatively thick gelatin layer over the image, one of several possible techniques can be adopted. The simplest would be to print the image through the base of the emulsion, a procedure that is possible only if the base is composed of a transparent substance. Another and more useful possibility lies in the use of silver solvents in the developer, compounded to have a fairly high initial appearance time. This means that hypo should be added. Or potassium iodide can replace the hypo, which, as was indicated in the chapter on Processing Screen Plates, also drives an image deep into the gelatin layer.

These are not the only considerations involved. The extreme potency of the complex mordant to absorb basic dyes, makes the use of normal images highly undesirable. The writer has at one time made a determination of the ability of this type of mordant to absorb dyes To this end a gray scale was copied upon a lantern plate. After development, fixation, washing, and formaldehyde tanning, one-half of the scale was covered with rubber cement. This formed a water-insoluble and impermeable coating which prevented any action of the bleach and dye bath upon the silver beneath it. After completely processing the plate to a final dyed image, the rubber cement was removed. This left every step in the gray scale in silver and in color. The relationship between the silver and dye was determined densitometrically, by reading both through a filter complementary to the dye With astraphloxine FF and rhoduline sky blue as the dyes, the following results were obtained, all other conditions being identical

ASTRAPHLOXINE FF

5-minute development			*3-minute development*		
Silver Density	*Dye Density*	*Intensification Density*	*Silver Density*	*Dye Density*	*Intensification Density*
41	2.30	5 9	48	2.32	4.8
.28	2.07	7 4	.40	2 21	5.5
18	1.90	10 6	32	2 05	6 4
.15	1.67	11.0	.27	1.86	7 0
12	1.20	10 0	.17	1.56	9 1
07	0.70	10 0	.12	1.22	10.0
.04	0.25	6 3	04	0.68	17 0

RHODULINE SKY BLUE

3-minute development		
Silver Density	*Dye Density*	*Intensification Density*
.50	2 36	4 7
.40	2.28	5 7
.34	1.98	5 8
.26	1.60	6.1
.20	1.18	5 9
.14	0.70	5 0
.03	0 20	6 7

It must be kept in mind that the accuracy of the readings is very low because of the difficulties of heterochromatic densitometry, and the reading of very low silver densities. But even so some, very important points stand out. The ability of the mordant to fix dyes is dependent upon the method of formation. Thus, long development and short exposure give apparently better and more uniform intensification than long exposure and short development. This is apparent from a consideration of the results with astraphloxine. With five minutes development the intensification was almost uniformly 10.0, while with three minutes it varied from a low of 4 8 to a high of 10 (disregarding the value of 17 for a silver density of 0 04, since an error of reading at this point of 0.02 will be equivalent to an error of 50 per cent).

Let us compare the results for rhoduline sky blue with those for astraphloxine. The constancy of the intensification factor indicates that the dyeing was to approximately the same extent as in the five-minute astraphloxine experiment. But a generally lower value, 5.7 as compared to 10.0, gives an indication that every dye is absorbed to a different extent. This was verified for a number of other dyes. Other factors which affect the intensifications are the concentrations of the dye baths, and the concentration of potassium iodide in the bleach. In order to make consistent prints by this method, it becomes necessary to standardize the various operations very carefully The writer is very partial to dye toning as a method for making prints, and believes that the quality of reproduction is far superior to any of the other methods.

Since the intensification is so high (the presence of as little silver as is required to give a density of 0 04 already yielding middle tones), it is essential that the development be extremely low, and the fog level of the emulsion equally low. For paper prints, the highest density permissible is approximately 1 60 The silver density for a magenta image composed of astraphloxine, which will yield a dye image with a density of 1.60, is 0.16. This therefore is the maximum silver density allowable in the black-and-white stage of the process Only the very contrasty emulsions, process, superprocess, etc , will operate at a low enough toe level to give the final image sufficient brightness. The contrasty lantern-plate emulsion is also suitable. The problem arises then, how to concoct a processing technique which will give straight-line reproduction in a region limited between the values 0.00 and 0.16, which will be a true representation of densities ranging from 0.35 to 2.0 in the original. The most successful procedure to adopt would be to use specially compounded developers Those who are not susceptible to paraphenylenediamine poisoning, will be able to use this excellent agent. When compounded with glycin, as in the Sease No. 3 formula, it has fair keeping qualities

Paraphenylenediamine	10 parts
Sodium sulphite	90 parts
Glycin	6 parts
Water to	1000 parts

If one cannot work with this chemical, he can compound a glycin formula by leaving out the paraphenylenediamine, and adding just sufficient alkali (carbonate, Kodalk, borax) to give a density of 0 16 in the deepest shadows in five to seven minutes development at 70 F. Another, and perhaps more feasible solution, would be to use metol The basic formula is

Metol	5 parts
Sulphite	100 parts
Borax	10–15 parts
Boric acid	5–30 parts
Potassium thiocyanate	½ part
Potassium bromide	½ part
Hypo	½ part
Water to	1000 parts

The concentration of borax and boric acid will vary with the emulsion, but once established should not be changed as long as that material is being used.

By properly varying the boric acid content, it is possible to make solutions that will require as much as one hour to yield a top density of 0.16 in the deepest shadows, even with as contrasty a material as the Eastman Super Contrast Process Plate. In an effort to compound a fine-grain developer for negative materials, Joseph Friedman (*Amer. Phot*, Vol 33 (1939), p. 738) proposed the following solution:

Metol	2 parts
Sulphite	30 parts
Potassium metabisulphite	30 parts
Chrome alum	20 parts
Hydroquinone	5 parts
Formalin	25 parts
Boric acid	20 parts
Water to	2000 parts

This gave excellent results as far as detail in very low densities was concerned, although the deposit was not sufficient to allow the images to be printed. It would appear, therefore, to be suitable for the purposes of dye toning. The metabisulphite, reacting with formalin, releases one equivalent of alkali, which is buffered by the boric acid. The chrome alum is present to prevent too great a swelling of the emulsion layer, and it is converted into a complex salt by the sulphite. Hence it will remain in solution. The hydroquinone probably has no action at the low alkalinity present in this solution, but it acts as a preservative.

Regardless of what procedure is used to obtain the very low densities required, it is a safe practice to use enough solution to process a single plate, or set of plates, and to discard it Temperature controls are very necessary, at least until the operator can learn to judge the results in the dim red of the safelight. Since densities that are not normally even suitable highlights correspond to deep shadows, the safety of the light is very important. This should be tested by covering half the plate with a sheet of black paper, and exposing to the safelight for fifteen minutes, at a distance equivalent to that used during development. The processing of the plate should be in total darkness for the maximum time to be used in actual practice, say fifteen minutes. A short stop in one-half per cent acetic acid, followed by a rinse, precedes the fixation, which should be done in two stages. In the first stage the plate remains until the image clears. After a five-minute wash, the plate is again treated with fresh hypo for a further period of five minutes In both cases only plain hypo, or hypo to which 1½ per cent of sodium bisulphite or potassium metabisulphite has been added, should be used After another ten-minute wash, the plate is treated with a one per cent formaldehyde solution and immediately dried This can be greatly facilitated if it be first treated with 80 per cent alcohol containing 1½ per cent formaldehyde In this case the drying will be rapid. No heat should be applied, since this would have a tendency to drive off the formaldehyde.

After the plate is dried, it can be treated with the bleach. As stated above this is an iodine-iodide mixture containing from five to ten per cent of potassium iodide per liter of solution. Because of the solubility of silver iodide in potassium iodide, this solution should not be used too long. However, this tendency can be reduced to a minimum if the iodine solution is loaded with agents that will prevent the penetration of the solution into the gelatin layer. The diffusion of the salts out of the emulsion layer will also be greatly hindered Hence, even if the silver mordant does dissolve, because of the very limited mobility of the substance, it will not diffuse out of the film. A suitable bleach along these lines, can be compounded as follows:

Stock Iodide Solution:

Water	100 parts
Potassium iodide	100 parts
Iodine	25 parts

The best method of preparing this is to make an intimate mixture of the iodine and iodide, then add the water in small amounts The volume should then be brought up to 250 cc, making a 10 per cent solution of iodine The bleach solution is prepared from this as follows.

Water	750 parts
Acetic acid	25 parts
Sodium sulphate (anhydrous)	100 parts
Stock iodine solution	25 parts
Water to	1000 parts

The plate containing the silver image (fog test) is immersed in this solution for a time sufficient for the image to disappear. If it is correctly printed, this should not require longer than two or three minutes. At the end of this time, the plate is given a one-minute bath in a one per cent solution of sodium bisulphite or metabisulphite, then a two-minute wash in running water, after which it may be dyed The dye baths are compounded to contain approximately one-half to one per cent of dye in three to five per cent of acetic acid. If great purity is desired, the dye should be dissolved in 100 cc of alcohol, filtered, then made up to volume with water and acetic acid (30 to 50 cc per liter). The dyeing time is five minutes. The excess dye is removed by washing in running water, and from fifteen minutes to one hour should be allowed. Sometimes it is possible to wash out the last traces of non-image dye with weak acetic acid (one per cent) or alcohol (25 per cent).

Any of the basic dyes are suitable for this process, but the writer has had good success with astraphloxine FF for the magenta, rhoduline sky blue for the cyan, and auramin for the yellow. This last may be somewhat too far on the orange side, in which case thioflavine T, or some of the phloxines could be used. All of the dyes with the exception of auramin, can be prepared as stock solutions, to be used until exhausted. But this last named dye is unstable in solution, so must be prepared fresh each time It has a limited solubility, so that its preparation is a little tricky. To prepare it in stable form, ten parts of the dye are dissolved in 100 parts of alcohol, the requisite acetic acid added, and the solution made up to volume with water. Instead of astraphloxine FF for the magenta, the rhodamines such as B or 6G, could be used The shade of rhodamine B is probably the closest to theoretical requirements, but it does not wash out as readily as the other Rhoduline sky blue could be replaced by setopolin, thionine blue, or methylene blue, although the last named is the least worthy of the group

The best dye to use to detect whether the safelights are really safe, is astraphloxine. If, after complete processing of the plate, a line of demarkation is distinct between the exposed and unexposed sections of the plate, then the safelight should be replaced. Since the dye intensifies the image ten times, this test is at least ten times as severe as the one ordinarily used.

The Miller patent was assigned to the Brewster Color Film Corporation, and it formed the basic principle underlying the process. The entire scheme is disclosed in a series of patents all issued to P. D Brewster, the earlier ones (U.S P. 1308538, 1563959, 1580114 and 1580115), dealing with a two-color system, and the later ones (U S.P. 1992169 and 2070222, Eng. P. 449678, 449749 and 449750) with three-color. Since long reels of film must be processed at one time, the keeping qualities of the solutions are of great importance. The tendency of the Miller bleach to dissolve out some of the silver-iodide made that item very short lived. Not only did this give rise to a loss of highlight detail, but it muddied the whites since some of the silver iodide in the solution transferred to and was retained by the film. This absorbed dye as well as the image-bearing portions of the film. The Friedman modification, containing the anti-swelling or loading agents (sodium sulphate) greatly extended the life of the solution

Mr. Brewster devised another scheme which accomplished the same purpose, and with much less danger. He achieved this result by forming the bleach within the image layers The film after being tanned and dried, is treated with a priming solution which contains potassium iodide and sodium iodate. From this bath, the film is led into a gas chamber and exposed to acetic acid fumes. The iodate, iodide, and acid react to form iodine, in accordance with the following scheme,

$$NaIO + 5KI + 6HOAc \rightarrow 3I_2 + 5KOAc + NaOAc + 3H_2O$$

Thus it is seen that 2.0 parts of sodium iodate will react with 8 5 parts of potassium iodide, to yield 8.0 parts of free iodine. In order to form the proper image, there must be present 10 per cent of potassium iodide, and 0 4 per cent of iodine To develop this quantity of free iodine, there will be required 1.0 part of sodium iodate and 4 25 parts of potassium iodide per 1000 parts of solution. To this must be added 100 parts of potassium iodide. The final concentration is as follows:

Sodium iodate	1.0 part
Potassium iodide	104.25 parts
Water to	1000 parts

A neutral solution of potassium iodide, when exposed to light, decomposes to form free iodine, which immediately reacts with water to form acid. Therefore, after some time, the priming bath begins to turn slightly reddish. When the film is treated with this solution, the free iodine, however slight, will etch out some of the highlight detail. To prevent this from happening, the priming bath is maintained at a pH just on the alkaline side, at about 7.5. If it is made too alkaline, the acidity of the gas will be insufficient to set off the reaction. A few drops of borax or sodium acetate solution, enough to give a

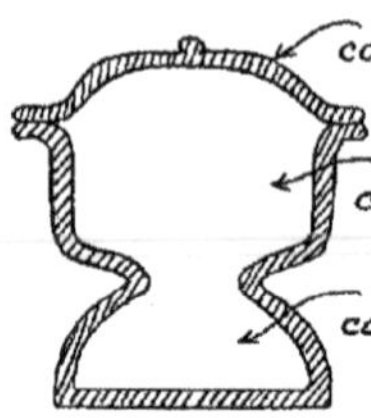

FIG. 108

definite indication of alkalinity, will suffice; or ammonia can be used. Now very little of the total concentration of the acid fumes will be used up to overcome the alkalinity of the priming bath. The use of a gas box is inconvenient for the technician without elaborate equipment, although a desiccator can be converted very easily into such. This is a piece of glass apparatus shaped as shown in Fig. 108. It is used by chemists to dry substances which are heat unstable. As they use it, concentrated sulphuric acid is placed in the bottom of the desiccator, in a thin layer. Calcium chloride or some other water-absorbing medium can replace the sulphuric acid. A perforated plate is placed across the indentations, and this forms a shelf upon which the material to be dried can be placed. To convert it into a gas chamber, a volatile acid replaces the drying substance. Care should be taken to allow the gas free access to the upper chamber.

If this is unhandy, it is possible to put the acid, in this case acetic or some other equally strong organic acid, into a solvent that does not wet gelatin and which is not miscible with water. A substance like benzene, toluene, or some other liquid hydrocarbon having a limited solubility in water, is ideal. In that case the hydrocarbon is saturated with a concentrated solution of the strong inorganic acid, or some acetic or other organic acid can be dissolved in it. After leaving the priming bath, the film is passed through this solution. The tendency will be for the gelatin to absorb the acid from the hydrocarbon solution, rather than for the hydrocarbon to remove the primer from the gelatin. Therefore the iodine will be formed in the gelatin layer, and no diffusion or loss of image will be possible. The further treatment of the film is the same as outlined above. A bisulphite bath removes the excess iodine, and a wash removes excess bisulphite This is followed by dyeing and removal of excess dye, after which the film is dried.

The Brewster process utilized a duplitized film with a yellow dyed emulsion on each side. This yielded two images, one of which was dyed a cyan, the other a magenta In the old days when two-color was acceptable in the motion-picture industry, this served well But since a revived Technicolor accustomed the public to the beauty of a three-color system, two-color no longer was satisfactory. In order to put a third color upon the duplitized film, Mr. Brewster recoated it with plain gelatin, then transferred an image of silver nitrate. This was immediately treated with 10 per cent potassium iodide to form the silver iodide hydrosol, which was then dyed with auramin. It was essential to put a layer of gelatin over the dyed images before transferring the silver nitrate, for otherwise this substance would react with the iodide ions adsorbed upon the silver iodide, to form a Traube type of image Not only would this give great opacity, but it would release the dye which is held by the mordant

This reaction could be used when it is desired to effect extreme intensification of a silver image By treatment with a Miller-type bleach, the silver could be converted into the hydrosol, so that at least three, and possibly more iodide ions will be held by each atom of silver. Upon treatment with an ammoniacal solution of silver nitrate, the excess iodide ions are converted into the corresponding silver salt A thorough wash, preferably with water made slightly alkaline with ammonia or with sodium sulphite, will remove the excess silver ions, especially those which would otherwise form silver-gelatin complexes (cf chapter on Processing Screen Plates) In this manner three or more silver atoms will be present where only one was present previously. The reduction to metallic state can be accomplished by treatment with sodium hydrosulphite.

The decomposition of the silver-iodide and potassium-iodide dye complex does not take place if copper replaces silver in the transfer. The latest Brewster technique makes use of this. The film, after drying, is treated with a mixture of copper, tannic acid, and chromium salts to completely fix the dyes in the film. A thorough wash removes the excess. Now there will be no interference between the yellow dye and the dyed image already present. Cuprous chloride is the substance transferred. To retain this in solution, it must be heavily charged with chlorides, either as hydrochloric acid, or sodium or ammonium chloride, or a combination of the three. It is also advisable to add some sodium sulphite or metallic copper, to prevent the oxidation of the copper to cupric salts After transfer, the cuprous chloride is converted into the iodide or thiocyanate by treatment with concentrated solutions of these ions

Before Brewster could successfully commercialize his product, several other pitfalls had to be overcome. One of these is common to all color processes, and that is the treatment of the sound track It is highly desirable that this be a black-and-white image Brewster accomplished this by applying to the sound track area only, a solution which destroyed the hydrosol, reforming silver iodide as a Traube-type of image. This was blackened by treatment with hydrosulphite. A suitable oxidizing agent was potassium permanganate, sodium chloride, and an acid Another problem was due to a defect in the duplitized emulsion, a defect that has now been corrected. This could not be detected except by the highly intensifying procedure used by Brewster. In order to eliminate the defect, the film was subjected to the action of bromine vapor, which completely removed any latent image existing in the film. Since a gas was used, no penetration took place into the depth of the emulsion, so that the destructive action was limited to the very surface. The oxides of nitrogen, chlorine, ozone, and other gases capable of exerting an oxidizing action upon the latent image, could also be used

The success achieved by Traube, Tauleigne and Mazo, and Brewster, soon centered considerable attention upon iodide as a mordant. H. D'Arcy Power (*Brit. J. Phot.*, Vol. 59 (1912), p. 41), proposed to use a bath in which the silver was oxidized by ferricyanide in the presence of potassium iodide.

Potassium ferricyanide	40 parts
Potassium iodide	20 parts
Water to	1000 parts

An opaque Traube-type of image was formed, and the further treatment was identical with that of Traube At approximately the same time C Wolf-Czapek proposed a much weaker bath, but containing both potassium salts. Dye also was present so that bleaching and dyeing were accomplished simultaneously.

Potassium ferricyanide	2 parts
Potassium iodide	3 5 parts
Dye solution, 2% solution	15 parts
Sulphuric acid, 10%	1 part
Water to	1000 parts

The dyes that were suitable for this process were auramine, chrysoidine, fuchsin, methylene blue, methyl violet, rhodamine, safranin, thionin blue, and Victoria blue It is interesting to note that Wolf-Czapek also claims the use of acid dyes, and he lists the following: tartrazine, Victoria yellow, naphthalin blue, acid violet, acid fuchsin, erythrosin, and rose Bengal These procedures yield the opaque type of image, so that the silver iodide must be removed from the final result by fixation in cyanide or hypo The dye must, however, be first precipitated by tannic acid before the mordant is removed.

The Tauleigne and Mazo technique is utilized by J H. Christensen (Eng. P. 132846 and 135477, U.S.P. 1447759). After treating the image with cuprous bromide, it can be simultaneously converted into a silver-iodide hydrosol and dyed, by treatment with:

Potassium citrate	71.5 parts
Potassium iodide	143 parts
Dye, to desired concentration	
Water to	1000 parts

It may be a little difficult to retain the dye in solution in the presence of so much salt, but this can be accomplished by the addition of acetic acid.

In the same disclosure Christensen describes a new mordant, one that is capable of great generalization. The ability of silver to form complex salts with thiourea has been well known for some time, and this and analogous substances have been proposed as fixing agents. Christensen disclosed that they may be used as mordants for basic dyes The complexes have the same high transparency that is characteristic of the Miller-type of hydrosol. The silver of the image is first converted into silver halide, and it is then treated with:

Potassium metabisulphite	7.8 parts
Thiourea	6 parts
Potassium iodide	3.1 parts
Potassium sulphocyanide	15 5 parts
Water to	1000 parts

The plate should remain in this solution until it appears to be cleared, after which it is rinsed in water and dyed. This has since been repatented by True Colour Film (Eng. P. 466710), where the mordant is generalized to include all thioamino compounds, of which thiourea and allyl thiourea are typical examples.

The Brewster-type of procedure was patented again by W T. Crespinel and Cinécolor (U.S.P. 2016666; Eng P. 459234 and 462353), and by A M. Gundelfinger and Cinécolor (U.S P. 2141354; Eng. P. 466290). F. Lierg (Eng P. 335930) disclosed some general methods for the formation of transparent iodide and other silver-salt-complexes that would act as mordants. H. Shorrocks (U.S.P. 1303506; Eng. P. 111054), shortly after Miller's disclosures suggested the use of a silver-iodide mordant for making a two-color picture. In a film containing both red and green positive images, the green silver deposits are protected from the action of a bleach This converts the red images into silver iodide. The protection is then removed, and the entire film subjected to the action of a green toning bath which contains a base red dye Since the green toner is chosen so as not to act as a mordant for the basic dye, the two act differentially W. V. D Kelley also used silver iodide for one of the images. The red negative was printed upon a positive film, then processed to form an image in silver iodide. The film was sensitized with dichromate and the green image printed This was dyed with a pinatype dye which would take only in the soft gelatin, after which the silver-iodide image was dyed with the appropriate color. M. S. Procoudin-Gorsky (Eng. P. 293038) iodized each component, then dyed in a bath containing hypo. He claimed that he obtained a tanned image in dyed gelatin that was free from silver. It is a little hard to follow this reasoning, as iodization, unless accomplished by a treatment with a solution containing a soluble iodide and acid dichromate, would not tan the gelatin. W. R Reid and H V A. Briscoe (Eng. P. 370999) also made individual color components which they proceeded to convert into mordant images These were dyed, then registered upon a single base. P. E F Lessertisseux (Eng P 420356) used duplitized film to form a three-color picture One image was printed upon each side of the film base, then converted into mordants and dyed. The entire film was resensitized with dichromate and exposed under a positive of the third separation. The resultant soft gelatin image was dyed with a pinatype color. These are dyes which stain soft gelatin only. The ability of silver iodide to fix dye was utilized by W. V. D. Kelley for the formation of gelatin filters. These consisted of dispersions of silver iodide plus basic dyes, in gelatin.

Instead of using silver images from which to form the mordants, R. Gschöpf (Eng. P. 279381, 311833) used a mixture of ferric oxalate and silver nitrate. This was light-sensitive, and upon exposure to light, formed metallic silver. The light acted upon the ferric salts to reduce them to ferrous condition. These reacted with the silver nitrate to form metallic silver. The image was then converted into cuprous thiocyanate by treatment with a mixture of cupric thiocyanate and ammonium oxalate. This was dyed with a basic dye. The plate or film was resensitized, and the procedure was repeated until three dye images were obtained Instead of mordanting basic dyes, the mordants can be made to act upon other constituents, which can then be converted into dyes. The silver-iodide complex takes on a negative charge, hence it will adsorb other positively charged particles whose sizes are such that true crystalloidal solution is improbable. Murray and Spencer (Eng. P. 363616) found that diazonium salts will attach themselves to the mordant, much in the same manner as basic dyes The chemistry of the diazonium salts is discussed at some length in the chapter on Diazotype Photography. In this disclosure, the light-sensitive properties of the diazonium salts are not utilized.

The silver is converted into a mordant image by any of the well-known methods. Thus upon treatment with cupric bromide, it is converted into silver and cuprous bromide. If this be treated with

Potassium iodide	20 parts
Diazonium salt	2 parts
Water to	1000 parts

the bromides become converted into the iodides which then absorb the diazonium salt. Upon treatment with alkaline solutions of coupling agents, azo dyes are formed and precipitated or mordanted directly upon the image. Hypo must be present to release the diazonium salt. If the diazonium salt is para-diazo-diphenylamine-sulphate, then these can be used as the couplers:

Magenta	
Borax	5 parts
Hypo	40 parts
Potassium hydroxide	0 5 part
Potassium citrate	1 part
J Acid	1 part
Water to	100 parts

Cyan

The J Acid is replaced by H Acid.

Yellow

Water	150 parts
Potassium hydroxide	5½ parts
Hypo	60 parts
Potassium citrate	30 parts
Meta cresol	saturate
Water to	200 parts

Quinone and naphthoquinone could also be used as mordants. This was disclosed by Seyewetz (*Brit J. Phot*, Vol. 71 (1924), p 611; cf. also Ger. P. 354434). A neutral solution must be used in order to form a mordant. The positive is bleached for 10 minutes in the following solution:

Benzoquinone	5 parts
Potassium chloride	120 parts
Water to	1000 parts

Wash for five minutes, after which the image can be dyed in a 0.1 per cent solution of a basic dye containing 0.5 per cent acetic acid. After a five-minute wash in water, the image can be cleared with 2 per cent sodium bisulphite. The potassium chloride can be replaced by 40 grams of the corresponding bromide. The benzoquinone could be replaced with twice the quantity of naphthoquinone The I.G (Eng. P 485861) utilized the oxidation product of hydroquinone as a mordant. The exposed plate is first developed in a mixture of equal parts of the following two solutions:

Solution A:

Hydroquinone	5 parts
Water	500 parts

Solution B.

Sodium carbonate	30 parts
Potassium bromide	1 part
Water to	500 parts

This yields a silver image plus one consisting of the oxidation products of hydroquinone, which is termed a "residual image." The rest of the unexposed, hence undeveloped, silver bromide is now exposed, then developed with a solution containing a very high concentration of sulphite. Therefore no residual image will be formed in this case. Upon converting all the silver to silver bromide by treatment with a mild oxidizing agent, the plate will take on a uniform sensitivity. If duplitized film is used, there will be present two residual images composed of oxidation products of hydroquinone. The third image is printed and developed normally The mordant power of the residual images allows this to be dye-toned, after which the silver image could be converted into the third color. Basic dyes, of course, are used.

Although this procedure is directly opposite to that first disclosed by Seyewetz, it is quite possible that the same mordant is used in both cases. When quinone in the presence of halide reacts with silver, this becomes reduced, not to hydroquinone, but rather to quinhydrone. When hydroquinone is oxidized in the presence of an excess of hydroquinone, quinhydrone is also the product formed. It might be mentioned that the ability of oxidized phenolic developers to mordant basic dyes has been known since 1920 when Lumière and Seyewetz published a paper describing this property (*Photo. Korr.*, Vol. 56 (1920), p 140) W. Eller (*Ber.*, Vol. 53 (1920), p. 1469) also disclosed that the air oxidation products of pyrocatechin, hydroquinone, or pyrogallic acid will tan gelatin, reduce ammoniacal solutions of silver, and form precipitates with basic dyes. A complete study of these substances was published by R. Jodl (*Zeit wiss. Phot.*, Vol. 37 (1938), p. 111).

Dr. Bela Gaspar, who has developed the successful silver-dye-bleach process which carries his name, made his first disclosures in the field of mordants (U.S.P 1956122; Eng. P. 369616). Here is disclosed a monopack containing two layers, each sensitized to a different portion of the spectrum. After exposure, development, and fixation, there are obtained two silver deposits, one in each layer. These are converted into mordants, then dyed with fuchsin The upper image is decolorized by treatment with nitrous acid, with the formation of a diazonium salt. The final step is to couple this with a coupling agent to yield a color complementary to that of fuchsin. Evidently diazotized fuchsin retains its basic characteristics and remains attached to the mordant image

CHAPTER 22

PRIMARY COLOR DEVELOPMENT

ONE of the most elegant solutions to the problem of forming a colored image, lies in the utilization of the products formed by the action of the developer upon the latent image. By this means there is formed a dye image whose intensity follows closely that of the silver. This possibility was first realized by Dr. B. Homolka not long after the significance of the group relations in an organic developer was disclosed by the Lumières, Seyewetz, and Andresen. In order to have a clear and concise view of the matter, a review of the fundamentals would not be out of place.

Photography, as it is practiced today, can be traced back to Talbot and the Calotype process, rather than to Daguerre and the Daguerreotype process. This was disclosed in 1840. A sheet of paper, sensitized with silver iodide plus silver nitrate and gallic acid, after exposure, was washed with a solution of silver nitrate and gallic acid. Here was grasped the idea of the development (physical) of a latent image. Several years later, R. Hunt discovered that ferrous sulphate could replace the gallic acid. In 1847 Blanquart-Evrard found that it was not necessary to give the plate the forebath, but that all the steps of development could take place after exposure. In 1851 Regnault and Liebig pointed out that pyrogallic acid could replace gallic. In these experiments, acid pyro was used, together with silver nitrate, so that it was physical development that was being practiced. In 1862 (*Brit J Phot.*, Vol. 9, p. 425) Major Russell disclosed the use of alkaline pyro as a chemical developer for the latent image. Two stock solutions were prepared, one containing pyro and citric acid, the other containing ammonia or some other alkali. The two were mixed just before use. Once mixed, the solution had no keeping qualities, so that it had to be discarded immediately after use. About 1881, H. B. Berkeley discovered that the addition of sulphite to the pyro solution gave the developer keeping qualities. Since then, all developers have been compounded with much sulphite present, except when this substance interfered with certain desired actions. The developing property of hydroquinone was discovered by Abney in 1880. In 1887 Eder and Toch disclosed pyrocatechin as a developer. The next year Andresen gave us p-phenylene diamine, and shortly after that p-amido-phenol.

It was generally recognized that when a developer acted upon a latent image, the developing agent became oxidized. What the photographic chemists did not realize was that the oxidation product of the amine or phenol was a dye capable of staining the gelatin This realization came relatively late, approximately in 1910, when J. Desalme wrote a paper in which he discussed the probable reaction that took place (*Ch. Ztg.* (1910), p. 953).

Among other things, he had the following to say: "The oxidation products of the organic developers are not quinones, but condensed (polymerized) quinone bodies. Thus paraphenylenediamine, by oxidation by air, ferricyanide, or peroxide in alkaline solution, does not yield the quinone-imide

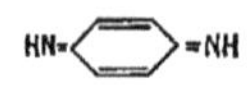

but yields instead, tetramido-diphenyl-para-azo-phenylene

$$(H_2N)_2{=}C_6H_3{-}N{=}C_6H_4{=}N{-}C_6H_3{=}(NH_2)_2$$

These oxidation products are, as a rule, dyes that stain gelatin. Because of this tendency to stain, these substances could not be used as developers without the addition of other compounds, such as sulphite, which would prevent the dye formation By development with a solution containing para-amido-phenol and meta-toluylene diamine, there results a blue coloration due to the oxidation of the amino phenol, and subsequent formation of indaniline. The leuco derivatives of the indophenols, indamines, indanilines, and the diphenyl-amine dyes in general, can be used as developers.

It is rather a sad fact that this was not realized earlier, and to make it worse, there is no reason why this discovery should not have been made In 1856 Perkins succeeded in oxidizing a mixture of aniline and toluidine to make the first synthetic dye Within a decade, this reaction or one similar to it, was used photographically This was in the Willis Aniline Process (Eng P. 2800/64) A paper was sensitized with a mixture of dichromate and phosphoric acid After drying, it was exposed under a copy. Where the light acted upon the dichromate, this oxidizing agent became reduced, hence had no effect upon aniline vapor with which the paper was fumed. If the acid content was low, the formation of a dye image was rather slow, and reddish brown tones were obtained. If the acid content was high, much faster action resulted, with green or blue tones. Toluidine, pyrrol, or their salts could replace the aniline

Almost simultaneously with this came a disclosure by E Kopp in the *Photographic News* (Vol 8 (1864), p. 147). A paper is sensitized with a mixture of dichromates. After exposure, it is washed free of unexposed salts, then treated with aniline, naphthalene derivatives, etc It is claimed that the reduced chromic oxides have associated with themselves chromic acid, which oxidizes amines to form dyes. This paper was published also in *Chemical News* (Vol. 9 (1864), p. 296; Vol. 10, p 28), and in the *Photographic News* about fourteen years later (Vol 22, (1878), p. 467).

These and analogous processes were discovered and rediscovered with great regularity, but no one appears to have made the rather obvious observation that the reaction could serve as a basis for color. Among the last to patent the idea, were Gusserow and Andresen of the Agfa Company of Germany (Ger. P. 116177; Eng. P. 12313/00). The sensitized paper was exposed, then washed free of unreacted dichromate.

It was developed by treatment with:

Water	600 parts
Paraphenylenediamine	1 part
Sodium bisulphite	1–2 parts

A dark brown image resulted. Other colors were obtained if the p.p.d was replaced by other amines and phenols Suitable for use were the dimethyl derivative of p.p.d, the corresponding toluene derivatives, 1:5 di-amino-naphthalene, 1:5 di-oxy-naphthalene, para-amino-phenol, metol, ortol, amidol, pyrogallic acid, para-diamino-diphenyl-amine, aniline, and di-methyl-aniline This was in 1900.

The next year they made a real contribution (Eng. P 5879/01) They discovered that by mixing several of the substances together, dye images of the indamine and indo-phenol class would be formed. This disclosure was the final one which fixed completely the chemistry of color development. It is immaterial whether the oxidation of the ingredients is accomplished by a latent image residing upon silver halide grains, or upon a reduced chromic oxide. In either case the same dye is formed. It is a rather curious type of astigmatism that must have afflicted Andresen, when he failed to recognize that these solutions would be capable of developing a silver image. After all, he was the discoverer of the developing properties of the diamines and amino phenols, and he had by this time already fully disclosed the structural requirements for developer action. Gusserow and Andresen seemed to lay considerable stress upon the fact that it is the reduced dichromates which serve as the oxidizing agent. They claimed this to be an original discovery, forgetting completely that more than thirty-five years before them, E. Kopp disclosed the identical phenomenon.

In the meantime the practical photographers were also tackling the problem. Liesegang noted (*Phot. Archiv.*, Vol. 36 (1895), p. 115; *Phot. Chem. Stud*, Vol 2 (1895), p 28) that the color of the image developed with pyro was much browner than the one produced by ferrous oxalate The next year A Watkins, who devised the factorial system of development, proved that the brown stain was not silver, and that it was proportional to the image density (*Phot. J.*, Vol. 36 (1896), p 245) He developed an image with a sulphite-free pyro developer, then removed the silver by treatment with cupric bromide and hypo. Luppo-Cramer proved that the stain was due to an organic dye (*Phot. Korr.*, Vol. 42 (1906), p 319; Vol. 43, p. 242). By this time the publications of Andresen (*Farbenindustrie* (1889), p. 187; *Phot. Mitt.*, (1891), pp. 124, 286, 296, *Jahr. Phot.*, Vol. 7 (1893), p. 418; *Phot. Korr.*, Vol. 36 (1899), p. 635; Vol. 37 (1900), p. 185) and of the Lumières and Seyewetz

(*Jahrbuch*, Vol 9 (1896), p. 62; Vol 12 (1898), p. 100), Vol. 13 (1899), p. 306; Vol. 18 (1904), p. 99; *Bull. Soc. franç. Phot.*, II, Vol 14 (1898), p. 158; *Brit. J. Phot.*, Vol. 56 (1909), p. 627), completely outlined the structural chemistry of the developers in the benzene series. It remained for Dr. B. Homolka to combine the theoretical findings with the practical (*Phot. Korr.*, Vol. 44 (1907), p. 55). He recognized that the essential group relationship that must exist in developing agents was present in the leuco derivatives of most dyes, hence these should act upon a latent image with the subsequent formation of a dye. Although he failed to find any leuco bases which gave insoluble dye images, he did disclose the developing properties of indoxyl and thio-indoxyl, and the subsequent formation of dye images composed of indigo and thioindigo respectively. The solutions he used were the following:

Blue image

Sodium sulphite, 6% solution	10 parts
Potassium bromide	0.5 part
Indoxyl	1.5–20. parts
Water to	100 parts

Red image

Sodium sulphite, 6% solution	10 parts
Sodium hydroxide, normal	10 parts
Thio-indoxyl	1 5 parts
Water to	100 parts

Several years later R. Fischer patented the practical application of Homolka's discovery, although instead of using indoxyl and thio-indoxyl he used the corresponding carboxylic acids. The —COOH group split off during the reaction, yielding the dyes indigo and thio-indigo for the final images. The solutions Dr. Fischer suggested were as follows (Eng. P. 15055/12; Ger. P. 257167, U S P. 1055155):

Yellow image

Pyrogallic acid	1 part
Potassium carbonate	5 parts
Water to	100 parts

Magenta image

Thio-indoxyl-carboxylic acid	0.5 part
Acetone	5 parts
Potassium carbonate	5 parts
Water to	100 parts

Cyan image

Indoxyl-carboxylic acid	0 5 part
Acetone	5 parts
Potassium carbonate	2 parts
Water to	100 parts

In another patent issued simultaneously with the German patent mentioned above, and assigned to the Neue Photographische Gesellschaft, Fischer utilized these developers to form a screen plate. A gelatin-silver-bromide plate was exposed under a black-and-white matrix, whose transparent areas were one-third the size of the opaque ones. It was next developed with indoxyl, thus converting the exposed regions to a blue color. It was then exposed again, but this time in a manner which formed a latent image in half of the areas previously left unexposed. Development with thio-indoxyl gave a red dye deposit. The emulsion was finally exposed completely, forming a latent image in the remaining clear areas. Development with chlor-indoxyl gave a green image The silver was removed, leaving only stained gelatin behind, upon which could be coated a panchromatic silver bromide emulsion suitable for screen plate processes.

In the same disclosure, Fischer suggested that it would be possible to add the agents to the emulsions before coating. The indoxyl could be added to the red-sensitive emulsion, etc. These could then be coated upon a plate in the form of superimposed layers. It is also possible to tan the emulsions containing the agents. This would seriously restrict their mobility. The emulsion grains could then be mixed with the probability that the indoxyl would remain in the close vicinity of the red-sensitized grains, and not diffuse out to the green- or blue-sensitive grains. Upon development, indoxyl will act only upon the grains exposed to red light. Since it is proposed to use thio-indoxyl to form the primary red required in screen plates, and the magenta required in subtractive processes, it can be imagined that it was not suitable for either of these purposes. The same is true with indoxyl. Perhaps that is why nothing further seems to have been done along these lines.

The chemistry of developers and the developing agents plays a great role in color development. The constituents of an ordinary developing solution are the developing agent, sodium sulphite, potassium bromide, and alkali. The silver bromide that contains a latent image becomes reduced to metallic silver, forming sodium or potassium bromide at the same time. Hence, it becomes possible to control the reduction of the silver salts by the concentration of bromide ions present in the original solution. The potential of the developer will vary inversely with concentration of bromide. Since the action upon non-image portions is also dependent upon the potential, the fogging tendency of a developer can be controlled by the bromide content. Negative developers are compounded with a minimum of bromide present, since here it is important to obtain the last ounce of action from the solution. Positive developers are compounded with relatively large quantities of bromide present, to insure the complete absence of fog.

Although the action of pyrogallic acid had been known since 1851, it was not until approximately thirty years later that it was made stable by the addition of sodium sulphite The brown discoloration that was typical of pyro solutions became completely eliminated when sulphite was present. It was well-known that the brown color was due to the oxidizing action of air upon alkaline solutions of pyrogallic acid, hence it was popularly assumed that sulphite had greater affinity for air than alkaline pyro. This belief persisted for some time, but it was attacked by Andresen (*Phot. Korr.*, Vol. 35 (1898), p. 445; Vol. 36 (1899), pp. 396 and 635; Vol. 37 (1900), p. 185); Bogisch (*Phot. Korr.*, 37 (1900), pp. 89 and 272); Luther and Leubner (*J. prakt. Chem.*, Series II, Vol. 85 (1912), p. 289; Vol. 86 (1913), p. 41; Vol. 22 (1922), p. 72; Vol. 27 (1930), p. 536; Vol. 98 (1918), p. 81); and by Seyewetz and Szymson (*Bull. Soc. Chim. franç.*, Series IV, Vol. 53 (1933), p. 1260). According to Andresen, the sulphite became oxidized, so that the sulphur changed from a quadrivalent to a hexavalent state. But it was not sulphate that was formed, but rather a sulphonated oxidized developer, thus:

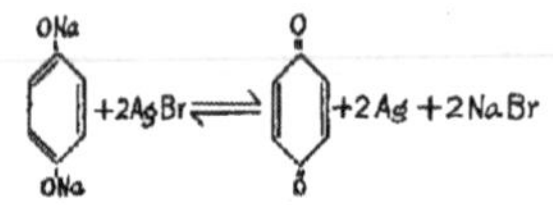

Di-sodium hydroquinonate Quinone

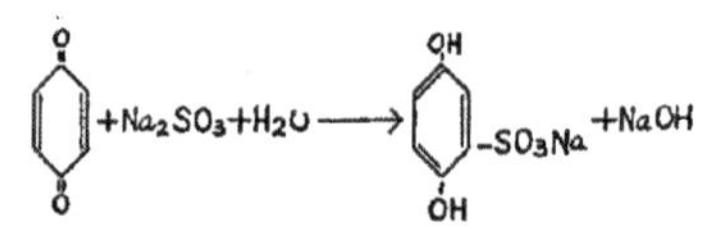

Quinone Sodium hydroquinone sulphonate

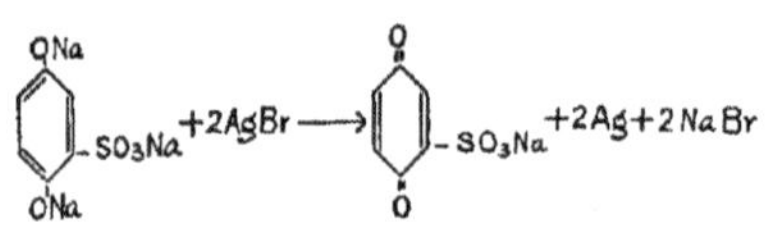

Tri-sodium hydroquinone sulphonate Sodium quinone sulphonate

Combining the three steps, the reaction may be written:

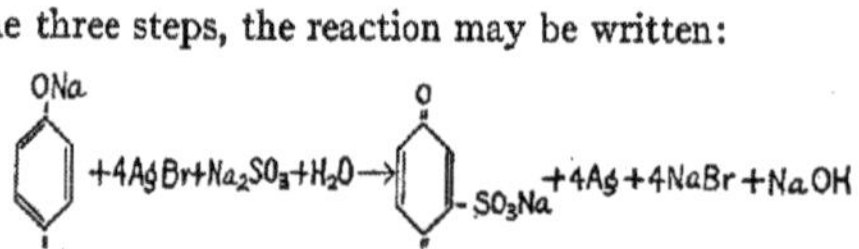

This would indicate that four molecules of silver bromide are utilized by every molecule of hydroquinone. The later work of Pinnow and Seyewetz and Szymson indicates, however, that the final product of the reaction is not quinone sulphonate, but hydroquinone monosulphonate and disulphonate. These can act as developers at the pH of caustic soda solutions, but not at that of carbonates.

When developers are used without sulphite present, the reactivity of the oxidized developer makes itself felt in an entirely different manner. In the absence of any other disturbing substances, polymerization takes place to yield brown amorphous residues A study of this type of developer has been made by R. Jodl (*Zeit. wiss. Phot.*, Vol. 37 (1938), p. 111). It had previously been found that sulphite-free pyrogallic acid, pyrocatechin, and hydroquinone, formed substances by their oxidation by means of the latent image, which tanned gelatin (Ger. P. 309193, 358093 and 358166, issued to G. Koppmann; and 565111, issued to F. Leiber). Koppmann in Germany, and the Technicolor Motion Picture Corporation in the United States (U.S.P. 1535700; Eng P. 204034; Ger P 400951, Fr P. 570076) have made this reaction the bases of color processes. The Lumières and Seyewetz noted that the oxidized developer products were able to mordant basic dyes (*Phot Korr*, Vol. 56 (1921), p 140) This was later made the basis for a color process by the I.G (cf. chapter on Dye Toning). F. Leiber then disclosed (Ger. P 565111) that it was also able to reduce silver nitrate, a property that could be used to intensify a silver image.

The air oxidation products had the same properties, a fact that was first pointed out by W. Eller (*Ber.*, Vol. 53 (1920), p. 1496). He called the polymers formed from phenolic developing agents, huminic acids. They could be precipitated from solution by the addition of aniline, quinoline, pyridine, etc., with which they formed insoluble salts. They united with gelatin to form leather, and with basic dyes to form lakes. They also reduced silver salts and Fehling's solution. When treated with diazonium salts, they formed azo dyes, all more or less brown in shade. Eller assigned the empirical formula $(C_6H_4O_3)_x$ to the huminic acids from pyrocatechin (ortho-dioxy-benzene), and hydroquinone (para-dioxy-benzene). It is evident, therefore, that an atom of oxygen is absorbed by each molecule of developer. The type of union between the molecules has not as yet been established. The potassium and barium salts have the empirical formulas $(C_{12}H_7O_6K)_x$, $(C_{12}H_7O_5BaOH)_x$ respectively. This would indicate that the unit of structure was $C_{12}H_7O_5 \cdot OH$. It is very probable that this is the substance formed when a developer is used which contains no sulphite or other substances that can attach themselves to the extremely reactive position formed within the molecule. It is to be recalled that Desalme (cf. above) proposed a similar type of reaction for the phenylene diamines.

Although we know practically nothing concerning the reaction that takes place when no sulphite is present, we do know that one or more of the positions in the benzene ring become extremely reactive. If any substances are present which contain active or labile hydrogens, coupling takes place and the oxidized developer ions unite with the "coupler" to form a new substance, which in many cases is highly colored and is able to stain the gelatin. Color developers, as we know them today, are compounded with practically no sulphite present. Instead, molecular equivalent quantities of "coupling" agents are added. These unite with the oxidized developer before that substance has a chance to polymerize.

The structural requisites for a derivative of benzene to be a developer, were outlined by the researches of the Lumières and Seyewetz in France and Andresen in Germany. By their very nature, developers must be reducing agents. But not all reducing agents are photographic developers. There are many inorganic substances which are capable of acting in this capacity, notably ferrous citrate, oxalate, fluoride, cuprous ammonium oxalate, hydrosulphite (under special conditions), hydrazine, hydrogen peroxide, and hydroxylamine. The last three have great theoretical interest, although little practical value since during their action they evolve a gas which causes blisters to form within the emulsion layer. They have the structures as follows:

$H_2N—NH_2$,	HO—OH,	$H_2N—OH$
Hydrazine	Hydrogen peroxide	Hydroxylamine

Here two amino, two hydroxy groups, or one of each, are attached to each other. These groups must also be present in the benzene molecule in order for it to have developing properties, and their location within the molecule must correspond to certain definite rules. The molecule of benzene has the structure

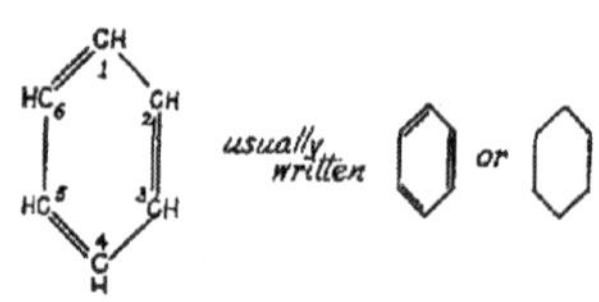

This arrangement of alternating single and double bonds between the carbon atoms of a hydrocarbon, is termed conjugation. In an unsubstituted hydrocarbon of this type, the positions within the molecule have no special significance. But consider the case where two of the hydrogens are replaced by other groups such as amines or hydroxyl radicals. Three different types of substitution are possible, namely:

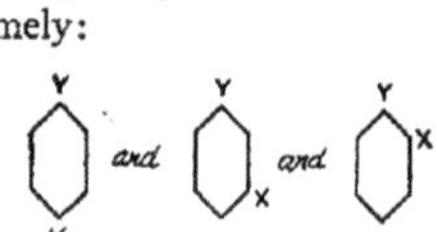

Para Meta Ortho

It is only the ortho and para substituted compounds which can be used as developers.

There are three possible types of tri-substituted derivatives,

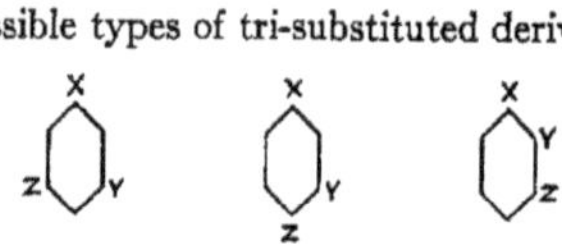

1:3:5 1:3:4 1:2:3

Of these, it is only the 1:3:5 substituted compound that does not have developing properties.

This was as far as the disclosures of the Lumières, Seyewetz, and Andresen went. In 1907 Dr. B. Homolka (cf. above) established that indoxyl and thio-indoxyl had developing properties. He also suggested that the leuco derivatives of di- and tri-phenyl methane dyes had the requisite structures, hence should be capable of developing a latent image. Lumière and Seyewetz tested several leuco tri-phenyl methane dyes and failed to notice that they had any developing properties. This was in keeping with a study which they made upon the effect of a ketonic group upon the developing properties of a substance (*Brit. J. Phot.*, Vol. 44 (1897), p. 665). In general, they found that a ketone group by itself had no effect, provided an aliphatic radical was present on one side of the molecule, and a group with developing characteristics on the other. Thus

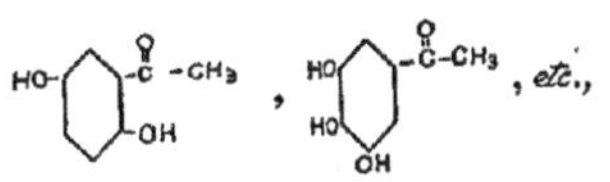

develop vigorously. If an unsubstituted phenyl group replace the methyl, the compound still has developing properties. The substance

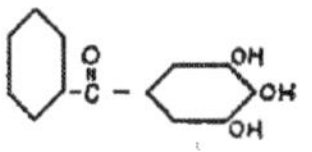

tri-oxy-benzophenone develops quite vigorously, but not as well as the corresponding aceto-phenone. But if any amino or hydroxyl group is present in both of the phenyl groups, the compound loses its developing power. Since most of these substances are colored, their application to color development is immediate. It does not appear, however, that they were studied from this point of view.

In some later work, Homolka extended the number of odd substances which developed a latent image and deposited at the same time insoluble dyes (*Phot. Korr.*, Vol. 51 (1914), p. 256 and 471; Vol. 53 (1916), p. 201; Vol. 56 (1919), p. 387; Vol. 59 (1922), p. 29). These were oxy-iso-carbostyril, whose structure is

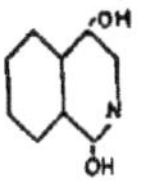

and symmetrical di-methoxy-pyrogallol.

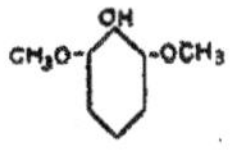

This last is very interesting in that it is apparently an exception to the rules established above. It would merit some study.

All the other substances mentioned also appear to be outside the limits of the established rules. They all have a common grouping however, of the type

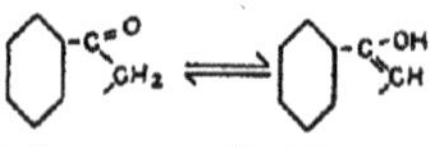

Keto form Enol form

These exist in a type of isomerism known as keto-enol tautomers. It is interesting to note that in the enol form the two carbon atoms have the conjugated linkage that is also present in the ring itself. In indoxyl an —(NH)— group is attached to the end carbon, and also to the benzene nucleus to form a fused indole ring. Now again we have a conjugated system in which adjacent carbons have a hydroxyl and a substituted amino group present. In thio-indoxyl, it is a substituted thiol group (SR) which is attached to the end carbon. This would mean that a thiol group, in which the sulphur atom is firmly attached and in no danger of splitting off, also can endow a substance with developing properties. As a rule such compounds give up the (SH) group very readily, forming hydrogen sulphide, which promptly reacts to form silver sulphide. In oxy-iso-carbo-styril, a similar situation exists. An (NR) group is attached to the end carbon, endowing the molecule with developing properties. If this were not sufficient, then we can consider the molecule from another point of view. It has two hydroxyl groups separated from each other by four atoms, linked together by means of a conjugated chain, hence presenting a hydroquinone type of grouping.

There is one other property common to all of these substances. The dyes which they form are all well-known. They all consist of two identical groups linked together by a double bond. Indoxyl, for instance, yields the dye indigo

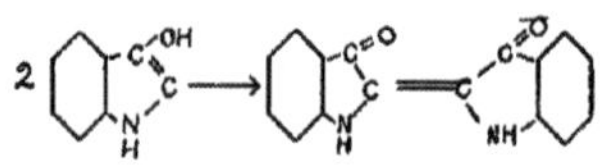

Thio-indoxyl yields the dye thio-indigo

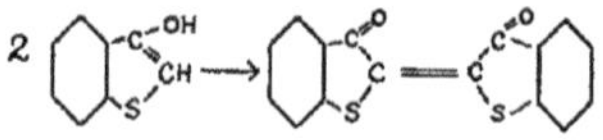

Oxy-iso-carbostyril gives the dye karbindigo

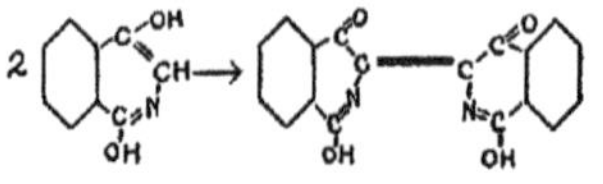

Similarly, symmetrical di-methoxy pyrogallol and para methoxy-alpha naphthol react as follows:

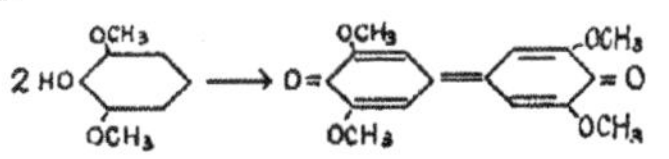

Di-methoxy pyrogallol Coerulignone

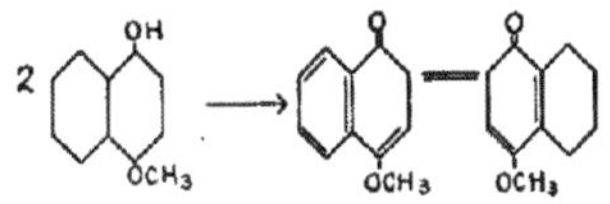

Methoxy alpha naphthol Russig's Blue

These reactions all yield well-known products, hence their structures are determined. In this respect they may furnish a clue as to the nature of the polymerization which takes place when the simpler developing agents like hydroquinone, metol, pyrogallic acid, pyrocatechin, etc., are used.

The work of Homolka was generalized by J. D. Kendall (*IX[e] Cong. int. Phot. sc. appliq.*, (1935), p. 252) in a paper read before the 9th International Congress at Paris. In the more general form, a substance to have developing action must possess a conjugated carbon chain,

$$-\underset{H}{\underset{|}{C}}=\underset{H}{\underset{|}{C}}-\underset{H}{\underset{|}{C}}=\underset{H}{\underset{|}{C}}-\underset{H}{\underset{|}{C}}=\underset{H}{\underset{|}{C}}-.$$

Two of the carbons in this chain must contain hydroxyl or amino substitutions, which must be separated by an even number of carbon atoms, thus

$$X-(\underset{H\ \ H}{\underset{|}{C}=C})_n-Y$$

The number n can be anything from zero up, X and Y represent amino or hydroxyl groups. Thus if n is zero, we have the inorganic series hydrogen peroxide, hydrazine, or hydroxylamine. The carbons can be part of a ring structure. This structural generalization has recently received striking confirmation when K. Maurer and G. Zapp (*Phot. Ind.*, Vol. 33 (1937) p. 90), and J. Rzymkowski (*Phot. Ind.*, Vol. 33 (1937), p. 91) disclosed that Vitamin C and oxytetronic acid could develop

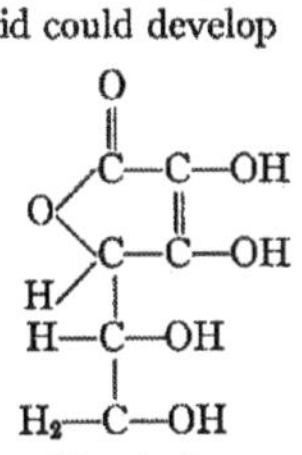

Vitamin C

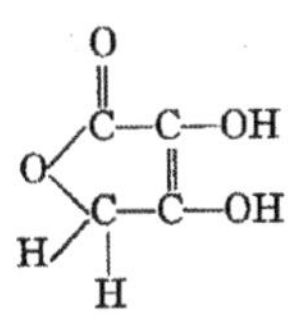

Oxytetronic acid

A partial application of this was patented by the I.G. (Eng. P. 459665, Ger. P. 646516; Fr. P. 807002). Whenever a ketonic group is adjacent to an amino methene group, —(HC—NH_2), the compound has developing properties, and yields a dye image together with the silver. Such a grouping gives rise to the possibility of a keto-enal tautomerism

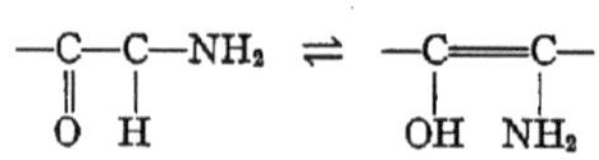

Keto form Enol form

and this, as was indicated above, satisfies the structural requirements for developing action Such developers need not always have alkali present to energize them. An example in the aliphatic series, which is a weak developer, is di-ethyl-amino-acetone

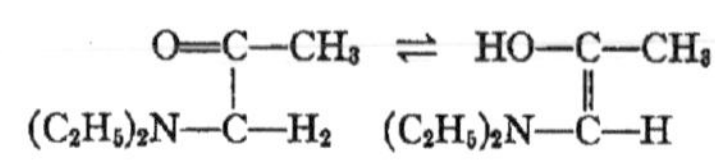

a better developer is amino-aceto-acetic ester

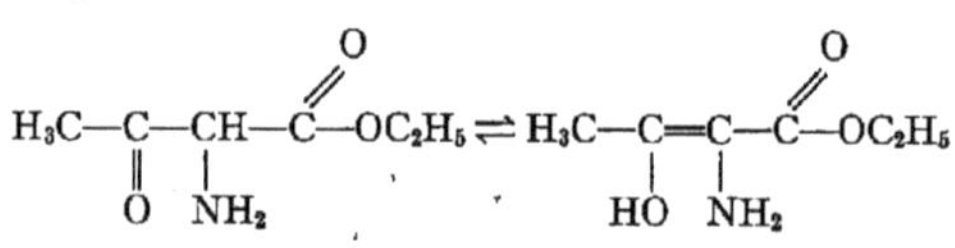

Of course the corresponding benzoic or other acid derivative would act in a similar capacity. Another possibility is 4-amino-5 pyrazolone

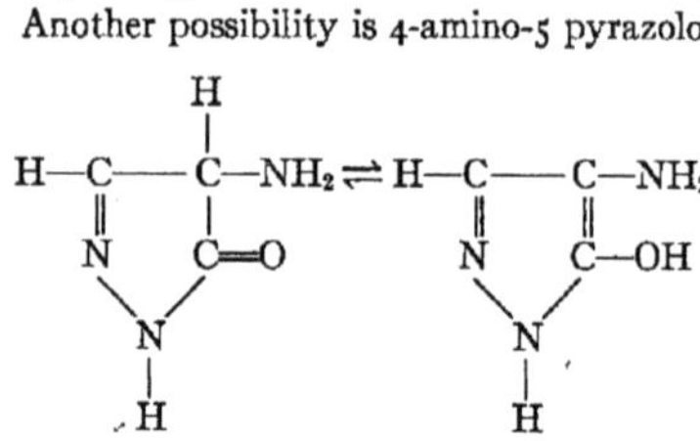

Keto form Enol form
4-amino-5-pyrazolone

Some typical examples of developer solutions are as follows:

1. Alpha-amino-aceto-acetic ester	6 o parts
Sodium sulphite	20.0 parts
Sodium carbonate	10 o parts
Potassium bromide	0.5 part
Water to	1000 parts
2. 1-phenyl-3-methyl-4-amino-5-pyrazolone	5.0 parts
Everything else as in the first example.	

3	1-p-chlor-phenyl-3-methyl-4-amino-5-pyrazolone	5.0 parts
	Sodium sulphite	5.0 parts
	Potassium bromide	0.5 part
	Water to	1000 parts

The last two solutions yield yellow dye images together with the silver.

Ortho-amino phenol has the structure

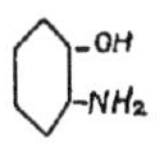

therefore it is a good developer, and capable of yielding dye images. It would appear that this compound and its substitution products are covered in the patent above, but the I G. made doubly sure by another patent (Eng P. 457326), issued a short time before the one discussed above. Yellow to red images are obtained. Typical examples are the following:

Yellow dye image	
4:5-di-methyl-2-methyl amino-phenol	1.0 part
Sodium hydroxide	0.8 part
Water to	200 parts
Orange image	
2-methyl amino-phenol	1 part
Potassium carbonate	10 parts
Water to	200 parts
Red image	
4-chloro-2-methyl amino-phenol	2 parts
Potassium carbonate	15 parts
Water to	200 parts

A further extension was made by the I.G. (Eng. P. 482652), when it disclosed that developers like pyrogallic acid, ortho-amino-phenol, etc., could be made into primary color developers by substituting a heavy residue into the molecule. Suitable for this purpose are groups such as diphenyl, stilbene, azoxybenzene, 2:3-oxy-naphthoic acid, diarylureas, benzthiazol, etc.

In 1936 and 1937 Karl and Ludwig Schinzel wrote a series of papers in the magazine *Das Lichtbild* (Vols. 11 and 12). In the first of these articles, the chemistry of primary color development is discussed (Vol. 11 (1936), p. 172; *Phot. Ind.*, Vol. 34 (1936), p. 942). The application of these findings has been protected by Karl Schinzel in a series of disclosures assigned to the Eastman Kodak Company (Eng. P 498869, 498870, 498871, and 498875). They found that hydroquinone, and naphth-hydroquinone can yield color images directly if heavy substitutions are placed within the molecule. Lemon-yellow images can be obtained if 2:5-diaryl-, 2:5-di-phenoxy-, 2:5-diphenetyl-hydroquinone, or 2-phenyl-1:4-dioxy-naphthalene be used as the developing agent.

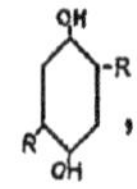, 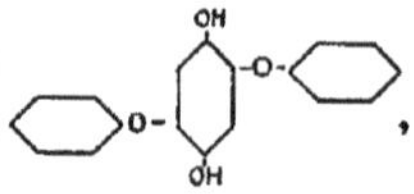, 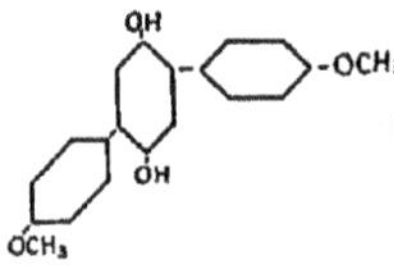, 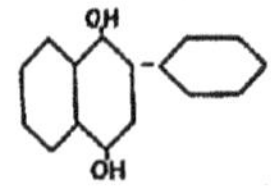

R is any aryl group

Orange or red dyes are obtained if acylamino groups are the substitutions. Examples of this are:

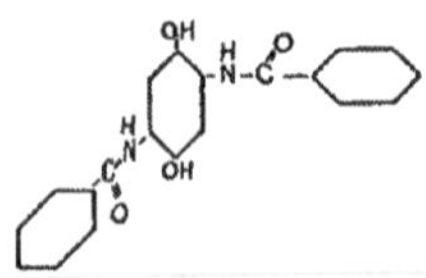

2:5-benzoyl amino-hydroquinone

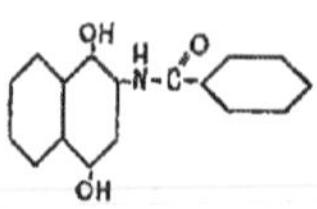

2-benzoyl amino-1:4-dioxy-naphthalene

The presence of an azo group in a molecule evidently does not affect the developing properties, for the deep blue sodium salt solution of 4-phenyl-azo-1:2-dioxy-naphthalene can act in the capacity, yielding at the same time a lemon-yellow dye image. This substance has the structure:

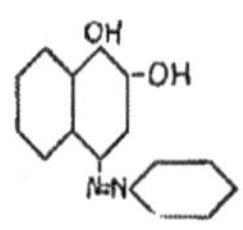

and can be formed by coupling benzene diazonium chloride with 1:2-dioxy naphthalene.

The generators of the lignone dyes can act as primary color developers. Several instances of these have already been mentioned. The symmetrical di-methoxy-pyrogallol is one, and 4-methoxy-alpha-naphthol is another. The beta-methoxy-alpha-naphthol gives a purplish red, beta-phenyl-alpha-naphthol a purple, and tetra-methoxy-alpha-naphthol a blue.

Substituted ortho-amino-phenols and naphthols are again mentioned (Eng. P. 498871). A yellow image is obtained from 3:5-dimethyl-2-amino-phenol. The corresponding di-chloro, bromo, and cyano derivatives can also be used. Ortho-amino-meta-brom-cresol gives reddish-yellow images, as does ortho-amino-para-xylenol. Rose to purple colors can be had using alkoxy ortho-amino-phenols, alpha-phenyl-amino-beta naphthol, or beta-phenyl-amino-alpha-naphthol.

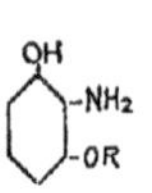 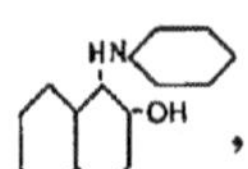, 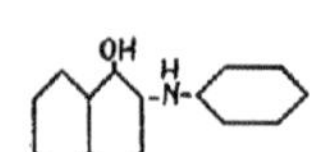

R is an alkyl group

It has been noted above that Homolka called attention to the fact that the leuco derivatives of many dyes should be developers. The action of leuco indamines, indo-anilines and indo-phenols, was long known. These are all derivatives of diphenyl amine

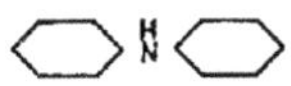

so that if the ortho or para positions in either of the phenyls be occupied by an amino or a hydroxy group, that portion of the molecule would contain the configuration necessary for developer action. Some of the more complicated leuco di-phenyl-amine dyes are quite stable, since it has been proposed to add them to the emulsion before coating (cf. Dieterich, Allison, and Detracolor in chapter dealing with Monopacks). Upon oxidation by means of the latent image the corresponding dye is formed. Fischer patented the use of these substances as color developers (U.S.P. 1102028; Eng. P. 2562/12; Ger. P. 253335), but, as noted above, Homolka mentioned their use in this respect in 1907, and Desalme in 1910 (cf. above). In their articles, and in the English patent 498875, the Schinzels turn to the leuco derivatives for color developers. They carefully exclude the leuco indophenols, indoanilines, indamines, and azomethines, as these have been previously disclosed. But they do list the leuco thio-indigos, seleno-indigos, etc. In using these substances, all air must be excluded. A slight excess of hydrosulphite should be present to act as a preservative.

The fact that the leuco derivatives of the vat and diphenyl methane dyes have developing properties, does not mean that all such substances have like properties. Thus Seyewetz and the Lumières were unable to find these among the leuco derivatives of the tri-phenyl methane dyes. The azo dyes form hydrazo compounds by reduction under controlled conditions, compounds which are derivatives of hydrazine. This, as was indicated above, is a developer, albeit an impractical one. Phenyl hydrazine also is a developer, a fact pointed out by E. Votocek (*Brit. J. Phot.*, Vol. 45 (1898), p. 633). This has the structure:

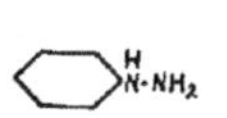

The hydrazo compounds have the structure:

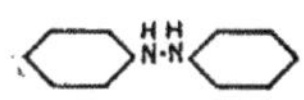

If we place an amino group in the ortho or para positions, we obtain:

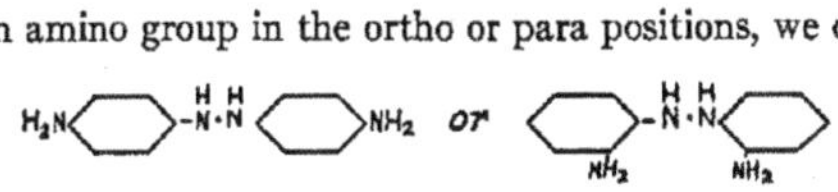

In either case, both portions of the molecule have developing properties, and upon oxidation by the latent image there should be formed the corresponding azo dyes

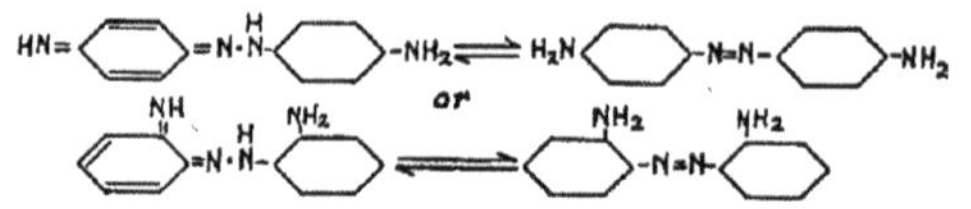

This reaction opens up the entire field of azo dye chemistry for possible application to color development. It may be that the latent image does not have a sufficient potential to oxidize the hydrazo compound. In that case, perhaps the quinones formed by the action of the latent image upon hydroquinone would serve. These are relatively strong oxidizers, especially in the presence of halides, which would serve to remove the silver from solution. The hydrazo compounds can be formed by the controlled reduction of azo dyes, usually by means of alkaline alcohol and zinc dust, sodium amalgam, etc. They can also be prepared by the reduction of nitro compounds with zinc dust and alkali.

$$R{-}N{=}N{-}R' \xrightarrow[\text{alcohol}]{Zn + KOH} R{-}\overset{H}{\underset{|}{N}}{-}\overset{H}{\underset{|}{N}}{-}R'$$

$$R{-}NO_2 \xrightarrow{Zn + KOH} R{-}\overset{H}{\underset{|}{N}}{-}\overset{H}{\underset{|}{N}}{-}R$$

In the first reaction, unsymmetrical hydrazo compounds are formed. In the second, symmetrical compounds are formed. Another possibility lies in the use of the leuco di- and tri-phenyl methanes, together with hydroquinone. The quinones that are formed should oxidize the leuco derivative to the dye.

If this is insufficient, then it is possible to convert the silver into a substance that is capable of oxidizing action. The disclosures of Willis and Kopp who oxidized aniline and other organic substances by dichromate or dichromate reduction products, have already been discussed. The production of dyes by such a procedure was suggested by Gusserow and Andresen (cf. above). These experimenters did not utilize a silver image, but one composed of chromic and chromous oxides formed by the action of light on dichromate sensitized emulsions. The Neue Photographische Gesellschaft in a series of disclosures (Eng. P. 18370/03, 10898/04, and 21584/06; Ger. P. 157411, 180947, and 180948) showed how a silver image could be converted into one of manganese oxide. This could then be made to react with amines or phenols to form colored residues. The silver image is first treated with one of the following:

A.	Potassium ferricyanide, 0.5% solution	100 parts
	Manganous sulphate, 2% solution	20 parts
	Potassium bromide, 10% solution	15 parts
B.	Potassium ferricyanide, 0.5% solution	100 parts
	Manganous sulphate, 2% solution	25 parts

C	Manganous ferricyanide, saturated solution	200 parts
	Potassium bromide, 10% solution	10 parts

After bleaching the silver, the print is washed and treated with:

Potassium ferricyanide, 2% solution	9 parts
Sodium hydroxide, 4% solution	10 parts

In this solution an image composed of manganese oxide is formed. This is finally treated with the color formers.

The catatype process of Ostwald and Gros (*Jahrbuch.*, Vol 17 (1903), p 519) operated along a similar idea A silver image is toned so that it becomes converted into one of platinum. If this be brought in contact with a paper that is sensitized with pyrogallic acid and potassium bromate, the pyro will be oxidized in contact with, and to an extent proportioned to, the image density, forming a stain. Copper sulphate is also useful as a catalyst. If an image of silver or platinum is flooded with peroxide, this substance will be decomposed in situ with the metal. The other portions will remain intact. By this means a peroxide negative image is left. The peroxide can then be made to oxidize amines or phenols to form dyes.

E. R. Bullock bleached the silver image with a mixture of ferricyanide and chromic acid or permanganate (U.S.P. 1279248) By this means there was formed an image of silver ferricyanide. The reduced manganous salts could be removed by washing with a five per cent oxalic acid solution Great care must be taken that no halides are present as otherwise silver halide will be formed After a thorough wash, the bleached image is treated with amines Benzidine gave a strong blue, ortho-tolidine or dianisidine gave a green, and paraphenylenediamine or alpha naphthylamine, a purple. If the bleached image be treated with manganous bromide, silver bromide and manganous ferricyanide would be formed, making the subsequent oxidation of the amines easier to carry out The silver can be fixed out with hypo to give greater brilliance.

A similar idea is utilized by Dr. Bela Gaspar (U.S.P. 1956017, Eng. P. 379679). The esters, ester salts or ethers of the leuco bases of dyes are incorporated into an emulsion. These are not affected by the operations of exposure, development, fixation, or wash. The silver image is next converted into a substance that is capable of regenerating the dye A photographic emulsion is prepared to contain diacetyl indigo white. After exposure, development, and fixation, the silver is converted by well known means into lead chromate. As long as no free chromic acid is formed, no action will take place with the leuco dye To accomplish the formation of lead chromate, the image is first treated with lead salts plus potassium ferricyanide in the presence of ions like citrates, lactates, etc. The lead ferrocyanide is then treated with neutral dichromates or chromates When an image composed of lead chromate is acidified, chromic acid is formed, which reacts with the leuco dye to yield the insoluble blue dye, indigo. The unreacted leuco dye as well as the lead can be removed by treatment with fixing agents and acetone

A red color can be formed if indigo white be replaced with the sulphuric ester of the leuco compound 6:6′ di-brom-di-methyl-bis-thio-naphthene-indigo. Yellow is formed from an ester of the leuco derivative of helindon yellow.

The fact that substances such as 4-methoxy-alpha-naphthol, and 2:6-di-methoxy-phenol

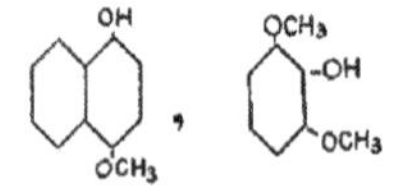

are developers, yielding dyes whose structures are the following:

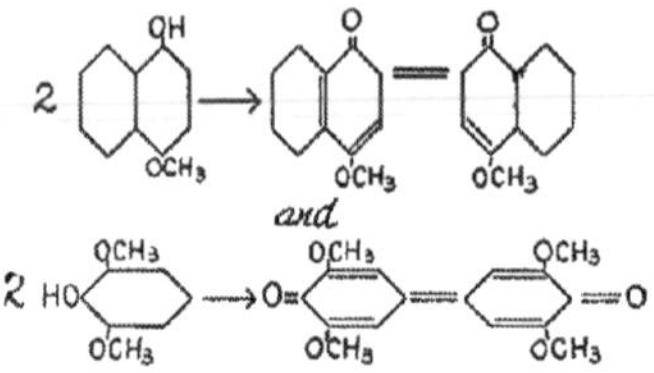

gives rise to the possibility that it may be possible to make other developers that cannot form quinone imide structures by oxidation, but form, rather, an indigoid type of structure. Since para methoxy-phenol is not a developer, whereas the di-methoxy compound is; and since alpha naphthol is not a developer, but para-methoxy-alpha-naphthol is; the inference may be drawn that in heavy molecules the structural requirements for the presence of developer power are different from what they are in the simpler compounds. It is well known, for instance, that phloroglucinol

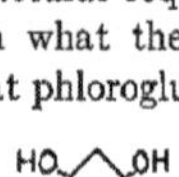

cannot act as a developer, but that tri-methyl-phloroglucinol

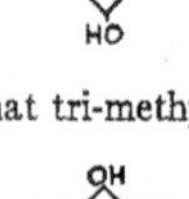

is a developer. Also it is well established that resorcin does not reduce exposed silver halide grains, but tri-methyl resorcin

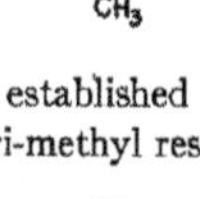

can develop the latent image. In these compounds there is no possibility for the formation of ortho- or para-quinoid structures, nor is there the possibility that the carbon ortho or para to a hydroxyl group can become highly reactive in the same manner as in methoxy-alpha-naphthol. It would be extremely interesting to determine whether symmetrical di-methoxy-phenol

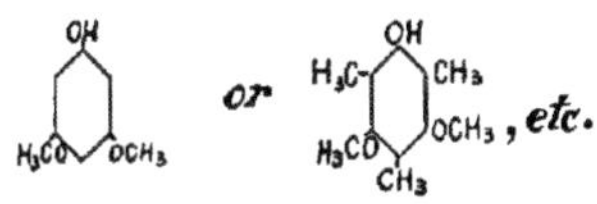

will develop, and if so, whether dye formation does not also take place simultaneously.

Another possibility lies in the compounds of the type

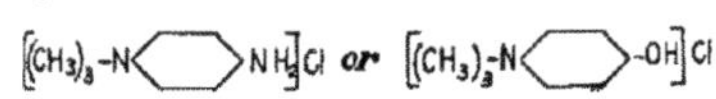

Here there is destroyed any likelihood that para-quinoid structures

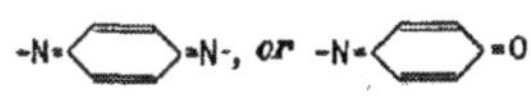

can be formed. But that does not preclude the absence of developer action, since there always remains the possibility that two oxidized residues will couple to yield a quinoid structure such as:

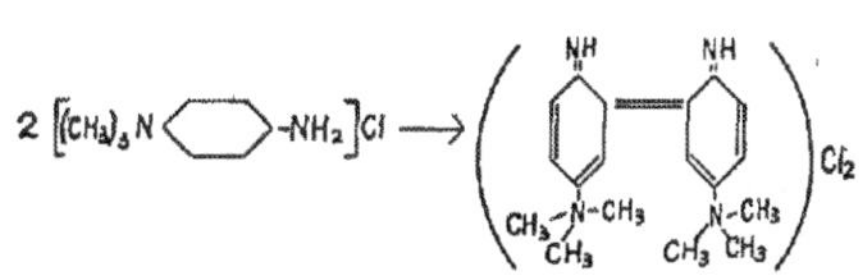

It can reasonably be supposed that the equivalent naphthalene compound would act in this manner, since we have the evidence with methoxy-alpha-naphthol. The methoxy group is strictly a neutral one in so far as giving a compound developing power is concerned. The quaternary ammonium nitrogen may not be so neutral.

CHAPTER 23

COUPLING COLOR DEVELOPMENT

IN the preceding chapter we discussed primary color development, in which the dye image is formed by the direct oxidation of the developer itself. Although this method is very simple and most direct, and although it was introduced some time before all other methods, it is not the technique which is being favored at the present moment. The fact that an oxidized phenylenediamine can unite with other amines and phenols was known for a long time, for the indophenol, indamine and indaniline dyes were prepared in that manner. But their application to color photography did not come until 1901 when Gusserow and Andresen amplified their disclosure of the previous year. In the first patent (Eng. P. 12313/00; Ger. P. 116177) they disclosed that amines and phenols become oxidized to colored substances by the product of the reaction between light and dichromates. The list of chemicals which could be used were as follows:

Para-phenylene-diamine	Amidol
Di-methyl-para-phenylene diamine	Pyrogallic acid
Para-toluylene-diamine	1:5 Dioxy-naphthalene
1:5-Di-amino-phenol	Para-diamino-diphenyl-amine
Para-methyl-amino-phenol	Aniline
Ortol	Di-methyl-aniline

The paper, sensitized with a strong solution of ammonium dichromate, is exposed under a negative It is washed free of unreacted dichromate, then treated with:

Amine or phenol	1 part
Sodium bisulphite	1–2 parts
Water to	600 parts

The different substances give different colors. In this form, the procedure offers no novelty over the one proposed by E. Kopp in 1864 (cf. preceding chapter) But in the next disclosure (Eng. P. 5879/01; Ger. P. 123292) a real advance was made. Instead of having present but one of the agents, several were used, one of which was paraphenylenediamine or an aminophenol. Now upon treatment with the exposed and washed plate, a dye image of the indophenol, indamine or indaniline was formed.

In 1908 Henri-Raymond Vidal treated paraphenylenediamine with dichromate and obtained a color image (Fr. P. 391465). He, as well as Gusserow and Andresen, failed to notice that these solutions could be used as developers until after Fischer made his disclosures and together with Siegrist published a full account of the chemistry and properties of such solutions. In 1914, a year after the fact was made known generally, Vidal made the discovery that his solutions also had developing power (Fr. P. 468537). Instead of using pure dichromate as the sensitive medium, A. Thiebau (*La Phot.* (1908), p 227, *Brit. J Phot.*, Vol 55 (1908), p. 738), suggested the following as being more sensitive

Ammonium dichromate	90 parts
Copper sulphate	45 parts
Manganese sulphate	10 parts
Water to	1000 parts

After exposure, the paper was washed, then immersed in a 5 per cent solution of one of the following agents, slightly acidulated with sulphuric acid

Aniline hydrochloride
Phenols
Pyrogallic acid
Cresols
Naphthols
Para-amino-phenol
Para-phenylene-diamine
etc.

In 1912 Dr. Rudolph Fischer disclosed the fact that the latent image in a silver halide emulsion could replace the reduced chromium oxide images utilized by Kopp, Gusserow and Andresen, Vidal, Thiebau, etc. Whether or not he was familiar with the work of these people is a question open to debate, for neither in his basic patents (Ger. P. 253335; Eng P. 2562/13, 5602/13; U.S.P. 1079756 and 1102028) nor in the article which he wrote together with Siegrist (*Phot. Korr.*, Vol. 51 (1914), p 18) does he mention it. But he does discuss the disclosures of Homolka on primary color development (cf. preceding chapter). The article covers the fundamentals so thoroughly that it well merits the detailed abstraction which follows. It is entitled "The Preparation of Dyes by Oxidation by Means of the Latent Image."

This subject has received but scant attention because it was very difficult to isolate and purify the dye formed. But the phenomenon is well known The brown stain of a pyro-developed image is due to an oxidation product, and this allows itself to be isolated from the silver. In 1907 Homolka showed that indoxyl and thio-indoxyl would develop a latent image and yield the dyes indigo and thio-indigo together with the silver. This brings to mind the agents para-amino-phenol, and para-phenylene-diamine, which upon oxidation in the presence of amines and phenols, yield the dyes of the indamine, indo-phenol, and indaniline classes The leuco derivatives of these dyes have already been proposed as developers, but their use has been restricted to the preparation of silver images, completely disregarding the fact that insoluble dyes are formed also. This was probably due to the fact that the solutions were compounded with large quantities of sulphite present to act as preservatives, a fact which would completely prevent the dye formation. Here is disclosed their use to yield dye images rather than silver. The fundamental reactions are as follows:

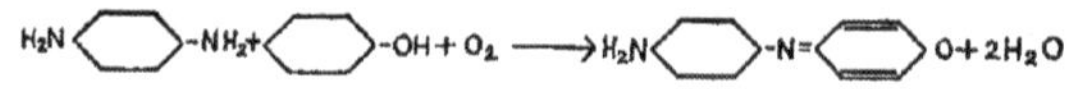

Para-phenylene-diamine Phenol Indoaniline

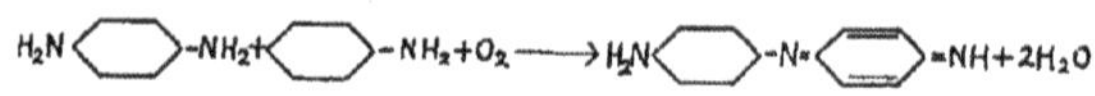

Para-phenylene-diamine Aniline Indamine

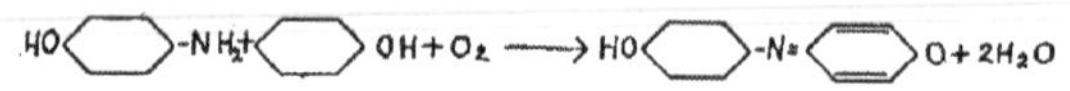

Para-amino-phenol Phenol Indophenol

Instead of oxygen as the oxidizing agent, the exposed silver bromide could be used.

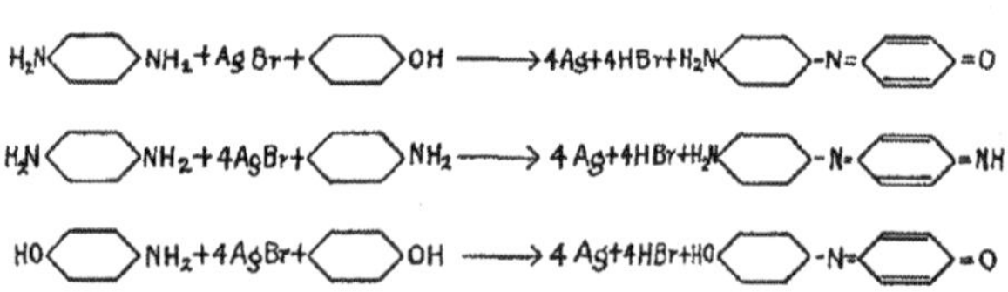

Since hydrobromic acid is formed during the reaction, it will proceed best in the presence of alkali, which will neutralize the acid as fast as it is formed. The amino group in para-amino-phenol, and one of them in the diamine, must be free of substitutions. The corresponding naphthalene derivatives could also be used. Thus instead of para-phenylene-diamine, 1:4 hydrobromic-naphthalene could serve, and instead of phenol or aniline the corresponding naphthylamine or naphthol could be substituted.

Fischer and Siegrist gave the name Color Development to this process and they termed the second agent present, couplers. Thus phenol is the coupling agent in the reaction where indophenols or indoanilines are formed, and aniline is the coupler in the third reaction. By reducing the silver halide grain, the developing agents are oxidized probably to form quinoid compounds with the hypothetical structures

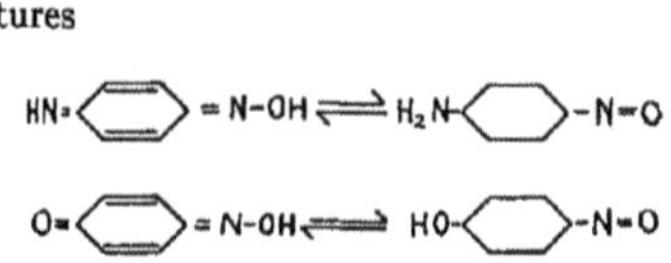

The form on the left is a hydroxyl amine derivative, while its tautomer on the right is a nitroso compound. These substances could couple or condense with compounds that have reactive hydrogens. In aromatic chemistry it is well known that the hydrogens in the ortho or para position to an hydroxyl, amino, or substituted amino group, are very reactive. We can conceive the reaction to be the following:

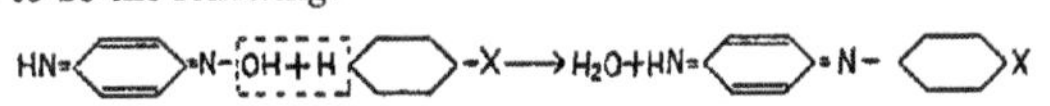

Here X represents an hydroxyl, amino or substituted amino group. This scheme sounds quite plausible when it is recalled that methods of formation of these dyes have been proposed in which nitroso-phenols or amines are used,

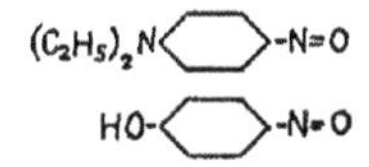

These substances can be very readily prepared by the action of nitrous acid HO—N═O, upon di-ethyl aniline or phenol

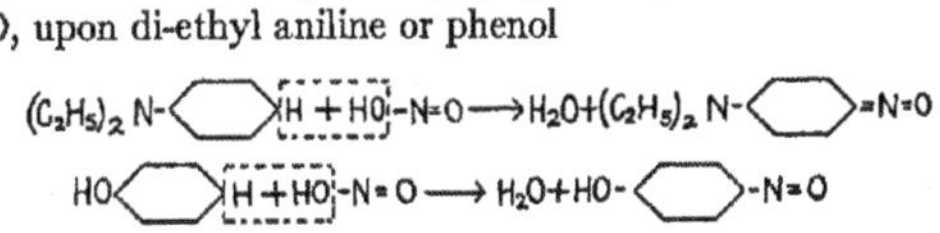

In order to form this hypothetical compound from the diamine or amino-phenol, two atoms of oxygen must be used up, thus

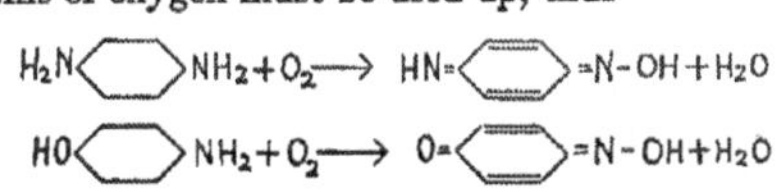

This means that a change of four valence units takes place. When silver bromide is reduced to silver, with the liberation of bromide ions, a change of only one valence unit occurs. Therefore four molecules of silver bromide must be reduced in order to supply the requisite electrons for a four-fold change in valences. This is discussed in some detail by A. G. Tull (*Brit. J. Phot.*, Vol. 85 (1938), p. 627).

The aromatic amines and phenols are not the only substances that can be used as couplers. Any compound which has a reactive methine group, $—CH_2—$, can be used. Such a group is formed when in methane two of the hydrogens are replaced by strongly polar groups, to form $R—CH_2—R'$, R and R′ being groups that have strong electric charges. Such groups are phenyl, cyano, carbonyl, acetyl, etc. Thus a substance such as phenyl-aceto-nitrile, 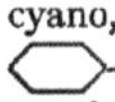$—CH_2—CN$, contains a very reactive $—CH_2—$ group. Other examples are the aceto-acetic-esters,

$$CH_3—\underset{\underset{O}{\|}}{C}—CH_2—\underset{\underset{O}{\|}}{C}—OR,$$

aceto-acetanilides,

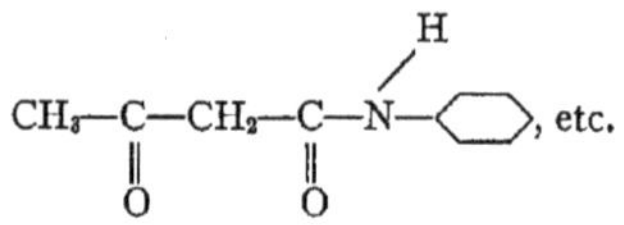

With such compounds azo methine dyes are formed

Not only did Fischer and Siegrist outline the fundamental chemistry of the reaction involved, but they also discussed rather fully the effect of substitutions within the molecules used, either for developing or for coupling They left practically nothing to be discovered, except tricky and complicated substitutions within the molecules, in places where no effect would be had upon the chemistry of the reaction. These merely modified the chemical and physical properties of the dyes formed, made their spectral absorptions correspond more closely to theoretical requirements, made them more insoluble, and substantive to the gelatin medium in which they were used, etc. No new chemical configurations were developed that would couple with the oxidized developer.

The substitution of a methyl or ethyl group into the developer molecule deepens the color In a series of tests in which the same coupler, di-chlor-alpha-naphthol, was used, and the developing agents varied, the results were as follows:

Developing Agent	*Color of Dye Image*
Para-phenylene-diamine	Pinkish or purplish hue
Para-toluylene-diamine	Blue
Para-di-methylamino-aniline	Cyan
Para-di-ethylamino-aniline	Cyan

The same type of color change results when the coupler is varied. This is indicated in the following series of experiments, in which para-di-ethyl-amino-aniline was used as the developing agent.

Coupler	*Color of the Image*
Phenol	Blue with a greenish tint
Ortho-cresol	Cyan
Meta-cresol	Cyan
1:4:5 Xylenol	Cyan
Alpha-naphthol	Blue
Di-chlor-alpha-naphthol	Cyan
Tri-chlor-alpha-naphthol	Greener cyan
Penta-chlor-alpha-naphthol	Green

These give only blue and blue-green shades. In order to obtain yellows and red, it is necessary to turn to the active methine group and the azine dyes. The same situation holds with these substances that was true with the aromatic amines and phenols

Using para-nitro-phenyl-aceto-nitrile, O_2N—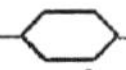—CH_2—CN as the coupling agents, the following variation in colors was obtained by the substitution of methyl and ethyl groups within the molecule of the developing agent.

Developing Agent	*Color of the Dye Image*
Para-phenylene diamine	Orange yellow
Para-toluylene diamine	Reddish yellow
Para-ethyl-amino-aniline	Bluish red
Para-di-ethyl-amino-aniline	Magenta

Using the same developing agent, the color of the dye image in the aceto-acetic ester group also deepens.

Coupler	*Color of the Dye Image*
$CH_3-\underset{\underset{O}{\Vert}}{C}-CH_2-\underset{\underset{O}{\Vert}}{C}-OC_2H_5$ Aceto-acetic-ester	Yellow
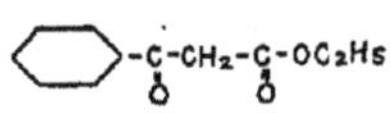 Benzoyl-acetic-ester	Reddish yellow
$H_2N-CH_2-\underset{\underset{O}{\Vert}}{C}-CH_2-\underset{\underset{O}{\Vert}}{C}-OC_2H_5$ Alpha-amino-acetic-ester	Orange
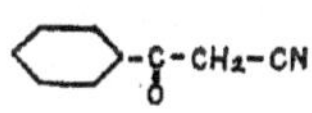 Cyan-aceto-phenone	Red
$NC-CH_2-CN$ Methylene-cyanide	Magenta

If the methine group, —CH_2—, is part of a ring structure, the color is also much deeper.

Coupling Agent	*Color of the Dye Image*
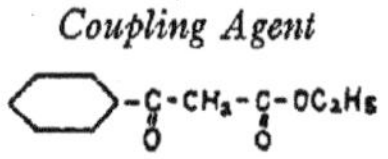 Benzoyl-acetic-ester	Reddish yellow
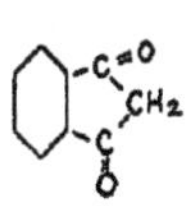 Diketo-hydrinden	Blue

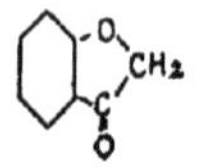

Coumaranon

Red

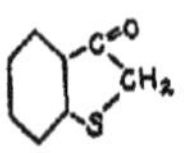

Thioindoxyl

Magenta

The azo-methine dyes have much more stability toward light and acids than the indophenols, indoanilines, and indamines. Strong acids decompose the dyes into the respective quinone or quinone-imides and the couplers. Therefore under no circumstances should strong acids be allowed to come in contact with the dye images Acid short stops and acid fixing baths of the conventional type should not be used. Being well aware of these difficulties, Fischer in his disclosures suggests other and more convenient working methods The three-color separations are first printed as ordinary black-and-white prints, on some stripping material. The silver of the images is next converted into silver ferrocyanide by treatment with potassium ferricyanide. This last could then be treated with coupling developers. The troubles that might arise from acid short stops and acid fixing baths are completely eliminated, since at this stage of the process no dye images yet exist.

Fischer and Siegrist commercialized their findings by marketing a self-toning paper which contained the coupling agents as an integral part of the emulsion. By developing a paper with paraphenylenediamine, a toned print was obtained immediately. In this work, they anticipated by a full generation the later work of the I.G. whose Agfa Color contains emulsions with the couplers present. The earlier efforts failed mainly because the appreciable solubility of the coupling agents caused them to diffuse out of the emulsion in sufficient quantity to affect the developer characteristics. Thus a developer became contaminated immediately after use. The I.G. remedied this defect by placing substitutions within the coupling molecule, which made that an extremely heavy and immobile compound despite relative high solubility in alkaline solutions Diffusion out of a gelatin layer was extremely slow. To all intents and purposes, the coupling agent behaved as a colorless "dye" that was mordanted to or was substantive to the gelatin The importance which the I.G. attached to this particular phase of the subject may be gathered from the fact that no fewer than fifteen United States, and thirteen English, patents cover it. In general, a very heavy molecular residue is attached to the coupler in a position where it will not interfere with the coupling qualities. Strictly speaking, from a chemical point of view, this procedure is merely like substituting an ethyl group for a methyl, within a compound which does not depend upon either of these groups for a determination of its chemical properties. From a patent and legal point of view, the justification is that a desired modification in the physical properties is achieved, this modification and its importance being fully described in the patent specifications Since these disclosures were discussed at some length in Chapter 11, they need only be mentioned here

A polyvinyl maleic acid residue is attached to a coupling molecule by means of an amino group present within that molecule Thus 1-para-amino-phenyl-3-methyl-5 pyrazolone is made to react with a polyvinyl-maleic acid anhydride to form

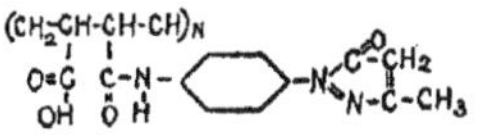

1-(polyvinyl-maleic-anilido)-3-methyl-5-pyrazolone

This is disclosed in United States patent 2179234 (Eng. P 468894; Fr P. 811541)

Other heavy groups that can be used are stilbene, azoxybenzene, diphenyl, oxy-naphthoic acid amide, benzthiazol, amino phenols and phenols substituted in the 3:5 position (U.S.P. 2179238; Eng. P. 458400; Fr P 803566). The residue can consist of a hydrocarbon with a minimum of five carbon atoms in the chain. This can be linked to the molecule by a homopolar bond (U.S.P. 2186849; Eng. P 465823; Fr P 810410), through an acid amide radical (U S.P 2186735; Eng. P. 489164; Fr P 828603), or by a straight substitution for one of the hydrogens attached to a carbon (U.S.P. 2186731; Eng. P. 488048; Fr. P. 822166). Resins (U.S P 2186733; Eng. P 489274; Fr. P. 827625), carbohydrates (U.S.P. 2186732; Eng. P 483000; Fr P 824878), polypeptides such as gelatin, albumen, or their degradation products (U.S.P. 2179244; Eng. P. 484098), sterol or the bile acids (U.S P. 2186851; Eng. P. 489093; Fr. P. 827626), polymeric carboxylic acids such as polyglycuronic acid or polyacrylic acid (U S P. 2178612; Eng P. 479838; Fr P 807792), and hydrogenated aromatic or heterocyclic compounds (U S.P. 2186719; Eng P. 491958) are some of the other substitutions that have been suggested. Very useful in this respect is the molecule 1-hydroxy-2-naphthoic acid, which can be made to react with aromatic amines such as dianisidene to yield cyan couplers (U S.P 2179228). Two or more molecular residues, each of which is capable of coupling, can be condensed to form a single molecule (U S P 2186734; Eng P. 489161; Fr. P. 828579).

The first world war stopped the further development of the subject. In the early nineteen-twenties, the Schinzels turned their attention to color development, but they apparently waited until 1936 before they made public any of their findings (*Lichtbild*, Vol. 12 (1936), p. 19). They pointed out that Fischer and Siegrist had proceeded under the mistaken notion that an appreciable solubility was necessary in order for the reaction to take place. But they found that this was not so. For instance leuco naphthol blue is extremely insoluble in alkaline solutions. Yet an emulsion prepared with this substance present, gave a good image when it was merely bathed in soda after exposure. They therefore centered their attention upon the building up of heavy coupling agents whose solubility in developer alkalinity would be very slight. To accomplish this, they adopted approximately the same dodge used by Ansco and the I.G., substitutions within the coupling molecule that made it extremely heavy. Very useful were amino groups that could be converted into an acid amide by treatment with a compound containing a free COOH radical, or vice versa. It must be borne in mind, that whereas the I G. chemists sought high solubility coupled with extreme immobility, the Schinzels strove for extreme insolubility.

Color development of the secondary type did not become popular until the Eastman Kodak Company adopted it as a processing technique for monopack film. The first patents issued to Mannes and Godowsky of this company which mentioned color development, were in 1932 (Eng. P. 376794, 376795, and 376838). The corresponding United States patent (1954452) was not issued until two years later. Dr. M. W. Seymour, another member of the Eastman staff had also interested himself in this procedure about this time (U.S.P 1900869 and 1900870), as did Capstaff (U.S P. 1954346 and 1969452) and Burwell (U S P. 1966330). These all disclosed various monopack schemes (cf. chapter on Monopacks) and contributed nothing not previously discussed by Fischer and Siegrist.

The first patent dealing with couplers that was issued to the Eastman Kodak Company, came in 1934, and was issued to Dr M. W. Seymour (U S.P. 1969479) This disclosed the pyrazolones as possibilities for the formation of magenta images. The pyrazolones could be prepared by the action of beta ketone esters upon hydrazines Thus when aceto-acetic-ester reacts with phenyl-hydrazine, the reaction that takes place is as follows:

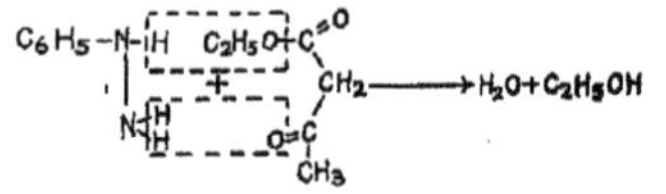

Phenyl hydrazine Ethyl-aceto-acetic-ester

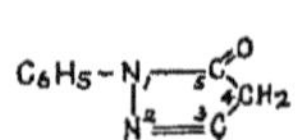

1-phenyl-3-methyl-5-pyrazolone

When prepared in this manner, the compound is characterized by the presence of a methine group between two polar carbon atoms, hence the hydrogens attached to this are extremely active. Not only will they couple with oxidized paraphenylenediamine, and amino-phenols, but also with diazonium salts.

Dr. Seymour gave several formulas which could be used, of which the following is a typical example.

Solution A.

Para-di-methyl-amino-aniline-monohydrochloride	0.5 part
Sodium sulphite	7.5 parts
Water to	250 parts

Solution B.

1-Phenyl-3-methyl-5-pyrazolone	0 5 part
Acetone	10 parts

Add *B* to *A*.

Several years later, the Eastman company was granted several more general patents covering the pyrazolones. In the first of these (Eng. P. 478990) a heterocyclic group could be attached to the molecule in the number-one position. In the number-three position, furyl, quinolyl, benzthiazolyl and like groups, or hydroxy and carboxy groups can be present. The ketone structure could be replaced by the equivalent thio-ketone or carbimide radical. In a patent issued still later (Eng P 496196) there is disclosed the use of two pyrazolone molecules linked para to each other through a phenyl group.

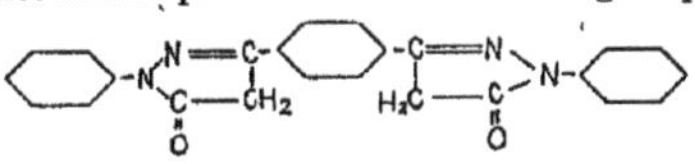

The phenyl groups can be replaced by amino-phenols, -cresols, -naphthols, and their alkyl substitution products. The starting point for the compounds of this family is the substance

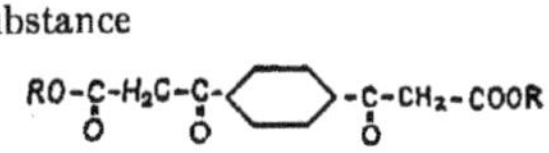

Terephthaloyl-bis-acetic-ester

This upon condensation with two molecules of phenyl-hydrazine, yields para-di-(1-phenyl-5-pyrazolone) benzene.

Not to be outdone, the I.G. prepared a pyrazolone derivative starting with di-ethyl-malonate (Eng P 502665) This has the structure

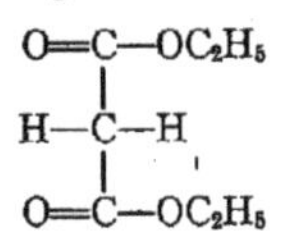

When this is treated with stearoyl chloride, there is formed:

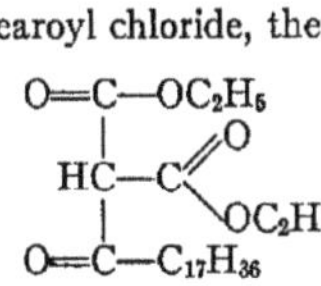

In this configuration the molecule was rearranged slightly to put a stearoyl radical along the straight chain Upon treatment with phenyl-hydrazine-3-carboxylic acid, a pyrazolone is formed:

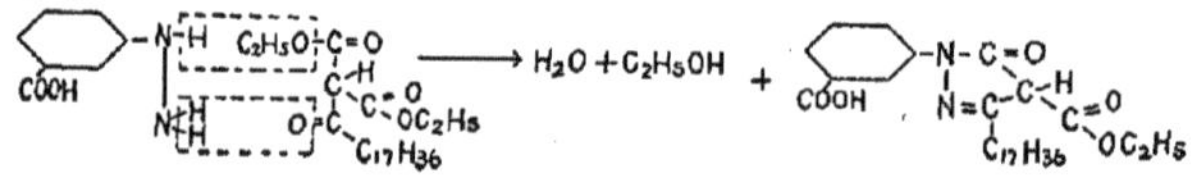

Upon heating with acids, ethyl alcohol and CO_2 split off, in accordance with a well-known reaction, leaving 1-(3′-carboxy-phenyl)-3-heptadecyl-5-pyrazolone

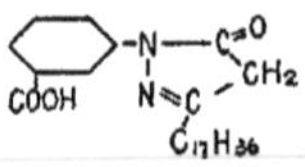

These substances yield red to magenta dye images. The molecule, incidentally, is rather interesting. Coupling properties are due to the CH_2 group within the pyrazolone molecule Solubility in alkali is attained since an acid group, COOH, is present. This is attached to the phenyl group, which plays no part in the chemical activity of the molecule. Very low mobility and diffusion through gelatin are achieved by the presence of a very heavy group, $C_{17}H_{36}$, and by a very high molecular weight, 443. A molecule as heavy as this cannot exist in solution except as a colloid, whose diffusion into and out of gelatin is very, very limited.

One bad feature of color development is that the solutions compounded with a minimum of sulphite present have no keeping quality. To improve this, E. E Jelley, of the Kodak, Ltd. staff has suggested the use of sulphoxylates (Eng. P. 462140) These are compounds formed by the action of formaldehyde upon sulphites and hydrosulphites. The active group becomes masked by union with the formaldehyde. Rongalite C is such a union of formaldehyde and sodium hydrosulphite. The sulphoxylates will preserve the developer somewhat against air oxidation, but will not interfere to any extent with the reaction between oxidized developer and the coupling agent. A typical example is the following:

Solution A

Para-diethyl-amino-aniline hydrochloride	3.0 parts
Sulphoxylate	5 0 parts
Sodium carbonate	50 parts
Potassium thiocyanate	0 5 part
Water to	1000 parts

Solution B.

Ortho-hydroxy-diphenyl	2.5 parts
Acetone	100 parts

Add solution *B* to *A* just before use. A cyan dye image is obtained with this solution. If the hydroxy-diphenyl be replaced with naphthoyl-acetonitrile, a magenta color would be obtained

It is to be noticed that the stock solution *A* contains potassium thiocyanate. This is a silver solvent, whose addition to developer solutions is desirable in reversal processes (cf. chapter on Processing Screen Plates) More recently it began to appear as an important addition to fine-grain developers such as DK-20. The substance was put to a third use by Mannes and Godowsky (U.S.P. 2191713) who found that its presence gave a developer solution a very pronounced boost in potential.

The disclosures of Fischer and Siegrist have described rather completely the chemical requisites for a substance to act as a coupler So fully did they cover the field that, with the possible exception of pyrazolone and its derivatives, no new chemical configurations have since been disclosed, but merely substitutions made in the old that left the reactive portion of the molecule intact. Even in the case of pyrazolone there is present a methine group, —(CH_2)—, which has the other two valences satisfied by strongly polar linkages, such as a carbonyl, (O=C), on one side, and a carbimide on the other, (—N=C). This, as all chemists can immediately foresee, makes the methine hydrogens very reactive and replaceable. To make matters still more complicated, the original papers amplified the chemistry of the process and discussed the effect which substitutions would have upon the shade of the resultant dye image

The patent office does not as a rule grant protection where the only change made is the substitution of an ethyl group for a methyl, since this only modifies the physical properties of the compound, without affecting the chemical But this substitution of an ethyl for a methyl group (using these terms now in a generic sense rather than in a literal) can be made slightly complicated. For instance, Mannes and Godowsky disclosed that hydroxy-diphenyls could be used as coupling agents (U S.P. 2039730; Eng. P. 458665). In the original Fischer patent phenol, cresol, xylenol, and naphthol are mentioned These have the constitutions

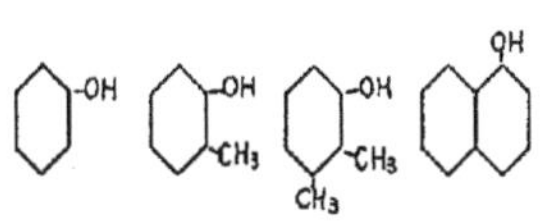

Phenol Cresol Xylenol Naphthol

Any hydroxy aromatic compound that has the para or ortho positions free, can be used. If one or more of the hydrogens are replaced by other groups, coupling is still possible, provided the coupling positions are left vacant. Ortho-hydroxy-diphenyl has the composition

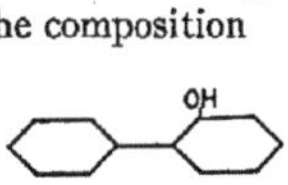

It is, therefore, merely a phenol in which the hydrogen in the ortho position has been replaced by a phenyl group. This merely modified the physical properties of the substance, in so far as the reaction under discussion is concerned, hence represents a replacement of a methyl by an ethyl group, figuratively speaking. All the other substitutions mentioned in this disclosure fall into the same category. These are:

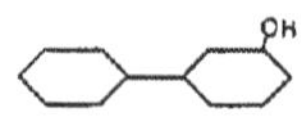

Meta-hydroxy-diphenyl

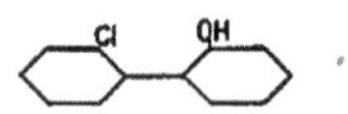

Ortho-hydroxy-ortho′-chlor-diphenyl

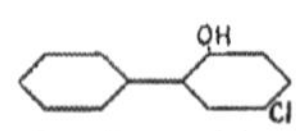

Ortho-phenyl-para-chlor-phenol

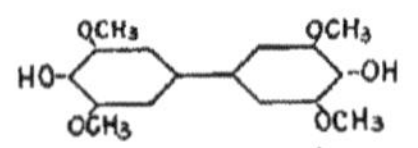

Hydrocoerulignone

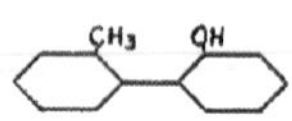

Ortho-tolyl-phenol

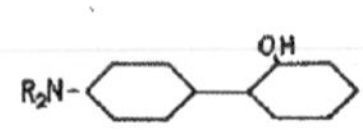

Para (ortho′hydroxy-phenyl)-di-alkyl-aniline

This is not the only disclosure in which the patent bars were let down a bit. Practically every patent issued in the field of couplers suffers from this defect, although the substitutions no longer are as simple as the ones indicated above. It must be recognized that in all cases the patentee starts with a molecule that contains coupling characteristics, then proceeds to put into that molecule substitutions of such a character that the chemical properties are retained in toto. No mention is made, with the exception of the series of patents issued to the I.G. and discussed in detail above, that any new and desirable properties are endowed upon the molecule.

The phenol molecule is the starting point in several other patents. The hydrogens can be replaced by halogen (Eng. P. 478984), even in the coupling positions. In that event, a halogen acid is formed during coupling. Ortho or meta amino phenols can be used, in which case the activity of the amino group is masked by acetylation, or substitution with thio-urea radicals, phenyl groups, etc. (Eng. P. 478985). Some of the compounds falling into this category are:

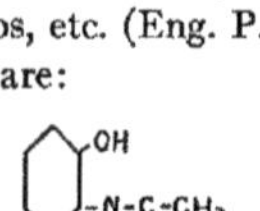

Acetyl-ortho-amino-phenol

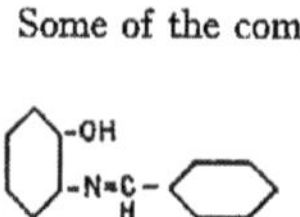

Ortho-nitro-benzal-ortho-hydroxy-aniline

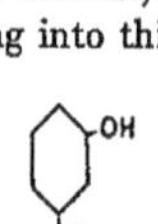

Meta-di-ethyl-amino-phenol

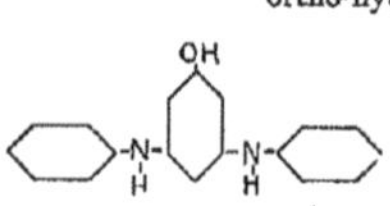

3:5 di-anilino-phenol

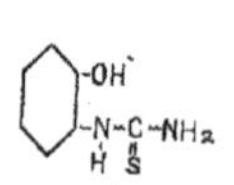

Ortho-hydroxyphenyl-thiourea

These all give blue to cyan dye images.

In English patent 478991, ortho and para substitutions are mentioned, all of which are either types such as —OCH_3, —OCH_2R, and —OCH_2—C(=O)—R.

It is to be noted that the methine group in these cases is not active, since no polar groups satisfy the other valences. Salicylaldehyde can be used to form substituted phenols (Eng. P. 496195). This is ortho-hydroxy benzaldehyde

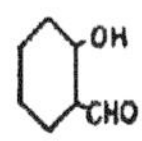

and by treatment with acid amides forms salicylidene-acid-amides. Thus with acetamide ($CH_3CO \cdot NH_2$) there is formed

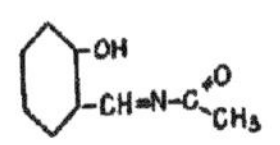

Salicylidene-acetamide

and with benzamide 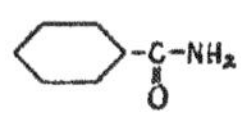 there is formed

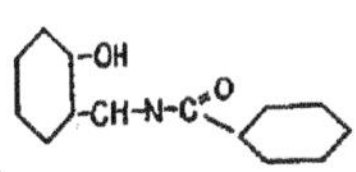

Salicylidene-benzamide

These also give blue to cyan colors. Somewhat more complicated is the British patent disclosure bearing the serial number 496245. Two ortho cresol molecules are connected to each other by means of a cyclohexanone group,

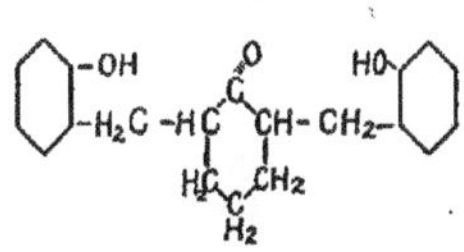

2:6 di(ortho-hydroxy-phenyl)-cyclohexanone

A styryl group can form the substitution. This is disclosed by Mannes, Godowsky, and Peterson in United States patent 2126337; English patent 478989. These have the general formula:

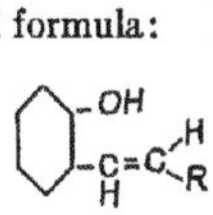

where *R* is a heterocyclic ring or forms a ring with the carbon to which it is attached, thus:

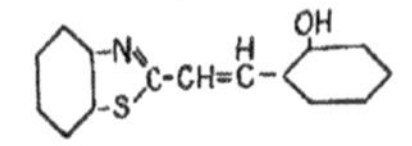

1-(ortho-hydroxy-cinnamenyl)-benzthiazol

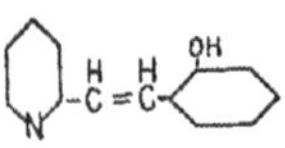

2-(ortho-hydroxy-cinnamenyl)-pyridine

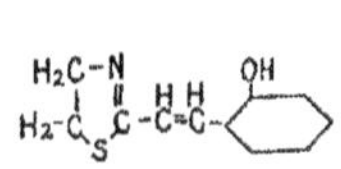

2-(ortho-hydroxy-cinnamenyl)-thiazoline

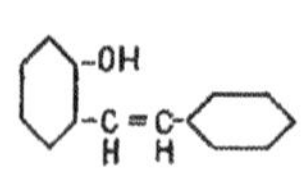

Ortho-styryl phenol

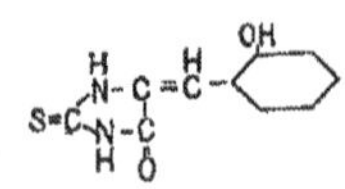

5-(ortho-hydroxybenzal)-2-thio-hydantoin

All of these patents are assigned or issued to the Eastman Kodak Company. They yield blue to cyan dye images, as would be expected when a phenol couples with oxidized paraphenylenediamine.

The I.G. was granted protection for the formation of naphthamide derivatives (U.S.P. 2156821). They started with the acid chloride of alpha-hydroxy-beta-naphthoic acid

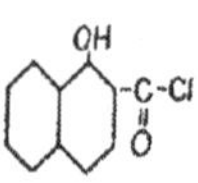

This was condensed with amines like benzidine, diamino-stilbene, diamino-azoxybenzene, amino-benzthiazol, and diamino-diaryl ureas. The reactions are to form hydroxynaphthamides, as typified by the reaction with benzidine

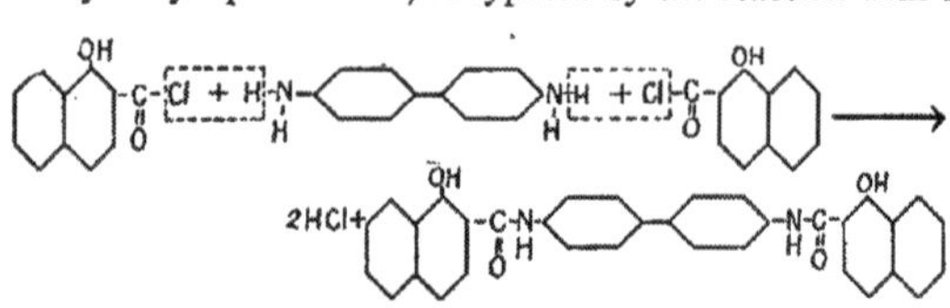

The molecule is extremely heavy, hence will not diffuse greatly. Solubility in alkaline solutions is conferred by the presence of hydroxyl groups. These also make the molecule a coupler.

DuPont was issued a very restricted patent which covered the mono-ethers of resorcin (Eng. P. 512542). The ether group is restricted to hydrocarbons, containing at least eight carbon atoms. The mono-ethers of ortho and para dioxy compounds had previously been disclosed by Eastman (cf. above), so that only the meta derivative, resorcin, remained unprotected. The use of heavy long-chained hydrocarbons was previously patented by the I.G., although its disclosures appeared to cover everything but ether formation.

That an active methine group, $—CH_2—$, confers coupling properties, was well-known to Fischer and Siegrist, who covered this property in their original and basic patent. Chemists are well aware that such a group is obtained by satisfying the other two valences on the carbon with polar groups, of which a carbonyl radical, $>C{=}O$, is a good example. Thus the compound aceto-acetic ester, a beta ketonic ester,

$$CH_3{-}\underset{\underset{O}{\|}}{C}{-}CH_2{-}\underset{\underset{O}{\|}}{C}{-}OC_2H_5$$

contains a $>CH_2$ group between two $>C{=}O$ groups The hydrogens on this central carbon atom are highly reactive, in fact sufficiently reactive to be replaced by metals. This means that they dissociate to form hydrogen ions. With some metals, silver, etc., the molecule acts as if this substance is in tautomeric equilibrium with the hydroxy substance

$$CH_3{-}\underset{\underset{OH}{|}}{C}{=}CH{-}\underset{\underset{O}{\|}}{C}{-}OC_2H_5$$

This is indicated by the conversion of the silver salt into

$$CH_3{-}\underset{\underset{OCH_3}{|}}{C}{=}CH{-}\underset{\underset{O}{\|}}{C}{-}OC_2H_5$$

With other metals, sodium, potassium, etc, the molecule behaves in the normal manner, and treatment with RI yields

$$CH_3{-}\underset{\underset{O}{\|}}{C}{-}\underset{\underset{R}{|}}{CH}{-}\underset{\underset{O}{\|}}{C}{-}OC_2H_5$$

This reactivity makes it very interesting from a coupling point of view. The interest has been translated in the issuance of a great many patents each covering the same basic idea, but worded in a slightly different manner so that the layman would fail to see the recurrent underlying principle. This is exemplified by the presence of a central acet-carbonyl group

$${-}CH_2{-}\underset{\underset{O}{\|}}{C}{-}$$

where the methine structure already has attached to it one polar radical, and needs but one other, attached to the other valence of the atom, to give it coupling properties To complete the molecule, a group must be attached to the vacant valence of the carbonyl. Thus to complete the structure, it is essential to add two groups *X* and *Y*:

$$X{-}CH_2{-}\underset{\underset{O}{\|}}{C}{-}Y$$

The many patents differ from each other in the nature of the *X* and *Y* groups. In aceto-acetic ester, *X* is an acetyl group, $CH_3{-}\underset{\underset{O}{\|}}{C}$, and *Y* is an ethoxy group, OC_2H_5. This last is relatively non-polar and adds little or nothing to the reactivity of the compound The other $CH_3C{=}O$, is a strongly polar group, and it makes the hydrogens on the CH_2 very reactive. It is possible, of course for *Y* to be a group of the type $-CH_2Z$, where Z is strongly polar. Then *X* can be a non-polar group, for the central $-CH_2{-}\underset{\underset{O}{\|}}{C}$ will confer activity to the $-CH_2Z$ methine group.

Mannes and Godowsky suggested the group of compounds in which *Y* is a substituted or unsubstituted amine (U.S.P. 2108602; Eng. P. 458664). The *X* must be a strongly polar group, in order for the resultant molecule to be a coupler. This is achieved if *X* is a cyano, or an aceto group. In the first case there is formed the cyan-acetamides

$$CN{-}CH_2{-}\underset{\underset{O}{\|}}{C}{-}NHR$$

These are derivatives of cyan acetic acid, formed by the action of KCN upon chloracetic acid

$$CH_2Cl{-}COOH + KCN \rightarrow KCl + CN{-}CH_2{-}COOH$$

This is easily converted into the cyan-acetyl-chloride, $CN{-}CH_2CO\ Cl$, and upon treatment with ammonia or an amine, the desired cyanacetamide is formed In the second case, there is formed acetacetamide

$$CH_3{-}\underset{\underset{O}{\|}}{C}{-}CH_2{-}\underset{\underset{O}{\|}}{C}{-}NHR.$$

This, among other things is a beta ketonic acid-amide, and upon treatment with hydrazines should yield interesting pyrazolone derivatives

In a later disclosure (U S.P 2113330; Eng. P. 493952) Mannes and Godowsky change the *Y* from an amine to an alkyl or acyl group, so that the basic structure becomes

$$X{-}CH_2{-}\underset{\underset{O}{\|}}{C}{-}R$$

a ketone. In order to establish coupling properties, the *X* must be one of the following:

Aceto	$CH_3{-}C{=}O$
Cyano	CN
Sulphonyl	SO_2
Carbonyl	$C{=}O$

In all cases the oxygens can be replaced by sulphur. Examples are:

$$CH_3-\underset{\underset{O}{\|}}{C}-CH_2-\underset{\underset{O}{\|}}{C}-CH_3,$$

Acetyl-acetone

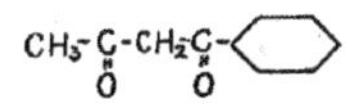

Benzoyl-acetone

Typical solutions with these ingredients present are:

1.	Para-di-ethylamino-aniline-hydrochloride	2 parts
	Sodium sulphite	5 parts
	Sodium carbonate	30 parts
	Water to	1000 parts

To this, just before use, add:

Benzoyl-acetone	2 parts
Acetone	100 parts

2.	Para-methylamino-aniline-sulphate	1 part
	Sodium sulphite	2 parts
	Sodium carbonate	30 parts
	Water to	1000 parts

To this should be added, just before use,

Acetyl-acetone	5 parts
Alcohol	100 parts

A third variation of the same basic structure was disclosed by Mannes and Godowsky in United States patent 2115394. The *X* is now restricted to a cyano group,

$$CN-CH_2-\underset{\underset{O}{\|}}{C}-R$$

and *R* can be any of a large variety of hydro-carbons or ethers, such as:

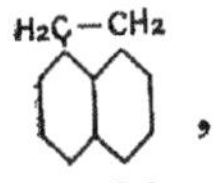

Acenaphthene

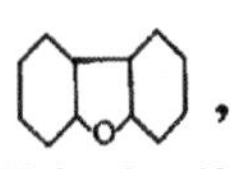

Diphenylenoxide

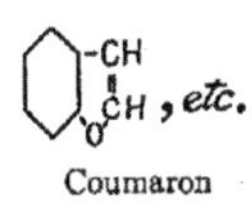

Coumaron

In several English patents issued to Kodak Ltd. (Eng. P. 474353 and 478942) other examples are given, thus:

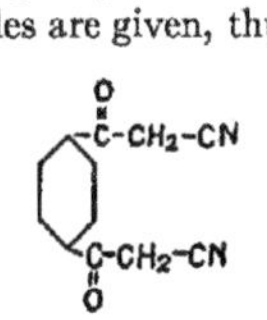

1:4-di(cyano acetyl)-benzene

CH_3COCH_2CN

Cyan acetone

With the exception of cyanacetone, which is a yellow, the colors obtained are all red to magenta.

The beta-ketones and the hydrazones formed from them by the action of hydrazine, is disclosed in English patents 478933 and 478934 These have the general structures

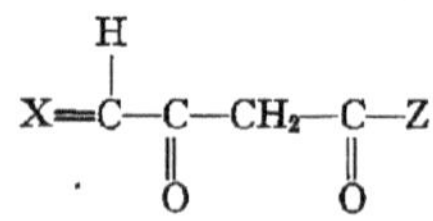

where *Z* can be an oxalkyl, *OR*, or alkyl group, and *X* can be hydrogen, halogen, alkyl, etc , and

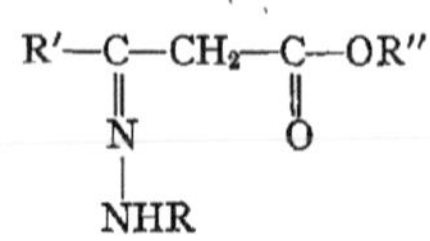

the *R*, *R'*, and *R''* can be any hydrocarbon group. The CH_2 can also be a member of a ring structure, as it is in:

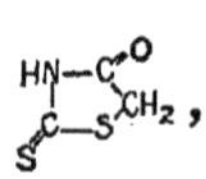

Rhodanine

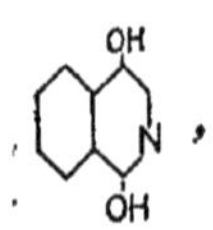

4-oxy-iso-carbostyril

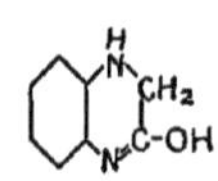

Dihydro-2-hydroxy-quinoxaline

The indoxyl structure, previously utilized by B Homolka for primary development, and by Fischer for coupling purposes, was generalized by Eastman Kodak Co to yield a large variety of coupling agents (Eng P. 478983). The general structure is

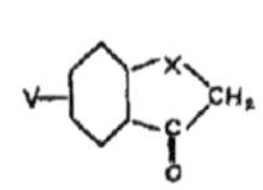

where *V* can be either a ring substitution or ring fusion. *X* can be oxygen, in which case the compound oxindole is formed. Or it can be NH or NR, which yield indoxyl and indoxyl derivatives. If it is sulphur, then thio indoxyl is the compound. The rhodanines

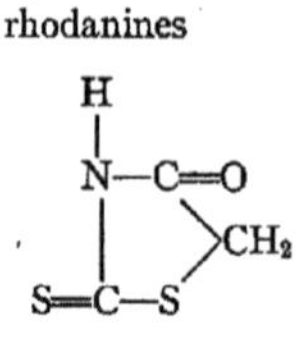

previously mentioned as an example in another patent, and the N-alkyl and acyl derivatives are suggested in English patent 509707.

This covers the work done by the members of the Eastman Kodak American and London staffs. But they were not the only ones who worked in this field or along these lines. DuPont, for instance, also started with the general formula (Eng. P. 497698)

$$\begin{array}{c} Y\text{—}CH_2\text{—}\underset{\underset{\displaystyle O}{\|}}{C}\text{—}R \end{array}$$

and made *R* an aryl or heterocyclic substituted amino group, and *Y* any electro-negative group, thus

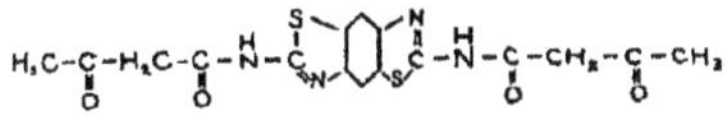

μ μ-di-aceto-acetamino-1:2·4:5 benzo-bis-thiazol

The corresponding selenazol can also be used. These are aceto-acetamide derivatives, despite the very complicated nature of the substitution. The same base, acylacetamine, is utilized in another disclosure issued to Dr. E. B Middleton and A. B. Jennings of the DuPont organization (U.S.P. 2133937; Eng P 497463), although the patent is restricted to aryl derivatives of morpholine.

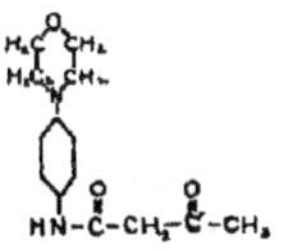

Aceto-acetamino-phenyl morpholine

In another disclosure (U.S.P. 2182815) the same men utilize the cyan-acetamino-bis-azoles These have no effect upon the characteristics of an emulsion, so that the couplers could be added to the emulsion rather than to the developer

The use of resin residues attached to a coupler molecule to give it substantive properties, was previously disclosed by the I.G. An idea along similar lines is disclosed by M Martinez (Eng. P. 505834), but he forms loosely held double salts of the resin with the coupler. J. H. Reindorp discloses (Eng P. 518017) a derivative of malonic acid as the coupling agent. Malonic ester, whose structure is

$$\begin{array}{c} O{=}C\text{—}OC_2H_5 \\ | \\ H\text{—}C\text{—}H \\ | \\ O{=}C\text{—}OC_2H_5 \end{array}$$

already contains the coupling characteristics, and is itself covered by many of the previously discussed disclosures. Evidently, in order to obtain further protection, a very limited field could be covered, and this is

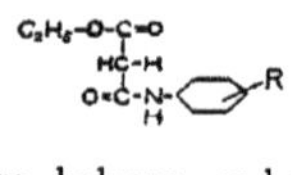

The *R* can be a methoxy, nitro, halogen, or benzene group, all of which are trivial substitutions as far as the nature and character of the couplers are concerned A glance at the basic structure shows the presence of a methine group whose two other valences are satisfied by a polar carbonyl on one side, and by a carbox-amide group on the other side. In so far as coupling is concerned, that is all that counts, the remaining portions of the molecule being in the nature of the particular suit of clothes that is used to dress up the material for public inspection. Of course it is not quite fair to single out this patent disclosure in order to make the comment, for practically every disclosure made up to now, and most of the disclosures still to be considered, fall in this category Thus in the disclosure of J D. Kendall and R. B. Collins (Eng P. 517197) the same basic structure

$$Y{=}N{-}\underset{\underset{O}{\|}}{C}{-}CH_2X$$

is met. The *Y* in this case is a heterocyclic nitrogen-containing residue, and *X* is a cyano or esterified carboxyl group, thus forming either cyan acetamide or malonic ester amide The Reindorp disclosure (cf above) issued but slightly later than this one, is a good example of the last type.

H D Murray, and the Veracol Film Syndicate suggested the use of coumaronones as coupling agents (Eng. P. 500047) These substances are prepared from halogenated hydroxy acetophenones.

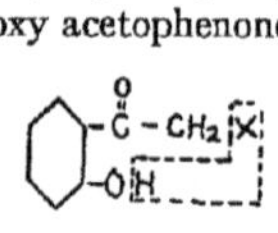

HX is split off to yield coumaronon

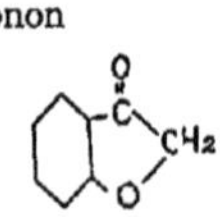

In another disclosure (Eng. P. 507611) Dr. Murray reverts to the beta-ketonic-acetamides

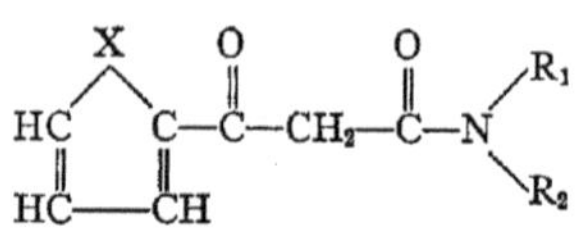

The atom *X* can be oxygen or sulphur. In the former case, the group attached to the carbonyl group is furane, and in the second case it is thiophene. The groups attached to the amino nitrogen, R_1 and R_2, may be hydrogen, alkyl, aryl, benzyl, cyclo-hexyl or benzthiazol radicals.

The I.G. and the General Aniline and Film Company, have also been granted a number of patents, some of which go beyond the stereotyped patterns indicated above. For instance, not all compounds containing the active methine group, will couple. Diphenyl-methane, cyclo-hexanone, indene, dihydroresorcine, fluorene, and benzo-fluorene, all containing the CH_2 radical, do not couple. But they can be converted into couplers if one of the hydrogens on the methine group is replaced by oxalic ester

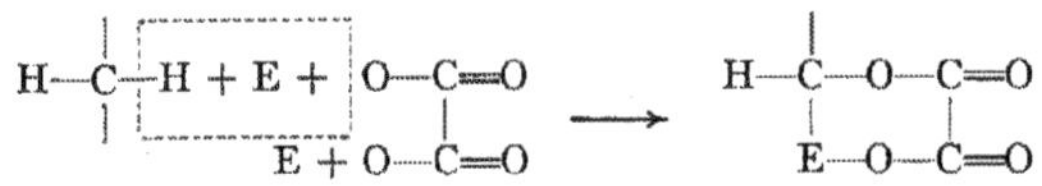

This is disclosed in United States patent 2186850 (Eng. P. 472224; Fr. P. 818388). The heterocyclic bases that contain an alpha methyl group can also be used as couplers (U.S.P. 2186685 and 2186736; Eng. P. 503318; Fr. P. 839998). Examples of this are

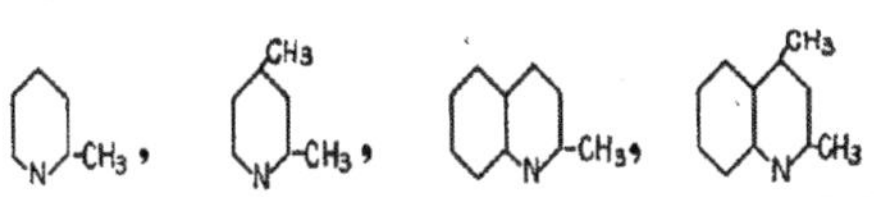

Picoline Lutidine Quinaldine 2:4-di-methyl-quinoline

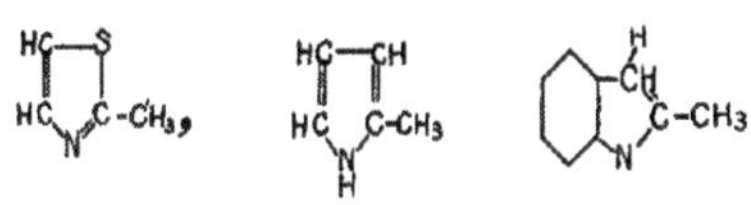

2-methyl-thiozal 2:methyl-pyrrol 2-methyl-indol

It should be noted that in all of these cases there is a methyl group attached to the carbon atom adjacent to the ring nitrogen. The hydrogens on this methyl group are well-known to be very reactive, hence their ability to serve as couplers need not create too much surprise. Much more conventional are the disclosures which suggest that alpha indolenone and its substituted products can be used (U.S.P. 2186045), or the oxindoles (Eng. P. 511790), the oxazolones (U.S.P. 2124612; Eng. P. 460599), and the pyridine derivative in which a pyridine group is attached to a methyl group already containing a ketonic substitution (Eng. P. 504376), thus:

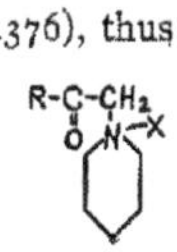

Here *X* can be any negative ion such as chloride, bromide, etc, and R an aryl, alkyl, or an arylalkyl residue In this substance, coupling properties are due to the active CH_2 group, for one valence is satisfied by a ketonic substitution and the other by pyridine, both very strongly polar.

It was mentioned above that di-phenyl-methane

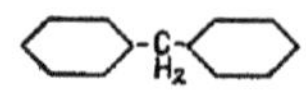

despite the presence of an active methine group in the molecule, does not couple, but that the replacement of one of the methine hydrogens by an oxalic ester residue overcame this defect. Evidently the two phenyl groups are not sufficiently polar to activate the hydrogens to a point where they will readily be absorbed by (OH) ions P. L. J. R Merckx and W. K A Körber of the Gevaert Company accomplish the same result by placing a polar group within one of the phenyl groups, thus increasing its polarity (U S P. 2197311).

The number and type of developing agents suitable for coupling received but little attention until now. But the rather complete coverage of the coupler field has begun to force the attention to other phases Fischer, in his basic patents, suggested that paraphenylenediamine, its substitution products (provided one amino group was left free), its homologues, and para-amino-phenol and its homologues could be used. It was soon found that of these, the best action was obtained from the unsymmetrically dialkyl substituted phenylene or toluylene diamines. These are the well-known developing agents para-di-ethyl and di-methyl-amino-aniline or toluidine. But their use left much to be desired. First and foremost they had a limited solubility in water, especially when alkaline. Secondly they cause severe skin irritations. Of course the last could be overcome by the constant use of gloves, but that is a nuisance which at times becomes more irritating than the skin irritation. Third, there is a decided decrease in developing potential, necessitating either excessively high pH's or long developing times. Dr. B Wendt discovered that by making the substitution upon the nitrogen, an hydroxy-alkyl group, the potential of the developing agent would be greatly increased (U.S.P. 2108243; Eng. P 460580) Examples of such developers would be

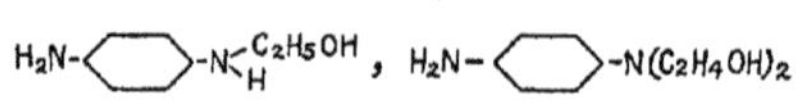

Para mono and di-hydroxy-ethyl amino-aniline

In a later patent, also issued to the I.G. (Eng. P. 481275), it is suggested that if the alkyl substitution on the amino group contain a carboxyl or sulphonic acid group, greater solubility and a decrease in the skin irritability would be obtained. If a heavy group is placed there, then the dye would be quite insoluble, and the loss of definition by diffusion made much less likely The groups suggested for substitution are:

$—CH_2—CH_2—O—CH_2—CH_2—O—CH_2—CH_2—OH$, or

The Eastman Kodak Company, through A. Weissberger, was also granted a patent along these lines (U.S.P. 2193015). This time the substitution is a sulphonamido-alkyl residue $—CH_2—SO_2 \cdot NH_2$.

Para-aminophenol, although usable as a coupling developer, possesses too low a potential to be of practical use. This can be considerably improved if the molecule is halogenated (Eng. P. 467087). If singly substituted, the halogens can be in an ortho or meta position,

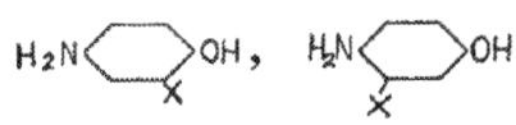

and if there are two halogen substitutions these may be in the 2:5, 2:6, and 2:3 positions

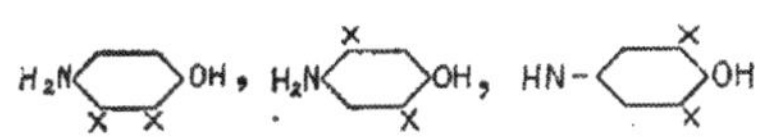

The *X*'s represent halogen atoms.

Very early in the history of color development, Homolka (cf. chapter on Primary Color Development) showed that the presence of a group of the type

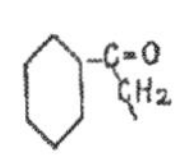

conferred developing properties upon a molecule. Dr. Homolka was a little hasty in his conclusions, the correct structural requirement being

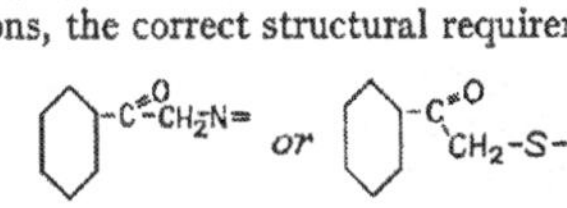

This grouping is present in indoxyl, thioindoxyl, and the iso-carbostyril compounds which he showed to have developing action. In indoxyl, the nitrogen is attached again to the benzene nucleus

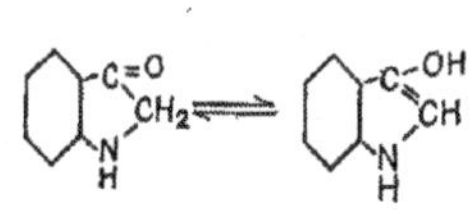

but it retains one valence which is satisfied by hydrogen. In isocarbostyril

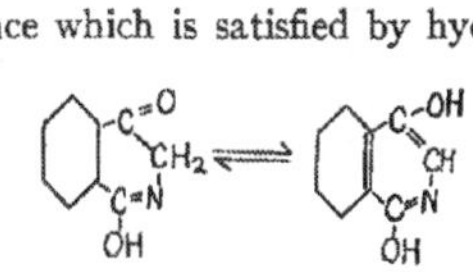

the nitrogen contains no hydrogen attached to itself, and the compound is still a developer. This is possible not only by virtue of the grouping

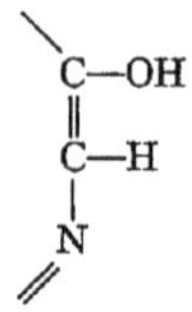

but also because of the grouping:

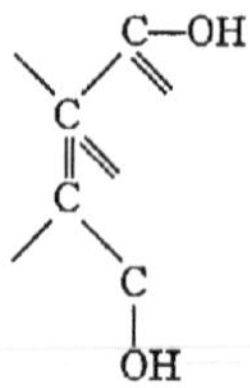

which, as was indicated by Kendall, would give a substance developing power. Therefore the question whether a nitrogen completely saturated as far as its primary valences are concerned, and still a member of a heterocyclic chain, can yield developing properties is not answered A compound of this type has been suggested as a coupler

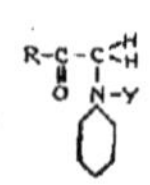

Here the nitrogen is quaternary (Eng. P. 504376). But this structure also appears to satisfy the Kendall condition for developer action, since it can also be written in the tautomeric form:

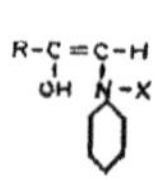

Here two carbons with a double bond between them contain an hydroxyl and a substituted amino group. Of course there is the offsetting fact that the nitrogen is in the quaternary form, which perhaps cannot endow developing properties (cf. preceding chapter).

But this discrepancy does not exist in the group of substances covered by W. D. Peterson, of the Eastman Kodak Company (U.S.P. 2196739). These are the heterocyclic compounds which contain a tertiary nitrogen within the ring, and an unsubstituted amine group on the benzene nucleus fused to the heterocyclic ring, thus:

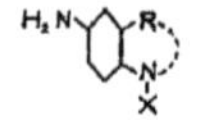

X represents an alkyl, hydroxy-alkyl, or allyl group. The $\left.\begin{matrix}R\\N\end{matrix}\right]$ can be any of a number of groups, which are all completely hydrogenated, thus:

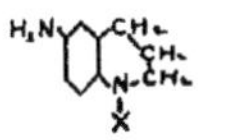

6-Amino-N-alkyl-tetrahydroquinoline

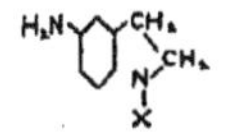

5-Amino-N-alkyl indolene

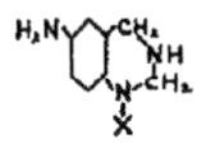

6-Amino-N-alkyl-phenmorpholine

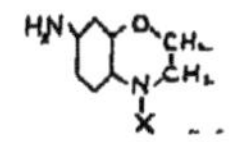

6-Amino-N-alkyl-tetra-hydro-quinazoline

These substances are all rather complicated derivatives of paraphenylene-diamine, hence no surprise need be felt that they can replace that substance in coupling-developer solutions.

Along these lines, are the compounds described by the I.G (Eng. P. 478345). Here also substituted paraphenylenediamines are used, and the substitution is in the form of a heterocyclic ring fused to the benzene ring. Here also the fused ring is completely hydrogenated, and the nitrogen in the ring is either ortho or para to the amino nitrogen in the benzene portion of the molecule. Examples given are:

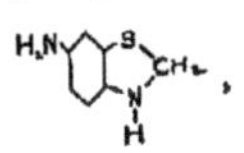

6-Amino-benz-thiazoline

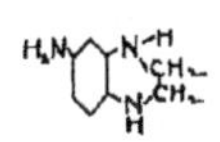

6-Amino-tetra-hydro-quinoxaline

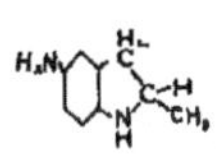

5-Amino-dihydro-2-methyl-indole

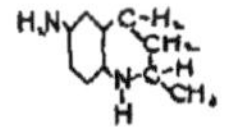

6-Amino-1.2'3:4 tetra-hydro-quinaldine

These are practically identical with the Eastman compounds, except that they are mono-substituted phenylene-diamines, while the others are di-substituted amino derivatives. In so far as the chemistry of the developing action is concerned, this added substitution plays no role.

Substitutions have also been made in the alkalis suitable for use in coupling developers. Since it is the pH of the solution which determines largely the potential of the developer, and not the agent which creates that pH, perhaps the substitution of methyl and di-methyl-amine for ammonia does not represent true invention. Then neither should the substitution of hydroxy-alkyl groups be considered true invention. In color development, Mannes and Godowsky of the Eastman Kodak Company (U S P. 2191037) suggested primary aliphatic amines of which ethylene diamine $H_2N—CH_2—CH_2—NH_2$, is an example. Being non-volatile it is very much to be preferred to ammonia, which it closely resembles This would be expected from a consideration of the structure. Not to be outdone by Eastman, or perhaps the situation is exactly the other way around since their patent came first (U S P. 2181941, Eng. P. 488370, Fr. P. 830642), the I G through Goldacker, Maiser, and Schmitz-Hillebrecht, of their staff, suggested mannamine, lactamine, and glucamine. The alkalinity is in all cases due to the presence of an amino-group.

In June 1937, the article by K. and L. Schinzel in *Das Lichtbild*, was abstracted by J. S. Friedman (*Am. Phot.*, Vol 31 (1937), p. 446). In the discussion which followed the abstract, the chemistry of color development was reviewed and several other possible reactions suggested Thus it was pointed out that the leuco derivatives of dyes like methylene blue, fuchsine, etc., although without any action upon the latent image, can be oxidized with great ease by even mild oxidizing agents Quinone, in the presence of halide is a rather strong oxidizing agent. It was suggested that the latent image be developed with a sulphite-free hydroquinone developer which contained the leuco bases of suitable dyes The development of the latent image would produce bromide and quinone which would act upon the leuco salt to produce the dye. Many of the leuco bases are quite stable, and Allison and Dieterich have proposed their addition to emulsions (cf. chapter on Monopacks) Another possibility lay in the addition of hydrazo compounds to a sulphite-free hydroquinone developer, and by virtue of a reaction such as discussed above, formation of an azo dye would take place in situ with the silver image

A third possibility was also suggested at that time In 1898 E Votocek (*Phot Korr.*, Vol 35 (1898), p. 458; *Brit. J. Phot*, Vol 45 (1898), p. 633) disclosed that many hydrazines possessed developing power. Tolyl hydrazine 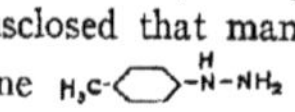, diphenyl hydrazine 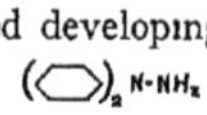, naphthyl hydrazine

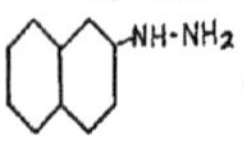

, and hydrazo-benzene 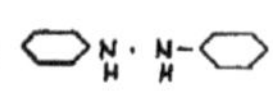, all have some action upon a latent image. In the case of the hydrazo compound, the product of the reaction would be an azo dye In the case of the aromatic hydrazines, the product of the reaction should be the corresponding diazonium salt. This last possibility is extremely interesting. The diazonium salts $R—N_2Cl$, or in this case, $R \cdot N_2 \cdot OH$, can unite with aromatic amines and hydroxy derivatives, to yield azo dyes. It becomes necessary, therefore, to oxidize the hydrazine in the presence of an alkaline solution of an amine or phenol to achieve dye images The developing action of the hydrazines is not very pronounced, hence Friedman advised the use of a sulphite-free hydroquinone developer, and in that way, cause oxidation to take place by the action of quinone.

Some months after this article appeared in the United States, Dr. A. Marriage of the Kodak Ltd. company made application for a patent which wa issued in 1939 in Great Britain, and 1940 in the United States (U.S.P. 2196734; Eng. P. 502960; Fr. P. 841225). Here is disclosed substantially the same idea with but one exception. Evidently hydroquinone cannot be used, but the naphthalene equivalents can. The developer is compounded with 1:4 or 1:2-dioxy-naphthalene and phenyl, tolyl, or quinolyl-hydrazine. The hydrazines have a tendency to reduce even unexposed silver halides, so it is recommended that the image be first developed and fixed, then converted into silver ferrocyanide, and finally treated with the hydrazine coupling developer. Dr. Marriage recommended the following solution:

Hydrazine	8 parts
Sodium sulphite	½ part
Naphth-hydroquinone	4 parts
Sodium carbonate	5 parts
Water to	1000 parts

In one of their articles, the Schinzels disclose that the deep blue alkaline solution of 4-phenyl-azo-1:2-dioxynaphthalene

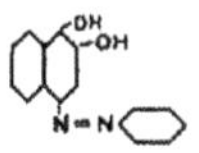

can develop a latent image, and yields a yellow dye-image with the silver. It is quite clear that the structure of the yellow dye is

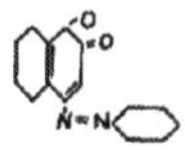

The phenomenon is extremely interesting since it indicates that the presence of an azo group within the molecule does not destroy the developing properties of that molecule. In this case the presence of two hydroxy groups ortho to each other, makes the molecule a developer of the pyrocatechin class. Since the color of the dye can be changed merely by changing the nature of the group attached to the azo nitrogen, this principle offers the technician a wide variety of possibilities with regard to primary and coupling development. Since the dye itself is a developer, it can reasonably be supposed that its hydrazo derivative would act in a similar manner, and upon oxidation would yield the azo dye, rather than the oxidation product of the azo dye. Or failing the use of the hydrazo compound, the original developer can be compounded to contain both the azo dye and some other hydrazine, to yield a hydrazone of the yellow dye, thus:

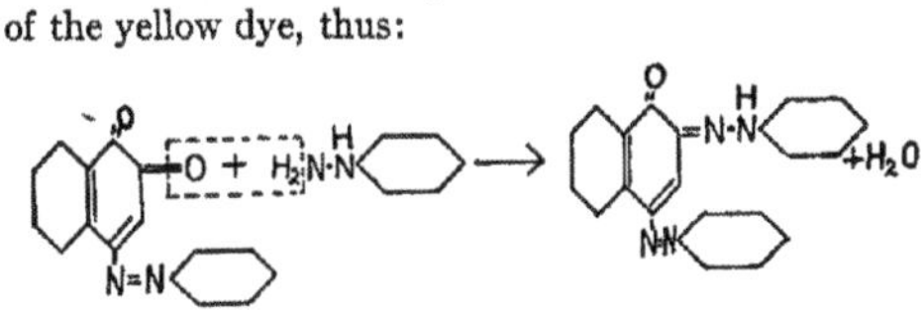

But this last can be written in the form

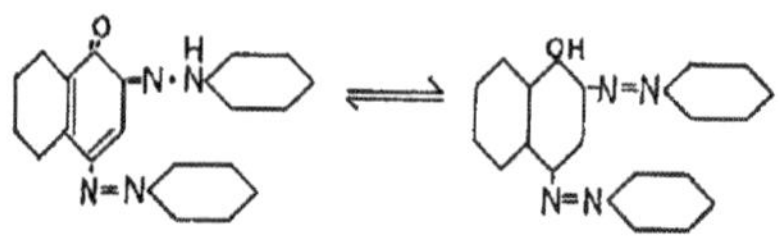

This is no longer an oxidized dye, so should be highly colored. Since the yellow dye is insoluble, it might be possible to convert it into the hydrazone by treatment with hydrazines after development rather than during development.

The possibility that the presence of an azo group does not affect developing action, merits further study. The Schinzels mention but one agent, 4-phenyl-azo-1:2-dioxy-naphthalene. If this is a general phenomenon, then it might be possible to use 2-phenylazo-1:4-diamino-benzene

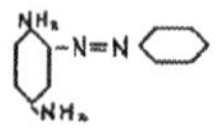

which should not only develop a latent image, but should also couple with amines and phenols. It should be possible to diazotize paradi-ethyl-amino-aniline, and couple it with some more para diethyl-amino-aniline, to form the dye

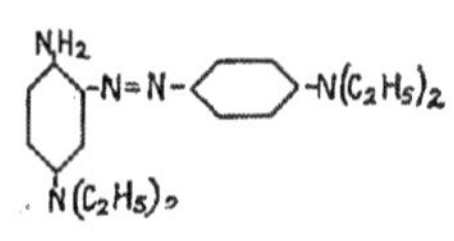

Either this, or the hydrazo derivative made from it, should have an action upon the latent image. In the presence of coupling agents, the above should couple to form azo-indo-anilines, azo-indophenols, azo-indamine, and azo-methine-azo dyes, the duplication of a color-forming group within the molecules giving deepening of the resulting color. If such compounds do not develop, then their hydrazo compounds might be used, yielding the original dye upon oxidation by means of the latent image.

The chemistry of the indamines and the related compounds offers other possibilities. These substances are usually prepared by the action of para-nitroso amines and phenols upon amines and phenols, thus:

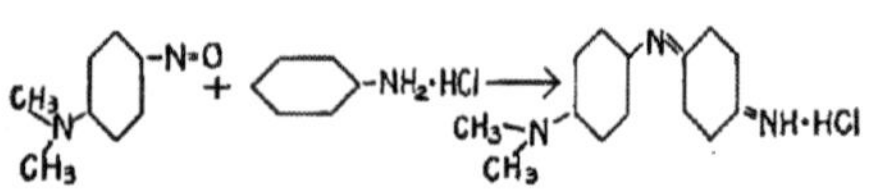

Para-nitroso-di-methyl-aniline — Aniline — Indamine

Fischer has demonstrated that these reactions can be duplicated by an amino group placed where the nitroso group is positioned, plus an oxidizing agent, more specifically, a latent image. The inference is, therefore, that the developing action is the preliminary formation of a para nitroso group,

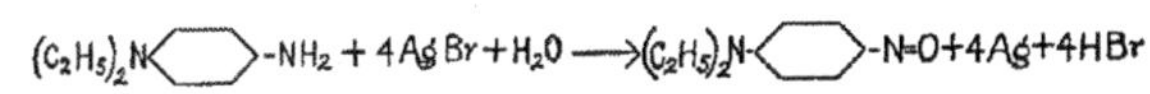

and this immediately couples with the coupler to form a dye. But dye chemists are well aware of the fact that the indamines can be oxidized in the presence of amines to form azine and safranine dyes, thus:

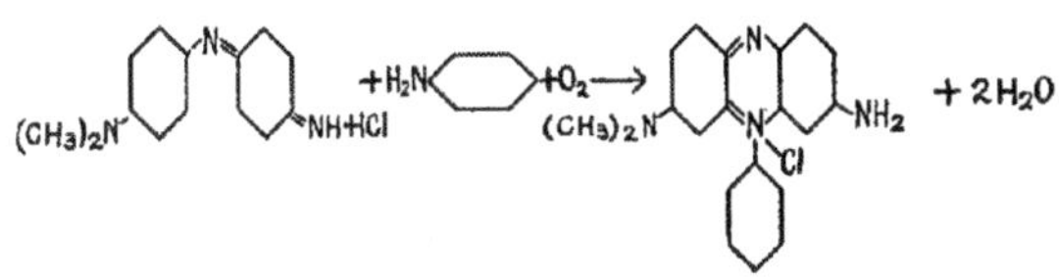

Methylene violet

True, these reactions require heat and the presence of solvents that are completely free of water, but the conversion of the nitroso-compound into the indamine also requires very rigid conditions, which are overcome when the corresponding amine is used. In fact, it is extremely difficult to prevent the formation of the indamine dye when coupler and developer are mixed in alkaline medium, and kept reasonably free from sulphite. It becomes an open question, then, whether the latent image, or its conversion product such as silver ferricyanide, manganic oxide, lead chromate, etc., cannot serve as the oxidizing agent in the conversion of the indamine to a safranine. Thus a latent image is first developed with a coupler developer to yield an indamine or indophenol. The dye plus silver image can then be treated with aniline hydrochloride and an oxidizing agent, such as potassium ferricyanide, etc. This should convert the indamine to a safranine dye image.

Another possibility lies in the use of meta-di-amino or di-hydroxy benzenes to form azine and oxazine dyes. In the industry these are formed by the action of para-nitroso-di-methyl aniline upon meta-toluylene-diamine, or resorcin

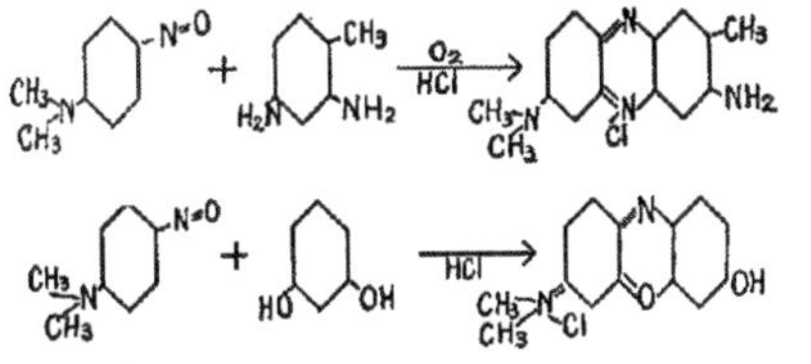

It may be that the latent image is not a sufficiently strong oxidizing agent to cause this reaction to take place, in which case it may be possible to first

develop the image in an ordinary manner, convert it into silver ferricyanide or some other oxidizing agent, then redevelop with para-di-methyl-amino-aniline in the presence of meta-toluylene-diamine or resorcin. The aromatic diamines or dioxy compounds must be so chosen that the resultant dye is insoluble.

When an aromatic amine reacts with formaldehyde, a peculiar reaction takes place.

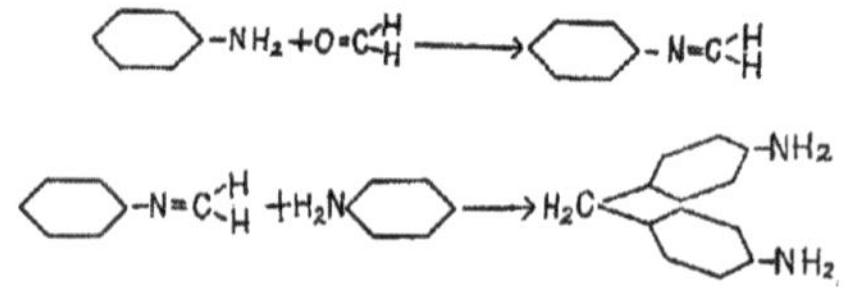

The substance di-amino-diphenyl-methane should be a very able coupling agent, that could possibly be used in conjunction with hydroquinone, naphth-hydroquinone etc., to yield tri-phenyl methane dyes, thus:

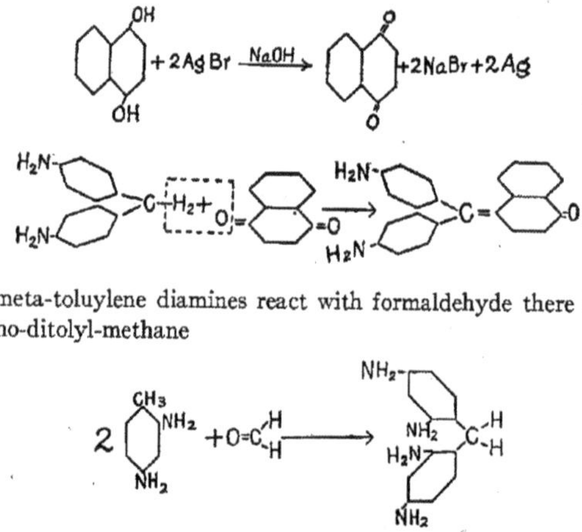

When meta-toluylene diamines react with formaldehyde there is obtained tetra-amino-ditolyl-methane

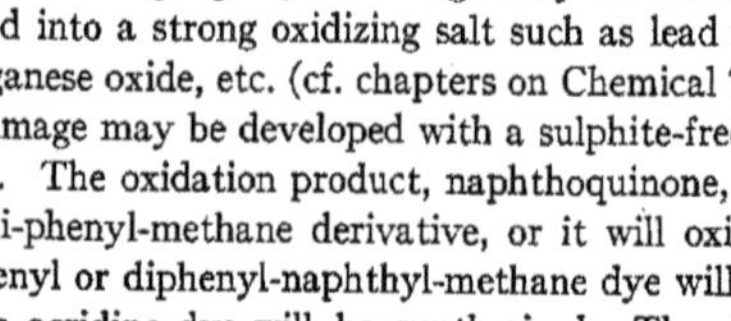

This upon oxidation, yields an acridine dye. If the latent image is not a sufficiently strong oxidizing agent, the image may be developed normally, and then converted into a strong oxidizing salt such as lead chromate, silver ferricyanide, manganese oxide, etc. (cf. chapters on Chemical Toning and Dye Toning). Or the image may be developed with a sulphite-free naphth-hydro-quinone developer. The oxidation product, naphthoquinone, will then either couple with the di-phenyl-methane derivative, or it will oxidize it. In the first case, a tri-phenyl or diphenyl-naphthyl-methane dye will be formed. In the second case an acridine dye will be synthesized. The dye flavinduline is made by the action of ortho-phenylamino-aniline upon phenanthrene-quinone,

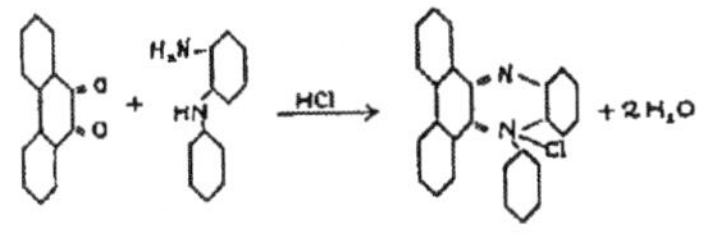

Phenanthrene quinone Ortho-phenyl-amino-aniline Flavinduline

This reaction offers several possibilities. We can recognize in phenanthrene-quinone the oxidized form of the corresponding di-oxy derivative. We know that naphth-hydroquinone is a more potent developer than hydroquinone, and that 1:2 dioxy-naphthalene is a better developer than pyrocatechin, the corresponding benzene derivative. We can assume then, that the phenanthracene dioxy compound could also behave in the same manner, and that by oxidation by means of the latent image it would form phenanthrene quinone

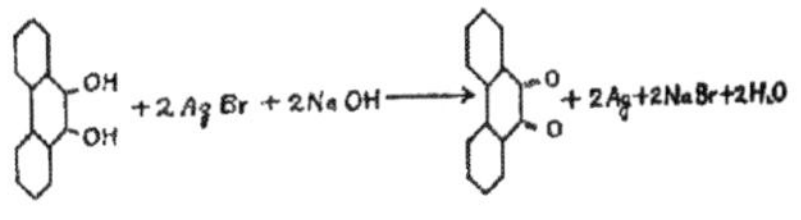

This oxidation product could then condense with ortho-phenyl-amino-aniline to form flavinduline.

The compound ortho-phenylene-diamine

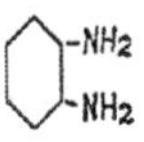

should be a good developer. The substitution of a phenyl group for one of the amino-hydrogens should not destroy the developer action. Upon oxidation by the latent image in the presence of the dioxy-phenanthrene, the dye should form.

These "paper reactions" are not being mentioned as schemes that have already received laboratory verification, but as a series of exploratory procedures, to determine the limits of color-forming developers.

CHAPTER 24

GASPARCOLOR AND THE SILVER-DYE-BLEACH PROCESS

FINELY divided silver can act as a catalyst. It has been proposed to utilize this property in the destruction or the formation of dyes, in situ with the image. These efforts culminated in the successful Gasparcolor process, although as utilized by Dr Gaspar it is doubtful if a truly catalyzed reaction is involved. There is little doubt, however, but that the historical development proceeded in that manner. Probably the first use of the catalytic property of silver was in 1889, when E. Howard Farmer disclosed the action of a silver image upon strong dichromate solutions (Eng. P. 17773/89). When a plate or film, containing a silver image, is immersed in a 20 per cent solution of ammonium, sodium, or potassium dichromate, the gelatin immediately surrounding the silver grains becomes tanned, the silver itself remaining apparently unaffected. As Farmer described the action, the dichromate and gelatin react under the influence of the catalyst silver, so that chromium salts are formed. These combine with the gelatin to form a tanned form of that colloid The action is extremely rapid. We will discuss this reaction in greater detail in a later chapter, when the subject of Wash-Off Relief is taken up.

In 1897 R E Liesegang disclosed another somewhat similar action, this time with ammonium persulphate (*Phot. Archiv.*, Vol. 32 (1897), p. 161), but now instead of forming a tanned image, there is formed an image of soft gelatin The action of persulphate was to soften the gelatin in situ with the silver. An improvement in this procedure was introduced the following year by M Andresen (Ger. P. 103516). He found that hydrogen peroxide, especially in the presence of the halogen acids, greatly accelerated this action. The further development of both this and the Farmer disclosure, appears to have been restricted to the preparation of matrices, and we will leave until we come to that subject the more detailed discussion of these reactions. Now we are merely interested in the fact that even before the turn of the twentieth century, the catalytic action of the metallic image was already noted.

A further extension, one that is closer to the form of the reaction in which our present interest lies, was made about 1903 by Ostwald and Gros (*Jahrbuch*, Vol. 17 (1903), p. 519), in a paper describing their "Catatype Process" They pointed out that the oxidation of pyro by potassium bromate was tremendously accelerated by platinum. If a sheet of paper, sensitized with a mixture of pyro and potassium bromate be squeegeed to a platinum print, and the two left in contact from 45 to 60 minutes, a brown image will be formed in the paper, corresponding to the platinum image in the print. This reaction can be further catalyzed by copper sulphate. In the same paper they note also that if a silver or platinum image be flooded with peroxide, nascent oxygen will be liberated in situ with the metallic image, thus indicating a destruction of the peroxide at these points By this means it becomes possible to form a negative image composed of peroxide which can be made to undergo other reactions. It is interesting to note that this scheme, although not proposed for the formation of color images, could be utilized for that purpose If peroxide is destroyed in situ with the silver image, then oxygen must be released at these points, and this oxygen could be utilized to form a color image by its action upon leuco dye bases, leuco ester salts of the vat dyes, or upon mixtures of paraphenylenediamine developers and coupling agents (cf. chapters dealing with Toning and Color Development processes). The same is true with the action of bromic acid or bromates.

Shortly after this article appeared, Dr Karl Schinzel proposed a complete process for the making of color prints, utilizing the catalytic destruction of dyes by the oxygen released from peroxide in contact with a silver image (*Brit. J. Phot.*, Vol. 52 (1905), p. 608, Aust P. 42478; *Phot. Woch.*, 1905) The disclosure is important from another point of view. It is one of the first patents which contains a complete description of a monopack. A plate was coated with three emulsion layers, one on top of the other, and separated from each other by plain gelatin layers. The entire group formed a single inseparable unit. Each emulsion layer was sensitized to but a single primary color, and was dyed in mass to a color complementary to its sensitivity. Thus the top layer, sensitive to the blue rays, would be dyed yellow. The central layer, sensitive to the red, would be dyed cyan. The bottom layer, sensitized to the green, would be dyed magenta. Therefore each layer completely removed the light to which it was specially sensitized, making for complete and accurate color analysis · The dyes that were used were stable to the action of water, alkaline developers, and fixing baths, so that after exposure, development, fixation, and washing they would remain intact in the gelatin layers, together with a silver image depicting the densities due to the individual primaries. The final step was to immerse the plate in a peroxide solution. Where this substance came in contact with the silver, oxygen was released This bleached the dye immediately about the silver. Since the amount of oxygen released depended upon the amount of the silver, the destruction of the dye followed the image density Where there was a heavy deposit of silver, there most of the dye became bleached Highlights in the original were recorded, therefore, as highlights in the dye image. The process gave a direct positive.

As long as one did not examine the procedure too closely, it was an excellent solution to the problem of making color prints, especially from other color transparencies such as Autochromes, etc. But the practice left much to be desired At the time the idea was proposed, the available dyes did not have the stability to peroxide that the procedure called for, so that it was extremely difficult to prevent the bleaching of the dyes at non-image portions of the layers, a fact pointed out by R. Neuhauss almost as soon as the idea was proposed (*Phot Rund*, Vol. 19 (1905), p. 239). This was admitted by Schinzel in a second paper in which he discussed several other highly theoretical procedures (*Chem. Ztg*, Vol 32 (1908), p. 665). Ideas along these lines were also advanced by F. Sforza (*Phot. Coul.*, Vol. 4 (1909), pp 23, 101) and R. Luther (*Phot. Rund*, Vol. 25 (1911), p. 1). But the procedures for the isolation of the dye image differed from that of Schinzel. Sforza, for instance, converted the silver into a dye mordant, thus fixing the dye in the form of a silver-salt complex Upon treatment with hypo, this dissolved out, leaving a positive image behind Of course all of the ideas expressed were hypothetical, as no reduction to practice was indicated by any of the gentlemen. When the Schinzel disclosure was cited as a prior art against Dr Troland, he answered that Schinzel never reduced his art to practice, and since the Troland monopack patent (cf. chapter on Monopacks) was issued, it may be inferred that this argument was acceptable. But to Schinzel must go the credit for being the first person to suggest the catalytic destruction of a dye for the formation of a color print. This suggestion culminated in the successful Gasparcolor process.

In the Schinzel scheme, the dye was apparently destroyed by oxidation. The reverse reaction, dye destruction by reduction, was outlined by Christensen in 1918 (U.S P 1517049; Eng. P. 133034; Ger. P. 327591; *Jahrbuch*, Vol. 29 (1920), p. 164) He found that certain dyes would be destroyed by hydrosulphite, at room temperature, only in the presence of finely divided silver. After exposure, development and fixation, a film may be dyed with any of the following dyes

Oxamin echt rosa	Diamine fast red F
Aurophenine	Benzoazurine G
Dianil pure blue	Rosophenine SG
Congo pure blue	

After being uniformly dyed, the film was treated with a solution containing from one to three per cent of sodium hydrosulphite or stannous chloride. The dye was bleached only in situ with the silver image, and to an extent depending upon the density of the image It is possible to add the dye to the emulsion, or to bathe the film immediately after the exposure. In this event, development and dye-bleaching could take place simultaneously by treating with

Sodium hydrosulphite	20 parts
Potassium bromide	20 parts
Water to	1000 parts

The silver could be removed by treatment with Farmer's reducer. A scheme such as this could be utilized with advantage in those processes where three layers containing the color part-images are superimposed to form the complete color print. The Defender Chromatone stripping paper, or some similar material, could be used.

Almost contemporary with the Christensen disclosure was the one made by George Pascal Joseph Schweitzer (Fr. P. 476213). He suggested that the silver image be converted into lead chromate, after which the film was dyed in mass. When this was washed with acid, it was found that chromic acid was released, which destroyed the dye in its immediate vicinity. By this means a direct positive was obtained — highlights in the original were reproduced as highlights in the colored image. Suitable dyes were tartrazine, aniline green, orchil, safranine, methyl blue, and methyl violet In a later disclosure (Eng P. 249530) he extended the scope of the reaction. The dye could be included in the emulsion. Three layers could be coated one on top of the other, in the form of a Schinzel monopack. After exposure, development and fixation, there would be obtained a silver image in each of the dyed layers. A final treatment must be given in a bath such as

Sodium bromate	15 parts
Sulphuric acid (concentrated)	10–20 parts
Water to	200–300 parts

In this bath the dye becomes destroyed in situ with the silver image, which acts upon bromic acid to decompose it, probably releasing nascent oxygen.

In another modification, it becomes possible to effect just the opposite result. The monopack is exposed and developed, but not fixed. Upon treatment with

Iodic acid	1 part
Sulphuric acid (concentrated)	3–5 parts
Alcoholic iodine, 25%	10–15 drops
Water to	200 parts

the dye becomes destroyed only in those places where the silver bromide exists. It is left undisturbed in situ with the silver image A black-and-white positive becomes converted into a color positive. There is some advantage to such a procedure, since the amount of dye that remains at each point depends upon the original silver image The dye is destroyed at all other places.

In German patent 396485 R. Luther and K von Holleben made a slight variation from the above general procedure The dye that was to form the final image was incorporated in the emulsion. After exposure, development and fixation, the silver image was converted into vanadyl ferrocyanide. The vanadyl ion acted as an oxygen carrier in the next step, which consisted in treating the dyed layer with chromic or hydrobromic acid The dye was destroyed in situ with the ferrocyanide image. To make positives, the silver image should be a negative, so that printing was to be done from positives. This makes it convenient as a duplicating material, especially when Kodachrome transparencies are to be duplicated. The one disadvantage is that the image itself is what remains, after exposure and development. This means that absolute uniformity in coating is required But this is a problem that had to be solved to a high degree of perfection during the last two decades, since the same problem exists in all reversal processes. Years later Dr. Gaspar revived the use of vanadium ions as a catalyst in a different type of oxidation, this time in the oxidation of leuco ethers, esters, and ester salts of the vat dyes (cf chapters on Toning)

In 1921, Mr. Crabtree of the Eastman Kodak Laboratories disclosed another procedure by which dyes were destroyed by reduction, in situ with a silver image (Communication No. 97, Eastman Kodak Laboratories; *Photo Era*, 1921). Dyes that were easily reduced to the leuco form, such as methylene blue, methylene green, fuchsine, etc , were bleached in situ with a silver image, if the dyed image layer were treated with

Hypo	5 parts
Acid hardener	2½ parts
Water to	100 parts

The acid hardener is made by dissolving 56 parts of alum, and a like amount of sodium sulphite, in 1000 parts of 10 per cent acetic acid. The time of treatment is from three to five minutes, after which the layer should be thoroughly washed so that the leuco dye bases are completely removed. If this is not done in a thorough manner, the unremoved leuco salts will reform the dye when the plate or film is treated with Farmer's reducer to remove the silver. It was also suggested that the leuco derivatives could be mordanted to the gelatin by some means that is not effective upon the dye In that case it becomes possible to wash the film free of the unreacted dye, then treat it with ferricyanide to regenerate the color. By this means the final dye image is directly related to the silver image, and not to what is left behind after the silver image has been removed. This scheme is really worthy of further study. For one thing, an attempt should be made to expend the reaction to those colors which form stable leuco derivatives that are soluble in alkali and so can be washed out readily. As a rule, strong reducing agents, such as alkaline hydrosulphite, zinc-acid, zinc-alkali, etc., are required for the reduction. But possibly the catalytic action of the silver image would allow milder agents.

After Crabtree, the idea appears to have become dormant until Dr. Bela Gaspar tackled it in a thorough and painstaking manner. After developing the original reaction (the reduction of dyes in situ with a silver or silver salt image), to a usable state, Dr Gaspar made a thorough study of the many other secondary variables whose previous non-uniformity was the stumbling block upon which the commercial application tripped. Problem by problem, Dr. Gaspar overcame these difficulties, until he was ready to launch a full utilization of the procedure to make prints in color from color transparencies.

There are at least four different phases to the successful application of the silver-dye-bleach processes. First of all, the fundamental reaction, the destruction of the dye in direct proportion to the silver image, must be made completely foolproof and applicable over a fairly wide range of variations in solution composition Motion-picture work requires millions of feet to be processed continuously, hence means must be found to guarantee the life of the solutions, so that results at the head and tail ends of a run will be uniform. The action must be fairly rapid, hence as great a differential as possible must be maintained in the reactivity of the solution upon dyes in the presence and in the absence of silver

A second problem is to diffuse the color uniformly through the gelatin layer. If some color is heavier at one spot, then regardless of how proportional the reaction may be, the result will be non-uniform, since there will be a disproportionate amount of dye left in the more concentrated regions. The dye must be very finely dispersed in the gelatin, otherwise the resultant image will be coarse and grainy. It must be remembered that the projected motion-picture image represents an enlargement of more than four hundred diameters, especially in the larger theatres where a forty-foot screen is used. The dye must be thoroughly localized and have either no solubility, or no mobility in the solutions used in processing. This problem we have met before, in our discussion of the Agfa version of Kodachrome.

A third problem relates to the proper construction of the monopack layer The original scheme formulated by Schinzel was to dye each layer the exact complementary to the spectral sensitivity of the layer. Thus the top layer, being blue-sensitive, would be dyed a yellow. One result of such a procedure would be to limit each silver image to a thin upper portion of each layer, making the final dye print flat. For copy material, this type of spectral distribution is unnecessary. Dr Gaspar has developed a special type of spectral distribution that allows full penetration of the printing light through the entire depth of each layer, and yet does not interfere with other layers. The fourth major problem is the formation of a sound track, equal in quality to the normal black-and-white product. In the present discussion, the Gaspar patents have been classified in accordance with the above system. We will discuss these in detail, since a study of their contents reveals a pattern for the successful solution of intricate and delicate procedures

Dr. Gaspar's first efforts in color were devoted to mordant and toning processes. These evidently have taught him that the silver in the normal black-and-white image could be made to influence other reactions, such as oxidations or reductions He quickly realized that either of these could be made to act on dyes to decolorize them. From a realization of this fundamental principle to the utilization of it for the making of color prints, was a very obvious extension.

The chemistry of the reaction is outlined in United States patent 2020775 (Eng P 395718, 397158, 397188, Fr. P 727168). The presence of a non-leuco-forming dyestuff which is uniformly diffused through the gelatin layer, and a metal image are essential for picture formation The metal image is, of course, the usual silver image produced by exposure, development and fixation of a normal photographic emulsion. The non-leuco-forming properties limit the selection of the dyes somewhat, but not seriously. Strictly speaking, there is no such thing as a non-leuco-forming dye. What Dr. Gaspar means is that the formation of the leuco form is extremely difficult under normal conditions, so that destruction of the dye rather than leuco formation takes place. The azo dyes fall into this classification, for the formation of hydrazo compounds is extremely difficult. Even when formed they are very unstable. Unlike other leuco dyes, they would probably undergo what chemists term the benzidine or semidine rearrangement. The resultant substituted benzidines, or amino diaryl amines, would be colorless substances capable of being washed out of the emulsion Dyes of the di and tri phenyl methane series, the indigoes, and the other vat colors, all form leuco derivatives, which easily reoxidize to the original dye. Unless the leuco forms are completely removed, the danger is always present that clear and clean-cut images will be difficult to obtain.

The dyes that are suitable for such destruction are of the substantive and acid-azo class, although some basic vats and alizarines are also available. Mentioned specifically are

Heliotrope BB, No 321
Chlor-amine light red 7BL (Sandoz)
Diamine rose G, No 119
Diamine rose BBF (Casella)
Diamine pure blue FF, No. 424
Naphthamine light blue 4 B (Kalle & Co)

The number beside the dye refers to its listing in the fifth edition of Schultz's "Farbstoff-tabellen" The chemical constitution, and the name of the manufacturer, together with all the trade names under which the dye is sold, are given in the tables.

The destruction of the dye can be accomplished either by oxidation or reduction The actual agents that attack the dyes are formed and act while the finely divided metal forming the image is being acted on by the treating agent. These are divided into two classes, "destructive" and "non-destructive" Reagents which are destructive can attack the dye even in the absence of a silver image, hence are undesirable Potassium permanganate, bromic acid, and hydrogen peroxide are oxidizing substances in this group. It is interesting to note that Schinzel first proposed to use peroxide, and Schweitzer suggested bromic acid (cf. above). Reducing agents of this class are sodium hydrosulphite (Christensen, cf. above), and stannous chloride. Concentrated solutions of sulphuric acid, and of sodium and potassium hydroxides, acting as solvents for the dyes, can also be classified as destructive, in that they act upon the dye generally. The fact that an accelerated action takes place in the presence of the silver image, brings all of these chemicals into the scope covered by this patent.

Of the other type of agent, there exists quite a variety. These, as has been pointed out above, act first to form silver salts and products which can reduce the dye, thus destroying it in direct proportion to the intensity of the silver image. Or the silver salts can form complexes which act upon the dye. In either case the reaction follows closely the image density.

Sulphur-containing compounds that can form complex silver salts, are especially useful in this respect From this point of view, an article by Dr. G Schwarz, director of the Gevaért Photo-Producten N.V., is of some interest It is titled "Photographic Silver-Gelatin as a Reagent in Spot Analysis," in *Industrial and Engineering Chemistry* (Vol. 12 (1940), p. 369) It is a well-known fact that when a silver image is immersed in water, then dried, the image loses density in the regions that were wet Dr Schwarz found that this decrease in density could be completely negated if the water contained any one of a fairly large series of organic compounds, in concentrations varying in some cases to one part in 100,000. The reaction was recommended as a spot test for the detection of minute quantities of specific materials in solution. Its value lies in the fact that organic chemists have an easy routine to determine whether or not a given reaction mixture still contains undesired material.

To carry out the procedure, a sheet of photographic paper is given an overall exposure to light, then developed to gamma infinity in

Metol	2.0 parts
Hydroquinone	5.0 parts
Sodium sulphite	50.0 parts
Sodium carbonate	50.0 parts
Potassium bromide	1.0 part
Water to	1000 parts

It is fixed in a 20 per cent hypo bath containing 2 per cent of sodium bisulphite, washed, dried, and finally cut into strips. Each of the strips contains a uniform silver density. When a test is to be made, a drop of the solution is placed on the test strip, and is allowed to evaporate to dryness. This should not take long, since most of the water will be absorbed by the gelatin. When dry, the entire strip is placed in hot water, at a temperature between 80 and 90 C. A positive test will be had if the area covered by the drop is appreciably darker than its surroundings. To us the interesting feature of this phenomenon is that all the reagents that give a positive test are those which contain a labile hydrogen, and which can therefore form simple or complex silver salts. This is also a condition that appears to be a requisite for the Gaspar type of dye-bleach solution. Dr. Schwarz details his results with a large number of substances, which by inference, at least, should be usable in Gasparcolor. It is interesting to note that most of the substances mentioned in the Gaspar patents, give positive results.

Some typical solutions that will destroy the dye in situ with a silver image, are the following:

1.	Thiourea	10 parts
	Citric acid	5 parts
	Water	200 parts

A film, dyed diffusely with one of the dyes mentioned above, and containing a silver image, is treated in the above solution. The dye will be destroyed only in the places where a silver image exists If this be a negative, then a positive dye image remains. Therefore to obtain a positive, the film must be printed through a positive.

2	Semi carbazide	5 0 parts
	Sulphuric acid	1.0 part
	Water to	100 parts
3.	Thio semi-carbazide	5.0 parts
	Sulphuric acid	1 0 part
	Water to	100 parts

Guanidine and amido-guanidine could replace the agents mentioned above.

4	Sodium sulphide	5 0 parts
	Metol	as desired
	Water	100 parts
5.	Thiodiglycolic acid and sugar	5 0 parts
	Water to	100 parts

The chemistry of the reaction was extended in a later patent application, which oddly enough was issued before this one in the United States (U.S P. 2004625; Eng P. 419810; Fr. P. addition 43049 to 727168). Here is disclosed the fact that the silver image could be developed and the dye destroyed simultaneously Ordinarily the developer will not have a sufficient potential to reduce azo dyes, but evidently the catalytic action of the silver makes the reduction possible. Two solutions are given:

1.	Amidol	1 0 part
	Sodium bisulphite	1 0 part
	Sodium sulphite, crystals	8 0 parts
	Water	200 parts
	and	
2.	Sodium hydrosulphite	0.5 part
	Potassium bromide	1 0 part
	Sodium bisulphite	3 0 parts
	Water	100 parts

The second solution differs but slightly from the one offered by Christensen (cf. above). The most important difference, and one which may be an indication of a truer understanding of the fundamental chemistry involved, is the inclusion of sodium bisulphite, making the solution more acid than previously. Dr. Gaspar, in several of his patent specifications states that the fundamental reaction is

$$Ag^0 + H^+X^- \leftrightarrows Ag^+X^- + H^0$$

This reaction proceeds most generally to the left. The presence of silver ions in the solution would force the reaction to the left, so that under ordinary conditions, the formation of nascent hydrogen by the action of an acid upon metallic silver, would never take place. The need for the presence of an agent which removes silver ions from solution, now becomes evident. When this happens, positive silver is removed as fast as it is formed, thus forcing the reaction to the right Hydrogen has a very limited solubility in water, so that its concentration is a minor influence However, this also is removed when an easily reduced dye is present Hence in Gasparcolor, the conditions are just ripe for forcing the reaction to the right. Nascent hydrogen is an excellent and extremely powerful reducing agent. Since its formation is dependent upon metallic silver, and this is removed during the formation, the production of hydrogen will continue only until the silver is used up.

Amidol is one of the few developing agents which can act even in acid media. But the action under such conditions is extremely slow. Dr. Gaspar suggests, therefore, that the development be started in a normal amidol developer, then finished in an acidified solution This can be accomplished if a few drops of concentrated hydrochloric acid be added to the original. The amidol could be replaced by pyrogallol, metol, glycin, etc., and HCl can be replaced by other acids. When hydrosulphite is used both as a developer and as a dye destroyer, it must be present in low concentrations, and its activity must be further curbed by the presence of mild acids (strong acids will decompose hydrosulphite) and fairly large concentrations of bromide.

While the formation of nascent hydrogen may be the true explanation when the solutions contain acids and silver-salt complex formers, this cannot be the true explanation in the case just discussed. Here we have only a very mild acidity, and no silver complex formers to remove silver ions from solution. Perhaps the adsorption theory of development provides a clew According to this theory, the metallic specks forming the latent image act as centers about which the developing ions, such as metol, amidol, etc , adsorb As a result of this adsorption, the local concentration of the reducing agent is increased to a point where its reducing power becomes sufficiently high to attack the silver bromide, and in the present case, the dye Since sodium hydrosulphite and peroxide can also act as developers, this explanation must not be overlooked as a possibility in the Schinzel and the Christensen techniques.

In the specifications of this patent, Dr Gaspar hints at another type of reaction. Instead of having the reaction products between the silver image and the bleach solution act on dyes, they can act upon dyestuff-forming substances, whereby the dyestuff-forming properties become destroyed. The very obvious extension, the reduction of nitro-bodies to amines, is not mentioned in this patent. Under such conditions non-dye-forming compounds become converted to dye-forming substances. One very obvious advantage of this type of reaction is that the intensity of the final image becomes directly proportional to the original silver image, rather than to its complement.

In English patent 397159, several new bleach formulas are given

1. Potassium thiocyanate	3 parts
Citric acid	3 parts
Water to	100 parts
2 Cystein hydrochloride	5 parts
Metol	5 parts
Sulphuric acid	3 parts
3. Phenyl hydrazine hydrochloride	8 parts
Hydrochloric acid	3 parts
Water to	100 parts

All the formulas listed above act upon the dye as reducing agents. In several other disclosures (Eng. P. 397188, 397192), oxidizing solutions that bleach dyes are listed. Here also are included the compositions of the dyed layers. A monopack contains a bottom layer dyed diffusedly with diamine pure blue FF, a central layer colored by diamine fast pink G, and a top layer dyed yellow with mordant yellow G. After exposure, it is developed, then treated with either of the following solutions.

1. Sodium chlorate	5 parts
Hydrochloric acid, 20%	5 parts
Water to	75 parts
or	
2 Potassium bromate	5 parts
Sulphuric acid	2 parts
Potassium iodide, 10%	1 part
Water to	100 parts

To this was added either 0.2 part copper sulphate or 0.1 part vanadium chloride to act as a catalyst. In these solutions, the dye becomes destroyed only in situ with the undeveloped silver halide salts, hence the importance of not fixing the emulsion after development. The decomposition of chloric or bromic acid into free chlorine or bromine takes place only in the presence of huge quantities of halide ions in accordance with the reaction

$$5NaCl + NaClO_3 + 3H_2SO_4 \text{——} 3Cl_2 + 3H_2O + 3Na_2SO_4$$

We recall that Mr. Brewster used the equivalent iodide reaction for the formation of his Miller-type silver iodide mordant (cf. chapter on Dye Toning). With bromic acid, a similar action takes place. In the present instance, silver bromide takes the place of NaCl or NaBr, thus localizing the reaction to the immediate vicinity of the insoluble salt. The bleaching action of free halogen is well known

Another possibility is outlined in these patent specifications. The monopack containing the silver image, can be treated with

Bleaching powder	2 parts
Acetic acid	2 parts
Water to	100 parts

Now the dye destruction will take place in situ with the silver image In this case it is possible to fix the emulsion before treating it with the bleach solution These solutions are quite reminiscent of the Schweitzer disclosures, where two baths are given, and the claim made that one solution gives dye destruction in situ with silver, and the other one in situ with the unfixed silver halide.

Instead of converting the silver into a substance which will act on the dye to bleach it, it is possible to convert it into a salt that will react with the bleach and thus prevent its action on the dye (Eng. P. 424563). The dye will in that case be bleached most where the least silver deposit is present. Here again there will be formed a negative dye image.

In compounding a bleach it is extremely desirable to have a solution that will act rapidly, for if the time of reaction be unduly prolonged there will be bound to be some action on non-image portions of the layers. In such cases it is usual to look for catalysts. These may serve two purposes. First, they may increase the rate of the general reaction, the reduction of the dye by the agent either present in the solution, or formed by its interaction with silver or silver halide. Secondly, they may increase the differential in the reaction rates between image and non-image portions. In either event the time required for image formation will be considerably decreased. When a thiourea bleach is used, it has been found (Eng. P. 496558) that substances like metol, hydroquinone, etc., are excellent activators, especially in the presence of organic solvents which probably act as solvents for both dye and dye-reduction products. Three solutions are given·

1	Thiourea	19 parts
	Hydroquinone	16 parts
	Hydrochloric acid (conc)	2 parts
	Ethyl alcohol	30 parts
	Water to	100 parts
2.	Thiourea	19 parts
	Hydroquinone	16 parts
	Hydrochloric acid (conc.)	2 parts
	Acetone	30 parts
	Water to	100 parts
3.	Thiourea	16 parts
	Metol	3 parts
	Sulphuric acid, 20%	1 part
	Methyl alcohol	30 parts
	Water to	100 parts

It is evident from the examples that only water-miscible solvents are used. In an extension of this patent, it is pointed out that the ortho hydroxy azo dyes, which are insoluble in alkali, are especially useful (Eng. P. 500098).

A more positive type of catalyst is disclosed in English patent 490451 (cf.

U.S.P. 2183395 for a method of synthesis). This also is to be used with the thiourea type of bleach. The substance phenazine has the structure

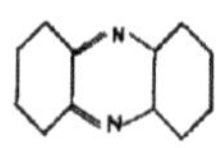

Here two benzene groups are bridged together by two amino nitrogens, forming a new six-membered azine ring. If there is present an amino or an oxy group in either of the benzene rings, the result is a dye. Safranine, one of the very first known practical desensitizers, has the structure

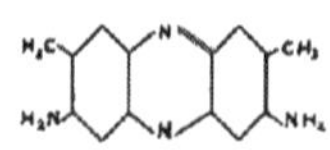

Phenosafranine, another excellent desensitizer, has the structure

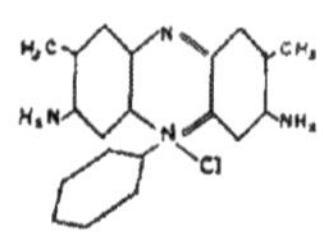

Both of these substances act as catalysts for Gasparcolor. Other phenazines that can be used are 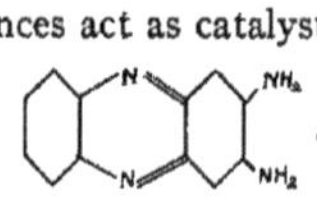 and 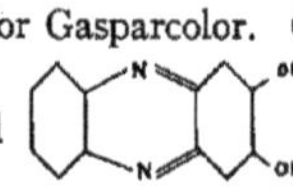

2:3 di-amino-phenazine 2:3 di-oxy-phenazine

Also dyes such as Janus blue, methylene blue, and induline scarlet can be used. They also act as desensitizers for the photographic emulsion. Another common property is that they bleach very readily when exposed to light, especially if thiourea and certain thiourea derivatives are present. In the bleached state they are fairly strong reducing agents, being capable of reducing silver nitrate to metallic silver. It may be inferred therefore, that these substances act as hydrogen carriers, becoming reduced readily by the action of the bleach solution, and then reforming the dye by reaction with the non-leuco-forming dye present in the emulsion layer. In general, derivatives of the following type can act in this manner

X can be *N*, *S*, or *O*.
Y can be *N*, *S*, or *O*.

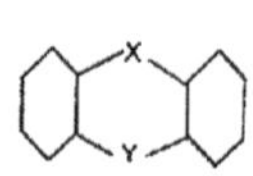

If *X* and *Y* are nitrogen, the compounds formed are azines (safranine, phenosafranine, etc.). If *X* is *N*, and *Y* is *S* the compounds are thiazines (methylene blue). If *X* is *N* and *Y* is *O* the compounds are oxazines. All the members of these classes of dyes have desensitizing properties, are easily bleached to leuco derivatives by the action of light (an action which is highly catalyzed by thiourea and its derivatives), and they strongly fog photographic emulsions when these are treated with the dyes. In this cycle of common properties may lie the explanation for the catalytic action of the substances in Gasparcolor. Also mentioned are di-methyl-phenyl-benzyl-ammonium chloride (leucotrope O), and quinoline-ethyl-sulphonate.

The second problem which Dr. Gaspar had to solve was to dye the gelatin layer uniformly. The dye must be completely localized, and must not diffuse away from the positions where it is placed. This usually means that the dye must be insoluble in the gelatin and in the solutions into which the gelatin layers might be placed. If this method is adopted for the localization of the dye particles, then another problem arises. The sizes of the dye particles must be made sufficiently fine to insure an image that will not be grainy. One solution would be to colloidally disperse the dye in gelatin. In order to accomplish this, it is desirable to start with some derivative of the dye which is soluble in water. After solution in the gelatin emulsion, the derivative can be treated so that the original insoluble dye becomes reformed. Under such conditions, especially if gelatin be present, extremely fine dispersion can be made. One method of accomplishing this is to start with a hydrazo compound. These compounds may be considered as leuco azo dyes. By a process of oxidation they become converted into the dye form. As oxidizing agents Dr. Gaspar suggests ferric chloride or nitrous acid (U.S.P. 2041827; Eng. P. 430991; Ger. P. 601572; Fr. P. 766192). In the specifications of this patent, there is suggested that the hydrazo compounds might serve as toning agents. In this case, the silver image must first be converted into lead chromate, which upon treatment with an acid will release chromic acid, a powerful oxidizing agent.

When an azo group is ortho to an hydroxy, as in the dyes of the Naphthol AS series, complete insolubility is achieved even though there is ostensibly present a solubilizing oxy group. This lack of solubility conforms to a hydrazone structure for the dye, thus

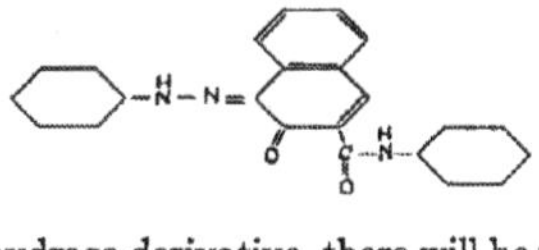

Upon reduction to the hydrazo derivative, there will be formed a true hydroxyl group which would be capable of forming soluble sodium salts

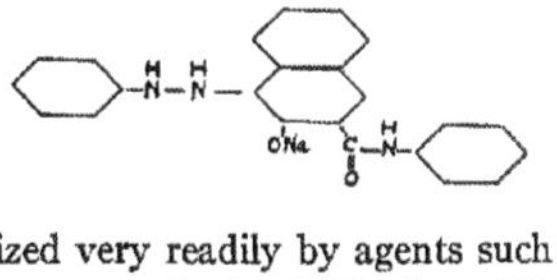

This form will be oxidized very readily by agents such as nitrous acid, ferric chloride, chromic acid, etc., to the insoluble dye. Methods of converting a silver image into an oxidizing agent have been described in the chapter on chemical toning.

The insoluble azo dyes, especially those containing an hydroxy group ortho to the azo, can be solubilized by forming a bisulphite addition compound (U.S P. 2172307, 2172308; Eng P 496559, 498461). Para red, formed by coupling para-nitro-benzene diazonium chloride into beta naphthol

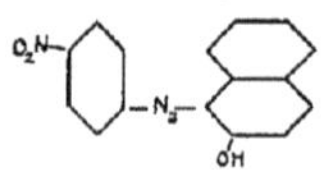

can be converted into a soluble product by the following method One gram of the dye is refluxed in a solution containing 9 grams of bisulphite, 35 cc of water, 35 cc of alcohol, and 25 cc of chloroform, until the red dye has disappeared. The solvents are partially distilled off, whereupon yellow crystals are precipitated These can be recrystallized from water

If the coupling agent is an amine, it is possible to achieve solubility by converting it into the omega sulphonic acid, by treatment with bisulphite-formaldehyde. The omega salt can then be coupled A dye omega sulphonate will be formed, which is soluble After dissolution in gelatin, the dye can be precipitated in exceedingly fine state, by treatment with alkali. Instead of the dye, the coupling agent may be made soluble in this manner, and the dye formation carried out after dispersion in gelatin.

A further extension of this idea is contained in United States patent 2178167 (Eng. P. 503873). Nitro or nitroso bodies are dispersed in the gelatin or emulsion layer. After exposure, development, fixation, and washing, the film is treated with sodium hydrosulphite, which will reduce the nitro or nitroso group to an amine, which can then be diazotized and coupled The resultant dye could finally be bleached in situ with the silver image by treatment with any of the solutions mentioned above.. Dr. Gaspar makes an obvious extension of the process in this disclosure. Instead of converting the nitro group generally into an amino body, this conversion is made to take place in situ with the silver image. This can be accomplished if the film is bathed with halogen acids, but a preferred bath is

Water	100 parts
Thiourea	7 parts
Sulphuric acid	1 part
Hydroquinone	6 parts

The time of treatment is ten minutes After a thorough wash, the film is treated with a solution containing one-half of one per cent of nitrous acid (made by dissolving 5 grams of sodium nitrite in one liter of water), then acidifying with hydrochloric acid This treatment will convert the amine into a diazonium salt Upon treatment with an alkaline solution containing a phenol, beta naphthol, or naphthol AS body, a dye will be formed, in those places where a silver image existed previously.

In another disclosure (U.S.P. 2071688; Eng. P. 416566, 416660; Fr P. 747252) Dr. Gaspar describes methods of forming other than azo dyes, in a gelatin medium Thus various metal salts may be dissolved in the gelatin solution, which by treatment with other salts, will yield pigments Ferrous salts can be dissolved in the gelatin, and this can later be treated with potassium ferricyanide. By interaction between the two, the cyan pigment Prussian blue is formed in true colloidal dispersion. The ferrous salt may be substituted by lead, and the potassium ferricyanide by potassium dichromate. The net effect will be to form the extremely efficient yellow pigment lead chromate, again in the form of a colloidal dispersion in gelatin. If the emulsion, colored either by lead chromate or Prussian blue, contains a silver image, treatment with one of the baths noted above will cause an imagewise reduction of the pigment to a soluble and colorless form.

It is not important that the diffusely dispersed material be a colored substance It is possible, for instance, to diffusely disperse zinc ferrocyanide in the emulsion layer. If the latent image be developed with a ferrous oxalate developer, ferric ions will be formed wherever silver is deposited. The ferric ions will immediately react with the ferrocyanide to form Prussian blue. In the specifications, Dr Gaspar states that zinc ferricyanide must be dispersed in the gelatin This is an obvious error or misprint. Prussian blue is formed by the interaction of ferric salts with ferrocyanides, and ferric salts will be formed from the action of ferrous oxalate upon the latent image Hence it is ferrocyanide that must be diffusely dispersed within the gelatin layer.

It is possible to form many organic dyes in a gelatin medium. To form an oxazine dye, resorcin is allowed to act on a nitroso-di-alkyl amine, in the presence of tannins. Many other examples are given. Suitable for this purpose are many of the developable dyes These are substances that have affinity for the medium in which they are dispersed, so that dyed gelatin is formed. The dyes contain free amino groups which can be diazotized. The dye affinity localizes the diazonium salt, and subsequent coupling forms a new dye that is very substantive

There are other methods of dying gelatin with dyes that will not diffuse out. It is possible, for instance, to start with dyes that are soluble, but which can be precipitated in the gelatin by colorless agents. Nitrogenous organic bases (U S P 2046067, 2075190, Eng. P. 415756, 428158, 516883, Fr. P. 746645, addition 44754 to 746645), such as guanidine, 2 phenyl-4-amino-quinoline, or biguanidines derived from aromatic polyamines, will form insoluble complexes with many dyes, especially if sulphonic acid groups be present. If the precipitation is allowed to take place in gelatin, exceedingly fine or truly colloidal dispersions may be formed

The dye may be made to react with the salt of a weak acid, and in that manner form a lake (U.S P. 2107605; Eng. P 434305). The alkaline earth metals, magnesium, the nitrogenous bases (compounds containing a trivalent nitrogen as part of a heterocyclic ring), etc., form suitable cations to react with dye-acids. The weak organic acids can serve as anions to unite with dye-bases. The dyes suitable for this procedure need not have any substantive properties for gelatin It is also possible to form metal complexes of many dyes, complexes sold under the names Neolan or Lanasol dyes (U.S.P. 2055407; Eng. P 445806; Fr. P. 785665) The metal ions are bound to the dye by means of chelate structures. Such dyes are immobile, and can be used directly. To illustrate the procedure, Dr. Gaspar gives the following example. A silver halide emulsion which contains 0.5 per cent Neolan yellow R, is coated on a film base. On top of this another emulsion layer dyed with 0.5 per cent Neolan pink G is coated. The yellow-dyed layer is green-sensitive, while the pink layer is red-sensitive. After exposure, development, and fixation, dye images can be produced by treatment with a thiocarbamide bleach bath, such as one of the solutions disclosed above. In a three-color process the third layer could be dyed with Neolan green BR To help disperse the dyes or dye formers in gelatin, wetting agents can be added (Eng. P 514639). In many cases the dye is soluble in an organic solvent such as alcohol In that case a coarse dispersion of the dye in gelatin could be treated with alcohol. A fine dispersion will result (U.S.P. 2080041; Eng. P. 458256, 458304).

Instead of adding dyes or color formers to the gelatin, it is possible to add specific precipitants (U.S P. 2137336; Eng. P. 478735, 480854, 516883). After exposure, the emulsion could be treated with dyes which will combine specifically with each precipitant. It has been found, for instance, that a gelatin layer containing di-phenyl-guanidine acetate will allow the penetration of a one per cent solution of diamine pure blue (Schultz No. 426, 5th edition) The dye will react with the guanidine to form an insoluble complex which, however, will not interfere with the further diffusion of another dye. If the treatment with the blue dye be interrupted and then continued with a solution of xylene light yellow 2G (Schultz No. 22), the yellow will diffuse through the blue dye precipitate and will undergo a like reaction in the region below where the blue formed. In this manner the layer can be dyed in strata.

The solution of the first two phases of the general problem taught Dr. Gaspar how to convert a silver image into a colored one. The next problem is the practical application of the technique to color photography and color reproduction To this end it is essential to prepare a three-layered monopack, whose separate entities will fulfill the requirements of subtractive-color synthesis. This means that each layer should be capable of registering a single color primary, and should yield a monochrome image which is the complement of the primary so registered. Offhand, these stipulations should not create much hardship. The blue-sensitive layer should be colored yellow, the green-sensitive portion should be colored magenta, and the red-sensitive stratum should be colored cyan. If the three layers are superimposed in the order yellow, magenta, cyan, each layer will register the complementary primary, and allow the other colors to pass practically unhindered to the next layer, minus the blue light which would otherwise severely interfere with proper color selection. Where the film is to be used in the camera, this order and correspondence must be followed. The quality of the image formed is considerably below par, however, under such conditions.

Consider the effect of exposing a yellow-dyed emulsion, with blue light. An ordinary negative emulsion contains approximately equal weights of gelatin and silver salts. However, silver bromide has a specific gravity of 6.47 while gelatin has a specific gravity of about 1.00. This means that the relative volume occupied by the silver is one-seventh that of the gelatin, so that in any one direction, the ratio of the path of the light traveling through the dyed gelatin to that through the silver halide is more than two to one. When blue light is incident upon such a layer, a considerable length of gelatin must be traversed before the light reaches the light-sensitive elements. During this passage, the light is absorbed by the dye, so that when the silver-halide layer is reached, the intensity of the blue has been reduced considerably. The net effect is that no density can be developed that will correspond to a deep black, if we are dealing with positives, or a highlight if we are dealing with negatives. The contrast of the image becomes reduced to a degree that makes good images practically impossible. For the same reason, considerable emulsion speed is lost, for the light absorbed by the gelatin is of no value whatsoever for image formation.

The obvious solution in the case where negatives are to be made by this means, is to dye the film after the exposure has been made, so that no light would be lost during the exposure stage. How this can be accomplished was outlined in the discussion above. In the main, the procedure is to add colorless dyestuff-formers to the emulsion, and, after the exposure, treat them to form the dye. Often such after-treatment may interfere with the latent image. In that case the dyestuff-formers can be stabilized against developing and fixing baths, and dye formation made to take place after the silver image has been formed.

When the film is to be used as a copy material, an entirely different story is true. First of all, color correctness is not essential in the master from which the copies are to be made. It is important only that the differential absorptions and transmissions of the three part images be such that they print in different layers in the copy material. Since the coloring and sensitization can be controlled at will, it can be arranged that the top yellow-dyed layer be made red- or green-sensitive. These colors will not be absorbed by the yellow, hence will produce a latent image throughout the entire depth of the layer. Thus there is no great loss of speed or of contrast. In order for the exposing light not to affect the layer underneath, that layer must be dyed with a color which will absorb the red or green used to expose the top layer. By careful choice of dyes and sensitizers, it can be arranged that each layer in the pack will be exposed by a light that will be transmitted by that layer and absorbed by the layer beneath. The method for doing this is disclosed in United States patent 1985344, and its extension to printing from lenticular and screen plate originals is disclosed in United States patents 1986054 and 1988891. The basic principles are discussed in the first mentioned patent (cf. also Eng P. 408991, 409287, 415040, 441411).

The arrangements of the layers are such that consideration is paid not only to the absorption and transmission of each of the layers, but also to the relationship which must exist between all the layers. Thus in one embodiment of the invention, three silver halide layers are poured one on top of the other, the bottom layer being colored cyan, the middle magenta, and the uppermost yellow This last is made green-sensitive by the addition of pinaflavol or erythrosin The magenta layer is made red-sensitive, while the bottom cyan layer is sensitized to the infrared. Most blue and green dyes transmit beyond 680 mμ quite freely. Each of the colored layers acts also as a protective filter for itself and for the layers underneath. Thus the yellow dye in the top layer acts as a minus-blue filter for the entire emulsion pack. The magenta layer in the center prevents the green printing light used to form an image in the uppermost emulsion layer from registering in the central layer, which, if sensitized by means of pinacyanol will have a weak green sensitivity in the regions 500 to 520 mμ and 575 to 600 mμ. In the same manner the cyan dye in the bottom layer will act as a barrier to whatever red light may spill over the exposure of the central layer. All three of the dyes freely transmit the infrared so that there will be no barrier to its passage Only the bottom layer has infrared sensitivity, so only this layer will register an image

A pack of this type is ideal when printing is done in stages from separation positives It can also be used for printing from a colored master positive. This can be done if the blue-filter separation is converted into a color which will transmit red and infrared, but which will be modulated by green. A magenta or red is such a color. The green-filter image must be printed by red light, but must be transparent to green and infrared. A cyan color would serve here, if it is transparent to the infrared. But then most dyes are. The red-filter image must be printed with infrared light, and be transparent to red and green. The patent specifications mention naphthol green for this, and the claim is made that, in somewhat weaker concentration, this dye has high transmissions from 650 mμ downward. This is a rather broad statement, and somewhat questionable, since the green character of the dye is indicative of red absorption. The "Handbook of Chemistry and Physics" (Chemical Rubber Publishing Company, 13th edition, p. 951) gives this dye a maximum transmission of 36 per cent at 540 mμ, dwindling down to one per cent at 640 mμ, and only seven per cent at 600 mμ. However, there are no doubt many substances which will absorb only in the infrared, and which would therefore serve.

When the material is to be used for printing from lenticular positives, the banded series of filters must not be the familiar red, green, and blue set. The blue must be replaced by a green filter which is opaque to the infrared, the green sector must be replaced by a red which is opaque to the infrared, and the red by an infrared which is opaque to the visible (U.S.P 1986054) In making duplicates from screen plates, where the screen is separated from the emulsion, as in the Finlay rather than the Dufaycolor techniques, a separate copying screen is used, with a pattern that is identical to that of the original, but having filter elements transmitting green, red, and infrared, rather than blue, green, and red (U.S P. 1988891; Eng P 369616, 406294). No mention is made as to how such a screen could be prepared.

Another attack on the problem of correlating the spectral sensitivity of the layer with the color of the dye dispersed within that layer is made in United States patent 2075191 (Eng. P. 446206; Ger. P. 636185; Fr. P. 784518). Instead of shifting the sensitivity of each layer toward the red, the layers are dyed weakly, and instead of having the emulsions on one side of the base, they are coated on both sides, each side containing the three layers. There is insufficient yellow dye to prevent the blue light from reaching through the entire depth of the yellow layer, and a similar condition holds with the magenta and cyan layers and green and red light. But instead of printing one image, two identical images are printed on each side of the base. When the two weakly colored images are combined, the effect will be that of a strongly colored image.

It may be easier to utilize a duplitized monopack, in which two layers are coated on one side of the base, and a third layer on the other side (U S.P. 2183393). The two outer layers are colored magenta and cyan, while the central layer is colored yellow. This means that two of the layers could be printed by means of blue light, and since both the magenta and cyan transmit blue freely, no loss of contrast would be had. Of course, each printing must be done separately, but this is a preferred method anyway. The central yellow layer forms a barrier for the further passage of any blue rays that may spill through the magenta or cyan layers. The yellow layer could be sensitized to the infrared, or to the red Many other arrangements of sensitizations could be had, which would allow the differential copying of the three partial images.

The preparation of a monopack suitable for two-color work, has also not been overlooked (U S.P. 2028279; Eng. P. 412950, Fr. P. 746644). But instead of coloring each layer with a single dye, two are used. Thus the orange-red layer will contain pyramine orange and azo fuchsin, or azo fuchsin and mordant yellow, while the green layer will contain benzo pure blue and pyramine orange or benzo pure blue and metanil yellow. The rate at which the two dye components are acted on by the bleach solutions varies with the dyes. Thus it becomes possible to obtain dichroic effects in each layer, orangy highlights with deep red shadows in the orange-red layer, and sky-blue highlights with deep green shadows in the other It becomes possible in this manner to obtain pleasant flesh and sky renditions, and at the same time, maintain true blacks in the middle tones and shadows. Such a process could be termed "two and one-half color."

A specific and detailed study of the entire problem of the relationship between the sensitivity of a given layer and the spectral absorption of the color it must have in order to retain good contrast and balance, is contained in English patent 485552. Other types of monopacks are outlined in United States patent 2193931 and in English patents 445959 and 503330. The last is especially interesting in that it takes advantage of the difference in the spectral sensitivities of silver bromide and silver chloride emulsions. The first has a sensitivity going to 520 mμ, while the last has a limit at 435 mμ. If a silver chloride emulsion is made green-sensitive, it will have a sensitivity gap from 435 to approximately 520 mμ. It becomes possible, then, to print through a yellow filter which absorbs the light up to 435 mμ. The range from 435 to 520 will serve to print on to an unsensitized or color-blind silver bromide emulsion, while the range beyond 520 will act only upon the sensitized silver chloride.

A monopack that is suitable either for use in the camera, or for the making of a master positive for subsequent printing, is disclosed in United States patent 2166049 (Eng P. 483366, 483463, 483464). The layers are coated in the following manner: A blue-sensitive emulsion is coated on to a celluloid base The emulsion is not dyed, but contains dye intermediates which can easily be converted into a yellow dye at a later stage. Upon this is coated a layer containing a yellow filter dye, then a green-sensitive emulsion containing colorless intermediates for the formation of a magenta dye, and finally a red-sensitive emulsion After the exposure, the pack is treated to form the dyes in the blue and green-sensitive layers. The top layer, which is undyed, contains a precipitant for a cyan dye, so that this layer can be dyed without affecting the other two Thus a colorless pack receives the exposures so there is no loss of speed nor of contrast. The formation of the dyes and the preferential dying of the uppermost layer is accomplished by the methods outlined earlier in this chapter. It is to be noted that the blue-sensitive emulsion is on the bottom. This means that the pack is to be exposed through the carrier side. Since the processing yields a direct positive, there is obtained an inversion of right and left. This is rectified by exposing through the base, rather than in the normal manner.

Dr Gaspar also suggested that the dye-bleach monopack could be used as one element of a Troland bipack Here, it may be recalled, a bipack is formed with a two-layered monopack as one of the elements. Several different possibilities suggest themselves as to the arrangement of layers. In five of the six arrangements, two of the layers are separated by the thickness of one of the supports. In these, one of the elements is a single-coated film, the other contains coatings on both sides of the carrier. Obviously this leads to poor definition and a possible loss of registry for the layer that is so separated. The sixth arrangement is the conventional one where the two supports form the outside surfaces, and the three emulsion layers are one directly behind the other . The front element contains a single emulsion layer, and is colorless. The rear element is a two-layered monopack, dyed and processed in accordance with the Gasparcolor technique (U.S.P. 2183394, Eng. P. 446392, 450685)

A procedure as complicated as this usually involves some special technique to make it work. Thus it has been found desirable to print the silver images very deep, much deeper than is required for the destruction of the dye. This enables the technician to cut down the time of treatment in the dye-bleach bath The excess silver could then be removed by treatment with

Copper sulphate	20 parts
Sodium chloride	20 parts
Nitric acid	1 part
Water to	100 parts

or

Cupric chloride	30 parts
Nitric acid	1 part
Water to	100 parts

For some reason or other this was considered of sufficient importance to protect by patent (U S P. 2042253; Eng. P. 416666; Fr. P. 751932). Another source of trouble lay in the creeping of the dyes in the bottom layer into the support or the backing. To offset this it was proposed (U.S P. 2088523; Eng. P 444669; Fr. P. 785525) to add a layer of colloidal silver or exposed silver halide between the bottom layer and the support. What dye creeps in will now be destroyed in the dye-bleach

The improved character of the image when a black-and-white key plate is present, has also been noted To take advantage of this, a silver halide layer dyed black, and sensitized to a region of the spectrum different from the other three layers, is incorporated into the film. This can also be used for the formation of a black-and-white sound track (U.S P. 2125015). The corresponding sound track area in the other three layers could be given overall unmodulated exposures to produce a uniform destruction of the yellow, magenta, and cyan dyes, thus leaving only a black dye image In another disclosure (U S.P. 2132154) it is proposed that the pack be exposed and developed, but not fixed. It is then treated with the dye bleach to form the color images The remaining unexposed silver salts could then be converted into a positive black-and-white key plate. If a silver sound track is desired, the three colored emulsions could be given a uniform exposure in the sound track area, developed and processed to destroy all the dye in this region, then rehalogenized to reform silver bromide. This can now be exposed to the sound negative and processed to a black-and-white silver image. Sound track problems are involved in the following disclosures

United States	*English*	*French*
2025658	412949	745934
2062304	413688	746426
2136143	432464	
2155894	468508	
	468509	
	472644	
	472981	

After Dr. Gaspar demonstrated that silver-dye-bleach processes were entirely feasible, other experimenters began to play with it. Chief among these were Agfa, and, more lately, the Eastman Kodak Company. Agfa had already solved the general problem of dispersing a substance evenly throughout a layer (cf. chapter on Ansco Color). It may be recalled that their method consisted in adding extremely heavy groups to the molecule to make it substantive, or at least non-diffusing A complete specification for a monopack is disclosed in English patent 488853 The red-sensitive layer contains the 3-amino-benzoyl derivative of H acid

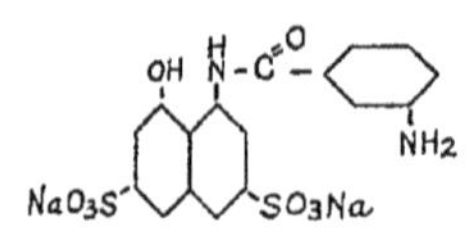

The green-sensitive layer contains a stearoyl-amino phenyl derivative of pyrazolone,

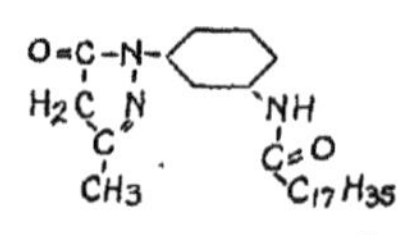

The blue-sensitive layer contains, besides a yellow filter dye, di-(aceto-acetyl)-benzidine

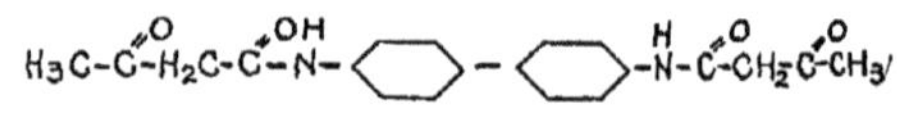

These substances are colorless, hence have no effect upon the exposure. After exposure and development, the film is treated with tetrazotized benzidine. The substituted H acid couples to form a cyan dye, the pyrazolone compound will form a magenta, and the benzidine couples to yield a yellow, all the colors diffusely coloring each layer. These dyes are next treated with a bleach solution, compounded by mixing equal parts of *A* and *B* (U.S.P. 2100594; Eng. P. 375338, 401340)

Solution A

Potassium iodide	33 parts
Iodine	17 parts
Sulphuric acid, concentrated	525 parts
Water to	6250 parts

Solution B

Sodium sulphite	33 parts
Thiourea	33 parts
Water to	6250 parts

Dyes suitable for this procedure, beside the ones formed above, are

Congo pure blue
Sirius ruby violet R
Sirius ruby B
Sirius yellow
Chrysophenine G

and any other azo dyes which can be readily reduced by sodium hydrosulphite to yield colorless products.

A more normal type of monopack is disclosed in English patent 454088. This is a duplitized type of monopack, containing a blue-sensitive layer on one side of the carrier, which has been dyed cyan with Chicago blue On the other side is coated a red-sensitive emulsion dyed magenta with Sirius ruby. On top of this is coated an uncolored blue-sensitive layer. Thus it is possible to print two separations on the two outer layers by means of blue light, and the central layer by means of red light. After exposure and development, the top uncolored layer is dyed yellow with chrysophenine yellow, after which the dye is bleached in situ with the silver image in accordance with the methods outlined above. The danger of dyes diffusing from one layer to another is minimized by dyeing each layer with a mixture of acid and basic dyes in such proportion that mutual precipitation takes place (U.S.P. 1954294; Eng. P. 372620).

In another disclosure, a monopack built along duplitized film pattern is described (U.S.P. 2020607; Eng. P. 379934). The cyan layer is colored with brilliant benzo fast green, the magenta with Sirius red violet R, and the yellow with benzo light yellow RL, or chrysophenine G extra. After exposure and development, the pack is not fixed, but is treated with the dye-bleach bath. The unused silver is then removed, and the unfixed silver halide exposed and developed to yield a black-and-white key plate (U.S.P. 2169320, Eng. P. 506359). It is quite surprising how close these procedures are to those disclosed by Dr Gaspar. The method for forming a sound track is disclosed in English patent 483052

The Eastman Kodak Company, especially the English subsidiary, has been issued a series of patents that deal generally with monopacks, whose processing is a combination of several techniques, including silver-dye-bleach (Eng. P. 468560, 475784, 475786, 477524). A patent issued to Dr. M. W. Seymour of the same company would utilize the vat dyes for coloring the layers (U.S P 2184022). Gaspar had first proposed to do this. But Dr. Seymour extends the list considerably. Indanthrene yellow (Schultz No. 1220), algol pink BBK (No. 1221), algol red BTK (No. 1261), indanthrene blue 5G (No. 1238), and caledon blue 3G (No. 1232) are some specific examples. For a three-color system, it is possible to use indigo for the cyan, algol pink BBK for the magenta, and indanthrene golden yellow or algosol golden yellow for the yellow

After exposure, development, and fixation the dye can be bleached by treatment with one or the other of the following solutions:

1. Potassium sulphide	2½ parts
Sodium hydroxide	2½ parts
Water to	100 parts
2. Potassium cyanide	5 parts
Pyridine	5 parts
Water	100 parts
or	
3. Stannous chloride	8 parts
Sodium hydroxide	10 parts
Triethanolamine	10 parts
Anthraquinone	0.0025 part
Water to	100 parts

The anthraquinone is present probably as anthrahydroquinone. Its presence helps to keep the highlights clear

CHAPTER 25

CARBON AND CARBRO

ACCORDING to E. J. Wall ("History of Three-Color Photography," p 339) Ducos du Hauron was the first person to make a print in color The method he used was not based upon silver halides, for at that time the conversion of the silver of a black-and-white image into color, was not well known. Abortive attempts at colored monochrome images had already been made. But no one had yet conceived the possible marriage between these and the ideas promulgated in 1857 by Clerk Maxwell, that is, nobody except du Hauron, who published his thoughts in 1869 (*Bull. Soc. franç. Phot.*, Vol. 11 (1869), pp. 122, 144, 155, 177; Vol. 12 (1870), p. 68, *Phot. News* (1869), p. 319; *Phot. Korr.*, Vol. 6 (1869), p. 169). To make his three-part images, du Hauron utilized the light-sensitive properties of gelatin that had been impregnated with soluble dichromates.

The technique is as old as photography, but it was not until 1864, when Sir Joseph Swan disclosed his method, that it had reached a sufficiently high degree of stability and perfection to allow its general use. Hexavalent chromium salts are light-sensitive, and are easily reduced to the trivalent form. This last has the property of raising the setting (melting) point of many colloids, the most important of which are gelatin, albumen, shellac, and gum arabic. The light-sensitivity of the chromium is considerably increased if the exposure be made in the presence of the colloids. Thus, dichromated gelatin, exposed under a stencil or a negative, will yield a positive that is composed of gelatin whose dissolution temperature has been considerably heightened By processing with water at a temperature just below that required to melt or dissolve away the "exposed" portions, the unexposed portions can be removed, leaving an image composed of "tanned" gelatin. This can be treated with dyes or pigments to yield colored pictures

Tanned gelatin has other properties besides a higher melting temperature It will not imbibe water. Upon this property is based a color technique known as pinatype. If portions of the gelatin will not imbibe water, these portions will remain uncolored when the whole is treated with water in which certain coloring matter has been dissolved. The ability to repel water could also be used in another way. The plate containing a tanned gelatin image, when treated with water, will absorb water only in the unexposed portions. The exposed portions will remain relatively dry. When the wet plate is treated with linseed oil or greasy inks, these will be repelled by the moist portions, but retained by the dry Collotype, oil, and bromoil are three reproduction techniques based upon this property. Photolithography, and other photo-mechanical procedures are also based upon the action of light upon dichromated gelatin, albumen, or shellac. From this, some fair idea of the importance and generality of the reaction may be had.

The history of carbon is told very precisely by Mr. Wall in another of his publications ("Carbon Printing," 1898). The fact that chromium is light-sensitive was first noted by Vauquelin in 1798 (*Ann. de Chim*, Vol 25 (1798), p. 21). He noted that the brick-red color of silver chromate turned purple after exposure to light He evidently made no effort to follow this lead, and the matter lay dormant for about thirty years At that time, according to Eder (*Handbuch*, Band I, Heft I, p 95), Suckow concluded that dichromates, when exposed to light in the presence of organic matter, became reduced. Seven years later, in 1839, the year in which Daguerre made public the methods of Daguerreotype, and Fox Talbot laid the foundation for silver-halide photography, Mungo Ponton, a Scot, proposed the dichromate reaction as a method of photography (*New Phil. J*, 1839, p. 169). Ponton proposed to impregnate a sheet of paper (cellulose) with dichromate and then expose it under a negative. The paper was next washed free of all unreduced dichromate. It acted not only as the organic matter that aided the reduction of the dichromate (acting as an acceptor in the photo-chemical reaction), but also as a base or carrier for the final image The visibility of the reduced dichromate image was extremely low, but despite this, Ponton allowed the matter to rest

In the next few years, several changes were made. E. Becquerel (*Compte rend*, Vol 10 (1840), p. 469) suggested starch, rather than paper Upon exposure to light, the dichromated starch became insoluble, and could no longer be washed away. The water-insoluble residue, upon treatment with iodine, gave the intense blue coloration typical of the starch-iodine complex. This was a great improvement over the previous methods since it gave an image that was capable of yielding deep densities Robert Hunt (*Brit Ass Adv Science*, Section B, Aug. 17, 1843; "Researches on Light," 1854, p. 175) improved the sensitivity by adding copper salts.

The application to the photo-mechanical printing procedures was made by Fox Talbot in 1853. He coated the sensitized gelatin upon steel plates Under the action of light, the image portions became tanned, and thus water-insoluble. Treatment with hot water removed the non-image sections, laying bare the metal at these points. When acids or other chemicals able to etch steel were applied, the image portions, protected by the water-repellant coating of tanned colloid, remained unaffected. The other portions, not having such protection, became deeply etched or engraved. After removal of the tanned colloid, there resulted an image composed of raised steel, which accepted greasy ink. In the main, very little improvement has been made in the fundamentals since Talbot's day

As practiced up to 1855, the principal problem involved in the use of dichromated colloids was to make the image visible. Becquerel (cf. above) had already made a good advance in this direction when he replaced gelatin by starch, and utilized the intense blue-violet coloration of the starch-iodine complex for the visible image. But the complex lacked permanence, and was otherwise unsuited for a final image. It easily decomposed, leading to a bleaching of the image. The obvious solution did not come until fifteen years later, in 1855, when A. L. Poitevin added an inert opaque material (powered carbon), to the gelatin. The individual carbon particles, encased in dichromated gelatin, acted as the units which composed the final image. Upon exposure, the particles lying in the image portions became encased in tanned and insoluble gelatin, so that after removal of the unexposed portions, there remained an image composed of carbon. For this reason the tissue and the technique were called "carbon."

Before the process could really become useful, one further development was necessary. When the sensitized gelatin was exposed, the tanned image lay upon the upper surface of the layer. Only the shadows had enough exposure to tan the gelatin sufficiently deep to cause adhesion to the carrier

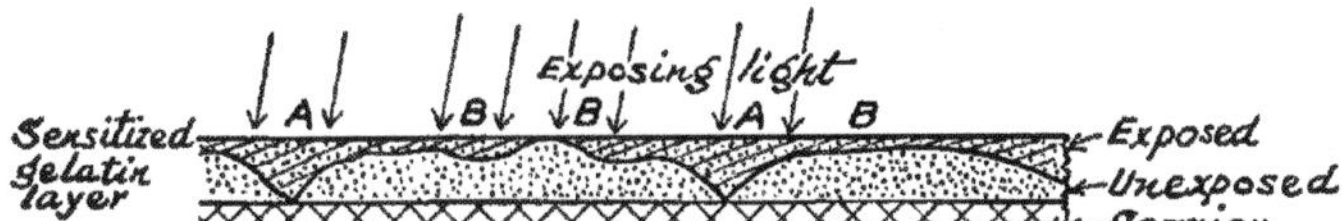

FIG. 109

This is illustrated in Fig. 109. A layer of sensitized gelatin coated upon an opaque carrier is exposed under a negative, which will modulate the intensity of light that reaches the sensitive layer underneath. At certain points (marked *A* in the diagram) the light intensity will be high, at other points (*B*) the intensity will be low. Where the intensity is high, the light will be able to penetrate very deeply into the depth of the sensitive layer; where it is low the penetration will be correspondingly less. The degree of penetration of the light is illustrated by the shaded portion of the sensitized gelatin layer. Since the gelatin becomes tanned only to the extent of its light absorption, the shaded portions in the diagram will correspond to the image. It is seen, therefore, that only in the regions marked *A* will the image remain attached to the carrier. This corresponds to the shadows. The highlights do not penetrate to the base, hence will become unattached after the untanned gelatin has been removed. The loss of middle tones and highlights can now be readily understood.

Today the reason for the faulty results appears elementary, but not so in 1855. It was not until 1858 that the Abbé Labord (*Bull. Soc. franç. Phot.*, 1858, p. 213) pointed this out. Fargier (*Bull. Soc. franç. Phot.*, 1860, p. 314) made a similar observation. But neither of them could offer a solution. For this we are indebted to J. C. Burnett (*Phot. J.*, Vol. 5 (1858), p. 84) who made the obvious suggestion that the exposure should be made through the support. This increased tremendously the exposure time, since the paper backing was only slightly translucent. It also superimposed the pattern of the paper grain upon the image. W. Blair got around this by proposing to treat the paper with waxes and oils to make it transparent (*Phot. Notes*, Vol 4 (1859), p. 331. Risler (*Bull. Soc. franç Phot.*, Vol. 10 (1864), p. 271; Eng P. 2954/63) suggested the transparent substance mica as a base. This was evidently the first use of a completely transparent material to serve as a carrier for the gelatin. Soon afterward Placet and Despaquis (*Bull. Soc. franç. Phot.*, Vol. 13 (1867), pp. 170, 227) proposed collodion, a material also suggested by du Hauron in 1869 (cf above).

The final step that made carbon completely acceptable as a print medium came in 1864 when Sir Joseph Swan published his procedure not only for the preparation of the tissue, but also for processing the material (*Phot News*, 1864, p 85) In order to give the tissue pliancy, he advised the addition of sugar to the gelatin, a practice that is used to this day, although it could be replaced by other polyalcohols such as glycerin, etc. The gelatin is prepared free of sensitizer, which was to be added just prior to coating. A typical formula as suggested by Swan, was the following:

Gelatin	2 parts
Water	8 parts
Sugar	1 part
Coloring matter to suit	

This solution could be coated upon paper, in which case the tissue was to be sensitized by bathing and drying just prior to use. If it was desired to coat a sensitized paper, then to ten parts of the gelatin solution was added one part of saturated dichromate. This was done just before coating. The unsensitized paper would keep indefinitely under proper conditions, whereas the sensitized tissue would keep only a few days or a week.

After drying, the tissue was exposed by contact. Swan's real contribution to the art lay in the next step He discovered that the tanned gelatin image would adhere to a polished surface. Therefore by mounting the exposed tissue upon a polished support so that the polished surface was in contact with the exposed surface of the tissue, he was able to wash away all the untanned gelatin, and retain the tanned image with all highlight detail intact, upon the new support. This technique is utilized to this day. The Swan disclosures were absorbed by the Autotype Company.

While carbon was being developed, the same procedure and chemistry were utilized by other people. In 1858 John Pouncy sensitized a piece of paper by brushing it with a solution of dichromated gelatin In this technique, the gelatin was later replaced by gum arabic, and the procedure became known as gum-bichromate In 1873 A. Marion (*Brit J. Phot.*, Vol. 20 (1873), p. 242, Vol. 47 (1900), p. 709) introduced a new wrinkle. He exposed a sensitized tissue under a negative, then placed it in contact with another tissue that was not sensitized After remaining in contact for a period of ten hours, it was found that an image could be developed in the second tissue. A transfer of the reduced dichromates had taken place. In 1898 T. Manly (Eng. P. 10026/98, Ger. P. 117829) improved the Marion technique by addition of manganese sulphate to the dichromate This apparently improved the sensitivity of the tissue. He also changed the development procedure. Whereas Marion merely placed the exposed dichromated tissue in contact with unsensitized pigment, Manly washed the exposed tissue in water, then treated it with an acidulated solution of ferrous sulphate, hydroquinone, or other reducing agent. This evidently was a considerable improvement over the Marion process, judging from the considerable attention that was paid it Pamphlets on the subject were written by A von Hubl ("Die Ozotypie," 1903) and many others However, it proved to be merely a slight flurry, for the process never attained any wide following. It was called "ozotype" because Manly had the mistaken notion that ozone was the product of the primary photo-chemical reaction.

Somewhat later, Manly introduced a further development. He found that the silver image could be utilized to reduce the dichromate, a fact previously disclosed by Howard Farmer (Eng P. 17773/89; *Phot J.*, Vol. 32 (1892, p. 30) This he combined with the transfer idea he used in ozotype He was accordingly able to print his negatives on an ordinary bromide enlarging paper, develop a normal silver image, then bring this image-bearing paper into contact with a pigment tissue saturated with a solution capable of reacting with metallic silver. In its present form, this technique is called "carbro," indicating that carbon images are made by means of bromide prints.

Another application of the use of dichromated gelatin sprang from an observation by Poitevin (cf above). He found that a gelatin, tanned by the action of light upon the dichromate dispersed within itself, imbibed water very sparingly and to an amount determined by the degree of tanning effected. Since this is directly proportioned to the amount of light absorbed, he quickly realized that images could be prepared in this manner The tanned gelatin, imbibing but little water, would repel greasy inks to the extent that it refrained from wetting An area receiving considerable light will be tanned to the point of becoming waterproof, and this area will absorb a maximum of printing ink An intermediate exposure will result in a milder tanning and these areas will imbibe considerable water. The amount of ink absorbed by such an area will be less than that absorbed by a fully tanned section Where very little or no light has been absorbed, practically no tanning results Such areas will imbibe water to saturation, and consequently will repel the ink completely. Thus where it is desired to print heavily, the exposure must be correspondingly heavy, and where it is desired to print lightly the exposure must be correspondingly light. This process is called "collotype" or "photo-gelatin" printing.

Exactly in the manner that carbro is related to carbon, bromoil is related to collotype. An ordinary bromide enlargement is treated with a solution that causes a reaction between the silver of the image and the dichromate. This forms chromic salts in situ with the image, causing a local image-wise tanning. The tanned portions will absorb printing inks, while the non-tanned portions will repel the ink. Pinatype is the exact reverse of this, for in pinatype the tanned portions repelling or not absorbing water will remain relatively uncolored when treated with colored aqueous solutions. In this scheme, where it is desired to have blacks, it is necessary to have little or no silver, and where whites are desired, it is necessary to have considerable silver To make positive prints by this method the image that is to be treated with the dichromate solution must be a negative, hence the printing should be done from positives, unless the original exposure could serve.

The study of carbon could be divided into three distinct sections. One section could deal with the preparation of the tissue A second section would deal with sensitization The third section would deal with the application to reproduction processes

The first attempts utilized plain gelatin It was soon discovered that gelatin is a variable substance and that if any semblance of regularity was to be obtained, other additions would have to be made. It was pointed out above that Sir Joseph Swan added sugar to give the gelatin some desired properties This was more or less a fixture afterward, although corn syrup and other polyhydric alcohols could also be used In his description of the technique used for making the first photograph in color ever to be made, Ducos du Hauron (cf. above) did not give any detailed information concerning the preparation of the tissue. He described it as consisting of a film of pigmented dichromated gelatin coated on a transparent base such as mica or collodion. The printing was done by contact, through the base· In 1897 ("La triplice photographique des Couleurs et l'Imprimerie," 1897, p 261) the brother of the du Hauron who did all the work, published a book on color reproduction, dealing with his brother's contributions Du Hauron noted that the blue monochrome image printed much deeper than the other colors, and he correctly attributed this to the fact that this tissue did not restrain the printing light as much as did either the red or the yellow. To overcome the defect he added a yellow dye, which was water-soluble, and which would be removed in toto upon development of the image He was quite impressed with the improvement this step made in his pictures, and he took out a patent in order to fix the date of his discovery (Fr P. 173012, December 18, 1885) The idea of adding non-actinic, light-restraining dyes to the tissue was patented time and time again Considerably later, F E. Ives and E. J Wall carried on quite a controversy on the matter of priority (*Brit. J Phot.*, Vol. 69 (1922), pp 27, 119, 206, and 286). The Lumières suggested that silver halide salts could act in the same manner (Eng. P. 7188/95; Fr. P. 245948, Ger. P. 94052) Von Hubl made the same suggestion in his book "Die Dreifarbenphotographie" (1897) It appears again in the disclosures of L. Vidal (*Bull. Soc. franç Phot.*, Vol. 41 (1899), pp 306, 486, 538), in his recommendation that Eastman film could be used. A somewhat different use of silver halide was suggested by A. Hoffmann (Ger. P. 113982). He made the salts serve as actinometers for the carbon printing, a fact that was previously disclosed by V. Matthieu and F. Dery (U.S.P. 624837; Eng. P. 17758/94; Bel. P. 138556, 138557, 138558, 138559)

The self-preparation of pigmented tissue is now no longer necessary, since the material is being supplied by several large firms. However, as supplied today, the pigmented tissue contains relatively coarse and not too transparent coloring matter. This introduces serious problems that are only partially solved by the technique of masking Efforts are constantly being made to improve this, but up to this writing little progress seems to have been made. It appears that the manufacturer of pigmentt issue has centered his attention upon the preparation of frill-proof material, accepting the pigments made for the printing-ink industry There are several hints, however, that at long-last the chemical aspects of the problem are receiving attention Until there is available tissue having the transparency of a film that has been dyed with a substantive color, the problem cannot be considered solved Prof. Wall is quite partial to the technique outlined by J. C. Arch (*Brit. J. Phot*, Vol 67 (1920), Color Supp., p. 33; Wall's "History of Three-Color Photography," p 331), for the general method of preparing the tissue.

The requisite quantity of pigment (40 grains chrome yellow for the yellow, 18 grains alizarin crimson for the magenta, and a mixture of 4 grains of Prussian blue and 6 of ultramarine blue for the cyan) is dispersed in one ounce of water, by the slow addition of water to the pigment, followed by vigorous shaking These colors are then put aside for several hours, with an occasional shaking to prevent flocculation. The dispersed pigment is finally added to a solution of four ounces of water containing 60 minims of glycerin and a half ounce of gelatin, that had been soaking in the mixture for several hours The gelatin is melted by warming on a hot water bath, after which the solution is filtered through muslin. Water is added to make a final volume of five ounces. Since the solution will not keep well, it should be used within a few days of preparation. It is coated upon a paper base, using 3½ ounces for every 100 square inches of surface.

In this formula no use was made of a light-restraining dye, since the tissue was to be sensitized by bathing prior to use. The light-restrainer could be added to the sensitizing solution The Lumière brothers exhibited some carbon prints in the Paris exhibition of 1900, and the following year gave full details as to the method they used for the preparation (*Bull. Soc. franç Phot*, Vol. 43 (1901), pp. 204, 303, 441). At this point our interest lies in the tissue itself.

A sheet of glass was polished, then coated with a film of collodion prepared as follows:

Pyroxylin (gun cotton)	10 parts
Castor oil	2.5 parts
Alcohol	500 parts
Ether	500 parts

After drying, the collodion film was placed in a solution of 7 per cent gelatin, together with a sheet of the paper that served as the base. The two were drawn out together, squeegeed, and allowed to dry. The paper was then given a coat of shellac, and dried again. The sensitized dichromate solution was coated over the shellac. This was prepared as follows: 120 parts each of glue and gelatin were soaked in 100 parts water for 12 hours, then melted by heating to 50 or 60 C. The solution was cooled to 35 C, and 60 parts of ammonium dichromate added, followed in turn, after complete solution, by 10 parts of neutral potassium citrate, one of cochineal red, and 500 of alcohol. After filtering, it was coated on the paper, 65 cc being allowed for every 1000 square centimeters After drying, which should be at a temperature not higher than 20 C the paper could be stripped from the glass plate. Drying should be as even as possible, as otherwise the sensitivity of the emulsion would be uneven

The use of pigment dispersions yields tissues that have relatively large particle sizes A much better procedure would be to dye the gelatin with a color that would be insensitive to the processing chemicals. One method of accomplishing this is to disperse a mordant in the gelatin solution, then treat with a basic dye This will give a tissue composed of dyed gelatin rather than one containing a dispersion of pigment particles in gelatin Two patents along this line were issued to Dr Merrill Seymour and assigned to the Eastman Kodak Company (U S.P. 1984090, 2043905). Two solutions are needed.

Solution A

Gelatin, 12½% solution	40 parts
Water	30 parts
Basic dye, 1% solution	20 parts
Silver nitrate, 10% solution	15 parts

Solution B

Potassium iodide, 10% solution	18 parts
Water	22 parts

Solution *B* is added slowly to Solution *A* This yields a silver-iodide emulsion prepared in the presence of an excess of iodide ions. For that reason it is somewhat hard to understand why the halide solution is added to the silver nitrate For the emulsion to be substantive to basic dyes, it is necessary for the grains to have a negative charge, such as is obtained when they are formed with an excess of halide ions present. In the above case, this condition will hold only toward the end of the addition. Previous to that the grains will be formed in the presence of silver ions, so will carry a positive charge and will not react with basic dyes. After mixing, the emulsion is set, shredded, washed, melted, then coated so that 10 cc will cover an area 5 by 7 inches.

A mordant that is much more efficient than silver iodide is copper thiocyanate. If it is prepared in the presence of a ten per cent solution of thiocyanate, it remains as a true colloidal dispersion that is practically completely transparent If silver iodide be prepared under the same conditions, a similar situation holds The ability of such silver salt hydrosols to fix basic dyes, is enormous; and the dyed gelatin is completely transparent. Hence their use for the formation of pigment tissue should be of great interest All the information obtained in the dye-toning processes becomes applicable here. Especially useful would be the indigosols or other soluble salts of the esters of the vat dyes. The soluble salts could be dissolved in the gelatin solution. In such cases a true solution of the dye-former is made. By treatment with proper agents the insoluble vat dye will be precipitated in an extremely fine dispersion. B. Wendt disclosed a technique along these lines when he dispersed the ester of the leuco form of a dye in a dichromated carrier (Ger P. 499481; Fr P. 696641) O Loisa dispersed a mordant and dye in the dichromated emulsion, along the lines of the Seymour disclosure (Ger. P. 465459). Applicable here are all the dodges outlined by the I G, Ansco, Dr. Gaspar, and by the other technicians who developed diffusedly colored monopack layers.

The keeping qualities of a sensitized gelatin layer are very poor, therefore it is best to sensitize the tissue a short time before use. The sensitivity of a film varies considerably the first eight or ten hours, hence a safe rule is to let the tissue age at least twelve hours before use. What change takes place after that will be gradual and within reason The simplest method for sensitizing a gelatin layer is to bathe it for several minutes in a dichromate solution varying in strength from two to ten per cent. The weaker bath yields a more contrasty, though slower, emulsion. Any salt of the dichromate ion could be used, but potassium or ammonium appears to be the most popular. Somewhat better results are obtained if the solution is treated with ammonia in a quantity sufficient to turn the orange into a lemon yellow, or until the odor of ammonia becomes quite discernible. Better keeping qualities result if some citric acid is present, although the improvement is obtained at the expense of the speed A good working formula along these lines is given in Wall and Jordan's "Photographic Facts and Formulas" (1940), page 235:

Potassium dichromate	20.0 parts
Citric acid	5.0 parts
Ammonia sufficient to give a distinct odor	
Water to	1000 parts

Sensitize for three minutes at 60 F

To overcome the lengthy time required for soft gelatin layers to dry, it has been proposed to add substances to the sensitizing bath which would evaporate very quickly A six-per-cent solution of dichromate is diluted with alcohol or acetone to make a final dichromate concentration of 2.4 per cent Since this solution is imbibed very much more slowly than a pure water solution, the time of sensitization should be increased to five or, preferably, ten minutes. The new bath will not keep for any length of time, so it should be prepared just before use, then discarded.

The sensitivity of a dichromated gelatin is very low, about that of a printing-out paper. This is not to be wondered at, since the final product is exactly that which is formed by the photo-chemical reaction. There is no great intensification factor such as is obtained in developing-out emulsions, where a silver halide grain containing at least 20,000,000 molecules of silver halide becomes developable by the absorption of approximately 200 quanta of light. The developing technique thus intensifies the direct photo-chemical reaction by a factor of 100,000. Fast negative emulsions will have a factor of 10,000,000.

Many efforts were made to increase the sensitivity of the dichromate, either by some addition to the sensitizing solution, or by some secondary chemical reaction which involved the products of the primary photo-chemical action. This has not been studied in any great detail, and not too much is known concerning the mechanism But this much is well established. The chromium in a dichromate ion is in the hexavalent condition and is reduced very easily to the trivalent form In vitro this is accomplished in acid solution by very mild reducing agents. It is therefore not surprising that light also could effect such a reduction, especially if other oxidizable substances are present. In such cases the solution no longer need be acid, but can be neutral or mildly alkaline. When the desired secondary reaction is the tanning of gelatin, albumen, shellac, etc., by the trivalent chromium formed by the light action, it is highly desirable that the pH be not on the acid side which favors the decomposition $Cr^{6+} \rightarrow Cr^{3+}$. The degree of tanning of the organic colloid is a maximum when the pH is above 7.0. The optimum conditions for the two conditions are antagonistic, so that only a compromise could be achieved between maximum photo-chemical sensitivity and maximum tanning of the gelatin.

Such a compromise could be achieved by the addition of salts to the sensitizing bath, which will intensify the secondary reaction. Sometime in the eighteen-fifties, Robert Hunt suggested the addition of copper sulphate. Benham (*Photogram*, Vol. 6 (1899), p. 24), and Phillipe (Fr. P. 112072) also used a similar combination, not in an effort to aid the tanning of gelatin, but rather to increase the light-sensitivity of the sensitized film. A. Thiebau (*La Phot.* (1908), p. 227) used both copper sulphate and manganese or cobalt salts, thus

Ammonium dichromate	90 parts
Copper sulphate	45 parts
Manganese sulphate	10 parts
Water to	1000 parts

or

Potassium dichromate	100 parts
Cobalt chloride	80 parts
Manganese sulphate	20 parts
Water to	1000 parts

As with the previous disclosures, these sensitizing solutions were not meant for the formation of tanned gelatin images, but for the aniline process. However, the effect of adding copper salts to a dichromate solution very often results in the formation of a much firmer tanned image. Much more recently W. Wadhams, A. Ziehm, H. A. Sonderman, and P. Worthe (Eng P. 228377) disclosed several sensitizing formulas that gave much higher sensitivities The first contained only inorganic substances, while the second contained aniline hydrochloride, concerning which more will be said below.

1.	Potassium dichromate	30 parts
	Magnesium chloride	10 parts
	Sodium acid phosphate	5 parts
	Water to	1000 parts
2.	Aniline hydrochloride	2 parts
	Sodium acid phosphate	5 parts
	Magnesium chloride	10 parts
	Water to	1000 parts

After everything is completely dissolved, add thirty parts of potassium dichromate.

After a study of the dichromate process, E. Valenta and J. M. Eder (*La Procede*, (1919), p. 132) and I. Cherney (*Phot. Kino. Chem. Ind*, (1935), p. 28), came to the conclusion that the sensitivity is increased considerably by the addition of small quantities of cupric salts. R. Namias (*Bull. Soc. franç Phot*, (1919), p. 331) claims that the keeping properties are very much improved if carbonate is added

The effect of organic bases was studied by George Hauberrisser (*Phot. Korr.*, Vol. 44 (1907), p. 225), a full generation before Wadhams, Ziehm, Sonderman and Worthe (cf. above). A solution of potassium dichromate was first treated with ammonia until the orange color turned into a yellow. Then substances such as aniline, etc, which contained amino nitrogens, were added. In all cases there was obtained an increase in sensitivity, but always accompanied by a considerable reduction in the keeping properties. His exact procedure was the following: To a four per cent potassium dichromate solution was added sufficient ammonia to turn the color to a yellow To this was added an organic base. The substances, and the corresponding amounts used (per 1000 parts of solution), were

Alpha-naphthylamine	19 20 parts
Beta-naphthylamine	19 20 parts
Pyrazol	9 40 parts
Aniline	12 0 parts
Methyl amine	4.1 parts
Pyridine	10.7 parts

When diamines were used, the keeping qualities became impossible. Twenty-eight years later, the work was repeated by G. Maillet (*Bull. Soc franç. Phot.*, series 3, Vol. 22 (1935), p. 202, U S P. 2025996; Fr. P. 770593), but with some slight modifications. Either from ignorance, or purposely, no mention was made of the previous work. To make matters still worse, the paper was read before the Ninth International Congress of Photography in Paris, and no one remembered the previous work, or at least the discussion failed to bring any mention of it.

The clue which guided Mr. Maillet in his work was that slightly better results were obtained from ammonium dichromate than from the other salts He immediately ascribed the effect to a difference in the degree of hydrolysis which the various salts underwent. One of the products of the hydrolysis is chromic acid, a substance which is capable of destroying many organic substances. The problem was therefore to find bases stable to chromic acid Many of these were known, but not all of them could be used, since some formed very insoluble addition products with the acid. His search was therefore very much limited, and he finally centered his attention upon pyridine and quinoline.

It is possible to form several different complex salts of these bases with chromic acid, the exact type of complex being determined by the concentration of the substances used These were found to yield tissues requiring from half to a quarter of the exposure of the normal solution The particular combination of pyridine and chromic acid which Mr. Maillet adopted he called pyrax Equivalent concentrations of pyrax and ammonium dichromate gave pH's of 1.75 and 4.00 respectively, indicating that pyrax hydrolyzed to a much greater degree than did ammonium dichromate. However, pH is not the whole answer, for buffering an ammonium dichromate solution to the same pH did not give identical results It may be that the actual photochemical reaction has been increased, but that the tanning action has been decreased; whereas in the case of pyrax, this tanning action is favorably affected by the pyridine. The best solution adopted was to add 15 cc of a 20 per cent pyridine solution and 30 cc of an 8 per cent pyrax solution, to 200 cc of a 5 per cent albumen solution The mix must be prepared just before use, as its keeping qualities are poor This solution does not differ markedly from the disclosures of Hauberrisser Also the disclosure by Wadhams, Ziehm, Sonderman, and Worthe, especially in their second and more sensitive formula, appears to follow along the same lines of reasoning. Both of these preceded the Maillet work.

Outside of the problem of general sensitivity, comes the problem of color sensitivity. This was solved for the photographic emulsion by Vogel, who discovered that many dyes united with the silver halide grain to yield light-sensitive systems whose range of action has been extended beyond 520 mμ, the limit of silver bromide sensitivity. Two papers by G. O't Hooft (*Phot Korr.*, Vol. 67 (1931), p. 72; *Zeit. wiss. Phot.*, Vol 28; *Brit J. Phot.*, Vol. 85 (1938), p 229; cf also J. S. Friedman, *Am Phot*, Jan 1939) deal with this subject In the second paper, Hooft describes a procedure for the color sensitization of a dichromated gelatin If a gelatin layer sensitized by dichromate be bathed with a solution of malachite green containing one gram of dye in three liters of water, the plate will become red-sensitive, and the exposure time will be approximately one-tenth that of the untreated plate.

In the other paper Mr. Hooft discusses some work previously reported by A. A Meisling (cf. "Eder's Ausführliche Handbuch der Photographie," (1917) Band 4, Teil 7). It is claimed that a gelatin layer bathed with a 0.1 per cent solution of auramine or erythrosin will become light-sensitive, a tanning taking place where light is absorbed. It is claimed that under the influence of light, formaldehyde is formed by the photo-chemical destruction of the dye This unites with the gelatin to form leather. Hooft tested a series of dyes by bathing a fixed plate with a 1:5000 dye bath, containing one cc of concentrated ammonia per 500 cc of solution. The exposure should be made while still wet, since then the sensitivity is a maximum. The results of these experiments are tabulated below, the number indicating the step that is just visible after processing as in carbon.

Victoria blue	0	Brilliant acid green	7
Uranin	2	Ethyl violet	8
Guinea fast red	3	Naphthaline green	9
Malachite green	3	Brilliant silk blue	9
Fuchsin	4	Erythrosin	10
Auramin	4	Eosin	11
Acid violet	5	Methylene blue	11
Ethyl cyanine	6	Rose bengal	11
Pinatype green D	7	Rhodamine	11

Many of these dyes contain free or substituted amino groups, hence should form complexes or salts with ammonium dichromate or chromic acid, much in the manner of naphthylamine or pyridine. The increased sensitivity in a carbon emulsion due to bathing with malachite green may well be due to some such action. Or it is possible that a sort of supersensitizing effect is obtained such as has been reported by Mees for the case of normal photography. He found that by mixing two sensitizing dyes of special type, he obtained an increase in total sensitivity far beyond the amount obtained were the dyes used individually. If the supersensitization idea is the correct one, then dyes such as rose bengal, rhodamine, methylene blue or eosin should be even more effective than malachite green

This reaction has been utilized to yield direct positives, a procedure described by Hooft in his *British Journal of Photography* article. He sensitized a silver-halide emulsion, specifically a sheet of enlarging paper, with ammonium dichromate and exposed it under a negative. After washing and drying he gave the entire sheet a flash exposure and developed normally in a paper developer. An image identical with the negative resulted. It appeared that the original exposure under the negative created insensitive or desensitized spots, which did not form a latent image when flash-exposed Hence the developed image corresponded to the original.

Several explanations were offered to explain this phenomenon It might be supposed that as a result of the exposure a tanned gelatin image resulted which prevented the absorption of developer solution, hence prevented the formation of a silver image This explanation has some experimental proof in the practice of the pinatype process, and in many procedures for the preparation of screen plates (cf chapter on Screen Plates). In these techniques a dichromated gelatin is exposed to light and the exposed portions become incapable of absorbing aqueous solutions of certain dyes This effect is definitely due to the tanning of gelatin since tanned gelatin has properties identical with light-exposed dichromated gelatin However, alkaline solutions will penetrate even into highly tanned gelatin, so it would not be expected that the loss of imbibing power would apply to a very strongly alkaline developer solution

Another explanation, and one favored by Hooft, is that one product of the photo-chemical reduction of dichromates is free chromic acid, which in this case would immediately destroy the sensitivity centers of the silver halide emulsion Thus, a subsequent exposure to light would prevent the formation of a latent image in these areas. In a discussion of this phenomenon J. S. Friedman (*Amer. Phot*, Jan. 1939) pointed out that if this theory is correct, a better procedure would be to give the silver halide emulsion a flash exposure first, an exposure sufficient to give as deep a black as is required were it processed normally. The sheet containing an over-all latent image is then sensitized with dichromate and exposed under a negative. Now the latent image will act as an acceptor for the chromic acid This should be very favorable for the reaction since one of the products would be constantly and immediately removed. The intensifying action of malachite green could be utilized in connection with this technique

The photo-chemical reaction plays only a small part in photography, but it is an extremely important reaction in the photomechanical industry. Most of the work has been done with photoengraving in mind. The interested reader should turn his attention to the work done in this field, to learn the latest developments.

The application of carbon procedure to photography is manifold As pointed out above it was only after a technique that retained all highlights was worked out, that a successful application could be obtained. This was accomplished when it was discovered that tanned gelatin would be retained by clean surfaces By bringing the exposed surface in contact with a polished one it became possible to dissolve away non-image portions which had not been tanned. It was also desirable to be able to remove the tanned image from this surface. This was achieved by polishing the support with wax. Many formulas have been listed for such a polishing wax, and a very useful one has been published by Wall in several of his publications.

Beeswax	20 parts
Resin	20 parts
Turpentine	1000 parts

The wax should be melted in a water bath, and when completely liquid, the resin is added, after which the turpentine is put in. A clear solution should result.

The polished surface upon which the image is transferred is a celluloid sheet approximately ten to twenty thousandths of an inch thick, and several inches larger than the tissue. Just before use it is given a wax polish When it is to be used for the first time it is washed with soap and water, then dried. It is finally given a wax polish by rubbing in a half-teaspoonful of the waxing solution per 16 by 20 inch celluloid.

The manipulations of actual picture formations are exceedingly simple. The exposed tissue and the waxed cell are brought together under water, the two withdrawn, and the tissue is squeegeed thoroughly upon the cell. Care should be taken to insure that it is the exposed side of the tissue that is in contact with the cell. After the squeegeeing, the combination is set aside for a period of ten to twenty minutes. During this time the tissue dries out somewhat The image-bearing portions, being formed of tanned gelatin, probably dry out sufficiently to become quite polished and the adhesion between the two is probably closely akin to that which exists between two highly polished surfaces in contact, such as in Johannsen blocks. The water used for bringing tissue and cell together should be as air-free as possible, for otherwise there will be formed a mottling which is caused by air suddenly released from the moist tissue.

After being in contact for about twenty minutes the combination is placed in hot water at a temperature of approximately 120 F (50 C) After resting there a short while, the pigment will be seen to ooze out along the edges. At this point the paper backing is removed, and the hot water wash continued until a clean image remains. A rinse in cold water sets the image, and the celluloid is put up to dry in a clean place. The drying should be uniform, otherwise the image will have a tendency to shrink or stretch differentially.

Three such images are prepared, one in each of the fundamental colors. The next step is to assemble them upon the same piece of white paper, in exact registry. There are two procedures in common use, one called the single-transfer, the other the double-transfer method. In the single-transfer technique, the permanent support, a sheet of paper carrying a layer of tanned gelatin, is soaked in water for half an hour. The celluloid carrying the most opaque of the three images is placed in the same water, and the two are withdrawn together, with the gelatin side of the support in contact with the image on the cell. The intervening water is squeegeed out carefully, the pressure being very light for the first few strokes, then increasing in intensity. After the squeegeeing is complete, the sandwich is set aside to dry. The contraction that takes place when the paper dries, is sufficient to cause the tanned image to transfer to the paper. What is more probable is that a fusion takes place between the gelatin of the support and the gelatin of the image, so that the force of contraction of the drying paper is transferred to the image and it is actually pulled away from the waxed celluloid. The dried support carrying the first image is rubbed over lightly with turpentine to remove any adhering wax. The procedure is repeated with the other two images in succession.

In the double-transfer process, the only difference is that the paper carries a soft gelatin layer. In this condition it is known as a temporary support. Now, instead of using the most opaque of the images for the first transfer, it is the most transparent that is used. When all three images have been assembled and dried, the surface of the image is again treated with turpentine to remove any adherent wax, and a thoroughly soaked sheet of permanent support (paper carrying a tanned gelatin layer) is placed in contact with the image. After twenty minutes of contact, during which time considerable drying takes place, the new sandwich is placed in hot water, and after a while the paper backing of the temporary support is removed

It is not surprising to note that the carbon process has been patented to death and that the same idea or modification has been claimed time and time again, making it extremely difficult to determine the true originator of any single device. However, it is quite safe to say that du Hauron recognized and pointed out most of the little tricks that others claimed at later periods. He was the first to make a print in color in carbon, so it must not be wondered at that he should be the first to realize the faults and to suggest remedies. He specifically mentions the use of a light-restrainer for the tissues other than the yellow, realizing that too deep a penetration of the printing light will cause too high a relief. He used a water-soluble yellow dye, fuchsin yellow or yellow corallin, for this purpose. The dye washed out during processing so that it did not interfere with the magenta and cyan images. Ives later claimed priority in this field because he used it for the preparation of colorless reliefs, using unpigmented tissues, whereas du Hauron used pigmented tissues. But this is a trivial modification.

The Lumière brothers (cf. above) utilized a silver-halide emulsion rather than pigmented gelatin, the silver halide acting as a light-restrainer. Here again we have a trivial modification of an old idea, and one which does not accomplish its purpose as well as the other. One could see some originality were the silver halide later used for image-forming purposes, either by dye or chemical toning, or by color development, but this very interesting possibility seemed to have escaped the experimenters of that period The quality of a carbon image is remarkably fine. The colors used in pigmenting the tissues are extremely poor. But dyes are and were then known that were far superior to any of the available pigments What could be simpler than to print a lantern plate by the dichromate process, form an image composed of silver bromide imbedded in tanned gelatin, convert the silver bromide to silver iodide or metallic silver, and then tone chemically or by means of a mordant?

The other possibility, that of forming a relief image, removing the silver halide entrapped in the relief, then dyeing with gelatin staining dyes, was suggested early and often. H C Bond made the suggestion in his English patent 13,301/88. The Lumières showed some prints at the Paris Exhibition of 1900 which created quite a sensation. These were made by dyeing colorless reliefs. Their directions called for the following baths:

Magenta	
Erythrosin J, 3% solution	25 parts
Water to	1000 parts
Cyan	
Diamine blue F pure, 3% solution	50 parts
Hard glue, 15% solution	70 parts
Water to	1000 parts
Yellow	
Chrysophenin G	4 parts
Water	1000 parts
Dissolve at 70 C, then add alcohol	200 parts

With the exception of the yellow, the dye baths are very weak, and it is small wonder that hours were required for complete staining After dyeing, the part images were given a bath in 5 per cent copper sulphate solution to fix the dye, then they were dried, stripped, and assembled.

L Didier (*Phot. Revue*, Vol. 12 (1900), p. 73) introduced a new wrinkle, also quite trivial, when he used printing-out paper for his tissue The paper was first given an over-all exposure to light until it was chocolate-colored. The colloidal silver image served as a light-restrainer in the next step, sensitization with dichromate. After exposure, the paper was etched to yield a brown image of colloidal silver in tanned gelatin. He also missed a point when he failed to utilize the silver for color formation. He preferred to remove it with ferricyanide and hypo, after which he dyed the colorless reliefs with auramin for the yellow, Prussian blue for the cyan, and rhodamine for the magenta.

Some idea of the position that carbon occupied in the field of color reproduction might be inferred from the voluminous literature on the subject. The patent literature could be discounted to a large extent in so far as any practical disclosures are concerned. They rehash old ideas, dressing them up in some fancy clothes. Ives was a prolific patentee, and, according to Wall ("History of Three-Color Photography") he claimed priority in several phases of this subject without regard to the previous history (U S P. 960939, 980962, 1122935, 1145143; Eng. P 21410/09, 17799/13; Ger P. 305752; Fr. P. 461078). However, his disclosures stamp him as a keen student of color photography, and as a person whose views merit study. In 1894 (*J. Cam. Club*, Vol. 9 (1894), p. 63) he proposed the use of unpigmented gelatin coated on celluloid, and exposed through the back. After development by hot water, the relief image was dyed up. This simple procedure soon proved impractical. The celluloid base was not completely shrinkproof, and had a tendency to buckle when superimposed, especially when used as lantern slides. A second flaw arose from the fact that the reliefs were too heavy to give pleasing contrasts after dyeing. The first flaw was apparently overcome by the use of amyl acetate base rather than nitro cellulose. This contained no camphor which evaporated slowly, hence did not shrink unevenly. The relief problem was partly solved by the use of fish glue, although he later solved this completely by the incorporation of non-actinic light-absorbing substances, such as silver-halide salts, yellow dyes, etc. He also claimed that an after-treatment of the relief with chromic acid gave improved sharpness. The reliefs were dyed in Neptune green, rhodamine and eosin, and brilliant yellow for the cyan, magenta, and yellow images respectively.

Another person whose opinions were worthy of note was von Hubl, who published probably the best description of the carbon process (*Phot. Rund.*, 1899, *Brit. J. Phot*, Vol 46 (1899), p. 409, 470, 537; "Three-Color Photography" (1915)). Here again gelatin, to which is added an inert material such as silver bromide, is used for the tissue. This, mixed with dichromate, is coated on paper, dried, exposed, transferred, and developed in the normal manner of a carbon print The silver bromide which is retained in the carbon relief, is fixed out with hypo after a treatment with ferricyanide, since the long exposure required must of necessity have formed photolytic silver. Von Hubl recognized that the dyeing of gelatin was something more than mere absorption by a spongy material, for he soon discovered that not all dyes were capable of permanently staining this colloid. The eosins, rhodamines, and most of the sulphonated dyes stained gelatin well, especially from an acidulated bath.

The dye baths which von Hübl recommended were the following:

Magenta	
Erythrosin	0.5 part
Alcohol	100 parts
Water to	1000 parts
Cyan	
Bluish fast green	1.0 part
Alcohol	100 parts
Acetic acid	6 parts
Water to	1000 parts
Yellow	
Naphthol yellow SL	0 5 part
Alcohol	100 parts
Acetic acid	6 parts
Chrome alum, saturated solution	50 parts
Water to	1000 parts

Weak dye baths were preferable since the more concentrated solutions stained the whites long before the shadows were sufficiently dyed.

It was mentioned above that most of the patent literature did not give much new material, but merely dressed up old stuff in new clothes. However, some of the disclosures give ideas that might be worthy of some consideration, while others are obviously intended to build up a certain position in the industry. The opacity of the pigments used for making the tissue was quite bothersome, and resulted in considerable falsification of colors. Pfenninger and Townsend (Eng. P. 26608/10) attempted to improve this by putting down a fourth impression made from a combination of the separation negatives. Thus, if the greens come too dark and the reds too light, a fourth impression is made from a negative that is the combination of the green and blue separations. This is an obvious attempt at masking, although a faulty one. It must be realized that this may give better reds, but at the expense of everything else

Another scheme to obviate the mistakes arising from the lack of transparency, was made by J. Sury and E. Bastyns (Eng. P. 2128/09). These men perforated the three part-images, then, after assembly, put the print under pressure. This forced the pigment of one part-image into the holes in the others, giving a mixing of the colors. But they overlooked one important thing. The perforations formed a sort of half tone so that after pressure had been applied a mosaic of juxtaposed color dots formed the final image. To the extent that these dots did not overlap, the procedure operated along additive rather than subtractive principles, and to that extent falsification of color reproduction took place. A more direct procedure along the same lines was disclosed by L. C Lesage in 1902 (Fr P. 326298) He printed his carbon images through a halftone screen. Now the printing could be deep enough to extend to the base of the tissue, hence it was no longer necessary to print from the back side. The mixture of subtractive and additive processes made this technique as false as the other.

Other special techniques were described by J. W. Bennetto (Eng. P. 28920/97) who used a tissue with three wide color bands. The images were printed upon the bands, which were then folded over toward the centre to form the composite picture. A. Gleichmar (Eng. P. 148737, Dan. P. 27784) had a similar idea. A Blachorovitsch used three carbon tissues superimposed upon each other (Fr P 353420) in the form of a monopack, to be exposed in the camera. Since at that time (1905) it was not possible to color-sensitize carbon tissue, this disclosure was of only theoretical interest. In a companion patent (Fr P. 355385) he incorporated a silver halide emulsion with the pigment and utilized the light-sensitive properties of the silver for exposing. Development with pyro ammonia gave a tanned gelatin image Here again the three tissues were superimposed to form a monopack, but here again he failed to incorporate sensitizing dyes to make his emulsions color active. Hence a very good idea fell flat. R. Krayn used carbon for making colored lantern slides. Two images were printed on glass, the third one on a thin base of celluloid (Eng. P. 10003/00; Ger. P. 123016). This minimized the separation in space of the part-images, making for crisper pictures. H. C. J. Deeks commercialized a carbon process under the name of Raylo (U.S.P. 1430059, 1430060, 1430061;

Eng. P. 189844, 190424; Fr. P. 533633; Ger. P. 378960). About the only thing of note is that he took a lesson from the makers of screen plates, forming his pigments by atomizing dyed alcoholic solutions of gum. A. R. Lawshe (U S P 1248139, Eng. P. 131319) used a bipack negative which he printed on two carbon tissues coated on celluloid These were cemented together to form the final image. Much later, Technicolor adopted a similar idea, but used a silver-halide emulsion to form the relief. E. A. Burchardt (*Brit. J. Phot.*, Vol 54 (1907), Col. Supp., p. 25; Vol. 59 (1912), Col. Supp., p. 26) used a sensitive size which he brushed over the paper. This size was made of

Sugar	152 parts
Water to	1000 parts

To this was added 42 parts of hard gelatin. After swelling, the mixture was heated on a water bath to melt the gelatin. To this was added a paste containing the pigments. The cyan had the composition

French blue	23 5 parts
Aureoline	15 7 parts
Ammonium dichromate	15.7 parts
Glycerin	62 parts

For the magenta he replaced the pigments listed above by alizarin crimson (5.25 parts) and French blue (1.75 parts). For the yellow he replaced the pigments with aureoline (15.7 parts) and aurora yellow (5.25 parts).

The paper was sensitized by brushing with one of the above mixtures. After exposure it was developed in water at 32 C, dried, and then painted with the following solution

Uncolored gelatin-sugar solution (cf above)	666 parts
Water	334 parts
Ammonium dichromate	11 parts

The next "color" size was then brushed on, and the procedure repeated until three images were formed

Burchardt was not the first one to suggest the repeated recoating of a carbon tissue G. Selle (U S P. 604269; Eng P. 7104/95, Fr P 246517; Ger. P. 101132), (cf also U S.P 654776; Eng. P. 4290/99; Ger. P 117134) had suggested this as far back as 1895, and doubtless he was not the first In English patent 12517/99 he proposed that the exposed and tanned gelatin could act as a mordant for certain dyes (cf. chapter on Dye Toning) The idea cropped up several more times, E. R. Clarke (Eng P 9184/02), B. Bechtler (Ger. P. 272666), Sury and Bastyns (Bel. P. 209468, 212155), and Ives (cf above) all utilizing the same technique, modifying it sufficiently to pass the rather sympathetic hearts of patent examiners.

No description of the carbon process could be complete without mention of the work of L. Vidal who exhibited some remarkable prints at a very early date in "carbon" history. His procedure was described enthusiastically by

T. Sutton in the *British Journal of Photography* (Vol 20 (1873), pp. 385, 464, 488, 521; Vol. 24 (1877), p 6, Vol. 25 (1878), p. 84; U.S.P. 178210; Fr P. 97446, 102415). But Eder in his *Handbuch*, Vol. 4 (1917), part II, page 204, claimed that these were chromolithographs with a carbon gray key plate over them. The method for making his tissues was described in the *British Journal of Photography*, Vol. 49 (1902), page 1002. The team of Sury and Bastyns has done considerable work in carbon They used carbon in combination with other techniques, especially cyanotype for the cyan image (Bel. P. 215338, 215339, 223732, 224641, 246084). This had been previously suggested by many others, among whom were W. A. Brewerton (*Phot. Mitt.*, Vol 34 (1901), p 468), W. C South (U.S P 769773, 827188; Eng P 128/03; Fr. P. 328228), Volback (Ger. P 360631, 361679), and A Wohler (Ger. P. 367928) C. S. Forbes modified this somewhat by toning one of the images (Eng. P 198245). L. Dufay, of Dufaycolor fame, first printed one image in silver, toned it, then sensitized with dichromate for the other two images (Fr. P. 571111). L. J. B. Didier (U.S.P. 1790978, Eng. P. 306328, Fr. P. 664803 to Splendicolor), used a duplitized film having a silver emulsion on one side and a plain gelatin emulsion on the other One image was formed by means of the silver, after which the two layers were sensitized with bichromate and the remaining two images printed by the carbon technique. Evidently the coloring itself was accomplished by the use of pinatype dyes. P. Lessertisseux (U.S P. 2008457) also used duplitized film, but he had silver-halide emulsions on both sides. The third color he put on by means of a dichromate printing. Others using double coated film were C. Roehrich (U S P. 1843001), the Projector A. G. Company of Germany (Ger. P. 489228, 536402), and K. Wahl (Eng. P. 306026).

A different use of the dichromate reaction was utilized by M G Bizot (Eng. P. 440448, Fr. P. 775222). He claimed that after exposure the exposed portions were unable to act as a mordant for certain dyes

Substances other than gelatin, gum arabic, etc , could be used in connection with the carbon process. W. T. L. Becker and L W. Oliver (U.S.P. 1927356, Eng. P. 317909; Fr. P. 673816) proposed to use cellophane. The Colour Phot. Company of France also disclosed a similar idea (Fr P. 708638), as did J. Karafiat and J. Cerny (Eng. P. 409134). L Cristiani (Eng. P. 367386), proposed to sensitize cellulose hydrate, while S. G S. Decker (Eng. P. 379715) utilized viscose. He found that dyes such as alizarin S took only in the unexposed portions.

Interesting studies of the dichromated gelatin processes were published by many people, some of which are: "Density Law in Bichromated Gelatin Processes", Richter, (*Zeit wiss Phot*, Vol 23, p 61), "A Study of Bichromated Gelatin", H. M. Cartwright, (*Phot. J.*, 1923, p. 265); "Tanning of Bichromated Gelatin by Light", R. E. Liesegang, (*Phot. Korr.*, Vol. 62 (1926), p. 77); and "Sensitometry of Dichromated Gelatin", A. C. Hardy and F. H Perrin, (*Jour Frank. Inst.*, Vol. 205 (1928), p 197).

Closely allied to carbon is carbro. As mentioned above, its beginnings could be traced to Marion who found that the light-formed tanned gelatin image was transferable from the tissue in which it was formed, to another. In 1889 Howard Farmer disclosed that the silver of a photographic image was able to act upon dichromate to form a tanned gelatin image in situ with the silver. Manly combined this with the idea of image transfer, and succeeded in developing a new printing technique He merely replaced the action of light by a silver image. This enabled him to overcome the extreme slowness of dichromate printing, since he first printed his images upon ordinary enlarging paper. The bromide was then brought into intimate contact with a carbon tissue that contained dichromate and other chemicals capable of reacting with the silver The net result was that the silver in the bromide became oxidized or bleached, and an imagewise transfer of reduced dichromate was found in the tissue. The two were separated, and from this point on the tissue was treated exactly as if it were a carbon print. The "sensitizer" disclosed by Manly (Eng. P. 10026/98; Ger. P. 117829) was the following:

Potassium dichromate	6 6 parts
Potassium ferricyanide	6 6 parts
Potassium bromide	6 6 parts
Alum	3 3 parts
Citric acid	1 0 part
Water to	1000 parts

Manly called his procedure ozobrome. It did not immediately achieve success and soon died out. Later a similar procedure was introduced under the name Raydex, but again the technique did not receive much attention. In its third appearance, under the name carbro (carbon prints via bromide enlargements), the process became very popular, and in the period between World Wars I and II, was recognized as the finest color-print procedure in use. Its merited popularity is best attested to by the fact that at least five organizations made pigment tissues solely for this technique

As it is practiced currently, some changes were made in the sensitizing formula. Two schools of thought exist One uses a two-bath system for sensitizing the tissue, while the other uses a single bath However, the two-bath system appears to be losing out. In this scheme, the tissues are first soaked in a solution containing potassium ferricyanide and bromide, for several minutes, then after a slight draining off of excess liquid they are bathed for a half minute in a second solution containing potassium dichromate, chromic acid, and chrome alum The Autotype Company, a pioneer in this field, recommends stock solutions of the two be made

Stock Solution A

Potassium ferricyanide	100 parts
Potassium bromide	100 parts
Water to	1000 parts

Stock Solution B

Potassium dichromate	40 parts
Chromic acid	8.5 parts
Chrome alum	10–20 parts
Water to	1000 parts

For use, dilute each with four parts of water. It is seen that the chemicals present in the sensitized tissue are not far different from the ones originally disclosed by Manly. Instead of citric acid, we now have chromic, and instead of alum we have chrome alum. It is possible to change the quantity of acid to obtain flatter or more contrasty results.

Practically the same chemicals are involved in the one-bath system, which is compounded from three stock solutions, mixed just before use

Stock Solution A

Potassium ferricyanide	50 parts
Potassium dichromate	15 parts
Potassium bromide	50 parts
Water to	1000 parts

Stock Solution B

Chromic acid 1% solution

Stock Solution C

Formalin	50 parts
Water to	1000 parts

The working bath contains 200 parts of solution *A*, 125 parts of solution *B* and 20 parts of solution *C*. Only enough solution is mixed at any one time to process one set of tissues. The work can be made a routine. The tissues are introduced into the sensitizing baths at one-minute intervals. They are removed at one-minute intervals This time is sufficient to bring the tissue and bromide into intimate contact, or to transfer the tissue on to the celluloid Working in this manner it is possible to complete a set of images in a little more than one hour

The reactions that are involved in carbon or carbro are not very well understood, and it is mainly for that reason that no real study has been made of the chemistry involved It goes without saying that the end result is a union of chromic salts with gelatin, and that this probably has definite conditions for best results. The photographic technician contributed but little to a determination of these conditions, but these contributions could help in a determination of what is desirable. The problem involved here is different from that met when a chrome fixing bath is to be prepared, although here also we are dealing with chrome tanning. Before discussing the few clues offered by photography, it might be well to turn to the leather chemists and see what they have to offer. These men have made an intensive study of the problem This is discussed in a monograph written by E. W. Merry, entitled "The Chrome Tanning Process," and published in London by A. Harvey. There is an excellent elementary discussion of chrome tanning in a book by

John Arthur Wilson called "Modern Practice in Leather Manufacture," published by the Reinhold Publishing Corporation.

Any discussion of chrome tanning must be preceded by a résumé of the chemistry of the trivalent chromium salts. This is indeed complex But the effect of salts like oxalates, sulphites, etc., upon tanning, can only be understood when the effect upon the chromium ion is understood. Leather is tanned mainly by treating the hide with chrome liquors that have been made "basic." This has a peculiar technical meaning. The salts $CrCl_3 \cdot 6H_2O$, $CrCl_3 \cdot 5H_2O$, and $CrCl_3 \cdot 4H_2O$, according to the empirical chemical formula, should not differ from each other when dissolved in water. In each case we would expect that treatment with three equivalents of silver nitrate would bring down a precipitate of silver chloride that would correspond to three mols of chloride. This is true only for the first body, hexaquo chromi chloride. The second body will precipitate only two of the three chloride ions, while the third body will precipitate only one halogen, the other halogens existing in non-ionic or non-dissociable form. Compounds such as $CrCl_3 \cdot 5H_2O$ and $CrCl_3 \cdot 4H_2O$, show all three types of chemical bonds, ionic, co-valent, and co-ordinate. The union between the un-ionized halogens and the chromium is by means of a shared electron pair to which the chromium and the halogen each contribute one electron, hence this bond is co-valent. The union between the water and the chromium is also by means of an electron pair, but now the pair is contributed solely by the oxygen atom in the water molecule, hence this is a co-ordinate bond The complex ion composed of the chromium to which are attached six other groups by co-valent or co-ordinate bonds is held to the ionized or dissociable chloride ions, by means of electrovalences or ionic bonds.

Before the advent of the quantum theory, Werner proposed to explain the chemistry of those complexes by the statement that chromium has a co-ordinate number of 6, meaning that the trivalent chromium ion could attach six units that are either neutral or negative ions. The new complex so formed would act as a new "atom" whose charge would be the algebraic sum of the charges on the chromium and the attached groups. Today we explain the existence of co-ordinate number by means of the quantum theory. The trivalent chromium ion can add a shell of twelve electrons to achieve a stable electronic structure. These electrons can be contributed by the adsorption of electron-saturated bodies which have at least one pair of electrons that are not utilized in a chemical bond Water is such a body, the oxygen atom containing four electrons that are not utilized. This substance can attach itself to the chromium ion, the point of attachment being one of the electron pairs, which in that way forms a co-ordinate bond between the oxygen and the chromium. Six molecules of water attached to chromium satiate its desire for electrons, forming, at the same time, the new unit

$$\left[\begin{array}{ccc} H_2O & \searrow \quad \swarrow & OH_2 \\ H_2O & \rightarrow Cr \leftarrow & OH_2 \\ H_2O & \nearrow \quad \nwarrow & OH_2 \end{array}\right]^{+++}$$

which carries a charge of plus three, since water is electrically neutral We have drawn arrows from the oxygen atoms to the chromium to indicate that the chromium is the "acceptor" and oxygen the electron "donor" atom

The essential thing in the above process is that the chromium has achieved electronic stability by the accumulation of a shell of twelve electrons It is immaterial that the twelve electrons were contributed by six molecules of water. The contribution could be made by ions that are electronically stable. For instance, the chloride ion has an outermost shell that is complete, and stable, since the configuration is that of argon. Six such ions could form the shell that is required for stability, forming the complex

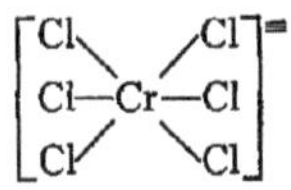

The chloride ion with its completed shell has a charge of minus one, so six chloride ions would contribute six negative charges to the complex. The chromium ion carries a charge of plus three, making the net charge on the complex to be minus three The union between the chromium and the six chloride ions is by means of shared electrons, by co-ordinate bond, so in solution the chloride ions will not be dissociated, hence not precipitable as silver chloride. Therefore, when a solution of tri sodium hexa chloro chromate, $Na_3[CrCl_6]$ is treated with silver nitrate, no precipitate of silver chloride will be formed.

Between the two extremes $[Cr6H_2O]^{+++}$ and $[CrCl_6]^{\equiv}$, we can have all the other possible structures. We can replace one of the water molecules by a chlorine to obtain the unit

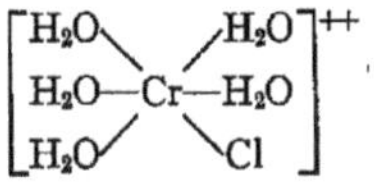

which carries a plus two charge, since the chlorine neutralizes one of the positive charges. We meet this structure in the compound $CrCl_3\ 5H_2O$, which should really be written $(CrCl \cdot 5H_2O)Cl_2$ The compound $CrCl_3\ 4H_2O$ should be written $(CrCl_2\ 4H_2O)Cl$. Now we can see just why but one of the halogens can be titrated with silver nitrate in the last compound named, and why two can be titrated in the pentaquo-compound.

The chemistry of the complexes is mainly the chemistry of an ion that has the electronic configuration as indicated above But superimposed upon this is a group of properties arising from the fact that the co-valent bonds between the chromium and the groups attached to it are not inviolate. The groups can be replaced by others, and in general give rise to a complicated equilibrium, changes in which give rise to apparent inconsistent reactions Many of the extreme points of view expressed by various leather technicians arise merely because of a failure to realize this possibility. The apparently diametrically opposite techniques adopted by many tanners is another manifestation of this phenomenon. We read statements that high acidity is needed for tanning, and yet we read that it is possible to tan with chromate salts, where the solutions are relatively alkaline.

One important reaction, from the tanner's point of view, is the replacement of one or more of the groups within the complex by hydroxy groups. The most general salt used for tanning is chrome alum, whose empirical formula is $Cr_2(SO_4)_3$ K_2SO_4 $24H_2O$. The tanning part of the molecule is $Cr_2(SO_4)_3$ $12H_2O$ and this can be broken down again in the following manner

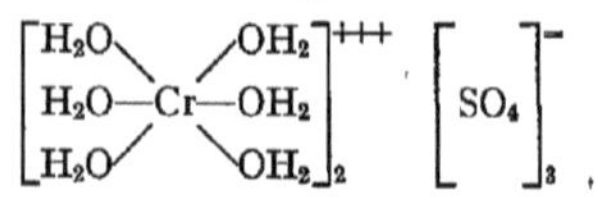

When chrome alum is freshly dissolved in water we have these ionic species present, and the pH of the solution in one per cent strength, is 2.81. Upon standing for four weeks, the pH of the solution falls to 2.12, and free acid can be detected. This free acid arises from a partial hydrolysis

$$[(H_2O)_6Cr]_2[SO_4]_3 \longrightarrow 2[(H_2O)_5CrOH]SO_4 + H_2SO_4$$

and the new complex has the structure

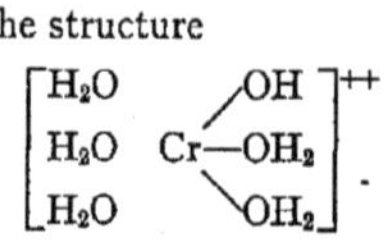

It is possible to neutralize the acidity that was formed by the hydrolysis, by adding alkali, and it is found that the released acid corresponds exactly to the equation given above. The substance chromic oxide, Cr_2O_3 is insoluble and it is formed as a gray precipitate when alkali is added to a solution of a chromic salt. Three equivalents of NaOH are required per equivalent of chromium In the case of chromic sulphate or chrome alum, we are dealing with two chromium ions, and it should require six equivalents of alkali to precipitate all the chromium. In the equation above, one molecule of sulphuric acid was liberated from one molecule of chrome alum. Since sulphuric acid is di-valent, and since chrome alum contains two chromium ions, one equivalent of acid was released per mol of chromium. After the neutralization of the released sulphuric acid, the solution is called $33\frac{1}{3}$ per cent basic, since the molecule is now $33\frac{1}{3}$ per cent along its path to conversion to Cr_2O_3.

The $33\frac{1}{3}$ per cent basic chrome alum solution upon standing will again generate acid, this time in accordance with the formula

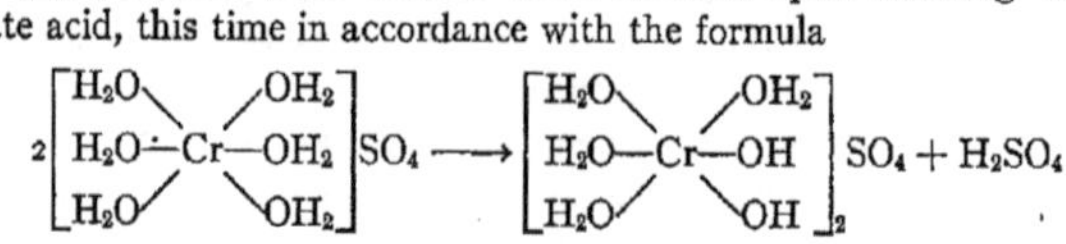

This acid can again be neutralized by the addition of alkali, and now the solution is called 66⅔ per cent basic. This procedure could be repeated again until the solution is from 86 to 90 per cent basic. The pH at this stage is about 4.0 The importance of this phenomenon is that most tanners agree that at least one, and preferably more, hydroxy groups must be present within the chromium complex for that body to have tanning properties, and it is essential in compounding solutions that this condition be fulfilled

When the tanner prepares his chrome bath, he fixes conditions so that the resultant solution will be between 33⅓ and 66⅔ per cent basic John Arthur Wilson, in his book mentioned above, states that the vigor of the combination of chrome liquor with hide increases with increasing basicity of the chrome solution up to a value of 66⅔ per cent. Beyond this point, precipitation of chromic oxide begins, thus removing the possibility of reaction But the tanner has one problem that the photographer does not meet. The hide that he must treat is about one hundred times as thick as the gelatin layer. He has the problem of even distribution of the tanning liquor throughout the depth of the skin. The higher the pH, the less the chrome liquor will penetrate into the leather, hence his solutions must represent a compromise between ease of diffusion and maximum absorption of chromium by hide protein. That is why he sometimes uses a bath with a relatively low pH. However, after he has achieved penetration, he neutralizes his solution to just below the point where chromic oxide is precipitated, that is to a pH of approximately 3.0, when no other salts have been added.

If salts are added to a chrome alum solution, some of the water molecules will be replaced by the negative ion of the salt. The substitution is not effected with equal ease in all cases. The resultant substance undergoes a hydrolysis, but the equilibrium conditions attained are different for each salt Wilson and Kern (*Jour. Amer. Leather Chem. Ass'n*, Vol. 12 (1917), p. 445) titrated 10 cc of a standard chrome liquor in the presence and absence of neutral salts, which were added to give a concentration of 0.02 molar with respect to that ionic species. Their results were as follows:

Salt	*cc* 0.1N NaOH	*Salt*	*cc* 0.1N NaOH
None	3.7	$NaCl$	5.4
KBr	3.9	$MgCl_2$	6.2
KCl	4.0	$MgSO_4$	10.5
KNO_3	4.2	Na_2SO_4	11.4
NH_4Cl	4.5	$(NH_4)_2SO_4$	11.6

This would indicate that the degree of hydrolysis or formation of chromium complexes containing hydroxy groups, is greatest in the presence of sulphate ions, and least with the halogens and nitrates. This had an effect upon the tanning properties of the chrome liquor. In the book on "Modern Practice in Leather Manufacture," Dr. Wilson describes a series of experiments on tanning in the presence of neutral salts. In all cases, a series of experiments were made in which the pH of the tanning liquor was varied. The maximum absorption of chromium took place when the pH was highest, but this varied with the specific salt used In the presence of NaCl, the maximum pH was about 3 0, at higher pH's chromic oxide was precipitated. When sodium formate was added, the allowable pH became higher, and the amount of chromium absorbed per unit of hide, became higher. With a concentration of 59 6 pounds of sodium formate per 100 gallons of chrome liquor and the pH adjusted to a point just below the precipitation of chromic oxide (pH 6.6), the absorption of chromium was at a maximum. This information should be of value to the fine-grain enthusiast who must toughen his negatives to the absolute maximum. The use of an acid stop with an indiscriminate pH leads to trouble when the film is transferred to hypo. But a pH between 5.0 and 6 0 is sufficient to stop development and is well above the point where danger threatens the fixing bath. Such a solution could serve as an ideal short stop.

When oxalate was added to the chrome bath, the tanning properties reached a maximum at a pH about 5 0, but the amount of chromium fixed was much less than in the other cases. When the pH went above 5 0, the chromium absorption became sharply reduced. In this case it is interesting to note that the formation of chromic oxide became permanently inhibited. Evidently chromate formation takes place when the pH becomes higher than 5 0, and the chromium available for tanning purposes becomes considerably diminished. Oxalate is not the only ion that acts in this manner. Tartrates and acetates behave likewise. This means that an acid short stop made up of acetic acid should never be used in conjunction with a chrome fixing bath.

We learn, therefore, from the leather chemist, that for best results in chrome tanning, we must compound a solution containing no acetate, tartrate or oxalate ions, since these will yield only a very mild tanning In the absence of sodium formate we must limit our pH to a value of 3 0, as otherwise chromic oxide will be formed. In the presence of large quantities of sodium formate, we can operate at a pH of 6.6, at which point there will be a maximum of tanning.

The entire subject of relief formation by carbon and carbro was reviewed by Joseph Friedman in a series of papers which appeared in *American Photography* (Vol 35 (1941), pages 437, 517, 589, 657, 716, 789, Vol. 36 (1942), December, p 34) The first half of this series dealt with carbon, the latter portions with carbro Since the dichromate must be reduced by silver, the carbro sensitizing agent must be acid and must contain a silver precipitant The need for this second substance was a rather surprising discovery made in a costly manner. At one time the writer was making a matrix of considerable length and used a bleach compounded from equal quantities of sulphuric acid and ammonium dichromate. When the matrix came out of the etching bath only celluloid remained, no trace of a relief being present Salt was then added to the bleach solution, and this cleared up the situation directly Evidently when no salt is present, the chromium does not form a solution with a basicity of $33\frac{1}{3}$ or $66\frac{2}{3}$ per cent, or the pH is so low that very little rise in the melting point of gelatin occurs Since the acidity was of the order of 5 grams of sulphuric acid per 1000 cc, the pH was about 1.0, and our leather chemists (cf. above) have shown that at this pH, the union of chromium with gelatin is very slight. It may also be due to the fact that acid is used up during the reaction with dichromate, which proceeds along these lines:

$$6Ag + Na_2Cr_2O_7 + 7H_2SO_4 \rightarrow Cr_2(SO_4)_3 + 7H_2O + Na_2SO_4 + 3Ag_2SO_4$$

In accordance with this equation, almost 700 grams of sulphuric acid will be required for 262 grams of dichromate, which is much more than equal weights When reduction took place, the acid was completely used up locally, so that instead of $Cr_2(SO_4)_3$, chromic oxide was formed, and this is incapable of action upon gelatin. Hence no tanning. But when there is present a considerable quantity of salt, the tanning could take place at much higher pH's, since chromic oxide will not be formed so readily in this case. Therefore some tanning action will result. If this theory is correct, it is hard to see why any tanning takes place when neutral or slightly alkaline dichromate is reduced photo-chemically. And yet it is under such conditions that the tanning action is at an optimum. It might be pointed out that in general it is not necessary to add salt to an acid dichromate solution before it has tanning properties Any ion which precipitates silver is sufficient.

The third important ingredient in the carbro sensitizing bath is dichromate, and some other agent capable of oxidizing silver. The oxidation of silver is most probably accomplished by the ferricyanide plus bromide rather than by the dichromate, although this probably does enter into the reaction to some extent But to this degree it probably interferes with the formation of the tanned image in the pigment layer, since to this extent there will be a tanning of the gelatin in the bromide with a consequent reduction of the diffusibility of the chromic salts from those regions, and a reduction of the total quantity of tanning material that can transfer to the tissue The desired reactions can therefore be written in the following manner:

1. $4Ag + 4K_3Fe(CN)_6 + 4KBr \rightarrow 4AgBr + 4K_4Fe(CN)_6$
2. $6K_4Fe(CN)_6 + Na_2Cr_2O_7 + 7H_2SO_4 \rightarrow Na_2SO_4 + 3K_2SO_4 + 7H_2O + Cr_2(SO_4)_3 + 6K_3Fe(CN)_6$

The first reaction takes place in the bromide, after the ingredients transfer from the tissue. The freed ferrocyanide transfers back to the tissue and there institutes the second reaction, thus causing a local imagewise (slightly diffused by the transfer) tanning of the gelatin, which takes place in the presence of considerable bromide concentration. To the extent to which dichromate transfers from the tissue to the bromide, there will be a loss of tanning, since to this extent both reactions will take place in the bromide

The sufficiency of the above conditions can easily be proven. It is merely necessary to separate the sensitizing solution into its two supposed functions This was done by the writer. The bromide was bleached in a ten-per-cent solution of potassium ferricyanide. This converted the silver image into one composed of silver ferrocyanide. A thorough wash removed all oxidation products The bleached bromide was next brought into contact with a tissue sensitized in a bath from which the ferricyanide was absent. The reactions that took place were as follows:

1. $Ag_4Fe(CN)_6 + 4KBr \rightarrow 4AgBr + K_4Fe(CN)_6$
2. $6K_4Fe(CN)_6 + Na_2Cr_2O_7 + 7H_2SO_4 \rightarrow Na_2SO_4 + 3K_2SO_4 + 7H_2O + 6K_3Fe(CN)_6 + Cr_2(SO_4)_3$

Here again the first reaction took place within the bromide, and the second reaction within the tissue. The density scale of the image was lengthened in both directions. The highlights corresponded very closely to the original silver deposit, and the shadows were carried a full step beyond the normal.

This experiment only shows the sufficiency of the hypothesis outlined above. It does not prove its necessity This might be accomplished by substituting some other oxidizing agent for the ferricyanide, which will not yield a product capable of taking part in the second reaction

It was mentioned above that one improvement obtained by the new technique was a more faithful reproduction of the highlight densities. This is quite a problem for the carbro technician. It makes necessary the over-printing of the bromides, especially in the highlights, so that after the loss incident to the normal technique, there will still be left the desired detail. This in itself is not so serious, since one can overcome the defect by printing the bromides somewhat heavier. What is serious is that the loss is not the same with all brands of paper Normal bromide enlarging paper is made with a very thin overcoating of plain gelatin This is to eliminate the danger of abrasion marks and other defects But in bromides that are to be used in carbro, the overlay must be eliminated, since it gives rise to a peculiar mottling in the highlights. Besides it occasions a severe loss of image since a good part of the reaction number two will take place in the overlay rather than in the tissue Paper is made specially for carbro without the overlay. Despite this, the amount of highlight detail retained when using one brand of paper is greater than when using another, even though both papers were made specifically for carbro.

Since all other conditions are constant, the difference between the two papers must be in the quality of the gelatin used for the emulsion. It was argued that the softer the gelatin, the less the possibility of hindrance of the transfer of the potassium ferricyanide. This could be tested easily by artificially softening the gelatin of the bromide by treatment with alkali salicylates, followed by thorough wash and acid treatment to restore the pH to its original value. J. S Friedman found (*Am. Phot.*, Vol. 35 (1941), p. 718) much greater highlight detail was obtained from this paper than from the untreated A similar result was obtained when Wash-Off Relief matrix film was substituted for the bromide. This, however, introduced mechanical difficulties due to the film base as opposed to a paper base, that made its use unwarranted.

Another attack upon this problem of loss of highlights was made by Leonard L. Perskie of the Defender company staff, and reported in the *Defender Trade Bulletin* (Vol. 26 (1942), No 1, p 4). Mr. Perskie worked on the assumption that the normal half-hour wash as recommended by most technicians, does not remove all the hypo from the bromides, and this hypo in conjunction with some of the sensitizing solution acted as a reducing bath, locally destroying some image A test with much greater washing time soon indicated that loss of highlights was either completely eliminated or greatly diminished, but the minimum time of washing was at least two and a half hours. Mr. Perskie next applied the technique used by Joseph S. Friedman in the processing of the Friedman monopack (cf. chapter on Monopacks). This consisted in fixing with a 2½ per cent solution of potassium iodide, followed by a wash Now it was found that the wash time was immaterial, and that no loss of highlight detail could be detected. While fixation with hypo dissolved out the silver bromide not used in image formation, the potassium iodide treatment converted it into the inert silver iodide, which could safely be left within the emulsion. Since no hypo was used, the danger of hypo acting in conjunction with ferricyanide to form Farmer's reducer locally, was obviated.

This procedure appears to take care of a more accurate duplication of the silver in the bromide. The character of the image is, however, the same as that of the one produced in the normal manner. It was pointed out above that the maximum absorption of chromium by gelatin is brought about by low acidity. The image formed in carbon, where the pH approaches a value of 7.0, is so tough that it can be scrubbed without harm. The carbro image is so tender that it must be handled very gingerly, otherwise it will be damaged. With this in mind Friedman (cf above) replaced the relatively strong chromic acid by boric acid. It is essential that the acidity be sufficient to allow the dichromate to act on silver. A quick test is to compound the bleach without potassium ferricyanide, and see if this will bleach the silver. The toughest image that the writer has ever encountered was made in this manner. The bromide was first bleached in ten per cent potassium ferricyanide The tissue was sensitized with:

Ammonium dichromate	15 parts
Potassium bromide	50 parts
Boric acid	10 parts
Borax	10 parts
Water to	1000 parts

Tissue and bromide containing the silver ferrocyanide image were kept in contact for fifteen minutes, after which the tissue was transferred to a polished celluloid and processed in the normal manner.

More recently there has been developed a carbro technique that made the problem of registry of the images much simpler. The bromides are printed upon a stripping film This is a paper emulsion coated on a very thin film base, which itself is pasted on to a paper base. During the processing, the film leaves the paper. Since the film is exceedingly thin, three such layers can easily be superimposed without harm The working technique is as follows: The thin film is placed upon a sheet of plate glass, gelatin side up, and after the surface moisture is wiped away, it is fastened to the glass by means of scotch tape or rubber cement If scotch tape is used, further wetting will cause the celluloid film which forms the base of the tape, to float away, leaving the cement adhering to the stripped film and the glass. From this point on the processing is normal. The sensitized tissue is squeegeed to the "bromide" and left in contact for fifteen to thirty minutes, after which the sandwich could be developed in hot water The carbro pigment image will be formed directly on top of the silver image Fixation removes the silver bromide, leaving a clear pigment image on a strip-film base. After drying, the three strip films can be assembled upon a paper base

The fact that it is possible to develop the carbro image directly upon the surface bearing the silver image, gave several people the inspiration needed to apply carbro technique to motion-picture film Capstaff of the Eastman staff recoated with gelatin a film carrying a silver image, and then applied an ozobrome bleach which caused an imagewise tanning of the recoated gelatin. If this contained leuco dye bases, dye regeneration took place simultaneously (Eng. P. 371077) Others who had a similar idea, but used pigmented gelatin for recoating, were D A. Spencer, H. D. Murray, and L. W. Oliver (U.S.P. 1939026, Eng P. 377706), H D. Murray and D. A. Spencer (Eng. P. 406743), J. E. Thornton (Eng. P. 417640, 422375, 422379) and Mr. Thornton in combination with Messrs Murray and Spencer (Eng. P. 405356).

CHAPTER 26

THE TRANSFER PROCESSES

UNDER this heading could be grouped all the processes in which a color image is transferred from a matrix to another surface. The most successful uses of the technique are to be found in the Technicolor process for the making of color motion pictures, and the Eastman Wash-Off Relief process for the making of color prints. The study of the process is the study of the procedures for the preparation of a matrix. This is a scheme by which it becomes possible to differentiate image-bearing from non-image-bearing portions of a surface. For instance, we can treat a layer with a resist so that certain sections will not absorb dye or ink. The resist may be a tanning agent which prevents the imbibition of an aqueous solution. Or, it can be an agent which will cause a greasy ink to adhere. Matrices of this type are called planographic Instead of treating portions of the surface to cause them to act differentially toward stains, the non-image portions could be completely removed. Matrices of this type are called reliefs. We will discuss the planographic matrices first.

About 1867, E. Edwards was concerned with the preparation of photo-gelatin transfer plates He took out a number of patents in which he described the general method for their preparation and use (Eng P. 2201/68, 2543/69, 2485/70, and 73/72). Generally, a gelatin layer was sensitized with dichromates, then exposed under a negative. The exposed portions became water-repellant, but ink-absorbent. This constituted the matrix In a subsequent disclosure (Eng P 2799/71) he suggested that if the water (which was absorbed by the untanned portions and made them ink-repellant), contained aniline dyes, curious two-tone effects could be obtained, and both ink and dye would transfer. This was probably the first disclosure on record that a dye would transfer Mr. Edwards recognized that he made a valuable contribution to the art, but outside of taking out a few more patents to secure his right to fame (U.S.P. 150946; Eng. P. 1362/75, 3453/75), he let the matter rest at this point.

The next advance came from Charles Cros (Fr. P. 139396) who rediscovered the idea, apparently in complete ignorance that it had been previously proposed He called the procedure "Hydrotypie," indicating the use of aqueous solutions for the staining baths. The technique was further developed by L. Didier and commercialized by the German dye firm Meister, Lucius and Bruning (U.S P. 885453, Eng P. 7557/05; Fr. P 337054; Ger P. 176693) under the name "Pinatype."

In practice, a gelatin layer was sensitized by means of dichromate (cf Chapter 25), then exposed under a positive The exposed portions of the layer became tanned and water-repellant, so they would not imbibe water or certain dyes dissolved in the water Hence the image corresponded to the unexposed portions. The sections which received partial exposure became partially tanned and these imbibed the water and dye to a corresponding degree. After staining, the matrix was brought in contact with a fresh gelatin surface. After a time the stain transferred to the new surface. Three such transfers in superposition gave the final color print. The matrices could be re-stained, and thus duplicate copies made.

Not all dyes could be used for this purpose It must be remembered that as prepared above, the matrix consisted of an image of soft or untanned gelatin impressed upon a layer of hard gelatin The dyes must stain the soft gelatin, but not the tanned, or if the staining is general, then the stain in the tanned portions must be readily removed while that in the soft portions must be relatively permanent. There are many dyes which have this property. A collection of such colors was at one time sold by the I.G. under the designation of Pina dyes, but their sale was discontinued about 1930 The chemical structure or the trade name of the dyes was never disclosed. The Eastman Kodak Company utilized similar dyes in their old discarded Kodachrome process (not to be confused with the present-day product of that name), but they also did not disclose the nature of the dyes However, the patent files do give some information. The original Didier paper gives the following classes of dyes as suitable.

1. The Mikado dyes obtained from p-nitro-toluol-sulphonic acid,
2. Dyes made from dihydrothiotoluidin or primuline and their substitution products,
3. Sulphonated nigrosines and indulines,
4. Natural carmine,
5. Dianil dyes, and the
6. Arylido anthraquinone sulphonates

More specifically, natural carmine and the dye obtained when diazotized primuline sulphonic acid was coupled into naphthol disulphonic acid, could be used for the magenta, dianil yellow R for the yellow, and fast blue or induline sulphonic acid for cyan

Special studies were made to determine what relationship existed between chemical constitution and the ability to stain gelatin F. Curtis and P Lemoult (Wall's "The History of Three-Color Photography," p. 397) found that the presence of sulphonic groups led to gelatin substantivity, while nitro groups had the opposite effect. Unfortunately, rhodamine and auramin were listed as nitro-containing dyes, which is not the case They are basic dyes with no affinity for gelatin. A more practical solution was offered by L. Lemaire (*Brit. J. Phot.*, Vol. 58 (1911), p. 969). He recommended lanafuchsin 6B or brilliant lanafuchsin SL for the magenta, alizarin cyanol BF for the cyan, and paper yellow M or solid yellow 2GL and quinoline yellow for the yellow The dyes were in one per cent solution. They were brushed on the matrices Other dyes which have this preferential staining action, or dyes which would stain tanned gelatin in preference to the untanned, are disclosed in some of the patents dealing with the formation of screens (cf. Chapters 12 and 13).

Complete working directions for pinatype were contained in the "Pina Manual," a pamphlet issued by the Agfa company. The separations are first converted into positive transparencies. These, with the exception of the yellow, should be very soft, hence they might be made upon a color-blind negative material. The yellow image should be developed fairly hard If it is desired to use transparency plates, then, the developer should be compounded along the lines outlined by J. S. Friedman (cf. discussion of the Brewster process, Chapter 21).

The printing plates are specially coated gelatin plates, but there is no reason to doubt that almost any plate or film could be used, if the silver halide emulsion were first fixed out with plain hypo, then washed thoroughly to remove all traces of this agent. If the transparencies are somewhat hard, it might be preferable to leave the emulsion in the film This will control the penetration of the printing light into the print plate. Sensitization is accomplished by bathing in 2½ per cent ammonium dichromate, or in any of the baths mentioned in Chapter 25. The time of treatment is three to five minutes at 15 C, after which they should be drained thoroughly, and put up to dry. This operation can be carried out in diffused yellow light

The exposures are made through the positive transparencies, the source of illumination being an arc light or bright sunlight Mazda light would prolong the time unduly. The plates are fixed by merely washing them in water until all the unexposed dichromate is removed, after which they may either be dried, or immediately stained. If the material used still contains silver bromide, this may be fixed out by plain hypo, followed by a thorough washing.

The matrices are stained in suitable dye baths, which are as follows:

Cyan

Pinatype blue F	2–3 parts
Water	100 parts

Magenta

Pinatype red F	3–4 parts
Ammonia	3–5 parts
Water	100 parts

Yellow

Pinatype yellow F	3 parts
Water, hot	100 parts
Cool before using.	

The matrices are treated in these baths for a period of ten minutes. The excess is washed in running water. Washing should be continued until the whites are clean. The image is best examined by placing it on a white surface, such as a white opaque glass or an enameled tray. Too low a contrast may be due to too short an exposure which did not harden the highlights to enable the shadows sufficient time to absorb enough dye. Overexposure leads to loss of highlight detail.

After dyeing and washing to satisfaction, the matrix is brought into contact with a thoroughly wet sheet of transfer paper. A process of preparing such a paper is described below, when the subject of Wash-Off Relief is discussed. Contact between the two is established quickly, but absolute care must be maintained that once contact is established, there should be no relative motion between transfer paper and matrix The dye transfer starts immediately, and if any motion occurs, a blurred image will result The time should be sufficient to allow a complete transfer of the dye. Any air bubbles will be indicated by white specks in the print After transfer, the matrix should be re-dyed This time a much shorter period is required both for dyeing and for transfer. It is best to leave the yellow transfer for the last, since then registry will be easier. After the three transfers have been made in registry upon the same sheet of transfer paper, it can be treated with a three-per-cent solution of copper sulphate. This will tend to mordant the dye in place.

These disclosures evoked a considerable interest, but most of the published and patented modifications dealt with slight variations in the formulas, or with the use of this procedure in combination with some other. However, some writers did contain themselves and dealt only with pinatype. L. Vidal (*Brit. J. Phot.*, Vol. 53 (1906), p. 390; Vol. 54 (1907), *Col. Supp.*, p. 9) suggested a procedure which he claimed gave more brilliant results. A glass plate is first coated with collodion, then with gelatin. The gelatin layer is sensitized, exposed, washed, then freed from the brown chromium stain by a treatment with bisulphite, washed, and finally dried. The dry plate is stained and washed in the manner described above, after which it is dried, then recoated with gelatin, sensitized, printed in registry through a second separation, fixed, stained, etc., until three images have been formed. The final act is to coat again with gelatin, set, and bring in contact with a sheet of gelatinized backing paper. When this is dried, the print can be stripped from the glass by merely cutting around the edges with a sharp knife. If plate glass is used, the print will have a high polish. If a ground glass is used, the finish will be mat

L. Didier (*Jahrbuch*, Vol. 19 (1905), p 343; *Brit. J. Phot.*, Vol. 54 (1907) *Col. Supp*, p. 43) made an interesting modification. The separation negatives were converted into normal separation positives. These should be fairly dense, with clean whites The yellow should be printed heavier than the other two. Development is effected in a non-tanning developer. The positives are then sensitized with dichromate placed in contact with a sheet of printing-out paper, and exposed until details appear in the shadows. The printing-out paper serves merely as an actinometer It is readily seen that by this procedure the gelatin in situ with the silver remains soft to the extent of the image density After washing the plate free from unreacted dichromate, the silver is removed by the action of Farmer's reducer, leaving a pinatype matrix of pure gelatin

Another novelty was proposed by G. Engelken. He did for this procedure what Manly did for carbro He tanned the gelatin in situ with the silver by treatment with an ozobrome bleach (cf. Chapter 25) The tanned portions become immune to the action of pina dyes (*Jahrbuch*, Vol 21 (1906), p. 453; *Brit J Phot.*, Vol. 56 (1909), *Col Supp.*, p 36). F W Donisthorpe accomplished the same result with an uranium toner, which also tanned the gelatin in situ with a silver image (U S P 923030, 1517200; Eng. P. 13874/07, 5641/08, 7087/08, 158021, Ger P. 219188, 360550; Fr P. 518229) Several alternative baths were given. The negative silver image was first treated with

Uranium nitrate	1 part
Potassium ferricyanide	1 part
Water	45 parts

for ten minutes, after which it was treated with

Ferric chloride	1 part
Glycerin	1 part
Water	50 parts

Another possibility was to bleach the image in

Lead nitrate	4 parts
Potassium ferricyanide	6 parts
Acetic acid	2 parts
Glycerin	1 part
Water	100 parts

for ten minutes, then bathe in 2½ per cent sodium sulphide solution until completely toned The preferred bath, however, was the following:

Vanadium chloride	2 parts
Potassium ferricyanide	2 parts
Ferric chloride	1 part
Glycerin	1 part
Ferric oxalate	1 part
Saturated oxalic acid	100 parts
Water	900 parts

If the dye did not take very evenly a remedy was to add more oxalic acid

A similar idea was utilized by J. E. Thornton (U.S.P. 1921050; Eng P. 25084/12, 339296). He disclosed several bleach formulas that tanned the gelatin sufficiently to be suitable for use with pinatype dyes. The image can be treated with any of the following:

1	Potassium dichromate	10 parts
	Potassium alum, 10% solution	5 parts
	Water	250 parts
2	Copper sulphate	2 parts
	Potassium bromide	1 part
	Potassium dichromate	1 part
	Water	100 parts
3.	Cupric bromide	50 parts
	Potassium dichromate	1 part
	Water	1000 parts
4	This is formed by mixing equal parts of *A* and *B*	
(*A*).	Potassium ferricyanide	$37\frac{1}{2}$ parts
	Potassium bromide	$36\frac{1}{4}$ parts
	Potassium dichromate	$37\frac{1}{2}$ parts
	Acetic acid	10 parts
	Water to	1000 parts
(*B*)	Potassium alum	50 parts
	Water to	1000 parts

It is to be noted that the first bath is a typical carbro sensitizer, while the second is a typical bromoil bleach. After bleaching, the print is washed in running water for one minute, treated with a ten per cent sodium sulphite solution, fixed in acid hypo, washed well, then stained with pinatype dyes such as platinum black or nigrosine For color, the proper secondaries should be used

Much along the same lines was the process Eastman tentatively introduced shortly after World War I, under the name of Kodachrome This is not to be confused with the Kodachrome of 1935, which adopted the old name, but which bore no other resemblance to that process The first Kodachrome was the invention of J. G Capstaff (U.S P 1196080, Eng P. 13429/15; Ger. P. 279802, Fr. P 479796, 479798). The printing must be done through positives. The negative silver is developed with an MQ developer, after which it is washed for ten minutes. It is then bleached in a solution made by mixing equal parts of *A* and *B*:

(*A*)	Potassium ferricyanide	37.5 parts
	Potassium bromide	56.25 parts
	Potassium bichromate	37.5 parts
	Acetic acid	10 parts
	Water to	1000 parts
(*B*)	Potassium alum	50 parts
	Water to	1000 parts

Fixation should be in an acid, but alum-free hypo A further wash of twenty minutes is followed by a bath of five per cent ammonia for three minutes, then a wash for five minutes, after which the plate was dried. Drying was the ticklish part of the procedure, and success or failure hinged on the ability to achieve this in a uniform and thorough manner. Special dyes known as Kodachrome red and Kodachrome green were used for staining, these being evidently pinatype colors since only the non-tanned portions of the plate absorbed them But the names or formulas were never disclosed.

Somewhat later, Capstaff modified the procedure In the original Kodachrome the non-image portions of the plate were tanned. This meant that printing was to be done from positives, a handicap since it involved another remove from the original. In the newer technique, the image was the silver-bearing portion of the plate To accomplish this, Capstaff utilized an idea that had already found application in the photomechanical printing trade. Gelatin printing surfaces were prepared by sensitizing a gelatin-coated plate with ferric chloride and tartaric acid This treatment tanned the gelatin so that it became completely ink-receptive and water-repellant. Upon exposure to light under a negative, the ferric ion became reduced to the ferrous state. This no longer had any specific action on the gelatin (Eng P 586/63, cf. also article by J. Joe, *Brit. J Phot*, Vol. 60 (1913), p. 250). By this means an imagewise de-tanning of the gelatin took place. Formulas and working directions for the technique are described in the chapter titled: "The Iron Processes" in Wall and Jordan's "Photographic Facts and Formulas"

The Capstaff modification consisted in treating a normal positive image with a bleach containing ferric chloride and tartaric acid. It was not necessary to fix the plate after development, since another fixation is required after the bleach. As recommended by Capstaff, the procedure was as follows (U.S.P. 1315464). Positive images were printed from separation negatives. These were developed, washed, then bleached in

Ferric chloride	100 parts
Tartaric acid	30 parts
Water to	1000 parts

After bleaching, the plates were fixed, washed, and dyed, using presumably the Kodachrome dyes or their equivalents, the pinatype dyes

In more recent times J. E. Thornton utilized a planographic matrix and pinatype dyes, for the preparation of color films (U.S P 1921050; Eng. P 339296). The negative silver images, formed on a duplitized film stock, are developed in a non-tanning developer, then bleached in a bromoil bleach or a carbro sensitizing solution, such as the one made by mixing equal parts of *A* and *B*.

(*A*).	Potassium ferricyanide	37 5 parts
	Potassium bromide	36 25 parts
	Potassium dichromate	37.5 parts
	Acetic acid	10 parts
	Water to	1000 parts

(*B*). Potassium alum	50 parts
Water to	1000 parts

The bleached prints are washed, then fixed in a bisulphite hypo made by mixing equal parts of 25 per cent hypo and 40 per cent sodium bisulphite solution Washing and drying prepares the film for the dyeing operation. In accompanying patents, Mr. Thornton discloses the preparation of the duplitized material (Eng P. 339319, 339321). In other patents (Eng P 316331, 316367) he mentions pinatype procedure for making one or more of the part images.

A somewhat different approach to this problem is disclosed by L. T Troland (U S P. 2013116, Eng. P. 377033). The matrix is hardened generally, but is softened imagewise This is accomplished by the use of either of the following bleaches:

1. Copper sulphate	20 parts
Potassium bromide	1 part
Nitric acid	2 parts
Potassium perborate	5 parts
Water to	1000 parts
or	
2 Potassium ferricyanide	1 part
Potassium permanganate	1 part
Water to	100 parts

If the second of the bleaches is used, the film must be cleared first in dilute hydrochloric acid, then in 10 per cent sodium bisulphite. Here it is the image bearing portions which are softened, hence the matrix silver image must be a positive. The I.G. (Eng. P. 447488) did just the opposite. The matrix was first given a general tanning, then the areas carrying the silver image were further tanned so that these portions would not absorb the dye. Hence the silver matrix image must be a negative

Bromoil and the photo-gelatin processes also use planographic matrices. But now it is the tanned gelatin portions which become stained. The coloring matters used are special greasy inks, litho or collotype Wall and Jordan's "Photographic Facts and Formulas" devotes a section to this subject, and many books have been published which deal exclusively with bromoil and bromoil transfer, so we will not go into any great discussion of the technique at this point But we must mention one modification described by Wall. The print or enlargement should be developed with a non-tanning developer fixed in plain hypo, washed, then bleached in

Potassium bromide	10 parts
Copper sulphate	15 parts
Potassium dichromate	5 parts
Water to	1000 parts

To this should be added just sufficient hydrochloric acid to form a clear solution. A large excess of acid is to be avoided for the reason noted in the chapter on carbon and carbro. When completely bleached, the paper is washed well, then treated with a one per cent sulphuric acid solution. This will remove any residual yellow stain in the film. Wash to remove excess acid, fix in plain hypo, wash well to remove excess hypo, then swell differentially by treatment for ten minutes with

Glycerin	1 part
Water	2 parts

The matrix is placed face up on a glass plate, and it is rolled down with a squeegee. This removes the surface excess of water. The inking is done with a roller.

So much for the planographic procedures. We now turn our attention to the relief matrices. Here image density is translated into gelatin thickness. Four distinct methods are available to accomplish this. One is patterned after carbon, the others tan the gelatin imagewise in connection with a silver image, but all of them utilize a silver-halide emulsion. Certain developing agents, when oxidized, unite with gelatin to tan it. This rather direct method is the basis for the Technicolor process. On the other hand, Eastman, in its Wash-Off Relief procedure, treats the silver image with acid dichromate, and achieves imagewise tanning at the same time. It is also possible to achieve imagewise detanning as was pointed out above.

Carbon technique for the preparation of a relief matrix was first suggested by E. Sanger-Shepherd and O. M. Bartlett (U.S.P. 728310; Eng. P. 24234/02; Fr. P. 329526; Ger. P. 161519). A sheet of celluloid was coated with gelatin and sensitized with dichromate It was exposed through the support, under a negative After exposure, it was developed in hot water. The unexposed, hence untanned gelatin, dissolved away, leaving an image on the celluloid in the form of a relief composed of tanned gelatin. This was stained with aniline dyes, and the stained side brought in contact with a sheet of gelatinized paper, previously soaked in water. After a while it was found that the aniline dye transferred from the matrix to the "blank," as the gelatinized paper was called. The men also pointed out in their disclosure that duplications become simple by this procedure As L. Vidal pointed out (*Mon. Phot.*, Vol 42 (1913), p 6), this technique differs from that of Cros only in the minor detail that a relief matrix is used, while Cros utilized a planographic matrix.

Once the idea of carbon reliefs was proposed, others began to use it. J. H. Smith and W. Merckens (Eng. P. 7217/07; U.S.P. 885066; Fr. P. 376062; Ger. P 209444) transferred to a collodion surface instead of gelatin. Ives, especially, did considerable work in this field, mainly in the development of simple dodges to give better control, to extend the range of the available dyes, etc. His patents and writings could well serve as a text on this subject (U S.P 1106816, 1160288, 1121184; Eng. P. 15823/14, Fr. P. 463737; Ger. P. 308030). He evidently was the first person to treat the gelatin in the blank with a dye-acceptor or mordant. He also emphasized the influence of the pH of the dye bath upon the contrast of the dyed matrix, a fact previously disclosed by von Hubl (*Brit. J. Phot.*, Vol. 46 (1899), p. 409, 470, 537) These ideas are now standard practice in all imbibition schemes

Making the matrix by the carbon technique severely restricted the scope, since only contact printing was permissible. It is not surprising, therefore, to find that this application of carbon did not become popular, nor affect in any way any of the other schemes which allowed the use of a normal silver image Some of these preceded carbon by a considerable time One such scheme was the developed relief, a technique brought to a high degree of precision by Technicolor.

Wall traces its history back to J. W. Swan, who prepared photo-relief plates by development with pyro-ammonia in 1879 (Eng. P. 2969/79), but these were evidently not relief images It was L. Warnerke who first made relief matrices in this manner (Eng. P 1436/81) He used a standard pyro-ammonia developer, but left all the sulphite from the bath. In the absence of sulphite, the oxidized pyro reacted with the gelatin, to tan it. Some time later *Silbermann* pointed out that the degree of tanning could be controlled by the addition of some sulphite (*Silbermann*, Vol. 2, p. 141). He also pointed out that other developing agents had similar properties. Hydroquinone and amidol gave strong reliefs. Metol and diaminophenol gave weaker ones, while glycin gave no relief at all.

Before discussing the details of such procedures it would be well to examine the characteristics of the matrix emulsions This must be a fine-grained silver-halide emulsion, suspended in soft gelatin The matrix material must wash away from non-image portions, leaving no trace of substance capable of absorbing color In the pure whites, the matrix gelatin must leave bare celluloid or substratum. This creates a problem, for the ordinary substratum contains tanned gelatin G. F. Nadeau (U S P. 2169004) suggested a low dye-retaining substratum. Another problem which arises from the fact that most substrating solutions contain acetic acid, is that the acid destroys the sensitivity of the emulsion in that region. This means that the emulsion adjacent to the film base is least sensitive, and it is highly desirable that it be most sensitive there M. W. Seymour (U.S.P. 1946640; Eng. P. 381787) discussed this phase of the problem, which, however, need not concern the average technician since matrix material is an article of commerce

The control of the contrast of the final image can be accomplished in the manufacture of the matrix The use of yellow dyes to insure a very low relief has been long recognized. The Jos Pé company sought to control the shape of the H & D curve, especially the toe regions, by mixing five per-cent of a fast negative emulsion to the slow matrix (Eng. P. 327283). This was achieved by E. A. Weaver by pre-exposing the emulsion to just below fog level (Eng. P. 263331) Another important control of relief depth was obtained by Technicolor in the following manner (U S.P. 2044864; Eng. P. 385293). The yellow dyed emulsion was sensitized to the green When high contrasts were desired, the printing was done with green light. By judicious choice of filters it became possible to get any contrast between the two extremes.

This dodge was by no means novel with Technicolor. It was disclosed first by R. Fischer in 1912, but in a slightly different form He mixed a very contrasty color-blind emulsion with a flat orthochromatic one. By a choice of filters, it became possible to obtain any contrast between the two extremes. Varigam paper of more recent times utilizes the same principle.

Other methods to control the contrast of the dye image were to add photographically inert substances to the emulsion. H. Piloty (U.S.P. 1586697) added agents which retarded the dye transfer from the matrix. The opposite effect was achieved by F. Janzen (U.S.P. 1613515) who added substances which increased the ability of the matrix to absorb dyes. The I.G. added pigments (U.S.P. 2181485; Eng P. 443111, 499758). The Jos Pé Company added dyes (Eng. P. 330997).

In tanning development the degree of tanning could be controlled by the amount of sulphite present in the developer. This was a general phenomenon that was independent of the particular agent used. Different experimenters preferred different developing agents, but soon the field narrowed down to two agents, pyrogallol and pyrocatechin. For some reason Wall showed a strong preference for hydroquinone, but in this he was practically alone. In his excellent book, "Practical Color Photography," he gives the following formulas for developers that tan the gelatin in situ with the developed image.

1.	Metol	1 5 parts
	Hydroquinone	1 5 parts
	Sodium sulphite	2 0 parts
	Sodium carbonate	17.5 parts
	Potassium bromide	1 5 parts
	Water to	1000 parts
2.	Hydroquinone	4 0 parts
	Sodium sulphite	2 0 parts
	Sodium carbonate	15 5 parts
	Potassium bromide	1 0 part
	Water to	1000 parts

In this formula the carbonate could be replaced with six parts of caustic soda.

3.	Pyrocatechin	2 0 parts
	Sodium sulphite	2.0 parts
	Sodium hydroxide	1 5 parts
	Potassium bromide	1.0 part
	Water to	1000 parts

Mr. Wall gives a pyro formula which contains a relatively large quantity of sulphite:

Pyrogallol	2 0 parts
Sodium sulphite	16.0 parts
Sodium carbonate	8 0 parts
Potassium bromide	0.5 part
Water to	1000 parts

Mr. Wall had an excellent opportunity to observe the action of pyrogallol at the Technicolor Laboratories. This organization brought the art of matrix making by the use of tanning developers to a high degree of precision. The formula used by Technicolor was disclosed in a patent issued to Dr. L. T. Troland (U.S.P. 1535700, Eng. P. 204034, Fr. P. 570076, Ger. P. 400951).

Pyrogallol	8 2 parts
Citric acid	0 2 part
Potassium bromide	4 0 parts
Sodium hydroxide	3.4 parts
Ammonium chloride	1.7 parts
Water to	1000 parts

This is a somewhat more contrasty developer than the one disclosed in a later patent issued to L T Troland and R D. Eaton (U S P 1919673; Eng. P 392785), which described the entire matrix procedure The developer formula was:

Pyrogallol	8 0 parts
Sodium hydroxide	3 0 parts
Ammonium chloride	1 5 parts
Potassium bromide	1 5 parts
Citric acid	0 2 part
Water to	1000 parts

The working bath was compounded from two stock solutions, one containing the caustic soda, the other containing the remaining ingredients except ammonium chloride. This was added to the developer in the form of a powder. Since the keeping qualities of pyrogallol are very poor, except in strongly acid solutions, the stock containing this ingredient was made up in a highly concentrated form, which required at least a twenty-fold dilution for use. The high acidity was obtained by addition of citric acid, which explains its presence in the formula Mr. Wall, in his discussion of this formula ("History of Three-Color Photography," p. 356), points out the lack of originality in the use of a mixture of ammonium chloride and caustic. He writes: "Obviously this is nothing more than Warnerke's original developer when it acts. The setting free of ammonia from a halide by caustic alkali has been known for many years." But the action of a developer compounded with straight ammonia is quite different from one in which the ammonia is generated by the action of an alkali upon an ammonium salt The reaction

$$NaOH + NH_4Cl \rightarrow NaCl + NH_4OH$$

requires the presence of forty parts of alkali for fifty-two parts of sal ammoniac. But in the two formulas disclosed by Dr. Troland, the alkali is present in much greater proportions The alkalinity of such a bath would be much greater than in one containing only ammonia. Also the change in alkalinity as the ammonia evaporated would be made less Therefore the solution is somewhat stabilized against change should it be used for an appreciable length of time. There may therefore be definite advantages in the use of a Troland type of developer over that of Warnerke. From experiences gained while a member of the Technicolor staff, I can say that cleaner reliefs result from the Troland formula. If there should be any criticism leveled at the formula, a better one would be the failure to use ammonium bromide instead of potassium bromide. This would obviate the need to use potassium bromide as a restrainer. The presence of chloride ions is practically of no value in a developer that is intended for use with iodobromide emulsions

After development of the silver image, the matrix was washed for a definite length of time in water, whose temperature was controlled to close limits. The tanning is a result of the reaction that takes place near the places where the pyro is oxidized, i.e , adjacent to the silver of the image. It has always been considered that this reaction is an instantaneous one, occurring at the time that the oxidized pyro is formed. It has also been assumed that the reaction between the two is complete. However, against these ideas, may be brought the fact that the tanning action continues to take place during the wash period following development This can be tested by the growth of the relief image with increased time of washing Such image growth can be detected even after twenty-four hours. Whether the growth is dependent upon the diffusion of the oxidized pyro from the locus of its formation, or whether it is an "age" effect, has never been determined For this reason it is very important that the elapsed time from entrance into developer to entrance into the hot water etch bath be strictly controlled

The further processing of the matrix is open to a great variety of procedures Where it is important to recover the silver, the matrix is bleached, washed, and fixed before it is etched Otherwise, it can be etched immediately after the developer wash. The bleaching is accomplished by use of an oxidizing agent. Technicolor prefers to use a fourteen per-cent solution of potassium ferricyanide to convert the silver into fixable form. This is very convenient for continuous long-time operation, but becomes expensive when only occasional matrices are made. If some bromide be added, the concentration of ferri can be materially reduced, a suitable solution being:

Potassium ferricyanide	15 parts
Potassium bromide	15 parts
Water to	1000 parts

It is also possible to use acid dichromate or cupric chloride solutions, but the ferricyanide baths are the most convenient. The bleach is followed by a wash, then by plain hypo, after which it is treated to form the relief.

This is done by placing the matrix in hot water whose temperature is maintained at 120 F. After a minute, the untanned gelatin will dissolve away. It should be kept in this bath until no more dissolution of the gelatin takes place If the matrix has not been fixed out before the hot water etch, it becomes easy to determine the end point, when no more cloudy material is washed away Otherwise, trial and error will set a time limit. At this stage the remaining gelatin, in the form of a relief image, is swollen and very delicate. It must be set immediately. In carbro, the technique of setting is to plunge the image into cold water A much better practice is to dehydrate it by treatment with strong alcohol, thus setting it chemically.

Procedures for the preparation of matrices using tanning developers are disclosed also by the Daylight Film Corporation (Eng P. 187638, Fr. P. 539828), R. John (U S.P 1374853, 1417328, 1778139), the I.G. (U S.P 1453258, Eng P 172342; Fr P. 518526), and the Jos Pé Company, who operate under the Koppmann disclosures (Ger P 309193, 310037, 310038, 358093, 358149, 358165, 358166, 358167, 358193, 395805). Most of these add nothing new to the practice, but Mr. Koppmann introduced one variation which has been also propounded by J. G. Capstaff (U S P. 1525766) This was to expose the matrix in the normal manner, develop with a non-tanning developer, expose the remaining grains, and develop these with a tanning developer. The gelatin beneath the primary image becomes tanned Since this corresponds to a reversal, the primary image must be a negative, hence the exposure must be made through positives, or the original negatives could be used

Tanning developers were never used to any great extent by the amateur technician. He preferred to use the tanning bleach processes Probably this was due to the fact that Eastman introduced him to Wash-Off Relief, which utilized an acid dichromate bleach to yield imagewise tanning of the gelatin The reactions are identically those involved in carbro, except that the relief image is treated as a matrix Historically we can trace the technique to E. Howard Farmer (Eng P 17773/99) who discovered that dichromate solutions acted upon a silver image to form chromic salts, which then united with the gelatin to form insoluble gelatin in situ with the silver. This was a remarkable discovery, one of the few really basic reactions known to photographic chemists. He described the reaction as catalyzed by the silver. If a plate or film containing a silver image be immersed for a few seconds in a twenty per cent ammonium dichromate solution, an imagewise tanning of the gelatin results. These tanned images show all the properties of a light-reduced dichromate sensitized material.

The importance to photographers of this observation by Farmer lies in the fact that it now became possible to duplicate with silver all the effects produced by light upon dichromate sensitized tissue Carbon has been universally recognized as one of the finest of reproduction media. Its use was limited considerably by the fact that only contact printing was possible. With this discovery it became possible to obtain carbon print quality from a normal silver image Coupled with carbro, it makes it possible to replace light by a silver image. This can be an enlargement from a small negative. Carbro and its predecessor, the Raydex process, obviously were based upon this discovery.

Immediately after this disclosure an animated discussion arose as to the exact chemistry involved. This has never been quite cleared up to the satisfaction of everyone, but there is little doubt that the same principles are involved here as in the tanning of leather. This we have discussed in detail in the chapter dealing with carbon and carbro, so there is no need to repeat it at this point.

Farmer failed to mention that the silver-image-bearing film could be pigmented This remarkably original discovery came considerably later, to be exact in 1902, when Riebensahm and Posseldt were issued a German patent covering this extension (Ger P. 153439). A corresponding English patent was granted curiously enough to Riebensahm and Koppmann (Eng. P. 808/04). There does not seem to be an American patent, which somehow restores one's faith in our patent system. To overcome the loss of speed incident to the use of pigmented gelatin as a carrier for the silver bromide, the same inventors proposed to color-sensitize the emulsion (Eng. P. 24290/04; Ger. P. 158517).

Some extensions to the chemistry of the bleach solution were made by the Neue Photographische Gesellschaft (Ger. P. 196962), the Plastographische Gesellschaft Pietzner & Co. (Ger. P. 117530, 196769; Fr. P. 363584), J. Mezaros (Fr. P. 352815), and F. E Ives (U S P. 1186000; Eng. P 15823/13), who acidulated the bleach solution, and added bromide to it. The addition of these components made the action visible, for a simultaneous bleaching of the silver image took place. As was pointed out in the chapter on carbon and carbro, the presence of some silver ion precipitant is essential for the gelatin tanning to take place. These few references do not by any means exhaust the list of people who patented some slight inconsequential changes in the bleach solution. The historically minded reader is referred to the patent files for a fuller discussion

The most popular procedure utilizing the tanning bleach principle is the one Eastman introduced in the middle nineteen-thirties, under the name of Wash-Off Relief. It is an excellent process, capable of giving very good results. It deserves, therefore, some detailed consideration. A yellow-dyed positive emulsion is used for the matrix material. To control the depth to which the printing light can go, it was advised to print through a C5 filter. Development was to be in DK-50, which is a modified borax formula

Metol	2.5 parts
Sulphite	25.0 parts
Hydroquinone	2.5 parts
Kodalk	10.0 parts
Potassium bromide	0.5 part
Water	1000 parts

Kodalk could be replaced by an equal quantity of sodium metaborate, its equivalent. The recommended time of development was five minutes at 65 F. After a wash, which must be quite thorough, the matrix is bleached in acid dichromate. This is compounded from two stock solutions

A.	Ammonium dichromate	20 parts
	Sulphuric acid	7 2 parts
	Water	1000 parts
B.	Sodium chloride (Common table salt)	45 parts
	Water	1000 parts

In compounding solution *A* the ammonium dichromate should first be dissolved in the water, which should be cold. The sulphuric acid is then added cautiously. Never add the solution to sulphuric acid.

The working bath is made by mixing equal parts of *A* and *B*, then diluting with six parts of water. After the matrix has been in the bleach for one minute, it is safe to turn on the white light. The time of treatment should be sufficient to cause the complete disappearance of the silver image, plus one minute When finished, the relief image is developed in hot water at a temperature of 120 F. The etch is finished when no more cloudy wash water runs off the matrix As a rule from three to five minutes treatment should be sufficient. If a continuous supply of hot water is not available, four or five changes, each one minute in duration, could be used

At this point, the gelatin relief is very delicate. It is necessary to set it This can be done by placing it in cold water, then fixing in alum hypo. After a final wash, the matrix is dried An alternative method is to set the gelatin in cold alcohol. This dehydrates and toughens the image directly. After allowing the alochol to dry, the matrix could be fixed, washed, and dried again

This delicacy of image is the one weak point of the entire processing. To overcome it, the writer changed the developer somewhat. The sulphite was reduced to a bare minimum consistent with fair keeping qualities, and pyro was added. Obviously this is capable of considerable variation, and it becomes possible to go all the way from a non-tanned image to a completely tanned one. A successful formula was

Pyro	2 parts
Sodium sulphite	15 parts
Hydroquinone	8 parts
Sodium carbonate	10 parts
Potassium bromide	2 parts
Water	1000 parts

The addition of copper sulphate to the bleach solution likewise adds toughness to the image. This was a feature of the Brewster procedure for a long time The bromoil technicians were the first to use copper salts in the bleach baths Their need was for an image that approximated the dichromate-light-reduced images in toughness The same is true for the technician who desires to make multiple transfers from the same matrix. It was this need that led Technicolor to the use of a pyro matrix, which is second only to carbon for toughness Next in line comes carbro, then finally Wash-Off Relief using a tanning bleach.

The last general procedure for the preparation of matrices softens the gelatin in situ with a silver image. This process is based upon a finding by Liesegang (*Phot Archiv.*, Vol 32 (1897), p 161) When a gelatin layer containing a silver image is placed in a bath containing ammonium persulphate, the gelatin immediately surrounding the silver becomes soft, or with prolonged treatment, dissolves away. A year later Andresen (Ger. P. 103516) suggested that hydrogen peroxide produced the same effect, especially if hydrochloric acid were present. The bath used by Andresen contained three per cent peroxide and two per cent hydrochloric acid Apparently in ignorance of this work, Houzel published a procedure for the making of carbon prints by this technique (*Phot. Woch*, Vol 48 (1902), p. 386) He attempted to remove dichroic fog from some prints, so he placed them overnight in a solution of hydrogen peroxide The next morning he discovered that all the parts containing silver were etched away or dissolved He then covered the whole surface of the etched print with ink, and dried it. A warm water bath now dissolved the gelatin relief, carrying with it what ink was on top This left a correct image consisting of ink. Koppmann patented a variation of this in 1924 (Ger. P. 400663)

The application to the making of matrices was suggested by E Coustet (*Mon. Phot*, Vol 42 (1903), p 251). He developed the silver image in ferrous oxalate, then treated the negative with persulphate solution until complete bleaching resulted. The softened gelatin he removed by gentle friction — a not very satisfactory procedure. The relief was then tanned by treatment with alum, and dried, after which it was dyed and transferred. Mr. Coustet marketed a bleach solution under the name of "Bioxhydro," which was very suggestive of hydrogen peroxide. Valenta identified the active ingredient of the bath to be peroxide (Wall, "History of Three-Color Photography," p. 357). The Coustet technique was applied by H. S. Schnauss (*Phot. Rund.*, Vol. 13 (1903), p. 282), directly to the separation negatives, thus obviating the necessity of making positives from which to print. But this meant that the original was destroyed, a cardinal sin in photography.

The chemistry of the etch solution was studied by Lüppo-Cramer (*Phot. Korr.*, Vol. 48 (1911), pp 466, 608) He found that silver acted catalytically, and that presence of silver ions in the solution retarded the reaction with gelatin. This explains the necessity for the presence of halogen ions in the bath, for these would precipitate the silver ions, thus removing them from the solution as fast as they are formed E J Wall ("History of Three-Color Photography," p 357) and Belin and Drouillard (Fr. P. 423150;

Ger. P. 230386) discovered, independently of each other, that the addition of copper salts also aided the reaction Wall suggested ("Practical Color Photography," p. 91)

Hydrogen peroxide	30 parts
Copper sulphate	20 parts
Nitric acid	5 parts
Potassium bromide	0 5 part
Water to	1000 parts

He was very partial to the procedure. This was because the bleach bath operated at room temperature, obviating the need of a hot-water etch, and removing the danger of bad registry due to unequal stretch of the matrix material. The bad feature of the process is that it is a reversal. The final image is the complement rather than the direct result of the initial exposure.

It required no stroke of genius to remedy this trouble Riebensahm and Posseldt made the necessary variation in their application of the technique to pigmented emulsions (Ger P 144554). After the exposed paper was developed, the silver image was removed by well-known means, such as treatment with acid dichromate or acid permanganate. The residual silver bromide was then exposed and developed completely, and finally treated with the peroxide bath. This removed the gelatin and silver formed in the second development. A similar procedure was again disclosed a full generation later by W Frankenburger and G Rossler (U S.P. 2178338) The application to the making of matrices suitable for motion pictures, was made by L. E. Taylor (U.S P. 1518945, 1518946)

To be of use, the matrix must be capable of staining with a dye that will later transfer to another gelatin surface brought in contact with it. By the very nature of its formation, the gelatin in the matrix is highly tanned The gelatin in the blank which is to receive the dye transfer, is only partially tanned. In this differential most probably lies the reason for the movement of the dye from matrix to blank For a dye to stain gelatin, it must be a member of the class known as acid dyes. The dye anion forms a union with gelatin, especially in the presence of weak acids. Too low a pH, indicative of high acid content, will usually precipitate the dye. An alkaline solution will not fix the dye to the gelatin. These facts are utilized to control the extent to which the matrix is stained As pointed out above, this knowledge comes to us mainly from the disclosures of F. E Ives. In Eastman's Wash-Off Relief system, the dyes are sold in powder form. It is quite possible that the powders have been cut with buffering agents, but no definite knowedge of this has ever been published

The dye baths are prepared by dissolving the powder in distilled water. The strength of the dye bath can be judged only from the fact that one ounce of the powder will make 170 fluid ounces of solution. This is in the ratio of 25 to 5000, or one to 200. The contrast of the dye image can be controlled by the addition of acetic acid With the Eastman dyes, a saturation point is reached when 30 cc of 28 per cent acetic acid has been added to 500 cc of dye solution. Beyond this acidity no further increase in dye absorption can be noted. It is well not to juggle the acid strength of the bath each time a matrix is to be dyed. A better plan would be to have three or four baths ready, which differ from each other only in the acid content. If a dyed matrix is seen to be too flat, it can be discharged by washing in a one per cent solution of ammonia, after which it is washed in plain water to remove the ammonia. The matrix can finally be re-dyed in a bath containing more acid than the first. It is of course desirable to know the relationship between contrast and acid content. This can be determined by measuring a dyed wedge through a complementary filter

This method of control of image contrast may be suitable for the technician who makes a single print, and so can spend considerable time in manipulations. However, the commercial laboratory cannot do this. It is not surprising, therefore, to note that Technicolor loads its formulas with acetic acid (U S.P. 1807805, 1807809, 1900140; Eng P. 270279). By this means a variable is fixed, and it can no longer plague the technician with possible irregularities. A two-color system utilized the following baths:

Red

Fast red S, 3% solution	10 0 parts
Acid magenta BN, 6% solution	4 5 parts
Metanil yellow	0 03 part
Acetic acid	0 9 part
Water to	18 parts

Green

Pontacyl green SN, 4½% solution	6 parts
Metanil yellow	0.022 part
Acetic acid	0.6 part
Water to	18 parts

The stock dye solutions were purified by a special treatment with egg albumen (U.S P. 1735142; Eng. P. 270279). The dye was dissolved in warm water To this was added egg albumen, after which the solution was brought to a boil. At this point 50 cc of glacial acetic acid per liter of solution was added, the solution brought to a boil to coagulate the albumen, cooled, and filtered. The colloid took down with itself the heavy metal salts and other impurities which had a deleterious effect upon the matrix.

For three colors the following may serve (U.S.P. 1900140):

Yellow

Anthracene yellow GR or	
Sulphone yellow R	0 090 part
Acetic acid	0 45 part
Water to	18 parts

Magenta	
Acid magenta 2B, 6% solution	4.0 parts
Acid magenta BN, 6% solution	0.3 part
Fast red S, 3% solution	1.5 parts
Acetic acid	0.6 part
Water to	18 parts
Cyan	
Pontacyl green SN, 4½% solution	5.7 parts
Fast acid green B, 3% solution	2.8 parts
Acetic acid	0.6 part
Water to	18 parts

It was mentioned above that the art of contrast control by means of acid could be traced to F. E. Ives. This is disclosed in his English patent 15823/13. His recommendations were as follows:

Cyan	
Alizarin blue AS	1 part
Citric acid	1 part
Potassium citrate	1–3 parts
Water to	1000 parts
Magenta	
Alizarin rubinol 3g	1 part
Citric acid	1 part
Potassium citrate	1–3 parts
Water to	1000 parts
Yellow	
Sulphone yellow R	1 part
Citric acid	1 part
Potassium citrate	1–3 parts
Water to	1000 parts

This disclosure contained several other features now standard practice in Wash-Off Relief technique. The dyed matrices were rinsed with strong (ten per cent) acetic acid solution. This prevented or minimized the diffusion of the dye into the wash water. By this means it became possible to remove only the dye solution adhering to the surface of the matrix. It also enabled the technician to judge the balance more accurately, for the dyed matrices could be superimposed on the bottom of a white tray containing ten per cent acetic acid solution. After proper balance has been achieved, the matrices could be left in the acid until needed for transfer. This removes the danger of drying

A survey of the textile dyes that could serve for imbibition purposes was made by J. S. Friedman (*Am. Phot*, Vol. 34 (1940), p. 531). The dyes were prepared as a two per cent solution in five per cent acetic acid. A step-wedge matrix was stained and transferred upon a fixed-out piece of film. Since these tests were made with a view to the preparation of transparencies, the transfer density was much heavier than would be required for paper prints. This decrease could be achieved either by the use of much more dilute dye baths, or by the preparation of much thinner matrices The following dyes appear to be interesting possibilities for a three-color process:

Magentas

Pontacyl light red 4BL	Alizarin rubinol R
Pontacyl carmine 2g	Acid magenta 2B (conc)
Violamine RR	Fast fuchsine g
Pontacyl carmine 2B	Fast crimson 6BL

Cyans

Pontacyl green S	Wool green B
Pontacyl green SN	Patent blue (conc)
Alphazurine 2g	

Yellows

Pontacyl light yellow 3g	Fast wool yellow 3gL
Pontamine fast yellow NN	Azo yellow
Pontamine yellow CH (conc)	Aceko fast light yellow Ex
Tartrazine O	

To achieve a better control in the multiple staining of matrices, the Uvachrome Company controlled the dispersity of the dye particles in the staining bath (Eng. P. 333392) This was accomplished by fractionating the solutions by means of dialysis, ultra filtration, etc. Technicolor found that when a matrix has been used for many transfers, the dyes begin to build up, especially in the shadows This causes an appreciable loss in the tone scale which the matrix could cover. To eliminate this trouble, the matrix was given a bath after transfer, in a two per cent ammonia-alcohol-water solution (Eng P. 322173).

It was mentioned above that F. E. Ives suggested as far back as 1913 that the gelatin surface receiving the transfer be treated to aid it in absorbing and retaining the dye. Technicolor found that it was very desirable to control the ability of gelatin to imbibe dyes, and developed a system of determining the capacity of the blank to do this The film or blank was dipped into a specially compounded green dye bath, at a temperature of 18 C, for a period of fifteen seconds, after which it was rinsed in water at the same temperature for a like period and dried. A gelatin that was suitable for use in their process had a dye absorption between two limiting values. These values were determined by trial and error Every piece of film that was to be used was tested in this manner, and all film was sorted into a number of classifications. It was usually found that when the dye absorption was too large, the definition of the image suffered. When it was too low, the contrast suffered. Hence the two limits Contrasty matrices could be saved by transferring them upon a hard blank; soft matrices upon a soft blank, that is, one which had a high index of dye absorption This was determined by reading the dyed test strip in a densitometer through a red filter

Before the advent of sound-on-film, it was possible for Technicolor to make the blank specially for their purposes If the gelatin is left untanned, it will be able to absorb the dyes with extreme ease, but the definition will be extremely poor, since the transferred dye will diffuse in the blank almost as well as it diffuses out of the matrix Tanning of the gelatin with chromium naturally suggested itself immediately. F. C. Atwood suggested that a dichromated gelatin be cast upon the base, and the film be subjected to SO_2 fumes, which would reduce the dichromate to chromic salts (U.S.P. 1801478). J. F Kienninger suggested that the dichromated film be bathed with sulphites (U.S.P 1851166, Eng P 288146) Mrs. B. S. Tuttle discovered that for best results the dichromate should be acidified with acetic acid, and that the reduction should be accomplished by the gelatin itself, at an elevated temperature (U S.P. 1939738; Eng P. 270280) When sound-on-film was introduced, Technicolor printed and developed the sound as a silver track The remaining silver halide was fixed, the film then washed thoroughly and treated finally with a five per cent basic chrome-alum solution By maintaining rigid controls all along the line, it was possible to obtain a blank with a surprisingly uniform dye absorption index. The procedure for accomplishing this was outlined by L. T. Troland in his English patent 344026 (U.S.P. 2085877), and also by Mrs Tuttle (U S P. 2079470; Eng. P 484411),

Eastman recommends treatment of the blank with aluminum sulphate or potassium alum. Almost any photographic paper could be used except those with rough surfaces. The best papers are the mat or semi-mat type These must first of all be fixed out in a fresh alum-hypo fixing bath such as Eastman formula F–5:

Hypo	240 parts
Sodium sulphite, desiccated	15 parts
Acetic acid, 28%	47½ parts
Boric acid	7½ parts
Potassium alum	15 parts
Water to	1000 parts

The paper is then washed thoroughly, after which it can be treated with the special mordanting baths The first of these is prepared by the slow addition of a solution which contains 40 parts of desiccated sodium carbonate in 500 parts of water, to another which contains 200 parts of aluminum sulphate in 1000 parts of water. When the addition is made, a white precipitate is first formed, but this redissolves upon stirring. When all the carbonate has been added, a clear solution should result If there is any precipitate left it should be removed by filtration. The paper is bathed in this solution for five minutes, after which it is washed for five minutes. It is then bathed in five per cent sodium acetate for five minutes, and followed by another wash If the paper is to be used immediately, it need not be dried; but if it is dried and stored away, it should be soaked in water for a period of at least five minutes.

When the blank was made from a fixed-out film or bromide, it was found that a freshly prepared sheet acted differently from one that had aged more than twenty-four hours It appears that the action of alum or chromium on the gelatin continues for a while. In a typical case, where the fixed-out film was prepared by giving a final bath in seven per cent titrated chrome alum, the following results were obtained:

Age of Blank	*Dye Absorption Index*
1 hour	66 0
6 hours	64 0
20 hours	61 0
44 hours	59.1
70 hours	59.0

The age of the blank was calculated from the time the film came out of the drier to the time the dye-absorption test was made. This was done by measuring the amount of dye absorbed by the film in fifteen seconds, followed by a rinse in water The index is the reading on a Martens densitometer, so that it represents degrees These are related to density by the equation $\log \tan^2 \theta =$ density, where θ is the angle determined in the Martens densitometer. The dye used was a green, and the reading was made through a red filter. Upon conversion into densities, the dye absorbed by the same material, differing only in age, was the following.

Age in Hours	*Density*
1	0.70
6	0.62
20	0 52
44	0 44
70	0.44

From this it is seen that in the first day the ability of the blank to absorb dye dropped rather fast. A slow drop continued to take place for the next twelve to twenty-four hours, after which constancy was obtained.

It is not at all certain that there is any reaction between the dyes and the chrome or other alums, during staining. It is possible to replace the alum with formaldehyde, and for best results, the formaldehyde bath should contain some urea to control the swelling factor, and some acid. The fixed and washed film was bathed for five minutes in

Formaldehyde 40% solution	25 parts
Urea	10 parts
Acetic acid	5 parts
Water	1000 parts

It was dried immediately after treatment. The results were as follows:

Age in Hours	*Dye Absorption Index*	*Density*
1	62.3	0 558
3	62 2	0 554
16	62.0	0.548
40	61 5	0.530
100	61.4	0 526
200	61 2	0.518

Now it is seen that the blank is practically at equilibrium from the first hour, and that the change over almost two weeks is negligible. These variations must be kept in mind when large amounts of transfer paper are prepared at one time and stored away for future use

Instead of transferring dyes, it has been proposed by F. Lierg to transfer a component, which would later be converted into color (U.S.P. 2036945). Thus a nickel salt could be transferred to a blank, and this treated with dimethyl-glyoxime to form the normal magenta obtained by chemical toning. Or a ferrous salt could be transferred, and the transfer treated with ferricyanide. The variations to this technique are manifold, and the many variations have been duly patented G. Szasz transferred a stabilized diazonium salt. This could be converted into the dye by a treatment with the proper coupling agent (Eng. P 451190; cf also 341154 and 384312). Brewster patented the transfer of a silver or copper salt which he later converted into the iodide This last is finally treated with a basic dye which becomes mordanted to the silver or copper iodide hydrosol (U.S P. 2070222)

The direct transfer of the extremely brilliant basic dyes was first proposed by R von Arx (U.S.P. 1643529; Eng. P. 245163). The general theory of this technique is that the matrix is treated with some solution such as silver iodide which will cause it to fix the dye in proportion to the image density. The dyed matrix is then brought into contact with the blank. This is made to contain a much stronger dye mordant than is present in the matrix. Under these conditions the dye will transfer from the relatively weak mordant in the matrix to the strong mordant in the blank. There are several advantages to this procedure The images are sharper, since no diffusion takes place after the dye becomes fixed in the blank. The dyes are more brilliant, since the basic dyes are the finest available when only shade, brilliance, and purity are considered. The disadvantages are the lack of stability of the dye images, and the long times required to effect transfer.

This procedure necessarily requires different matrix material from the others. F. Lierg did quite a bit of work along these lines (U.S.P 2054261; 2073212; Eng. P. 353819, 344365). The matrix emulsion was made to contain substances which would fix the dyes loosely. Basic dyes could be fixed by alkali, acid dyes by acids. Or the matrix could contain albumen which would have a high affinity for some dyes. The blank would then contain substances that would release the dye, and other substances that would fix the dye once it transfers to the blank The agent that releases the dye must be capable of diffusion out of the blank and into the matrix. The agent that fixes the dye once it transfers, must be non-diffusing. It might be stated that it was in these experiments that Mr. Lierg discovered how to make substances non-diffusible, which he later applied to monopacks.

The blank must be specially prepared, and a number of experimenters have tackled this phase of the problem F J. Tritton, in a general patent dealing with imbibition (Eng. P. 330199) describes the preparation of the blank. It is made to contain magnesium salts and is tanned with formaldehyde It is also possible to use aluminum hydroxide, zinc oxide, ferric hydroxide, meta-stannic acid, antimony or bismuth oxychloride, lead or barium sulphate, lead molybdate, etc. A typical gelatin casting solution is

Gelatin	20 parts
Water	150 parts
Magnesium sulphate, 20% solution	50 parts
Ammonia	5.7 parts
Saponin	6 0 parts
Formaldehyde, 2½% solution	1 part

The blank is suitable to receive both acid and basic dyes, hence could be used in all imbibition procedures. R Gschopf (Eng. P. 430823) suggested that the gelatin contain the complex acid such as phospho-tungstic, silico tungstic or antimony tungstic acids These are excellent pigmentary agents for basic dyes, and are used in that capacity by the pigment manufacturer. The same inventor, in conjunction with K Pokorny disclosed the use of organic acids like oxy naphthoic acids (U S P 2124371). The use of silico tungstic acid was also disclosed by A Jasmatzi (Eng. P. 481822) and by L O. A. Pollak (Eng. P. 504790). In the last disclosure, a casting solution was prepared by dissolving 30 parts of a hard (tanned) gelatin in 500 parts of warm water. At a temperature between 60 and 70 C there was added 15 parts of silico-tungstic acid dissolved in 100 parts of water. A white gummy precipitate was formed This was washed thoroughly in cold water, dispersed in hot water, and cast upon a paper base.

CHAPTER 27

DIAZO PHOTOGRAPHY

THE light-sensitivity of diazonium salts was first noted by the French chemists Berthelot and Vielle in 1881. The phenomenon was studied quite fully by later chemists who were mainly interested in the properties of such systems. The first to utilize the procedure photographically was West who, in 1885, showed pictures made by this procedure ("Ergebnisse der Angewandten Physikalischen Chemie," Vol. V, p. 376). For some reason his disclosure passed unnoticed, and it remained for others to rediscover the photographic applications. Hence most historians ascribe to Feer and to Green, Cross, and Bevan the honor of being the initiators of this important technique. West's finding was only recently uncovered. Although a dye image is the final result of a diazotype print, the procedure has not been successfully applied to the making of color prints. It has been exceedingly successful, however, as a copy material. When light is absorbed by a system containing diazonium salts, one of several reactions can take place. If the salt is a chloride, and water is present, the diazonium group becomes converted into an OH. The unreacted diazonium salt can then be developed by conversion into a dye. This procedure yields a direct positive, since whites yield whites, and blacks yield the maximum dye density obtainable. If the diazonium salt is a cyanide, a reactive type which can couple to form dyes becomes converted, by the absorption of light, into an unreactive type, which no longer can be changed into a dye. Here, again, a direct positive is formed. If the salt is a sulphonate which is unreactive, and cannot couple to form a dye, absorption of light converts it into a reactive form that can undergo dye formation. In this technique we have a negative process, since whites now yield the dye in maximum intensity, while blacks yield no dye deposits. We see, therefore, that in order to understand and realize the possibilities of the technique, we must understand the chemistry of the changes that take place

Diazo chemistry is very complex. Several very interesting and important texts have been written in the English language dealing with this subject, and the interested reader is referred to these for detailed information Probably the best reference is the book by K. H. Saunders, published in 1936, and titled "The Aromatic Diazo Compounds." Here we will give only a streamlined discussion of the pertinent facts.

If an aromatic amine be treated with nitrous acid at a low temperature, the amino group becomes converted into a diazonium group in accordance with the equation

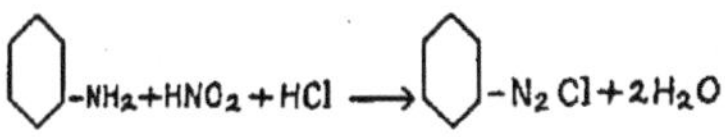

Nitrous acid can be generated in situ by the interaction between the stable sodium nitrite salt and hydrochloric acid. It is seen that one mol of hydrochloric acid is also used up so that the reaction neutralizes two molecules of acid. In practice, the amine is dissolved as the hydrochloride, an extra molecule of acid added, the solution cooled with ice to below 5 C, and the theoretical quantity of sodium nitrite added in the form of a concentrated solution. Reaction is practically instantaneous and usually quantitative. In fact so near perfect is the reaction, that it is used to determine the presence of amines quantitatively. This procedure serves to convert the simple amines into diazonium salts The carboxylated, nitrated, sulphonated or otherwise substituted amines may need special treatments that are specific for specific bodies. In some cases it is sufficient to dissolve the amine in concentrated sulphuric acid and diazotize with nitrosulphuric acid made by dissolving sodium nitrite or nitrous oxide in concentrated sulphuric acid In other cases, where solution of the amine can be obtained in the form of a sodium salt, a solution containing it and the requisite quantity of sodium nitrite is added to hydrochloric or sulphuric acid. These and other procedures for the formation are discussed in detail in the book noted above.

The diazonium salts are complex bodies. For a long time there raged a heated discussion concerning their structure, but it is now fairly universally accepted that the structure is a complex mixture of different tautomers and isomers, the predominant type depending upon the conditions. In strong acid solutions, the accepted structure of the diazonium salt is the following.

$$[R-N^{+}\equiv N]Cl^{-}.$$

In this form one of the nitrogens is quaternary, as in the ammonium type salts, hence the "ium" ending to the name. If *R* is a benzene group, the compound above would be called benzene-diazonium chloride.

If the solution is made less acid, or slightly alkaline, the chloride ion becomes replaced by an hydroxyl group to yield:

$$[R-N^{+}\equiv]OH$$

a body whose existence has been proven, but which immediately undergoes a tautomeric change into the diazo form:

$$R-N=N-OH$$

This form differs materially from the other. Benzene diazonium hydroxide $[R-N^{+}\equiv N]OH$, being the hydroxide of a quaternary nitrogen, is a very strong base. The other form is a derivative of nitrous acid, $[R-N=N-OH]$ and it would be expected to be acidic This is proven by conductivity, ionization, and other tests This form of the molecule undergoes a very important reaction termed coupling It unites with aromatic amines or phenols to form azo bodies which are highly colored, and which are the azo dyes of industry. The reaction proceeds in accordance to the scheme:

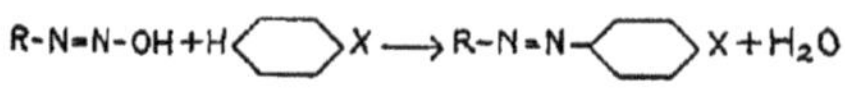

Here X represents an amino or hydroxy group. It is this reaction which is utilized as a developer in diazo photography.

If benzene diazonium chloride be added to a neutral solution of sodium sulphite, a reaction occurs whereby the chloride becomes replaced by a sulphurous acid group. There are two possibilities here. First we can have the formation of a diazonium sulphite:

$$[R{-}N^{+}{\equiv}N]Cl + Na_2SO_3 \rightarrow [R{-}N^{+}{\equiv}N]SO_3Na + NaCl$$

This body would be no different in its behavior toward coupling agents than the diazonium chloride. After the solution stands for a while, it loses its capacity to couple. This might be explained by a tautomeric change in accordance with the scheme:

$$[R{-}N^{+}{\equiv}N]SO_3Na \rightarrow R{-}N{=}N{-}SO_3Na$$

The diazonium sulphite became transformed with a diazo sulphonate This body is no longer expected to couple since we no longer have an easily removable hydroxy group. The situation is further complicated by the fact that the diazo sulphonate can exist in two forms which are stereo isomers of each other, thus:

$$\begin{array}{rcl} R{-}N & \leftarrow & R{-}N \\ \| & \rightarrow & \| \\ NaO_3S{-}N & & N{-}SO_3Na \end{array}$$

Syn or normal form Anti or iso form

Two forms of the compound are known, whereas three are indicated Hantsch and all the other scientists believe the two forms to be the stereo isomeric syn and anti bodies. One of these is reactive, and can couple readily, the other is unreactive and cannot couple. When the unreactive form is exposed to ultraviolet light, it becomes converted into the active form that can couple This reaction, first discovered by Feer (Ger. P. 53455), was formulated by him for use in textile printing, where a design was printed by exposure under a stencil. The activated diazo sulphonate was then made to couple to form a dye in the exposed regions K. Noack (*Brit. J Phot.* Vol. 45 (1898), p 822) applied this procedure to make the magenta print in a three-color process, using a lead chromate image for the yellow, and a cyanotype for the cyan The cloth or paper was impregnated with a solution containing the diazo-sulphonate coupling agent and alkali. Upon exposure, dye formation took place instantaneously Fixation was achieved by washing to remove the sensitive material from the unexposed portions.

This procedure was utilized for the making of three-color prints by Valette and Feret (Fr P 457446). Three sensitizing solutions were required, one for each of the secondary colors. The yellow sensitizer contained phenol and benzene-diazo-sulphonate. The magenta sensitizer was a mixture of beta-naphthol and para-nitro-benzene-diazo-sulphonate. The cyan sensitizer was a mixture of tolidine-tetrazo-disulphonate and alpha-naphthol. The carrier was sensitized in one of the baths, dried, and exposed under the proper negative It was then washed in acidified water to remove all unexposed diazo body, resensitized, dried, and the cycle repeated until all three images had been formed

Another process using a similar technique was disclosed by Langguth and Hummel (Eng P. 274129). The solutions they suggested were the following:

Cyan	
Dianisidine-tetrazo-disulphonate	1 part
Sodium hydroxide, 3% solution	2.5 parts
Alcohol	400 parts
Glycerin	3 parts
H acid	1 part
Water	200 parts
Yellow	
2 methyl-benzidine-tetrazo-disulphonate	4 parts
Alcohol	200 parts
Water	200 parts
Glycerin	20 parts
Aceto-acetic ester	2 parts
Magenta	
Anisidine-diazo-sulphonate	2 parts
Sodium hydroxide, 1% solution	200 parts
Alcohol	100 parts
Glycerin	3 parts
Beta-oxy-naphthoic acid	2 parts

If the diazonium chloride is treated with cyanide, there is formed a diazo cyanide. Here again we have one of three possibilities. We may have a replacement of the chloride ion by the cyanide, to yield a diazonium cyanide

$$[R—N^{+}{\equiv}N]Cl + KCN \rightarrow [R—N^{+}{\equiv}N]CN + KCl$$

In this form we would expect to retain all the properties of a diazonium salt Another possibility is the formation of the tautomeric diazo-cyanide, thus:

$$[R—N^{+}{\equiv}N]Cl + KCN \rightarrow R—N{=}N—CN + KCl$$

This would not be a diazonium salt, which is a derivative of a quaternary nitrogen. It would be the nitrile derivative of a substituted nitrous acid nitrogen As a matter of fact, three derivatives have been isolated, one of which is colorless and shows all the characteristics of a diazonium salt, while the other two are colored, indicating a true azo grouping Hence these two have been formulated to be the syn and anti diazo-cyanides

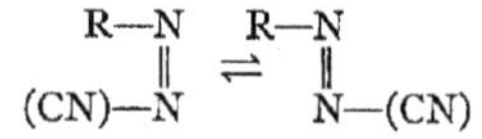

Syn form Anti form

When a diazo-cyanide which is in the form that is capable of coupling, is exposed to light, the exposed portions lose this property. Hence upon treatment with a coupling agent, dye formation will take place only in the unexposed areas. No one has yet disclosed a color process based on this reaction.

The diazonium chlorides are notoriously unstable to heat and to light. This has greatly limited their use in printing pastes in the textile industry. But the chemist's ingenuity has found a way to overcome this defect. He has discovered a method whereby he can stabilize the salt against heat deterioration. To prevent the action of light, he merely keeps the material away from light This stabilization he accomplished by forming double salt complexes of the diazonium body with zinc chloride, borofluorides, naphthalene sulphonic acids, potassium alum, etc Such stabilized double salts can be kept for months where the untreated materials would decompose in a matter of hours. This stabilization was not always extended to the reaction with light, so that it is possible to utilize a heat-stabilized diazonium double salt as the light-sensitive element for the production of prints. This has been the direction in which the later efforts of the diazotype processes traveled. The patent literature is quite ample in this phase

The application to color has been made only in a few instances. Many factors had to be taken care of. The usual practice was to mix the coupling agent with the diazonium salt, together with a sufficient content of an organic acid to prevent reaction between them. After exposure, treatment with an alkali allowed the non-exposed diazonium salt to form the dye. A color process along these lines was disclosed by Kalle and Company (Eng P. 299010). The sensitizing baths were as follows:

Cyan	
4-ethylamino-3-methyl benzene-diazonium borofluoride	1.2 parts
Tartaric acid	4 parts
H acid	1.9 parts
Water	100 parts
Magenta	
1-diazo-2-naphthol-4-sulphonic acid	1 0 part
Aluminum sulphate	3 0 parts
Resorcin	0 6 part
Water	100 parts

Yellow

4-ethyl-amino-3-methyl-benzene-diazonium-borofluoride	1.2 parts
Tartaric acid	4 0 parts
Phenol	0.5 part
Water	100 parts

If a two-color image is desired, the cyan image above is combined with one made using the following orange-red sensitizing solution:

1-diazo-2-naphthol-4-sulphonic acid	1 5 parts
1-phenol-3-methyl-5-pyrazolone	0 9 part
Sulphuric acid	7 2 parts
Water	100 parts

Instead of using acids to prevent coupling, it is possible to mask the phenolic group in the coupling agent until after exposure, then release it. This procedure was disclosed by Van der Grinten. The masking was accomplished by use of hydroxylamine which united with the hydroxyl group to form an oxime. At the proper time, treatment with alkali regenerated the phenol, and allowed dye formation to take place. Another advantage gained is that the masking of the reactive hydroxyl group also prevented deterioration by oxidation, hence purer colors result. For further details on this as well as on many other dodges utilized to yield clean whites, stabilized storable light-sensitive materials, etc , one should examine the patent literature dealing with diazotype copying processes in general

The reactions involved in diazotype were of sufficient importance to interest the chemist, and he has made a study of the reactivity of the group and the manner in which this reactivity was influenced by substitutions within the molecule. Ruff and Stein reported a rather extensive study (*Ber* Vol 34 (1901) p. 1668) Their results were reclassified by Spencer to have greater application to photography (*Phot. J.* Vol. 68 (1928) p. 490). Strips of paper were sensitized by bathing in equimolar quantities of various diazonium salts, then were given a time-wedge exposure The time required for complete destruction was noted

Diazotized amine	*Time required for complete destruction*
p Amino phenol	100
p Nitro aniline	125
p Amino benzoic acid	150
p Chlor aniline	175
p Toluidine	200
m Toluidine	125
o Toluidine	200
Benzidine	75
Diamino fluorene	29
Diamino carbazol	32

Orton, Coates and Burdett (*J. C. S.* Vol. 91 (1907), p. 35) and Ljaschenko and Kerner (*Anilinokros Prom.* Vol. 4 (1934), p. 272) made similar tests, the latter using a mercury-quartz lamp for illumination A comparison of the results indicated that ultraviolet light was the most effective.

Since the decomposition is brought about by the absorption of energy, it would be thought that the light and heat instabilities of the diazonium salts should follow parallel paths. In general, the opposite is true. The substances showing the maximum heat stability are the most light-sensitive, and vice versa. This is a fortunate circumstance since it enables the preparation of high sensitivity with simultaneous good keeping properties. Negative groups substituted in the ortho and para positions usually give greater sensitivity than positive groups substituted in the same position. Thus p-nitraniline requires less time than p-chloraniline for complete destruction. A study of the rate of decomposition of the double salts of the diazo bodies with ferric, cadmium, zinc and mercurous chloride was published by Schmidt and Maier (*Ber.* Vol. 64 (1931), p 767).

Another anomaly was disclosed in the patents issued to the Philips Gloelampenfab. (Eng P 433586, 434761; Fr. P. 783321, 783415). The degradation product of the light or heat reaction was a phenol. This should be capable of dye formation if treated with a diazonium salt. This firm found that the phenols formed by photolysis reacted much more readily than did the phenols formed by pyrolysis, despite the fact that the two are identical chemically. Schoen (Ger. P. 111416) utilized the fact that coupling agents are the result of the light exposure, by causing the photolytic phenol to combine with the excess unreacted diazonium salt. He used ortho amino salicylic acid, and 1–2–4 amino-naphthol-sulphonic acid as his starting materials.

An interesting use to which this reaction can be put is in the making of relief images Using amino phenols the reaction products become dioxy derivatives, and by secondary reactions, these can be made to effect an imagewise tanning of the gelatin. Another possibility lies in the fact that if para or ortho amino phenol be diazotized, the reaction product is either hydroquinone or pyrocatechin If silver ions be present, then a secondary reaction occurs which deposits metallic silver. This reaction is discussed by Kogel and Steigmann at some length (*Zeit. wiss. Phot.* Vol. 24 (1926), pp. 18, 171; *Phot. Ind.* (1925) p. 860; Eng P. 391963, 401898).

The use of a monopack film containing the diazonium salts has been proposed by Langguth and Hummel, Kalle and Co. (cf. references above) and the I.G. (Eng. P. 436587). But they did not explain how to make the diazonium salts sensitive to light of wavelength beyond 5000 A. Gaspar suggested the use of colored diazo bodies, on the assumption that the absorbed visible light would also be effective in the decomposition (Eng. P 417588). This is a point that has to be proven. Although no light which is not absorbed by a system can effect a chemical change in the system, not all the absorbed light is equally effective.

The use of the diazonium salts as toning agents has been discussed in a previous chapter.

CHAPTER 28

BLEACH–OUT PHOTOGRAPHY

THE term "Bleach-Out" is used to designate those processes which utilize the light sensitivity of dyes for the primary action. The image is formed of the residual unaffected dye remaining after the exposure has been made. They are therefore the most direct of all save the micro spectra procedures It was not long after the development of the dye industry, that the fugitive character of dyes was noted, and immediately proposed for photographic purposes The very fundamental Grotthus-Draper law was formulated by these scientists when they noted that natural coloring matter bleached when exposed to light.

The ability to absorb light is one of the most fundamental optical properties of matter. Under modern concepts, this absorption is to be identified with an absorption of energy, hence can be identified with some change in the absorbing material. To put it to useful purposes, it becomes necessary merely to identify the exact nature of the change, and develop means to convert it into a visible form. In the normal photographic procedure, the absorption of light produces a speck of metallic silver of colloidal size, that is adsorbed upon the silver halide grain. This constitutes the "latent image" which, under the action of certain agents, enables one to reduce completely all the silver ions in the crystal lattice of the grain. There is therefore, a dual function to the silver salts in a photographic emulsion. The first function is to allow the formation of the metallic speck by a direct action of light upon the light-sensitive medium. The second function is to furnish silver ions for the formation of the visible end product. It is merely a coincidence in nature that, with the silver halide emulsion, both functions are carried out by the same material. But this is not necessarily essential. One possible application of bleach-out photography may be found in this respect, an application first propounded by Kogel and Steigmann (*Zeit wiss. Phot.* Vol 24 (1926) p. 18, 171).

A silver halide emulsion was bathed with a weak solution of methylene blue. The plate was then exposed to a wedge which also contained some color patches. After exposure, one plate was treated with a one per cent solution of silver nitrate, then with sodium chloride, after which it was subjected to a metol developer. Another plate, similarly sensitized and exposed, was developed without the silver nitrate and sodium chloride treatment. An image was developed only in the case of the first plate. Where the silver and chloride baths were omitted, no action except general fog was obtained. The color patches also indicated that red light was the effective light in the image formation.

In this experiment, the two roles which an emulsion plays have been separated. The light-sensitive system was not that of silver halide but of methylene blue. The dye was bleached by the absorbed light, forming leuco methylene blue This was anchored at those parts of the layer where the light absorption took place. The red rays being the ones that were absorbed by the dye, the action was noted only under the red patch. When the emulsion was treated with silver nitrate, the leuco dye became oxidized by the silver ions, forming metallic silver in situ with the leuco methylene blue. But the silver is adsorbed upon the silver halide grains, hence the net result is the formation of silver halide grains that have metallic silver adsorbed upon them. This constitutes a latent image It is no wonder, therefore, that the grains receiving an original red-light exposure become developable after treatment with silver nitrate The bath in sodium chloride is necessary to remove the excess silver ions, for these are spontaneously reducible

The Grotthus-Draper law states that in a system that absorbs light, only that light is active photo-chemically, that is absorbed by the system. Let us consider the consequences of such a law when applied to dye systems A yellow dye appears such because the ultraviolet and blue rays are absorbed, and the green and red rays are transmitted unaffected A yellow dye will fade, therefore, only when it is exposed to blue or ultraviolet light. A magenta dye will absorb the green rays, hence its sensitivity will be limited to the green range. A cyan dye will absorb the red rays, so its sensitivity will be confined to that region. If a yellow, cyan, and magenta dye be mixed in equivalent portions, the yellow will absorb the blue, the magenta will absorb the green, and the cyan the red Together, they will absorb all the visible light If the dyes are fugitive and bleach upon exposure, a very interesting phenomenon results Suppose we expose the mixture to blue light. This will affect only the yellow dye, since only that will absorb blue (we assume ideal dyes), and thus only the yellow dye will fade or bleach, dependent upon the length and intensity of exposure. If all the yellow dye be bleached, there will remain an equivalent mixture of the cyan and magenta dyes The cyan will absorb the red primary and transmit the blue and green The magenta will absorb the green primary and transmit the other two Only the blue primary will be transmitted by both acting simultaneously. Thus an exposure to blue will yield blue A similar analysis will show that, regardless of what the color of the exposing light is, the resultant image will be as close an approach to it as is possible under a three-color subtractive system utilizing these dyes as secondaries.

There is one other fact to be disclosed before we can determine the utility of dye-bleach for photographic purposes We saw that the reproduction of color is direct. We must now determine how tones will be reproduced. To this end a film or paper is sensitized by treatment with a balanced mixture of three dyes, then is exposed to "white" light under a gray scale. The lightest step in the scale will transmit the most light. Hence at the corresponding point in the sensitized sheet, there will be the maximum effect Light areas become reproduced as light grays or white, while dense areas become reproduced as deep grays or blacks. Tone reproduction, like hue, is therefore direct. This makes the procedure an ideal printing process for the duplication of Ansco Color, Kodachrome, Dufaycolor or other types of color transparencies. It is no wonder, therefore, that interest in dye-bleach processes follows fairly closely the historical development of successful transparency processes.

It was the brilliant German scientist, Liesegang, who was the first to point out this ideal situation (*Phot. Archiv.* No. 633 (1889) p. 382). It was immediately seized upon by a whole series of scientists who spent considerable time and effort to make it more than a laboratory curiosity This enthusiastic approach to a theoretical solution of the color problem is quite analogous to the hopes aroused by the Lippmann Process, the lenticular film procedures, and the screen plates. It is with some sorrow that one must acknowledge that, despite the elegance of the solution, the successful application of the principles involved still remains unsolved

We can divide the work done in this field into two historical periods. The first takes in the period up to the great deluge known as World War I During this time such eminent chemists as Vallot, Neuhauss, Worel, Szczepanik, Limmer and Smith devoted a lot of attention to the solution. The war period 1914–1918 appeared to have definitely stopped most of the work, and it was not until about 1925 that Koenig, Steigmann, Mudrovcic, Wendt and others, resurrected it for another brief period. One still runs across a reference in the current (1943–1944) literature to the bleach-out procedure, but by and large, it has been abandoned.

The work of the first period is best summarized in a booklet by Limmer, termed "Das Ausbleichverfahren," published in 1911 at Halle. Here are listed all the dyes then known to be suitable for this purpose, together with a discussion of the various sensitizing agents that could enhance or even impart light-sensitivity to the dyes. Limmer himself tested a large series of dyes for their stability to light in the presence or absence of various chemical agents, and various binding agents such as gelatin, nitrocellulose, etc. He was able to classify the dyes into four classes. In Class *A* he listed the dyes that were stable to light in nitrocellulose solutions In Class *B* were listed those that were light-sensitive per se. In Class *C* were listed the dyes that became light-sensitive upon the addition of various sensitizing agents. In Class *D* were listed the dyes that had their light-sensitivity enhanced by the presence of nitrocellulose. The number beside each dye is the Schultz number in the edition of the *Farbstofftabellen* then (1911) available.

The dye was dissolved in water or alcohol in the ratio of one part of dye to 50,000 parts of solvent. The solution was exposed for one hour to the light of a Siemens lamp, in the presence and absence of the sensitizers, binding agents, etc., and the notation made as to whether or not fading took place. This type of trial-and-error experiment was quite typical of the work done in the first period.

Class A

Martin yellow	4	Crystal violet	428
Victoria blue 4BS	42	Fast acid violet 10B	438
Tartrazine	95	Victoria blue R	461
Brilliant yellow	100	Victoria blue B	462
Congo	219	Rhodamine S	471
Orange 2		Uranine	487
Benzo blue 2B	282	Eosin A	489
Chicago blue RW	309	Brilliant alizarin blue R	595
Benzo pure blue	311	Phenosafranine	611
Sulfonazurine	340	Rhoduline violet	620
Columbia black FB	376	Chinoline red	...

Class B

Thiazol yellow	15	Chrome violet	420
Chrysoidine A	.	Fuchsin	424
Congo rubine	236	Aniline blue	433
Direct orange G	267, 291	Acid fuchsin B	434
Benzo purpurin 4B	268	Water blue 3B	452
Benzo azurin 3G	314	Methylene blue	588
Auramine 2G	401	Mimose	648
Malachite green	403	Pinaverdol	.
Brilliant green	404	Pinachrome	..
Acid green G	410	Dicyanine	..
Chrome green	419	Orthochrome T	...

Class C

Benzo purpurin 10B	304	Rose bengal	500
Methyl violet 2B extra	427	Auracin G	...
Erythrosin	494		

Class D

Thiazol yellow	15	Benzo purpurin 10B	304
Benzo purpurin 4B	268	Auracin G	...

Dr J. H Smith made the greatest technical advances in this period. About 1910 he introduced a paper-print procedure based on dye-bleach technique. The material was called Utocolor paper. Speaking before an English group at the time the paper was introduced, he outlined the problems that were inherent in the procedure (*Phot. J.* Vol. 50 (1910) p. 141).

He said in substance:

The use of Utocolor paper behind Autochrome plates led to failure because the problems inherent in color reproduction by additive processes became superimposed upon those met in subtractive processes. The failure to obtain pure whites in dye-bleach methods caused a considerable loss of color contrast. This led to a degradation of color in the final print. Therefore Dr. Smith suggested that it is best to use hand-colored transparencies as originals. The greatest problem in bleach-out was due to the unequal rates at which the different dyes bleached. Most dyes bleached more rapidly when exposed to blue than to the other colors. This may seem to be a contradiction of the Grotthus-Draper law, but no dye exists which does not have an appreciable blue and ultraviolet absorption. The first problem to solve, therefore, is to find dyes whose action along the entire spectrum range would be uniform.

The nature of the reaction between light and the dye was commonly supposed to be that of oxidation, but the mechanism was obscure. It was possible to distinguish at least three different reactions. Methylene blue, for instance, becomes reduced upon exposure to light, forming leuco methylene blue This was not an oxidation. Another type of reaction was that described by Stobbe (*Ann.* Vol. 359 (1908) p 1), and termed pseudo bleaching by Smith. He found that when the fulgides were exposed to light, an internal rearrangement of the molecule took place with a resultant color change. Several other reactions took place before a final bleaching was obtained. This chain of events is typical of many other dye systems. Such dyes were unsuitable for bleach-out processes.

Some dyes worked well when pure, but became unsuitable when mixed with other dyes. For instance, when an acid dye was added to a basic dye, interaction took place which caused a mutual precipitation of both. Szczepanik segregated the two types. Thus acid dyes were used in gelatin media, and basic dyes were used in collodion. But even so it was not possible to completely isolate them from each other. Smith was rather partial to the use of gelatin He dispersed his dyes in this binding medium, and added thiosinamine to the mixture to increase the sensitivity This was the really great advance which Dr. Smith achieved, for thiosinamine proved to be a very effective sensitizing agent. In this respect it is interesting to note that fifteen years later, Dr S. E Sheppard of the Eastman Kodak Research Laboratories, isolated a related compound from gelatin and demonstrated that it was a powerful sensitizer for the silver-halide emulsion.

The tremendous enthusiasm which gripped the photographic technicians when Utocolor paper was announced turned into as great a disappointment when results failed to even approach the high hopes expected. A reaction set in that was typified by the editorial which appeared in an issue of the *British Journal of Photography* of that period The editors stated that bleach-out processes had little merit, and they decried the usefulness of further research. The firm of Meister, Lucius and Bruening, who specialized in the manufacture of dyes for photographic purposes, stated in their "Pina Manual" (page 55), that the bleach-out processes were of no practical value. They listed a series of dyes which they stated gave clear whites. These were

Brilliant green	Naphthol yellow
Malachite green	Naphthol green
Victoria blue	Erioglaucine
Erythrosin	Acid violet

This attitude and the first World War combined to give the process a bad name. But after a while a new group of scientists appeared and they approached the problem from a more scientific point of view. Their aim was to determine the nature of the reaction, rather than to develop a marketable product. These men disclosed a large number of facts, and established a curious cross-connection between dye-sensitizer systems and dye-silver-halide systems. One of the difficulties mentioned by Smith was the failure of dyes to bleach at a uniform rate, and that pure dyes reacted differently from their mixture. Neuweiler (*Zeit. wiss. Phot.* Vol. 25 (1928) p 127) studied the photo-chemical bleaching of a large number of dyes in the presence of zinc oxide and eosin. Both these substances sensitized the reduction of dyes to an extensive degree. Eosin is a dye closely related to erythrosin, one of the best dyes known for the bleach-out processes. In the presence of "anodic depolarizers" (reducing agents, substances which readily give up electrons) such as cane sugar or glycerin, the dye Victoria blue becomes reduced to the leuco form upon exposure if either eosin or zinc oxide is present. These last do not suffer any change. Azo dyes become irreversibly reduced to amines under analogous conditions. Thus photo-chemical reduction rather than oxidation takes place. Eosin is itself a highly light-sensitive body, yet under the above conditions, it remains unchanged Thus in the mixture of eosin and Victoria blue, two dyes of extremely low light fastness, only the blue dye remains active.

To explain this phenomenon, Neuweiler adopted the Baur concepts. The reaction can be formulated schematically in the following manner

$$\text{Eosin}\begin{cases} \oplus + \text{Anodic depolarizer} \rightarrow \text{oxidation of depolarizer} \\ \ominus + \text{Victoria blue} \rightarrow \text{reduction of dye} \end{cases}$$

Translated, this reads that upon the absorption of light, the dye eosin undergoes an internal rearrangement. An electron in the molecule becomes displaced, thereby making the remainder of the molecule relatively positive. In the presence of substances that readily give up electrons, the eosin residue absorbs electrons, returning to its original state. The anodic depolarizer, having given up an electron, is oxidized. In the meantime, the released electron from eosin becomes absorbed by the dye Victoria blue, which thus becomes converted to the leuco base. Thus, the dye eosin sensitized the photo-chemical reduction of Victoria blue. For this to be true, the light that is active is the light absorbed by eosin and not by Victoria blue, for its bleaching is merely a secondary reaction, not the primary one. It is very interesting to note that the same dye eosin is a fair sensitizer for the photolysis of silver halides, and here it has been proven that the activity is limited to the range of colors absorbed by eosin Now gelatin takes the place of the cane sugar or other anodic depolarizer.

$$\text{Eosin}\begin{cases} \oplus + \text{gelatin} \rightarrow \text{oxidized gelatin} \\ \ominus + Ag^{+} \rightarrow Ag^{0} \end{cases}$$

A somewhat analogous reaction, with the shoe on the other foot this time, was disclosed a year later by Mudrovcic, another disciple of Baur. He reported (*Phot Ind* Vol. 27 (1929) p. 1318) that the polymethine dyes such as pinacyanol or pinachrome, bleach much more readily in the presence of other dyes such as Victoria blue, methylene blue, Laut's violet, Rosinduline yellow, Capri blue, or safranine, than in their absence. The experimental procedure was to place the dye in a concentration of one to 20,000 in water or 50% alcohol, in a test tube, add the sensitizing dye, seal the tube to prevent access of air, then expose to light. In the absence of any sensitizer, it required five hours to bleach pinacyanol. Upon the addition of one drop of 1 : 20,000 methylene blue the bleach time was reduced to several minutes. In another experiment a mixture contained one-third volume methylene blue (1 : 10,000) and two-thirds volume pinacyanol (1 : 5000). In three minutes the pinacyanol bleached completely, leaving the methylene blue untouched. Upon further exposure, this dye also began to bleach, but in a reversible manner The pinacyanol was bleached irreversibly. The reversible bleaching of the methylene blue indicated that this dye was reduced to the leuco form. According to Mudrovcic, the other dye, pinacyanol, became oxidized

We have here a curious cycle. The dye eosin sensitizes the bleaching of the dye Victoria blue, when reducing agents are present Here eosin becomes a sort of electron carrier, donating an electron on the one hand to the dye, and receiving it on the other, from cane sugar. Eosin is a sensitizer for the silver-halide emulsion, causing a photolytic decomposition to take place under the influence of light other than the blue Pinacyanol, another sensitizer for the silver-halide emulsion, under somewhat different conditions (no anodic depolarizer present) when mixed with Victoria blue, is itself oxidized while the Victoria blue remains untouched Of course it is quite possible that in the presence of an anodic depolarizer like cane sugar, pinacyanol would itself be left untouched, and the Victoria blue would be bleached. The two reactions are not exclusive, but appear rather to be complementary. If silver nitrate is added to a pinacyanol solution, there is evidence that simultaneously with the bleaching of the dye, reduction of the silver ions takes place (Mecke and Semerano, *Zeit. wiss. Phot.* Vol. 36 (1937) p. 25, Steigmann, *Zeit wiss Phot.* Vol. 27 (1929) p. 113) It is also interesting to note that pinacyanol is a basic dye while eosin is an acid dye

Another parallel of bleach-out with normal silver bromide is the fact that both systems are highly sensitized by thiourea and thiourea derivatives. But here also the analogy must not be carried too far, for the sensitization of dyes by thiourea is not a general phenomenon It is true for dyes like Victoria blue, methylene blue, Capri blue, phenosafranine, etc. These dyes are also sensitized by eosin, zinc oxide, and pinacyanol. But the polymethine dyes act differently. They are actually desensitized by the presence of thiourea. The difference may be explained by the fact that the first group of dyes bleach by conversion to the leuco form, that is, they undergo photo-reduction reactions, while the polymethine dyes, as pointed out by Mudrovcic (cf above) and before him, by Lasareff (*Trans. Far. Soc.* Vol. 21 (1925) p 475; *Zeit. Phys. Chem.* Vol. 78 (1912) p 657) undergo photo-oxidation.

A more detailed study of the bleach-out processes was made by Mudrovcic in 1929 (*Zeit. wiss. Phot.* Vol. 26 (1929) p. 171). Here a study was made not only of the dyes but also of the sensitizing agents The dyes tested included

Capri blue	Flavinduline O	Malachite green
Cresyl blue	Erythrosin	Patent blue
Rhoduline red B	Rhodamine S	Tartrazine
Rosinduline B	Methylene blue	

Very few of the sensitizing agents tested were without effect upon methylene blue. The action of the thiourea derivatives was governable to a great extent upon substitutions within the molecule. This molecule has two amino groups, each containing two hydrogens

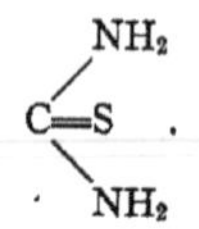

All but one of the hydrogens can be replaced before the sensitizing action is lost. When the substitution was a phenyl or a naphthyl group, only a slight increase in activity over that of the parent substance was noted. An entirely different order of sensitivity was obtained, however, when an allyl group, $CH_3—CH{=}CH_2$, replaced the hydrogen. Thiosinamine, the sensitizing agent that made Utocolor a salable product, was allyl thiourea

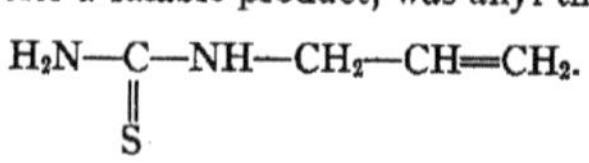

According to Victor Henri ("Études des Photochimie," p. 186) this was due to the fact that the allyl radical was a very efficient absorber of ultraviolet light, which would infer that it was the ultraviolet absorption that was mainly responsible for the light sensitivity of the system, a fact that no one has pointed out as yet, probably because no one has thoroughly investigated it. If the amino group that contained the allyl substitution remains with one free hydrogen, and the other be ethylated, another tremendous boost in sensitivity occurs A. Just disclosed that the most powerful sensitizing agent he was able to prepare, was N . N diethyl : N′ allyl-thiourea. Placing an acetyl group in place of one of the hydrogens, reduced the sensitizing action somewhat.

These facts were utilized by Mudrovcic to prepare a balanced pack. Flavinduline served for the yellow, Capri blue G ON for the cyan, and rosinduline 2B for the magenta, all in a concentration of one per cent. The flavinduline was dissolved in collodion, and since it bleached so much more readily than the others, it was sensitized with acetyl thiourea. The other two were dissolved in gelatin solution and sensitized with diethyl-thiosinamine. The sensitizers were present in double the concentration of the dyes. The whites did not bleach very clean, so that screen-plate transparencies were not suitable for copy purposes The exposures needed were approximately fifteen minutes in a June sun.

The patent literature is not very extensive in this field By far the greatest number of patents issued in the post World War I period were made to the I.G and to Ansco. From these disclosures it is apparent that the dyes used are those of the xanthonium type, dyes that are quite stable ordinarily, but become light-sensitive when treated with sensitizing agents To fix the images, the material is treated with agents which destroy the sensitizer (U.S.P. 1850162; Eng. P. 341371; Ger. P. 506100). Sulphurous acid is especially effective in this respect. Since this treatment requires bathing in aqueous solutions, it is necessary to first treat the layers with dye precipitants such as $NaBF_4$ or its free acid (U.S.P. 1871830, Eng. P. 348102, Fr. P. 690386) In U S patent 1880573 are listed many other dyes that are suitable. All of these are characterized by the groupings

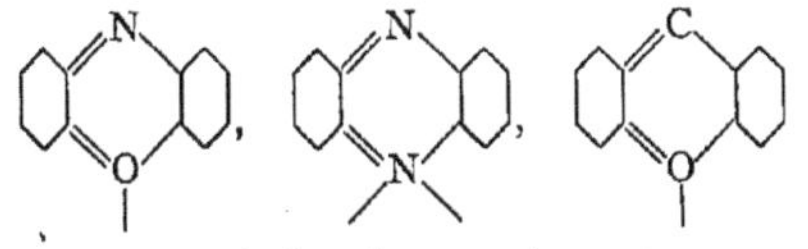

where the rings that are attached to the central structures, may be substituted benzene or naphthalene residues, containing amino or hydroxy groups. They may also contain other groups which serve to equalize the rate of bleaching. These factors are discussed in some detail in a number of patents (U.S P 1880572, 1850220; Eng. P. 348232, 352196; Ger. P. 500502, 518065). Various binding agents are suggested as carriers for the light-sensitive systems in U S. patent 1916779 (Eng. P 341151). These are gelatin, nitrocellulose, acetyl cellulose, the cellulose ethers, or preferably mixtures of all From one to three milligrams of dye, one gram of binder, and from 0 06 to 0 12 gram of sensitizing agent are used for every hundred square centimeters of surface to be coated.

That seasoned color worker, Dr Gaspar, also dabbled in this field (U.S.P. 2049005). He proposed to use acid dyes instead of basic. To do this, he found it necessary to add some "activating" agent to the usual sensitizer. A useful bath is either of the following:

A	Water	100 parts
	Thiosinamine	5 parts
	$NaHSO_4$	5 parts
	Metol	1 part
B.	Water	200 parts
	Rongalite	5 parts
	Thiocarbamide	5 parts

The following solution will cover one square decimeter of surface

Gelatin, 4% solution	4 cc
Dye, 1%	½ cc
Sensitizer	½ cc

Tartrazine can be used for the yellow image, fast red D for the magenta, and patent blue A for the cyan.

From the above analysis, it is seen that the bleach-out processes are still laboratory curiosities. This is a great pity, for the procedure does offer an elegant theoretical solution to the problems of color photography. There are several extremely interesting things that may be pointed out. First and foremost, a bleach-out system is the least expensive process as far as light-utilization is concerned. This is because the effective light is the light absorbed by the system. Since our system contains a mixture of three dyes, and since these have mutually exclusive absorptions (in theory at least) all the light absorbed by the system can be utilized for image formation. In normal three-color processes we divide a light beam into three parts, then pass each sub-beam through a filter which absorbs a minimum of two-thirds of the light energy in the beam, and may, as with the C5 filter, absorb more nearly 80 per cent of the energy. Thus only a small fraction of the energy entering the lens, is utilized for image formation.

Even with the more modern monopacks and tripacks, we lose considerably. Theoretically in these cases, no light should be lost, since each emulsion layer utilizes the light of but a single primary, and passes the remainder to the other layers. But here again, practice is far behind theory. The first layer is sensitive to, and therefore absorbant of, the blue rays. Unfortunately this layer does not absorb blue light with any great efficiency. Were this so, a normal color-blind emulsion would appear to be a brilliant yellow instead of a gray with a slight tinge of yellow. To insure against the unused or unabsorbed blue light acting upon the layers beneath, it is necessary to place a yellow filter between the top and the other layers. This filter has to have a density of at least 2.00 to effect a good separation. This is indicative of how intense the transmitted blue rays are relative to the overall green and red sensitivities of the other layers Similarly it is necessary to place a red filter between the red- and green-sensitive layers, to absorb the unused green rays

This problem is one which, curiously enough, has little or no mention in the current literature, and yet herein lies a great possible advance in emulsion-making We must learn to make a blue-sensitive emulsion which is colored minus blue or yellow, for such an emulsion must absorb the blue rays. Perhaps this can be done by some system of optical sensitization of a silver-halide emulsion The so-called methylene blue effect, disclosed by Kogel and Steigmann and mentioned early in this chapter, offers another possibility. In this system, the light-sensitive element is no longer silver bromide, but an easily reducible dye. The reduced dye is adsorbed upon silver-halide grain, so that when it is made to react with silver nitrate or other easily reduced metallic ion, a speck of metal will be formed which will be adsorbed at the same spot on the grain. This makes that grain developable. The red-light absorption of a silver-halide grain dyed with methylene blue, is considerably better than one dyed with pinacyanol, hence we should expect more efficient use of the incident light. That, of course, is the goal, not the present achievement. One other advantage which such a system gives is that a silver-halide grain containing adsorbed methylene blue, becomes considerably desensitized to the blue rays. We thus have a possible system whereby a light-sensitive element yielding a silver image is insensitive to the blue rays If such an element could be developed to yield a reasonable speed, we could make a tripack with a front element which is sensitive to red and considerably more transparent to green and blue than the silver-halide emulsion is to green and red. The blue-sensitive emulsion, yielding the yellow-colored part image, could then be made the rear element. Definition would be considerably improved.

From the description we gave above, the methylene blue effect had a speed that was comparable to that of a contact paper. But the experiments of Mudrovcic, Neuweiler, Smith, etc., have shown how bleach-out layers based on photo-reduction reactions could be made considerably more sensitive. The entire circle of photo reactions of the photographic sensitizing and desensitizing agents need thorough re-examination with the methylene blue effect in mind

LIST OF PERIODICALS AND ABBREVIATIONS

Abr Sci Pub	Abridged Scientific Publications from the Kodak Research Laboratory
Am. Phot	American Photography
Anilinokros Prom	Anilinokrosochnaya Promyshlennost
Ann	Liebig's Annalen
Ann de chim	Annales de chimie
Ber.	Berichte der deutschen chemischen Gesellschaft
Brit Ass Adv Sci	British Association for the Advancement of Science
Brit J Phot	British Journal of Photography
Bull. soc chim franç.	Bulletin de la société chimique de France
Bull soc franç phot.	Bulletin de la société française de photographie
Bu. Stand. J. of Res	Bureau of Standards Journal of Research
Bu. Stand. Sci.	Bureau of Standards Scientific Papers
Chem Rev.	Chemical Reviews
Chem. Ztg.	Chemiker-Zeitung
Compte rend.	Compte rendus hebdomadaires des sciences de l'Académie des sciences
Defender Trade Bull.	Defender Trade Bulletin
Handbuch	Eder's Handbuch der Photographie
Ind. Eng Chem	Industrial and Engineering Chemistry
Jahrbuch	Eder's Jahrbuch der Photographie und Reproduktionstechnik
J Amer Leather Chem Ass'n	Journal of the American Leather Chemists Association
J Frank Inst.	Journal of the Franklin Institute
J Cam Club	Journal of the Camera Club (English)
J. Optical Soc Am	Journal of the Optical Society of America
J Phys Chem	Journal of Physical Chemistry
J Prakt Chem.	Journal für praktische Chemie
J Soc Mot. Pic. Eng.	Journal of the Motion Picture Engineers
Kol. Z	Kolloid-Zeitschrift
La Phot	La Photographie
Lichtbild	Das Deutsche Lichtbild
Mon Phot.	Moniteur de la Photographie
New Phil J.	New Philosophical Journal
Phot. Almanach	Photographische Almanach
Phot Archiv	Photographisches Archiv
Phot Chem Stud	Photo chemische Studien
Phot Coul	La Photographie des Couleurs
Phot Ind	Photographische Industrie
Phot J.	Photographic Journal
Phot Kino Chem Ind	Photo-Kino Chemical Industry (USSR)
Phot Korr.	Photographische Korrespondenz
Phot. Mitt.	Photographische Mitteilung
Phot News	Photographic News
Phot. Notes	Photographic Notes
Phot. Rund	Photographische Rundschau
Phot Tech	Photo Technique
Phot. Times	Photographic Times
Phot Woch	Photographisches Wochenblatt
Rev franç phot cinémat.	Revue française de photographie et de cinématographie
Silbermann	Fortschritte auf dem Gebiete der photo- und chemigraphischen Reproduktionsverfahren
Trans Far Soc	Transactions of the Faraday Society
Trans. Roy Soc Edin.	Transactions of the Royal Society of Edinburgh
Zeit. anal Chem	Zeitschrift für analytische Chemie
Z. anorg. Chem.	Zeitschrift für anorganische Chemie
Zeit phys Chem.	Zeitschrift für physikalische Chemie
Zeit. tech Physik.	Zeitschrift für technische Physik
Zeit. wiss. Phot	Zeitschrift fur wissenschaftliche Photographie
Zeit phys Chem	Zeitschrift für physikalische Chemie

INDEX

Ingram Content Group UK Ltd.
Milton Keynes UK
UKHW021001130623
423366UK00006B/273